STANDARDS-BASED SCHOOL MATHEMATICS CURRICULA

What Are They?
What Do Students Learn?

STUDIES IN MATHEMATICAL THINKING AND LEARNING

Alan H. Schoenfeld, Series Editor

For more information on LEA titles, please contact Lawrence Erlbaum Associates, Publishers, at www.erlbaum.com.

STANDARDS-BASED SCHOOL MATHEMATICS CURRICULA

What Are They?
What Do Students Learn?

Edited by

Sharon L. Senk
Michigan State University

Denisse R. Thompson
University of South Florida

LAWRENCE ERLBAUM ASSOCIATES, PUBLISHERS
Mahwah, New Jersey London

Senior Acquisitions Editor:	Naomi Silverman
Assistant Editor:	Lori Hawver
Cover Design:	Kathryn Houghtaling Lacey
Textbook Production Manager:	Paul Smolenski
Full-Service Compositor:	TechBooks
Text and Cover Printer:	Sheridan Books, Inc.

This book was typeset in 10/12 pt. Times Roman, Bold, and Italic.
The heads were typeset in Americana and Americana Bold.

Lawrence Erlbaum Associates, Inc., Publishers
10 Industrial Avenue
Mahwah, New Jersey 07430

This book was prepared with the support of NSF grant 9729228.
However, any opinions, findings, conclusions, and/or recommendations
herein are those of the authors, and do not necessarily reflect views of NSF.

Library of Congress Cataloging-in-Publication Data

Standards-based school mathematics curricula : What are they? What do
   students learn? / edited by Sharon L. Senk, Denisse R. Thompson.
      p.   cm.—(Studies in mathematical thinking and learning)
   Includes bibliographical references and index.
   ISBN 0-8058-4337-X (case : alk. paper)
   1. Mathematics—Study and teaching—United States—Standards.   2. Academic
achievement—United States—Evaluation.   I. Senk, Sharon Louise, 1943–
II. Thompson, Denisse Rubilee, 1954–   III. Series.

QA13 .S72   2003
510′.71′073—dc21   2002010672

Contents

PART V: FINAL COMMENTARY

Preface

Most Americans, whether they are parents, caregivers, business leaders, or professional educators, care deeply about what children learn in school and how children are educated. However, in many subject areas, people sometimes disagree about what should be taught and how it should be taught. In mathematics education these disagreements have usually focused on what skills are needed for productive citizenship and on students' abilities to apply their knowledge in everyday life, the workplace, or higher education.

In 1989 the National Council of Teachers of Mathematics, the largest organization of mathematics teachers in the world, issued the *Curriculum and Evaluation Standards for School Mathematics* outlining a vision of both mathematical content and pedagogy for grades K–12. Between 1989 and 1991 the National Science Foundation (NSF) issued calls for proposals to develop instructional materials at the elementary, middle, and high school levels to reflect the visions of school mathematics described in the *Standards* document. By the mid-1990s the instructional materials developed by projects funded by the NSF were being field tested in hundreds of schools across the United States. Revised editions of these materials became available from commercial publishing companies in the late 1990s, and by the 1999–2000 school year, several million American school children were studying mathematics from these so-called *Standards*-based or *Standards*-oriented materials.

It is natural to ask "How well do these *Standards*-based instructional materials work?" The desire to answer this question was our rationale for developing this book. To investigate the relations between mathematics curricula and student achievement, we invited people who had conducted research on the outcomes of *Standards*-based curriculum development projects to describe how use of the instructional materials affects students' learning and other outcomes, and to provide evidence for any claims they make. In particular, we asked the authors to identify content on which performance of students using *Standards*-based materials differed from the performance of students using more traditional materials, and content on which performance of these two groups of students was virtually identical. Additionally, we invited four scholars not involved with any of the materials development projects to write critical commentaries on the work reported in the other chapters.

This book is organized into five sections. The first section consists of only Chapter 1. In it we provide some historical background to place the current curriculum reform efforts in perspective, and a summary of recommendations to reform school mathematics made during the 1990s. We also discuss issues that arise when conducting research on student outcomes.

The second, third, and fourth sections are devoted to research on mathematics curriculum projects for elementary, middle, and high schools, respectively. The first chapter in each section sets the stage for the chapters that follow it. It provides summary data on student outcomes in mathematics at this level of schooling and an overview of the specific recommendations in the *Standards* for this level. Each introductory chapter is followed by three to five chapters describing the curriculum of a single elementary, middle, or high school mathematics project and reporting the results of that project's research about students' achievement in mathematics. The last chapter in each section is a commentary on the chapters about the curriculum projects in that section by a scholar with experience in mathematics education research and teacher education: Ralph Putnam (elementary school), Michaele Chappell (middle school), and Jane Swafford (high school). These authors were asked to comment on common themes that cut across all curriculum chapters, to discuss strengths and weaknesses of the research reviewed, and to outline some directions for future research.

The fifth section consists of only Chapter 20. It is a commentary by Jeremy Kilpatrick, Regents Professor of Mathematics Education at the University of Georgia, on the research reported in this book. It provides a historical perspective on the use of research to guide mathematics curriculum reform in schools, and it makes additional recommendations for further research, including comments about the need for articulation between grade levels.

A research bibliography consisting of references not cited in the individual chapters is provided at the end of the book.

Authors of the chapters about research on individual curriculum development projects worked independently of each other but with feedback from us, the book editors. Similarly, the authors of the three school-level reaction chapters developed their reactions independently of each other, having had access only to the curriculum chapters on which they commented. Professor Kilpatrick wrote the first draft of Chapter 20 having had access only to Chapter 1 and the chapters about research on individual curriculum development projects. However, we later shared copies of all other chapters with him. Thus, the version of Chapter 20 in this book is a reaction based on all of Chapters 1–19.

We hope this book is useful to teachers, parents, principals, and other school administrators who want to learn about *Standards*-based mathematics curricula available for students in their district. Knowledge of any of the particular programs and the results of the research described in this book might help them decide whether that program should be adopted. However, knowledge of the broader issues about curriculum research discussed in this book will help them evaluate other proposed changes in school mathematics programs as well.

Although this book is concerned primarily with student outcomes, as we all know and as many authors have noted, teachers are an integral part of students' learning. We hope that this book encourages teachers, teacher educators, and researchers to think more about the relations between teachers, curriculum materials, and students' achievement.

We hope this book also will be used by professors and graduate students interested in curriculum, program evaluation, or the history of education. The results of the research reported in this volume contribute to our knowledge of what students know and can do when they study from *Standards*-based mathematics curricula. The commentaries by Professors Putnam, Chappell, Swafford, and Kilpatrick critique the methodologies used by the curriculum researchers and suggest ways in which other researchers might build upon the work described here. By collecting information about 12 sets of curriculum research studies in one volume, we hope to make it easier for the next generation of curriculum researchers to take advantage of the lessons learned by these authors.

Finally, we hope that this book might be of use to the policymakers and others who participate in the discussions about school mathematics taking place daily in meetings at the local, state, and national levels, and in newspapers, on the radio, the television, or the Internet. As we describe in Chapter 1, some of those discussions result in name-calling, e.g. *fuzzy math* versus *parrot math*. We encourage all participants in discussions about school mathematics curricula to base their opinions on facts. We hope that both the empirical evidence and the educational values discussed in this book encourage readers to engage in *civil discourse* in the future.

ACKNOWLEDGMENTS

The initial development of this book was supported by grant number ESI-9729228 from the National Science Foundation to Michigan State University with a subcontract to the University of South Florida. We appreciate the support and encouragement of John (Spud) Bradley at the Foundation for our work. The opinions expressed herein, however, are those of the chapter authors and do not necessarily express the position or support of the Foundation or of our universities.

We wish to acknowledge Karen D. King, who at that time was at San Deigo State University, and James W. Wilson at the University of Georgia who reviewed the original book proposal and encouraged publication of this volume.

We are grateful to Pamela Moses for help with the initial processing of the manuscript and to Stephen Hwang for his research assistance and other valuable help. We also thank Susan Beal, Pamela Drummond, Barbara Ferguson, Robert Floden, Marian Fox, Richard Hill, and Gladis Kersaint for helpful comments on the first two chapters of this book. Special thanks go to Joan Ferrini-Mundy for reading more than one version of the introductory chapters. Thanks also to Alan Schoenfeld for critical reading of and suggestions for the entire manuscript, and to Naomi Silverman and Lori Hawver for editorial support. Cara Brooks, Gabriel Cal, Jennifer Jones, and Joan Simmons deserve thanks for their help in proofing the author and subject indexes.

We also acknowledge Paul Hunt and Lori Hudson of Michigan State University and Ken Preston, Wendy Davis, and Lisa Bonilla at the University of South Florida for their assistance in working with Lawrence Erlbaum Associates in obtaining a contract for the publication of this volume.

Lastly, we thank our friends, colleagues, and families for tolerating our long absences while we worked on this book.

Sharon L. Senk
Michigan State University

Denisse R. Thompson
University of South Florida

Author Biographies

Susie Alldredge, Assistant Director of a curriculum development project at the Developmental Studies Center, has been in education for fifteen years as an elementary classroom teacher, curriculum developer, and staff developer. She received her Master's in Education in Mathematics, Science, and Technology from the University of California, Berkeley, where her research focused on instructional strategies to enhance students' number sense. She co-authored the *Number Power* program, and also was a project lead and writer of the *MathLand* program.

Glenn Allinger, Professor Emeritus of the Department of Mathematical Sciences at Montana State University—Bozeman, was Co-Chair of the Professional Development Committee for the SIMMS Project and was Co-Director of the SIMMS IM Project.

Victor Battistich, Deputy Director of Research at the Developmental Studies Center in Oakland, California, received his doctorate in Social Personality Psychology from Michigan State University in 1979. His primary research interests include school reform, social context of education, and positive youth development.

Janet Beissinger, Research Assistant Professor at the Institute for Mathematics and Science Education at the University of Illinois at Chicago, holds a doctorate in Mathematics from the University of Pennsylvania. Dr. Beissinger was a senior author of *Math Trailblazers* and is currently a member of the TIMS research team. She has taught mathematics to a variety of students, from seventh graders to graduate mathematics majors, as well as preservice and in-service elementary and secondary school teachers. Her research interests are in mathematics education and in the mathematics field of combinatorics.

Rick Billstein, Professor of Mathematics at the University of Montana in Missoula, has worked in the areas of mathematics education and technology education for the past 30 years and is a coauthor of a popular mathematics textbook for elementary teachers. He served as Director of the Six Through Eight Mathematics (STEM) Project and is now working with the Show-Me Project and several other teacher education projects.

Maurice Burke, Associate Professor in the Department of Mathematical Sciences at Montana State University—Bozeman, was Co-Director of the SIMMS Project. He is currently teaching for the department full time. He was Editor of the *2000 Yearbook* of the National Council of Teachers of Mathematics.

Bill Carroll, mathematics teacher at St. Ignatius College Preparatory High School in Chicago, directed research and evaluation for the elementary component of the University of Chicago School Mathematics Project (UCSMP) from 1991 to 1997. He also worked on Northwestern University's longitudinal study of students using *Everyday Mathematics*.

Andy Carter, Assistant Professor in the School of Science and Mathematics and in the College of Education at Roosevelt University, previously taught for 14 years in Chicago Public Schools. He also worked as a Program Associate for the TIMS Project at the University of Illinois at Chicago and as a staff developer and contributing author for *Math Trailblazers*. Carter earned a doctorate in Curriculum and Instruction at the University of Illinois at Chicago in 1999. His research interests include school change and the roles of inquiry and teacher authority in the development of student autonomy.

Michaele F. Chappell, Professor at the Middle Tennessee State University, received her doctorate in mathematics education at Florida State University. During the development of her chapter for this book she was on the faculty of the University of South Florida. Her research interests include the mathematics achievement of minority students and the professional development of teachers. She has worked as an investigative researcher for the Quantitative Understanding: Amplifying Student Achievement and

Reasoning (QUASAR) Project. She is active in a number of research-related activities of the National Council of Teachers of Mathematics and has authored several book chapters and journal articles.

Donald Cichon, an independent consultant and program evaluator based in Dover, New Hampshire, directed the evaluation of the **MATH** *Connections* curriculum. He also has evaluated numerous other educational and social service programs in New England and the Midwest.

Astrida Cirulis, Assistant Professor of Mathematics Education at National-Louis University, received her doctorate in mathematics from the University of Illinois at Chicago. She is a former high school teacher and works with many school districts in efforts to improve mathematics instruction at the elementary and secondary levels. Her interests focus on in-service elementary and secondary teacher education. She is a senior author of *Math Trailblazers*.

June Ellis, Director of MATHconx and the **MATH** *Connections* Implementation Center, holds a doctorate in Educational Research and Statistics from Florida State University. From 1990 to 1997 she was Executive Director of the Hartford Alliance for Mathematics and Science. Previously she worked for the Hartford Insurance Group as Director of several departments, including Information Management Systems and Technical Education. She also has taught mathematics in junior and senior high schools in Miami, Florida, and at the University of Hartford and Southern Connecticut State University.

Marty Gartzman, Director of Outreach for the University of Illinois at Chicago's Institute for Mathematics and Science Education, is a senior author of *Math Trailblazers* and has been associated with many of the University of Illinois at Chicago's mathematics and science professional-development and materials-development projects.

Christian R. Hirsch, Professor in the Department of Mathematics at Western Michigan University and Principal Investigator of the Core-Plus Mathematics Project, was a member of the original National Council of Teachers of Mathematics Commission on Standards for School Mathematics and chaired the Curriculum Working Group for Grades 9–12. Professor Hirsch is a former member of the Board of Directors of the National Council of Teachers of Mathematics and of the Board of Directors of the School Science and Mathematics Association.

James Hirstein, Professor, Department of Mathematical Sciences at the University of Montana, was Co-Chair of the Assessment Committee for the SIMMS Project. He currently is both teaching and is Chair of the department.

Mark Hoover, a graduate student at the University of Michigan, studies teaching, learning to teach, teacher education, and mathematics education. In his current research, he analyzes classroom practice in an effort to map both the work of teaching mathematics and the role of mathematical understanding in this work.

Andy Isaacs, currently Director of the UCSMP Everyday Mathematics Center and an author on the second edition of *Everyday Mathematics*, has worked for UCSMP since 1995. Before joining UCSMP, Isaacs worked for 10 years with the TIMS Project at the University of Illinois at Chicago. Previously he taught fourth and fifth grades for 8 years in public schools in suburban Chicago.

Catherine Kelso, Co-Director of the TIMS Project at the University of Illinois at Chicago, is a senior author of *Math Trailblazers*, Principal Investigator on the TIMS95 Teacher Enhancement grant, and Co-Director of the Math Trailblazers Implementation Center.

Jeremy Kilpatrick, Regents Professor of Mathematics Education at the University of Georgia, joined the faculty in 1975. Before then he taught at Teachers College, Columbia University. He has taught courses in mathematics education at several European and Latin American universities and has received Fulbright awards for work in New Zealand, Spain, Colombia, and Sweden. He recently chaired the National Research Council's Mathematics Learning Study. His present scholarly interests include mathematics curricula, research in mathematics education, and the history of both.

Diana Lambdin, Associate Dean for Teacher Education and Associate Professor at Indiana University, teaches mathematics education courses, codirects a masters-level teacher certification program, and is a frequent presenter of in-service workshops for mathematics teachers. Active as a project evaluator, author, and editor, she was on the writing teams for *Assessment Standards for School Mathematics* (NCTM, 1995) and *Principles and Standards for School Mathematics* (NCTM, 2000), and she also has authored numerous papers and book chapters about mathematical problem solving, assessment, standards, and teacher education.

Johnny W. Lott, Professor in the Department of Mathematical Sciences at the University of Montana, was Co-Director of both the SIMMS Project and of the SIMMS IM Project. He is currently teaching for the department and is working for the National Council of Teachers of Mathematics on the Figure This! grant. He became President Elect of the Council in 2001.

Michael Lundin, Assistant Professor in the Department of Mathematics at Central Washington University, was Co-Chair of the Professional Development Committee for the SIMMS Project.

Jan Mokros, TERC's principal researcher for the *Investigations* curriculum during its development, directed the project's evaluation efforts, coauthored several curriculum units, and designed teacher development workshops to accompany the curriculum. Dr. Mokros has written materials for parents about doing mathematics with their children, including the book *Beyond Facts and Flashcards* (Heinemann, 1996). She is directing a project involving mathematical outreach to parents through the workplace. She also is conducting a project to infuse a strand on gender equity into professional development workshops for teachers who are using *Standards*-based elementary mathematics curricula.

Dean Preble, formerly the Co-Chair of the Materials Development Committee for the SIMMS Project, also worked with the SIMMS IM Project and taught at Forsyth High School in Montana until his untimely death in November 1998.

Ralph Putnam, Associate Professor in the Department of Counseling, Educational Psychology and Special Education, Michigan State University, received his doctorate from Stanford University and did postdoctoral work at the University of Pittsburgh. Dr. Putnam's teaching and research focus on cognitively oriented studies of classroom teaching and learning. His recent research has examined the teaching and learning of mathematics in elementary school classrooms, especially the knowledge and beliefs of teachers as they strive to teach mathematics for understanding and the different ways that students learn about mathematics from various kinds of instruction. Dr. Putnam serves as editor for the journal *Cognition and Instruction*.

James Ridgway, Professor of Education at the University of Durham, England, is an applied psychologist whose interests include assessment, educational change, and educational uses of Information and Communications Technology. Professor Ridgway is a director of the Mathematics Assessment Resource Service, which provides practical support to states, cities, and districts in the United States on all aspects of assessment, ranging from the design of complete assessment systems through teacher professional development. He also directs a major project in the UK focused on identifying high-attaining students in science, mathematics, and technology.

Thomas A. Romberg, Bascom Professor and Professor Emeritus in Education at University of Wisconsin—Madison, served as Director of the National Center for Research in Mathematical Sciences Education from 1988 to 1996 and of the National Center for Improving Student Learning and Achievement in Mathematics and Science from 1996 to 1999. Professor Romberg has worked in mathematics curriculum reform since the 1960s and served as Chair of NCTM's *Curriculum and Evaluation Standards for School Mathematics* in the 1980s and of NCTM's *Assessment Standards for School Mathematics* in the 1990s. He currently directs an NSF-funded study of the impact of *Mathematics in Context* on student achievement.

Mary C. Shafer, Assistant Professor of Mathematics Education at Northern Illinois University, co-directs a National Science Foundation funded study of the impact of *Mathematics in Context* on student achievement. Her research interests include teachers' pedagogical decisions and classroom assessment practices.

Harold L. Schoen, Professor of Mathematics and Education at the University of Iowa, has been Co-Director of the Core-Plus Mathematics Project since 1992 with the main responsibility for developing the curriculum-embedded assessments and directing the project's formative and summative evaluation. Professor Schoen was a member of the Curriculum Working Group for Grades 9–12 of the NCTM's 1989 *Curriculum and Evaluation Standards* and chair of the 1989 Task Force on Implementing the Standards. He is former Co-Chair of the AERA Special Interest Group for Research in Mathematics Education.

Sharon Senk, Professor in the Department of Mathematics at Michigan State University, received her doctorate from the University of Chicago in 1983. Since 1987 she has been Co-Director of the Secondary Component of the University of Chicago School Mathematics Project. Previously she was a faculty member at Syracuse University and the University of Chicago. She also taught mathematics for more than 12 years in secondary schools in Illinois, Massachusetts, and Michigan, and at two universities in Colombia. Her major research interest is secondary school mathematics, including issues of curriculum, teaching, learning, and assessment.

Terry A. Souhrada, Visiting Assistant Professor in the Department of Mathematical Sciences at the University of Montana, was Co-Chair of the Materials Development Committee for the SIMMS Project and the SIMMS IM Project.

Jane Swafford, a retired Professor of Mathematics from Illinois State University, where she was involved in teacher education, department administration, and research on the development of algebraic reasoning and teacher change, most recently served as Study Director for the Mathematics Learning Study at the National Research Council in Washington, DC. She also has been a faculty member at Northern Michigan University and Michigan State University and a Program Officer at the National Science Foundation.

Denisse R. Thompson, Associate Professor of Mathematics Education at the University of South Florida, has been on the faculty since 1991. Her present position involves teaching mathematics methods courses, K–12, to both undergraduate and graduate students. Prior to her present position, she taught at both the high school and community college levels. Dr. Thompson became interested in curriculum development through her involvement with the University of Chicago School Mathematics Project, first as an author on *Advanced Algebra* and then as an editor on *Precalculus and Discrete Mathematics* while completing her doctoral studies. She has also chaired the editorial panel of *Mathematics Teaching in the Middle School.*

Ineko Tsuchida, an educational researcher in the San Francisco Bay Area, earned her doctorate in education at the University of California, Berkeley, in 1990. Since then she has conducted qualitative and quantitative studies comparing U.S. and Japanese school systems. Her research has examined student responsibility and learning, student–teacher interactions, teachers' instructional and management statements, research lessons, and differences between U.S. and Japanese elementary science textbooks.

Philip Wagreich, Professor of Mathematics and the Director of the Institute for Mathematics and Science Education at the University of Illinois at Chicago, is also co-founder of the TIMS Project. Professor Wagreich directed the development of *Math Trailblazers.* He is also a Principal Investigator of the UIC–Community College Collaborative for Excellence in Teacher Preparation. He was a member of the writing group for NCTM's *Principles and Standards for School Mathematics.*

Sharon Walen, Associate Research Professor, Department of Mathematics at Boise State University, was Co-Chair of the Assessment Committee for the SIMMS Project. She is currently teaching and doing research in mathematics education.

Norman Webb, Senior Research Scientist at the Wisconsin Center for Education Research at the University of Wisconsin—Madison, works primarily in evaluation and assessment in mathematics education. He is Principal Investigator on two NSF-funded projects, the Strategies for Evaluating Systemic Reform Team for the National Institute for Science Education (NISE) and the Study of the Impact of Statewide Systemic Initiatives, and is Co-Principal Investigator of the Study of Systemic Reform in Milwaukee Public Schools. Currently, he is editing a book on the evaluation of systemic reform for NISE. He was an author of the NCTM's 1989 *Curriculum and Evaluation Standards.*

Jim Williamson, Visiting Assistant Professor of Mathematics at the University of Montana in Missoula, has been involved in mathematics education for 30 years and has taught mathematics at all levels from fourth grade through university. He was awarded a Presidential Award for Excellence in Mathematics Teaching in 1984. He chaired the writing team for the STEM Project and is now working with the Show-Me Project.

Judith Zawojewski, Associate Professor in Purdue University's Department of Curriculum and Instruction, is interested in teaching and learning mathematics in the context of the classroom experience. In addition to teaching mathematics education courses, her professional activities include development and evaluation in the areas of assessment, algebraic thinking, and problem solving for both students and their teachers. She has chaired the editorial panel of *Mathematics Teaching in the Middle School*, is currently serving on the Educational Materials Committee for the National Council of Teachers of Mathematics, and has been an author in many of the Council's journals and publications.

PART I

Introduction

1

School Mathematics Curricula: Recommendations and Issues

Sharon L. Senk
Michigan State University

Denisse R. Thompson
University of South Florida

Who of all the boys in the Boston Grammar and Writing schools, shall hereafter be city assessors, when not one of them can tell what tax shall be levied on a hundred thousand dollars, when all the conditions are given, with perfect precision and clearness? Who of all the boys, aye, or girls either, shall cast the interest on a note, either as borrower or lender, when not one of them knows there is any difference between the value of a note for $200 payable in six months, and the value of two notes of $100 each,—one payable in three and the other in nine months!

—The Common School Journal (October 1, 1845)

Concerns about what mathematics students learn in school have been raised repeatedly since Horace Mann, Secretary of the State Board of Education in Massachusetts, wrote the words above (Caldwell & Courtis, 1925, p. 265). Toward the end of the 20th century, students' performance in school was linked not just to their ability to be effective employees or consumers, as Mann suggested, but also to the economic vitality of the United States as a whole. The National Commission on Excellence in Education (1983) reports:

Our Nation is at risk. Our once unchallenged preeminence in commerce, industry, science, and technological innovation is being overtaken by competitors throughout the world. . . . The educational foundations of our society are presently being eroded by a rising tide of mediocrity that threatens our very future as a Nation and a people. (p. 5)

Invariably, concerns about student outcomes in mathematics give rise to recommendations about what to teach in schools and how to teach it. Advocates of reform often attempt to influence classroom practice, and hence, student achievement, by means of changes in textbooks. As noted by Edward G. Begle (1973), the director of one of the largest mathematics curriculum development projects in the history of the United States,

The textbook has a powerful influence on what students learn. . . . The evidence indicates that most student learning is directed by the text rather than the teacher. This is an important finding, since the content of the text is a variable that we can manipulate. In fact, it seems at present to be the only variable that on the one hand we can manipulate and on the other hand does affect student learning. (p. 209)

Surprisingly, until recently, there had been relatively little research to extend our understanding of the effects of textbooks on students' learning of mathematics.[1]

In 1989 the National Council of Teachers of Mathematics published the *Curriculum and Evaluation Standards for School Mathematics*, a set of recommendations for mathematics curricula for Grades K–12 that stimulated a nationwide discussion of standards for school mathematics. This book examines the effects of 12 sets of *Standards*-based mathematics textbooks on students' achievement and other outcomes of schooling.[2]

This chapter provides background information for understanding the goals of the curriculum reform projects, and the research they conducted. We begin with a brief history of earlier efforts to reform the school mathematics curriculum. Then we describe the visions of school mathematics presented in documents developed by the National Council of Teachers of Mathematics, and how those documents led to the development of so-called *Standards*-based school mathematics curricula. Next we summarize some of the debates that have taken place about the directions of school mathematics that have been sparked by the development and use of these curricular materials in the United States. Lastly, we discuss some issues that one needs to keep in mind when trying to understand or interpret results of studies of the effects of mathematics curricula on students.

THE EVOLUTION OF SCHOOL
MATHEMATICS

In the early days of the United States, education was neither universal nor free. By the end of the 19th century, most cities and states had established publicly supported elementary schools, but few had established publicly supported high schools. In 1900 a majority of Americans aged 7 to 13 years attended school. However, only 1 in 10 remained in school beyond the age of 14, and fewer than 7% of 17-year-olds graduated from high school. By the close of the 20th century, access to public education in the United States was virtually universal. In the year 2000, more than 8 in 10 young adults had a high school diploma; more than 6 in 10 enrolled in college immediately after graduation (Olson, 2000, p. 4).

While access to education in the United States was expanding, the mathematics curriculum in schools was also evolving. In the following sections we summarize how the mathematics studied in school evolved during the 19th and 20th centuries.

19th Century School Mathematics

In the 19th century, the mathematics taught in elementary schools consisted of arithmetic with whole numbers, fractions, decimals, and percents, augmented by work with measures of length, area, and volume. In early arithmetic textbooks, each topic was usually introduced by stating a rule followed by an example of how to apply the rule; then a set of exercises was given. Typically instruction involved demonstration of procedures by the teacher and oral recitation by students of work that had been memorized.

During this time, the prevailing view of how students learned was based on a theory called mental discipline. Advocates of the mental discipline theory believed that the mind was a muscle, and like any muscle, it needed exercise to develop. Doing mathematics, particularly practicing difficult arithmetic computations, was thought to be good exercise and crucial to improving one's reasoning ability, even in other domains (Grouws & Cebulla, 2000; Jones & Coxford, 1970).

However, as the citation from Horace Mann that begins this chapter suggests, the level of performance in arithmetic was disappointing to Mann and his contemporaries. Mann called for school reform, particularly for greater emphasis on teaching thinking, not just memorization (Caldwell & Courtis, 1925; Kilpatrick, 1992a). By the late 19th century many educators expressed general uneasiness about the rigidly formal methods of instruction employed in all subjects, but especially in arithmetic, which was "the chief source of non-promotion in the elementary school" (Buswell & Judd, 1925, p. 7, as quoted in Kilpatrick, 1992b).

During the first half of the 19th century, secondary schools were rare, primarily serving as college preparatory academies for males from privileged families. The best academies offered algebra and geometry; mathematics beyond geometry was generally not studied in secondary schools.[3]

By 1890 vocational and commercial high schools had been developed to offer preparation for skilled employment. In the 1890s the high school mathematics curriculum for the college-bound student consisted primarily of algebra and geometry, with trigonometry taught in some of the larger or more elite academies; bookkeeping and technical arithmetic were taught in business and vocational schools.

In the 1890s dissatisfaction with the proliferation of secondary schools prompted the National Education Association to appoint a Committee of Ten on Secondary School Studies. The report of the Committee of Ten was the first report in the history of the United States by a professional association of educators that commented on the curriculum for secondary schools. The subcommittee appointed by the Committee of Ten to investigate mathematics in schools found that both the elementary and high school mathematics programs were inadequate. To strengthen elementary school programs, they recommended that work with arithmetic in Grades 5–8 be supplemented by informal work in algebra and geometry. To strengthen secondary school programs, they recommended that 1 year of algebra be required of all high school students. For Grades 10 and 11 they recommended that the geometry course incorporate more work with logic and proof, and that geometry and advanced algebra each meet $2\frac{1}{2}$ hours per week over 2 years (Jones & Coxford, 1970; National Education Association, 1893).

School Mathematics: 1900–1950

Despite the calls by the Committee of Ten and numerous other commissions to broaden the content of the mathematics taught in Grades K–8, mathematics in elementary school continued to be dominated by arithmetic during the first half of the 20th century.[4] However, both theories of learning and the methods of instruction in arithmetic evolved during this period.

In the first half of the 20th century, many psychologists, including Edward L. Thorndike, Charles Judd, and John Dewey, conducted research on how students learn arithmetic. Space does not permit a thorough review of the research on learning theories in this volume. Readers interested in the evolution of these theories are encouraged to consult Kilpatrick (1992b), Mayer (2001), and Schoenfeld (2001) for more details. Thorndike's work on how mental connections are reinforced by practice was one of the forerunners of the behaviorism that dominated American psychology in much of the

20th century. Arithmetic textbooks influenced by Thorndike's work (1922) emphasized a systematic approach to teaching arithmetic, with careful sequencing of tasks designed to accumulate bits of knowledge. Drill on number facts and computation was dominant; little attention was paid to the interests of the child or to the practical uses of mathematics.

In contrast, Judd (1927, 1928), like McLellan and Dewey (1895) before him, argued that the concept of number develops out of a child's activity. He contended that Thorndike's view of arithmetic as a tool subject was false and that, instead, arithmetic is a general mode of thinking. Later, Dewey (1916, 1933) argued that the main goal of education was to develop students' abilities to think. He believed that thinking developed in social situations involving both reflection by the individual learner and interaction with a community of other learners. Thus, advocates of these more child-centered views recommended that the teaching of mathematics should involve engaging students in activities from which the teacher, through discussion with students, could help students reflect on fundamental ideas and develop powerful habits of mind, such as comparing and contrasting or generalizing. The Progressive Education Association (PEA), which was founded in 1919, supported many of these views. Further, the PEA advocated that only content that was interesting or useful to the child should be studied (Committee of the PEA, 1940). Arithmetic textbooks sympathetic to the line of work begun by Dewey, Judd, and the PEA emphasized solving practical problems and doing project work, with little attention paid to systematic drill.

The high school curriculum became even more fragmented during the first half of the 20th century. Those few students who were hoping to attend college could take 2 years of algebra and 1 year of geometry. The bigger or better high schools offered a fourth year of mathematics, usually a semester each of trigonometry and solid geometry. Because the college-preparatory curriculum did not seem to meet the needs of all students who wanted a high school education, many high schools created different curricula for students in different tracks. Some large public high schools offered as many as four tracks. In addition to the academic track, there were commercial (or business), vocational (with options for industrial or home economics specialties), and general tracks (Olson, 2000). The mathematics offerings in such tracks included business mathematics, mathematics for the shop, consumer mathematics, and general mathematics. Most of these courses taught arithmetic. Influences of the progressive movement can be seen in some textbooks of this era in the work with formulas and graphs related to the practical needs of a particular track (Osborne & Crosswhite, 1970).

The induction testing of military recruits for World War II revealed that many youths and young adults were ill prepared in mathematics. Mathematics was seen as an important component of success in the engineering and technical support needed by the war effort. However, the prevailing view of the general public in the late 1940s was that there was no need for students to study much mathematics unless they planned to become scientists, engineers, or mathematicians.

School Mathematics Since 1950

In 1950 the U.S. Congress established the National Science Foundation (NSF) to develop a national policy for the promotion of basic research and education in the sciences, including mathematics. Until 1957 the major contribution of the NSF to education in Grades K–12 was the support of summer institutes for teacher training in mathematics and science. However, in 1957 the launch of Sputnik by the Soviet Union sparked an interest in the race to conquer space. This, in turn, kindled a desire to strengthen instructional programs in school mathematics and science, particularly the curricula for the college-intending student. Soon thereafter, the NSF began to fund programs to create high-quality teaching materials for mathematics in elementary and secondary schools.

Among the mathematics curriculum development projects funded by the NSF during the late 1950s were the University of Illinois Committee on School Mathematics (UICSM) and the School Mathematics Study Group (SMSG). The UICSM developed textbooks for a strong high school mathematics program to enable more students to study engineering or science in college. The SMSG began with the goal of developing instructional materials for college-capable high school students, defined to be the top third of each grade level. However, by the time SMSG ended its work in the early 1970s, it had produced sample textbooks for grades K–12, including some for average students. Teachers' manuals to accompany the students' textbooks, materials for the preparation of teachers, and programmed materials for students were also produced.

The instructional materials developed during the period between 1957 and 1970 became known as *modern mathematics* or *the new math*. At elementary school the new math programs included more work with geometry and graphs than other instructional materials for Grades K–6. The materials for high school introduced work with inequalities, solid geometry, and trigonometry earlier in the high school curriculum, and they included textbooks for teaching probability and statistics and matrix algebra in high school. The director of the SMSG (Begle, 1970) commented that

> The chief difference between the old and new programs is the point of view toward mathematics. No longer is computational skill the be-all and end-all of mathematics. Now there is an equal emphasis on understanding the basic concepts of mathematics and of their interrelationships, i.e., the structure of mathematics. (p. 1)

In both elementary and secondary schools the concepts of set and mathematical structure served as unifying ideas, precision in the use of mathematical language was emphasized, and guided discovery was encouraged as a teaching technique. Consistent with their goal of creating a curriculum for talented students, the authors of the UICSM and SMSG materials included problems to challenge the best students.

Controversy about the new math began shortly after the introduction of the prototype materials in classrooms in the United States. Critics claimed that the new math was too theoretical, used language that many teachers and parents did not understand, and did not pay sufficient attention to basic skills (Kline, 1973). Hence, critics were concerned that students' achievement in mathematics might suffer. However, as Usiskin (1985) and Kilpatrick (Chapter 20 of this volume) point out, the use of the modern mathematics curricula did not have a negative impact on student outcomes.

In the early 1970s, a strong back-to-basics movement emphasizing arithmetic computation and algebra skill developed in reaction to the new math. The mathematics textbooks written by proponents of the back-to-basics movement had few references to mathematical principles, very little to read, and thousands of exercises to practice skills. There were virtually no problems showing how mathematics is used in daily life or in other fields, and no challenging problems in these texts.

In 1969 the National Assessment of Educational Progress (NAEP) was initiated by an act of Congress to monitor the performance of American children in school subjects. The first administration of tests by the NAEP in 1972 on reading and mathematics established a baseline for future examinations, but the levels of performance by 9-, 13-, and 17-year-olds were considered quite low by many educators and parents.

Soon thereafter, the back-to-basics movement was criticized for defining *basic skills* too narrowly. In response, the National Council of Supervisors of Mathematics (NCSM, 1977) issued a report that called for defining basic skills more broadly than numerical computation and algebraic skill. The report advocated 10 basic skills including problem solving, applying mathematics, number sense, geometry, and data analysis. In 1980 the National Council of Teachers of Mathematics (NCTM) published *An Agenda for Action* (1980), which called for similar changes in school mathematics curricula, with problem solving as the fundamental goal of school mathematics. Both the NCSM and NCTM reports noted that what is basic must change as society and technology change. Each called for the use of calculators and computers in school mathematics.

The National Commission on Excellence in Education (1983) cited poor performance on tests administered by the NAEP, declining SAT scores, and an increase in remedial courses by colleges, businesses, and the military as evidence of a "rising tide of mediocrity" in schools in the United States. In their report, *A Nation at Risk*, the committee called for increased requirements for all high school graduates, including 3 years of mathematics. They also called for developing equally challenging programs for both college-bound and non-college-bound students (National Commission on Excellence in Education, 1983).

In 1987 the results of the Second International Mathematics Study (SIMS), which had been conducted in 20 countries from 1981 through 1982, were released, adding to the pessimism reported in *A Nation at Risk*. In the United States approximately 12,000 randomly chosen students from Grades 8 and 12 in approximately 250 public and private schools participated in the SIMS. In their 1987 report, *The Underachieving Curriculum*, McKnight and his colleagues (McKnight et al., 1987) report that on no test administered by SIMS did the U.S. students score significantly above the international average; on many tests, U.S. students scored substantially below the international average.

The United States had also participated in the First International Mathematics Study in 1964. On a common set of 36 items from the two international studies, the overall U.S. achievement of eighth-grade students dropped from 48% correct to 45% correct, with a drop of 6% in both arithmetic and geometry. Hence, the back-to-basics movement of the 1970s was not necessarily effective in improving computational proficiency in arithmetic and thus would not serve as an effective model for curricular revision in the 1980s and 1990s (McKnight et al., 1987).

For 12th-grade students, there was an overall increase of 6% on the 20 common items from the First International Mathematics Study to the SIMS. For the most part, this increase was due to enhanced performance on the functions and calculus items, perhaps reflecting the increase in enrollment in calculus in high school from 8,000 in 1964 to 32,000 in 1982.

The data cited in *A Nation at Risk* and *The Underachieving Curriculum* led people to search for explanations for the poor levels of performance of mathematics students. McKnight et al. (1987) suggested that the intended mathematics curriculum in the United States was a major determinant of American students' poor showing on the international tests. They claimed that the American curriculum was fragmented and had lower expectations than the curricula in other developed countries. For instance, whereas the eighth-grade curricula in France and Japan concentrated on geometry and algebra, respectively, the eighth-grade curriculum in the United States concentrated on arithmetic. Because their analysis of classroom processes had confirmed that "commercially published textbooks serve as the primary guide for instruction," the SIMS researchers argued that "any significant reform must take this fact into account" (McKnight et al., 1987, p. xiii).

STANDARDS FOR SCHOOL MATHEMATICS

Efforts to reform school mathematics education in the United States in the last 2 decades of the 20th century have been led by the NCTM.[5] In 1989 the NCTM published the *Curriculum and Evaluation Standards for School Mathematics* with recommendations about goals for school mathematics and specific content that should be part of school mathematics in Grades K–12. As Kilpatrick and Stanic (1995) note, "by using the language of standards, the NCTM could lay out its goals and its hopes for change in a form that would speak to the profession about a vision for school mathematics and to the politicians and public about improved learning" (p. 13).

What Do the *Curriculum and Evaluation Standards* Recommend?

The authors of the 1989 *Standards* document were mathematics teachers at all levels from kindergarten through college, mathematics supervisors, researchers, and teacher educators. In the *Curriculum and Evaluation Standards*, five goals for all students are articulated: "(1) that they learn to value mathematics, (2) that they become confident in their ability to do mathematics, (3) that they become mathematical problem solvers, (4) that they learn to communicate mathematically, and (5) that they learn to reason mathematically" (NCTM, 1989, p. 5).

Statements in the *Curriculum and Evaluation Standards* support the view that *all* students need to develop mathematical power. Furthermore, the authors argue that "*what* a student learns depends to a great degree on *how* he or she has learned it" (NCTM, 1989, p. 5, italics in the original).

Four standards that should guide mathematics instruction at all levels are identified: problem solving, communication, reasoning, and mathematical connections. In addition, at each of three grade-bands (K–4, 5–8, and 9–12), seven or eight content standards list specific mathematical content, including both skills and concepts that should be part of the mathematics program at that grade-band. Topics that have traditionally been taught in school mathematics are among the specific content listed, including number and operations at Grades K–4, measurement at Grades 5–8, and geometry from a synthetic view in Grades 9–12. However, in each grade-band, topics that were not generally part of the curriculum in most schools in the late 20th century also are recommended, such as statistics and probability in Grades K–4, patterns and functions in Grades 5–8, and probability in Grades 9–12. More specific information about the curriculum standards for each grade-band is given in Chapters 2, 8, and 13.

The authors of the *Curriculum and Evaluation Standards* (NCTM, 1989) argue that at all grade levels there should be less emphasis on memorization of facts and rules, and greater emphasis on active engagement and problems set in realistic contexts that have meaning for students. They also claim the following:

> Because technology is changing mathematics and its uses, we believe that appropriate calculators should be available to all students at all times; a computer should be available in every classroom for demonstration purposes; every student should have access to a computer for individual and group work; students should learn to use the computer as a tool for processing information and performing calculations to investigate and solve problems. (p. 8)

Soon after publishing the *Curriculum Standards*, the NCTM published two companion volumes: the *Professional Standards for Teaching Mathematics* (NCTM, 1991) and the *Assessment Standards for School Mathematics* (NCTM, 1995).[6]

The *Professional Standards for Teaching Mathematics* proposes standards for teaching mathematics, the evaluation of the teaching of mathematics, the professional development of teachers, and the support and development of mathematics teachers and teaching. Included in the standards for teaching mathematics are specific guidelines for worthwhile mathematical tasks, the teacher's role in discourse, the students' role in discourse, and tools for enhancing discourse.[7]

The authors of the *Assessment Standards for School Mathematics* (NCTM, 1995) note that assessment can be used for various purposes, including monitoring students' progress, making instructional decisions, evaluating students' achievement, and evaluating programs. They suggest that "several shifts in program evaluation may be necessary: [including] toward making program decisions based on high-quality evidence from multiple sources and away from relying on over-simplified evidence from a single test or test format" (NCTM, 1995, p. 67). For instance, "short-answer or multiple-choice tests (or other machine scoreable tests) can elicit some information on skills if the balance among topics is appropriate for the intended purposes. In addition, performance assessment tasks can indicate how well students are able to integrate their knowledge of mathematics and apply this knowledge in different situations if the contexts are familiar to students" (NCTM, 1995, p. 68).

According to Willoughby (2000), some people interpreted the NCTM *Standards* documents as suggesting that most traditional skills be eliminated, and that schools should concentrate all their efforts on teaching problem solving and other higher-order thinking skills. However, no such recommendations are actually made. In fact, as noted in the previous paragraph, the authors of the *Assessment Standards* call for testing both skills and the integration and application of knowledge. When discussing the standards for middle grades, the authors of the *Curriculum Standards* claim that "the thirteen standards promote a broad curriculum for students in Grades 5–8. Developing certain computational skills is important but constitutes only a part of this curriculum" (NCTM, 1989, p. 66).

According to Lappan and Briars (1995), ideas about teaching and learning mathematics expressed in the *Standards* recognize that children build their own mathematical knowledge from their experiences, and that what they learn is fundamentally connected with how they learn it. Lappan and Briars suggest that learning occurs best through dialogue, discussion, and interaction. These views, which are similar to the beliefs expressed by Dewey (1916, 1933) earlier in the 20th century about the importance of context and social interaction in learning, are consistent with psychological theories such as *situated cognition* (Greeno, 1997) or philosophical approaches such as *constructivism* (Davis, Maher, & Noddings, 1990).

Impact of the *Curriculum and Evaluation Standards*

Ferrini-Mundy notes "the *Curriculum and Evaluation Standards* was designed to speak to those very close to decisions about mathematics curriculum— teachers, supervisors, and developers of instructional materials" (2000, p. 39). Unfortunately, there has been little systematic accumulation of data to determine what features from the *Standards* documents seemed to have the most impact on classroom practice. Case studies directed by Ferrini-Mundy and colleagues (Ferrini-Mundy & Schram, 1997) suggest that pedagogical features of the *Standards*, such as an emphasis on cooperative groups, writing in the mathematics classroom, or discussion and discourse "were more readily taken up by teachers than some of the mathematics-content features" (Ferrini-Mundy, 2000, p. 39).

As the *Curriculum and Evaluation Standards* were being developed, and following their release, many states and local communities began to develop and modify their own standards and curriculum frameworks for school mathematics to be consistent with the recommendations of the NCTM (Council of Chief State School Officers, 1995). Concurrent with the launching of the mathematics standards movement by the NCTM, the NSF initiated systemic reforms in states, cities, rural areas, and other local regions. In the requests for proposals for early systemic initiatives, the NCTM *Standards* documents were cited as the mathematics curriculum framework that was to be promoted in systemic reforms.

The *Standards* were also used as a guide for NSF-supported programs for designing instructional materials. By 1991 the NSF had issued calls for proposals that would create comprehensive instructional materials for

TABLE 1.1
Instructional Materials Development Projects Participating
in the Gateways Conferences

Elementary school
    Teaching Integrated Math and Science
    University of Chicago School Mathematics Project Elementary
    Investigations in Number, Data, and Space
    Cooperative Mathematics Project

Middle school
    Connected Mathematics Project
    Mathematics in Context
    Six Through Eight Mathematics (STEM)
    Middle Grades Mathematics Through Applications Project
    Seeing and Thinking Mathematically

High school
    Core-Plus Mathematics Project
    Interactive Mathematics Program
    MATH Connections
    Systemic Initiative for Montana Mathematics and Science, Integrated
      Mathematics Project (SIMMS IM)
    Applications/Reform in Secondary Education (ARISE)
    Connected Geometry

Grades 7–12
    University of Chicago School Mathematics Project Secondary Component

---

elementary, middle, and high schools consistent with the calls for change in the *Curriculum and Evaluation Standards* and other major policy reports. It was expected that "supported projects will represent a range of complete but different options" for the target grade levels (Directorate for Education and Human Resources, 1991). Ultimately the NSF funded more than a dozen projects to develop *Standards*-based instructional materials for the study of mathematics at multiple grade levels.

Between 1992 and 1998 the NSF held a series of annual conferences at which representatives of instructional materials development projects for mathematics in Grades K–12 were invited to discuss issues of common concern. The projects with representatives attending these Gateways Conferences are listed in Table 1.1.

With the exception of the University of Chicago School Mathematics Project (UCSMP) Secondary Component, all the projects listed in Table 1.1 were funded by the NSF.[8] When we began to develop this book we surveyed the directors of all projects listed in Table 1.1 about the extent of the research conducted on the impact of use of the materials they developed on students' achievement in mathematics. Four projects were unable to contribute chapters to this book because they did not have sufficient data on student outcomes: Middle Grades Mathematics Through Applications Project, Seeing and Thinking Mathematically, ARISE, and Connected Geometry.[9] Representatives of all other projects listed in Table 1.1 wrote chapters for this book.

Each of the *Standards*-based mathematics curriculum projects described in this book was developed over 4 to 6 years by large teams of people, including teachers from both schools and universities. As described in subsequent chapters, each curriculum development team designed its own process for writing, piloting, and field-testing materials. Each team established a relationship with a commercial publishing house to publish and market its materials.

Maurer (2000) estimated that in 1999 more than 300,000 high school students in the United States were studying from mathematics textbooks developed by the five NSF-funded high school projects listed in Table 1.1. Another 3 million students in U.S. elementary, middle, and high schools were using materials developed by the UCSMP.

Many of the *Standards*-based materials differ markedly from the traditional content and approaches that most Americans remember from their own schooling experiences (Robinson, Robinson, & Maceli, 2000). For instance, as compared with the so-called traditional textbooks, the *Standards*-based materials have far more problems set in realistic contexts and far fewer exercises requiring only arithmetic or algebraic computation. On certain questions the *Standards*-based materials ask students to use calculators or computers; in the traditional textbooks, there is little or no mention of using calculators or computers. When classes use traditional textbooks, typically teachers demonstrate how to do something and students work individually to reproduce what the teacher has shown them. In contrast, in classes using *Standards*-based materials, teachers often pose problems for students to work on in small groups, and that might be solved by using various strategies. Ability grouping or tracking is strongly embedded in many American middle and high schools. However, most *Standards*-based mathematics curricula are designed for use in heterogeneously grouped classes. Thus, the *Standards*-based materials challenge strongly held beliefs about what mathematics is most important as well as how it is taught and learned most effectively.

CONTROVERSIES ABOUT STANDARDS-BASED SCHOOL MATHEMATICS

As policymakers, parents, teachers, mathematicians, and the mathematics education community began to read the *Standards*, and to examine the instructional materials that were being developed based on the *Standards*, heated debates often arose. Through articles and editorials in newspapers and professional journals and in discussions on the Internet, many mathematicians, educators, and parents have challenged the recommendations of the *Standards* and the principles upon which many of the *Standards*-oriented instructional materials are based (see, for example, Addington & Roitman, 1996; Clayton, 2000a; Hartocollis, 2000; Kilpatrick, 1997; Wu, 1997; http://mathematicallycorrect.com).

The disagreements about the nature and process of recent reform efforts have often been so strident and acrimonious that they have been dubbed the *Math Wars*. Those who are concerned that the content and instructional strategies recommended by the NCTM will lower mathematics achievement have applied terms such as *fuzzy math* to reform-oriented instructional materials (Hartocollis, 2000). In particular, critics of the *Standards* worry about what they perceive to be an overemphasis on the process of obtaining an answer, rather than on the answer itself. They are concerned that encouraging students to invent solutions and algorithms, rather than emphasizing use of traditional algorithms, will lead to a decline in basic skills (Klein & Milgram, 1999). The use of calculators, particularly in the elementary grades, is also seen as a threat to the development of basic arithmetic skills (Andersen, 1998). The use of cooperative learning and discovery approaches instead of direct instruction has raised concerns that either teachers are not teaching or that only some children are learning mathematics. In some school districts, parents with these concerns have organized groups to protest the use of reform-oriented materials, fearing that their children would not be academically competitive (Chaddock, 2000; Clayton, 2000a, 2000b).

In contrast, people who generally support mathematics education reform often object to the *drill and kill* that characterizes many traditional mathematics programs. O'Brien (1999) used the term *parrot math* to decry the emphasis on numerical and symbolic manipulations performed by rote memorization without any understanding. Some advocates of reform believe that critics of reform are applying a double standard when studying the effects of various school mathematics curricula. Critics of new curriculum materials often suggest that reform curricula must be *proven* to work, yet traditional curricula are *assumed* to work (Hiebert, 1999). Advocates of reform also point to the fact that much of the public and many students dislike mathematics and believe they cannot be successful at it. Moreover, they contend that traditional instruction has failed large portions of the population (Colvin, 2000). For instance, in 1999 Glenda Lappan, who at that time was President of the NCTM, stated that "We've had the longest running experiment in human history about whether rote memorization of facts and skills works. And it doesn't. Students are coming to universities and into the workplace not understanding math. Why wouldn't I want to try something new?" (Schulte, 1999, October 17). In addition, advocates of reform argue that the *Standards*-based instructional materials have a broader scope than traditional textbooks. For individuals on this side of the debate, the recommendations in the *Standards* offer hope to a new generation by suggesting ways to help *all* students develop mathematical power.

In October 1999, the United States Department of Education published a list of 10 Exemplary and Promising Mathematics Programs (Mathematics and Science Expert Panel, 1999). The process of identifying high-quality school mathematics programs was part of a new evaluation system mandated by Congress in 1994. Recommendations were made after review in several stages by national panels of teachers, mathematicians, statisticians, program evaluators, and others. This book includes chapters about six of these mathematics programs. Three are designated Exemplary (the Connected Mathematics Project, the Core-Plus Mathematics Project, and the Interactive Mathematics Program), and three are designated Promising (Everyday Mathematics, Number Power, and the University of Chicago School Mathematics Project secondary curriculum).

The publication of the list of Exemplary and Promising Mathematics Programs seemed to propel the controversies about mathematics reform to new heights. Soon after the release of the list, approximately 200 prominent research mathematicians and scientists signed an open letter appearing in the *Washington Post* to then Secretary of Education Richard Riley requesting that the list of Exemplary and Promising Mathematics Programs be withdrawn (1999, November 18). In January 2000 Secretary Riley responded to the open letter by noting that it was important to find areas where all participants in the debates were in agreement. Among the areas of agreement he noted were that "the very best mathematics programs must include mastery of basic skills and the use of those skills in solving complex problems" (Riley, 2000). In the following chapters of this book, authors specifically address the extent to which students using various curricula master basic skills and how well they are able to apply those skills in a variety of settings.

ISSUES IN CONDUCTING CURRICULUM RESEARCH

Researchers investigating the effects of a curriculum face many issues, including the following: what questions to ask, what type of research design to employ, how to ensure that students using various curricula are comparable at the start of their experience, how to determine the extent to which teachers implement the curriculum, and what measures to use to determine the effects of the curriculum. In order to help the reader interpret and evaluate the quality and results of comparative research studies reported in this book, we examine these issues briefly. The issues are complex, and they overlap considerably.[10] The discussion that follows is not meant to be exhaustive.

Rather, it is meant to describe some facets of these issues that are particularly related to the curriculum research reported in this book and to point out how the authors have dealt with these issues.

Research Questions

Research about the effects of mathematics curricula can potentially address questions about students' achievement relative to a particular curriculum, or comparisons of students' achievement relative to different curricula. Students' achievement might be examined on different content (arithmetic, geometry, etc.) or different processes (using algorithms, solving nonroutine problems, etc.) or over different periods of time.

Research on the effects of curricula can also address questions about the nature of classroom discourse, students' attitudes toward mathematics, or the effects of a particular mathematics curriculum on the number of students who continue to study mathematics once it is no longer required. In addition, as Romberg and Collins (1999) suggest, studies of *Standards*-based curricula also might investigate the critical instructional features in classrooms that promote understanding for all students, the role of teachers in such classrooms, or the organizational characteristics in the school or larger community needed to support the development of classrooms that promote high levels of understanding.

Researchers studying the effects of the 12 sets of instructional materials that are the subject of this book have examined questions about virtually all of the issues mentioned in the previous paragraphs. However, because of limits on their resources, no single project could examine all the issues mentioned. Furthermore, because of space limitations, not all research conducted by any one set of researchers could be described in this book. Specifically, we asked authors to limit their discussions to research on *student outcomes*.

Authors of all chapters examine the extent to which students who use *Standards*-based instructional materials learn fundamental mathematics skills. At early elementary grades, computation with whole numbers is of primary concern. Studies in the upper elementary and middle grades examine computation with fractions. Studies of high school achievement examine skill in working with algebraic expressions and equations.

However, none of the authors reports just on basic skills. To be consistent with the vision articulated in the *Curriculum and Evaluation Standards*, the authors also examine the nature and extent of students' achievement on content other than arithmetic and algebra, and on processes other than the use of algorithms. For instance, Carroll and Isaacs report on achievement in geometry; Mokros reports on students' ability to solve word problems; Ridgway and his colleagues describe achievement on open-ended problems;

Hirsch and Schoen report on results of a test of quantitative reasoning; and Webb reports on students' achievement on statistics questions.

In each chapter some studies of 1 year's duration are reported. However, in the chapters by Carroll and Isaacs, Battistich and colleagues, Ridgway and colleagues, Romberg and Shafer, Billstein and Williamson, Hirsch and Schoen, and Senk, the results of longitudinal studies are reported.

Additionally, Billstein and Williamson, and Cichon and Ellis both provide data on students' attitudes. Carter and his colleagues and Cichon and Ellis report on classroom discourse.

Research Design

Researchers studying the effects of curricula employ varied methodologies. Some studies are true experiments in which students are randomly assigned to classes and teachers to curricula (Campbell & Stanley, 1963). Pretests and posttests are administered; quantitative analyses of the data are performed. Other investigations use qualitative research methods, for instance a case study of how a curriculum is implemented in one school, or an anthropological study of how a curriculum affects the nature of classroom discourse among teacher and students (Romberg, 1992).

Schoenfeld (1994) noted a shift in the late 20th century away from quantitative methods and toward qualitative research methods in mathematics education. Since then researchers have continued to debate the relative merits of various research methods and what should count as evidence in research in mathematics education (Carnine & Gersten, 2000; Lester & Wiliam, 2000). In particular, Carnine and Gersten (2000) call for greater use of well-controlled quantitative experimental studies in mathematics education.

However, as Cline and Mandinach (1999) point out, experiments in schools involve many more variables than laboratory experiments; and schools are more complicated settings than laboratories. In some schools it is impossible to control all the prior, independent, intervening, and outcome variables. In other cases, even though the experimenter believes he or she has controlled all the significant variables, circumstances during the school year undermine the research design. For instance, classes that were supposed to be kept intact have students move in and out during the year, teachers' assignments are changed, the teacher of the comparison class decides to use some features of the new curriculum, and so on.

Although most studies in this book are not true experiments with random assignment to groups, most research studies reported in this book use quantitative methods to report achievement of students using *Standards*-based and traditional materials. Thus, in every chapter the reader will note references to mean scores on pretests or posttests or to the percent of students who got a particular item correct. However, in some chapters, authors also report results from qualitative studies. For instance, Carter and his colleagues report on classroom interactions of students and their teacher. Lott and his colleagues and Webb report comments of students about the instructional materials used.

Comparability of Groups

In order to conclude that end-of-year differences in students' mathematics achievement can be attributed to differences in the mathematics programs used in their classes, one must know whether or not students' knowledge of mathematics was comparable at the beginning of the year. Many researchers suggest that random assignment of students and teachers to treatments will ensure groups of equal ability (Campbell & Stanley, 1963; Carnine & Gersten, 2000).

The studies reported in this book all make use of comparison groups, but most do not involve random assignment of students to classes. Beyond first grade, random assignment of students to classes is not possible in most schools. In the early grades, administrators and teachers often use reading proficiency and social skills to determine assignments to classes. In later grades, students' participation in singleton courses such as band, creative writing, or foreign language, as well as prior achievement in mathematics, determines what section of a mathematics course a student might take.

Virtually all authors of chapters in this book report how investigators tried to control for possible initial differences in prerequisite knowledge of mathematics. For instance, Senk reports studies in which classes of students were tested for prerequisite knowledge, and if and when the pretest scores of classes did not match, those classes were eliminated from the study. Both Ridgway and his colleagues and Lott and his colleagues used an analysis of covariance as a statistical technique to adjust for initial differences in students' prerequisite knowledge.

When no comparison groups could be found, researchers used data from national or international studies for comparison. Hirsch and Schoen compare the achievement of students using Course 3 of the Core-Plus curriculum to that of a sample from the 1992 NAEP. Senk reports data comparing the achievement of students using the UCSMP *Precalculus and Discrete Mathematics* textbook to the achievement of students in the U.S. precalculus and calculus samples of the SIMS.

Fidelity of Treatment

The extent to which a curriculum is used in the way it was intended is sometimes called the fidelity of the treatment. Each of the projects whose work is described in this book had to attend to this issue.

Certainly, one cannot expect all teachers to use a particular set of instructional materials in exactly the same way. Although the *intended curriculum* is embodied in the instructional materials and curriculum guide given to the teacher, as Ball and Cohen note, "the *enacted curriculum* is actually jointly constructed by teachers, students, and materials in particular contexts" (1996, p. 7; italics not in original).

In this book many authors, including Battistich and colleagues, Romberg and Shafer, Hirsch and Schoen, and Cichon and Ellis, report on how they visited classrooms, or how they asked teachers to complete surveys or keep diaries about their teaching during the year. Such data enable investigators not only to determine the fidelity of the treatment but also to look for explanations of what instructional practices might account for observed differences in students' achievement. In many cases, space limitations do not allow authors to provide much detail about the enacted curriculum. However, readers interested in this issue are encouraged to consult the research reports cited at the end of each chapter or at the end of this book for explanations of how teachers may have supplemented, omitted, or adapted the instructional materials used in a particular study.

How To Measure Students' Achievement

The instruments used to measure the outcomes of a research study must be consistent with the questions posed initially by the investigator. Thus, if the only outcome of interest to an investigator is students' computational skill, the instruments used need only test computational skill. However, a test of computational skill is not an appropriate instrument to answer questions about students' acquisition of concepts or students' abilities to solve multistep problems set in realistic contexts. Investigators studying the effects of the 12 sets of instructional materials described in this book raised questions about students' achievement in multiple domains. Thus, it was necessary to use multiple instruments.

To satisfy the public's interest in students' performance on standardized tests, many authors report scores on such tests, including the Iowa Test of Basic Skills in elementary grades and the PSAT or SAT in high school. However, standardized tests give only a limited picture of what students know about mathematics (Kilpatrick, 1999; Romberg & Wilson, 1992). Thus, in each section here, authors also report results of students' achievement on other instruments that more accurately measure other intended outcomes, such as the ability to solve open-ended problems. Mokros, Carroll and Isaacs, Ridgway and colleagues, and Hirsch and Schoen report results on instruments developed by other researchers to measure conceptual understanding or problem solving in other domains. Battistich and his colleagues, Lott and his colleagues, and Senk report on instruments developed by their own

projects' staffs when no suitable instruments for measuring a particular outcome could be found.

Whenever instruments are used to compare the achievement of two or
more groups, one should raise the question of whether or not the instruments are fair to each group. For instance, to what extent are students' test
results influenced by the opportunity to learn provided by their curriculum
and teacher? How do gender or social class influence test performance?
A few authors deal with the fairness issue explicitly; most leave it unstated—
an issue for the reader to ponder.

USING THE RESEARCH ON STUDENT OUTCOMES

For more than 150 years concerned citizens in the United States have raised
questions about the mathematical performance of students in school. In the
1980s the desire to improve students' mathematics achievement led professional organizations to publish recommendations about what mathematics
to teach in school and how to teach it. Among the most influential of the
documents advocating reform in school mathematics education during this
period was the *Curriculum and Evaluation Standards for School Mathematics* published by the NCTM in 1989. This so-called *Standards* document influenced
curriculum frameworks developed by state and local education authorities,
funding priorities at the NSF, and the development of textbooks and other
instructional materials.

In this volume we bring together information about 12 *Standards*-based
mathematics materials development projects. In so doing, we hope to provide insights into both the process of doing research about the impact of
mathematics curricula on achievement, and the results of that research.
We hope that insights into both the process and results of research will
help mathematicians, educators, parents, and other interested citizens make
sense of debates about the direction of school mathematics, and to evaluate
current and future proposals for mathematics curriculum reform in schools.

The following chapters paint a first picture of the mathematics achievement that occurs when *Standards*-based curriculum materials are used in
schools. Note that in each of the chapters about a particular set of *Standards*-
based instructional materials, the new curriculum is compared with a more
traditional curriculum. Notice that none of the research that is reported in
this book compares one *Standards*-based curriculum with another.

Although each study described in this book may have its own limitations,
readers are encouraged to consider the results across studies. If the results
across studies are similar, regardless of research paradigm or differences
in controls, then perhaps the message about achievement results can be
considered robust.

Choosing, using, and evaluating instructional materials involves deciding what goals are most important and figuring out which materials and instructional practices are most likely to help students achieve those goals. As Hiebert (1999) points out, decisions about which materials to use or which teaching methods to employ often involve taking into account *values*, as well as empirical *facts*. For instance, if researchers find that students using two different sets of instructional materials perform differently on some mathematical tasks, the people charged with choosing instructional materials for a school or district will have to decide how important that difference in students' performance is to *them*.

In the following chapters of this book we present facts about student outcomes. We hope that this presentation of facts will also help readers clarify their values about what mathematics is most important for students to learn in school. When parents, educators, mathematicians, business leaders, and other interested citizens have accurate facts and well-articulated values, we can have reasoned dialogue about the direction of school mathematics education in the future.

REFERENCES

Addington, S., & Roitman, J. (1996). Who is Dick Askey and why is he so upset about the Standards? *Mathematics Teacher, 89,* 626–627.

Andersen, N. (1998, December 11). State school board oks back to basics for math. *Los Angeles Times,* p. A1.

Ball, D., & Cohen, D. (1996). Reform by the book: What is—or might be—the role of curriculum materials in teacher learning and instructional reform? *Educational Researcher, 25,* 6–8, 14.

Begle, E. G. (Ed.). (1970). *Mathematics education: The sixty-ninth yearbook of the National Society for the Study of Education.* Chicago: The National Society for the Study of Education.

Begle, E. G. (1973). Lessons learned from SMSG. *Mathematics Teacher, 66,* 207–214.

Bogdan, R. C., & Biklen, S. K. (1982). *Qualitative research for education: An introduction to theory and methods.* Boston: Allyn & Bacon.

Borg, W. R., & Gall, M. D. (1987). *Educational research: An introduction* (4th ed.). New York: Longman.

Caldwell, O. W., & Courtis, S. A. (1925). *Then and now in education, 1845–1923: A message of encouragement from the past to the present.* Yonkers-on-Hudson, NY: World Book.

Campbell, D. T., & Stanley, J. (1963). *Experimental and quasi-experimental designs for research.* Chicago: Rand McNally.

Carnine, D., & Gersten, R. (2000). The nature and roles of research in improving achievement in mathematics. *Journal for Research in Mathematics Education, 31,* 138–143.

Chaddock, G. R. (2000, May 23). In math education, who decides what works best? *The Christian Science Monitor,* p. 14.

Clayton, M. (2000a, May 16). If this is math, then we're at war. *The Christian Science Monitor,* p. 16.

Clayton, M. (2000b, May 23). How a new math program rose to the top. *The Christian Science Monitor,* p. 15.

Cline, H. F., & Mandinach, E. B. (1999). The corruption of a research design: A case study of a curriculum innovation project. In R. Lesh & A. Kelly (Eds.), *Handbook of research design in mathematics and science education* (pp. 169–189). Mahwah, NJ: Lawrence Erlbaum Associates.

Colvin, R. L. (2000, March 17). Debate over how to teach math takes a cultural turn. *Los Angeles Times*, p. A1.

Committee on the Function of Mathematics in General Education of the Commission on the Secondary School Curriculum of the Progressive Education Association. (1940). *Mathematics in general education*. New York: Appleton-Century.

Council of Chief State School Officers. (1995). *State curriculum frameworks in mathematics and science: How are they changing across the states?* Washington, DC: Author.

Davis, R., Maher, C., & Noddings, N. (Eds.). (1990). Constructivist views on teaching and learning mathematics. *Journal for Research in Mathematics Education* (Monograph Series No. 4). Reston, VA: National Council of Teachers of Mathematics.

Dewey, J. (1916). *Democracy and education*. New York: Macmillan.

Dewey, J. (1933). *How we think*. Lexington, MA: Heath.

Directorate for Education and Human Resources, National Science Foundation. (1991). *Instructional materials for secondary school mathematics, program solicitation and guidelines*. Washington, DC: National Science Foundation.

Dossey, J., & Usiskin, Z. (2000). *Mathematics education in the United States 2000*. Reston, VA: National Council of Teachers of Mathematics.

Ferrini-Mundy, J. (2000). The standards movement in mathematics education: Reflections and hopes. In M. J. Burke & F. R. Curcio (Eds.), *Learning mathematics for a new century* (pp. 37–50). Reston, VA: National Council of Teachers of Mathematics.

Ferrini-Mundy, J., & Schram, T. (1997). The recognizing and recording reform in mathematics education project: Insights, issues, and implications. *Journal for Research in Mathematics Education* (Monograph Series No. 8). Reston, VA: National Council of Teachers of Mathematics.

Greeno, J. (1997). Theories and practices of thinking and learning to think. *American Journal of Education, 106*, 85–106.

Grouws, D. A., & Cebulla, K. J. (2000). Elementary and middle school mathematics at the crossroads. In T. Good & M. Early (Eds.), *American education: Yesterday, today and tomorrow* (pp. 209–255). Chicago: University of Chicago Press.

Hartocollis, A. (2000, April 27). The new, flexible math meets parental rebellion. *The New York Times*, p. A1.

Hiebert, J. (1999). Relationships between research and the NCTM Standards. *Journal for Research in Mathematics Education, 30*, 3–19.

Jones, P. S., & Coxford, Jr., A. F. (1970). Mathematics in the evolving schools. In P. S. Jones & A. F. Coxford, Jr. (Eds.), *A history of mathematics education in the United States and Canada* (pp. 11–89). Washington, DC: National Council of Teachers of Mathematics.

Judd, C. H. (1927). *Psychological analysis of the fundamentals of arithmetic* (Supplementary Educational Monographs No. 32). Chicago: University of Chicago Press.

Judd, C. H. (1928). The fallacy of treating school subjects as "tool subjects." In J. R. Clark & W. D. Reeve (Eds.), *Selected topics in the teaching of mathematics* (Third Yearbook of the National Council of Teachers of Mathematics) (pp. 1–10). New York: Columbia University, Bureau of Publications.

Kelly, A. E., & Lesh, R. A. (1999). *Handbook of research design in mathematics and science education*. Mahwah, NJ: Lawrence Erlbaum Associates.

Kilpatrick, J. (1992a). "America is likewise bestirring herself": A century of mathematics education as viewed from the United States. In I. Wirszup & R. Streit (Eds.), *Developments in school mathematics around the world* (pp. 133–146). Reston, VA: National Council of Teachers of Mathematics.

Kilpatrick, J. (1992b). A history of research in mathematics education. In D. A. Grouws (Ed.), *Handbook of research on mathematics teaching and learning* (pp. 3–38). New York: Macmillan.

Kilpatrick, J. (1997). Confronting reform. *American Mathematical Monthly, 104*, 955–962.

Kilpatrick, J. (1999). The role of research in improving school mathematics. Paper presented at the Joint Meetings of the American Mathematical Society and the Mathematical Association of America, San Antonio, TX.

Kilpatrick, J., & Stanic, G. M. (1995). Paths to the present. In I. M. Carl (Ed.), *Prospects for school mathematics* (pp. 3–17). Reston, VA: National Council of Teachers of Mathematics.

Klein, D., & Milgram, R. J. (1999, September 17). L.A.'s math program just doesn't add up. *Los Angeles Times*, p. B7.

Kline, M. (1973). *Why Johnny can't add: The failure of the new math.* New York: St. Martin's Press.

Lappan, G., & Briars, D. (1995). How should mathematics be taught? In I. M. Carl (Ed.), *Prospects for school mathematics* (pp. 131–156). Reston, VA: National Council of Teachers of Mathematics.

Lester, F. K., & Wiliam, D. (2000). The evidential basis for knowledge claims in mathematics education research. *Journal for Research in Mathematics Education, 31*, 130–137.

Mathematics and Science Expert Panel. (1999). *Exemplary and promising mathematics programs.* Washington, DC: U.S. Department of Education.

Maurer, S. (2000). College entrance mathematics in the year 2000—What came true? *Mathematics Teacher, 93*, 455–459.

Mayer, R. (2001). Changing conceptions of learning: A century of progress. In L. Corno (Ed.), *Education across a century: The centennial volume* (pp. 34–75). Chicago: University of Chicago Press.

McKnight, C., Crosswhite, F. J., Dossey, J., Kifer, E., Swafford, J. O., Travers, K. J., & Cooney, T. J. (1987). *The underachieving curriculum: Assessing U.S. school mathematics from an international perspective.* Champaign, IL: Stipes.

McLellan, J., & Dewey, J. (1895). *The psychology of number.* New York: Appleton.

McLeod, D. B., Stake, R. E., Schappelle, B. P., Mellissinos, M., & Gierl, M. J. (1996). Setting the standards: NCTM's role in the reform of mathematics education. In S. A. Raizen & E. D. Britton (Eds.), *Bold ventures: Vol. 3. Case studies of U.S. innovations in mathematics education* (pp. 13–132). Boston: Kluwer.

National Commission on Excellence in Education. (1983). *A nation at risk: The imperative for educational reform.* Washington, DC: U.S. Government Printing Office.

National Council of Supervisors of Mathematics. (1977). Position paper on basic skills. *Arithmetic Teacher, 25*(1), 19–22.

National Council of Teachers of Mathematics. (1980). *An agenda for action.* Reston, VA: Author.

National Council of Teachers of Mathematics. (1989). *Curriculum and evaluation standards for school mathematics.* Reston, VA: Author.

National Council of Teachers of Mathematics. (1991). *Professional standards for teaching mathematics.* Reston, VA: Author.

National Council of Teachers of Mathematics. (1995). *Assessment standards for school mathematics.* Reston, VA: Author.

National Council of Teachers of Mathematics. (2000). *Principles and standards for school mathematics.* Reston, VA: Author.

National Education Association. (1893). *Report of the committee on secondary school studies.* Washington, DC: Author.

O'Brien, T. C. (1999). Parrot math. *Phi Delta Kappan, 80*, 434–438.

Olson, L. (2000). Opening the doors. In *Lessons of a century: A nation's schools come of age* (pp. 1–31). Bethesda, MD: Editorial Projects in Education.

Osborne, A. R., & Crosswhite, F. J. (1970). Forces and issues related to curriculum and instruction, 7–12. In P. S. Jones & A. F. Coxford, Jr. (Eds.), *A history of mathematics education in the United States and Canada* (pp. 155–297). Washington, DC: National Council of Teachers of Mathematics.

Patton, M. Q. (1980). *Qualitative evaluation methods.* Beverly Hills, CA: Sage.

Riley, R. W. (2000, January 6). Letter of response to the open letter in *The Washington Post*. Available: http://www.ed.gov/News/Letters/000106.html.

Robinson, E. E., Robinson, M. F., & Maceli, J. C. (2000). The impact of Standards-based instructional materials in mathematics in the classroom. In M. J. Burke & F. R. Curcio (Eds.), *Learning mathematics for a new century* (pp. 112–126). Reston, VA: National Council of Teachers of Mathematics.

Romberg, T. A. (1992). Perspectives on scholarship and research methods. In D. A. Grouws (Ed.), *Handbook of research on teaching and learning mathematics* (pp. 49–64). New York: Macmillan.

Romberg, T. A., & Collins, A. (1999). The impact of standards-based reform on methods of research in schools. In R. Lesh & A. Kelly (Eds.), *Handbook of research design in mathematics and science education* (pp. 73–85). Mahwah, NJ: Lawrence Erlbaum Associates.

Romberg, T. A., & Wilson, L. D. (1992). Alignment of tests with the standards. *Arithmetic Teacher, 40*, 18–22.

Schoenfeld, A. H. (1994). A discourse on methods. *Journal for Research in Mathematics Education, 25*, 697–710.

Schoenfeld, A. H. (2001). Mathematics education in the 20th century. In L. Corno (Ed.), *Education across a century: The centennial volume* (pp. 239–278). Chicago: University of Chicago Press.

Schulte, B. (1999, October 17). Divided on Connected Math: For some parents and experts, curriculum doesn't add up. *The Washington Post*, p. 1.

Scriven, M. (1967). The methodology of evaluation. *Perspectives on curriculum evaluation* (AERA Monograph Series on Curriculum Evaluation, No. 1, pp. 39–83). Chicago: Rand McNally.

Thorndike, E. L. (1922). *The psychology of arithmetic*. New York: Macmillan.

Usiskin, Z. (1985). We need another revolution in secondary school mathematics. In C. R. Hirsch (Ed.), *The secondary school mathematics curriculum* (pp. 1–21). Reston, VA: National Council of Teachers of Mathematics.

Usiskin, Z. (1999, Winter). Which curriculum is best? *UCSMP Newsletter, 24*, 3–10.

Willoughby, S. S. (2000). Perspectives on mathematics education. In M. J. Burke & F. R. Curcio (Eds.), *Learning mathematics for a new century* (pp. 1–15). Reston, VA: National Council of Teachers of Mathematics.

Worthen, B. R., & Sanders, J. R. (1987). *Educational evaluation: Alternative approaches and practical guidelines*. White Plains, NY: Longman.

Wu, H. (1997). The mathematics education reform: Why you should be concerned and what you can do. *American Mathematical Monthly, 104*, 946–954.

ENDNOTES

1. Usiskin (1999) found that during 1995 and 1996 less than 2% of the research studies reported in the *Journal for Research in Mathematics Education* were about the effects of textbooks. Both Usiskin and Ball and Cohen (1996) call for more research on the effects of textbooks.

2. Technically, *textbooks* are special types of *instructional materials*. A textbook is a set of instructional material bound in a single book for use by students. In the United States, school mathematics textbooks typically are designed for a single academic year of study. Other types of instructional materials include modules containing smaller amounts of mathematical content, workbooks in which students can write their solutions to problems, and computer software to be used as a tool for solving problems. In many mathematics classrooms, teachers use a textbook and additional instructional materials. Despite the technical distinction between textbooks and instructional materials, many people use the terms synonymously.

Sometimes people also use the term *curriculum* synonymously with textbook or instructional materials. We use the term *curriculum* to refer to the mathematical content of the textbook or instructional materials. However, even this word has many meanings. The mathematical content specified in a set of recommendations or in a set of instructional materials can be viewed as the *intended curriculum*. The mathematical content actually studied in an individual classroom can be viewed as the *enacted curriculum*. The mathematical content actually learned by the students can be viewed as the *achieved curriculum*.

3. Jones and Coxford (1970, p. 27) report that algebra was first required for entrance into Harvard in 1820, Yale in 1847, and Princeton in 1848. Geometry was first required for entrance into Yale in 1865; Cornell, Michigan, and Princeton in 1868; and Harvard in 1870.

4. Dossey and Usiskin (2000) list 27 reports on school mathematics issued by professional organizations or national commissions between the years 1890 and 2000.

5. The NCTM is a professional organization of mathematics teachers founded in 1920. At the end of the 20th century, most of its members taught in elementary, middle, or high schools. However, a large minority worked in colleges or universities, state or local educational agencies, or in research, publishing, or test development.

6. In April of 2000 the NCTM published a fourth Standards document, *Principles and Standards for School Mathematics* (PSSM). This volume updates recommendations about curriculum made in the *Curriculum and Evaluation Standards for School Mathematics* (NCTM, 1989). Because PSSM was published after the research reported in this volume was conducted, we do not discuss it here.

7. For a detailed history of the development of the *Curriculum and Evaluation Standards*, see McLeod, Stake, Schappelle, Mellissinos, and Gierl (1996).

8. The UCSMP Secondary Component, with funding from the Amoco Foundation and others, had begun working on a mathematics curriculum for Grades 7–12 prior to the publication of the *Curriculum and Evaluation Standards*. During the years of the Gateways Conferences, staff of the UCSMP Secondary Component worked on a second edition of UCSMP materials.

9. Some NSF-funded projects listed in Table 1.1 were funded to conduct formal evaluation studies of the instructional materials, but others were not.

10. Some useful resources for evaluation and research are Bogdan and Biklen (1982), Borg and Gall (1983), Kelly and Lesh (1999), Patton (1980), Scriven (1967), and Worthen and Sanders (1987).

PART II

Elementary Grades
Curriculum Projects

2

Elementary School Mathematics Curriculum Reform

Denisse R. Thompson
University of South Florida

Sharon L. Senk
Michigan State University

This part of the book reports research on what students know and are able to do when they study from *Standards*-based elementary school mathematics curricula. To place the research and development done by these curriculum projects in context, this chapter describes the typical elementary mathematics curriculum in the 1980s, and it reports results from both national and international studies of mathematics achievement of elementary students at that time. This chapter also summarizes the recommendations for Grades K–4 in the *Curriculum and Evaluation Standards for School Mathematics* (National Council of Teachers of Mathematics, 1989). It closes with a description of efforts by the National Science Foundation to fund the development of instructional materials for the elementary grades that would seek to implement the reform recommendations.

THE ELEMENTARY SCHOOL MATHEMATICS CURRICULUM

Most mathematics in elementary schools takes place in so-called self-contained classrooms, where one teacher gives instruction in language arts, mathematics, science, and social studies. Unlike middle schools or high schools where a master schedule dictates how many minutes each class meets per week, in elementary schools the teacher has more flexibility in determining how much time to spend on mathematics. Elementary teachers also determine what is taught in school (Porter, Floden, Freeman, Schmidt, & Schwille, 1988, p. 96).

Several bodies of research give insights into the curricula and instructional practices used in elementary classrooms in the decade prior to the publication of the *Curriculum and Evaluation Standards*. In 1987 Weiss reported the results of a 1985–1986 national survey of more than 600 elementary school teachers about their instructional practices. In 1988 Porter and his colleagues summarized a series of studies they had conducted during the late 1970s and 1980s that collected both survey data and data from in-class observations.

Weiss reported that the average amount of time spent per day on mathematics was approximately 40 minutes in Grades K–3 and 50 minutes in Grades 4–6. Porter and his colleagues found large variations in the allocation of time devoted to mathematics. Some classes averaged as little as 20 minutes per day (Porter et al., 1988, p. 106).

Porter et al. found that elementary teachers spent approximately 75% of their mathematics time teaching computational skills. The remaining time was distributed between teaching conceptual understanding or applications of mathematics. Teachers tended to cover a large number of topics in the time not devoted to computation. Seventy to eighty percent of the topics taught during the school year received 30 minutes or less of instructional time. Students were rarely ever asked to formulate a problem for themselves (Porter et al., 1988, p. 106).

Weiss' survey asked teachers to indicate the degree to which they emphasized certain objectives in their mathematics classes. The most heavily emphasized objective was to "know mathematical facts, principles, algorithms, or procedures," supported by 81% of the K–6 teachers. Other heavily emphasized objectives (emphasized by at least 70% of teachers) were to perform computations with speed and accuracy, to develop a systematic approach to problem solving, and to become aware of the importance of mathematics in daily life (Weiss, 1987, p. 44). In contrast, only about half of the teachers in Grades K–6 emphasized developing inquiry skills or learning to communicate mathematical ideas effectively.

The findings by Porter et al. and by Weiss support Lambdin Kroll's (1989) observation that instruction in elementary mathematics classrooms in the 1980s showed strong evidence for both the drill and practice advocated by the behaviorists and the work with meaning and applications advocated by the progressives. The findings do not suggest strong support by K–6 teachers for objectives valued by the developers of the new math of the 1960s.

Elementary school teachers reported using a variety of classroom activities every day, including lectures and discussions with the whole class, work in small groups, and individual work. The individual work by students was usually seatwork assigned from the textbook. Approximately 63% of teachers in Grades K–3 and approximately 31% of teachers in Grades 4–6 reported using hands on, manipulative, or laboratory equipment in the class that was surveyed (Weiss, 1987, p. 49).

More than 90% of the K–6 teachers said they used a published textbook for teaching mathematics. Of those using mathematics textbooks, most teachers reported covering the majority of the book: 39% of K–6 teachers said they covered 75% to 90% of their mathematics textbooks, and 50% of the teachers said they covered at least 90% (Weiss, 1987, pp. 31, 39). However, the studies conducted by Porter and colleagues found that elementary school teachers viewed their mathematics textbooks as resources to be drawn from and added to as seems appropriate. Porter et al. (1988) claimed that "most teachers cover only a fraction of their textbook's content" (p. 102). The apparent contradiction between the two studies may be due to differences in the questions the researchers asked. In Weiss' study, the teachers estimated the amount of the textbook they planned to cover. In contrast, Porter et al. asked teachers to go through the text and tell what they covered or to keep a log of content coverage throughout the year.

In addition to examining classroom practices, Porter and his colleagues analyzed the content of four widely used fourth-grade mathematics textbooks. They found that 19 topics formed the core curriculum in all four texts; approximately half the exercises in each book were focused on those topics. The other parts of the books were idiosyncratic in their topic coverage, suggesting that in the 1980s there was considerable variation in what was defined to be fourth-grade mathematics (Porter et al., 1988, p. 97).

Flanders (1987) analyzed the content of three popular series of mathematics textbooks for Grades K–8 to determine the extent to which the content taught in each grade was *new*. He found that on average approximately 75% of the content was new in first grade (that is, it was not in the book for kindergarten). In Grades 2–6 roughly 40% to 65% of the pages contained new content, which was "an equivalent of new material two or three days a week" (p. 20). On average, the first half of the books for Grades 1–8 had 35% new content, whereas the second half of the books had 60% new topics (pp. 20–22). Flanders (1987) concluded that

> The net result is that early in the year, when students are more likely to be eager to study, they repeat what they have seen before. Later on, when they are sufficiently bored, they see new material—if they get to the end of the book. (p. 22)

ELEMENTARY STUDENTS' ACHIEVEMENT
ON THE NATIONAL ASSESSMENT
OF EDUCATIONAL PROGRESS

The Fourth National Assessment of Educational Progress (NAEP) was conducted in 1986. In contrast to the results of the first three assessments, which had been conducted in 1973, 1978, and 1982, the results of the fourth NAEP were widely publicized. Dossey (1989) claims that the media attention given to the fourth NAEP "contributed to the growing awareness of Americans that the emphases in mathematics education needed to shift from the narrow view based on facts and computational procedures to a broader vision of mathematics that recognized the importance of problem solving" (p. vii).

To allow for a study of trends over time, the NAEP administered a number of secure items to 9-year-old students, as this was the age at which earlier NAEP assessments occurred. For the fourth NAEP, elementary assessments were also administered at Grade 3, with roughly 18,000 third-grade students participating in the assessment.

The trend data showed that "the overall performance of 9-year-olds, which had showed little change from 1973 to 1982, improved significantly between 1982 and 1986" (Carpenter & Lindquist, 1989, p. 160). In analyzing levels of proficiency, the NAEP found that 98% of 9-year-old students were at or above the level at which they know basic addition and subtraction facts, can add two-digit numbers without regrouping, and can identify addition and subtraction situations. At this age, 74% were at or above the level at which they had beginning skills and understandings, meaning that they have "considerable understanding of two-digit numbers. They [students] can add two-digit numbers, but are still developing an ability to regroup in subtraction. They know some basic multiplication and division facts, recognize relations among coins, can read information from charts and graphs, and use simple measurement instruments" (Dossey, Mullis, Lindquist, & Chambers, 1989, p. 118). Only 0.6% of 9-year-old students were able to deal with moderately complex problems involving computations with decimals and fractions.

At the third grade, the NAEP assessed students' achievement in seven broad content areas: numbers and operations; fundamental methods of mathematics; discrete mathematics; data organization and interpretation; measurement; geometry; and relations, functions, and algebraic expressions (Carpenter, 1989, p. 1). Kouba, Carpenter, and Swafford (1989) report the results of students' use of whole numbers. Specifically, "over 80 percent of the 3rd-grade students could perform simple two-digit addition and subtraction computation with whole numbers, but fewer than half of them were successful in problems with more than two addends" (p. 65). Further, "about 60

percent of the 3rd-grade students were successful on two items involving pic-
torical representations of multiplication" (p. 69). In addition, "a little over
half of the 3rd-grade students could do the simpler multiplication problem
[31 × 3], but only about one in ten could correctly multiply a three-digit
number by a two-digit number [213 × 12]" (p. 72). Also, they report that students at the elementary grades "were more successful on one-step word problems containing whole numbers than on two-step word problems. Students
generally tried to solve two-step problems by using only one step" (p. 65).

In other content areas, Kouba et al. (1989) report that "slightly more than
half of the 3rd-grade students could identify what fractional part of a figure
was shaded [See Fig. 2.1]" (p. 79). Lindquist and Kouba (1989) report that
approximately 60% of 3rd-grade students could select the unit to measure
the length of a pen but only 35% could select the unit to measure the length
of a house.

Which show 3/4 of the picture shaded?

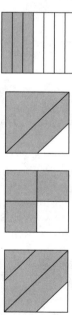

FIG. 2.1. Third-grade NAEP item dealing with fractions. *Note.*
From *Results from the Fourth Mathematics Assessment of the
National Assessment of Educational Progress* (p. 80), by M. M.
Lindquist (Ed.), Reston, VA: National Council of Teachers of Math-
ematics. ©1989 by National Council of Teachers of Mathematics.
Reprinted with permission. All rights reserved.

The results of the 1986 NAEP revealed that many concepts and skills had been learned at a superficial level. Despite improvement in overall achievement, Carpenter and Lindquist (1989) caution against complacency because of the deficiencies in understanding highlighted by the NAEP results:

> The emphasis on computational skills that has generally characterized mathematics instruction has left many students with serious gaps in their knowledge of underlying concepts. As a result, students have not learned many advanced skills and frequently they cannot apply the skills they have learned. Moreover, the skills they have learned are in danger of becoming obsolete as technological advances alter the mathematics that adults need to function productively in society. Students' lack of flexibility in applying the mathematics they have learned may leave them unable to adapt to these demands. (p. 169)

Furthermore, results of surveys from teachers and students found that "mathematics instruction in 1986, as in previous years, continues to be dominated by teacher explanations, chalkboard presentations, and reliance on textbooks and workbooks. More innovative forms of instruction—such as involving small group activities, laboratory work, and special projects—remain disappointingly rare" (Dossey, Mullis, Lindquist, & Chambers, 1988, p. 10).

CROSS-CULTURAL COMPARISONS OF MATHEMATICS IN ELEMENTARY SCHOOLS

Between the time of the second and fourth NAEP, two sets of international comparisons directed by Professor Harold Stevenson at the University of Michigan shed additional light on the state of mathematics achievement in elementary schools. In the first study, conducted in 1978–1979, a representative sample of first- and fifth-grade classrooms in Sendai, Japan and Taipei, Taiwan was compared with a similar sample from the Minneapolis metropolitan area. Achievement on individually administered items in Grade 1 slightly favored the Asian students. However, by Grade 5, the Asian advantage was huge. On a test of mathematics achievement covering arithmetic computation and geometry, Stevenson, Lee, and Stigler (1986) reported that the highest scoring U. S. fifth-grade classroom did not score as well as the lowest scoring Japanese classroom, and it outperformed only one of 20 Chinese classrooms.

A second study conducted in 1985–1986 compared mathematics achievement in kindergarten, first, and fifth grades in Sendai, Japan and Taipei, Taiwan with a sample from the Chicago metropolitan area. Students were tested on word problems, operations, number concepts, estimation, mental calculation, geometry, graphing, visualization, and mental image transformation. Some preliminary results of this study were given by Stigler and Perry in 1988, with more technical research papers appearing in 1989 and 1990. The results of both the first and second Michigan studies were summarized in Stevenson and Stigler (1992). Overall, the achievement of Japanese children was higher than that of American children beginning as early as kindergarten, and the gap between their achievement widened as students passed to higher grades. The achievement of the Chinese students was similar to that of American students in kindergarten; but by Grade 5 the Chinese students also achieved significantly higher scores than the Americans.

Stigler and Perry (1988) reported large cross-cultural differences in the beliefs held by parents, teachers, and children about the nature of mathematics learning. Differences in beliefs about academic expectations might help us to understand how gaps between the mathematics achievement of American and Asian children develop. For instance, in the study by Stevenson et al. (1986) mentioned earlier, U. S. mothers were significantly more likely than Japanese mothers to believe that ability (as opposed to effort) underlies children's success in elementary mathematics. As Stigler and Perry point out, "if innate ability is believed to determine success in mathematics, then there are always limits on what one could expect a particular child to achieve in school mathematics" (1988, p. 196).

Other studies have identified substantial differences in the grade placement of mathematics topics. U. S. elementary textbooks of the 1980s introduced large numbers at a slower pace than did books from Japan, China, or the Soviet Union. They also delayed the introduction of regrouping in addition and subtraction considerably longer than did books from the other countries (Fuson, Stigler, & Bartsch, 1988). The fact that children in other countries do so well with curricula that are more demanding than ours suggests that our beliefs about curricula might also be questioned.

Different cultures also have different beliefs about the best methods for teaching. For example, many U. S. teachers believe that young children need concrete experiences in order to understand mathematics, and some even believe that concrete experience will automatically lead to understanding. In contrast, Japanese teachers seem to believe that concrete experience must be accompanied by reflection in order for understanding to follow (Stigler & Perry, 1988, p. 197). During the 1980s, expert mathematics teachers in the United States were believed to be those who could "get though 40 problems in a single class" (Stigler & Perry, 1988, p. 215). However, in elementary mathematics classes in China and Japan, teachers often spent an entire 40-minute mathematics class on the solution of only one, two, or three problems. Stigler and Perry hypothesize that by discussing fewer problems during a class period, Asian teachers are able to develop greater coherence in their lessons and that this, in turn, leads to greater comprehension by students.[1]

ADDITIONAL RESEARCH ON ELEMENTARY STUDENTS' MATHEMATICS LEARNING

In many areas the research base concerning mathematics learning in elementary school is extensive and deep; in others it is still in its infancy. Much is known about how young children learn addition and subtraction; less is known about the learning of multiplication and division, geometry, and statistics. Space does not permit a thorough review here of the research on the mathematical capabilities of elementary school children. In this section we review selected studies that seem to have been particularly influential in the development of the curriculum projects whose work is examined in this book.

Although the results of the NAEP and the international studies painted a somewhat grim picture of the capabilities of elementary children on tasks beyond low-level ones, results from other research studies suggested that young children were capable of much more higher-order thinking in mathematics than was often assumed. For instance, cognitive research conducted at the University of Wisconsin has shown that young children can analyze and solve simple addition and subtraction word problems by using their own informal modeling and counting strategies (Carpenter, Hiebert, & Moser, 1983; Carpenter & Moser, 1982). Furthermore, when appropriate tools are available, children can solve word problems beyond their expected level of ability (Carpenter & Moser, 1984). Peterson (1988, p. 7) pointed out that the traditional mathematics curriculum has been based on the assumption that computational skills must be learned before children are taught to solve even the simplest word problems. However, she claims that the research by Carpenter and his colleagues suggests that word problems should form the basis for the mathematics curriculum.

Peterson's own work (cited in her 1988 chapter) has established the effectiveness of various small-group learning techniques to help students learn elementary mathematics. She claims that small groups are effective because they increase opportunities for students to learn different strategies for solving problems. Also, by explaining to others why an answer is incorrect, students deepen their own understanding.

In the late 1980s Carpenter, Fennema, and Peterson developed an instructional model called Cognitively Guided Instruction (CGI) for first-grade teachers, based on increased emphases on the following classroom practices:

- building on the informal knowledge base first-grade students bring to school as active learners and "constructors" of knowledge;
- teaching meaning of addition and subtraction concepts and using students' understanding of problems to build competence with number facts;
- encouraging students to use and verbalize specific strategies, such as "counting on" or "derived facts" to solve word problems (Peterson, 1988, pp. 22–23).

In the 1990s a large body of research would show that teachers' use of the CGI approach led to improved problem solving and higher-order thinking by students in early elementary grades.

Furthermore, Kamii (1985) demonstrated that young children are capable of inventing computational algorithms, and in so doing, they develop greater facility with place value, estimation, and mental computational skills than students who are explicitly taught the traditional algorithms.

NCTM'S RECOMMENDATIONS FOR CURRICULUM CHANGE AT THE ELEMENTARY SCHOOL LEVEL

Similar concerns about mathematics curriculum and instruction at the elementary level were raised in the *Curriculum and Evaluation Standards for School Mathematics*, published by the National Council of Teachers of Mathematics (NCTM, 1989):

> A long-standing preoccupation with computation and other traditional skills has dominated both *what* mathematics is taught and *the way* mathematics is taught at this [elementary] level. As a result, the present K–4 curriculum is narrow in scope; fails to foster mathematical insight, reasoning, and problem solving; and emphasizes rote activities. Even more significant is that children begin to lose their belief that learning mathematics is a sense-making experience. They become passive receivers of rules and procedures rather than active participants in creating knowledge. (p. 15; italics in original)

According to the authors of the NCTM *Standards*, a K–4 curriculum should have three goals. It should "*address the relationship between young children and mathematics*" ... to encourage "the exploration of a wide variety of mathematical ideas in such a way that children retain their enjoyment of, and curiosity about, mathematics." It should also "*recognize the importance of the qualitative dimensions of children's learning*" ... to realize that "how well children come to understand mathematical ideas is far more important than how many skills they acquire." Further, it should "*build beliefs about what mathematics is, about what it means to know and do mathematics, and about children's view of themselves as mathematics learners.*" (NCTM, 1989, pp. 16–17; italics in original)

The actual content of the K–4 *Standards* (NCTM, 1989) is based on six assumptions:

1. *The K–4 curriculum should be conceptually oriented.* . . .
2. *The K–4 curriculum should actively involve children in doing mathematics.* . . .
3. *The K–4 curriculum should emphasize the development of children's mathematical thinking and reasoning abilities.* . . .
4. *The K–4 curriculum should emphasize the application of mathematics.* . . .
5. *The K–4 curriculum should include a broad range of content.* . . .
6. *The K–4 curriculum should make appropriate and ongoing use of calculators and computers.* (pp. 17–19; italics in original)

The goals and assumptions of the authors of the K–4 *Standards* are consistent with a curriculum that would help children understand concepts through exploring, investigating, and communicating mathematics. The curriculum would also help children see the usefulness of mathematics and foster their confidence in their ability to do mathematics.

In addition to four standards that were common across all grade levels (problem solving, communication, reasoning, and connections), nine content standards were also specified:

- Estimation
- Number Sense and Numeration
- Concepts of Whole Number Operations
- Whole Number Computation
- Geometry and Spatial Sense
- Measurement
- Statistics and Probability
- Fractions and Decimals
- Patterns and Relationships

For each standard, specific recommendations were made. For instance, in the Whole Number Computation standard, students were expected to "model, explain, and develop reasonable proficiency with basic facts and algorithms; use a variety of mental computation and estimation techniques; use calculators in appropriate computational situations; and select and use computation techniques appropriate to specific problems and determine whether the results are reasonable" (p. 44).

The K–4 *Standards* recommend decreased attention to "rote practice, rote memorization of rules, one answer and one method, use of worksheets, written practice, and teaching by telling." In contrast, increased attention was to be given to "use of manipulative materials, cooperative work, discussion of mathematics, questioning, justification of thinking, writing about mathematics, problem-solving approach to instruction, content integration, and use of calculators and computers" (pp. 20–21).

THE DEVELOPMENT OF *STANDARDS*-BASED ELEMENTARY MATHEMATICS CURRICULA

The changes advocated by the K–4 *Standards* required that new instructional materials be available to those interested in attempting to reform curriculum. In response to the developments leading to the *Standards*, the National Science Foundation solicited proposals for the development of comprehensive curriculum materials for the elementary grades that would be consistent with recent recommendations to improve the teaching and learning of elementary school mathematics. The first two comprehensive elementary curriculum development projects funded were *Investigations in Data, Number, and Space: An Elementary Mathematics Curriculum* at the Technical Education Research Center (TERC) and *A Modern K–6 Mathematics Curriculum Based on Integrating Mathematics and Science* (currently *Math Trailblazers*) at the University of Illinois at Chicago. Both programs ultimately developed curriculum materials for Grades K–5. Later, two other projects received support: *Everyday Mathematics* at the University of Chicago, and *Cooperative Mathematics Project* (which developed the *Number Power* program) at the Developmental Studies Center in Oakland, CA. *Everyday Mathematics* developed a complete curriculum for Grades K–6. *Number Power* developed a supplementary program for Grades K–6 to replace 30% to 60% of the typical curriculum.

As readers study these four chapters on elementary grades curriculum, they will undoubtedly notice similarities and differences among the chapters, both in their curriculum emphases and in their research emphases. For instance, all discuss basic skills computational facility. Some discuss achievement on content knowledge in geometry or with estimation skills. Still others describe the role of the teacher and classroom discourse. Such commonalities and differences and implications for further research are discussed in Chapter 7 by Ralph Putnam.

REFERENCES

Carpenter, T. P. (1989). Introduction. In M. M. Lindquist (Ed.), *Results from the fourth mathematics assessment of the national assessment of educational progress* (pp. 1–9). Reston, VA: National Council of Teachers of Mathematics.

Carpenter, T. P., Hiebert, J., & Moser, J. M. (1983). The effects of instruction on children's solution of addition and subtraction problems. *Educational Studies in Mathematics, 14*, 56–72.

Carpenter, T. P., & Lindquist, M. M. (1989). Summary and conclusions. In M. M. Lindquist (Ed.), *Results from the fourth mathematics assessment of the national assessment of educational progress* (pp. 160–169). Reston, VA: National Council of Teachers of Mathematics.

Carpenter, T. P., & Moser, J. M. (1982). The acquisition of addition and subtraction concepts. In R. Lesh & M. Landau (Eds.), *The acquisition of mathematical concepts and processes* (pp. 7–14). New York: Academic Press.

Carpenter, T. P., & Moser, J. M. (1984). The acquisition of addition and subtraction concepts in grades one through three. *Journal for Research in Mathematics Education, 15*(3), 179–202.

Dossey, J. A. (1989). Foreword. In M. M. Lindquist (Ed.), *Results from the fourth mathematics assessment of the national assessment of educational progress* (pp. vii–viii). Reston, VA: National Council of Teachers of Mathematics.

Dossey, J. A., Mullis, I. V. S., Lindquist, M. M., & Chambers, D. L. (1988). *The mathematics report card: Are we measuring up?* Princeton, NJ: Educational Testing Service.

Dossey, J. A., Mullis, I. V. S., Lindquist, M. M., & Chambers, D. L. (1989). What can students do? (Levels of mathematics proficiency for the nation and demographic subgroups). In M. M. Lindquist (Ed.), *Results from the fourth mathematics assessment of the national assessment of educational progress* (pp. 117–134). Reston, VA: National Council of Teachers of Mathematics.

Flanders, J. R. (1987). How much of the content in mathematics textbooks is new? *Arithmetic Teacher, 35*, 18–23.

Fuson, K., Stigler, J. W., & Bartsch, K. (1988). Grade placement of addition and subtraction topics in Japan, Mainland China, the Soviet Union, Taiwan, and the United States. *Journal for Research in Mathematics Education, 19*, 449–456.

Kamii, C. K. (1985). *Young children reinvent arithmetic.* New York: Teachers College Press.

Kouba, V. L., Carpenter, T. P., & Swafford, J. O. (1989). Number and operations. In M. M. Lindquist (Ed.), *Results from the fourth mathematics assessment of the national assessment of educational progress* (pp. 64–93). Reston, VA: National Council of Teachers of Mathematics.

Lambdin Kroll, D. (1989). Connections between psychological learning theories and the elementary mathematics curriculum. In P. R. Trafton & A. P. Shulte (Eds.), *New directions for elementary school mathematics* (pp. 199–211). Reston, VA: National Council of Teachers of Mathematics.

Lindquist, M. M., & Kouba, V. L. (1989). Measurement. In M. M. Lindquist (Ed.), *Results from the fourth mathematics assessment of the national assessment of educational progress* (pp. 35–43). Reston, VA: National Council of Teachers of Mathematics.

National Council of Teachers of Mathematics. (1989). *Curriculum and evaluation standards for school mathematics.* Reston, VA: Author.

Peterson, P. L. (1988). Teaching for higher-order thinking in mathematics: The challenge for the next decade. In D. A. Grouws, T. J. Cooney, & D. Jones (Eds.), *Effective mathematics teaching* (pp. 2–26). Reston, VA: National Council of Teachers of Mathematics.

Porter, A., Floden, R., Freeman, D., Schmidt, W., & Schwille, J. (1988). Content determinants of elementary school mathematics. In D. A. Grouws, T. J. Cooney, & D. Jones (Eds.), *Effective mathematics teaching* (pp. 96–113). Reston, VA: National Council of Teachers of Mathematics.

Stevenson, H. W., Lee, S. Y., & Stigler, J. W. (1986). Mathematics achievement of Chinese, Japanese, and American children. *Science, 231*, 693–699.

Stevenson, H. W., & Stigler, J. W. (1992). *The learning gap: why our schools are failing and what we can learn from Japanese and Chinese education.* New York: Summit Books.

Stigler, J., & Hiebert, J. (1999). *The teaching gap: best ideas from the world's teachers for improving education in the classroom.* New York: Free Press.

Stigler, J. W., & Perry, M. (1988). Cross-cultural studies of mathematics teaching and learning: Recent findings and new directions. In D. A. Grouws, T. J. Cooney, & D. Jones (Eds.), *Effective mathematics teaching* (pp. 194–223). Reston, VA: National Council of Teachers of Mathematics.
Weiss, I. R. (1987). *Report of the 1985–86 national survey of science and mathematics education.* Research Triangle Park, NC: Research Triangle Institute.

ENDNOTE

1. This hypothesis was confirmed more recently in studies of teaching practices in Grade 8 mathematics classes in Germany, Japan, and the United States conducted as part of the Third International Mathematics and Science Study (TIMSS). See the *Teaching Gap* by Stigler and Hiebert (1999) for details.

3

Student Learning and Achievement with *Math Trailblazers*

Andy Carter
Roosevelt University

Janet S. Beissinger
University of Illinois at Chicago

Astrida Cirulis
National-Louis University, Chicago

Marty Gartzman
University of Illinois at Chicago

Catherine Randall Kelso
University of Illinois at Chicago

Philip Wagreich
University of Illinois at Chicago

The first edition of *Math Trailblazers: A Mathematical Journey Using Science and Language Arts* was completed in 1997. The roots of this curriculum, however, date back to the late 1970s and the work of Howard Goldberg, a particle physicist at the University of Illinois at Chicago (UIC). Building on the work of Robert Karplus and others, Goldberg developed a framework for adapting the scientific method for elementary school children and applied that framework within a series of elementary laboratory investigations (Goldberg & Boulanger, 1981). Goldberg was joined in 1985 by UIC mathematician Philip Wagreich, and they, together with others, formed the Teaching Integrated Mathematics and Science (TIMS) Project.

Thus, the motivation for TIMS came from two sources, one with roots in science and one with roots in mathematics. The scientific impetus stemmed from the desire to teach science to children in a manner that reflects the practice of scientists. Modern science is fundamentally quantitative; therefore quantitative investigations should play an important role in children's science education. The mathematical impetus was to make mathematics meaningful to all children. Engaging children in quantitative investigations of common phenomena harnesses their curiosity and builds on their understanding of the natural world, to promote the study of rigorous mathematics (Isaacs, Wagreich, & Gartzman, 1997).

Until 1990, TIMS focused primarily on the development and implementation of a series of quantitative, hands-on activities, the TIMS Laboratory Investigations (Goldberg, 1997). The laboratory investigations continue the tradition of Dewey (1910) and others in focusing on the method of science and on exploring a relatively small set of fundamental scientific concepts in depth. To date, more than 140 experiments have been developed. Typically, the laboratory investigations are used as supplemental materials rather than as a full curriculum. Several studies provide evidence that the TIMS Laboratory Investigations are effective in promoting students' development of mathematics and science concepts (Goldberg, 1993; Goldberg & Wagreich, 1990; Teachers Academy for Mathematics and Science, 1995, 1996).

In 1990, the National Science Foundation (NSF) awarded the TIMS Project a grant to develop a comprehensive, elementary reform mathematics curriculum that would build on the foundations of the TIMS Laboratory Investigations.[1] The resulting curriculum, *Math Trailblazers* (Wagreich, Goldberg, & TIMS staff, 1997), is a full mathematics curriculum for kindergarten through fifth grade, with strong connections to science. Schools that select *Math Trailblazers* as their mathematics program may also use it to supplement or supplant part of their existing science program. The materials for Grades 1–3 became commercially available in the spring of 1996; those for Kindergarten and Grades 4–5 were first available in the summer of 1997.

THE CURRICULUM

In developing *Math Trailblazers*, the authors drew on research findings from a wide variety of sources, as well as from the broad experiences of the authoring group. The authors first identified the key mathematical concepts and skills to be developed at each grade level within the following mathematical strands: number and operation, including estimation; geometry and spatial sense; measurement; data analysis, statistics, and probability; fractions and decimals; and patterns, functions, and algebra. Problem-solving contexts that support student learning in these areas were then developed. Although *Math Trailblazers* employs a broad range of problem-solving contexts, a distinctive feature of the curriculum is its use of the TIMS Laboratory Investigations. Beginning with first grade, 8 to 10 TIMS labs have been adapted and integrated into the curriculum at each grade. The integrated investigations involve the use of a scientific method to study classification, length, area, volume, and mass in all grades; speed and density are also studied in fifth grade.[2] Table 3.1 contains an overview of the content across the mathematical strands for Grades K–2 and Grades 3–5.

Excerpts from three lessons are provided to illustrate how *Math Trailblazers* uses problem-solving contexts in science to develop and apply mathematical concepts and skills within different content strands. Two lessons, one from second grade and one from third grade, involve volume. The third example is from a fifth-grade lesson involving speed.

Place Value and Arithmetic in Context

In the lesson, "Marshmallows and Containers," students find the relative volumes of three containers by filling them with marshmallows and counting the marshmallows. The investigation is part of a second-grade unit within the number and operation strand that focuses on the development of place value concepts involving numbers through the hundreds. Students first draw a picture as in Fig. 3.1 to illustrate the procedures they will complete during the investigation. In counting the marshmallows, students arrange the marshmallows into groups of tens and "leftovers." To help with the grouping and counting, they use a modified egg carton that has spaces for ten groups of ten marshmallows.

Data are then collected, recorded in a data table, graphed, and analyzed as shown in Figs. 3.2 and 3.3. Each of these representations provides a tool for students to investigate and deepen their understanding of the numerical data. The investigation helps promote students' understanding of volume, such as the fact that the tallest container (the graduated cylinder) does not necessarily have the biggest volume. Data analysis also provides a context for practicing arithmetic through word problems, such as: What was the total number of marshmallows in all three containers? How many more marshmallows did the bowl hold than the cup? Which would hold more marshmallows, three cups or two bowls? How many more? The data are represented in the picture, in a data table, and in a graph.

"Fill 'er Up!" is a third-grade volume investigation. In this investigation, students devise a plan for using a graduated cylinder to find the volume in cubic centimeters of at least three containers. Students follow a process similar to that used in "Marshmallows and Containers"; that is, they draw a picture, collect the data and organize it into a data table, graph the data, and analyze it. Similarly, the investigation provides a context for applying arithmetic operations. Problems involving multiplication and division situations, important topics covered throughout the third grade, naturally

TABLE 3.1

Math Trailblazers Content Summary

Number and Operations		Patterns, Functions, and Algebra	Geometry and Spatial Sense	Measurement	Data Analysis, Statistics, and Probability
Number Sense and Whole Numbers	*Fractions and Decimals*				
Grades K–2					
Problem solving and applications involving all operations	Symbolic, pictorial, and concrete representations of fractions	Identifying patterns and describing them in words, pictures, and symbols	Properties and classification of two- and three-dimensional shapes	Measurement of length (including perimeter), area, volume, and mass by using standard and nonstandard units	Basic principles of experimental design and of scientific method
Number sense	Conceptual understanding of fractions	Using number patterns to make predictions and solve problems	Building three-dimensional objects with cubes and representing them in two dimensions	Use of measurement tools, including rulers, grids and tiles, graduated cylinders, two-pan balances, and cubes	Identifying experimental and controlled variables in an investigation
Partitioning numbers	Problem solving and applications involving fractions	Using tables and graphs to make generalizations and predictions	Maps, scales, and coordinates	Comparing measurements and examining relationships between different units of measure	Conducting surveys
Place value through the hundreds	Solving problems involving money	Function machines	Direction and distance on a number line		Making and interpreting bar graphs
Addition and subtraction facts			Line and rotational symmetry		Problem solving and making predictions based on collected data; justifying conclusions based on data
Mental arithmetic and estimation			Slides, flips, and turns		Finding the median values of collected data sets
Conceptual development for all operations					
Paper-and-pencil addition and subtraction involving two-digit numbers					

Choosing appropriate tools and methods to compute (e.g., mental math, estimation, paper and pencil, calculator)				Using numbers and units to report measurements Accuracy in measurement Fundamentals of telling time	Using samples to make predictions about larger populations
Grades 3–5					
Problem solving and applications involving all operations Basic math facts for all four operations Place value with large numbers Paper-and-pencil procedures for addition and subtraction with large numbers Multiplication and division concepts Paper-and-pencil procedures for multidigit multiplication and division with two-digit divisors	Problem solving and applications involving fractions and decimals Symbolic, pictorial, and concrete representations of fractions and decimals Conceptual understanding of fractions and decimals Ordering fractions and decimals Place value for decimals through thousandths Equivalence between fractions, decimals, and percents	Mathematical and scientific investigations involving variables Making connections among graphs, tables, symbols, and real-world situations Using tables and graphs to make generalizations and predictions Investigating how change in one experimental variable affects another variable	Cartesian coordinates Maps and scales Dividing and combining shapes Building three-dimensional objects and representing them in two dimensions Properties and classification of two- and three-dimensional shapes Congruence and similarity Line and rotational symmetry	Measurement of length (including perimeter), area (including surface area), volume, mass, time, density, and speed by using metric and "customary" units Angle measurement Use of measurement tools, including rulers, grids, graduated cylinders, balances, stopwatches, and protractors	Experimental design and scientific method Variables in an investigation or survey Problem solving and making predictions based on collected data; justifying conclusions based on data Making and interpreting line, bar, and circle graphs Using samples to make predictions about larger populations Drawing best fit lines and using them to make predictions

(Continued)

49

TABLE 3.1
(Continued)

Number and Operations		Patterns, Functions, and Algebra	Geometry and Spatial Sense	Measurement	Data Analysis, Statistics, and Probability
Number Sense and Whole Numbers	Fractions and Decimals				
Factors, multiples, primes, and square numbers Choosing appropriate tools and methods to compute (e.g., mental math, estimation, paper and pencil, calculator)	Estimating sums, differences, and products involving fractions and decimals Paper-and-pencil procedures for addition, subtraction, and multiplication with fractions and decimals Scientific notation	Developing proportional reasoning using tables, graphs, and symbols Function machines Using formulas Order of operations Powers of ten and exponents Introduction to negative numbers Investigating rates of change	Slides, flips, and turns Constructions	Analysis of error and accuracy in measurements Elapsed time; telling time	Mean, median, and mode Error and accuracy in data Basic principles of probability Experimental and theoretical probability Probabilities expressed as fractions and decimals

Note. Problem solving, reasoning, and communication are pervasive throughout, with an emphasis on justification of solution strategies. There are extensive connections among mathematical topics and between mathematics and other subjects, especially science and language arts. Most topics begin by developing conceptual understanding and then proceeding to more formal, abstract work.

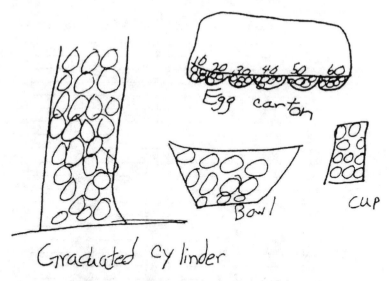

FIG. 3.1. Samantha's picture for the second-grade investigation "Marshmallows and Containers." Students were asked the following question from the lesson guide: *What could you do to find out which container holds the most marshmallows?* Here is one student's work.

Container	N Number of Marshmellov units
Graduated cylinder	133
Cup	121
bowl	181

FIG. 3.2. Samantha's data table for "Marshmallows and Containers."

emerge from the investigation. A student's response to one of the lesson's questions is shown in Fig. 3.4.

The student's work illustrates how this investigation of volume provided a physical context that helped the student visualize the problem and connect it with the operations of addition, multiplication, and division. Multiple

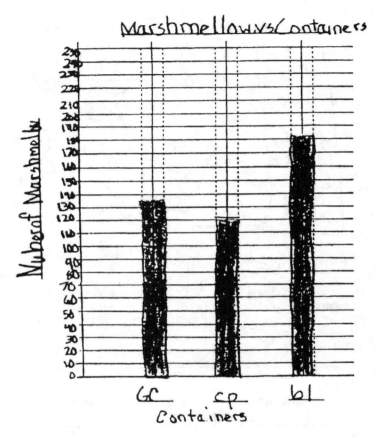

FIG. 3.3. Samantha's bar graph for "Marshmallows and Containers" (note that GC stands for graduated cylinder, cp for cup, and bl for bowl).

representations of the mathematical situation—words, pictures, symbols—are evident in the student's explanation. This is typical of the approaches used throughout *Math Trailblazers*. Students are asked to devise their own solutions to problems, communicate how they solved them, and then represent their solutions with number sentences.

Using Data in Developing an Understanding of Fractions

"A Day at the Races" is the second of two fifth-grade laboratory investigations involving speed, and it further develops concepts and skills in the fraction and decimal strand. In the earlier investigation, students explore the ratio

Mimi has a small jar with a volume of 40 cc and a bigger
jar with a volume of 230 cc.

A. How many *full* small jars of water can Mimi pour
    into her big jar? Show your work.

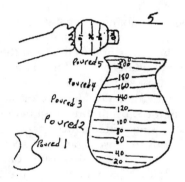

B. How much more water does she need to fill the big
    jar to the top? Show your work.

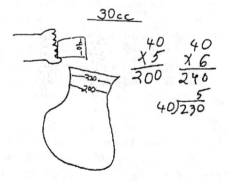

FIG. 3.4. Student solution for a problem from the third-grade lab
"Fill 'er Up!"

TABLE 3.2
Data for a 6-Yard Race from the Fifth-Grade Investigation
"A Day at the Races"

Name	Activity	D	t	S
John	Running	18	2.33	18/2.33
Nila	Crawling	18	10.25	18/10.25
Jessie	Walking backward	18	4.64	18/4.64
Arti	Walking	18	3.40	18/3.40

Note. D = distance in feet; t = average time in seconds; S = speed in feet/seconds.

of distance to time for a person walking at a constant speed. The data collected by students yield a straight-line graph that goes through the origin. By examining points along the line, students find that the ratio of distance to time (D/t) is the same at all points on the line. The physical context of people traveling at a constant speed is represented mathematically as patterns on a data table (when the time doubles, the distance doubles), as a straight line that goes through the origin on a distance versus time graph, and as equal ratios expressed as equivalent fractions.

"A Day at the Races" extends the investigation of speed and of fraction concepts. Students conduct two races. They first collect data for a 6-yard race, in which students travel 6 yards in different ways (e.g., running, crawling, and walking backward). Student data for the 6-yard race are shown in Table 3.2. The graph of that data is shown in Fig. 3.5.

The last column of the data table shows four ratios, each expressed as a fraction with a common numerator. John, who traveled the 18 feet in the shortest time, was the fastest; Nila, who took the longest to travel the 18 feet, was the slowest. On the graph, the data take the form of a family of lines with different slopes. John's data have the steepest incline; Nila's have the most gradual incline. The 6-yard race provides a concrete means to compare fractions that have a common numerator, encouraging students to look at the denominator to determine which fraction is larger or smaller; the smaller denominator yields the larger fraction. The graph provides another means for comparing the fractions because the largest fraction is represented by the line with the steepest slope.

Students then collect data from a 3-second race, in which they determine how far they can travel in 3 seconds. The data from this race allow students to compare fractions with common denominators (3 seconds). Students can easily grasp that the person who traveled the farthest in 3 seconds was the fastest. In the data table this translates into the fraction (speed in feet per second) with the largest numerator. The graph again shows that the line with the steepest incline represents the greatest speed.

Finally, students compare the speeds from the same activity (e.g., running) in the 3-second race and the 6-yard race to see who was faster. The

TABLE 3.3
Comparing Running Speeds in the Fifth-Grade Investigation
"A Day at the Races"

Name	Activity	D	t	S
John	Running	18	2.33	18/2.33
Nila	Running	30	3	30/3

Note. D = distance in feet; t = average time in seconds; S = speed in feet/seconds.

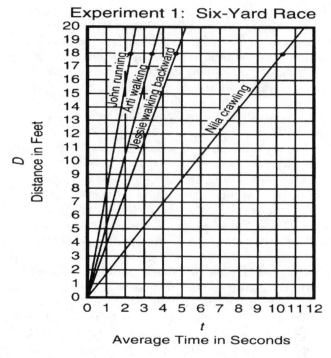

FIG. 3.5. Graphical representation of data from the 6-yard race in the fifth-grade investigation "A Day at the Races."

running data for John and Nila are shown in Table 3.3. Because there is no common numerator or denominator, students need a different strategy to compare the ratios, such as graphing the data. The data also serve as a source for other questions that encourage the use of proportional reasoning: In the 3-second race, how far did you travel in 1.5 seconds? How far would you travel in 6 seconds if you traveled at the same speed?

In each of the three sample lessons, a physical science investigation provided a context for inquiry. In addition to science investigations, other problem-solving contexts are integrated throughout *Math Trailblazers*. Each context is used to develop and to apply specific mathematical concepts and skills that are built into new and increasingly challenging problems as the curriculum builds on itself both within and across grade levels.

STUDENT OUTCOMES

The complete K–5 *Math Trailblazers* curriculum has been available only since the summer of 1997. Therefore much of the data collection investigating the effectiveness of the curriculum is still in its early stages. Through a Teacher Enhancement grant from the NSF, the TIMS Project worked with all Chicago-area schools that were early adopters of *Math Trailblazers*.[3] As a result of their involvement in the Teacher Enhancement grant, these schools received implementation support directly from TIMS staff members who were involved in writing *Math Trailblazers* and were also deeply committed to its success. Thus, most of what we currently know about the effectiveness of *Math Trailblazers* comes from schools receiving extensive support from the TIMS project staff.

For the purposes of this chapter, we report data from several completed investigations with Chicago-area schools and we report both quantitative and qualitative data regarding student outcomes. We first discuss two studies of student performance on two different standardized tests. In both studies, we report data collected from all schools that fit the criteria of the study, namely schools that had used *Math Trailblazers* for 2 years. We then discuss three case studies that focus on specific schools and that provide comparative data with schools not using *Math Trailblazers*: two provide details about the impact of *Math Trailblazers* on student achievement in urban schools; and the third provides student achievement data on an open-ended assessment. In order to provide a balanced view of student performance in *Math Trailblazers* classrooms, we conclude with qualitative data taken from a 1-year case study of a school's implementation of *Math Trailblazers*. A specific classroom episode, taken from the study, is presented to provide expanded insights into the complex social interactions that occur in classrooms using a reform curriculum.

Results from the Illinois Goals Assessment Program

Most public school students in Illinois are required to take the Illinois Goals Assessment Program (IGAP) test.[4] Therefore, the IGAP provides an opportunity to compare student achievement on a widely administered achievement test. The mathematics section of the IGAP was administered to third-, sixth-, and eighth-grade students during the years of this study.

Because *Math Trailblazers* is a K–5 curriculum, we report only third-grade IGAP results. In order to provide as broad a view as possible of the performance of *Math Trailblazers* students and at the same time control important variables, we report IGAP results from all eight Chicago-area schools that met the following criteria: all third-grade classrooms in each school used *Math Trailblazers*, each school had been in existence 4 years prior to the curriculum's adoption, and the school did not use *Math Trailblazers* field-test materials so that each school had exactly 2 years of experience with the curriculum in the spring of 1998.

Six of the schools (A–F) are Chicago public schools; two of the schools (G and H) are the only two elementary (K–6) schools in a K–12 school district in a middle-class suburb west of Chicago. Schools A–F share similar demographic characteristics with high percentages of minority and low-income students. In 1998 the percentage of minority students in these schools was 99%, ranging from 98% to 100% across the six schools. The percentage of low-income students was 86%, ranging from 61% to 98% across these six schools. Between Schools G and H, approximately 12% of the students were minority, predominantly Hispanic, and approximately 13% were low income.

The data in Table 3.4 and the corresponding graph in Fig. 3.6 compare each school's performance on the IGAP before and after the implementation of *Math Trailblazers*. In the spring of 1997, third-grade teachers and students had only 1 year of experience with *Math Trailblazers*. In the spring of 1998, third-grade students had 2 years of instruction with the curriculum and third-grade teachers had 2 years of experience teaching *Math Trailblazers*. Table 3.4 and Fig. 3.6 report the percentage of third-grade students in each school who met or exceeded the state goals in mathematics.[5] To assist in the comparison, we have calculated a "historical average" for each school by averaging the school's IGAP mathematics scores for 4 years prior to its use of the published *Math Trailblazers* materials. Presenting the data in this way provides a means of comparing a school's performance before and during implementation of *Math Trailblazers*.

After the first year of implementation, six out of the eight *Math Trailblazers* schools had a higher percentage of students meeting or exceeding the state goals than their historical averages. By the end of the second year, all eight schools were at levels above their historical averages, regardless of the initial level of student achievement. That is, *Math Trailblazers* is effective in schools that are initially low achieving and in schools that are initially high achieving.

Results from the Iowa Test of Basic Skills

Another widely used standardized test is the Iowa Test of Basic Skills (ITBS). Because all Chicago public elementary schools are required to administer

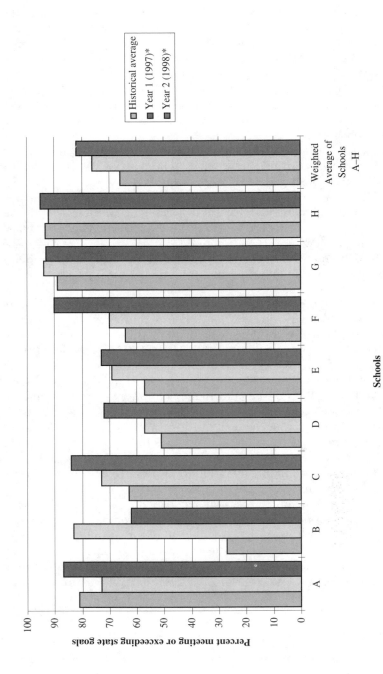

FIG. 3.6. Percentage of students who met or exceeded state goals in mathematics on Grade 3 IGAP. *IGAP scores are after 1 year of *Math Trailblazers* implementation (1997) or 2 years of implementation (1998).

TABLE 3.4

Percentage of Students Meeting or Exceeding State Goals on Grade 3 IGAP

School	1993	1994	1995	1996	Historical Avg.	Year 1 (1997)	Year 2 (1998)
A	70	86	86	78	81	73	87
B	25	27	43	15	27	83	62
C	49	68	74	64	63	73	84
D	49	41	45	70	51	57	72
E	57	63	50	60	57	69	73
F	60	63	67	69	64	70	90
G	85	90	88	93	89	94	93
H	87	92	96	98	93	92	95
Weighted avg. of A–H	60	66	69	68	66	76	82

Note. IGAP scores are after 1 year of *Math Trailblazers* implementation in 1997 or 2 years of implementation in 1998.

the ITBS, it also provides a comprehensive view of student performance on a standardized test of basic skills. Hence, we examine data from the six Chicago public schools (Schools A–F) that had 2 years of experience using the published *Math Trailblazers* materials in the spring of 1998 and that had historical data.

The data in Table 3.5 and Fig. 3.7 are based on results from the mathematics section of the ITBS. To establish a baseline level of school performance on the ITBS, we again developed a historical average for each school by averaging the school's percentage of students at or above national norms for the 4 years prior to *Math Trailblazers* implementation.

After the first year of *Math Trailblazers* implementation, three of the six schools showed increases in the percentage of students performing at or above national norms when compared with their historical averages. By the end of the second year of implementation, all six schools showed an improvement when compared with the previous year's performance; five of the six schools were at levels above their historical averages. The performance of Chicago-area *Math Trailblazers* students on both the IGAP and ITBS illustrates that a balanced, problem-solving curriculum, such as *Math Trailblazers*, can prepare students for traditional standardized tests at least as well, if not better, than traditional non-*Standards*-oriented curricula.

Case Studies in Specific Schools

In this section we discuss results from three case studies of schools that have adopted *Math Trailblazers*. The first two involve schools that participated in the early development of *Math Trailblazers* and thus have had extensive

TABLE 3.5
Percentage of Students Scoring at or Above National Norms in Mathematics
on Grade 3 ITBS

School	1993	1994	1995	1996	Historical Avg.	Year 1 (1997)	Year 2 (1998)
A	50	57	46	44	49	21	41
B	22	11	16	13	16	25	28
C	31	37	30	12	26	13	36
D	30	22	20	28	25	26	35
E	28	34	17	24	25	18	30
F	21	22	25	34	25	26	33
Weighted avg. of A–H	28	29	24	27	27	22	34

Note. ITBS scores are after 1 year of *Math Trailblazers* implementation in 1997 or 2 years of implementation in 1998.

experience with the curriculum. The last is a comparative study of student achievement data from a school within a school. All school names used in these studies are pseudonyms.

Sandburg School

Sandburg School is a K–8 neighborhood school located on the far north side of Chicago. Sandburg has a "United Nations" flavor, with student backgrounds representing over 30 cultures and languages. Two Sandburg teachers began piloting *Math Trailblazers* materials in 1991. Feedback from these and other teachers helped guide development of field-test materials that were piloted at Sandburg in Grades 1, 2, and 3 in 1994–1995 and in Grades K and 4 in 1995–1996. The newly published *Math Trailblazers* was first implemented in Grades 1–3 in 1996–1997 and in Grades K, 4, and 5 in 1997–1998. During these years, Sandburg teachers were able to participate in professional development workshops and take advantage of in-school support activities provided by the TIMS Project. In addition, the school's principal instituted policies and administrative practices designed to support teachers in their implementation of *Math Trailblazers*.

Each public school in Chicago is governed by a Local School Council. Curriculum decisions are made at the local-school level by individual Local School Councils, and thus, math curricula vary from school to school. This made it possible to compare the student achievement scores at Sandburg with those of the nearby Truman School, which was not using *Math Trailblazers*. We chose to compare student performance at Truman and Sandburg because both schools had similar patterns of academic achievement in the years before Sandburg adopted *Math Trailblazers* (see Fig. 3.8). Also,

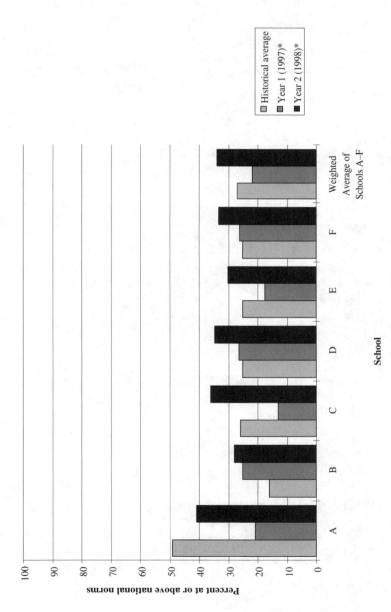

FIG. 3.7. Percentage of students scoring at or above national norms in mathematics on Grade 3 ITBS. *ITBS scores are after 1 year of implementation (1997) or 2 years of implementation (1998).

Grade 3

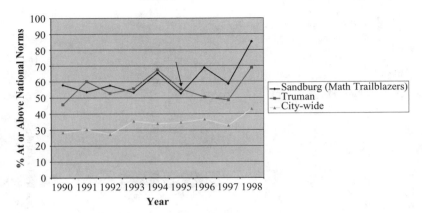

Grade 4

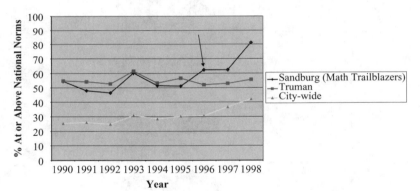

Grade 5

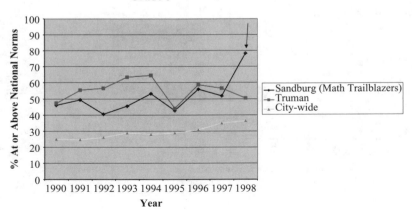

TABLE 3.6
Demographic Data for Sandburg and Truman

Demographic Char.	1990		1998	
	Sandburg	Truman	Sandburg	Truman
Enrollment	896	1052	1048	1498
Low income (%)	23.9	43.8	66.4	72.5
White (%)	53.8	51	46.6	40.1
African-American (%)	8.5	6	7.4	7.5
Asian (%)	22.4	29.3	23.9	33.7
Hispanic (%)	14.8	13.4	21.6	18.5

both schools exhibited similar trends on demographic indicators during this time, including number of students, percentage of low-income students, and the racial and ethnic makeup of the student body (see Table 3.6).

The graphs in Fig. 3.8 show trends in the percentage of Sandburg students scoring at or above national norms after all Sandburg students at a particular grade had studied from *Math Trailblazers*. Sandburg's percentages of students scoring at or above national norms are significantly greater than Truman's in third grade in 1996[6] and 1998,[7] in fourth grade in 1998,[8] and in fifth grade in 1998.[9] It is important to note that in 1998, many of the third-, fourth-, and fifth-grade students who began their academic careers at Sandburg had been using some version of *Math Trailblazers* for multiple years. Thus, the fact that Sandburg students scored significantly higher than Truman students at all three grade levels that year provides evidence that prolonged and consistent use of *Math Trailblazers* can have cumulative, positive effects on student achievement.

Further analysis of the ITBS data from Sandburg shows significant changes in the percentage of students scoring in both the bottom and top quartiles. These results are summarized in Fig. 3.9. Similar comparisons at Truman in these years show no significant decreases in the percentage of students in the bottom quartile. During the same years, the percentage of students in the top quartile at Truman decreased at all three grades. These results indicate that *Math Trailblazers* can benefit students at all ability levels by decreasing the percentage of students in the bottom quartile while increasing the percentage of students in the top.

FIG. 3.8. Percentage of students scoring at or above national norms in mathematics on ITBS: Sandburg, Truman, and Chicago public schools. (The arrow points to the first year that all students at a particular grade level had access to *Math Trailblazers* for a full year.)

National Quartile Comparisons

Sandburg Before and After *Math Trailblazers* Implementation at Sandburg

Percent in Bottom Quartile

- 3rd grade: decreased significantly from 14% in 1994 to 2% in 1998[a]
- 4th grade: decreased significantly from 26% in 1995 to 5% in 1998[b]
- 5th grade: decreased from 20% in 1997 to 12% in 1998

Percent in Top Quartile

- 3rd grade: increased from 39% in 1994 to 44% in 1998
- 4th grade: increased significantly from 26% in 1995 to 44% in 1998[c]
- 5th grade: increased significantly from 27% in 1997 to 47% in 1998[d]

Truman Before and After *Math Trailblazers* Implementation at Sandburg

Percent in Bottom Quartile

- 3rd grade: decreased from 18% in 1994 to 9% in 1998
- 4th grade: stayed constant at 25% in 1995 and 1998
- 5th grade: decreased from 23% in 1997 to 20% in 1998

Percent in Top Quartile

- 3rd grade: decreased from 41% in 1994 to 36% in 1998
- 4th grade: decreased from 30% in 1995 to 21% in 1998
- 5th grade: decreased from 22% in 1997 to 18% in 1998

FIG. 3.9. National quartile comparisons (The percentage in each quartile in 1998 is compared with the corresponding percentage from the year prior to the year in which all students at that grade used *Math Trailblazers*. [a]$z = -1.99, p < .025$; [b]$z = -3.45, p < .001$; [c]$z = 2.20, p < .025$; and [d]$z = 2.54, p < .01$.)

Test scores for third-grade students at Sandburg and Truman on the mathematics portion of the IGAP show patterns similar to those found on the ITBS data. From 1993 to 1996, the percentage of students meeting or exceeding state goals at both schools is within three or four percentage points of the Illinois state percentage. Then in 1997, the first year that the published version of *Math Trailblazers* was in use, Truman's percentage remained close to the state percentage. At the same time, Sandburg's percentage was 9 points higher than the state percentage and 11 points higher than Truman's percentage. Most notably, the percentage of students not meeting Illinois state goals at Sandburg dropped from 14% in 1993 to 2% in 1997.

The similar patterns found in student achievement on two different standardized tests at these two schools provide an added measure of confidence in the data that show increases in test scores at Sandburg following *Math Trailblazers* implementation. This is true despite an increase in the percentage of low-income students at Sandburg during the time of the study.

Jackson School

A second case study of a *Math Trailblazers* field-test school involves Jackson Elementary School, a school in a suburban district near Chicago. Jackson is one of eight K–6 elementary schools in the district. White students comprise approximately 67% of the 667 students and African-American students comprise approximately 26%. Income levels are diverse: Although most households are middle class, 8% of the students are categorized as low income. Pilot testing of *Math Trailblazers* materials in primary grades began at Jackson in 1991–1992. Field-test materials were used in Grades 1, 2, and 3 in 1994–1995 and in Grades 4 and 5 in 1995–1996. The *Math Trailblazers* curriculum was officially adopted in Grades 1, 2, and 3 beginning with the 1996–1997 school year and in fourth grade in 1997–1998.

The district tests its students in mathematics by using two standardized achievement tests, the IGAP and the *Stanford Achievement Test, Ninth Edition*. In the spring, third and sixth graders took the IGAP. Jackson School's third-grade math scores have traditionally been greater than or near the state average but below the district average; in 1995 and 1998, the scores were about the same as the district average. In the fall of 1996, the district began testing all students with the *Stanford Achievement Test, Ninth Edition*.

The "Stanford 9" offers a choice of assessment formats, including a traditional multiple-choice format and an open-ended assessment format. In 1997 the district elected to test students in third and fifth grades by using both the multiple-choice and the open-ended assessment components.

The multiple-choice format has two content clusters in mathematics. One, the problem-solving cluster, has 46 items, divided into subcategories based on the 1989 National Council of Teachers of Mathematics (NCTM) *Standards*: concepts–whole number computation, number sense and numeration, geometry and spatial sense, measurement, statistics and probability, fraction and decimal concepts, patterns and relationships, and problem-solving strategies. The second, the procedures cluster, has 28 items in three subdivisions: number facts, computation–symbolic notation, and computation in context.

The Stanford 9 Mathematics open-ended assessment consists of nine questions or tasks. Students are asked to explain their reasoning or show their work and the use of calculators is encouraged. Students' proficiency with three process clusters—problem solving, communication, and reasoning—is reflected in the resulting scores, as well as their proficiency with three content clusters—number concepts, concepts of shape and space, and patterns and relationships.

Because the Stanford 9 was first administered in the district in the fall of 1996, it is not possible to compare performance before and after the introduction of *Math Trailblazers*. However, the combination of multiple-choice format and the open-ended assessment given to third graders in the fall of 1997 provides an opportunity to expand our analysis of student achievement to include some areas not addressed when we look solely at results on multiple choice tests. It should be noted that third-grade students in the fall of 1997 had studied from *Math Trailblazers* for at least 1 year as second graders.

On the Stanford multiple-choice questions at Grade 3, 55% of Jackson's students scored at or above the National 50th Percentile Ranking, compared with 63% of the rest of the district's third-grade students who scored at this level. This is consistent with Jackson's relatively low ranking in the district on the IGAP. A notable difference, however, appeared in third-grade scores on the separate open-ended assessment. This format provides a "measurement of reasoning ability because students must use higher-order thinking to generate and justify their own responses" (Stanford, 1996, p. 259). On the open-ended test, 70% of Jackson's third-grade students scored at or above the National 50% Percentile Ranking, as compared with 64% of the rest of the district's students.

The open-ended test is scored on a 4-point scale, from 0 (essentially incorrect) to 3 (essentially correct). In each of the six content and process clusters, a higher percentage of Jackson students than other district students met the district standard by achieving a score of at least 2.[10] At the highest level, Jackson's student performance was even more impressive. The percentage of Jackson students and the percentage of other district students who scored 3 are displayed in Fig. 3.10. The differences in percentages were significant for the patterns and relationships[11] cluster and the communication[12] cluster.

The strong performance of Jackson students on the Stanford open-ended questions provides evidence that students using *Math Trailblazers* exhibit mathematical learning beyond what is measured on traditional multiple-choice tests. The results also suggest that, with a reform mathematics curriculum, program evaluations that are based solely on results from multiple-choice exams may provide a limited analysis of student achievement, which underrepresents student learning.

School Within a School

One Chicago-area school that adopted *Math Trailblazers* in the fall of 1996 is a school within a school. This "small school" is a distinct entity that resides

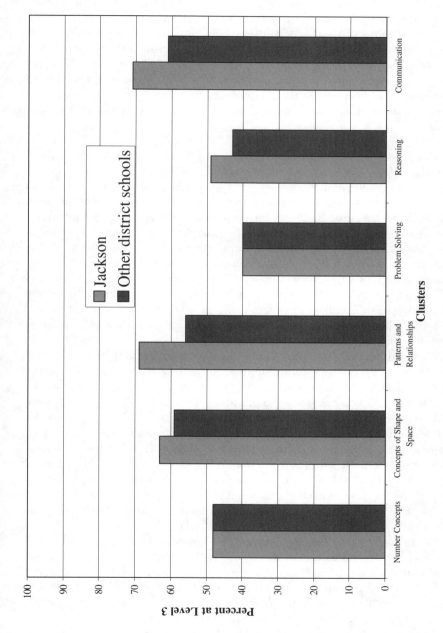

FIG. 3.10. Percentage of students scoring at the highest performance level (Level 3) on the Stanford open-ended assessment.

physically within a larger school and thus shares many of the same characteristics of the larger school. The larger school continued using a traditional mathematics curriculum, thereby creating an opportunity to evaluate the effectiveness of the *Math Trailblazers* curriculum by comparing student achievement in the small school to a similar population in the larger school.

The James School, part of the Eisenhower School, is part of the Teacher Leadership Academy, a support network of 12 small schools that was developed through grants from the Annenberg Foundation. It is also part of a loosely organized network of more than 50 small schools within the Chicago public schools.

The James School. The James School opened its doors to students in the fall of 1996. The school's origin, however, can be traced to 2 years earlier when a group of Eisenhower teachers began to meet and share ideas about how they could better educate their students. The small school began with one teacher per grade in kindergarten through third grade. A fifth teacher served as the school's lead teacher and also directed the school's science programs. One of the early decisions made by its teachers was the adoption of *Math Trailblazers*. James has an open enrollment policy and students are admitted to the small school in the order in which they apply. Thus, no preference in admission is given to students based on past school performance or other criteria. Both schools share similar demographic characteristics: 98% of their students are African-American and 90% of the students come from low-income families.

We examined mathematics scores on the 1996 ITBS in order to compare the levels of mathematics achievement for students at James and Eisenhower before the James students began using the *Math Trailblazers* curriculum. In the fall of 1996, incoming second-grade students at the Eisenhower School had an average grade equivalent of 1.8 years ($n = 21$, SD $= 0.51$) on the mathematics portion of the ITBS. Incoming James students had a higher average grade equivalent of 2.2 years ($n = 22$, SD $= 0.42$).[13] At the third-grade level, students at the Eisenhower school had an average grade equivalent of 2.3 years ($n = 33$, SD $= 0.56$) and the James students had a slightly higher average at 2.6 years ($n = 23$, SD $= 0.68$).[14] Although both second- and third-grade James students had higher incoming scores, the difference was statistically significant only at the second grade.

Because of these achievement differences between Eisenhower and James students, our comparisons of the two schools are based on individual student gains. We calculated each student's gain in grade equivalents during the 1996–1997 school year by subtracting their 1996 mathematics score from their 1997 score. We then averaged the individual student gains for the James and Eisenhower grade levels.

Second-grade students at James made an average gain of 0.78 years ($n = 22$, SD $= 0.46$) per student on the mathematics section of the ITBS.

The average gain for second-grade students at Eisenhower was significantly lower at 0.40 years ($n = 21$, SD $= 0.50$) per student.[15] Third-grade students at James made an average gain of 0.83 years ($n = 23$, SD $= 0.53$) in mathematics; the Eisenhower third-grade students had a significantly lower average gain of 0.41 years ($n = 33$, SD $= 0.73$) per student.[16] Although neither school averaged a full year of progress, their performance is consistent with other Chicago schools with high levels of low-income and minority students (Hess, 1995). It is, however, encouraging to note that the students at James who were using *Math Trailblazers* did average about twice the yearly gain in mathematics as their peers at the Eisenhower School who were using a traditional math curriculum.

The superior performance of James students relative to the performance of Eisenhower students also can be seen in the schools' IGAP data. On the third-grade mathematics section of the 1997 IGAP, the average score for James students was 245 ($n = 23$, SD $= 102$); the average score for Eisenhower students was significantly lower at 193 ($n = 37$, SD $= 68$).[17] The 52-point difference between James and Eisenhower students can be analyzed further by looking at the six areas of mathematics assessed by the IGAP as shown in Fig. 3.11.

James students scored significantly higher than Eisenhower students in the areas of measurement,[18] geometry,[19] and data collection.[20] Although the Eisenhower students did slightly better in the area of number concepts, the section of the test that deals most extensively with computation and math facts, the difference was not statistically significant.[21] Thus, the *Math Trailblazers* students scored approximately as well as the comparison group in computation sections of standardized tests while significantly outperforming the comparison group on most other sections. These results indicate that the higher levels of performance by *Math Trailblazers* students in the areas of math concepts and problem solving have not come at the expense of math facts and computation. These results are consistent with Hiebert's (1999) finding: "Instructional programs that emphasize conceptual understanding can facilitate significant mathematics learning without sacrificing skill proficiency" (p. 14).

Expanding Our View: A Look Beyond Standardized Tests

To expand our assessment of student outcomes beyond performance on standardized tests as recommended by the NCTM (1991), Perrone (1991), and Stake (1995b), we have examined students' classroom experiences and investigated the impact these experiences have on learning. In a study by Carter (1999), a school's first-, second-, and third-grade teachers were observed, videotaped, and interviewed during their first year of *Math Trailblazers* implementation to develop detailed descriptions of classroom processes.

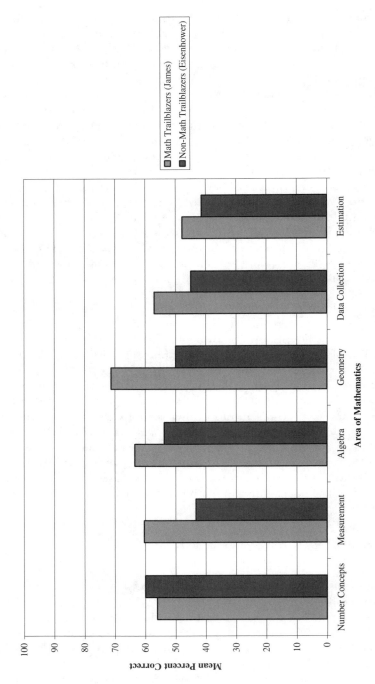

FIG. 3.11. Grade 3 IGAP scores at James and Eisenhower schools.

70

During the study, teachers participated in professional development workshops provided by the TIMS Project, including weekly visits by the researcher to assist teachers in curriculum implementation. These visits, together with formal and informal interviews, provided regular and sustained interactions, which fostered a level of trust between the researcher and teachers necessary to carry out this type of research project.

During March and April, each teacher was videotaped teaching at least one complete *Math Trailblazers* lesson. These tapes were transcribed and used to develop detailed descriptive narratives of the lesson. "Dialogical data gathering" (Carspecken & Apple, 1992, p. 531), in which teachers participate in data analysis, was accomplished by providing each teacher with the narrative and the videotape for each lesson. The narratives were discussed at length and revised to incorporate the teacher's input. The teacher's perceptions and input provide an important source of validity for the results (Stake, 1995a).

Ms. Padilla's Math Class

To highlight findings from Carter's study, we present an extended excerpt from a narrative describing a *Math Trailblazers* lesson in a first-grade classroom taught by Ms. Padilla.[22] Over the past 7 years, Ms. Padilla has developed a teaching style that is both caring and serious. At the same time she has also established high expectations for student participation in classwork and clear boundaries of acceptable student behavior. Although the interactions seen in this lesson are typical for Ms. Padilla's class, they reflect a 7-month evolution of social norms in a classroom where listening and cooperation are valued, modeled, and practiced on a daily basis.

In the lesson, students are asked to find the area of various shapes by covering them with tiles. Ms. Padilla begins the lesson by informing the class that they will use the full square-inch and half-square-inch tiles in Fig. 3.12 to cover shapes 1 and 3 in Fig. 3.13.

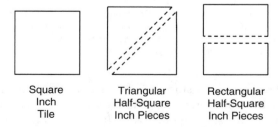

Square
Inch
Tile

Triangular
Half-Square
Inch Pieces

Rectangular
Half-Square
Inch Pieces

FIG. 3.12. Full square-inch and half-square-inch tiles for measuring the area.

Name_____ Date_____

Tiles 1

Find and record the area of each figure below. Use square-inch tiles and halves of square-inch tiles to help you.

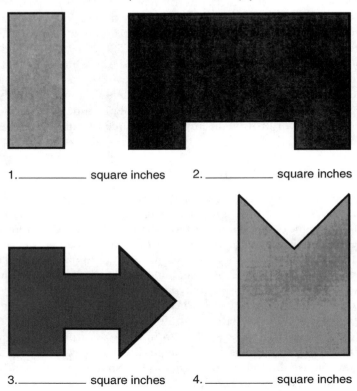

1._____ square inches   2. _____ square inches

3._____ square inches   4. _____ square inches

FIG. 3.13. Page from a first-grade *Math Trailblazers* lesson on the measurement of area. *Note.* From *Math Trailblazers: A Mathematical Journey Using Science and Language Arts*, by P. Wagreich, H. Goldberg, and TIMS Project Staff, 1997, Dubuque, IA: Kendall/Hunt. © 1997 by Kendall/Hunt. Reprinted with permission

The problem-solving situation used in this lesson helps first-grade students develop the conceptual foundations for the study of area and polygons later in the year and in subsequent grades. It also encourages students to participate actively in the process of doing mathematics and in communicating their results to others. An assumption in *Math Trailblazers* is that valuable learning takes place in discussions about the lesson—whole class discussion,

discussion among students in small groups, and discussion between the teacher and individuals or small groups of students.

After students demonstrate solutions for the first two problems, the teacher asks them to work with their groups to complete the final two. For the next 23 minutes, the class bustles with activity as the students work on the assigned problems. During this time, Ms. Padilla does not speak to the class as a whole but instead moves around the room assisting students. Most interactions are student initiated, one-to-one conversations in which Ms. Padilla listens carefully and responds directly to a student's ideas and questions. Often, other students who are nearby are also listening, watching, and sometimes participating in the exchange. The following is typical of the interactions between Ms. Padilla and her students.

> *(Sonia walks up to Ms. Padilla and tells her the answer she has found for Problem 4. Ms. Padilla responds, "Five and a half square inches? Wow! I am going to come right over, Sonia, so you can show me the five and a half square inches." When she arrives at Sonia's table, Ms. Padilla asks Sonia to show her the area by counting the tiles.)*

S: 1, 2—

T: Which ones are you counting? Can you point to which ones you are referring to?

S: 1, 2, 3, 4, 5, 6.

> *(In her count, Sonia does not distinguish between the square-inch tiles and the half-square-inch pieces and incorrectly gives the answer as 6 (in.^{2}) instead of 5 (in.^{2}). Ms. Padilla points to one of the half-square-inch tiles and asks if it is a square inch. When Sonia replies that it is, the teacher then points to a square-inch tile and a half-square-inch piece simultaneously and asks if they are the same, to which Sonia replies "yes." After verifying Sonia's misunderstanding, Ms. Padilla takes a more direct approach by placing one of the triangular-halves directly on top of a square-inch tile.)*

T: Let me put this one on top so you can see. Is it the same as this one? Is it the same?

S: No!

T: No, it is not. So is it ...

S: I can put it together to make a block (*pushes two triangular halves together*).

T: Yes, if you put in another one. But if it is by itself, is it one square inch? What is it?

> *(Here Ms. Padilla waits a long 8 seconds for Sonia to reply. When it becomes clear that Sonia is not willing to attempt an answer, Ms. Padilla explains that it is one-half square inch and reminds her that she made it by cutting one square inch into two equal pieces. Ms. Padilla then refocuses the discussion on the assigned problem.)*

T: ... Now let's count them again. Let's start with the square inches.
S: 1, 2, 3, 4 ...
T: Four and ...
S: And two halves.
T: What can you do with these two halves?
S: Put them together.
T: Put them together. Go ahead and put them together (*student puts two rectangular halves together*). Now how many square inches do you have? Count again so I can hear you.
S: 1, 2, 3, 4, 5.
T: How many square inches?
S: Five.

In addition to the teacher-to-student interaction, there is often sustained student-to-student interaction. For instance, later in the lesson from which the above excerpt is taken, Luis, Armando, and Hosea engage in a heated debate about one of the problems, and they begin questioning Ms. Padilla about the disputed answer. See Carter (1999) for further detailed examples.

Discussion of the Lesson.   One of the most striking aspects of this lesson is the sustained and sometimes passionate engagement of Ms. Padilla's students. One of the benefits of this level of engagement is the connection between emotion and learning. Although the idea that learning is strongly influenced by emotion is not new (Wolfe & Brandt, 1998), it is receiving renewed interest based on current brain research (Goleman, 1995). In addition, as Dewey (1938) noted, when students are intellectually engaged in an activity that they perceive as meaningful, there is little need for the teacher to exert "external control" over her students. Thus, the high level of involvement seen in this *Math Trailblazers* activity has the positive consequence of allowing the teacher to focus on promoting student learning rather than controlling student behavior.

The 23 minutes of uninterrupted work that occurred in this lesson allowed enough time for the teacher to engage her students in "mathematical conversations," during which the teacher listened to student solutions and engaged in dialogue directed toward deepening student understanding. The long duration of this period also allowed students to engage in self-initiated discussion of mathematical content with their peers. By participating in such discussions, students play an active role in developing shared mathematical understandings (Bruner, 1986; Voigt, 1996). Development of such understandings has been identified as an important part of the learning process (Bauersfeld, 1995; Cobb, Wood, Yackel, & McNeal, 1992). Additionally, these conversations provide the teacher with valuable informal assessment data. By engaging in conversations with her students,

Ms. Padilla modeled listening as a powerful and often underutilized tool for the construction of mathematical meaning (Davis, 1996).

During the course of the lesson, students moved freely about the room, comparing answers, working at the overhead, and occasionally being off task. But most, if not all, of these students also chose to return to their assigned work. Providing opportunities to make such choices has been shown to be a key factor in the development of student autonomy (Deci, 1995; DeVries, 1997; Glasser, 1998; Kamii, 1994; Kohn, 1993). In a review of current research, Rodgers (1998) observed, "Research indicates that more autonomous children have greater classroom competence and are less likely to act out in class. They also have higher achievement scores and grades" (p. 78).

Data from this study are consistent with results reported by Kelly, Perry, Lewis, and McConney (1999). When using *Math Trailblazers*, teachers consistently engaged in the types of focused, contextualized explanations that have been associated with Asian classrooms. The data also document students and teachers engaging in mathematical conversations, or what Bernstein (1992) has characterized as "dialogical encounters," in which "one begins with the assumption that the other has something to say and to contribute to our understanding" (p. 337).

SUMMARY AND CONCLUSIONS

Math Trailblazers: A Mathematical Journey Using Science and Language Arts is a complete mathematics curriculum for kindergarten through fifth grade. Its origins can be traced to the efforts of the TIMS Project to integrate the teaching of mathematics and science, and to the support of the NSF for the creation of mathematics curriculum based on the NCTM *Standards* (1989).

The student outcomes presented in this chapter are based both on standardized tests and on qualitative measures of what students have experienced in *Math Trailblazers* classrooms. The research reported here was conducted in both inner-city Chicago public schools with high percentages of minority students from low-income families and in schools from middle-class Chicago suburbs. In both types of schools, students using *Math Trailblazers* performed at least as well, and often better, on the IGAP and ITBS than students in those schools prior to implementation of this *Standards*-oriented curriculum. The consistent performance of *Math Trailblazers* students on such measures illustrates that a balanced problem-solving curriculum, such as *Math Trailblazers*, can be effective in preparing students for traditional standardized tests and can be successful in both urban and suburban schools.

Several case studies give additional evidence of the effectiveness of the *Math Trailblazers* curriculum. In particular, research in one study of an urban school suggests that the *Math Trailblazers* curriculum leads to a decline in both the percentage of students in the lowest quartile on the ITBS and the percentage of students not meeting state goals on the IGAP, with a concurrent increase in the percentage of students in the highest quartile on the ITBS and in the percentage of students exceeding state goals on the IGAP.

In another study of a suburban school, which had traditionally ranked in the bottom half among the district's schools on multiple-choice standardized tests, *Math Trailblazers* students outperformed the rest of the district in all six content strands on the open-ended portion of the Stanford 9 Test. This provides evidence that *Math Trailblazers* promotes mathematical learning beyond what may be measured on multiple-choice tests.

Finally, a qualitative study of classroom interactions provides insight into the factors that may be responsible for student performance with these materials. The extensive teacher-to-student and student-to-student interactions provide multiple opportunities for students to explain their thinking about mathematics. These interactions support the development of conceptual understanding and the ability to justify mathematical reasoning.

The *Math Trailblazers* curriculum is grounded in the belief that scientific investigations of everyday situations offer an ideal setting for learning mathematics. Although we are still in the early stages of data collection concerning the impact of *Math Trailblazers* on student achievement, the results accumulated thus far are encouraging. They indicate that the balanced problem-solving approach found in *Math Trailblazers* has been successful in improving student learning and achievement in mathematics.

REFERENCES

Bauersfeld, H. (1995). "Language Games" in the mathematics classroom: Their function and their effects. In P. Cobb & H. Bauersfeld (Eds.), *The Emergence of mathematical meaning: Interaction in classroom cultures* (pp. 271–291). Hillsdale, NJ: Lawrence Erlbaum Associates.

Bernstein, R. (1992). *The new constellation: The ethical-political horizons of modernity/post-modernity.* Cambridge, MA: MIT Press.

Bruner, J. (1986). *Actual minds, possible words.* Cambridge, MA: Harvard University Press.

Carspecken, P. F., & Apple, M. (1992). Critical qualitative research: Theory, methodology, and practice. In M. D. LeCompte, W. L. Millroy, & J. Preissle (Eds.), *The handbook of qualitative research in education* (pp. 507–553). San Diego, CA: Academic Press.

Carter, M. A. (1999). *Student autonomy and making meaning in an urban small school.* Unpublished doctoral dissertation, University of Illinois at Chicago.

Cobb, P., Wood, T., Yackel, E., & McNeal, B. (1992). Characteristics of classroom mathematics traditions: An interactional analysis. *American Educational Research Journal, 29,* 573–602.

Davis, B. (1996). *Teaching mathematics: Toward a sound alternative.* New York: Garland.

Deci, E. (1995). *Why we do what we do.* New York: Penguin.

DeVries, R. (1997). Piaget's social theory. *Educational Researcher, 26*(1), 4–17.

Dewey, J. (1910). Science as subject-matter and as method. *Science, 31*(787), 121–127.

Dewey, J. (1938). *Experience and education.* New York: Macmillan.

Glasser, W. (1998). *Choice theory: A new psychology of personal freedom.* New York: HarperCollins.

Goldberg, H. (1993). *A four year achievement study: The TIMS Program.* Chicago: University of Illinois at Chicago Institute for Mathematics and Science Education.

Goldberg, H. (1997). *The TIMS Laboratory Investigations.* Dubuque, IA: Kendall/Hunt.

Goldberg, H. S., & Boulanger, F. D. (1981). Science for elementary school teachers: A quantitative approach. *American Journal of Physics, 49*(2), 120–124.

Goldberg, H., & Wagreich, P. (1990). A model integrated mathematics science program for the elementary school. *International Journal of Educational Research, 14*(2), 193–214.

Goleman, D. (1995). *Emotional Intelligence.* New York: Bantam.

Hess, G. A., Jr. (1995). *Restructuring urban schools: A Chicago perspective.* New York: Teachers College Press.

Hiebert, J. (1999). Relationships between research and the NCTM standards. *Journal for Research in Mathematics Education, 30*(1), 3–19.

Isaacs, A., Wagreich, P., & Gartzman, M. (1997). The quest for integration: School mathematics and science. *American Journal of Education, 106*(1), 179–206.

Kamii, C. (1994). The six national goals . . . A road to disappointment. *Phi Delta Kappan, 75*(9), 672–677.

Kelly, M., Perry, M., Lewis, J. L., & McConney, M. (1999). Understanding the explanation: Effects of new mathematics curriculum on teacher explanations and student learning. Paper presented as part of the biennial meeting of the Society for Research in Child Development, Albuquerque, NM.

Kohn, A. (1993). *Punished by rewards: The trouble with gold stars, incentive plans, A's, praise, and other bribes.* Boston: Houghton Mifflin.

National Council of Teachers of Mathematics. (1989). *Curriculum and evaluation standards for school mathematics.* Reston, VA: Author.

National Council of Teachers of Mathematics. (1991). *Professional standards for teaching mathematics.* Reston, VA: Author.

Perrone, V. (1991). *Expanding student assessment.* Alexandria, VA: Association for Supervision and Curriculum Development.

Rodgers, D. B. (1998, May). Supporting autonomy in young children. *Young Children, 53,* 75–80.

Stake, R. (1995a). *The art of case study research.* Thousand Oaks, CA: Sage.

Stake, R. (1995b). The invalidity of standardized testing for measuring mathematics achievement. In T. Romberg (Ed.), *Reform in school mathematics and authentic assessment* (pp. 173–235). Albany, NY: State University of New York Press.

Stanford Achievement Test Series. (1996). *Compendium of instructional objectives* (9th ed.). San Antonio, TX: Harcourt Brace.

Teachers Academy for Mathematics and Science. (1995). *1995 IGAP Math Study.* Unpublished evaluation report, Chicago, IL.

Teachers Academy for Mathematics and Science. (1996). *1996 IGAP Math Study.* Unpublished evaluation report, Chicago, IL.

Voigt, J. (1996). Negotiation of mathematical meaning in classroom processes: Social interaction and learning mathematics. In L. P. Steffe, P. Nescher, P. Cobb, G. A. Goldin, & B. Greer (Eds.), *Theories of mathematical learning* (pp. 21–50). Mahwah, NJ: Lawrence Erlbaum Associates.

Wagreich, P., Goldberg, H., & TIMS Project Staff. (1997). *Math trailblazers: A mathematical journey using science and language arts.* Dubuque, IA: Kendall/Hunt.

Wolfe, P., & Brandt, R. (1998, November). What do we know from brain research? *Educational Leadership, 56*(3), 8–13.

ENDNOTES

1. NSF Grant MDR 9050226, "TIMS Elementary Mathematics Curriculum Project."
2. Mass is introduced formally in the second grade.
3. NSF Grant ESI 9550068, "TIMS95: School University Partnership for Improvement of Math Teaching and Learning."
4. In 1999 the name of the IGAP test was changed to the ISAT (Illinois Standardized Achievement Test).
5. The state of Illinois designates three criterion-referenced levels of performance on the IGAP. Level one is for students who do not meet state goals; level two is for students who meet state goals and level three is for students who are above state goals.
6. Percentage at Sandburg $= 68.9\%$, $n = 61$; percentage at Truman $= 50.4\%$, $n = 115$ ($z = 2.35$, $p < .01$).
7. Percentage at Sandburg $= 85.4\%$, $n = 41$; percentage at Truman $= 68.9\%$, $n = 74$ ($z = 1.95$, $p < .05$).
8. Percentage at Sandburg $= 81.3\%$, $n = 64$; percentage at Truman $= 55.8\%$, $n = 95$ ($z = 3.32$, $p < .001$).
9. Percentage at Sandburg $= 78.4\%$, $n = 74$; percentage at Truman $= 50.4\%$, $n = 119$ ($z = 3.87$, $p < .001$).
10. Percentage scoring at least 2 on the content strands: number concepts—93% at Jackson, 90% in rest of district; concepts of space and shape—95% at Jackson, 90% in rest of district; patterns and relationships—97% at Jackson, 94% in rest of district; problem solving—93% at Jackson, 88% in rest of district; reasoning—91% at Jackson, 91% in rest of district; communication—93% at Jackson, 89% in rest of district. For Jackson, $n = 98$; for the rest of the district, $n = 496$.
11. Percentage scoring 3: 69% at Jackson ($n = 98$), 56% in rest of district ($n = 496$), $z = 2.38$, $p < .01$.
12. Percentage scoring 3: 71% at Jackson ($n = 98$), 61% in rest of district ($n = 496$), $z = 2.01$, $p < .02$.
13. $t(41) = 2.99$, $p < .01$.
14. $t(54) = 1.82$, NS ($p = .075$).
15. $t(41) = 2.60$, $p < .02$.
16. $t(54) = 2.35$, $p < .03$.
17. $t(58) = 2.38$, $p < .03$.
18. Mean percentage at James $= 60.4\%$ (SD $= 24.8$), $n = 23$; mean percentage at Eisenhower $= 43.3\%$ (SD $= 20.4$), $n = 37$ [$t(58) = 2.91$, $p < .01$].
19. Mean percentage at James $= 71.3\%$ (SD $= 18.9$), $n = 23$; mean percentage at Eisenhower $= 50.0\%$ (SD $= 20.5$), $n = 37$ [$t(58) = 4.02$, $p < .01$].
20. Mean percentage at James $= 57.0\%$ (SD $= 22.9$), $n = 23$; mean percentage at Eisenhower $= 44.9\%$ (SD $= 20.2$), $n = 37$ [$t(58) = 2.14$, $p < .04$].
21. Mean percentage at James $= 56.1\%$ (SD $= 23.9$), $n = 23$; mean percentage at Eisenhower $= 60.0\%$ (SD $= 22.6$), $n = 37$ [$t(58) = 0.64$, NS].
22. A pseudonym was used.

4

Achievement of Students Using the University of Chicago School Mathematics Project's *Everyday Mathematics*

William M. Carroll

St. Ignatius Preparatory High School

Andrew Isaacs

University of Chicago

In 1983, the University of Chicago received a 6-year grant from the Amoco Foundation for a project to improve mathematics education for U.S. elementary and secondary students. Funding of the University of Chicago School Mathematics Project (UCSMP) reflected a growing consensus among educators, leaders of industry, and government agencies that the U.S. mathematics curriculum was failing to produce citizens literate in the mathematics needed for the 21st century. In 1985, after 2 years of feasibility studies with schools and teachers, the UCSMP Elementary Component began development of *Kindergarten Everyday Mathematics* (*KEM*), an ambitious program that built on students' informal, everyday knowledge of mathematics.[1]

Soon after the publication of *KEM* in 1987, it became apparent that *KEM* children would require a first-grade program more demanding than any available at that time. A decision was made to extend the program into the elementary grades. Funding from the GTE Corporation and the Everyday Learning Corporation made possible the development of *Everyday Mathematics* for first through third grades, published in 1989, 1991, and

79

1992, respectively. The success of the primary grade program led, in 1993, to a National Science Foundation (NSF) grant that made possible the completion of the curriculum through sixth grade. By 1996, *Everyday Mathematics* (*EM*) for K–6 was finished and available from the Everyday Learning Corporation.[2]

THE *EVERYDAY MATHEMATICS* PROGRAM

Principles for the Development of *Everyday Mathematics*

EM is based both on research in mathematics education[3] and on the curriculum developers' experience teaching mathematics and writing curriculum. The research basis and the developers' experience lead to the following principles for building a new curriculum.

First, children begin school with a great deal of mathematical knowledge and intuition. Rather than ignoring or suppressing this knowledge, the curriculum should build on it, aiming significantly higher than has been the case traditionally (Baroody & Ginsburg, 1986; Bell & Burns, 1981; Carpenter, Ansell, Franke, Fennema, & Weisbeck, 1993; Carpenter & Moser, 1984; Fuson & Hall, 1983; Gelman & Gallistel, 1978; Gelman, Meck, & Merkin, 1986; Hiebert, 1984; Resnick, 1983; Resnick, Lesgold, & Bill, 1990; Riley, Greeno, & Heller, 1983).

Second, the elementary school mathematics curriculum should be significantly broadened. Investigations in geometry, data and statistics, and algebra should begin in kindergarten and continue with growing sophistication throughout the grades (Begle, 1973; Bell, 1974; National Council of Supervisors of Mathematics [NCSM], 1977, 1988; National Council of Teachers of Mathematics [NCTM], 1989, 2000; Pollak, 1983/1987).[4]

Third, manipulatives are important tools in helping students represent mathematical situations. They support students' thinking and promote the development of problem-solving skills (Brownell, 1968; Bruner, 1964; Fennema, 1972; Hiebert & Wearne, 1992; Lesh, Post, & Behr, 1987; Post, Lesh, Cramer, Harel, & Behr, 1993; Suydam, 1984, 1986; F. Thompson, 1991; P. Thompson, 1994).

Fourth, although paper-and-pencil calculation is important, it is only one strand in a well-balanced computational curriculum. Flexible number sense, estimation and mental arithmetic skills, and good judgment about using calculators and other technology are as important as paper-and-pencil skills. The new curriculum should include practical routines to help build the arithmetic skills and quick responses that are so essential in a problem-rich environment (Coburn, 1989; Rathmell & Trafton, 1990; Reys, 1986; Schoen, 1986; Sowder, 1992; Sowder & Wheeler, 1989).

Fifth, although students actively construct their knowledge, the teacher and curriculum are important in providing a guide for learning important mathematics. Instruction should provide rich contexts and accommodate a variety of learning styles. Whole-class discussions, small-group explorations, individual practice, problem-solving activities, and guided instruction are all important in a balanced curriculum (Committee of Inquiry, 1982; Fraivillig, Murphy, & Fuson, 1999; NCTM, 1991; Stevenson & Stigler, 1992; Stigler & Perry, 1988; Stodolsky, 1988; Yackel, Cobb, & Wood, 1991).

Sixth, mathematical questions and observations should be woven into daily classroom routines—class attendance, temperature, and time and date—so that mathematics becomes a pervasive way of thinking rather than just another school subject (Anderson, Reder, & Simon, 1996; Bell, 1972; Dewey, 1902, 1938; Usiskin & Bell, 1983).

Seventh, assessment should be ongoing and should match the types of activities in which students are engaged. Teachers need a broad and balanced set of assessment tools and techniques (Lambdin, 1993; NCTM, 1995; Webb, 1993).

Eighth, reforms must take account of the working lives of teachers. Reforms often fail because they are not practical. The new curriculum should be manageable and should include suggestions and procedures that make teachers' lives easier, at least in the long run.

Based on these principles, *EM* was developed 1 year at a time so that feedback from field tests could inform the writing process and each grade could build on the mathematics in previous grades. Throughout its development, teachers have been involved in writing, testing, and revising *EM*. Each grade was tested in classrooms for at least 1 entire year and was then revised on the basis of observations, interviews, student and teacher comments, and assessment results. As this is being written, *EM* is undergoing another revision, so the development cycle continues.

The *Everyday Mathematics* Curriculum

KEM, the first year of the curriculum, supports approximately 100 hours of mathematics activities. The program emphasizes playful, verbal interactions and manipulative activities while laying the groundwork for symbolic understanding. The activities encompass a variety of mathematics strands, including simple and complex counting, numeration, operations, measurement, geometry, clock and calendar use, graphs, patterns, attributes, and function ideas. Common life applications are a feature of each strand.

Materials for Grades 1–3 build on and extend the concepts first studied in the previous grades, with progressively increasing attention to mental and symbolic arithmetic, measurement, geometry, the collection and use of data, and the beginnings of algebra. Strong emphasis is placed on formulating and solving "number stories" with information from day-to-day life, science, geography, and other curriculum areas.

The Grades 4–6 curriculum emphasizes "mathematical modeling" of situations from everyday life and other school subjects. It blends the mathematical strands introduced in previous grades with science, geography, sports, and architecture. For example, in a year-long project for fourth grade, called the World Tour, students "visit" a variety of countries, collecting and analyzing information about them. In a similar project for Grade 5, called the American Tour, students collect and analyze data about the United States.

Probably the best way to understand *EM* is to observe some lessons in a school where it is well implemented. In such a school, children will be engaged in a mix of small group, whole class, and individual work. Compared with children in classrooms using traditional textbooks, children will use tools such as hundreds grids and calculators more frequently. Teachers will commonly represent mathematical ideas in multiple ways and children will discuss their own solution methods. Arithmetic work will be more mental or tool based and less paper and pencil. There will be a balance of concepts, skills, and facts. Topics will be introduced earlier and will be revisited repeatedly in new contexts and at greater depth.

For instance, instead of learning to count and read whole numbers only up to 10 or 20, *KEM* students read and write whole numbers up to 100, and they create number stories for whole numbers and simple fractions. In Grade 2, *EM* students learn to skip count not just by 2s, 5s, and 10s up to 100 or 200, but to skip count to 10,000 by using other patterns. By the end of Grade 6, *EM* students not only have studied algorithms for addition, subtraction, multiplication, and division of fractions and decimals, they have also studied topics generally not covered in traditional curricula until later years such as using rates, ratios, and percents to solve problems, and reading and writing numbers in exponential and scientific notation.[5]

Two examples of the depth of study of geometry in *EM* are given in Fig. 4.1. The first is a geometry question from a set of first-grade mixed review exercises; the second is a fourth-grade assessment item. In both of these problems, the vocabulary and concepts are much more ambitious than those generally explored in early elementary school. Together they illustrate how far the *EM* curriculum progresses from first grade, in which entire figures are identified, to fourth grade, in which students must reason from geometric properties and relationships to identify the partially hidden figures. Typically, in class discussion of such questions, students are asked to explain their reasoning.

1.   A first-grade Math Box

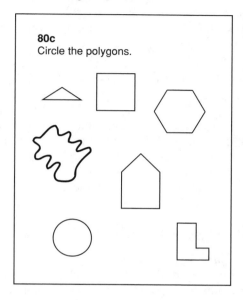

2.   A fourth-grade assessment item

Checking Progress

1. Part of each polygon below is hidden. One of the three polygons is a parallelogram, another is a trapezoid, and another a regular hexagon. Write the name of each polygon in the space provided.

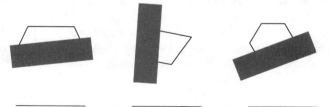

FIG. 4.1.   Sample geometry questions from *Everyday Mathematics*.

STUDENT ACHIEVEMENT STUDIES

Because of the curriculum's roots in research and a development process based on classroom trials, a large number of studies of *EM* have been conducted. These studies have been carried out by three principal groups: the Elementary Component of UCSMP, an NSF-funded group at

Northwestern University under the direction of Dr. Karen Fuson, and individual schools and districts using the curriculum.

Here we discuss representative studies employing different methodologies and investigating various grades.

Studies Conducted by the UCSMP Elementary Component

UCSMP has always devoted a significant portion of its resources to research and evaluation. Since 1987, the UCSMP Elementary Component has carried out numerous studies of the effects of *EM* on teachers and students. Although most of this research was intended only for internal use, a few reports have been made public at professional meetings and in various journals (Carroll, 1996a, 1996b, 1997, 1998).

The Third-Grade Illinois State Test

When *Third Grade Everyday Mathematics* was first published during the 1992–1993 school year, the opportunity arose to evaluate *EM* student performance on a state mathematics test, the Illinois Goal Assessment Program Test. The mathematics portion of the Illinois Goal Assessment Program (IGAP) is administered each April to all third-, sixth-, and eighth-grade students in Illinois public schools. Because the results are widely reported in the media and are used in evaluating individual schools, the IGAP is a high-stakes test. In 1993, the third-grade IGAP mathematics test employed a timed, multiple-choice format with no open-ended questions. No calculators or other tools were allowed.[6]

Although traditional in these respects, the 1993 IGAP, like many state tests, was influenced by the NCTM *Standards* (1989, 1991). Third-grade items covered six mathematical content strands: computation, measurement, algebra, geometry, data collection and analysis, and estimation. In alignment with the NCTM *Standards*, the computation subtest focused on number sense and problem solving rather than symbolic computation. Figure 4.2 gives two sample items from the computation subtest (Illinois Board of Education, 1989). Because of the inclusion of a broad range of mathematical topics not usually emphasized in primary school and the use of computation in context, the 1993 IGAP appeared to be a good fit with the *EM* curriculum.

Method. In 1993, IGAP test scores were reported at the school level and not for individual children or classes, so only Illinois public schools in which all third-grade students used *EM* were selected for this study. Curriculum supervisors were contacted at schools identified as using *EM* to confirm that all third-grade teachers had used the curriculum. Twenty-six

1. What are the missing numbers?

 7, 14, 21, 28, 35, __, __

 ☐ 28, 21

 ☐ 38, 41

 ☐ 40, 45

 ☐ 42, 49

2. There are 25 students in a third-grade class. There are 7 students absent today because they are sick. Which number expression below tells how many students are in class today?

 ☐ 25 − 7

 ☐ 25 + 7

 ☐ 7 − 25

 ☐ 18 + 7

FIG. 4.2. Sample computation items from the IGAP.

schools from nine districts with a total of 1,885 students met these criteria and were included in the study. These schools represented a cross section of suburban schools from the Chicago area. That is, the *EM* schools did not come from the districts with the highest socioeconomic status but instead represented a range of schools, including three schools with a sizeable low-income population. Third-grade students in 14 of these 26 schools had used *EM* since kindergarten. Third-grade students in the remaining 12 schools began using *EM* in second (four schools) or third grade (eight schools). No third-grade classes in the Chicago public schools were using *EM* during the year of this study.

Two measures are considered in this study, that is, the mean score and the performance of students relative to state expectations. To allow for comparisons of mean scores between schools or districts or across years, the state provides a confidence band of plus or minus two standard errors around the school or district mean score (Illinois State Board of Education, 1993). Scores that do not overlap within this confidence band are significantly different. Because the majority of the *EM* schools (65%) were in suburban Cook County and the remaining *EM* schools were from three other Chicago-area counties with similar demographics, the suburban Cook County score (not including Chicago city schools) on the IGAP was used along with the state score for comparison.

Results. The mean mathematics scores for the 26 schools using the *EM* curriculum ranged from 276 to 423, with an overall mean school score of 337. By comparison, the state mean score was 268 and the suburban Cook County mean score was 295. As shown in Fig. 4.3, all *EM* schools scored well above the state score, and all but three scored above the suburban Cook County score. When only those 14 schools whose third-grade students had been in the *EM* curriculum since kindergarten are considered, the mean scores ranged from 310 to 423, with an overall mean of 351.

Because of concerns about the performance of lower-income students in a *Standards*-based curriculum, the scores of three schools with sizeable low-income populations were examined separately. These schools (D, E, and O) had a substantial population of low-income students according to state guidelines (45%, 27%, and 18%, respectively).[7] Their mean scores were 325, 333, and 306, respectively, all well above the state and suburban Cook County mean scores.

The high performance of the *EM* students is more evident when performance relative to state goals is considered. At the 14 schools where students had used the curriculum since kindergarten, more than half of the students exceeded the state goals, and only 2% failed to meet the goals (Fig. 4.4). As shown in Fig. 4.4, as compared to the state and Cook County data, a much higher percentage of *EM* students exceeded the state goals, and a lower percentage failed to meet the state goals.

Mental Computation and Number Sense of Fifth Graders

Although mental computation is used more often than paper-and-pencil calculations in everyday situations, little attention has been given to it in the traditional U.S. curriculum (Hope, 1986). Without experience using appropriate mental methods, students are weak at mental computation, often mentally applying the standard paper-and-pencil algorithms rather than more effective methods (Reys, Reys, & Hope, 1993). Because *EM* encourages primary grade students to use their own solution methods during problem-solving activities, it is expected that *EM* students will develop a stronger number sense that will help them in mental computation.

A study by Reys, Reys, and Hope (1993) examined mental computation at several grades. Items from this study were used during the field test of *Fifth Grade Everyday Mathematics* to assess the mental computation of students who had been through several years of the curriculum.

Method. In the original study by Reys et al., 250 fifth-grade students from a suburban U.S. school district and a Canadian urban school district were tested. In both districts, students were using traditional mathematics

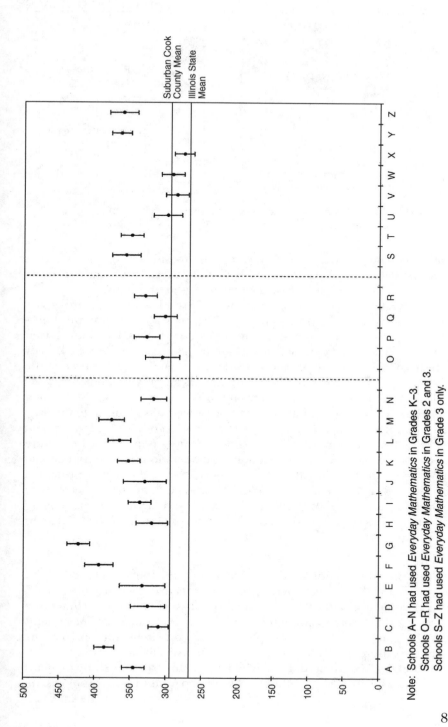

Note: Schools A–N had used *Everyday Mathematics* in Grades K–3.
Schools O–R had used *Everyday Mathematics* in Grades 2 and 3.
Schools S–Z had used *Everyday Mathematics* in Grade 3 only.

FIG. 4.3. Confidence bands (±2 SE) for 1993 third-grade IGAP scores.

87

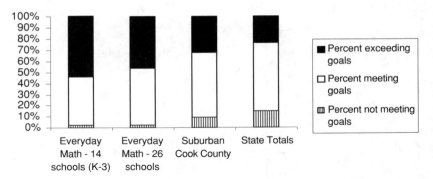

FIG. 4.4. Percent at each level of competence on the 1993 Illinois mathematics test.

textbooks. The purpose of the Reys study was twofold: to provide a snapshot of the mental computation of students in traditional curricula and to provide a benchmark for comparison with *Standards*-based programs.

For the current study, participants were 78 students in four fifth-grade classes using the field-test version of the *EM* curriculum during the 1994–1995 school year. These field test schools had used *EM* since kindergarten and were selected to be similar to the baseline group in the Reys et al. study in terms of age and type of school district (Reys et al., 1993). Three of the schools were in suburban districts, and one was an urban school.

Twenty-five items were selected from the Reys test and administered by a trained research assistant following testing procedures identical to the original study. Because classes were already involved in other tests for the field test of *EM*, only a subset of the original Reys items was used. The items were selected to include a range of mathematical operations and computational difficulty. As in the original study, problems were read orally or presented visually on the overhead (see Table 4.1), and students had 8 seconds to record their answers. All calculations were to be done mentally and a narrow piece of paper was provided on which answers were recorded. All items were scored as correct or incorrect.

Results.   Mean scores on the 25-item test for the four *EM* classes ranged from 41% to 50% correct. Overall, *EM* students had a mean score of 47% correct compared with 24% correct for the baseline group of students, a difference that is statistically significant.[8] As shown in Table 4.1, *EM* students scored higher than the Reys sample on all but one item, and on 16 of the items the differences in performance were statistically significant.

Although *EM* students did much better than the baseline group on many problems, especially large differences were apparent in story problems, on

TABLE 4.1
Mean Percent Correct on Mental Math Items

Presentation and Problem	Fifth Graders	
	EM ($n = 78$)	Reys et al. ($n = 250$)
Oral Presentation		
47 plus 29	62	35*
28 plus 75	63	34*
265 minus 98	8	6
Double 84	76	50*
60 multiplied by 70	63	33*
4000 multiplied by 100	50	17*
8 times 99	24	26
5 times 125	31	15
5 multiplied by 54	33	20
3800 divided by 10	72	12*
Visual Presentation		
68 + 32	81	53*
325 + 25 + 75	62	39*
75 + 85 + 25 + 2000	38	1*
426 + 75	58	37*
470 − 300	67	64
$20.00 − $11.98	19	10
7000 − 4000 − 300	42	18*
25 × 28	3	1
2 × 27 × 5	24	12
3500 divided by 35	53	16*
Story Problems		
Linda had $20. How much will she have left if she buys this scarf? (Picture of scarf for $12.85).	31	9*
Chuck's family lives 100 km from Chicago. They stop after driving 65 km. How much farther do they have to go?	86	32*
Kevin delivers 38 newspapers each day. How many newspapers does he deliver in 5 days?	49	26*
Five identical tapes cost $10.30. What does each tape cost?	21	4*
Total	47	24

Note. Story problems were presented both orally and visually. A Bonferroni correction was used to adjust the significance level for multiple planned comparisons. For each of the 25 tests the significance level was set at $\alpha = .05/25 = .002$.

*A chi-square test indicated a significant difference; $p < .002$.

multiplication and division involving multiples of 10 (e.g., 60×70), and on addition and subtraction problems that could be solved by transforming the problem in some way. For example, the problem $75 + 85 + 25 + 2{,}000$, which might be transformed as $[(75 + 25) + 85] + 2{,}000$, was solved by 38% of the *EM* students and by only 1% of the baseline group.

Given the focus of the *EM* curriculum on problem solving, alternative solution methods, and discussions of methods and answers, these results are not unexpected. Follow-up interviews showed that *EM* students used a variety of solution methods reflecting good number sense (Hope & Sherrill, 1987), including left-to-right addition or changing problems to make "friendly" numbers. Many of these methods were "invented" methods observed in the primary grades, and none of the interviewees used the standard paper-and-pencil algorithms mentally.

Geometric Knowledge of Fifth- and Sixth-Grade Students

Geometry is a major strand in the *EM* curriculum, with lessons guided by the van Hiele model of geometric thought (Crowley, 1987; Fuys, Geddes, & Tischler, 1988). In kindergarten and first grade, geometry lessons focus on recognizing, naming, and drawing figures. In higher grades, students analyze properties of figures and begin to make informal deductions based on those properties. As part of the field test of sixth-grade *EM*, the geometric knowledge of *EM* fifth- and sixth-grade students was compared with that of students in more traditional curricula.

Method.   Six classes using the field-test version of the sixth-grade *EM* curriculum and four classes using the published version of the fifth-grade *EM* curriculum were selected from six different districts, four in Illinois and one each in Pennsylvania and Minnesota. Three districts were suburban, two rural, and one urban. The sample included students from a wide range of socioeconomic and ethnic backgrounds, and half of the schools had a low-income population of 16% or greater. All classes in the *EM* sample were of mixed ability, and all students except transfer students had been in *EM* since kindergarten.[9]

Ten comparison classes were also selected; there were six at sixth grade and four at fifth grade. These classes were selected from districts that matched the participating *EM* schools on location and socioeconomic status (SES) variables. None of the comparison students had been in the *EM* curriculum at earlier grades. The comparison classes studied mathematics from traditional mathematics texts, generally a few years old. None were using *Standards*-based texts. In some districts the fifth- and sixth-grade classes were in the same school; in others they were in different schools. At sixth grade, most schools were departmentalized with students changing classes for mathematics. A paper-and-pencil computation test given to the fifth-grade classes (four *EM* and four comparison) found no difference between the *EM* and comparison fifth-grade students.

A geometry test, constructed by the first author and based on the van Hiele framework, was administered in each class in the fall and again in the spring of the 1995–1996 school year.[10] Prior to testing, a draft of the test was sent to three researchers outside the UCSMP Elementary Component who are familiar with the van Hiele model. Changes were made in accord with their suggestions.

Because of the age of the students, only Level 0 (Visualization), Level 1 (Analysis), and Level 2 (Informal Deduction) of the van Hiele model were assessed. The geometry pretest and posttest each consisted of 27 questions. Twenty-one of these questions assessed the van Hiele levels, with seven questions at each level. A criterion of at least five correct was chosen to indicate success.[11] Six questions that were not based on the van Hiele model were also included to assess other geometric topics, including two questions that required the students to discuss or illustrate their reasoning. Sample items for each of the van Hiele levels and one of the reasoning questions are shown in Fig. 4.5.

Only test scores of students who took both the pretest and the posttest are analyzed here; 75 fifth-grade students and 109 sixth-grade students in the *EM* group and 91 fifth-grade students and 137 sixth-grade students in the comparison group took both tests.

Results. At both grades, *EM* students outperformed the comparison students on both the pretest and the posttest, and *EM* fifth-grade students scored higher than comparison sixth-grade students (see Fig. 4.6). Because the *EM* students had studied a geometry-rich curriculum since kindergarten, they were expected to score higher than the comparison students at the beginning of each grade. Given the differences in pretest scores, an analysis of covariance (ANCOVA) was done on the posttest, using the pretest score as the covariate, group (*EM* and comparison) and grade as predictor variables, and the posttest as the response variable.[12] At the sixth grade, the gains of the *EM* and comparison students were large and virtually identical. At fifth grade, the comparison students showed much smaller gains than the *EM* students. Despite the fairly large gains made by the comparison sixth-grade students, *EM* fifth-grade students outscored them at both the beginning and the end of the year.

Most students (90% on the pretest and 95% on the posttest) had response patterns that matched those predicted by the van Hiele model.[13] In the comparison classes, nearly half of the fifth-grade students and nearly one fourth of the sixth-grade students scored below Level 0 at the end of the year.

Level 0: Visualization

What is the best name for the figure below?

a) Cube

b) Rectangular prism

c) Pyramid

d) Triangular prism

e) Cone

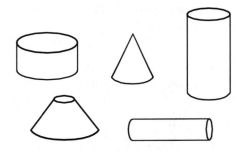

Level 1: Analysis

Circle all of the shapes below that are cylinders.

Level 2: Informal deduction

Which of the shapes below can be called rectangles?

(A) All can

(B) Q only

(C) R only

(D) P and Q only

(E) Q and R only

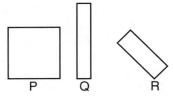

Sample reasoning question

Sheila said, "I can draw a triangle that has 2 right angles."

Do you agree with Sheila? _____ Explain your answer.

FIG. 4.5. Sample items from the geometry test.

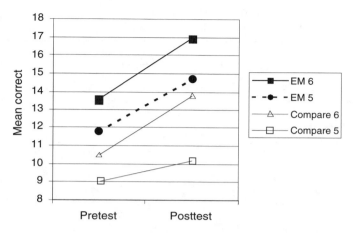

FIG. 4.6. Mean number of items correct on the geometry test. (Note: the maximum score possible was 25. The two reasoning items are not included.)

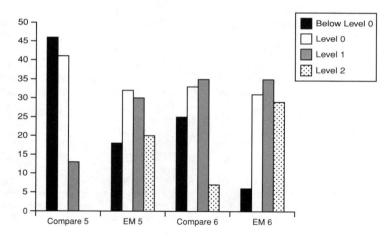

FIG. 4.7. Percent of students at each van Hiele level on the posttest. (Note: graph includes only students who matched one of the van Hiele levels—95% of sample.)

These students could not recognize or name common geometric figures. In contrast, at least half of the *EM* students at each grade were scoring at Level 1 (Analysis) or Level 2 (Informal Deduction) on the posttest (see Fig. 4.7). A Mann–Whitney nonparametric test showed that the van Hiele levels attained by the *EM* students on the test at each grade were significantly higher than the van Hiele levels of the students in the corresponding comparison group.

TABLE 4.2
Mean Percent Correct on Spring van Hiele Geometry Test Questions

| | Fifth Grade | | Sixth Grade | |
| | EM | Comp. | EM | Comp. |
Level and Question	($n=91$)	($n=75$)	($n=137$)	($n=109$)
Level 0: Visualization				
1. Identify rectangles	96	90	95	93
2. Name pyramid	74	75	69	68
3. Match time to right angle	91*	71	97	90
4. Identify triangles	80*	48	87*	66
5. Identify letter with parallel lines	78*	43	88	81
6. Find area (square units shown)	88	84	92*	76
7. Identify parallelograms	59*	16	66	47
Mean percent correct on Level 0 items	81	61	84	74
Level 1: Analysis				
1. Identify cylinders	78	63	81	80
2. Match angle to direction	82*	43	83*	59
3. Identify properties of rectangles	83	63	83	70
4. Find area of triangle in rectangle	57*	29	63*	43
5. Name parallel sides in square	42*	16	78	65
6. Properties of isosceles triangles	61	63	69	59
7. Identify properties of rhombi	25*	7	38	27
Mean percent correct on Level 1 items	61	41	71	58
Level 2: Informal Deduction				
1. Identify polygons with parallel sides	59*	34	74*	56
2. Which shapes are rectangles (incl. square)	30	25	46*	27
3. Find supplement of given angle	30*	0	50*	23
4. Identify cube from properties	49	58	68	64
5. Properties of parallelograms	33	27	34	25
6. Draw triangle of given area	29*	8	30*	15
7. Find base angle in isosceles triangle given vertex angle	34*	2	48*	24
Mean percent correct on Level 2 items	38	22	50	33

Note. A Bonferroni correction was used to adjust the significance level for multiple planned comparisons. For each of the 21 tests the significance level was set at $\alpha = .05/21 = .0024$.

*A chi-square test indicated a significant difference; $p < .0024$.

Mean correct scores on the 21 van Hiele items are shown in Table 4.2. The *EM* fifth-grade students scored significantly higher than the comparison fifth-grade students on 12 items; the *EM* sixth-grade students scored higher that the comparison sixth-grade students on seven items.[14] No differences favored the comparison groups.

Two questions on each test required written explanations about geometric concepts. For example, on both tests, the students were asked to explain whether a triangle could be drawn with more than one right angle. A total of 7 points, based on rubrics, were possible on the two reasoning questions (for rubrics and a further discussion, see Carroll, 1998). Mean scores on these two questions were 4.4 for *EM* sixth-grade students, 2.8 for comparison sixth-grade students, 2.9 for *EM* fifth-grade students, and 1.6 for comparison fifth-grade students.

Other UCSMP Studies

Along with the three studies described here, a number of tests, individual interviews, and classroom observations have been carried out as part of the field tests of the *EM* curriculum. At different grades, *EM* students generally score as well or better than comparison groups or normative samples on symbolic computation problems. However, these studies also show that *EM* students consistently perform higher than comparison students on mental computation, story problems, geometry, measurement, problem solving, and other areas that are underrepresented in more traditional mathematics programs.[15]

A Longitudinal Study Conducted at Northwestern University

In 1993, in conjunction with funding the development of the *EM* curriculum for Grades 4–6, the NSF commissioned a longitudinal study of students in the program. The purpose of this study was to provide information about student achievement in one curriculum aligned with the NCTM *Standards*. Other issues were also examined, including the implementation of such curricula, teacher belief and change, and the nature of classroom interactions in reform-based classrooms. Dr. Karen Fuson of Northwestern University directed this multiyear study.

When the longitudinal study began, only Grades K–3 of *EM* were completed. All schools chosen for the longitudinal study planned to adopt the *EM* curriculum at all grades. Participating districts were chosen to provide a cross section of sites with various levels of SES, in which *EM* was well implemented. This design provided an opportunity to evaluate the curriculum under favorable conditions. Specifically, the implementation of *EM* was fairly well supported by the school district, including providing opportunities for teacher in-service and for purchasing materials to support students' mathematical thinking.

The initial sample consisted of 496 first-grade students in five school districts, including urban and suburban districts in the Chicago area as well as one small town–rural district in Pennsylvania. In each year from first through fifth grade, the longitudinal sample was tested and interviewed. Participating teachers and classes were observed and videotaped. All teachers also took part in interviews and surveys pertinent to the implementation of a reform-based curriculum (see Fraivillig et al., 1999; Fuson, Carroll, & Drueck, 2000). Because of the large number of classes being observed and tested, the broad focus of the study, and the difficulty in finding comparable districts willing to commit to a multiyear study, comparison classes were not feasible. To provide for comparisons, tests and interviews in the study included items from recent national and international tests (e.g., the first- and fifth-grade study included items from Stigler, Lee, & Stevenson, 1990).

Multidigit Computation in Third Grade

Tests conducted during the second year of the longitudinal study showed that *EM* second-grade students scored higher than comparison samples of U.S. and Japanese second-grade students on a number sense test, but slightly lower on some standard computation problems (Fuson et al., 2000). In general, *EM* students did better on computation problems that were conducive to nonstandard solution methods (e.g., mental computation or counting strategies), but worse on multidigit problems that were presented in the standard vertical format.

Thus, third-grade tests were designed to investigate further the computational proficiency of *EM* students by including a larger number and a greater variety of computation problems, both symbolic and story problems. In particular, 22 third-grade items were selected from the Fourth National Assessment of Educational Progress (NAEP; Carpenter, 1989). NAEP items include three subtests: number and operation (11 items), geometry and measurement (4 items), and data analysis (7 items). An additional nine items were selected from a third-grade test developed for another research project (Wood & Cobb, 1989; Wood & Sellers, 1997).

The Wood and Cobb comparison sample included third-grade students in a traditional mathematics program and third-grade students using a problem-centered curriculum developed by the researchers. Items from this test were of interest because of their greater emphasis on conceptual understanding of mathematics, whereas NAEP items were selected to provide a range of mathematical topics.

Method.   Tests were administered to the longitudinal sample when students were in third grade ($N = 236$). Whole-class tests were administered in May by a researcher from Northwestern University. As a way to increase the number of topics assessed, four test forms were constructed, each consisting of 33 items (each question appeared on at least two forms of the test), and testing was planned so that the sample for each question included the range of student achievement levels and SES backgrounds. That is, each test form was administered so as to sample the range of school districts.

Administration took approximately 50 minutes. Chi-square tests were used to compare the performance of *EM* students to each sample on individual items.

Results. As indicated in Table 4.3, *EM* students significantly outperformed the NAEP comparison group on 55% of the number and operation items, 75% of the geometry and measurement items, and 71% of the data analysis items. *EM* students did not score significantly lower on any item. In fact, on three of the items (geometry 1a—finding the area of a rectangle, geometry 2b—finding the perimeter of a rectangle, and data 3—applying reasoning to a story situation), third-grade *EM* students did as well as or outperformed NAEP seventh-grade students.

Because second-grade *EM* students had performed lower than comparison students on symbolic computation, third-grade performance in this area was of particular interest. On the six multidigit symbolic addition and subtraction problems from the NAEP (items 3–8 in the Number and Operation subtest of Table 4.3), *EM* students had a correct mean score of 61% compared with 54% for the NAEP sample. However, the gap between the *EM* and NAEP sample was much higher on the three story problems, at 74% versus 52% correct.

Similar results were found on the items from the Wood and Cobb test (Table 4.4). *EM* students scored significantly better than the Wood and Cobb comparison sample on all six of the story problems, with a mean of 75% versus 52% correct. Eighty percent of the *EM* students and 59% of the comparison sample correctly completed $3 \times \_ = 27$, an item that assesses multiplication–division fact links. *EM* students also significantly outperformed the Wood and Cobb sample on one of the place-value questions. Overall, these results are in accord with previous studies that found that *EM* students are equivalent to normative samples on paper-and-pencil computation, but they are much better at applying computation in number stories, problem-solving activities, and more conceptual questions.

Finally, *EM* third-grade students' scores on two- and three-digit computation problems were compared with their results on second-grade longitudinal tests. Results indicated that *EM* students made good progress in this area. For example, 54% of the second-grade *EM* students correctly solved $296 + 604$. By third grade, 78% did so. Similarly, 38% of the second-grade versus 72% of the third-grade *EM* students correctly solved a two-digit subtraction problem requiring regrouping.

In addition to the two studies cited here, a large body of data has been collected and reported from the longitudinal study. Generally, these results paint a very positive picture of the implementation of *EM* and the mathematical development of *EM* students. For example, classroom observations show that *EM* teachers have implemented many of the ideas of the

TABLE 4.3
Percent Correct on Third-Grade NAEP Items

Question	EM[a]	NAEP[b]
Subtest: Number and Operation		
1. What digit is in the thousands place in the number 43,486?	67	45*
2. What number is 100 more than 498?	80	43*
3. $57 + 35$	79	84
4. $49 + 56 + 62 + 88$	60	48
5. $54 - 37$	72	70
6. $504 - 306$	38	45
7. $242 - 178$	62	50
8. If $49 + 83 = 132$, which of the following is true? (answer: $132 - 49 = 83$)	56	29*
9. Robert spends 94 cents. How much change should he get back from $1.00?	85	68*
10. Chris buys a pencil for 35 cents and a soda for 59 cents. How much change does she get back from $1.00?	59	29*
11. At the store, a package of screws costs 30 cents, a roll of tape costs 35 cents, and a box of nails costs 20 cents. What is the cost of a roll of tape and a package of screws?	77	58*
Mean percent correct on 11 number and operations items	67	52
Subtest: Geometry and Measure		
1. What is the area of this rectangle?		
a.	56	20*
b.	19	5*
2. a. What is the distance around a 4 by 7 rectangle?	23	15
b. What is the perimeter of this rectangle?	67	17*
Mean percent correct on 4 geometry and measure items	41	14

(Continued)

TABLE 4.3

(Continued)

Subtest: Data and Analysis		
1. Using a graph		
a. Read bar graph.	80	67*
b. Compare information from bar graph.	54	29*
c. Combine information from bar graph.	46	44
2. Using a table		
a. Read a table.	87	70*
b. Compare information in a table.	60	34*
c. Combine information in a table.	63	58
3. Four cars wait in a single line at a traffic light. The red car is first in line. The blue car is next to the red. The green car is between the white car and the blue car. Which car is at the end of the line?	64	29*
Mean percent correct on 7 data and analysis items	65	47
Overall mean percent correct (22 items)	62	44

Note. Because of the multiple comparisons made between scores on overlapping, but not identical, forms of the tests, the significance level used was $\alpha = .01$.

[a]Because different forms of the test were given, the number of *EM* students on each item varied from 107 to 119.

[b]Nationwide, a total of 18,033 third graders participated in the fourth NAEP. Only 10% to 15% of these students answered each item (Carpenter, 1989).

*A chi-square test indicated a significant difference; $p < .01$.

NCTM *Standards*, including providing a safe environment for students to investigate and discuss challenging mathematics (Fraivillig et al., 1999). An analysis of second- and third-grade observation transcripts showed that *EM* teachers were more likely to ask problem solving and conceptual questions than Japanese teachers or U.S. teachers using traditional textbooks (Fuson, Ding, & Perry, 1997).

School District Studies

Because *EM* is widely used, many school districts have looked at *EM* student achievement. Such school district studies typically report the results of paper-and-pencil tests, usually commercial norm-referenced tests or mandated state assessments. Surveys of teachers, parents, and students are also often included in these district program evaluations. Here we briefly discuss one such study, carried out in 1997 by the Hopewell Valley Regional School District (HVRSD), a high SES district that uses UCSMP in all grades, Grades K–12. This study is more thorough than most such program evaluations, but the results are typical.

HVRSD has approximately 1,750 K–6 students in three schools. In 1993, the district began using *EM* in first and second grades. In 1994, the *EM*

TABLE 4.4
Percent Correct on Items Developed by Wood and Cobb

Question	EM[a]	Comp. Sample[b]
Story Problems		
1. Paul planted 46 tulips. His dog dug up some of them. Now there are 27 tulips left. How many tulips did Paul's dog dig up?	68	49*
2. Sue had some crayons. Then her mother gave her 14 more crayons. Now Sue has 33 crayons. How many crayons did Sue have in the beginning?	76	50*
3. Ann and Stacy picked 31 roses altogether. Ann picked 17 roses. How many roses did Stacy pick?	79	52*
4. Mary, Sue, and Ann sold 12 boxes of candy each. How many boxes of candy did they sell in all?	74	49*
5. There were 48 birds in a tree. Then, 14 flew away and 8 more arrived. How many birds are in the tree?	70	51*
6. In school, 24 children play soccer. Each soccer team has 6 players. How many teams are there?	88	60*
Place-Value Questions		
7. There are 12 cubes hidden in the box. How many cubes are there altogether?	77	67

8. Some cubes are hidden in the box. There are 57 cubes altogether. How many cubes are hidden?	73	50*

9. $3 \times \underline{\hspace{1em}} = 27$	80	59*

Note. Because of the multiple planned comparisons made between scores on overlapping, but not identical, forms of the tests, the significance level used was $\alpha = .01$.

[a]Because different forms of the test were given, the number of *EM* students on each item varied from 107 to 119.

[b]In the Wood and Cobb sample, $N = 191$.

*A chi-square test indicated a significant difference; $p < .01$.

curriculum was extended to third grade, in 1995 to fourth grade, and in 1996 to fifth grade. A program evaluation study in 1996 indicated the program was a success, but the school board felt that further study was nonetheless indicated. As the 1997 evaluation report states, "Many teachers and parents believe that in comparison with more traditional mathematics curricula the program provides students with a more sophisticated understanding of math concepts, a better ability to write and talk about mathematics, and the capacity to more readily connect mathematics to everyday life. Other opinions, however, suggest that the program has undermined students' ability to compute quickly and accurately, that it has reduced the confidence of certain students regarding their understanding of math, and that it has placed an undue burden on many students to learn material independently" (Mathematics Evaluation Committee of the HVRSD, 1997, p. 1).

To plan the evaluation, the district formed a committee consisting of one principal, two parents, and 13 teachers representing all grades and schools. This committee designed and carried out a comprehensive study of HVRSD's mathematics curriculum, including standardized achievement tests and surveys of teachers, parents, and students. The standardized tests used were the Comprehensive Testing Program, edition 3 (CTP III) and the Metropolitan Achievement Test, edition 7 (MAT7). The MAT7 is a traditional standardized instrument published by the Psychological Corporation, a division of Harcourt, Inc. The CTP III is also a more challenging test favored by some private schools and high-achieving public schools because the publisher, Educational Records Bureau, provides special norms for suburban and independent schools.

HVRSD's grade-by-grade implementation of *EM* made possible a comparison involving 500 children in three schools over 2 years. In 1995–1996, none of the fifth-grade students in the district had ever used *EM*; in 1996–1997, all fifth-grade students had used *EM* since second grade. The report states the following (Mathematics Evaluation Committee of the HVRSD, 1997):

We administered the CTP III for the first time in the spring of 1996 to our fifth grade class. We administered the test again in the spring of 1997 to a new group of fifth graders. The two administrations of the test allowed us to compare the performance of fifth graders who never used the *Everyday Mathematics* program to the performance of fifth grade students who for 4–5 years were instructed almost exclusively with *Everyday Mathematics*. The results are impressive.

The mean score of the class without exposure to *Everyday Mathematics* was at the 85th percentile according to national norms. The mean score of the class taught with *Everyday Mathematics* was at the 94th percentile nationally. While both classes did well on a national scale, it is clear that the class with *Everyday Mathematics* placed significantly more of its students in the top stanine (42% as compared with 22%) (pp. 6–7) (see Fig. 4.8.).

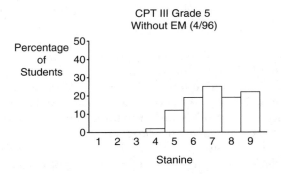

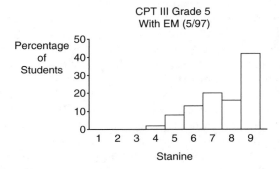

FIG. 4.8. Hopewell Valley Comprehensive Testing Program III results.

The two cohorts started out with comparable ability. The class without *EM* was at the 85th percentile nationally in first grade; the class that eventually had *EM* scored at the 84th percentile.

These CPT III results are particularly impressive considering that the *EM* fifth-grade students in the study had teachers every year since second grade who were using the curriculum for the first time. For many teachers, the first year teaching *EM* is difficult, so students who have a series of such teachers may not do as well as students whose teachers are more experienced.

The district's MAT7 results were also quite positive. In general, the findings were that concept scores rose consistently across the grades with each year of *EM* implementation, that computation scores were stable, and that there was no evidence that lower-achieving students were being adversely affected.

The committee also conducted surveys of teachers, parents, and students. Teachers had some concerns about the program—principally its effect on lower-achieving students and weakness in basic facts and computation—but overall, as the report states, "Despite their concerns, teachers continue to be strongly supportive of the UCSMP approach" (Mathematics Evaluation Committee of the HVRSD, 1997, p. 17). Parent support was weaker. Concerns centered on perceived weakness in basic facts and computation and parents wanted more information about the program and more guidance about how to help their children at home. Student surveys showed that they were very positive about mathematics.

Many school districts have carried out program evaluations of *EM* similar to HVRSD's.[16] It is certainly possible to find fault with some of these studies. Many are imperfectly controlled. Many have been carried out by the same people who decided to adopt the curriculum in the first place, so that the investigators are not always unbiased. Often the teachers were new to reform mathematics or did not have adequate training.

Nevertheless, there are clear patterns in the school district data. The preponderance of school district reports find that *EM* students maintain traditional levels of proficiency with paper-and-pencil calculation while they achieve at much higher levels in problem solving, geometry, mental arithmetic, data analysis, and logical thinking. When the *EM* curriculum is implemented, total mathematics achievement usually goes up, often dramatically. This is especially true when evaluations are conducted with assessment instruments that are aligned with the goals of *EM* and the NCTM *Standards*.

CONCLUSION

KEM was field tested in 1986–1987, with later grades appearing 1 year at a time through the publication of *Sixth Grade Everyday Mathematics* in 1997. Throughout this development period, researchers at UCSMP have conducted many formative and summative studies of the curriculum. Because *EM* became available before most other *Standards*-based curricula and has come into subsequent widespread use, a large number of studies have also been conducted by school districts using the curriculum. Finally, Northwestern University has carried out a longitudinal study of *EM*, investigating student achievement, classroom implementation, and teachers' attitudes. Across these studies, a wide range of instruments and methodologies have been used to measure students' progress and understanding, providing a broad perspective on the effects of the curriculum.

Generally, results indicate the following. First, on more traditional topics, such as fact knowledge and paper-and pencil computation, *EM* students perform as well as students in more traditional programs. However, *EM* students use a greater variety of computation solution methods. Students are especially strong on mental computation. Second, on topics that have been underrepresented in the elementary curriculum—geometry, measurement, data, and so on—*EM* students score substantially higher than do students in more traditional programs. *EM* students also generally perform better on questions that assess problem solving, reasoning, and communication. Third, although some districts report a decline in computation, especially in the first year or two of implementation, this is usually offset by gains in other areas. Many districts, moreover, report gains in all areas. On tests that are aligned with the NCTM *Standards,* such as the Illinois Goal Assessment Program, *EM* students nearly always show significant improvement over scores before the curriculum was adopted.

A variety of causal connections linking these positive results and the *EM* curriculum may be proposed. The emphasis in *EM* on "invented algorithms" in the early grades may be contributing to students' greater flexibility and competence in problem solving and mental arithmetic. The gains that many schools report on applications, conceptual understanding, and problem solving may be attributable to *EM*'s emphasis on students' devising their own solution methods and critically comparing multiple solutions. The positive results on higher-level thinking provide evidence that children who are regularly asked to think for themselves become more able to do so. The improved performance with *EM* on nontraditional topics may be the result of expecting students to learn more mathematics at an earlier age. Children are learning more of these things simply because they are in the *EM* books.

Research on *EM* supports the reforms outlined in the NCTM *Standards.* Although some critics decry the reform agenda as "fuzzy," these results show that gains can be made in understanding and problem solving without sacrificing important skills in traditional topics. *EM* is thus an existence proof that U.S. students can succeed in a much more ambitious elementary mathematics curriculum.

REFERENCES

Anderson, J. R., Reder, L. M., & Simon, H. A. (1996). Situated learning and education. *Educational Researcher, 25*(4), 5–11.

Baroody, A. J., & Ginsburg, H. P. (1986). The relationship between initial meaning and mechanical knowledge of arithmetic. In J. Hiebert (Ed.), *Conceptual and procedural knowledge: The case of mathematics* (pp. 75–112). Hillsdale, NJ: Lawrence Erlbaum Associates.

Begle, E. G. (1973). Some lessons learned by SMSG. *The Mathematics Teacher, 66*(3), 207–214.

Bell, M. S. (1972). *Mathematical uses and models in our everyday world: Studies in mathematics* (Vol. XX). Stanford, CA: School Mathematics Study Group. (ERIC Document Reproduction Service No. ED 143-557)

Bell, M. S. (1974). What does 'Everyman' really need from school mathematics? *Mathematics Teacher, 67,* 196–202.

Bell, M. S. (1976). Calculators in elementary schools: Some tentative guidelines and questions based on classroom experience. *Arithmetic Teacher, 23,* 502–509.

Bell, M., & Burns, J. (1981). Counting and numeration capabilities of primary school children: A preliminary report. In T. R. Post & M. P. Roberts (Eds.), *Proceedings of the Third Annual Meeting of the North American Chapter of the International Group for the Psychology of Mathematics Education* (pp. 17–23). Minneapolis: University of Minnesota.

Brownell, W. A. (1968). Conceptual maturity in arithmetic under differing systems of instruction. *Elementary School Journal, 69*(3), 151–163.

Bruner, J. S. (1964). Some theorems on instruction illustrated with reference to mathematics. In E. R. Hilgard (Ed.), *Theories of learning and instruction: The sixty-third yearbook of the National Society for the Study of Education* (pp. 306–335). Chicago: University of Chicago Press.

Carpenter, T. P. (1989). Introduction. In M. M. Lindquist (Ed.), *Results from the fourth mathematics assessment of the national assessment of educational progress* (pp. 1–9). Reston, VA: National Council of Teachers of Mathematics.

Carpenter, T. P., Ansell, E., Franke, M. L., Fennema, E., & Weisbeck, L. (1993). Models of problem solving: A study of kindergarten children's problem-solving processes. *Journal for Research in Mathematics Education, 24*(5), 428–441.

Carpenter, T. P., & Moser, J. M. (1984). The acquisition of addition and subtraction concepts in grades one through three. *Journal for Research in Mathematics Education, 15*(3), 179–202.

Carroll, W. M. (1996a). Use of invented algorithms by second graders in a reform mathematics curriculum. *Journal of Mathematical Behavior, 15*, 137–150.

Carroll, W. M. (1996b). Mental computation of students in a reform-based mathematics curriculum. *School Science and Mathematics, 96*, 305–311.

Carroll, W. M. (1997). Results of third-grade students in a reform curriculum on the Illinois state mathematics test. *Journal for Research in Mathematics Education, 28*, 237–242.

Carroll, W. M. (1998). Middle school students' reasoning about geometric situations. *Mathematics Teaching in the Middle School, 3*, 398–403.

Coburn, T. G. (1989). The role of computation in the changing mathematics curriculum. In P. R. Trafton (Ed.), *New directions for elementary school mathematics* (pp. 43–56). Reston, VA: National Council of Teachers of Mathematics.

Committee of Inquiry into the Teaching of Mathematics in the Schools. (1982). *Mathematics Counts (The Cockcroft Report)*. London: Her Majesty's Stationery Office.

Crowley, M. L. (1987). The van Hiele model of geometric thought. In M. M. Lindquist & A. P. Shulte (Eds.), *Learning and teaching geometry K–12* (pp. 1–16). Reston, VA: National Council of Teachers of Mathematics.

Dewey, J. (1902). *The child and the curriculum*. Chicago: University of Chicago Press.

Dewey, J. (1938). *Experience and education*. New York: Macmillan.

Everyday Learning Corporation. (1996). *Everyday Mathematics: Student achievement studies*. Chicago, Chicago: Author.

Everyday Learning Corporation. (1998). *Everyday Mathematics gets results: Student achievement studies* (Vol. 2). Chicago: Author.

Fennema, E. H. (1972). Models in mathematics. *Arithmetic Teacher, 19*(8), 635–640.

Fraivillig, J. L., Murphy, L. A., & Fuson, K. C. (1999). Advancing mathematical thinking in *Everyday Mathematics* reform classes. *Journal for Research in Mathematics Education, 30*, 148–170.

Fuson, K. C., Carroll, W. M., & Drueck, J. V. (2000). Achievement results for second and third graders using the standards-based curriculum *Everyday Mathematics*. *Journal for Research in Mathematics Education, 31*(3), 277–295.

Fuson, K. C., Ding, D., & Perry, M. (1997, March). Teacher questions in *EM* second-grade classes compared to teacher questions in Japanese, Taiwanese, and traditional U.S. classrooms. Paper presented at the annual meeting of the American Educational Research Association, Chicago.

Fuson, K. C., & Hall, J. W. (1983). The acquisition of early number word meanings: A conceptual analysis and review. In H. P. Ginsburg (Ed.), *The development of mathematical thinking* (pp. 49–107). Orlando, FL: Academic Press.

Fuys, D., Geddes, D., & Tischler, R. (1988). The van Hiele model of thinking in geometry among adolescents. *Journal for Research in Mathematics Education* (Monograph Series No. 3). Reston, VA: National Council of Teachers of Mathematics.

Gelman, R., & Gallistel, C. R. (1978). *The child's understanding of number.* Cambridge, MA: Harvard University Press.

Gelman, R., Meck, E., & Merkin, S. (1986). Young children's numerical competence. *Cognitive Development, 1,* 1–29.

Hiebert, J. (1984). Children's mathematical learning: The struggle to link form and understanding. *Elementary School Journal, 84*(5), 497–513.

Hiebert, J., & Wearne, D. (1992). Links between teaching and learning place value with understanding in first grade. *Journal for Research in Mathematics Education, 23*(2), 98–122.

Hope, J. A. (1986). Mental calculation: Anachronism or basic skill. In H. L. Schoen & M. J. Zweng (Eds.), *Estimation and mental computation* (pp. 45–54). Reston, VA: National Council of Teachers of Mathematics.

Hope, J. A., & Sherrill, J. M. (1987). Characteristics of unskilled and skilled mental calculators. *Journal for Research in Mathematics Education, 18,* 98–111.

Illinois State Board of Education. (1989). *Sample: 1989 Illinois goal assessment program, mathematics grade 3.* Springfield, IL: Author.

Illinois State Board of Education. (1993). *An overview of IGAP performance standards for reading, mathematics, writing, science, and social studies.* Springfield, IL: Author.

Lambdin, D. V. (1993). The NCTM's 1989 evaluation standards: Recycled ideas whose time has come? In N. L. Webb & A. F. Coxford (Eds.), *Assessment in the mathematics classroom* (1993 Yearbook of the National Council of Teachers of Mathematics) (pp. 7–16). Reston, VA: National Council of Teachers of Mathematics.

Lesh, R., Post, T., & Behr, M. (1987). Representations and translations among representation in mathematics learning and problem solving. In C. Janvier (Ed.), *Problems of representation in the teaching and learning of mathematics* (pp. 33–40). Hillsdale, NJ: Lawrence Erlbaum Associates.

Mathematics Evaluation Committee of the Hopewell Valley Regional School District. (1997). *Mathematics evaluation report: Year two.* Pennington, NJ: Hopewell Valley Regional School District.

National Council of Supervisors of Mathematics. (1977). Position paper on basic skills. *Arithmetic Teacher, 25*(1), 19–22.

National Council of Supervisors of Mathematics. (1988). *Essential mathematics for the 21st century: The position of the National Council of Supervisors of Mathematics.* Minneapolis: Author.

National Council of Teachers of Mathematics. (1989). *Curriculum and evaluation standards for school mathematics.* Reston, VA: Author.

National Council of Teachers of Mathematics. (1991). *Professional standards for teaching mathematics.* Reston, VA: Author.

National Council of Teachers of Mathematics. (1995). *Assessment standards for school mathematics.* Reston, VA: Author.

National Council of Teachers of Mathematics. (2000). *Principles and standards for school mathematics.* Reston, VA: Author.

Pollak, H. O. (1987). The mathematical sciences curriculum K–12: What is still fundamental and what is not. In T. A. Romberg & D. M. Stewart (Eds.), *The monitoring of school mathematics: Background papers* (Vol. 1). Madison, WI: Wisconsin Center for Education Research. (Original work published as a report from The Conference Board of the Mathematical Sciences, 1983.)

Post, T., Lesh, R., Cramer, K. A., Harel, G., & Behr, M. (1993). Curriculum implications of research on the learning, teaching, and assessing of rational number concepts. In T. Carpenter, E. Fennema, & T. A. Romberg (Eds.), *Rational numbers: An integration of research* (pp. 327–362). Hillsdale, NJ: Lawrence Erlbaum Associates.

Rathmell, E. C., & Trafton, P. R. (1990). Whole number computation. In J. N. Payne (Ed.), *Mathematics for the young child* (pp. 153–172). Reston, VA: National Council of Teachers of Mathematics.

Resnick, L. B. (1983). A developmental theory of number understanding. In H. P. Ginsburg (Ed.), *The development of mathematical thinking* (pp. 109–151). New York: Academic Press.

Resnick, L. B., Lesgold, S., & Bill, V. (1990). From protoquantities to number sense. Paper prepared for the Psychology of Mathematics Education Conference, Mexico City.

Reys, B. J. (1986). Estimation and mental computation: It's "about" time. *Arithmetic Teacher, 34*(1), 22–23.

Reys, B. J., Reys, R. E., and Hope, J. A. (1993). Mental computation: A snapshot of second, fifth, and seventh grade student performance. *School Science and Mathematics, 93*, 306–315.

Riley, M. S., Greeno, J. G., & Heller, J. I. (1983). Development of children's problem-solving ability in arithmetic. In H. P. Ginsburg (Ed.), *The development of mathematical thinking* (pp. 153–196). New York: Academic Press.

Schoen, H. L. (Ed.). (1986). *Estimation and mental computation: 1986 yearbook.* Reston, VA: National Council of Teachers of Mathematics.

Sowder, J. (1992). Estimation and number sense. In D. A. Grouws (Ed.), *Handbook of research on mathematics teaching and learning: A project of the National Council of Teachers of Mathematics* (pp. 371–389). New York: Macmillan.

Sowder, J. T., & Wheeler, M. M. (1989). The development of concepts and strategies used in computational estimation. *Journal for Research in Mathematics Education, 20*(2), 130–146.

Stevenson, H. W., & Stigler, J. W. (1992). *The learning gap.* New York: Simon & Schuster.

Stigler, J. W., Lee, S., & Stevenson, H. W. (1990). *Mathematical knowledge of Japanese, Chinese, and American elementary school children.* Reston, VA: National Council of Teachers of Mathematics.

Stigler, J. W., & Perry, M. (1988). Mathematics learning in Japanese, Chinese, and American classrooms. In G. B. Saxe & M. Gearhart (Eds.), *New directions for child development: No. 41. Children's mathematics* (pp. 27–54). San Francisco: Jossey-Bass.

Stodolsky, S. (1988). *The subject matters: Classroom activity in math and social studies.* Chicago: University of Chicago Press.

Suydam, M. N. (1984). Research report: Manipulative materials. *Arithmetic Teacher, 31*(5), 27.

Suydam, M. N. (1986). Research report: Manipulative materials and achievement. *Arithmetic Teacher, 33*(6), 10.

Thompson, F. (1991). Two digit addition and subtraction: What works? *Arithmetic Teacher, 38*(5), 10–13.

Thompson, P. W. (1994). Concrete materials and teaching for mathematical understanding. *Arithmetic Teacher, 41*(9), 556–558.

Usiskin, Z., & Bell, M. S. (1983). *Applying arithmetic: A handbook of applications of arithmetic.* Chicago: University of Chicago. (ERIC Document Reproduction Service Nos. SE 046 244, SE 046 245, and SE 046 246).

Webb, N. L. (Ed.). (1993). *Assessment in the mathematics classroom: 1993 yearbook.* Reston, VA: National Council of Teachers of Mathematics.

Wood, T., & Cobb, P. (1989). *The development of a cognitively-based elementary school mathematics test: Final report.* Lafayette, IN: Purdue University School Mathematics and Science Center.

Wood, T., & Sellers, P. (1997). Deepening the analysis: Longitudinal results of a problem-based mathematics program. *Journal for Research in Mathematics Education, 28*(2), 63–186.

Yackel, E., Cobb, P., & Wood, T. (1991). Small-group interactions as a source of learning opportunities in second-grade mathematics. *Journal for Research in Mathematics Education, 22*(5), 390–408.

ENDNOTES

1. Research conducted by the UCSMP Elementary Component was supported by National Science Foundation Grant ESI-9252984, the Everyday Learning Corporation, and the UCSMP Fund for Research in Mathematics Education. The Northwestern University Longitudinal Study was supported by the National Science Foundation under Grant ESI 9252984. The opinions expressed in this chapter are those of the authors and do not necessarily reflect the views of the funders.
2. Everyday Learning Corporation was purchased by McGraw-Hill in 2000. *Everyday Mathematics* is now published by SRA/McGraw-Hill.
3. For details, see "A Research Based Curriculum: The Research Foundations of the UCSMP Everyday Mathematics Curriculum" by Andrew Isaacs, William Carroll, and Max Bell. This paper is available on the UCSMP Everyday Mathematics web site, http://everydaymath. uchicago.edu, or from Mr. Isaacs at 5835 S. Kimbark, Chicago, IL, 60637.
4. In "What does 'Everyman' really need from school mathematics?" Max Bell (1974) outlined content for a new mathematics curriculum that would be more ambitious and more balanced than the Back-to-Basics curricula of the 1970s. Bell's proposed curriculum framework included ongoing investigations in measurement, geometry, algebra, and statistics, as well as in arithmetic. Although calculators were only beginning to become available as consumer products, it was clear that they should play a role in curriculum and learning (Bell, 1976). These ideas were taken up by many in the mathematics education community, contributing significantly to the evolution of the NCTM *Curriculum Standards* (1989).
5. Various materials describing *Everyday Mathematics*, including grade-level samplers, scope and sequence charts, and so on, are available from SRA/McGraw-Hill at (800) 382-7670.
6. The IGAP has recently been replaced by a newer test, the ISAT, with similar aims. The ISAT is largely multiple choice, like the IGAP, but it also includes some open-ended items.
7. Thirty percent of Illinois students and 17% of suburban Cook County students are classified as low income.
8. Two-proportion z test; $p < 7.5 \times 10^{-5}$.
9. The number of students transferring each year varied by school, with an average of approximately 8%. For reasons involving access to student records, it was not possible to drop students who had not been in *EM* since first grade. Furthermore, because students from lower-income households often move more frequently than higher-income students, dropping *EM* students who had not been in their schools since first grade could have biased the sample.
10. Sample items and further information about the test are available from the first author (william.carroll@ignatius.org).
11. A criterion of 6/7 correct showed nearly identical results.
12. This ANCOVA found that both group and grade were significant; $F(1, 408) = 26.61$ and $F(1, 408) = 23.5$, $p < .001$ in both cases. A group by grade interaction was also significant; $F(1, 408) = 5.06$, $p < .05$. This interaction was due to a mean gain between pretest and posttest that differed by grade (see Fig. 4.6).
13. A student who met the criteria for a higher level but missed the criteria for a lower level would be a mismatch. Because there were seven questions at each of the three levels, a student was considered to meet the criteria if he or she answered five or more questions at that level correctly.
14. Chi-square test; $\chi^2 = 3.841$, $p < .05$.
15. Contact the second author for a bibliography of research about *Everyday Mathematics*, including many unpublished UCSMP reports.
16. Collections of results from such studies are available from SRA/McGraw-Hill (800 382-7670).

5

Learning to Reason Numerically: The Impact of *Investigations*

Jan Mokros
TERC

Investigations in Number, Data, and Space[1] is designed to provide a coherent, comprehensive curriculum for Grades K–5 that allows all students to explore important mathematical ideas. Each of the four content strands (number, data, geometry, and the mathematics of change) is developed from kindergarten through fifth grade.

The number strand focuses on helping students learn about the number system and understand the relationships among operations. Students are expected to develop sensible approaches to solving problems, making use of their knowledge of the number system and how numbers are composed and decomposed. The standard algorithms for doing arithmetic operations are not explicitly taught; rather, students generate their own strategies based on their understanding of number relationships.

The *Investigations* curriculum also stresses the development of skills in describing and comparing data sets. Students pose their own questions, collect data, critique and refine their data-collection methods, represent and compare different ways of representing their data, and use the data they have collected to make reasoned interpretations. Some data units emphasize categorical data, in which the emphasis is on the process of classification and description; others emphasize numerical data, in which the emphasis is on examining variability, the shape of the data set, and indicators of center. Probability is examined in brief activities throughout the grades and in a separate unit at the upper grades.

The geometry and measurement strand provides opportunities for students to analyze their spatial environment, to describe characteristics and relationships of geometric objects, and to use number concepts in a geometric context. Students encounter polygons, polyhedra, symmetry, and geometric motions. They measure length and distance; perimeter, area, and volume; angles; and weight and capacity. The three-dimensional (3-D) geometry units emphasize spatial visualization, the construction and description of 3-D objects, and transformations between two-dimensional and 3-D objects.

Investigations recognizes that one of the driving forces of mathematics is to understand and predict change. Therefore, the curriculum emphasizes the description of change in many units. Students learn to represent and interpret graphs of changing populations, plant growth, geometric patterns, and motion. They use addition and subtraction sequences to describe situations of discrete change. Because the mathematics of change is often used to describe physical situations involving growth and time, integration between science and mathematics is an important focus of these investigations.

THE *INVESTIGATIONS* CURRICULUM

Goals of the Curriculum

Investigations aims to accomplish six major goals (Mokros, Russell, & Economopoulos, 1995).

First, the curriculum provides meaningful mathematical problems for students. The problems in *Investigations* are based on important mathematical ideas, are addressed to a wide range of students, require students to think mathematically, and encourage the use of different strategies by students with different learning styles. Problems sometimes have more than one correct solution, and they always have more than one approach that results in a correct solution. Sometimes, the problems in *Investigations* involve a real or fantasy context, but often they are purely numerical or geometric, demonstrating that mathematics can be aesthetically pleasing and satisfying in and of itself.

A popular example of an *Investigations* problem that is mathematically and aesthetically meaningful, but does not have a real-life context, is found in the fourth-grade unit, *Different Shapes, Equal Pieces*, which focuses on area models of fractions. Students are asked to divide "dot-paper squares" (paper versions of geoboards) into equal fourths and then to divide dot-paper rectangles

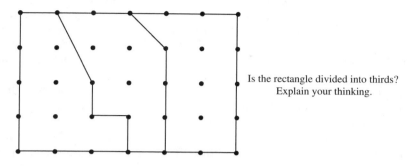

Is the rectangle divided into thirds?
Explain your thinking.

FIG. 5.1.   Assessment task dealing with area models of fractions.

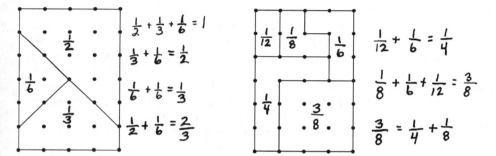

FIG. 5.2.   Student work showing fraction equations based on the diagrams.

into thirds and sixths. The emphasis is on understanding that equal parts of a whole must be equal in area, but do not need to be congruent. A sample assessment task, which follows several days' work with drawing and proving equivalence, is displayed in Fig. 5.1.

Second, the curriculum articulates a clear set of goals for mathematics learning. *Investigations'* primary goal is the development of powerful mathematical thinking, explanation, justification, and demonstration. The curriculum, which does not aim to cover all mathematical topics at each grade level, focuses on critical mathematical ideas. It identifies mathematical priorities for children of different ages, based on current research, anticipated mathematical needs of citizens and workers, and extensive work in classrooms.

For example, in the fraction unit previously discussed, fourth-grade students focus on a few central ideas about fractions. Although they do addition of fractions by using equations and area models, there is no use of prescribed algorithms to find common denominators. Rather, students practice finding combinations of fractions that equal one whole and write equations that correspond to ways they have divided up a whole, as illustrated by the student work in Fig. 5.2.

Third, the curriculum focuses on mathematical thinking. *Investigations* encourages sustained thinking by focusing on a small set of significant problems within each unit. In many cases, only one or two problems are studied during a single class session. Beginning in kindergarten, students are expected to develop their own strategies for solving problems, compare approaches with their peers, and engage in serious discussion about differences in their strategies and results.

For instance, in the fifth-grade unit *Name That Portion*, which continues the work with fractions begun in *Different Shapes, Equal Pieces*, students work in small groups, making a poster with different ways to explain why one fraction is bigger than another. Different teams have easier or harder fractions to compare. Figure 5.3 contains student work from one team, showing six different "proofs" that $2/3 > 2/5$.

Fourth, the curriculum is designed to provide both coherence and depth in mathematical content. *Investigations* takes a long-term view of the development of significant mathematical ideas. Students revisit ideas over a period of years from different perspectives because the authors believe that a major task of a curriculum is to articulate and demonstrate the coherence of mathematical ideas. In *Investigations*, units of study are developed in such a way that students can explore a few important, related mathematical ideas over a period of several weeks. Within each unit, contexts and problems build on each other. A unit is not a collection of activities to be pulled apart and used individually.

Consider the development of fractions as this topic is studied in *Investigations* during fourth and fifth grades. The area model, which is introduced prior to fourth grade, is developed and expanded upon first, because it is relatively easy for students to understand. As students develop a better understanding of equivalence, other models of fractions are introduced, building on a foundation of understanding about fractions and area. By fifth grade, students are linking their understanding of fractions to their understanding of decimals and percents, again using area as a foundation. This deep and interconnected understanding is evident in the student work shown in Fig. 5.3.

Fifth, the curriculum is designed to support teacher learning. *Investigations* units are written directly to teachers, with student sheets provided as reproducible masters at the end of each unit and as separate consumable workbooks. The curriculum provides teachers with explanations about each unit's central mathematical ideas, shows how classroom discussions might proceed, provides a variety of ways of assessing students' learning, and gives many specific examples of ways that teachers can support student learning through listening and questioning. Each unit in the curriculum can be viewed as a minicourse for teachers about a particular domain of mathematics in action with students.

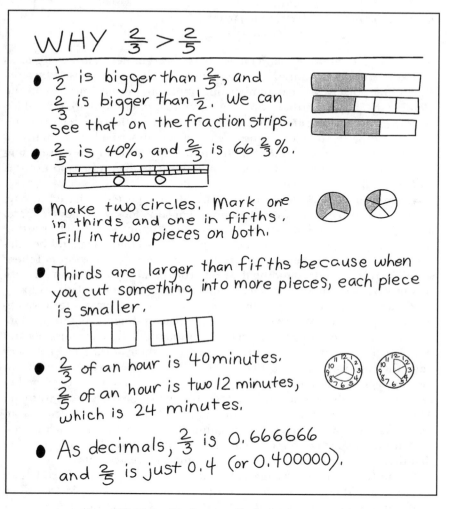

WHY $\frac{2}{3} > \frac{2}{5}$

- $\frac{1}{2}$ is bigger than $\frac{2}{5}$, and $\frac{2}{3}$ is bigger than $\frac{1}{2}$. We can see that on the fraction strips.

- $\frac{2}{5}$ is 40%, and $\frac{2}{3}$ is 66$\frac{2}{3}$%.

- Make two circles. Mark one in thirds and one in fifths. Fill in two pieces on both.

- Thirds are larger than fifths because when you cut something into more pieces, each piece is smaller.

- $\frac{2}{3}$ of an hour is 40 minutes. $\frac{2}{5}$ of an hour is two 12 minutes, which is 24 minutes.

- As decimals, $\frac{2}{3}$ is 0.666666 and $\frac{2}{5}$ is just 0.4 (or 0.400000).

FIG. 5.3. Student proofs that 2/3 > 2/5.

Sixth, the curriculum is designed to connect all students with mathematics. *Investigations* acknowledges and builds on the fact that within any classroom, the range of students' needs, interests, and strengths is typically wide. The curriculum intends to invite all students into mathematics—girls and boys; diverse cultural, ethnic, and language groups; and students with different strengths and interests. Fieldwork and anecdotal reports from *Investigations* teachers show that the curriculum is used in a range of settings, from special needs classes to classes for gifted and talented children. It is intended for a heterogeneous audience.

Investigations' Treatment of Number, Basic Facts, and Algorithms

Although other areas of mathematics are studied in depth in *Investigations* and are central to children's mathematical development, most educators (including ourselves) view number operations as a critical priority in the elementary grades. Furthermore, whole number operations are critical for work in geometry, statistics, and algebra. Thus, one of the research priorities for examining the impact of *Investigations* was to describe how students involved in this curriculum understand number operations. Before discussing achievement results related to number, a more detailed discussion of this content strand is provided.

When using *Investigations*, students are often expected to have two ways of solving a problem and to explain how their strategies work. For example, a fourth-grade student might explain that she computed 4×19 by starting with $4 \times 20 = 80$, then subtracting 4 to get 76. A second way might be multiplying $4 \times 10 = 40$, then adding the product of 4×9, or 36. Both of these solutions rely on understanding the properties of multiplication, in this case the distributive property, as well as understanding number relationships.

Students may use manipulatives and sometimes calculators to solve operational problems. Whether using manipulatives, fingers, pictures, or invented procedures, students often need considerable time to construct and double-check solutions. As students progress in their work, greater fluency and efficiency with strategies is expected. They are not expected to invent new strategies each time they do a problem; rather, they are encouraged to become more efficient at the strategies that make greatest sense to them. Throughout their work, students develop new and better strategies by articulating their own ideas and by listening to others' strategies. In all cases, students are expected to meet standards of mathematical rigor by proving that their strategies work and that their solutions are accurate.

In the early grades, *Investigations'* students develop their own strategies for solving addition and subtraction problems involving basic facts. The *Investigations* approach to basic facts is "strategies based," defined by Isaacs and Carroll (1999) as an approach that helps children "refine and extend their natural strategies for solving simple problems" (p. 509). They do this by building an understanding of the relationships between numbers and by examining different ways of composing and decomposing numbers. They often work with addition combinations that equal a given total. For example, a child who starts with $6 + 6 = 12$ might use this known quantity to reason that $7 + 5 = 12, 8 + 4 = 12$, and so on. As children build these understandings, they practice addition combinations, through the use of number games, daily classroom routines, and other activities.

The *Investigations* approach to mastery of basic facts involves building an understanding of number relationships and practicing these in different contexts. However, the curriculum is not limited to numbers of certain sizes. For example, students at third grade are expected to generate all the multiplication combinations that yield the number 36, including combinations such as 18×2 and $2 \times 3 \times 6$. In contrast, in a typical third grade, the only multiplication "facts" involving 36 are 9×4 and 6×6.

WHAT DO CHILDREN LEARN ABOUT NUMBER?

Three studies are described, one of which was conducted by TERC researchers and two of which were dissertations. These were the only rigorous studies of the *Investigations* curriculum that had been conducted at the time this chapter was written.[2]

The studies have several commonalties. Each poses word problems involving whole number operations and examines the accuracy and effectiveness of participants' methods of solving problems. Each involves an individual interview component, providing insight into how children are thinking about the mathematics. All involve both an *Investigations* group and one or more comparison groups. Finally, the studies provide data about the mathematics that actually was taught in each of the classrooms.

Third- and Fourth-Grade Students' Number Skills

This study, conducted during the 1992–1993 school year, was an evaluation of the impact of the *Investigations* curriculum on third- and fourth-grade students' understanding of number, data, and geometry (Mokros, Berle-Carman, Rubin, & Wright, 1994). The goal was to identify gains in mathematical understanding over the course of an academic year and to compare gains between *Investigations* students and students using traditional curricula.[3] Reported here are the study's results with respect to children's understanding of number.

Method

The study involved 96 students (56 third-grade students and 40 fourth-grade students) randomly selected from seven *Investigations* classrooms and five comparison group classrooms. Comparison and *Investigations* classrooms were selected on the basis of having equivalent socioeconomic characteristics. The classrooms were located in five Massachusetts communities, with schools in urban, suburban, and rural communities in each group. Students were diverse with respect to race, gender, background characteristics, first language, and mathematical skills. Eight randomly selected students from each classroom participated in the study.

Students were assessed at the beginning and end of the school year by use of a pretest–posttest design. There were two separate components to the assessment. One component was a written test of calculation skills, including all four operations; approximately 80% of the items were straightforward calculations and 20% were word problems. This test, consisting of 20 items (third grade) and 22 items (fourth grade), was designed by the researchers and was based on typical problems in textbooks at these grade levels. For example, third-grade items included a word problem asking students to determine the number of six-packs of cupcakes that could be made with 48 cupcakes. The comparable problem at fourth grade involved 150 cupcakes in packs of six. Third-grade students were asked to calculate $102 - 4$ and $129 + 35$; fourth-grade students were asked to calculate $1,259 + 350$ and $1,002 - 4$. The written test was administered to small groups of students on an untimed basis. There were no differences between *Investigations* students and comparison group students in the time needed to complete the test.

The second component of the assessment involved individual interviews, consisting of several tasks that each took approximately 5–8 minutes to complete. The tasks emphasizing number operations that were presented at each grade level are listed here. For third grade, they are as follows.

1. Determine how much candy there will be altogether if three people each get 39 pieces of candy.
2. Determine the possible ages of four people in a family, if their ages together are 101 years; then do the same problem given that the mother is 37 years old.

For fourth grade, they are as follows.

1. Estimate about how much 349×3 will be; then figure it out exactly.
2. Determine how many 60-pound dogs it would take to weigh the same as a 3,000-pound elephant.
3. Determine ways of "jumping" on a gameboard in same-sized jumps to land exactly on 20, to land exactly on 72, and to land exactly on 400. Determine how many jumps are needed in each case.

A holistic, 3-point rubric was developed for each of the interview items, with attention paid to the following factors:

High Response:

> These children are successful in conceptualizing and implementing both parts of the problem. They accurately solve both parts of the problem. They often make use of their knowledge of 100 to decompose the total into four parts. They understand the relationships between the numbers they are working with, as evidenced by their ability to make adjustments in the individual ages to make them closer to 101. Students may subtract from the total, may build up the numbers by adding, or do a combination of these approaches. They may use mental computation or pencil and paper.

Middle Response:

> These children solve the first part of the problem successfully, though they often take a few tries. They may approach the problem by trial and error, and often combine trial and error with a more effective strategy (such as adding/subtracting). The second part of the problem, in which they must solve it given that the mother's age is 37, poses significant difficulty for these students, and few are successful at solving it. Trial and error is usually the only approach they have for the second part of the problem.

Low Response:

> A main characteristic of these students is that they are not sure what to do with the numbers that are provided. They may try various operations with the numbers 101 and 4. In some cases, students try putting some numbers together to get to 101, but can't add effectively or don't know how many numbers they should add together. Also included in this category are students who fail to enter the problem at all.

FIG. 5.4. Rubric responses for third-grade task on family ages.

- the degree to which a student chose a strategy that worked;
- the child's explanation of how to solve the problem;
- completeness and accuracy of the solution; and
- the child's use of representation and tools.

The scorers were kept blind to student identity and to the curriculum being studied. Note that accuracy was not considered as a separate variable but instead was part of the overall scoring rubric. Each rubric consisted of a general set of questions to evaluate, a complete description of what constituted a high, medium, and low response, and two or more prototype responses in each category. Reliability of the scoring was at least 90% on all items.

The rubric for scoring responses to the third-grade item concerning four people in a family whose ages total 101 is given in Fig. 5.4.

Results and Discussion

Written Test of Calculation Skills. Scoring of tasks on this instrument was based on the number of correct answers achieved. Students in both third and fourth grades performed significantly better on the posttest than on the pretest, regardless of condition. For Grade 3, the time of testing was highly significant ($F = 53.38$, $p < .0001$), with no significant interaction

TABLE 5.1
Mean Number Correct on Written Computation Test:
Third and Fourth Grades

	Investigations			Comparison		
Grade	n	Pre	Post	n	Pre	Post
3	32	9.9	13.2	24	8.3	12.1
4	24	10.5	14.1	16	11.2	13.9

Note. For third grade, the maximum score is 20; for fourth grade, the maximum score is 22. Original data files are unavailable, so standard deviations are not available.

TABLE 5.2
Mean Number Correct on the Interview Tasks Dealing With Number
Operations: Third and Fourth Grades

Task	Investigations				Comparison			
	Pre	Post	Gain	p	Pre	Post	Gain	p
			Third Grade					
Candy, requiring comput. of 39 × 3	1.84	2.25	0.39	0.04	1.60	1.81	0.21	NS
Ages in a family	1.69	2.18	0.48	0.03	1.76	2.18	0.42	0.04
			Fourth Grade					
Estimation of 349 × 3	1.19	1.67	0.48	0.03	1.47	1.47	0	NS
Weight of dogs, requiring comput. of 3,000 ÷ 60	1.53	1.94	0.41	0.04	1.21	1.36	0.15	NS
Factors	1.36	2.18	0.82	0.0001	1.64	1.78	0.14	NS

Note. Maximum score on each task is 4.

between condition and time of testing. For Grade 4, the effect of time of testing was likewise significant ($F = 12.10$, $p = .0014$), but again there was no interaction between condition and time of testing. Mean scores for the two groups are provided in Table 5.1.[4]

Interview Tasks. During the interview, only two number tasks were administered at third grade and three at fourth grade. Hence, item analyses were conducted rather than a composite score determined. When the results for both third- and fourth-grade students were examined, *Investigations* students made significant gains on all five number tasks. The comparison group achieved a significant gain on only the item dealing with the ages in a family task; there were no gains on the other four interview tasks. Table 5.2 provides the mean scores for both groups of students on the interview tasks dealing with number operations.

An example illustrates the nature of the gains achieved by *Investigations* students. At the beginning of fourth grade, few children had a viable strategy for determining how many 60-pound dogs would weigh the same as a 3,000-pound elephant. It was difficult for most students to begin this task. A few children started adding up 60s, but most of these gave up. A good number of children asked the interviewer to tell them which operation to perform. As one child said, "Just tell me whether to add or subtract or divide or whatever, and then I can do it." (This child also believed that 3000/60 and 60/3000 were equally viable approaches.)

By the end of the year, many *Investigations* students, but few comparison students, had sound ways of thinking about this problem. Most *Investigations* students approached the task by building up chunks of 60s to arrive at 3,000. For example, one child, with an especially well-developed sense of number, explained that five 60s was 300 and that there were ten 300s in 3,000; therefore 5 × 10, or 50 dogs, would weigh as much as the elephant.

This study was conducted at an early time in the development of the *Investigations* curriculum, when the materials were in draft form and teachers did not have substantial time to review the curriculum before teaching it. Yet, despite the difficult teaching and learning conditions, *Investigations* students showed that their thinking about number was changing in significant ways, and that their understanding of number relationships was deepening.

Children's Construction of Number Sense in Traditional, Constructivist, and Mixed Classrooms

Anne Goodrow's 1998 dissertation examined the numerical reasoning of three groups of second-grade students. One of her goals was to determine how a constructivist mathematics curriculum (in this case, *Investigations*) would affect children's understanding of number composition and place value, as well as their knowledge of basic facts and two-digit addition and subtraction.

Method

Students were drawn from several public and parochial school classrooms studying from (a) a traditional textbook curriculum, (b) the *Investigations* curriculum taught as the developers envisioned, or (c) a "mixed" program in which *Investigations* was taught in a teacher-directed way. Goodrow conducted extensive classroom observations to determine the nature of instructional practices. In the traditional textbook group, children typically started math class with reviewing a procedure, which was followed by learning a new procedure and then completing one or two pages in a workbook. In the

Investigations group, the curriculum was used with an emphasis on constructing and sharing strategies for solving numerical problems. The mixed group used *Investigations*, but taught in a way that was teacher directed; further it is likely that children in this group were learning standard algorithms.

Forty-six children participated in the study, although not all children completed all tasks as a result of time limitations. The number of children completing different tasks ranged from 22 to 30. Each task was completed by roughly comparable numbers of students from each group. There was a range of abilities and understanding among the children in each classroom.

Goodrow interviewed children individually, asking them to do tasks involving addition and subtraction. Tasks included the following.

1. Write at least five number sentences for a particular number (selected by the student).
2. Identify the hidden part, given that you can see 7 tiles and there are a total of 16 tiles.
3. Group tiles by tens and ones, and write the corresponding numeral.
4. Count by tens and ones in the process of using chips to buy stickers.

Children were also asked to solve 12 two-digit addition problems and 12 two-digit subtraction problems on a worksheet and to complete another worksheet involving basic addition and subtraction facts. Problems were usually presented in vertical form, though a few were presented horizontally. All testing took place at the end of the school year, during a series of several 20-minute interviews with each child.

Results

Children's strategies and levels of accuracy were coded for all tasks. To determine whether there were group differences with respect to computation, Goodrow examined the two computation worksheets as well as the open-ended task that involved writing number sentences. On the number sentence task, children in the traditional textbook group produced 2.88 correct sentences; those in the mixed and *Investigations* groups produced 6.71 and 5.44, respectively, a difference that was statistically significant ($p = .0025$). Children in the traditional textbook group usually wrote sentences involving only addition, and all of these children used only two numbers and one operation in their equations (e.g., $9 + 4 = 13$). Children from the *Investigations* and mixed groups frequently used several numbers and more than one operation within the same sentence.

Included here are some responses that are representative of those produced by children in the traditional textbook group and the *Investigations* group.

Student from the traditional group
  Number chosen: 25. Sentences: $24 + 1$; $2 + 23$; $26 - 1$; 5×5; $25 + 0$.
Student from the *investigations* group
  Number chosen: 150. Sentences: 50×3; $70 + 60 + 20$; $500 - 400 + 50$; $50 \times 2 + 30 + 20$; $60 + 50 + 40$.

With respect to the addition and subtraction "basic facts" worksheets, there were virtually no differences between the three groups in terms of accuracy. Accuracy scores of the groups with respect to addition facts ranged from 95.8% to 97.5%. For the subtraction facts, accuracy scores of the groups ranged from 89.1% to 90.7%. All three groups performed better on addition facts than on subtraction facts.

Similarly, there were no significant differences among the three groups with respect to accuracy on two-digit addition items. Only on two-digit subtraction problems did significant differences emerge. On these problems, the *Investigations* group was most accurate (80% accuracy), the mixed group least accurate (60.8%), and the traditional textbook group falling between these two with respect to accuracy (69.2%; $p = .023$). A more detailed analysis showed that the differences emerged only on subtraction problems involving regrouping. Children in the *Investigations* group showed the greatest accuracy, and those in the mixed group showed the least. Table 5.3 reports the accuracy levels for the three groups on the addition and subtraction problems.

There were differences in the extent to which the three groups of children used standard algorithms to solve two-digit addition and subtraction problems, as reported in Table 5.4. Very few of the *Investigations* students solved these problems by using the typical computational algorithms.

Goodrow concludes that not only did the *Investigations* group rely on strategies that showed greater understanding of part–whole relationships, but they also performed better than other groups on the most difficult problems, specifically subtraction with regrouping. She confirms the conclusion reached by others that "children are more successful at computation when they rely on their own thinking about number rather than on taught procedures" (Carpenter, Fennema, & Franke, 1998, p. 8). In prior research,

TABLE 5.3
Percentage of Second Graders Who Were Correct on Addition
and Subtraction Problems

Type of Problem	Investigations	Mixed	Trad. Textbook	p
Two-digit addition	94	87	89	
Subtraction: no regroup.	72	66	74	>0.05
Subtraction: one regroup.	77	43	60	>0.023

Note. All three groups had roughly comparable numbers of students.

TABLE 5.4
Percentage of Second Graders Using Standard Algorithms
To Solve Addition–Subtraction Problems

Type of Problem	Investigations	Mixed	Trad. Textbook
Addition	0	60	93.65
Subtraction	3.77	48.33	85.71

Note. All three groups had roughly comparable numbers
of students.

this conclusion was based on constructivist teaching methods that are not based on a complete curriculum. In Goodrow's study, the finding is directly linked to the *Investigations* curriculum. Moreover, the study shows that it is not the *Investigations* curriculum itself that results in understanding addition and subtraction; rather, it is the consistent use of the curriculum to elicit, communicate, and build on students' own numerical strategies.

A Study of Proportional Reasoning As It Relates To the Development of Multiplication Concepts

In this dissertation study, Flowers (1998) studied the multiplication, division, and proportional reasoning skills of fourth-grade students who were using the *Investigations* curriculum. As in Goodrow's study, Flowers' research makes use of three groups: an *Investigations* group, which she labels Reform 1; a mixed group, which introduced students to a variety of procedures, including the standard algorithms; and a traditional group, which used a 1992 textbook that emphasized practice of standard algorithms. Teachers using *Investigations* and those in the mixed group received workshops about the curricula; those in the traditional group received no staff development.

Method

This study of fourth-grade students involved a pretest–posttest design and took place during the 1996–1997 school year. Students were from six classrooms in a suburban school district in the Midwest. There were two classrooms in each of the three groups; within each school, students were randomly assigned to classes. The schools using *Investigations* and traditional programs were similar, with low-middle to middle-level socioeconomic backgrounds. The mixed group was more varied in terms of socioeconomic characteristics, ranging from lower-middle to upper-middle class.

Classroom observations showed that instruction in the *Investigations* classrooms focused on students sharing their numerical strategies. Instruction in the mixed classrooms consisted primarily of teacher-directed instruction; students were encouraged to choose from a variety of procedures, including their own invented strategies as well as standard algorithms. In the traditional classrooms, students were introduced to computational procedures and then practiced and reviewed these procedures. Teachers were observed twice during the study and were interviewed to establish that instruction was aligned with the program being taught.

Flowers administered a 24-item written test at the middle and end of the school year. The items tapped multiplication, division, and proportional reasoning skills involving computation, word problems, and conceptual understanding. The written test was untimed and took approximately 45 minutes to complete. Tasks on the written test included the following:

- 14 multiplication and division computational problems, involving single, two digit, and three-digit numbers. The most difficult item was 112/8.
- 5 word problems involving multiplication and proportional reasoning. The most difficult item involved a ratio of three lions for every four tigers at a zoo, asking children to determine how many tigers there are if there are 36 lions.
- 5 conceptual understanding items, requiring students to explain the meaning of multiplication–division problems and to use a known fact to figure out a related problem, such as using 3×8 to determine 6×8.

In addition, Flowers interviewed six students from each of the three groups to assess their ability to use known facts to figure out related problems and to use proportional reasoning to solve word problems. Eight tasks were presented to each student, including the following four sample tasks.

1. How could you use the fact that $7 \times 12 = 84$ to help you find 14×12?
2. There is a drawing that shows three pizzas, which are to be shared among seven girls, and one pizza to be shared among three boys. Who gets more pizza, the girls or the boys?
3. Determine how many words you can read in 18 minutes if you can read 540 words in 4 minutes.
4. Determine the distance covered by a bicyclist in 4 hours if she travels at a steady speed and has traveled 20 miles in 3 hours, and 40 miles in 6 hours.

Results

For the written test, data were compared from pretest to posttest, with mean scores determined for each subsection of the test. As reported in

TABLE 5.5
Mean Percent Correct (and Standard Deviation) of Fourth Graders
on a Written Test by Group

Subtest	Investigations (n = 50)		Mixed (n = 47)		Traditional (n = 28)	
	Pre	Post	Pre	Post	Pre	Post
Computation (14 items)	71.9	77.9	77.0	81.4	58.7	72.2
	(16.5)	(14.9)	(17.0)	(15.9)	(17.3)	(17.5)
Word problems (5 items)	57.2	68.4	57.4	60.9	35.6	52.6
	(23.6)	(24.9)	(23.7)	(27.6)	(27.4)	(27.3)
Conceptual understanding	56.4	78.4	69.1	55.2	48.2	46.7
(5 items)	(26.1)	(24.5)	(27.9)	(26.7)	(31.0)	(33.3)
Composite Results	61.8	74.9	67.9	65.8	47.5	57.2
	(17.6)	(16.1)	(19.3)	(18.0)	(21.5)	(21.9)

Note. Each student's composite score was the average of his or her three subtest scores. This score is the average of those composite scores. Adapted from Flowers (1998, p. 46).

Table 5.5, the *Investigations* group made the greatest gains on the composite score, with particularly high gains in conceptual understanding. *Investigations* students achieved the greatest gain on the composite score, but this gain was not significantly different from that of the traditional group. It is interesting to note that the mixed group showed a slight, nonsignificant decline in the composite score from pretest to posttest. With respect to conceptual understanding, there were substantial differences between groups; although the pretest scores of *Investigations* students were comparable with those in the other two groups, the posttest scores of *Investigations* students were significantly higher ($F = 14.6220$, $p < .001$).

Despite the fact that the three groups were drawn from comparable populations, Flowers notes that their composite scores on the pretest were not comparable. Therefore, she conducted further analyses based on students' incoming score. Data were analyzed to determine the extent to which initially low-, medium-, and high-scoring children made gains over the course of the study. These results are reported in Table 5.6.

The posttest data showed that there were significantly higher conceptual scores for *Investigations* students, compared with those in the mixed or traditional groups, regardless of whether the *Investigations* students initially scored low, medium, or high in quantitative background. In other words, gain in conceptual understanding was significant for *Investigations* students of all ability levels, but there were no comparable gains over time in conceptual understanding for students from the other groups.

Flowers does not speculate about why the non-*Investigations* groups show little change or possibly a decline in conceptual understanding. The differences in curriculum may explain the differences in the scores. For instance,

TABLE 5.6
Pretest and Posttest Results of Fourth Graders on a Written Test
by IQB levels

IQB	Investigations		Mixed		Traditional		F	
	Pre	Post	Pre	Post	Pre	Post	Pre	Post
High	(n = 15)		(n = 23)		(n = 5)			
Computation	11.73	12.47	12.48	12.35	11.00	12.60	2.59	0.07
	(1.53)	(1.77)	(1.47)	(1.27)	(1.23)	(1.34)		
Word problems	4.00	4.07	3.74	3.70	3.80	4.20	0.65	0.75
	(0.85)	(1.03)	(0.62)	(1.19)	(0.45)	(0.84)		
Concept. und.	4.20	4.80	4.43	3.39	4.20	4.40	0.52	10.78
	(0.77)	(0.56)	(0.73)	(1.12)	(0.84)	(0.89)		*
Middle	(n = 27)		(n = 17)		(n = 10)			
Computation	10.00	10.19	9.65	11.00	8.60	10.20	2.12	0.74
	(1.88)	(2.19)	(1.70)	(2.30)	(1.96)	(2.53)		
Word problems	2.63	3.33	2.18	2.53	2.00	2.90	2.98	2.10
	(0.74)	(1.30)	(0.81)	(1.38)	(0.94)	(0.99)		
Concept. und.	3.00	3.63	2.48	2.41	3.10	2.60	2.59	7.56
	(0.87)	(1.15)	(0.94)	(1.06)	(0.88)	(0.97)		*
Low	(n = 8)		(n = 7)		(n = 13)			
Computation	7.13	9.88	7.00	8.00	6.62	9.31	0.20	1.11
	(1.89)	(0.84)	(1.83)	(3.46)	(2.02)	(2.56)		
Word problems	1.50	2.75	1.43	1.86	0.69	1.62	2.33	2.19
	(1.07)	(1.17)	(1.13)	(1.17)	(0.75)	(1.20)		
Concept. und.	1.38	3.62	1.00	1.00	1.00	1.31	0.56	9.12
	(0.74)	(1.30)	(0.58)	(0.82)	(1.00)	(1.60)		*

Note. IQB = incoming quantitative background. The computation section includes 14 items, the word problem section includes 5 items, and the conceptual understanding section includes 5 items. Adapted from Flowers (1998, p. 51).
$*p < 0.001$.

all five of the conceptual understanding items asked children to explain the processes of multiplication or division. Two examples are (a) "If you had to explain what 6×7 means to an alien who knows nothing about multiplication, what would you say?" and (b) "You know that 3×8 is 24. How can you use this information to figure out the answer to 6×8?" Students in *Investigations* routinely do these kinds of explaining problems. Those in the other groups were probably not expected to explain their processes regularly. It is possible that on the pretest, children from all groups made some attempts at explanation. By the posttest, children who had not had opportunities to explain multiplication–division in class may have more readily given up.

Flowers also examined the strategies employed by students to solve the problems and discovered striking differences. The traditional group used standard algorithms and other conventional procedures, showed little flexibility, and rarely explained their work. Those in the mixed group also used standard algorithms, but sometimes they used other strategies as well. However, they could not explain their work, especially for division problems. Students in the mixed and traditional groups were more likely to give up on problems if their initial approach did not work, whereas those in the *Investigations* group persevered in using different strategies.

On the interview tasks, the types of strategies used by students were analyzed. *Investigations* students used strategies based on number relationships 79% of the time, compared with 68% of the time for those in the mixed group and 59% of the time for those in the traditional group.

SYNTHESIS OF THE STUDIES

In this section, the results as they relate to some of the questions commonly asked about the *Investigations* curriculum are discussed.

1. Do children who use *Investigations* learn the "basics" as well as they would if they used another curriculum?

There are two kinds of "basics" addressed in these studies: (a) mastery of basic facts; and (b) mastery of operations with respect to problems involving larger numbers (e.g., addition–subtraction involving numbers beyond 20; and multiplication–division involving numbers beyond 50 or 100). In all three studies, students completed computational worksheets in which many problems were presented in the standard vertical manner. There were no differences between groups or trends with respect to composite scores on these computation tests.

The performances of children in the *Investigations* and comparison groups were similar, as were the gains made by children in these groups over the course of a school year.

In two of the studies (Flowers, 1998; Goodrow, 1998), detailed results from item analyses are presented along with composite scores. In these studies, there are indications that more difficult computation problems elicited more accurate responses from *Investigations* students compared with those of peers in other groups. Goodrow found better performance of *Investigations* students on subtraction problems involving regrouping. This finding may be attributable to the fact that *Investigations* students are encouraged to examine number relationships, especially with respect to "landmark" numbers of 10, 100, and 1,000.

There is little evidence in these studies regarding students' efficiency in solving computation problems, and it is important for future research to provide additional descriptive data concerning efficiency. Although observational data suggest that *Investigations'* students perform calculations relatively quickly, speed is not emphasized in the curriculum. It would be useful for researchers to operationalize their definitions of "efficiency" prior to engaging in the research and to indicate their criteria for acceptable speed. Consistent with the recommendations of the National Council of Teachers of Mathematics *Standards*, the emphasis should be on the attainment of an acceptable level of efficiency, rather than on determining who is fastest.

   2. Do *Investigations* students have a solid understanding of number and number relationships?

Here, the answer is clear and positive. In all of the studies, *Investigations* students performed better than their counterparts from other curricula with respect to word problems, more complex calculations embedded in word problems, and problems that involved explaining how an operation worked. For example, *Investigations* students generated more sophisticated solutions when asked to write number sentences resulting in a given number (Goodrow, 1998). *Investigations* students were also more successful on word problems in which there were multiple solutions and the choice of operations was not obvious, such as specifying the ages of four people in a family whose ages total 101 (Mokros et al., 1994). Furthermore, *Investigations* students were able to show deeper conceptual understanding when solving multiplication problems and to explain how the solution to one problem helped in solving a related problem (Flowers, 1998). Finally, *Investigations* students showed a better understanding of place value (Flowers, 1998; Goodrow, 1998).

Besides being more accurate with respect to solving complex problems, students in the *Investigations* groups showed qualitatively different ways of thinking about the operations than students in other groups. According to Flowers, procedures of *Investigations* students "displayed an understanding of the meaning of the operation, of the structure of multiplication and division, and of place value" (p. 20). She points out that, in contrast, students who used the standard algorithms did not connect the operation of multiplication with an understanding of place value. The deeper understanding of place value by *Investigations* students was also found by Goodrow, who concludes that these students, compared with those in either traditional or mixed groups, had a substantially more sophisticated knowledge of the base ten system. Although place value is taught as an explicit skill in most traditional curricula, the evidence presented in this chapter shows that students in these programs have a very limited understanding of this concept.

All of the researchers noted differences between *Investigations* students and other students with respect to their use of standard algorithms and with respect to inventing their own strategies. Consistently, *Investigations* students were less likely than other students to use standard algorithms; instead, they developed and used strategies that were matched to the particular problems they were solving. The flexibility of approach that was found in these studies is exemplified by a student's response to the question, "How would you solve a two-digit by one-digit multiplication problem?" This fourth-grade student responded, "It depends on what the problem was. Like if it was 13×9, I would do 13×10 and subtract one 13. And if it was 13×3, I would just add three 13s. But if it was 13×6, I would do 10×6 and 3×6 and add them together."[5]

    3. Does *Investigations* work with students who have different degrees of strength in mathematics?

Flowers (1998) found that *Investigations* worked equally well in improving the conceptual understanding of children with initially low, medium, and high levels of mathematical understanding. Students at these three levels made comparable gains over the course of a semester, though their starting and ending points were different. The Flowers study demonstrates that students at all levels of mathematical understanding develop their own effective strategies for solving number problems. Flower's work is a good beginning, and it should be followed with more research on how *Investigations* students with different learning styles, weaknesses, and strengths develop mathematical understanding.

    4. Is it beneficial for children to combine elements of the *Investigations* curriculum with more traditional programs, in order to obtain a "balanced" curriculum?

In the studies reported here in, there were different levels of use of the *Investigations* curriculum, and the curriculum was often used in conjunction with other materials or programs. In one case (Goodrow, 1998), *Investigations* was used in conjunction with a didactic teaching style in which the teacher herself presented prescribed strategies to students. This "mixed" approach was not always as effective an approach as the one that emphasized students' own development of strategies. In fact, Goodrow's mixed group, which used the *Investigations* curriculum, performed more poorly on more difficult subtraction problems than either the *Investigations* group or the traditional group.

Like Goodrow, Flowers (1998) and Mokros, Berle-Carman, Rubin, and O'Neil (1996) found that children in the mixed conditions did not perform as well as children who were consistently using *Investigations*. Flowers (1998) observed that students in the mixed group, who were encouraged to invent procedures and learn standard procedures, used standard algorithms to a much greater extent than invented strategies. However, those who used standard algorithms did not perform as well. It is possible that students have more success with their own strategies because these make more sense to the individual and are more easily remembered.

Goodrow (1998) hypothesizes that the differences between the mixed and *Investigations* groups in her study are attributable to different ways in which teachers implemented the curriculum, in particular with respect to the relative emphasis placed on class discussion and on children's own thinking and sense making. In the purely *Investigations* group, the teacher raised questions and insisted that children explain their methods for solving problems completely. In the mixed group, discussion was limited, sharing of students' strategies was infrequent, and students were given feedback primarily concerning the correctness of their answers. Thus, Flowers' and Goodrow's explanations reduce to the same message: children need to rely on problem-solving strategies that are based on their own solid understandings of number relationships. In other words, "Relationships cannot be put into children's heads from sources external to them" (Kamii & Joseph, 1988, p. 51).

All of the authors call for more examination of mixed approaches, in part because these methods are educationally appealing to the many parents, teachers, and administrators who want students to have the best of all mathematical worlds. Many educators use mixed approaches in the hopes of providing students with a wider mathematical repertoire. However, Mokros et al. (1994) and Goodrow (1998) caution against situations in which students may become confused about whether it is better to try to remember a taught procedure or to rely on one's own strategies. Mokros et al. also speculate that mixed curricula may preserve, rather than reverse, the characterization by the Third International Mathematics and Science Study of American mathematics programs being "a mile wide and an inch deep" (Schmidt, McKnight, & Raizen, 1997, p. 2). Further fragmentation is clearly an additional risk that has to be considered in using a mixed approach. The evidence presented suggests caution with respect to combining different approaches to learning mathematics.

5. How much of the variation in the studies of the impact of *Investigations* is attributable to the teacher or other factors, rather than directly to the curriculum?

Neither *Investigations* nor any other math curriculum can be viewed as an isolated educational intervention. Rather, the intervention in these studies involves an interaction among teacher, students, and curriculum. Goodrow's study, in which one of the *Investigations* (mixed group) classrooms performs poorly, indicates that the teacher's practices can override the curriculum itself. This finding is supported in studies by Cobb et al. (1991) and Carpenter et al. (1996) in which teachers received a great deal of support in helping children develop their own strategies, but did not have an extensive curriculum on which to build. In the Carpenter and Cobb studies, in which there were limited curricular resources for teachers to use, children in constructivist groups made substantial gains in their understanding of number.

This is not to say that the role of the curriculum is superfluous. It may well be that the *Investigations* curriculum, which encourages teachers to examine and build on children's thinking, has its greatest impact on students by effecting teacher change and by supporting teachers in their work. The curriculum provides a foundation and facilitates the work of a teacher who is striving to develop students' mathematical thinking. The teacher does not have to invent good problems, nor does he or she have to identify mathematical priorities and build a coherent program of study. That is the role of the curriculum. However, it is clear that there must be a partnership between the curriculum and the teacher to help children construct mathematical understanding.

Many teachers do not initially have well-developed skills in this area of examining children's thinking. Therefore, according to Russell (1997, p. 252), "the best use of good curriculum materials is in the context of a long-term staff development program which engages teachers in ongoing reflection about students' mathematical thinking." Oversimplifying the relationship between a mathematics curriculum and students' learning does not work. We must examine the impact of teacher practice combined with curriculum in order to understand how children learn mathematics.

REFERENCES

Carpenter, T. P., Fennema, E., & Franke, M. L. (1996). Cognitively guided instruction: A knowledge base for reform in primary mathematics instruction. *The Elementary School Journal, 97*(1), 3–20.

Cobb, P., Wood, T., Yackel, E., Nicholls, J., Wheatley, G., Trigatti, B., & Perlwitz, M. (1991). Assessment of a problem-centered second grade mathematics project. *Journal for Research in Mathematics Education, 22*(1), 3–29.

Flowers, J. (1998). *A study of proportional reasoning as it relates to the development of multiplication concepts.* Unpublished doctoral dissertation, University of Michigan, Ann Arbor.

Goodrow, A. M. (1998). *Children's construction of number sense in traditional, constructivist, and mixed classrooms.* Unpublished doctoral dissertation, Tufts University, Medford, MA.

Isaacs, A. C., & Carroll W. M. (1999). Strategies for basic-facts instruction. *Teaching Children Mathematics, 5*(9), 508–515.

Kamii, C., & Joseph, L. (1988). Teaching place value and double-column addition. *Arithmetic Teacher, 35*, 48–52.

Mokros, J., Berle-Carman, M., Rubin, A., & O'Neil, K. (1996, April). *Learning operations: Invented strategies that work.* Paper presented at the annual meeting of the American Educational Research Association, New York.

Mokros, J., Berle-Carman, M., Rubin, A., & Wright, T. (1994, December). *Full year pilot grades 3 and 4: Investigations in number, data, and space.* Cambridge, MA: TERC (available from the author).

Mokros, J., Russell, S. J., & Economopoulos, K. (1995). *Beyond arithmetic: Changing mathematics in the elementary classroom.* Palo Alto, CA: Dale Seymour.

Russell, S. J. (1997). The role of curriculum in teacher development. In S. N. Friel & G. W. Bright (Eds.), *Reflecting on our work: NSF teacher enhancement in K–6 mathematics* (pp. 247–254). Lanham, MD: University Press of America.

Schmidt, W., McKnight, C., & Raizen, S. (1997). *A splintered vision: An investigation of U.S. science and math education.* East Lansing, MI: Michigan State University, U.S. National Research Center for the Third International Mathematics and Science Study.

ENDNOTES

1. The *Investigations* curriculum was developed at TERC in collaboration with Kent State University and the State University of New York at Buffalo. The work was supported in part by National Science Foundation Grant ESI-9050210.
2. One additional study, "Learning operations: invented strategies that work," by TERC researchers is available but was not reported here because of a lack of baseline information on the comparison and *Investigations* groups to determine their initial comparability. In this study, significant differences attributable to condition were in all cases higher for the *Investigations* group.
3. Students in *Investigations* classrooms were using drafts of the various units.
4. At third grade, time of testing was a significant main effect ($F = 53.38$, $p < .0001$). There was no significant interaction between time of testing and curriculum condition. A similar result was found at fourth grade; the time of testing was significant ($F = 12.10$, $p < .005$) but there was no interaction between time of testing and curriculum used.
5. K. Economopoulos (*Investigations* author), personal communication, November 10, 1998.

6

Number Power:
An Elementary School
Program to Enhance
Students' Mathematical
and Social Development

Victor Battistich, Susie Alldredge,
and Ineko Tsuchida

Developmental Studies Center

Number Power: A Cooperative Approach to Mathematics and Social Development[1] is a *Standards*-based, K–6 mathematics program intended to support students' mathematical reasoning and number sense, as well as their development as fair, caring, and responsible individuals. Currently in use by elementary and middle school teachers in the United States, Australia, Canada, and Finland, the *Number Power* program supplements or replaces existing curricula and is aimed at developing number concepts. The program aims to enhance students' mathematical and social development through cooperative problem solving and by stimulating children's natural curiosity about numbers.

The development of number sense is a primary goal of elementary school mathematics education (National Council of Teachers of Mathematics, or NCTM, 1989). The *Number Power* program is built on the premise that children come to school with intuitive understandings about the meaning of numbers and about how numbers describe quantities, and that all children can and should go on to develop interconnected, flexible, and useful number sense during their elementary school years.

Aspects of number sense, as described by Thompson and Rathmell (1989), Hope (1989), and Sowder (1992), include understanding number meanings and relationships, thinking about numbers as quantities, and understanding the relative magnitude of numbers. For example, a student with number

133

sense may think of 24 as two 12s, almost 25, approximately half of 50, small compared with 93, and large compared with 3. Number sense also involves understanding the effects of operations on numbers; for instance, adding 4 to 24 results in a far smaller change to 24 than does multiplying 24 by 4. Further, number sense means the ability to establish and use referents for quantities and measures (e.g., How long is a foot? How far is a mile? How many is 1,000?). A person with good number sense can make reasonable estimates, use numbers to support an argument, detect errors, use a variety of calculation procedures and tools, and make judgments about the reasonableness of numbers in various situations.

Unfortunately, traditional mathematics instruction has often not fostered an inclination toward this kind of sense-making in mathematics among students (NCTM, 1989). Studies from national assessments show that many students have little real understanding of numbers and number relationships and are unable to apply mathematical skills they have learned to problem-solving situations (see Lindquist, 1989). *Number Power* attempts to address these issues by helping students develop the ability to reason flexibly with numbers as well as to develop the social skills they need to work well in collaborative settings. Students work together to investigate a broad range of mathematical concepts over time, in different contexts, and with a variety of materials. They learn and practice problem-solving skills and explore number concepts by using concrete objects and data they have collected. Students work with numbers in meaningful contexts and in relation to other strands of mathematics, including measurement, geometry, and data and statistics.

A cornerstone of the program is the belief that social and academic learning occur simultaneously. Students work in pairs or small groups to enhance their social development as well as their learning of mathematics. Group work equalizes the status of students because every group member's contribution is essential to the group's success. As students are encouraged to take responsibility for their own learning and behavior, as well as for the functioning and productivity of the group, they must negotiate, take initiative, rely on each other, and balance their own needs with the needs of others. As they reflect on how behavior affects others and on the underlying values that guide behavior, students begin to understand and act in accordance with basic social values of responsibility, fairness, and concern for others.

THE *NUMBER POWER* PROGRAM

Program Content

The *Number Power* program is contained in teacher resource books for each grade from kindergarten through Grade 6. Each resource book contains approximately 30 multiday mathematics lessons organized into three multiweek units. Each unit, if fully implemented, would replace approximately 10% of a typical year-long mathematics curriculum. There is one volume (three units) for each of kindergarten, first, fourth, fifth, and sixth grades, and two volumes (six units) for each of the second and third grades. Each volume contains detailed information about the philosophy and focus of the program, the development of number sense, and how to implement the program. Each makes suggestions for managing effective group work as well as developing and assessing students' conceptual understandings.

All of the units emphasize the central aspects of number sense. Throughout the lessons, students are encouraged to devise their own strategies and informal algorithms and to explain, discuss, and record their computations. They make estimates, use mental computation, decide when an estimate or an exact answer is appropriate, use numbers to support mathematical arguments, and make decisions about the appropriate use of different computational methods (e.g., calculator, pencil and paper, mental computation, or a combination of these). The progression of lessons within and across units provides in-depth exploration of number concepts over time, thereby helping students build on prior learning and reflect on their work.

Kindergarten Through Grade 3.   Units at the primary grades focus on whole number concepts and operations. In first grade, students compose and decompose numbers by looking for different ways to divide 10 objects between two bags, and by combining and taking away bags of 10 objects to make different numbers. In second and third grades, students describe patterns of 10 in the number system. They estimate, group, and count in different ways, including by 100s, 10s, 5s, and 1s; they add, subtract, multiply, and divide with two- and three-digit numbers; and they describe the magnitude of numbers relative to referents such as 100, 250, 500, and 1,000. At third grade, students explore relationships among powers of 10, including using paper money in denominations of 10, 100, 1,000, 10,000, 100,000, and 1,000,000 to solve problems and play trading games.

As students get to know the base ten number system during Grades K–3, they have opportunities to relate number concepts to other strands of mathematics. For example, in Grade 1, Unit 2, students work in pairs to measure the length, girth, capacity, and surface area of boxes, examining numeric relationships among the measurements through making comparisons, estimating, and computing. In Lesson 8 of that unit, students discuss relative magnitude by using numbers generated when they used tiles to find the surface area of their boxes. Written on self-stick notes, these numbers become the topic of class discussion as they are placed on 0–100 and 0–200 number lines, as illustrated in Fig. 6.1.

As another example of strand integration, many lessons call on students to collect, organize, and analyze data. Because the data points represent relevant quantities such as people, pets, money spent, and personal preferences,

FIG. 6.1.   Illustration of classroom activity on exploring the relative magnitude of numbers (Grade 1, Unit 2, Lesson 8).

students have opportunities to examine and describe relationships among numbers embedded in meaningful contexts.

Grades 4–6.   In the upper elementary grades, the program focuses on rational numbers. In fourth grade, two of the three units investigate fractions as relationships of part to whole, including identifying and describing fractions of regions and of sets, estimating the fractional value of parts of wholes, and identifying and describing fraction equivalency. This builds toward describing the relative magnitude of common and uncommon fractions by using referents such as 1/4, 1/2, 3/4, and 1 in fifth grade, and extending these understandings about fractions to include percents and decimals. In sixth grade, students connect knowledge about fractions, percents, and decimals to ratios as they describe equivalencies, compare quantities, and describe part–part, part–whole, and whole–whole relationships.

In the sixth grade lesson illustrated in Fig. 6.2, students discuss geometric relationships among triangles, squares, and parallelograms as they analyze ratio relationships among the areas of Tangram pieces. For example, the area of the medium-sized triangle to the area of a large triangle in a Tangram set can be described as having a 1:2 or a 2:4 ratio, depending on whether the unit of measure is the medium triangle or the small triangle, respectively. Using this understanding, students work in pairs to create designs with multiple Tangram sets and use ratios to describe part–part and part–whole relationships. In the illustration, partners work together to create a Tangram design based on ratio "clues" written by another pair of students.

FIG. 6.2. Illustration of classroom activity on exploring ratio relationships (Grade 6, Unit 2, Lesson 6). (Note: the tangram clue design reads as follows. The ratio of the area of one color to the area of the other color is 1:2. The ratio of the area of one color to the area of the design is 2:4. What might be the design?)

Social Development. Because students' social development is also an explicit goal of *Number Power*, the units and lessons have social as well as mathematical emphases. Students discuss and reflect upon their group work as it relates to both mathematics and social development. For example, an emphasis on "analyzing the effect of behavior on others and on the work of the group" might involve, at first grade, having students think about how they included each other or how they used the materials in a responsible way. At sixth grade, this same emphasis might involve asking students to reflect on how they are giving and receiving feedback in their group, and how they help each other feel comfortable in expressing their opinions.

Instructional Design

Several features of the instructional design of *Number Power* are intended to support students' thinking and help provide access to all students, including those who may be new to this way of learning mathematics or who are just beginning to develop their number sense. Throughout the program, students are asked to build on what they know by applying learned concepts to new situations. Big ideas about number, such as composition and decomposition (flexibly putting numbers together or taking them apart) or identifying rules to generate and extend number patterns, recur throughout the units and across grades. Thus, students have opportunities to develop concepts in increasingly sophisticated contexts. For example, students' understanding of fraction equivalency in fourth grade becomes the basis for comparing the magnitude of fractions such as 3/8 and 5/8 in fifth grade. What students know about the size of two fractions helps them make predictions about their sum; in the case of 3/8 and 5/8, understanding relative magnitudes helps students know if the sum will be more than, less than, or equal to one whole.

Number Power provides opportunities for students to reflect on what they have learned. Many units and lessons begin with a discussion of activities done previously, including what has been learned about numbers and mathematics in general. The rationale for each lesson is clearly explained to students, so they can use prior learning as well as make predictions based on what they know. Each unit ends with a transition lesson, in which students reflect on their mathematical learning and their social interactions with their partner or group during the unit. For example, in the transition lesson for Grade 5, Unit 3, students reflect on and apply what they have learned about part–whole relationships during the unit as they work in groups to create and play a "Concentration" style card game to find equivalents among fractions, percents, and decimals. Then students discuss, in groups and as a whole class, ways they think they worked fairly and responsibly over the course of the unit.

Open-ended teacher questions are an important feature of the program. Questions that begin with words such as *how, why,* and *what* probe students' underlying beliefs and understandings about numbers, challenging students to call on specific language and understandings in order to respond. Beyond producing a correct answer, students are asked to justify their solution by using mathematical reasoning. Such questions also serve assessment purposes, providing the teacher with information about each student's conceptual development that is a basis for making instructional decisions.

In addition to open-ended questions, the program supports teachers in promoting discourse among students in both the mathematical and social domains and provides information about the importance of doing so. *Number Power* provides detailed information about planning and introducing lessons, facilitating group work and discussion, helping students reflect on their work, and establishing a positive classroom environment. As a result, students realize they are discussing mathematical ideas with each other, not just with the teacher, and that they are each responsible for their own learning and contribution.

Finally, an important feature of the program is that the lessons are designed to provide a variety of "entry points" to solving a problem. Thus, the lessons are accessible to students who are just beginning to develop number sense while allowing students with more developed understandings to find multiple solutions to problems or extend the investigations. Students have opportunities to approach problems in a variety of ways, including building and manipulating models, drawing pictures and diagrams, and talking through their problem-solving strategies.

EVALUATING THE *NUMBER POWER* PROGRAM

A 2-year study was conducted to evaluate the effectiveness of the *Number Power* program among a sample of second- through fifth-grade students attending urban elementary schools.[2] A complete technical report on the evaluation is available from V. Battistich (Developmental Studies Center, 1996).

Evaluation Design

The 2-year evaluation was based on a quasi-experimental, pretest–posttest design with three conditions: (a) *Number Power* with staff development, (b) *Number Power* only, and (c) comparison. Teachers at six elementary schools, two schools from each of three different school districts, participated in the evaluation. For a school to be eligible to participate, at least two teachers each at Grades 2–5 had to agree to participate in the evaluation, regardless of the condition to which the school might be assigned. Two schools were randomly assigned to each condition, within the constraint that both schools from the same school district could not be in the same condition.

Prior to the introduction of *Number Power*, none of the schools or teachers were using a *Standards*-based mathematics program. One of the districts (one staff development and one comparison school) used the Silver Burdette texts, and another (one curriculum only, one comparison school) used Open Court. The third district (one curriculum only, one staff development school) did not have an adopted text, but the teachers at both schools used district-developed math activities. All teachers reported using a variety of additional mathematics materials from various sources (e.g., Marilyn Burns, *Math Their Way, Family Math*).

Number Power *With Staff Development Condition.* Each teacher in this condition (hereafter referenced as staff development) received staff development for *Number Power* in addition to a teacher resource book for his or her grade level and a resource kit containing manipulatives and other materials necessary to teach the units. During the first year, the staff development consisted of a 3-day summer institute at the beginning of the school year, with 2 follow-up days and two to three additional support visits during the school year. The summer institute was designed to (a) introduce the *Number Power* program, (b) help teachers explore the teaching approaches recommended by the *Standards*, (c) provide opportunities to experience and discuss lessons and to discuss students' number sense and social development, and (d) provide opportunities to discuss how to develop a classroom climate that supports students' abilities to work collaboratively and to solve academic and interpersonal problems. The 2 follow-up days provided opportunities for teachers to reflect on and discuss their experiences using the lessons, to deepen their understanding of mathematical and social development, and to receive assistance and advice from the program developers about their implementation of the *Number Power* lessons.

During the second year of the study, the teachers at each school received 1 day of staff development as a group at the beginning of the school year, followed by five to seven individual support visits by program staff during the school year. During the support visits, each teacher had the opportunity to choose from a variety of services, including reviewing individual lessons or key mathematical and social concepts or goals; discussing needs, approaches, or problems; and coplanning or coteaching a lesson with the program staff member.

Number Power Only Condition.   Teachers in this condition (hereafter referenced as curriculum only) received the teacher resource book for their grade level as well as the resource kit containing manipulatives and other materials necessary to teach the units. However, they did not receive any staff development services or other support from program staff during the course of the evaluation.

Comparison Condition.   Teachers in the comparison condition continued to teach their "regular" mathematics program during the course of the evaluation.[3]

Research Sites and Participants

Participants were second- through fifth-grade teachers and students at six urban elementary schools in the San Francisco Bay area. The schools served ethnically diverse student populations from working-class and middle-class families.

TABLE 6.1
Number of Participating Teachers by Grade
Level and Condition

Grade	Comparison	Curr. Only	Staff Dev.
2	4	3	7
3	5	3	4
4	4	5	5
5	4	3	3

A total of 50 teachers participated in the evaluation: 31 participated during both years, 8 participated only during the first year, and 11 participated only during the second year. Turnover resulted from teachers leaving the schools or moving to nonparticipating grades. Table 6.1 gives the number of teachers by grade and condition.

The teachers were predominantly female (92%) and White (73%), and they had considerable teaching experience (average of 18 years).

A total of 929 students participated in the evaluation. This includes 848 students at Grades 3–5 who completed questionnaires (571 during Year 1 and 539 during Year 2, with 262 students completing questionnaires both years), and 352 students at Grades 2–5 who were interviewed (234 during Year 1 and 228 during Year 2, with 110 students being interviewed both years). Approximately equal numbers of boys and girls participated. The students were 48% White, 5% African-American, 8% Hispanic, and 39% Asian–Pacific Islander (including Southeast Asians). Approximately 15% of the students had little or no English proficiency, 18% were eligible for subsidized school lunches, and 10% were receiving compensatory education. Slightly more than 30% of the students participated during both years of the evaluation.[4] The parents of all participating students provided written informed consent for their participation in the evaluation.

Instruments

Assessments included classroom observations, questionnaires, and interviews. Data on implementation were obtained from classroom observations, teacher questionnaires, and from teachers' reports of their experiences of using the curriculum during annual teacher interviews.

Effects on students' attitudes and experiences were assessed by questionnaire. The questionnaire included several multi-item scales:

- Efficacy at math (e.g., "I'm very good at math."),
- Enjoyment of math (e.g., "I like to figure out different ways to do math problems."),

- The quality of group interaction (e.g., "When I work with other students in my class we listen carefully to each others' ideas."),
- Enjoyment of group work (e.g., "I really like working with other students."),
- Positive outcomes of group work (e.g., "We work with other students because we can learn more things that way."), and
- Classroom supportiveness (e.g., "Students in my class work together to solve problems.").

Students responded to the items by using a three-point scale: 1 = not true, 2 = sometimes true, 3 = true.

Students' *number sense* was assessed by using individual, structured interviews, one for students at Grades 2 and 3 and a second for students at Grades 4 and 5. In the interviews, students were asked to perform a variety of tasks (e.g., estimate the number of objects in a container, compose and decompose numbers, divide objects into equal and unequal fractional parts, interpret data on a chart), to describe how they approached each task, and to justify their answers (i.e., "How do you know?"). The interviews provided information on students' number sense in several areas, including estimation, mental computation, relative magnitude of numbers, and composition and decomposition of numbers. Consistent with program emphases, the Grade 2–3 interview focused on whole number concepts and operations; the Grade 4–5 interview focused on rational numbers. All students were asked to do some tasks involving whole numbers and some tasks involving rational numbers; approximately one quarter of the interview consisted of identical tasks for all students.

Performance on each of the interview tasks was scored by using a 5-point rubric: 0 = unable to answer; 1 = poor answer; 2 = adequate answer; 3 = good answer; 4 = superior answer.[5] For example, in one of the common tasks, students were presented with numbers printed on cards and asked to answer questions about relative magnitude. Students were initially presented with the numbers 36, 120, 200, and 340 in random order. They were asked, "Which numbers are less than 150?" and "Which numbers are more than 100 but less than 300?" Students were then shown, in random order, the following eight numbers printed on cards: 120, 200, 340, 436, 480, 560, 700, and 850. They were asked "Which numbers are more than 450 but less than 800?" and "Which numbers are closer to 500 than to 400?" Students were free to rearrange the number cards as they wished and were asked to justify their answers to each question.

A student with a poor response would not be able to identify both numbers that are less than 150 and that are between 100 and 300, and that student would not be able to articulate a good rationale for his or her answers. He or she would have inaccurate or inconsistent responses to

(Interviewer questions are shown in abbreviated form within parentheses; HDYK? = how do you know?)

(a) Poor Response:

    (< 150?) *36. . . because 30 + 6 = 36 and. . . it's less than 150.* (> 100 and < 300?) *200, because it's between 100 and 300.* (others?) *No.* (> 450 and < 800?) *70. . . 700. . . and. . .* (HDYK?) *Because it's before 8.* (closer to 500 than 400?) *480. . . and. . . 436.* (HDYK?) *Because 480 is nearer 500 because 90 then 100, but the numbers are different.* (436?) *Because you have to put more numbers in to make 36, so it can't be near 400.*

(b) Adequate Response:

    (< 150?) *36 and 120.* (HDYK?) *120 and 36 comes before 150, so less.* (> 100 and < 300?) *120 and 200.* (HDYK?) *120 and 200 are more than 100 but less than 300.* (> 450 and < 800?) *560, 700, 480.* (HDYK?) [S restates original question as answer.] (closer to 500 than 400?) *480.* (HDYK?) *The middle is 450 and 480 is more than 450.* (others?) *No.*

(c) Good Response:

    (< 150?) *120, 36.* (HDYK?) *150 is higher than 120 because 50 is higher than 20 and they each have 100. And 36 is lower than 120, so it has to be less than 150.* (> 100 and < 300?) *200, 120.* (HDYK?) *20 + 100 = 120, so it has to be over 100, and 1 is less than 3, so it's less than 300.* (> 450 and < 800?) *480, 700, 560.* (HDYK?) *480 is more than 450 because 80 is more than 50 and they each have 400. 700 is over 480. 560 is over 480 also. 800 is greater than all of these numbers; 700 is 100 off, and 560 is a lot off of 700.* (Closer to 500 than to 400?) *480, 850, 700, 560, and that's it.* (HDYK?) *80 is just 20 off from 500 and 80 off of 400. 560, you have to minus 60. To be closer to 400, you have to minus 160. 700 has to be closer to 500 because it's higher than 560, and 850 is higher than 700, so it has to be.*

(d) Superior response:

    (< 150?) *120 and 36.* (HDYK?) *First of all, 36 isn't even 100, and 120, the 2 would have to be a 5.* (> 100 and < 300?) *120 and 200.* (HDYK?) *120 is over 100 but is not even close to 300, and 200 is right in the middle of 100 and 300.* (> 450 and < 800?) *480, 560 and 700. 700 is way more than 450 and it's under 800 because that* [points to the 7] *would have to be an 8. 560 is more than 450 but way less than 800, and 480 is a little over 450 but a long way from 800.* (Closer to 500 than to 400?) *480, 560, 700, and 850.* (HDYK?) *First of all, 560, 700 and 850 are* <u>more</u> *than 500 so they have to be, and 480 is only 20 away from 500 but 80 away from 400.*

FIG. 6.3.   Sample responses and scores to one interview task.

the questions involving larger numbers. See Fig. 6.3(a) for a sample response.

    A student with an adequate response would correctly identify the numbers less than 150 and those between 100 and 300, and possibly provide a satisfactory rationale. This student would have difficulty correctly identifying the numbers between 450 and 800 and those closer to 500 than to 400, or would not be able to articulate a good rationale. He or she would not realize that all numbers greater than 500 are closer to 500 than to 400. See Fig. 6.3(b) for a sample response.

A student with a good response would correctly answer virtually all of the questions, although one correct answer might be omitted out of carelessness, and this student would provide a good rationale for his or her answers. However, a separate rationale would be given for each number identified as being closer to 500 than to 400. See Fig. 6.3(c) for a sample response.

Finally, a student with a superior response would answer all of the questions correctly with an appropriate rationale and would recognize that all numbers greater than 500 must be closer to 500 than to 400. See Fig. 6.3(d) for a sample response.

In addition to the number sense score, students' overall responses to each of the interview tasks were scored for depth of mathematical understanding. A student received a low score if he or she displayed a very limited understanding of the mathematical principles and concepts relevant to the task, had difficulty answering the questions, and often was incorrect. When questions were answered correctly, the student appeared to possess a well-rehearsed algorithm, as suggested by puzzlement when asked for a rationale. The student generally was not able to provide coherent reasons for his or her responses or provided a rationale that consisted of a simple statement of fact.

A student who displayed some understanding of most of the mathematical principles and concepts relevant to the task received a moderate score for depth of mathematical understanding. He or she may have had some difficulty answering the more difficult questions, but his or her answers generally were correct and the student usually was able to provide a reasonable explanation for his or her responses. The dominant approach to the task may have been algorithmic or formulaic, but the student generally indicated some understanding of the underlying principles and concepts in justifying his or her answers.

A student received a high score for depth of mathematical understanding when he or she displayed an accurate, thorough, and elaborate understanding of the mathematical principles and concepts relevant to the task. This student easily answered all of the questions, was always correct, and provided a clear and reasonable justification for his or her answers. "Conventional" algorithms and formulas may have been used, but the student was readily able to construct alternative approaches to solving the problems and his or her justifications showed an understanding of fundamental mathematical principles.

Scores for both number sense and depth of mathematical understanding were highly correlated across the different interview tasks. Consequently, composite measures were constructed by averaging each student's scores for the separate interview tasks. Internal consistency reliability coefficients were .89 for the composite number sense scale and .90 for the composite depth of mathematical understanding scale. Intercoder agreement on the composite scores was $r = .96$ for number sense and $r = .91$ for depth of mathematical understanding.

Procedures

Each teacher in the staff development and curriculum only conditions was observed teaching a *Number Power* lesson on three occasions during each of the 2 years of the evaluation. The observations were conducted by research staff at a time arranged in advance with the teacher. To the extent possible, the three observations spanned the school year (i.e., fall, winter, and spring).

The teacher interviews were conducted in the spring of each year by the same researchers who conducted the classroom observations. The interviews were scheduled at a time convenient to the teacher and generally were conducted face to face at a location in the participating school, although several interviews during the second year were conducted by telephone. All of the interviews were audiotaped for later coding. Teacher questionnaires were distributed to participating teachers in the spring of each year.

The student questionnaires and interviews were administered in the fall and the spring of each of the 2 school years. The student questionnaires were administered to all students in Grades 3–5 whose parents had provided consent for their participation.[6] Two-member teams administered the questionnaires to students in their regular classrooms. While one administrator read the items aloud to students, the other circulated throughout the room to answer questions and provide individual help when needed.

For the student interviews, a sample of three boys and three girls was randomly selected from each participating second- through fifth-grade classroom in the fall of Year 1. All of these students who were still attending the same school were reinterviewed in the spring of Year 1. In the fall of Year 2, three boys and three girls were randomly selected to be interviewed from the cohort of newly entering second graders. Students in participating classrooms in Grades 3–5 who had been interviewed during the first year and were still attending the same school were interviewed again in the fall and spring of Year 2. Additional students were randomly selected to be interviewed from any classroom at Grades 3–5 in which there were fewer than three boys or three girls who had been previously interviewed during Year 1.

The student interviews were conducted by research staff. Students were individually interviewed at a school location outside of their regular classroom. The interviews were audiotaped for later scoring by research staff. Interviewers were aware of students' treatment condition. However, in an effort to keep the interview *coders* blind to condition, students were identified on the audiotape only by name and grade (i.e., information about school and teacher was removed from the tape label).

FINDINGS

Program Implementation

Teachers in the *Number Power* with staff development condition taught more of the lessons than teachers in the *Number Power* only condition during each of the 2 years. During their first year of using *Number Power*, teachers who had received staff development taught an average of 74% of the lessons, a significantly higher percentage than the average of 53% of the lessons taught by teachers in the curriculum only condition. During the following year, teachers in the staff development condition once again taught an average of approximately three-fourths of the lessons (73%), whereas teachers in the curriculum only condition taught 62% of the lessons, a difference that was not statistically significant.[7]

Effects on Students

Preliminary analyses of the student interview and questionnaire data revealed a number of grade and gender effects. Boys and older students generally scored higher than girls and younger students on attitudes about mathematics and number sense; girls and younger students generally scored higher than boys and older students on the measure of classroom supportiveness. However, these effects did not vary across the *Number Power* with staff development, *Number Power* only, and comparison groups, meaning that there were no significant interactions between gender or grade and condition. Consequently, the effects of *Number Power* on students were examined by using analysis of covariance (ANCOVA), controlling for student gender and grade.

Effects on Mathematical Performance. Mean number sense scores on the pretest (fall) and on the posttest (spring) for students in all three conditions for Years 1 and 2 are shown in Table 6.2. Scores for depth of mathematical understanding are reported in Table 6.3.

The adjusted mean number sense pretest scores were comparable for students in the staff development and comparison groups in both Year 1 and Year 2, but students in the curriculum only group had lower scores for both Years 1 and 2. Similarly, students in the curriculum only condition had lower adjusted mean pretest scores in both years for depth of mathematical understanding than students in the staff development or comparison conditions. These "baseline" differences in mathematical performance for the students in the curriculum only group should be kept in mind when the findings regarding program effects are interpreted.

TABLE 6.2

Mean Number Sense Scores (and SDs) by Condition, Grade,
and Time of Testing

Grade	n^a	Comparison				Curriculum Only				Staff Development		
		Fall	n	Spring	n	Fall	n	Spring	n	Fall	n	Spring
						Year 1						
2	18	1.48	17	2.11	19	1.25	15	1.86	21	1.78	18	2.22
		(0.54)		(0.75)		(0.48)		(0.57)		(0.81)		(0.86)
3	14	1.95	12	2.16	13	1.83	11	2.31	18	2.21	16	2.75
		(0.77)		(0.82)		(0.42)		(0.54)		(0.67)		(0.71)
4	16	1.88	16	1.89	19	1.50	16	1.77	20	1.90	16	2.67
		(0.92)		(0.87)		(0.62)		(0.60)		(0.87)		(0.62)
5	26	2.50	24	2.69	16	1.94	15	2.38	20	2.27	17	2.87
		(0.77)		(0.60)		(0.96)		(0.95)		(0.66)		(0.61)
Adj. mean^b	74	2.05	69	2.27	67	1.61	57	2.10	79	2.03	67	2.64
						Year 2						
2	18	1.62	16	1.97	12	1.18	12	2.01	24	1.55	23	2.19
		(0.80)		(0.67)		(0.54)		(0.69)		(0.56)		(0.64)
3	19	2.54	16	2.97	12	2.12	11	2.41	24	2.29	21	2.80
		(0.53)		(0.59)		(0.62)		(0.63)		(0.80)		(0.65)
4	25	1.89	24	2.20	18	1.79	18	2.43	21	2.29	20	2.77
		(0.75)		(0.76)		(0.62)		(0.43)		(0.65)		(0.62)
5	18	2.65	17	2.73	19	2.25	19	2.80	20	2.82	20	3.16
		(0.65)		(0.90)		(0.67)		(0.49)		(0.72)		(0.50)
Adj. mean^b	80	2.22	73	2.46	61	1.84	60	2.43	89	2.25	84	2.75

Note. Scale range = 0 (unable to respond) to 4 (superior); SD = standard deviation.

[a]Some students interviewed in the fall were not available for interviewing in the spring, resulting in minor differences in *n* from fall to spring. This initial random selection of students to be interviewed suggests that each sample is representative of the class from which it was drawn.

[b]Adjusted for gender and grade by using an analysis of covariance.

Changes over time in students' number sense scores are shown in Fig. 6.4. In both Year 1 and Year 2, students in the staff development condition improved twice as much on average between fall and spring in number sense ($M = .56$) as students in the comparison group ($M = .23$).[8] Students in the curriculum only group improved almost as much on average each year ($M = .54$) as students in the staff development group. However, the curriculum only group was smaller than the other groups and had greater variability. Hence, the improvement of the curriculum only group was not significantly greater than that of comparison students.[9] (Recall that the curriculum only students were lower on number sense than students in the other two groups at baseline. Although they improved more than the comparison students, their scores never exceeded those of the comparison group.)

TABLE 6.3
Mean Depth of Mathematical Understanding Scores (and SDs)
by Condition, Grade, and Time of Testing

Grade	n^a	Comparison Fall	n	Spring	n	Curriculum Only Fall	n	Spring	n	Staff Development Fall	n	Spring
						Year 1						
2	18	2.37	17	3.04	19	1.90	15	2.75	21	2.55	18	3.09
		(0.86)		(0.77)		(0.71)		(0.72)		(1.12)		(1.03)
3	14	2.85	12	3.06	13	2.64	11	3.16	18	3.04	16	3.64
		(0.71)		(0.90)		(0.63)		(0.58)		(0.91)		(1.02)
4	16	2.69	16	2.53	19	2.29	16	2.55	20	2.62	16	3.40
		(1.06)		(1.10)		(0.78)		(0.62)		(0.92)		(0.85)
5	26	3.20	24	3.54	16	2.64	15	3.17	20	3.20	17	3.73
		(0.91)		(0.78)		(1.01)		(1.23)		(0.72)		(0.88)
Adj. mean^b	74	2.80	69	3.11	67	2.40	57	2.94	79	2.88	67	3.49
						Year 2						
2	18	2.53	16	2.72	12	1.89	12	2.75	24	2.45	23	3.05
		(0.98)		(0.97)		(0.73)		(0.72)		(0.64)		(0.90)
3	19	3.50	16	4.00	12	3.01	11	3.45	24	3.09	21	3.80
		(0.61)		(0.73)		(0.88)		(0.76)		(0.96)		(0.73)
4	25	2.88	24	3.07	18	2.64	18	3.13	21	3.14	20	3.60
		(0.80)		(0.79)		(0.63)		(0.52)		(0.81)		(0.82)
5	18	3.55	17	3.71	19	2.90	19	3.61	20	3.63	20	4.18
		(0.76)		(0.91)		(0.76)		(0.68)		(0.88)		(0.57)
Adj. mean^b	80	3.16	73	3.39	61	2.61	60	3.29	89	3.09	84	3.67

Note. Scale range = 1 (low)–5 (high); SD = standard deviation.

^{a}Some students interviewed in the fall were not available for interviewing in the spring, resulting in minor differences in n from fall to spring. This initial random selection of students to be interviewed suggests that each sample is representative of the class from which it was drawn.

^{b}Adjusted for gender and grade by using an analysis of covariance.

The same pattern of effects was found for students in the 2-year longitudinal subsample; see Fig. 6.4(c).[10]

During both Year 1 and Year 2, students in the staff development condition improved more than twice as much on average between fall and spring in depth of mathematical understanding ($M = .60$) as students in the comparison group ($M = .27$). Students in the curriculum only group also showed substantial gains in depth of mathematical understanding each year ($M = .61$), but once again they did not differ significantly from comparison students.[11] Among the 2-year longitudinal subsample, however, students in both the staff development ($M = .62$) and curriculum only groups ($M = .53$) showed significantly greater increases in depth of mathematical understanding between the fall and spring of each year than comparison students ($M = .26$).[12]

(a) Full Sample, Year 1

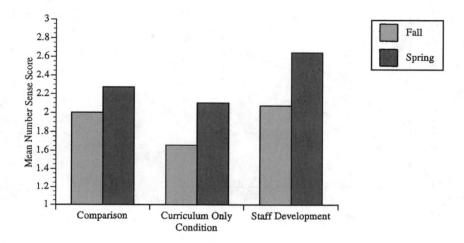

(b) Full Sample, Year 2

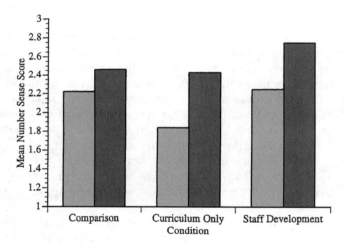

FIG. 6.4. Adjusted mean number sense scores over time for students in the three conditions.

Effects on Student Attitudes and Quality of Collaborative Work. Table 6.4 reports the mean scores on the attitude questionnaire scales for the entire sample; Table 6.5 gives the comparable results for the longitudinal subsample. There were differences between students in their attitudes and collaboration in the classroom. However, in contrast to the uniformly

(c) Two Year Longitudinal Subsample

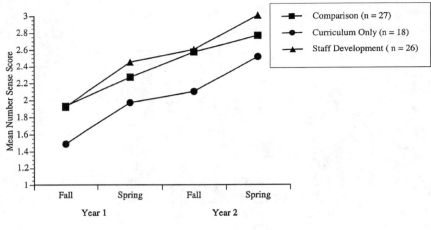

FIG. 6.4.   (Continued)

positive program effects on mathematical performance, the effects on student attitudes and collaboration varied by condition.

Scores for comparison students and for curriculum only students declined slightly between the fall and spring of each year in quality of group interaction, whereas scores for students in the staff development condition tended to increase slightly between the fall and spring of each year. Similarly, curriculum only students declined slightly in perceived positive outcomes of group work between Year 1 and Year 2. Students in the staff development condition had higher scores than comparison students for perceived positive outcomes of group work during both years.

Students in the staff development condition increased more between Year 1 and Year 2 in their sense of efficacy at math than comparison students. Students in the curriculum only condition did not differ from comparison students on this measure.

Students in the curriculum only condition also differed significantly from comparison students in their enjoyment of group work and their enjoyment of doing math problems with other students (single item). Curriculum only students decreased in both their enjoyment of group work and their enjoyment of doing math problems with other students between Year 1 and Year 2. Students in the staff development condition did not differ from comparison students on either of these measures.

Among the 2-year longitudinal subsample, students in the staff development condition differed from comparison students on quality of group interaction, perceived efficacy in math, and enjoyment of math.

Teacher Factors Associated With Differences Between Program Conditions

Based on analyses of the teacher interviews, we identified several factors that may help to explain the differences in program implementation and outcomes for students and teachers in the staff development and curriculum only conditions. These include not only the direct effects of staff development on teachers' preparedness to teach the lessons, but also indirect effects of receiving or not receiving staff development on teachers' attitudes toward the lessons. Differences in how well and consistently the lessons were implemented, and thus in the quality of students' experiences with the program, may account for the general pattern of positive effects on students' attitudes in the staff development condition and negative effects on these outcome variables for students in the curriculum only condition.

General Understanding of the Program. The instructional approach in the *Number Power* program represents a considerable departure from traditional approaches to teaching mathematics. Traditionally, teachers may have emphasized the learning and practicing of standard algorithms to obtain an answer. In contrast, *Number Power* emphasizes open-ended problems for which there may be multiple solutions, or problems with one right answer but numerous ways of finding it. Some teachers indicated that *Number Power* was very much like their "regular" mathematics program. However, some teachers indicated that the program was confusing and, in the words of one teacher, "didn't make a lot of sense." Comments by teachers in the staff development condition indicated that the workshops, discussions, and individual support provided by staff developers helped them understand the goals and objectives of the program:

> Certainly it made me more confident in going through the lessons because I have gone through the key points with [a staff developer].

Preparing for Lessons. Teachers in both the staff development and curriculum only conditions commented on the time required to prepare materials for the lessons. This may have represented the difficult shift for some teachers to a hands on, investigative approach to teaching mathematics that often requires class sets of concrete materials and manipulatives. Although such comments were made by teachers in both conditions, they were made more frequently by teachers in the curriculum only group, and they were expressed just as often by curriculum only teachers during the second year as the first year. In contrast, few comments about preparation time were made by teachers in the staff development group during the second year. Instead,

TABLE 6.4

Mean Student Questionnaire Scores (and SDs) by Condition and Time for the Full Sample

| | Comparison | | | | Curriculum Only | | | | Staff Development | | | |
| | Fall | | Spring | | Fall | | Spring | | Fall | | Spring | |
Questionnaire Scale	n	Mean	n	Mean	n	Mean	n	Mean	n	Mean	n	Mean
						Year 1						
Quality of group interaction	194	2.54 (0.31)	184	2.50 (0.32)	131	2.56 (0.29)	129	2.48 (0.34)	245	2.57 (0.28)	231	2.60 (0.33)
Enjoyment of group work	194	2.22 (0.51)	184	2.24 (0.52)	131	2.27 (0.46)	129	2.19 (0.48)	245	2.21 (0.43)	231	2.15 (0.46)
Positive outcomes of group work	194	2.41 (0.46)	182	2.43 (0.46)	131	2.50 (0.36)	129	2.45 (0.40)	245	2.53 (0.38)	231	2.57 (0.39)
Classroom supportiveness	194	2.33 (0.39)	182	2.27 (0.39)	131	2.26 (0.40)	129	2.17 (0.43)	245	2.37 (0.39)	231	2.38 (0.41)
Perceived efficacy in math	194	2.32 (0.52)	182	2.27 (0.51)	131	2.35 (0.50)	129	2.33 (0.47)	245	2.35 (0.47)	231	2.35 (0.46)
Enjoyment of math	194	2.28 (0.53)	182	2.17 (0.55)	131	2.37 (0.52)	129	2.31 (0.54)	245	2.29 (0.48)	231	2.20 (0.50)

					Year 2							
Quality of group interaction	180	2.55 (0.29)	183	2.47 (0.31)	121	2.43 (0.34)	117	2.39 (0.31)	177	2.57 (0.30)	179	2.60 (0.31)
Enjoyment of group work	180	2.29 (0.50)	183	2.26 (0.51)	121	2.15 (0.50)	117	2.13 (0.50)	177	2.23 (0.48)	179	2.15 (0.48)
Positive outcomes of group work	180	2.53 (0.42)	183	2.47 (0.44)	121	2.44 (0.44)	117	2.44 (0.36)	177	2.55 (0.40)	179	2.54 (0.41)
Classroom supportiveness	180	2.36 (0.39)	183	2.31 (0.37)	121	2.20 (0.36)	117	2.16 (0.36)	177	2.36 (0.36)	179	2.35 (0.37)
Perceived efficacy in math	180	2.31 (0.49)	183	2.33 (0.49)	121	2.39 (0.42)	117	2.32 (0.44)	177	2.45 (0.45)	179	2.51 (0.47)
Enjoyment of math	180	2.27 (0.49)	183	2.22 (0.52)	121	2.31 (0.48)	117	2.26 (0.56)	177	2.29 (0.48)	179	2.30 (0.48)

Note. Items on the questionnaire were scored 1 (not true), 2 (sometimes true), or 3 (true). The numbers in each cell vary as a result of missing data from students' being absent at the fall or spring testing, leaving the school before the spring testing, or failing to complete the entire questionnaire.

TABLE 6.5
Mean Student Questionnaire Scores (and SDs) by Condition and Time
for the Longitudinal Sample

Questionnaire Scale	Comparison		Curriculum Only		Staff Devel.	
	Fall	Spring	Fall	Spring	Fall	Spring
			Year 1			
Quality of group interaction	2.61	2.63	2.55	2.40	2.59	2.49
	(0.28)	(0.29)	(0.28)	(0.39)	(0.30)	(0.39)
Enjoyment of group work	2.29	2.30	2.28	2.20	2.19	2.02
	(0.53)	(0.52)	(0.55)	(0.51)	(0.48)	(0.50)
Positive outcomes of group work	2.48	2.48	2.52	2.44	2.57	2.46
	(0.47)	(0.40)	(0.38)	(0.44)	(0.40)	(0.45)
Classroom supportiveness	2.44	2.42	2.27	2.10	2.31	2.21
	(0.35)	(0.37)	(0.42)	(0.50)	(0.39)	(0.46)
Perceived efficacy in math	2.38	2.37	2.45	2.29	2.43	2.37
	(0.54)	(0.48)	(0.45)	(0.39)	(0.44)	(0.51)
Enjoyment of math	2.36	2.32	2.43	2.31	2.22	2.08
	(0.51)	(0.53)	(0.49)	(0.51)	(0.51)	(0.55)
			Year 2			
Quality of group interaction	2.47	2.47	2.39	2.31	2.48	2.51
	(0.31)	(0.29)	(0.40)	(0.35)	(0.30)	(0.35)
Enjoyment of group work	2.18	2.19	2.06	2.07	2.14	2.04
	(0.52)	(0.54)	(0.52)	(0.55)	(0.48)	(0.45)
Positive outcomes of group work	2.41	2.47	2.43	2.39	2.49	2.46
	(0.46)	(0.44)	(0.48)	(0.44)	(0.42)	(0.46)
Classroom supportiveness	2.35	2.34	2.17	2.18	2.29	2.29
	(0.41)	(0.41)	(0.38)	(0.38)	(0.40)	(0.41)
Perceived efficacy in math	2.23	2.36	2.40	2.28	2.48	2.56
	(0.52)	(0.53)	(0.39)	(0.44)	(0.43)	(0.44)
Enjoyment of math	2.18	2.16	2.33	2.30	2.27	2.24
	(0.52)	(0.59)	(0.50)	(0.56)	(0.49)	(0.49)

Note. Items on the questionnaire were scored 1 (not true), 2 (sometimes true), or 3 (true).
For the Comparison group, $n = 63$; for the curriculum only group, $n = 45$; and for the
staff development group, $n = 86$. SD = standard deviation.

they tended to emphasize how much easier it was to use the program a
second time.

Student Group Work and Perceived Importance of Social Development.
Placing students in small groups to work with materials such as interlock-
ing cubes and toy vehicles can pose classroom management challenges for
teachers. Several teachers in the curriculum only condition, in particular,
encountered problems related to student behavior in groups, which they
tied to the use of manipulatives:

When it's something that doesn't have to do with manipulatives it's easier. When it has to do with things you can touch, then we get into problems.

In contrast, teachers in the staff development group rarely mentioned student behavior problems. Rather, they more often described positive effects of the program on their students' interpersonal behavior and social development:

> I think what I most enjoy about *Number Power* is that we focused on what we were going to do socially.... My kids have surprised me—they've come up with some things in group situations that I ... wouldn't have expected it at fifth grade. If I say to the kids, "What are some ways we are going to make sure you include someone?", the kids will come up with ideas that are grown up ... if we followed them we'd have successful faculty meetings!

A number of curriculum only teachers, however, did not appear to see the integration of social and intellectual development as particularly important, and consequently they did not emphasize the social goals of the program.

> No, I don't [use the questions about social relationships], because I'm too busy getting the lessons together. I'm really not comfortable with ... reflecting on how we're working together. I don't think you can do that too much. I think they [students] get tired of it, or I get tired of it.

The fact that students' reported group experiences in the curriculum only condition were less positive than in the staff development condition may be due in part to less attention having been paid to the social development goals of the program by teachers in the curriculum only condition.

Collegiality, Support, and Perceived Importance of Staff Development. Teachers in the staff development condition commented extensively in the interviews about how the initial summer workshop helped to build a sense of collegiality and support among the staff that continued throughout the 2-year project and extended beyond their work with *Number Power.* These results are consistent with other research on the importance of membership in a "learning community" for supporting and sustaining teachers' changes in instructional practices (e.g., Lieberman, 1990; Little & McLaughlin, 1993). The comments of teachers in the staff development condition highlighted the importance of discussing lessons with their colleagues, working through problems collectively, and learning from one another about how to implement the program effectively:

> [The initial summer workshop] was mainly helpful to unify us and to get us to talk about what we were going to be doing and what we've done ... we just

don't have a time to get together and share with each other what's going on and what's working.

Teaching, as you know, can be a very lonely kind of profession . . . You're all alone in there wondering, "Gee, is this okay?" You hope you're doing the right thing, and just validating that you're professionals, getting the feedback . . . all of this is just invaluable as a teacher . . . Staff development not only gives the academic part of it, but it gives the emotional support that teachers need.

It is noteworthy that *all* of the teachers at each of the two staff development schools participated in the staff development and used the *Number Power* lessons. In contrast, although the *Number Power* books were offered to all teachers at the curriculum only schools, only those who agreed to participate in the evaluation actually tried to implement the program. Thus, not only did the teachers who received staff development develop a sense of common purpose through the summer workshop that was not experienced by the curriculum only teachers, but the curriculum only teachers were also isolated from their colleagues in their attempts to use *Number Power*. Several curriculum only teachers commented in their interviews on the importance of staff development for effective use of a program such as *Number Power*:

I felt very keenly the lack of any training from *Number Power* . . . I suspect that we were the guinea pigs, we were the ones that were given the materials, and it was a sink or swim situation . . . There were a lot of places where I fell through the cracks because . . . there were a lot of ways to approach it . . . It was not always the best lesson.

Mathematical Value of Lessons.   The evaluation data suggest that staff development helped to deepen teachers' understanding of the mathematical goals of the program and helped them recognize how the lessons formed a coherent sequence of experiences that progressively deepened students' understanding of number. The teachers who received staff development generally followed the lesson plans and taught most of the lessons in the order presented in the book, particularly during the second year. Curriculum only teachers more often altered the lessons and more often taught them out of sequence; they also taught fewer of the lessons overall. Differences in understanding of the mathematical development of the program may account for differences in how teachers viewed the value of the lessons. For example, a couple of teachers at each of the curriculum only schools commented that some of the *Number Power* lessons were "inappropriate" for their students or had too little "mathematical substance." In contrast, staff development teachers commented on the amount of growth in mathematical understanding among their students; although several were initially concerned that some of the mathematics was too challenging for their students, they were pleasantly surprised when their students were able to perform at a more advanced level than they expected:

> I feel that children were challenged to understand fractions, percents, and decimals in ways that they may not previously have been challenged. And I feel that they were able to achieve a certain level of success which, frankly, I don't think initially I would have predicted ... I was pleasantly surprised with the accessibility of some of what I felt to be fairly challenging.

> I really learned a lot about how children think. ... My expectations for some of these youngsters at the age of seven or eight were too limiting ... I think it's exciting to see the kids can take any kind of problem and deal with it ... if you allow them the time to think those through, and not limit their experiences.

External Factors. A final factor that may help to explain the differences in implementation between teachers in the staff development and curriculum only conditions is the fact that during the second year of the evaluation, the districts for both curriculum only schools and one of the staff development schools adopted a new year-long mathematics curriculum for district-wide use beginning the following school year. Faced with having to learn a new mathematics curriculum, and given the difficulties they encountered with *Number Power*, there was little reason for curriculum only teachers to continue investing time and energy in implementing the program during the second year of the evaluation. (The teachers at the staff development school facing a new mathematics curriculum for the coming school year also implemented somewhat fewer *Number Power* lessons during Year 2 than Year 1, but the quality of their implementation did not decrease.)

FINAL COMMENTS

The findings from the *Number Power* evaluation show that the program resulted in significant gains in mathematical understanding among students in both the *Number Power* with staff development and *Number Power* only conditions. They also provide evidence that the experiences of students were otherwise quite different in these two conditions. For students in the staff development condition, the program resulted in positive effects on their enjoyment of math and sense of efficacy at math, as well as on the quality of student collaboration in the classroom, and perceived benefits of working in groups.

The findings were mixed for students in the *Number Power* only condition. Although they had gains in mathematical performance comparable with those of students in the staff development condition, the observed effects on their attitudes and quality of collaboration were negative. This suggests that, even when not implemented extensively or with as much fidelity as expected, exposure to the kinds of mathematical experiences represented by the *Number Power* program can have positive effects on some aspects of students' mathematical abilities.

It is also worth noting that the teachers in the *Number Power* only condition who participated during both years of the evaluation improved in their implementation of the lessons during the second year. This suggests that, with additional time or a more supportive environment for undertaking a new approach to mathematics instruction, teachers are more likely to achieve quality implementation of the *Number Power* program without formal staff development. Clearly, however, the staff development provided during this 2-year evaluation made a substantial difference in implementation and student outcomes.

In conclusion, the findings from the 2-year evaluation of *Number Power* indicate that the kinds of changes in mathematics instruction recommended by the NCTM *Standards* can be accomplished by elementary teachers. When such practices are implemented, students benefit in a variety of areas, including number sense, sense of efficacy at mathematics, and enjoyment of mathematics. The findings also suggest that *Number Power* can lead to positive changes in the general social environment of the classroom. At the same time, the findings indicate that given the depth and breadth of instructional changes required by programs such as *Number Power*, improvements are much more likely to be achieved on a wide scale when teachers have the benefit of staff development that supports their efforts to alter their instructional practices.

REFERENCES

Developmental Studies Center. (1996, May). Findings from the evaluation of the *Number Power* mathematics program: Final report to the National Science Foundation. Oakland, CA: Author.

Hope, J. (1989). Promoting number sense in school. *Arithmetic Teacher, 36*(6), 12–16.

Lieberman, A. (1990). *Schools as collaborative cultures: Creating the future now.* New York: Falmer Press.

Lindquist, M. M. (Ed.). (1989). *Results from the fourth mathematics assessment of the national assessment of educational progress.* Reston, VA: National Council of Teachers of Mathematics.

Little, J. W., & McLaughlin, M. W. (Eds.). (1993). *Teachers' work: Individuals, colleagues, and contexts.* New York: Teachers College Press.

National Council of Teachers of Mathematics. (1989). *Curriculum and evaluation standards for school mathematics.* Reston, VA: Author.

Sowder, J. T. (1992). Making sense of numbers in school mathematics. In G. Leinhardt, R. Putnam, & R. Hattrup (Eds.), *Analysis of arithmetic for mathematics education* (pp. 1–51). Hillsdale, NJ: Lawrence Erlbaum Associates.

Thompson, C. S., & Rathmell, E. C. (1989). By way of introduction. *Arithmetic Teacher, 36*(6), 2–3.

ENDNOTES

1. The development and evaluation of *Number Power* was supported by grants from the National Science Foundation, the Stuart Foundation, and the Walter S. Johnson Foundation. The views expressed are those of the authors and not necessarily those of the funders. *Number Power* was developed by Laurel Robertson, Shaila Regan, Julie Wellington Contestable, Susie Alldredge, Carol Tensing Westrich, Marji Freeman, and Susan Urquhart-Brown. We also thank William Ruano for assistance with the evaluation.

2. At the time of the evaluation, the units for kindergarten and first grade had not yet been completed. The sixth-grade units were not evaluated because all of the participating schools had a K–5 configuration.

3. At the end of the 2-year evaluation, interested teachers in the comparison condition were provided with the curriculum and staff development, and interested teachers in the *Number Power* only condition were provided with staff development.

4. Fifth-grade students in Year 1 were no longer in the schools in Year 2, and all second-grade students in Year 2 were new to the study. The remaining turnover was the result of normal attrition, as well as students' moving from participating to nonparticipating classrooms between Years 1 and 2 at intervention schools in which not all teachers were participating in the study. No students moved from one study condition to another.

5. Copies of the interview protocol and scoring manual are available on request from V. Battistich.

6. Second-grade students were interviewed but did not complete any group-administered surveys.

7. For Year 1, $t(23) = 2.10$, $p < .05$. For Year 2, $t(21) = 1.51$, $p < .15$. The percentages of lessons taught were consistent across grade levels for each of the two conditions. Although the number of lessons taught varied across teachers, the variation was not systematic by grade.

8. The average change in number sense scores is found by averaging the differences in the adjusted means from fall to spring for the 2 years.

9. With the use of planned contrasts from group by time ANCOVAs, $t(868) = 2.56$ with $p < .01$ for the difference in the average change in number sense scores for staff development versus comparison. For curriculum only versus comparison, $t(868) = 1.80$ with $p < .18$. The degrees of freedom are based on the residual mean squares from the total number of cases analyzed, which ranged from 867 to 875 depending on missing data values.

10. For the longitudinal subsample, a statistical test on the average change in number sense scores yields $t(68) = 1.87$ with $p < .07$ for staff development versus comparison.

11. With the use of planned contrasts from group by time ANCOVAs, $t(868) = 2.51$ with $p < .02$ for the difference in the average change in depth of mathematical understanding for staff development versus comparison. For curriculum only versus comparison, $t(868) = 1.59$ with $p < .12$.

12. For the longitudinal subsample, a statistical test on the average change in depth of mathematical understanding yields $t(68) = 1.97$ with $p < .05$ for curriculum only versus comparison, and $t(68) = 3.05$ with $p < .01$ for staff development versus comparison.

7

Commentary on Four Elementary Mathematics Curricula

Ralph T. Putnam
Michigan State University

The four curricula in Chapters 3–6 share the goal of trying to create for students experiences of learning mathematics that are consistent with the *Curriculum and Evaluation Standards for School Mathematics* from the National Council of Teachers of Mathematics (NCTM; 1989). All focus in various ways on helping students develop conceptually powerful and useful knowledge of mathematics while avoiding the learning of computational procedures as rote symbolic manipulations.

The first striking thing to note about the chapters is the overall similarity in their findings. Students in these new curricula generally perform as well as other students on traditional measures of mathematics achievement, including computational skill, and they generally do better on formal and informal assessments of conceptual understanding and ability to use mathematics to solve problems. These chapters demonstrate that "reform-based" mathematics curricula can work. This is good news for schools and districts considering adoption of these and similar curricula in the face of concerns of parents, teachers, and community members about whether students' learning of traditionally valued arithmetic will suffer with these new curricula. The ability to make such claims about achievement is important, especially in the current climate of heated debate over the mathematics curricula in our schools.

161

However, focusing solely on such general outcomes masks important features that distinguish these curricula from more traditional elementary school mathematics teaching and learning, as well as important differences among the new curricula. Thus, I begin my discussion of these four chapters by considering a set of key assumptions—about mathematics, learning, and teaching—that they all share to some degree. Then I consider a number of factors that influence what we can learn from these and other studies of curriculum outcomes. Finally, I discuss three salient issues that arose for me as I thought about these elementary mathematics curricula and what students learn from them: the importance of teacher learning, the role of computational skill and fluency, and the role of technology in learning mathematics.

COMMON ASSUMPTIONS

Common to the four chapters and the curricula they depict is a general set of assumptions and emphases about mathematics curriculum, learning, and teaching. Because all the curricula were developed, at least in part, to be consistent with NCTM's *Curriculum Standards*, such similarities are not surprising, but there are also important differences in the assumptions— explicit and implicit—underlying these curricula.

Important Mathematics

Although they differ in how they define it, the four curricula emphasize important mathematics, attempting in various ways to move beyond the highly computational emphasis of traditional elementary mathematics curricula. Thus, the curricula represent new visions of the mathematics that children should learn and how they should know it, which is one important message of the *Standards*. There are differences, however, in what the curricula emphasize—their explicit or implicit definitions of important mathematics. *Everyday Mathematics* starts with the assumption that "the elementary school mathematics curriculum should be significantly broadened," expanding the range and sophistication of mathematical ideas that elementary school students encounter (see Chapter 4). *Math Trailblazers* emphasizes the use of mathematics in scientific investigations, with the goal of making the mathematics that children learn more meaningful, and having connections to science. *Investigations* focuses most explicitly on developing students' reasoning in the context of meaningful mathematical problems, de-emphasizing even more than the other curricula the teaching of traditional computational algorithms. Unlike the other three curricula, which were developed as comprehensive elementary school mathematics programs, *Number Power* focuses on a single, but crucial, aspect of children's mathematical understanding—their development of number concepts or number sense. These differing stances on what constitutes important mathematics are not mutually exclusive, but they do result in differing emphases among the curricula.

In addition to assumptions about what mathematics is important for children to learn, the curricula share important assumptions about how children learn mathematics and how the learning of powerful mathematics can best be facilitated. The next three themes focus on these assumptions about learning.

Build on Children's Current Understanding

Fairly prominent in the discussion of these curricula is the assumption or principle that meaningful mathematics learning entails building on students' existing understanding and thinking. For example, Battistich, Alldredge, and Tsuchida argue that "the *Number Power* program is built on the premise that children come to school with intuitive understandings about the meaning of numbers and about how numbers describe quantities, and that all children can and should go on to develop interconnected, flexible, and useful number sense during their elementary school years" (Chapter 6). This basic constructivist assumption pervades much current thinking about classroom teaching and learning and represents an important commitment to, as Dewey (1964) put it, bringing together the child and the curriculum.

Ground Learning in Meaningful Settings

All the curricula emphasize the importance of grounding the learning of mathematics in meaningful settings and problems. In contrast to using various "real-world" settings and "word problems" as a site for students to *apply* mathematics they have already learned, these curricula attempt in various ways to immerse students in meaningful problems as sites for *learning* important mathematics in the first place. There is some important variation here among the curricula. *Math Trailblazers*, for example, emphasizes investigations in which students explore some phenomena as they both develop and apply mathematical concepts and skills. In describing *Investigations*, Mokros points out that meaningful settings can involve real or fantasy contexts, but that settings can also be "purely numerical or geometric" (Chapter 5).

Informal To Formal

Intertwined with the assumptions that learning experiences should explicitly build on children's current understandings and in meaningful settings is the notion that meaningful learning of mathematics proceeds from informal, grounded understandings to more formal knowledge of the symbol systems of mathematics. As Carroll and Isaacs point out, *Everyday Mathematics* "emphasizes playful, verbal interactions and manipulative activities while laying the groundwork for symbolic understanding" (Chapter 4). Thus, rather than focusing first on the acquisition of symbolic and computational fluency, with the assumption that understanding and connections will come later, these curricula introduce formal terms, symbols, and procedures after students have developed an understanding of the concepts they represent.

The Teacher's Role

These three assumptions about learning—that meaningful learning builds on the learner's existing understanding, that it is grounded in meaningful settings, and that it proceeds from informal and idiosyncratic to more formal modes of knowing—represent a perspective on learning that is fundamentally different from the explicit and implicit views pervading many existing curricula and much of traditional school practice. Traditionally, for many teachers, ensuring students' success involves providing explanations, modeling, and practice of "basic" skills before moving on to the more "difficult" work of problem solving and application. In contrast, these new curricula, with varying degrees of explicitness, view the teacher as *guiding* students through discussions and learning activities as they build on their existing understandings and develop mathematical reasoning. Better understanding what it means for a teacher to serve as such a guide is one of the challenges for these new curricula and the mathematics education community as a whole.

STUDYING OUTCOMES: WHAT MATTERS?

These assumptions and perspectives make these new curricula quite different from traditional elementary school mathematics curricula. How have their developers set about determining the effects of these new approaches? Do students learn more mathematics with these new curricula? Is their learning somehow better or worse than before? These are the sorts of questions that the chapters in this book, with its emphasis on outcomes, seek to inform.

At first glance, evaluating the effectiveness of a new curriculum seems relatively straightforward: Try the new curriculum in a number of schools, measure what students learn, and compare this learning with the learning of students in schools without the new curriculum. This sort of evidence should provide answers to the questions we—as teachers, administrators, parents, and community members—would really like to answer: Which curriculum is best for our students? Do these curricula really work? Will students learn? As Hiebert (1999) has pointed out, we often turn to research to answer these sorts of questions. Unfortunately, as Hiebert argues, it is not that simple. Although research certainly can and should inform our decision making, it cannot *prove* what curriculum or instructional approach is best. There are too many complex factors at work to make simple prescriptions.

In assessing the outcomes resulting from a new curriculum, there are decisions to be made at every step of the way. What shall we count as "better" learning? What does it mean to learn "more" mathematics? Classrooms and schools differ on many dimensions; how do we decide where to assess the impact of the new curriculum? Decisions about each of these issues and more entail trade-offs in what we do and do not learn about the effects of a particular curriculum.

The researchers studying the curricula in these chapters made varied choices in assessing their impact. This diversity illustrates the complexity of assessing the effects of new curricula and raises a number of important issues about curriculum, teaching, and learning.

What Outcomes To Measure and How?

These curricula differ, both from more traditional curricula and among themselves, in what mathematics they consider important for students to learn. What mathematics learning, then, should be assessed when considering their impact? Should researchers develop assessments to measure the mathematics emphasized in the new curriculum—be it problem solving, mathematical reasoning, or number sense? Or should they use traditional mathematics achievement tests to enable ready comparison with existing curricula? The research reported in these chapters took a variety of approaches in what learning outcomes to measure and how.

Everyday Mathematics and *Math Trailblazers* were developed as comprehensive mathematics curricula for elementary schools. Thus, their developers chose existing standardized measures of mathematics achievement for their major outcome studies. Both reported studies using the Illinois state mathematics assessment, relying on overall scores to argue that students being taught with the new curricula scored as high as or higher than their counterparts in other schools. Both groups also reported studies using global scores on commercial standardized achievement tests. An advantage of using such existing measures of overall mathematics achievement is that they can demonstrate that students experiencing the new curricula are learning the mathematics represented by publicly accepted measures. This sort of documentation is important for allaying fears that students may not be learning the mathematics that has traditionally been considered important. In addition, standardized measures, whether developed at the state or national level, typically adhere to systematic criteria for measurement properties, such as reliability. Relying on standardized measures, however, is not without problems. For example, comparing the learning over time of two groups that start out at different levels—as in the *Math Trailblazers* case study of a school within a school—is difficult. Measurement experts consistently caution us that a change in the grade-level equivalent score at one grade level cannot be considered to represent the same amount of learning as the same change at another grade level (i.e., a change of 0.6 years at one grade level does not represent the same level of learning as a change of 0.6 years at another grade level).

A disadvantage in using standardized measures is that they often do not shed much light on the more complex mathematical understanding, reasoning, and problem solving emphasized in the new curricula. Using global scores also does not reveal differences in the nature of the mathematics students are learning, such as computational skills versus conceptual understanding. Nor do global scores reveal whether students are using the rich reasoning and variety of strategies these new curricula value and seek to nourish. An exception to this limitation is seen in the *Math Trailblazers* case study that included the open-ended format of the Stanford 9. It was this standardized, but nontraditional, measure that revealed superior mathematical reasoning and justification by *Math Trailblazers* students.

Additional studies of *Everyday Mathematics* and *Math Trailblazers* attempted to move beyond the content limitations of standardized measures by assessing more specific content and by measuring that learning with alternatives to standardized tests. One approach was to measure specific aspects of mathematics learning brought to the fore by the new curriculum. Two studies of *Everyday Mathematics*, for example, examined learning of mental computation and geometry, areas emphasized in the new curriculum, by using measures developed for research purposes. Another study used researcher-developed measures of computational skills because of concerns that the new curriculum might not be providing sufficient opportunities for students to develop in this area. The use of specific measures such as these helps provide a richer picture of the kinds of mathematics that students using the new curriculum are learning, enabling Carroll and Isaacs to support their claims that *Everyday Mathematics* students perform as well as other students on traditional topics and better in some areas. The measures typically do not have, however, the same sort of consistent measurement properties established in large-scale standardized instruments.

The studies of *Investigations* relied exclusively on evaluator-developed measures, with their concomitant strengths and weaknesses. The studies used assessments of calculation skills and understanding of number operations developed for the express purpose of studying the effects of the *Investigations* curriculum. These assessments relied on individual interviews with students as well as paper-and-pencil tests. The measures relied on a relatively small number of items (20–22 items on the written test) and were used with a small sample of students, making impossible the establishment of the reliability and other standard measurement characteristics expected for large-scale tests. The interview tasks required students to draw on the sorts of mathematical understanding and reasoning that are emphasized in the *Investigations* curriculum. These tasks enabled the researchers to show that *Investigations* students were indeed developing the sorts of knowledge and thinking the curriculum was intended to foster. However, the fact that the tasks were so similar to the sorts of activities in the *Investigations* curriculum, and so different from those in more traditional classrooms, leaves one wondering how the two groups of students would compare on measures of understanding and reasoning that were more curriculum neutral.

The 2-year study of *Number Power* also relied on researcher-developed measures, including interviews that focused on the specific aspects of number sense targeted by the curriculum. Again, an advantage of these measures is that they entail tasks that require students to use mathematics in various ways and can reveal their mathematical understanding and reasoning. A disadvantage is that such measures developed for particular studies lack the control and comparability afforded by widely used standardized measures. Because the *Number Power* evaluators were trying to assess number sense and understanding, which are not well captured by most standardized tests, they developed rubrics for judging students' number sense and depth of understanding. Although these measures were so highly correlated that the researchers formed a composite score from them, the two scores were used separately in the reported analyses, raising further questions about the nature of these measures.

Who Is Being Assessed?

Another important factor to consider in evaluating outcomes is who are the students and teachers using the new curriculum. Students, teachers, and schools differ in many ways that may influence how a new curriculum is received and the impact it has on student learning. As a set, the studies in these chapters represent a range of settings, from privileged suburban to low-socioeconomic-status urban schools. The researchers studying *Math Trailblazers* and *Everyday Mathematics*, in particular, worked to include a range of students and to examine the effects of the curriculum on typically disadvantaged students.

Giving a new curriculum a fair trial in diverse settings can be difficult. When a curriculum is new, its developers are likely to work closely with teachers and schools trying it out. Because it is often these "early adopters" who become the focus of studies of the effects of the curriculum, at least two problems can arise. First, the schools willing and able to do the intense work needed for early implementation of a new curriculum are likely to be schools that already work well and have successful students. Second, these early adopting schools are likely to develop strong connections to the developers of the curriculum, and they are apt to receive considerable support and guidance in their work with the new curriculum. Both of these factors may make the situations of the early adopting schools quite different from what happens when the curriculum is adopted more widely.

Compared To What?

Evaluating what students are learning from a new curriculum requires some basis for comparison. Ideally, one wants to know what a particular group of students learns with the new curriculum compared with what they would have learned with a different curriculum. Obviously this question cannot be answered directly, and coming up with reasonable alternatives is fraught with problems. The studies in these chapters took a variety of approaches to judging the impact of the new curricula by comparing the learning of students with other students or benchmarks.

The studies of *Math Trailblazers* compared students' performance after experiencing the new curriculum with the historical performance of students in the same school. By looking at performance on the same mathematics tests over time, the researchers were able to show the positive impact of the new curriculum. The consistent pattern of improvement across two measures after the introduction of the new curriculum into classrooms provided convincing evidence of increased learning in the targeted schools. The picture from this change across time was supplemented in the case studies, which compared the performance of *Math Trailblazers* students with that of students in a similar nearby school.

This comparing of students' performance with that of other students is another strategy for judging whether a new curriculum is having a positive impact. Some of the studies of *Everyday Mathematics* compared the average test scores in schools using the new curriculum to the overall performance of students across the district and the state. As long as no one has reason to believe that the *Everyday Mathematics* schools are not different from other schools in major ways, this strategy provides good evidence of the positive impact of the curriculum.

Yet another approach was to administer specific outcome measures to students from classes using the new curriculum and from classes chosen to be roughly comparable but using different curricula. This approach was taken in studies of *Investigations, Number Power,* and the geometric knowledge of students using *Everyday Mathematics*. Finally, some studies relied on existing data from previous studies as benchmarks against which to compare students using the new curricula. For example, the study of mental computation by *Everyday Mathematics* students relied on a measure of mental computation developed in a previous study and the findings of that previous study as the source of comparison.

None of these approaches is perfect. Each involves trade-offs. Comparing school or class performance to state or district averages begs the question of whether the schools with the new curriculum were already high-performing schools. Doing historical comparisons with the same school avoids this problem but leaves open the issue of whether it was the new curriculum or some other factor such as the energy and excitement of trying something new that was responsible for the improved scores. In using existing data for comparison, one can always question whether the students using the new curriculum were truly comparable with the students in the original research. The advantage of having a variety of studies using these different approaches, however, is providing confidence in general effects that emerge.

What Does It Mean To Implement a Curriculum?

Finally, there is the issue of what it means to say that the new curriculum has or has not been implemented. It would be silly, for example, to argue that a curriculum has been implemented if a school district buys new textbooks or other materials and places them in classrooms, but the new materials sit unopened on a shelf in the classroom. But what then does it mean to say that a particular curriculum has been implemented sufficiently to claim that it is having an impact on students' learning? The question becomes more complex in curricula such as those described in these chapters because they entail fairly major changes in what goes on in classrooms.

The developers of these curricula obviously recognize that adopting or implementing their curriculum means more than simply placing new instructional materials into classrooms. All of the authors speak to the importance of changes in what students and teachers actually do in classrooms— the exploring of problems, the sharing of various solutions, and the guiding of students' mathematical conversations and thinking by the teachers. Criteria for what counts as implementing the new curricula, however, vary. In the studies on *Math Trailblazers* reported by Carter et al., for example, we know only that the new curriculum was used in the classrooms studied. We do not know whether "using" the curriculum meant teaching occasional lessons from it, having students use the printed materials, or regularly carrying out the activities as described in the curriculum. In their case studies of student outcomes in individual schools, Carter et al. point out that teachers had opportunities for professional development and support in using the new curriculum, but again we do not know what actually went on in the studied classrooms. Carter et al. provide a partial window into classrooms through their study involving detailed descriptions of the classroom processes in a single school. The narrative description of Ms. Padilla's first-grade classroom richly characterizes aspects of teacher–student interaction around mathematics that the authors value. Note that it does not, however, shed light on how typical these valued interactions are in other *Math Trailblazers* classrooms.

In the first of the achievement studies reported by Carroll and Isaacs, we are told that curriculum supervisors were asked to confirm whether the classrooms being studied indeed used the *Everyday Mathematics* curriculum. Again, it is not clear what "using" meant to these supervisors. The more extensive longitudinal study Carroll and Isaacs describe included observation, videotaping, interviews, and surveys to document what went on in target classrooms. None of these data were presented, however, in discussing what students learned in the *Everyday Mathematics* classrooms, leaving us again unsure of the nature of teaching and learning.

The chapters on *Number Power* and *Investigations* do more to link what goes on in classrooms with the outcome data they report. Battistich et al. used an evaluation design that included three groups of classrooms: (a) the *Number Power* curriculum with staff development support, (b) the *Number Power* curriculum without additional support, and (c) comparison classrooms. They also used observations, questionnaires, and teacher reports to assess the teaching and learning in the studied classrooms. Including these data allowed Battistich et al. to make important observations about patterns in their outcome data, including the lack of implementation by teachers who did not receive opportunities for staff development with the new program.

In the first of the three studies on *Investigations* reported by Mokros, students were selected from seven *Investigations* classrooms. No information was provided on what constituted an "*Investigations* classroom." The two dissertation studies she describes, however, included extensive classroom observation and interviews, enabling the researchers to describe the nature of classroom instruction. This made it possible for Mokros, like Battistich et al., to address important issues, such as the recognition that using the *Investigations* materials with a didactic teaching style focused on prescribed strategies was not as effective as teaching as the developers intended—with a focus on students' development of sensible strategies.

It is important to attend to such implementation issues, because without information about how curricula are being implemented, it is difficult to know what is being compared in student outcome studies. Of course, as curricula are adopted more widely, the conditions in schools and districts are likely to vary widely. On a broad scale, it is important to know what happens to the learning of students in a range of schools and classrooms in which the new curricula have been adopted with all the variation that is bound to occur. However, to help inform districts, schools, and teachers in making decisions about adopting new curricula, it is imperative to know what changes are entailed and what is being compared in reported studies.

The variety of approaches taken to assess the effects of these mathematics curricula illustrate the complexity underlying apparently simple questions about what students learn when using a new curriculum. The trade-offs entailed by any decision about what to measure, whom to assess, the basis for comparison, and what it means to implement the new curriculum limit our ability to make strong conclusions on the basis of any single study. The diversity of approaches, however, can increase our confidence in general patterns that emerge. Again, the overall pattern here is that students experiencing these reform-oriented mathematics curricula do as well as or better than other students on traditional measures of mathematics achievement, including computational skill, and they generally do better on formal and informal assessments of their conceptual understanding and ability to use mathematics to solve problems. The collection of studies also supports two general conclusions reached by Hiebert (1999) when considering the relationships among research, standards, and instruction: First, "instructional programs that emphasize conceptual development, with the goal of developing students' understanding, can facilitate significant mathematics learning without sacrificing skill proficiency" (p. 14). Second, "one of the most reliable findings from research on teaching and learning [is that] students learn what they have an opportunity to learn" (p. 12). We see from these studies that new curricula can support students' learning of rich mathematical thinking, understanding, and problem solving.

ISSUES FOR THE FUTURE

In reviewing the chapters and thinking about what they helped us understand about the effects of these new curricula on student outcomes, three issues emerged for me as particularly salient. First is the central importance of teachers in current reform efforts and the need for curriculum to support their work and learning. Second is the ongoing issue of the role of computational skill, algorithms, and fluency in the elementary school. Third is the important but neglected role of new technologies in supporting mathematics teaching and learning.

Teachers

All of the chapters acknowledged in some way the important role of teachers in implementing these new curricula. Among the principles underlying

Everyday Mathematics, for example, is the assumption that "the teacher and curriculum are important in providing a guide for learning important mathematics" (Chapter 4). In the *Number Power* curriculum, "open-ended teacher questions are an important feature . . . providing the teacher with information about each student's conceptual development that is a basis for making instructional decisions" (Chapter 6). What it means, however, for the teacher to be a "guide" or to make "instructional decisions" is not always clear. Some of this lack of clarity results from authors' being asked to focus their limited space in these chapters on student outcomes—the topic of this book. It also reflects a more general need for the mathematics education community at large to understand better the changing roles of teachers and the changes in knowledge and perspective that these roles entail.

A subtle yet important difference in perspective on the teacher's role emerges from these chapters. One view is that the teacher plays a critically important role in properly implementing the tasks and activities of the curriculum. This perspective is implicit, for example, in Carter et al.'s description of *Math Trailblazers* activities intended to help students learn important mathematics grounded in meaningful scientific problems and activity. Carter et al. show how the various activities are structured to lead students to particular understandings and competencies. For example, the Fill 'er Up! "investigation of volume provided a physical context that helped the student visualize the problem and connect it with the operations of addition, multiplication, and division" (Chapter 5). As students work through these activities they "are asked to devise their own solutions to problems, communicate how they solved them, and then represent their solutions with number sentences" (Chapter 5). The teacher obviously plays a role here; indeed, the importance of the teacher engaging in "mathematical conversations" with her students is brought out in the case study later in the chapter. The explanations for student learning, however, focus on the curriculum's activities: The intellectually engaging activities create a positive connection between emotion and learning; the length of the activities allows students to discuss mathematics with their peers, and the student choice provided by the activities "has been shown to be a key factor in the development of student autonomy" (Chapter 3). The overall impression created here is that the activities of the *Math Trailblazers* curriculum, if implemented properly, lead to the desired student learning. The teacher plays the undeniably important role of implementing the activities and supporting students' engagement in these activities.

In contrast, in the *Investigations* curriculum as described by Mokros, "the curriculum provides a foundation and facilitates the work of a teacher who is striving to develop students' mathematical thinking" (Chapter 5). Rather than the teacher supporting the implementation of a particular curriculum, the curriculum supports the work of the teacher; learning is located more directly in the interactions among students and teachers. The activities and materials of the curriculum are important because they provide rich sites for students and teachers to interact around significant mathematical content. The importance of how teachers interact with students is highlighted by the findings of the case studies that teachers using the *Investigations* activities to teach prescribed strategies was not effective.

Like many distinctions, this contrast between teacher as important implementer of curriculum versus teacher being supported by curriculum should not be used rigidly. Indeed, each of the curricula described in these chapters likely contains shades of both perspectives. The distinction is important, however, because it highlights the relationship between a curriculum and what actually goes on in classrooms, as well as the fundamental nature of some of the changes being called for in mathematics classrooms.

Regardless of whether teachers are viewed as implementers of new curricular activities or as being supported by the curricula, working with these curricula entails significant learning by teachers. Teacher learning can be considered from at least two perspectives. First is the need for teachers to learn about the new curriculum and new pedagogical skills it might require. The questioning, guiding, and fostering of student discussion emphasized in all these curricula represent a significant departure from much traditional teaching; teachers must acquire new skills in interacting with students to implement them successfully. The importance of this learning is illustrated by the finding that teachers using *Number Power* without professional development opportunities were not effective in using the new curriculum.

Beyond the particular techniques and skills that teachers might need to implement these new curricula, however, lie deeper changes and learning that may be required by teachers to embrace these new curricula and the approaches to teaching and learning mathematics they represent. These reform-oriented curricula embody assumptions about what mathematics is important and how it is learned that are different, perhaps fundamentally different, from the implicit assumptions that pervade existing curricula and school culture. As I argued earlier, for many teachers, good teaching involves clear explanations and modeling, along with providing opportunities for students to practice what is being explained and modeled in various settings. For such teachers, the activities of these new curricula may conflict with their images of good teaching. Claims such as "students develop new and better strategies by articulating their own ideas and by listening to others' strategies" (Mokros, Chapter 5) may seem unreasonable and even raise questions about their role as effective teachers (Smith, 1996). Indeed, Battistich et al. reported that teachers who did not participate in professional development activities associated with *Number Power* failed to recognize the importance of various aspects of the program and thus failed to implement it fully.

All of this means that as these new curricula and others like them become more widespread, significant attention to teachers' learning is essential for successful change. The sorts of mathematical reasoning, communication, and problem solving recommended in the NCTM *Standards* and in these curricula demand thoughtful interaction among teachers and students around important mathematics. This interaction can be achieved only if teachers are supported in their efforts to learn new ways of teaching and thinking about mathematics and students. As Mokros argues about *Investigations,* the curriculum may well have "its greatest impact on students by effecting teacher change and by supporting teachers in their work. The curriculum provides a foundation and facilitates the work of a teacher who is striving to develop students' mathematical thinking" (Chapter 5). This statement makes explicit something that is implied at best in the other curricula: that supporting teachers' development of richer understandings of the mathematics to be taught is a key role of the curriculum.

Computational Skills, Algorithms, and Fluency

All of these chapters somehow addressed the issue of computational skill as a student outcome—not surprising, given public concern that reforms in mathematics education may be hindering students' learning of basic computational skills. Although the importance and role of computational skills in the curriculum is dangerous territory in today's vitriolic climate of debate about mathematics education, I would like to venture into that territory a bit to offer some perspectives on reasons we need to assess what computational skills students are or are not learning. At the risk of oversimplifying, let me offer three reasons to justify the inclusion of computational skills in the elementary mathematics curriculum.

1. *Tradition.* The ability to compute accurately and efficiently has long been a central component of the elementary school curriculum and is considered an important competency for any educated person. Arithmetic skill is valued in our society.[1] One reason for evaluators of new curricula to include assessments of students' computational skill is that these skills are outcomes the public expects.

2. *Utility.* A second justification for computational skills is that they are important for getting around in the world, being successful in the workplace, and so forth. When Thorndike (1922) wanted a systematic, scientific basis for deciding on the content of the elementary mathematics curriculum, he conducted an analysis of the arithmetic skills that people actually used in daily life. The importance of computational skills was obvious; they were needed in many facets of social and economic life. Similarly, we can argue

that certain computational skills are important for getting around in today's world. The widespread infusion of computers and other computational technologies into all facets of our lives, however, raises important questions for this line of thought.

3. *Foundational.*   Computational skills also play important roles in other mathematical competencies that we value. Some would argue that one cannot understand advanced mathematical concepts until after gaining fluent mastery of more basic computational skills. Others argue that conceptual understanding is an important foundation for the learning of efficient skills. It is clear, however, that some aspects of computational skill and fluency are essential to mathematical understanding and problem solving. In thinking about curriculum and outcomes, the question becomes, What aspects are important? Better understanding how computational skill and fluency are intertwined with and support mathematical reasoning and problem solving is a critical area for scholarship and research in a world in which new technologies are transforming the nature of computation almost daily.

Arguments from any of these three areas can provide strong warrants for including careful assessment of students' computational skills in evaluations of outcomes. What is important is that the researchers studying the effects of the curricula, and the people making use of these studies to make policy and instructional decisions, are thoughtful about why computational skills are important.

Is Technology Important?

Given that these curricula were so recently developed and the general value placed on the settings and tools with which students learn to think mathematically, I was struck with the limited attention in these chapters to the role of calculators, computers, and other new technologies in the teaching and learning of mathematics. Three of the chapters mentioned in their curricular goals the importance of students being able to "choose appropriate tools," including calculators, for computation. In describing a "typical" *Everyday Mathematics* classroom, Carroll and Isaacs pointed out that calculators are used more frequently than in traditional classrooms. These were the only mentions of new technologies. I do not point out this lack of attention to technology to criticize these curricula or these authors' trying to document what students are learning from them. One could certainly argue that these curricula are about learning mathematics, not technology, and there are plenty of important issues about mathematical content, learning, and pedagogy that the developers have been thinking about, without the added burden of trying to figure out where technology fits into all of this.

I raise the issue more as a pointer for the future. I believe that the role of new technologies in learning and teaching mathematics has to receive more explicit attention in curriculum development efforts like these for a number of reasons.

The 1989 *Standards* used the profound changes in our society brought about by new technologies as an important part of the rationale for rethinking how we teach and learn mathematics, and what mathematics should make up the curriculum. These ideas were extended in the *Principles and Standards for School Mathematics* (PSSM; see NCTM, 2000), where technology is the basis for one of six organizing principles: "Technology is essential in teaching and learning mathematics; it influences the mathematics that is taught and enhances students' learning" (p. 24). A chapter on outcomes of curricula is not the place for a thorough discussion of this topic, but here are four reasons that technology should be made a more explicit part of elementary mathematics curriculum. Three of these are outlined in PSSM; the fourth is not.

First, new technologies provide powerful new tools for enhancing the learning of mathematics. Computers and calculators provide new ways to represent abstract mathematical ideas, rich sites with realistic data for mathematical problem solving, and computational tools that can enable students to focus on "higher level" aspects of problem solving.

Second, these technologies can support teachers in their teaching of mathematics and their own learning (Putnam & Borko, 2000). The rapid expansion of electronic networks has made possible unprecedented opportunities for teachers to have access to information and interactions with others. Video and multimedia hold great potential for representing teaching and learning in rich ways that can serve as examples for others and support self-study and improvement.

Third, technology influences what mathematics is and should be taught. New technologies are transforming the way people use mathematics. As pointed out by the NCTM in the 1989 *Curriculum Standards*, calculators, computers, and related technologies have "dramatically changed the nature of the physical, life, and social sciences; business; industry; and government" (p. 3). These changes have implications for mathematics education in the elementary school that simply cannot be ignored. As I argued earlier, the widespread availability of calculators and other technology makes it increasingly difficult to support the need for having efficient computational skills. This does not mean that attaining computational skill and fluency is not important. Rather, it raises new questions about their role in the curriculum. What *is* the relationship between computational skill and other aspects of knowing mathematics? What does it mean to learn mathematics by using the tools that are now available?

Finally, capitalizing on the current wave of interest and resources for bringing new technologies into our schools may be an important opportunity for enacting more fundamental changes in teaching and learning. There is tremendous public pressure to incorporate new technologies into schooling—whether to ensure that our youth will be prepared for the world of tomorrow or because of a naïve belief that new technologies may be the silver bullets that will solve enduring educational dilemmas. The pressure for technology, like the pressure for accountability through standardized test scores, is an easy one on which the media and the public can focus. Thoughtful educators know that simple solutions are not to be had, but the pressure is real nonetheless. Mathematics educators and curriculum developers should be thinking hard about how they can incorporate these new technologies into curriculum and instruction.

CONCLUSION

These chapters have provided us with an important look at the impact of several reform-oriented elementary mathematics curricula on the nature of students' experiences and learning. The authors have revealed important assumptions—both implicit and explicit—about mathematics learning, teaching, students, and the role of curriculum in the instructional process. Although the individual studies had measurement and methodological weaknesses, as a set they provide strong evidence for the fact that teaching mathematics with an emphasis on understanding can result in the learning of valued computational skills and at the same time foster mathematical understanding and reasoning. I close with two important implications of this evidence.

First, teachers who choose to emphasize mathematical understanding do not have to do so at the expense of procedural proficiency. Teaching mathematics for understanding can result in students gaining conceptual understanding *and* procedural competence.

Second, in the current political climate of promoting excellence in schools by increasing accountability through high-stakes tests, we must encourage the use of assessments that capture the broad range of mathematical knowledge, skills, and dispositions we want our children to learn. In these chapters, traditional standardized assessments typically failed to capture the problem solving, strategy use, mathematical reasoning, and number sense the new curricula were designed to foster. Without alternatives to traditional standardized tests, much of the important learning of students experiencing these new curricula would have gone undocumented. If we want our students to understand and use mathematics, then our high-stakes assessments must be broad and diverse enough to capture the conceptual understanding and reasoning we value.

REFERENCES

Dewey, J. (1964). The child and the curriculum. In R. D. Archambault (Eds.), *John Dewey on education: Selected writings* (pp. 339–358). Chicago: University of Chicago Press.

Hiebert, J. (1999). Relationships between research and the NCTM standards. *Journal for Research in Mathematics Education, 30,* 3–19.

National Council of Teachers of Mathematics. (1989). *Curriculum and evaluation standards for school mathematics.* Reston, VA: Author.

National Council of Teachers of Mathematics. (2000). *Principles and standards for school mathematics.* Reston, VA: Author.

Putnam, R. T., & Borko, H. (2000). What do new views of knowledge and thinking have to say about research on teacher learning? *Educational Researcher, 29*(1), 4–15.

Smith, J. P., III. (1996). Efficacy and teaching mathematics by telling: A challenge for reform. *Journal for Research in Mathematics Education, 27,* 387–402.

Thorndike, E. L. (1922). *The psychology of arithmetic.* New York: MacMillan.

ENDNOTE

1. At the same time, mathematical competence has quite a different status in our society than does literacy. It is perfectly acceptable among educated company to say, "I can't balance my checkbook." It is much less acceptable to say, "I can't read the newspaper."

PART III

Middle Grades
Curriculum Projects

8

Middle School Mathematics Curriculum Reform

Sharon L. Senk
Michigan State University

Denisse R. Thompson
University of South Florida

This part of the book is devoted to research about *Standards*-based middle school mathematics curricula. Because not all students in a given grade in middle school take the same mathematics courses, we begin this chapter with a brief description of middle school mathematics course offerings. Then, as we did in Chapter 2, we summarize results of research on students' achievement in middle school mathematics that were reported in the 1980s. Later, we describe recommendations made for reforming the middle school mathematics curriculum in the *Curriculum and Evaluation Standards for School Mathematics* (National Council of Teachers of Mathematics [NCTM], 1989) and other documents. Finally, we describe the call from the National Science Foundation for proposals to develop new curricula to embody the vision outlined in the *Standards*, and that ultimately led to the curriculum projects whose work is described in the three chapters that follow this one.

MIDDLE SCHOOL MATHEMATICS COURSES

At the end of the 20th century, schools for young adolescents were configured in various ways in the United States. Some 13-year-olds attended elementary schools containing Grades K–8. Others were studying in junior

181

high schools containing Grades 7 and 8 or Grades 7–9. Still others were enrolled in middle schools containing Grades 6–8, 5–8, or 6–9. Unlike elementary schools in the United States, where students were generally taught mathematics in heterogeneous groups, many middle schools grouped students homogeneously, that is, by ability. Oakes (1985) found that among the 12 junior high schools studied intensively in the late 1970s, in 11 schools students were grouped homogeneously in mathematics. Some schools offered three tracks of mathematics: high, average, and low; others had four tracks: honors, academic, general, and basic. The mathematical content differed quite a bit across the tracks (Oakes, 1985):

> The low-track mathematics courses focused grade after grade on basic computational skills and arithmetic facts—multiplication tables and the like. Sometimes included in these classes were simple measurement skills and the conversion of the English system into the metric. . . . In the high track classes, topics . . . included mathematical ideas — concepts about numeration systems, mathematical models, probability, and statistics—as well as computational procedures which became increasingly sophisticated at the higher grades. (p. 77)

Average math classes were considerably more like the high-track classes in their content than like the low.

In a 1985–1986 survey conducted by Weiss (1987) of 348 schools with classes in Grades 7–9, 16% of the mathematics classes were considered high ability, 16% were considered low ability, 49% were considered average ability, and 19% were of widely differing abilities. Students designated as having high ability frequently took an algebra course in middle school. Usiskin (1987, p. 429) estimated that among the high school students graduating in 1985, 10% of the students had taken algebra in Grade 7 or 8.

Achievement of Eighth-Grade Students in the Second International Mathematics Study

During the 1981–1982 school year, approximately 7,000 eighth graders in the United States participated in the Second International Mathematics Study (SIMS). The eighth graders, who were chosen from the full range of mathematics classes from remedial mathematics through algebra, were tested on five major topics: arithmetic, algebra, geometry, statistics, and measurement.

U.S. eighth-grade students were slightly above the international average in computational arithmetic (calculation), and they were well below the international average in noncomputational arithmetic (e.g., problem solving). U.S. achievement in algebra and statistics was comparable with the international average. Achievement in geometry and measurement of the U. S. sample was among the bottom 25% of all countries, reflecting to a large extent teachers' lack of coverage of the subject matter (McKnight et al., 1987, pp. v–vii, 21).

An analysis of the textbooks used by students in the sample found that "the U.S. curriculum is characterized by a great deal of repetition and review, with the result that topics are covered with little intensity. By contrast, at this level France places a great deal of emphasis on geometry, and Japan provides an intense treatment of algebra." Furthermore, "the eighth grade curriculum in the U.S. tends to be *arithmetic driven*, resembling much more the end of elementary school than the beginning of high school" (emphasis in the original; McKnight et al., 1987, p. ix)

Teachers of the eighth-grade classes in the United States reported that students spent the majority of their time on individual seatwork or listening to explanations from the teacher. Very little time was spent in small groups. "Little place seems to have been given to guided, active discovery learning, in which students generated high-level questions and in which there was more of a balance between teacher and student subject-related talk" (McKnight et al., p. 73). Further, abstract and symbolic representations of content were the primary means of demonstrating content, facilitating a reliance on rote learning of procedures.

Noting a strong positive relation between students' achievement and their opportunity to learn the content, McKnight and his colleagues called for "a fundamental revision of the U.S. school mathematics curriculum" beginning at the early grades of the elementary school. In particular, they recommended that the curriculum of the junior high school "be broadened and enriched by the inclusion of appropriate topics in geometry, probability and statistics, as well as algebra" (McKnight et al., 1987, p. xii).

The SIMS researchers also expressed concerns over tracking in the middle grades.

> The practice of the early sorting of students into curricula with vastly different content leading to substantially different opportunities to learn mathematics in high school must be carefully re-examined. At present, significant proportions of U.S. students as young as 12 or 13 years are being sorted into mathematics curricula that offer little intellectual challenge, seriously limit their chances for success in many fields of study (in high school and beyond) and greatly restrict their career choices in today's society. (p. xiii)

Earlier, Oakes (1985) had remarked that although tracking is well intentioned, it "has some pretty hellish consequences" (p. 5). Although the topics taught in low-track mathematics classes are often desirable—consumer math skills, for example—the omission of other content—algebraic equations, for example—denies students the opportunity to learn material essential for mobility to higher tracks. This essentially denies students in low-track classes the opportunity to prepare for college entrance. Poor and minority students who are represented disproportionately in lower track classes seem to suffer most from tracking. Oakes reports that the content and intellectual processes used in heterogeneous classes are more like those in the high-track classes than the low-track classes. She recommended that schools eliminate or reduce their use of tracking, and she suggested that the use of cooperative learning could increase achievement and develop equity in secondary schools.

Achievement on the Fourth National Assessment of Educational Progress

The results from the Fourth National Assessment of Educational Progress (NAEP) conducted in 1985–1986 provided additional evidence about the mathematics achievement of students in the middle grades. The Fourth NAEP examined the performance of more than 23,000 middle grades students. Most students were in Grade 7; but data also were collected for students at age 13 to provide comparisons with earlier NAEP data on 13-year-olds.

In order to preserve the integrity of the trend data, no items from those tests are released. Instead, overall performance is reported. Virtually all of the 13-year-old students knew simple arithmetic facts and demonstrated a command of beginning skills and understanding. They could also add two-digit numbers, read information from charts and graphs, and use simple measurement instruments. Approximately 73% of the 13-year-olds had also developed an understanding of beginning problem solving. They could add, subtract, multiply, and divide multidigit whole numbers, compare information in graphs and charts, and were developing an ability to analyze simple logical relations. However, only approximately 16% of the 13-year-olds demonstrated moderately complex procedures and reasoning by computing with decimals, simple fractions, and commonly used percents; identifying geometric figures; measuring lengths and angles; and calculating areas of rectangles. Less than 1% of the 13-year-olds were able to do multistep problem solving and algebra (Dossey, Mullis, Lindquist, & Chambers, 1989, pp. 118–119).

Researchers reported that slightly more than half of the seventh-grade students could perform basic computations with fractions; approximately 60% could add and multiply decimals, whereas fewer than 50% could subtract and divide them. An extremely limited knowledge of fraction procedures was demonstrated by approximately one third of the seventh-grade students. Extremely limited knowledge of basic decimal concepts and skills was demonstrated by approximately 40% of the seventh-grade students (Kouba, Carpenter, & Swafford, 1989, pp. 79, 82).

Performance on specific topics or items gives additional insight into the level of mathematical understanding of seventh-grade students. According to Kouba et al. (1989),

> About 90 percent of the 7th-grade students correctly solved simple two-step word problems involving successive small additions or subtractions to a given starting number, such as in the following problem:
>> There are 31 birds on the fence. Six take off and 3 more land. How many are on the fence then? (p. 77).

In contrast, Brown and Silver (1989) found that less than half the students in Grade 7 could find the average of the ages of six children (p. 30). According to Swafford and Brown (1989), approximately 90% solved the open sentence $27 = \Box + 14$ correctly; approximately 60% solved $\Box - 8 = 8$ (p. 57). However, "few 7th-grade students could correctly identify the graph of the solution of the simple inequality $3x \geq 15$" (p. 59).

According to Lindquist and Kouba (1989), approximately half the students tested in Grade 7 could find the area of a rectangle when given the length of its sides or when shown a figure with the square units indicated. However, in Grade 7 many students confused area and perimeter. "The most common error made on the area items was choosing the perimeter, and vice versa" (p. 35). Lindquist and Kouba also found that approximately 40% of the seventh-grade students chose the best of the given estimates for the area of the irregular figure shown in Fig. 8.1 (1989, p. 41).

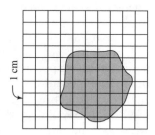

About how many square cm is the area of the shaded region?

FIG. 8.1. Item from the fourth NAEP used to assess seventh-grade students' abilities to estimate area. *Note.* From *Results from the Fourth Mathematics Assessment of the National Assessment of Educational Progress* (p. 41), by M. M. Lindquist (Ed.), Reston, VA: National Council of Teachers of Mathematics. © 1989 by National Council of Teachers of Mathematics. Reprinted with permission. All rights reserved.

Carpenter and Lindquist concluded that "the emphasis on computational skills that has generally characterized mathematics instruction has left many students with serious gaps in their knowledge of underlying concepts. As a result, students have not learned many advanced skills and frequently they can not apply the skills they have learned" (1989, p. 169).

OTHER STUDIES ABOUT MIDDLE SCHOOL MATHEMATICS

Many other research studies conducted during the 1980s dealt with issues related to teaching and learning middle school mathematics. Space does not permit a thorough review of that research here; below we report on several studies that appear to have had direct impact on the calls for changes in the middle school mathematics curriculum.

Flanders' (1987) study of three of the most popular textbook series in use in the mid-1980s showed that the repetition in the Grade 8 mathematics curriculum noted by the SIMS researchers characterized all of Grades 6–8. The average percentage of new content in these books was approximately 38% at Grade 6, 36% at Grade 7, and 30% at Grade 8. Further, much of the new material in the textbooks for Grades 6–8 was in the second half of the books, making it less likely that students encounter that new material if teachers begin on the first page of the text. Flanders noted that

> We say we want students to be active and creative problem-solvers yet we set up an environment that seems designed to discourage them from thinking about new ideas—in short, an environment designed to put them to sleep. (p. 23)

In contrast, Flanders found that in the textbooks for algebra, the course intended for most students in the ninth grade, 88% of the content was new. He suggested that the disparity between the low expectations with regards to new material at Grades 6–8 and the high expectations at Grade 9 might explain why many students have difficulty with algebra.

Usiskin (1987) cited data from a different popular textbook series for Grades 6–8 to argue that "for students who know sixth-grade mathematics, not much is new in seventh or eighth grade" (pp. 431–432). This was the first of six reasons Usiskin gave for why elementary algebra can, should, and must be an eighth-grade course for average students. However, the algebra course he recommended for eighth graders had four major differences from the algebra course typically taught at that time. Usiskin would replace contrived word problems by applications; reduce the emphasis on factoring trinomials; delete simplification of and operations with rational expressions; and emphasize solving quadratic equations by use of the quadratic formula.

Research indicates that the concepts of variable and equation develop in young students over time. As a consequence of early instruction in arithmetic, students often view the equal sign operationally, that is, as a signal to do something to get an answer. However, to be successful in algebra students need to view the equal sign as a symbol of equivalence or balance. Kieran (1981) pointed out that early adolescents' difficulties with understanding variables, expressions, and equations center on the meaning of letters, the shift to a set of conventions different from those used in arithmetic, and the recognition and use of algebraic structure.

It is generally agreed that the rational number system, with fractions, decimals, ratios, and proportions, is a core area of study for the middle grades. Fuson (1988) noted that research on learning about concepts and operations with rational numbers has identified many different meanings and interpretations for the same symbol, be it the multiplication symbol $\times$ or the rational number symbol a/b. She recommended that these multiple interpretations, as well as the relations between addition–subtraction situations and multiplication–division situations, be articulated more clearly both in the research literature and in middle school classrooms (pp. 261–262). Lesh, Post, and Behr (1988, p. 97) note how proportional reasoning is a watershed, because it is both a capstone activity of elementary arithmetic and measurement concepts and a cornerstone of algebra and other higher levels of mathematics. Further, Case (1988, p. 268) pointed out that "real-world" learning situations are a necessary ingredient for success in the study of middle grades mathematics, but their presence in the curriculum or in the classroom is no guarantee of success.

During the 1980s, research on learning geometry validated that students' thinking about geometry proceeded through a sequence of levels first identified by the van Hieles (Burger & Shaughnessy, 1986; Fuys, Geddes, & Tischler, 1988). The analysis of the geometry lessons in three series of K–8 mathematics textbooks done by Fuys, Geddes, and Tischler (1988) indicated that once a topic was introduced it tended to be reviewed every year. In each of the three sixth-grade textbooks the type of thinking required for the majority of geometry lessons was at the lowest level. Even in the textbooks for Grade 8, the majority of lessons was still at the two lowest of the five van Hiele levels.

STANDARDS FOR MIDDLE SCHOOL MATHEMATICS

The results from the SIMS, the National Assessment of Educational Progress, and the other research cited in the previous section were well known by the members of the mathematics education community in the late 1980s. Thus, it is not unusual that when citing the need for curriculum change, the writers of the *Standards* expressed themes that had been mentioned earlier (NCTM, 1989):

> Many students view the current mathematics curriculum in grades 5–8 as irrelevant, dull, and routine. Instruction has emphasized computational facility at the expense of a broad, integrated view of mathematics and has reflected neither the vitality of the subject nor the characteristics of the students. (pp. 65–66)

As a remedy to this situation, they called for a "broad range of topics that should be taught as an integrated whole, not as isolated topics" (p. 67). The authors of the *Standards* recommended a shift away from arithmetic toward a more balanced view of mathematics. They argued that basic skills in the future would require more than computational proficiency. Topics in geometry, probability, statistics, and algebra have become increasingly important and accessible to students through technology.

In addition to the standards for problem solving, communication, reasoning, and connections that were common to all grade levels, nine content standards were specified for the middle grades:

- Number and Number Relationships
- Number Systems and Number Theory
- Computation and Estimation
- Patterns and Functions
- Algebra
- Statistics
- Probability
- Geometry
- Measurement

For each of the 13 standards, the authors specified a short list of more specific topics that should be included. They also provided specific examples to illustrate how each standard might be implemented in a middle school classroom. Because middle grades students are "especially responsive to hands-on activities in tactile, auditory, and visual instructional modes," many examples illustrated how concrete materials, computers, or calculators could be used effectively (NCTM, 1989, p. 67).

Charts listing recommended changes in content and emphases were also given (pp. 70–73). For instance, authors called for *increased attention* to the following: pursuing open-ended problems and extended problem-solving projects; developing number sense; creating algorithms and procedures; using appropriate technology for computation and exploration; and assessing learning as an integral part of instruction. In contrast, they called for *decreased attention* to the following: practicing routine, one-step problems; memorizing rules and algorithms; finding exact forms of answers; drilling on paper-and-pencil algorithms; and testing for the sole purpose of assigning grades.

Finally, the authors noted that "mathematics educators and others must realize that this broad, rich curriculum is intended to be available to *all* students. No student should be denied access to the study of one topic because he or she has yet to master another" (NCTM, 1989, p. 69; italics in the original).

A CALL FOR MATERIALS FOR MIDDLE SCHOOL MATHEMATICS INSTRUCTION

Shortly after the publication of the *Curriculum and Evaluation Standards*, the National Science Foundation (NSF) issued a Program Solicitation entitled *Materials for Middle School Mathematics Instruction*. Preliminary proposals were due January 1, 1990, with June 1, 1990 set as the date for formal proposals. The poor performance of U.S. eighth graders on international comparisons and the great amount of repetition in the middle school curriculum of the time were cited as two reasons for proposing new middle school curricula.

According to the NSF (1989), projects responding to this program solicitation

> were expected to do most or all of the following:
> * prepare **course material** for a complete middle school mathematics curriculum;
> * explore and improve on **teaching methods**, possibly including new uses of technology and new applications of mathematics, appropriate for presenting the new material to middle school students;
> * develop **strategies and materials for teachers** to improve their understanding of mathematics and introduce them to more effective methods of instruction; and
> * formulate **assessment methods and materials** so that teachers can evaluate and adjust the learning environment to best suit the needs of the students. (p. 4; bold in original)

It was expected that "the new materials will be based upon sound mathematics appropriate to the middle school, and that new teaching materials will reflect solid research in the learning process" (NSF, 1989, p. 4).

Among the references about mathematics content and curriculum cited in the solicitation are the *Curriculum and Evaluation Standards* (NCTM, 1989), *Everybody Counts* (National Research Council, 1989), Flanders' (1987) analysis of textbooks, and the proceedings of an international conference sponsored by the University of Chicago School Mathematics Project (Wirszup & Streit, 1987). Citations about research on learning included a book on the learning of number concepts and operations by Hiebert and Behr (1988), and two articles on work in cognitive science (Brown, Collins, & Duguid, 1989; Davis, 1986).

STANDARDS-BASED MIDDLE SCHOOL MATHEMATICS CURRICULA

Four middle school curriculum projects were funded from this solicitation: the Connected Mathematics Project, The Development of an "Achieved" Curriculum for Middle School [currently *Mathematics in Context*], Seeing and Thinking Mathematically [currently *MathScape*], and Six Through Eight Mathematics [currently *Math Thematics*]. Of these, *Mathematics in Context* is a curriculum for Grades 5–8; the others focus on Grades 6–8.

When development for this book began, the developers of Seeing and Thinking Mathematically had only anecdotal information about the effects of their curriculum on students' achievement; hence, they did not meet the minimum requirements for inclusion in this book. Thus, only the Connected Mathematics Project, Mathematics in Context, and Six Through Eight Mathematics are the subjects of chapters in this volume. Research on the effects of these three *Standards*-based curricula is the subject of Chapters 9–11.

In Chapter 12 Michaele Chappell looks across all three chapters for similarities and differences in the research methodologies and achievement results reported. She also raises some questions for future research at the middle grades level.

REFERENCES

Brown, J. S., Collins, A., & Duguid, P. (1989). Situated cognition and the culture of learning. *Educational Researcher, 18,* 32–42.

Brown, C. A., & Silver, E. A. (1989). Data organization and interpretation. In M. M. Lindquist (Ed.), *Results from the fourth mathematics assessment of the national assessment of educational progress* (pp. 28–34). Reston, VA: National Council of Teachers of Mathematics.

Burger, W., & Shaughnessy, J. M. (1986). Characterizing the van Hiele levels of development in geometry. *Journal for Research in Mathematics Education, 17,* 31–48.

Carpenter, T. P., & Lindquist, M. M. (1989). Summary and conclusions. In M. M. Lindquist (Ed.), *Results from the fourth mathematics assessment of the national assessment of educational progress* (pp. 160–169). Reston, VA: National Council of Teachers of Mathematics.

Case, R. (1988). Summary comments: Developing a research agenda for mathematics in the middle grades. In J. Hiebert & M. Behr (Eds.), *Number concepts and operations in the middle grades* (pp. 265–270). Mahwah, NJ: Lawrence Erlbaum Associates.

Davis, R. (1986). The convergence of cognitive science and mathematics education. *Journal of Mathematical Behavior, 5,* 321–335.

Dossey, J. A., Mullis, I. V. S., Lindquist, M. M., & Chambers, D. L. (1989). What can students do? (Levels of mathematics proficiency for the nation and demographic subgroups.) In M. M. Lindquist (Ed.), *Results from the fourth mathematics assessment of the national assessment of educational progress* (pp. 117–134). Reston, VA: National Council of Teachers of Mathematics.

Flanders, J. R. (1987). How much of the content is new. *Arithmetic Teacher, 35*(1), 18–23.

Fuson, K. (1988). Summary comments: Meaning in middle grade number concepts. In J. Hiebert & M. Behr (Eds.), *Number concepts and operations in the middle grades* (pp. 260–264). Mahwah, NJ: Lawrence Erlbaum Associates.

Fuys, D., Geddes, D., & Tischler, R. (1988). The van Hiele model of thinking in geometry among adolescents. *Journal for Research in Mathematics Education* (Monograph Series No. 3). Reston, VA: National Council of Teachers of Mathematics.

Hiebert, J., & Behr, M. (Eds.). (1988). *Number concepts and operations in the middle grades.* Mahwah, NJ: Lawrence Erlbaum Associates.

Kieran, C. (1981). Concepts associated with the equality symbol. *Educational Studies in Mathematics, 12*, 317–326.

Kouba, V. L., Carpenter, T. P., & Swafford, J. O. (1989). Number and operations. In M. M. Lindquist (Ed.), *Results from the fourth mathematics assessment of the national assessment of educational progress* (pp. 64–93). Reston, VA: National Council of Teachers of Mathematics.

Lesh, R., Post, T., & Behr, M. (1988). Proportional reasoning. In J. Hiebert & M. Behr (Eds.), *Number concepts and operations in the middle grades* (pp. 260–264). Mahwah, NJ: Lawrence Erlbaum Associates.

Lindquist, M. M., & Kouba, V. L. (1989). Measurement. In M. M. Lindquist (Ed.), *Results from the fourth mathematics assessment of the national assessment of educational progress* (pp. 35–43). Reston, VA: National Council of Teachers of Mathematics.

McKnight, C. C., Crosswhite, F. J., Dossey, J. A., Kifer, E., Swafford, J. O., Travers, K. J., & Cooney, T. J. (1987). *The underachieving curriculum: Assessing U.S. school mathematics from an international perspective.* Champaign, IL: Stipes.

National Council of Teachers of Mathematics. (1989). *Curriculum and evaluation standards for school mathematics.* Reston, VA: Author.

National Research Council. (1989). *Everybody counts: A report to the nation on the future of mathematics education.* Washington, DC: Mathematical Sciences Education Board, National Research Council.

National Science Foundation. (1989). *Materials for middle school mathematics instruction: Program solicitation.* Washington, DC: Author.

Oakes, J. (1985). *Keeping track: How schools structure inequality.* New Haven, CT: Yale University Press.

Swafford, J. O., & Brown, C. A. (1989). Variables and relations. In M. M. Lindquist (Ed.), *Results from the fourth mathematics assessment of the national assessment of educational progress* (pp. 55–63). Reston, VA: National Council of Teachers of Mathematics.

Usiskin, Z. (1987). Why elementary algebra can, should, and must be an eighth-grade course for average students. *Mathematics Teacher, 80*, 428–437.

Weiss, I. R. (1987). *Report of the 1985–86 national survey of science and mathematics education.* Research Triangle Park, NC: Research Triangle Institute.

Wirszup, I., & Streit, R. (Eds.). (1987). *Developments in school mathematics education around the world.* Reston, VA: National Council of Teachers of Mathematics.

9

Student Attainment in the *Connected Mathematics* Curriculum

James E. Ridgway
University of Durham

Judith S. Zawojewski
Purdue University

Mark N. Hoover
University of Michigan

Diana V. Lambdin
Indiana University

The Connected Mathematics Project (CMP) was funded by the National Science Foundation to develop a complete mathematics curriculum with support materials for Grades 6, 7, and 8.[1] The development, piloting, and field testing of the materials spanned a 5-year period, during which a number of studies were conducted that evaluated students' achievement when using the curriculum. This chapter provides information about the program and reports on students' mathematics attainment when studying from CMP materials (now called *Connected Mathematics*; Lappan, Fey, Fitzgerald, Friel, & Phillips, 1998). It draws some conclusions about the successes so far, raises issues about implementation and evaluation of complex curriculum reform, and identifies challenges and questions in need of further investigation.

193

THE CURRICULUM

Connected Mathematics authors worked to write materials that would develop student knowledge and understanding of mathematics through attention to connections: between mathematical ideas and their applications in the world outside school; among the core ideas in mathematics; among the strands in a modern mathematics curriculum; and between the planned teaching–learning activities and the special aptitudes and interests of middle school students. They designed the curriculum with the hope that it would promote changes both in the mathematics content taught and in the teaching of that mathematics. The *Connected Mathematics* curriculum is organized around interesting problem settings—activities designed to involve groups of students with mathematical concepts and applications as well as in discourse and reflective writing about these same ideas. Students are expected to observe patterns and relationships, make conjectures, discuss solutions, and generalize from their findings. The goal is to immerse students in the mathematics and the mathematical thinking needed for success in high school and eventually college. To meet this goal, development of this problem-based curriculum relied heavily on mathematicians who advised the project and pushed the development team to keep mathematics in the forefront of all student activity.

At each grade level, the *Connected Mathematics* Curriculum comprises eight modules, each focusing on an important area of mathematics and emphasizing connections to previously learned content. Appendix A lists the modules and their content for each of the three grades. The treatment of number begins with an emphasis on concepts and operations with fractions, decimals, and percents in the sixth grade, and it progresses to formal treatment of proportional reasoning in seventh grade. A problem-centered approach to algebra begins in the seventh grade and becomes a primary emphasis in the eighth grade as students learn about linear, exponential, and quadratic functions. The students solve contextualized problems by using graphing calculators and learn to make connections among tables, graphs, equations, and verbal statements for functions. Geometry is addressed in all three grade levels, drawing on both Euclidean and transformational traditions and emphasizing the development of spatial reasoning. The content in measurement, statistics and probability is common to middle school curricula, but it is presented in a problem-centered manner that emphasizes the development of conceptual knowledge. Practice with computation and symbolic manipulation is embedded throughout units that build conceptual foundations for such skills. For example, number skills are used extensively in statistics and probability, and algebra is prevalent as students learn the various perimeter, area, and volume formulas.

The materials call for an instructional model in the classroom that encourages higher-level thinking and problem solving; the emphasis is on making sense of mathematics and its uses. *Connected Mathematics* teachers are expected to *launch* a lesson by ensuring students understand the context of a problem and, more importantly, the mathematical challenge within that context. During the time when students *explore*, teachers are encouraged to move about the classroom, observing, encouraging students, redirecting, and providing additional challenges. Finally, teachers are asked to *summarize* by initiating a class discussion of strategies used, mathematical ideas that arose, and connections that can be made. Teachers play a central role in guiding students by making explicit the mathematics typically elicited by the problem situation. Although the curriculum is problem centered, learning of mathematics content is not left to chance.

Problems were extensively field tested with students to ensure that they would give rise to the intended mathematics when explored appropriately in class. Appendix B provides a glimpse of the types of investigation and implementation that are characteristic of the *Connected Mathematics* materials. The vignette was taken from classroom observations done in *Connected Mathematics* classrooms during the pilot phase.

Evident in this vignette is the interaction between mathematical content and process that is key to the *Connected Mathematics* curriculum. In this case, students deal with the formula for the area of a triangle by reasoning through a concrete situation. Each investigation is accompanied by follow-up problems, called ACE (applications, connections, and extensions), which continue the emphasis on linking content and process. These range from application problems that provide opportunities to practice skills and concepts to lengthy problem-solving situations, as illustrated in Appendix C. In this particular unit of study, the subsequent investigations introduce the formulas for finding the area of a rectangle, parallelogram, and triangle, and they emphasize how each can be derived from the other.

Integrating mathematics content and processes was new to many of the *Connected Mathematics* teachers. They reported that implementing these materials was quite different than implementing conventional texts. In the early formative evaluation reports, there were anecdotal reports that students pressured teachers to "Tell us what to do!" and that teachers found it hard not to give away too much. It was a challenge to help teachers build confidence in their own abilities and the abilities of their students to handle larger problems and to develop deeper mathematical understanding from them. Professional development of the teachers involved at least a summer workshop offered at Michigan State University. During these sessions, teachers experienced the curriculum as students, and they had opportunities to share methods and techniques for their classroom implementation.

STUDENT ATTAINMENT IN *CONNECTED*
MATHEMATICS

Understanding what students learn in *Connected Mathematics* is a complex issue. Central to the study of students' attainment is the issue of alignment between the goals of the program and the construct validity of the assessment instruments. That is, do the tests assess what the program is designed to teach? *Connected Mathematics* aims to stimulate connections and to develop sound mathematical reasoning. Therefore, in addition to assessing attainment on a wide range of content, student performance in the areas of mathematical problem solving, reasoning, communication, and connections has to be documented.

Three major studies have been conducted to gather data related to these questions: What effect does the curriculum have on student learning? How much? In what ways? The first study is a large-scale study of overall student performance. The second study summarizes the effect of using *Connected Mathematics* in a *Standards*-based improvement effort in one school and reports the scores on the state test. The third study uses a subsample of the large-scale study and focuses on proportional reasoning. Each of these studies provides information about different aspects of student attainment. Together, they provide encouraging evidence on the robustness of the program across curricular topics and geographic locations.

The Overall Large-Scale Evaluation of Student Performance

A large-scale evaluation study was conducted in sixth and seventh grades during 1994–1995 and in eighth grade during 1995–1996. This evaluation served at least three purposes: first, to provide accountability to the National Science Foundation (NSF) on the effective use of the funding; second, to augment the ongoing formative evaluation that informed the materials development process, confirming or disconfirming apparent trends and highlighting areas of the curriculum in need of attention; and third, to obtain evaluation information that would be useful later in helping schools that adopted the curriculum to identify reasonable student achievement expectations.

Student Samples

Random assignment of students to treatments was not possible, so volunteer samples of *CMP* and non-*CMP* populations were sought. An effort was made to match the two groups as much as possible based on similar ability grouping, urban–suburban–rural designation, and diversity in student population. Nine sites across the country participated in the study: five were in the Midwest; two were in the West; and two were in the East. At five of the sites, only a small number of teachers were using the *CMP* curriculum, so comparison classrooms were identified locally. At the four other sites, all rural midwestern sites, *CMP* was the only curriculum taught in the middle school; so, an alternative rural location provided non-*CMP* comparison data.

During the second year of the study two sites dropped out, each of which had provided both *CMP* and non-*CMP* data during the previous year. A western site dropped out because all the eighth-grade students were to take a traditional algebra course. A midwestern site dropped out because no volunteer eighth-grade teacher was available to teach the *CMP* curriculum. Among the remaining seven sites, one midwestern rural site that had provided both *CMP* and non-*CMP* data the previous year decided to use *CMP* in all middle school grades. To respond to the loss of non-*CMP* comparison data, two small rural midwestern sites were combined to provide comparison data.

At each site, the *Connected Mathematics* group consisted of pairs of classrooms by grade level in a school in which *Connected Mathematics* was used as the core curriculum throughout the school year. It was assumed that the NSF-funded curricula represented a broader range of mathematical topics and processes than the commercially available texts at that time. Thus, for every pair of *CMP* classrooms, just one non-*CMP* classroom using commercially available texts was recruited. It was difficult to recruit non-*CMP* classrooms because many teachers felt overtested with district and state tests. None of the non-*CMP* teachers were involved in any reform efforts; in contrast, the *CMP* teachers were at least involved in the summer *CMP* institutes at Michigan State University. We offered each participating teacher the incentive of a gift certificate from a popular distributor of mathematics materials once all of the agreed-on tests were completed and returned.

No data exist about the mathematics textbook series used at the non-*CMP* sites. Nor are there data on the extent to which non-*CMP* classrooms were drawn from the algebra or prealgebra tracks. However, we attempted to match the volunteer classrooms and sites by having students from similar tracks in the *CMP* and non-*CMP* groups. Statistical analyses took any initial differences into account, using a standardized test score as a covariate.

As seen in Table 9.1, there were fewer sixth-grade students in the study than seventh- or eighth-grade students. We were able to assess more seventh-grade students because their teachers taught several math classes per day, but most sixth-grade teachers taught in self-contained classrooms. We learned during the first year of implementation that gathering complete data on students (requiring 4–6 testing days) was a more difficult feat than expected, so additional sites for the eighth-grade study were recruited for the 1995–1996 study. The non-*CMP* group for the eighth-grade study was smaller

TABLE 9.1
Number of Students in the Large-Scale Study

Group	Grade Level		
	6th	7th	8th
CMP	338	627	820
non-CMP	162	234	275

than intended because of an error in the distribution of appropriate grade-level tests to some of the comparison sites.

This study looked at comparative growth over 1 school year and was not intended to be longitudinal. No student was in both the sixth-grade sample and the seventh-grade sample. Because the eighth grade was assessed the following year and used some of the same geographic sites, a small number of students in the eighth-grade sample had also been in the seventh-grade sample the previous year.

Not all students in the study were in the *CMP* curriculum for the duration of their middle school experience. Approximately three fourths of the students using *CMP* were in schools where the program had been fully adopted (just over half of the sites), but in other situations a small number of volunteer teachers were using the curriculum. As a result, all of the sixth-grade students in the study were new to the curriculum and approximately three fourths of the seventh-grade and eighth-grade students in the study had used *CMP* in the previous year.

Procedures

At all three grade levels, two tests—one a measure of mathematical technique and one intended to assess a range of mathematical competencies—were administered as pretests and posttests. The former test, the Iowa Test of Basic Skills (ITBS) Survey Battery, was administered first in both the fall and the spring; the publisher's specified testing conditions were followed carefully. The test administration took approximately 50 minutes and could be split over 2 days. Students took the same test in September and April, with performance normed accordingly. Two of the five subtests were normed for calculator use, so calculators were distributed to students for those portions of the tests. Students worked individually and had no access to other classroom materials.

The latter test, the Balanced Assessment (BA) Test, was administered after the ITBS Survey Battery in both the fall and the spring by trained staff who used the same administration protocol. Although the test was expected to take approximately 45 minutes, students were given as much time as they needed to complete the test in one sitting, subject to schedule constraints of the teacher. Students were given the same BA Test in the spring as in the fall. Students worked individually on the tests, but they were given access to calculators, rulers, and other commonly available classroom tools.

The Testing Instruments

The authors and evaluators chose two different instruments because a close examination of the then-available standardized tests suggested that none included items to measure the higher-order thinking goals outlined in the *Curriculum and Evaluation Standards for School Mathematics* (National Council of Teachers of Mathematics [NCTM], 1989). Hence, the *Connected Mathematics* team collaborated with the Balanced Assessment Project to produce a test that would capture students' problem solving, reasoning, and mathematical communication as well as their ability to make connections among the mathematics topics in any curriculum.[2] A critical feature of the BA Test design (Balanced Assessment, 1999) was that the new tests should assess educational goals set out in NCTM *Standards* documents (1989, 1991, 1995). There was a deliberate decision not to create a "*Connected Mathematics* Test" linked to the *CMP* curriculum; that is, the BA Test did not mimic the language, format, or specific content of the *CMP* curriculum.

Test data come from the following sources:

- Five forms of 1-hour-long tests for each of the grades designed by the Balanced Assessment Project to assess reasoning, mathematical communication, connections, and problem solving in a balanced treatment of mathematics topics[3]; and
- The ITBS Survey Battery Form K (Levels 12, 13, and 14) mathematics sections to assess the technical concepts and skills typically found on commercially available, multiple choice, timed, standardized tests.

The BA Test and the ITBS Survey Battery were analyzed and found to differ in at least two important ways. First, the BA instrument tested a variety of curricular areas, whereas the ITBS Survey Battery primarily evaluated achievement with number and operations. Second, the BA test items took longer to complete because they were constructed-response items requiring a range of responses from short answer to extended responses; the ITBS Survey Battery used only tightly timed multiple-choice items.

Every item from the BA Test and the ITBS Survey Battery was examined by one of the authors of this chapter and classified by one of four content area emphases: number and operations, patterns and algebra, geometry and measurement, and statistics and probability. If there appeared to be an emphasis in more than one area, the item was given dual classification.

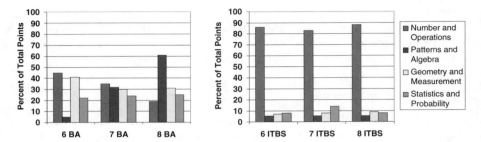

FIG. 9.1. Percent of total points classified by topic emphasis on the BA and ITBS tests (percents may add up to more than 100% because some items were simultaneously classified under two topics).

Then, each item was weighted by the number of points the item was assigned in the test scoring process. For the ITBS Survey Battery, each item counted 1 point; for the BA Test items, the items varied in points.

Figure 9.1 shows the consistency of topic emphasis over the grades on the ITBS Survey Battery and the shifts in emphases over the grades on the BA Test. The ITBS Survey Battery consistently emphasizes number and operations in each grade; the BA Tests provide a moderate emphasis on number and operations in the sixth grade, but that emphasis gradually decreases in seventh and eighth grade, giving way to an increased emphasis on patterns and algebra. Geometry–measurement and statistics–probability are given the same moderate emphasis on the BA Tests at all three grade levels.[4]

Although the five ITBS Survey Battery subtest titles (Concepts, Estimation, Problem Solving, Data Interpretation, and Computation) suggest a broad coverage of curriculum, an examination of the individual items in each subtest reveals an emphasis on number. Item 1 in Fig. 9.2 is typical of an item found in the Estimation section of the ITBS Survey Battery.[5] A student who uses a rule-based approach, "round to the lead digit and multiply," will respond correctly, as will students who use a number sense approach. However, if the second factor had been 8.47, instead of 8.67, the rule to "round and multiply" would produce an estimate that would *not* be the closest choice ($0.9 \times 8 = 7.2$, so select A). The actual product would be 7.9618, which is closest to 8. On this revised item, a student who used a number sense approach might think, "This is close to 1×8.47. Then if I adjust the product by subtracting off 10%, that would be about 7.6. But subtracting off 10% is too much, so the product must be even closer to 8." The modified item favors a number sense approach, but items like this revision are not included in the test.

Item 1.

Choose the closest estimate for .94 × 8.67

A. 7

B. 8*

C. 9

D. 10

Item 2.

Alex brought $11 to the movies. He spent $4 to get into the theater and $3 on a large tub of popcorn. He spent the rest of his money on three juice beverages. The extra large beverage cost twice as much as the two smaller beverages. **What additional information is needed to find out how much Alex spent on each juice beverage?**

A. The amount he spent in all.

B. The cost of the three beverages altogether.

C. The cost of the smaller beverage.

D. No additional information is needed. *

* Correct Response

FIG. 9.2. Multiple-choice items like those found on the ITBS survey battery.

Likewise, the Data Interpretation subtest emphasizes computational aspects of data analysis, such as finding the average rather than dealing with issues of sample selection. The Concepts subtest requires students to recognize definitions of number concepts; the Problem Solving subtest contains routine story problems that focus on multistep operations with number, as illustrated in sample Item 2 in Fig. 9.2.

The two tests differ not only in their content, but also in the topics and processes included within the content strands. Generally, the BA Test covered a broader array of topics and processes, as illustrated by the descriptions in Table 9.2.

The types of items and the expected time to complete them also vary. The BA Tests use constructed-response items, many requiring an extended explanation or demonstration of approach used; students are expected to interpret real-world situations, make connections among mathematical concepts, justify their answers, explain their approaches and strategies, and

TABLE 9.2
Differences Between BA and ITBS Tests for Specific Topics

Content Topic	BA	ITBS
Number & Operations	Uses computation as a tool in the context of solving problems; emphasizes flexible representation of number concepts and use of number sense	Emphasizes pure computations, rule-based procedures for estimation, and single & multistep story problems
Patterns & Algebra	Makes links among graphs of functions, tables of values, verbal descriptions of situations, and symbolic representations	Computes using order of operations and evaluates an expression by substituting a given value for the variable
Geometry & Measurement	Deals with Euclidean geometry, transformational geometry, and spatial reasoning	Deals with properties and definitions within the realm of Euclidean geometry
Statistics & Probability	Uses concepts and procedures as tools in the context of solving problems, e.g., evaluates the fairness of a game, makes predictions, models data with a function, and critiques sampling techniques	Emphasizes concepts and procedures of interpreting data and graphs, e.g., reads a bar or line graph, finds the mean of a small set of numbers, or determines the number of combinations for two classes of items

communicate mathematical thinking underlying decisions. In contrast, the ITBS Survey Battery comprises approximately 60 multiple-choice items that focus on specific concepts, skills, definitions, and procedures.

One seventh-grade BA task presents a situation organized around a table of data in which student work ranges from representing ratios as fractions, decimals, and percents to making decisions and providing mathematical explanations. An excerpt of this task is shown in Fig. 9.3 to provide an example of a middle-length BA Test item. The scoring rubric and sample student responses for this item are in Fig. 9.4; note that no score of 3 was possible on this item. (An illustration of a longer-time item can be found in Zawojewski, Robinson, & Hoover, 1999.) In this item, students not only interpret the information in the table but also connect the information to a real-world use of an estimate and explain whether or not that use is reasonable.

All seventh grade students at Holmes Junior High must choose between French or Spanish for their foreign language requirement. Below are the number of boys and girls enrolled in French or Spanish.

Language	Number of Boys	Number of Girls
French	29	75
Spanish	121	50

When asked to compare the popularity of French between boys and girls, Ms. Francois said, "One fifth of the boys take French while three fifths of the girls are enrolled in my French classes."

   (a) Did Ms. Francois answer the question appropriately?

   (b) Why did she report her answer in fifths?

   FIG. 9.3.   Excerpt from the French–Spanish BA test item.

Because students could complete only a relatively small number of BA items in a single test administration, five different test forms for each grade level were constructed. The five test forms were distributed in equal numbers across the *CMP* and non-*CMP* students to sample the student population across a broad base of content topics and to ensure that any differences in form difficulty would have no impact on the conclusions drawn from the study. Each form had two to four contexts, each with from 2 to 12 items; students responded to approximately 10 individual items.

Scoring

The ITBS Survey Battery tests were scored and analyzed by Riverside Testing Company, using the company's national norms. The BA Tests were scored under the direction of the BA and *CMP* staff. Scoring rubrics and training packages were developed from extensive review of student work, involving a cycle of one person drafting a rubric, two people applying the rubric, reconciling differences, and then revising the rubric. Rubrics were designed specifically for individual tasks, using both holistic and analytic techniques, as illustrated in Fig. 9.4.

At each grade level the tests were thoroughly mixed, combining tests given in fall and spring, and across sites; no student identification to indicate *CMP* or non-*CMP* group was visible to the scorers. Responses were double scored

Scoring Rubric and Sample Responses

4 pts   For an answer of **yes** with an explanation that the fractions used are either easier to understand or easier to compare than the "exact" fractions.

Illustrative Student Response A

(a) "Yes, because you can't say how many more girls went to French than boys because there are more boys than girls."
(b) "Because that was the same fractions she could get it down to, and most easiest to understand."

Illustrative Student Response B

(a) (blank)

(b) "Ms. Francois answered the question correctly. There is only $\frac{1}{100}$ difference between my $\frac{19}{100}$ and her $\frac{1}{5}$. She answered it in fifths because that was the smallest she could get the fractions and they could both be written in fifths."

2 pts   For an answer of **yes**, with reasoning based on the desirability of common denominators, without explicit discussion of the ease of comparison or understanding. (An argument based on the desirability of common denominators, suggests concern for comparability, but is insufficient.)

Illustrative Student Response C

(a) "Yes"
(b) "Probably because both totals can be divided by 5 and the fraction can too, if you round 29 to 30."

1 pt   For work that contains some reasoning about appropriate ratios, but either (1) provides significantly inadequate reasoning (e.g., simplest fractions), (2) is unclear about the fact that Ms. Francoisí statement is reasonable (including answers with "no"), **OR** (3) reveals significant misconceptions. (References to reducing, renaming, factoring, or "easier," are in this category.)

Illustrative Student Response D

(a) "No, because that's not the right fraction."
(b) "So it would be more understood, it's down as far as it can go. People understand lower numbers better than higher."

0 pts   For work that does not meaningfully articulate a reason for the situation. This includes work that nicely articulates and reasons about inappropriate ratios.

Illustrative Student Response E

(a) "No"
(b) "Because it's a fraction"

Illustrative Student Response F

(a) "Yes"

(b) "Because they have to decide what is bigger and/or less than $\frac{1}{2}$ to make it so they could be approx."

FIG. 9.4. Scoring rubric and illustrative student response for the item in Fig. 9.3.

in sets of 10 papers, until the pair of scorers were sure their scoring procedures were consistent. If a set of 10 responses could be scored so that at most one item score differed by more than 1 point, then the pair moved to single scoring (Herman, Aschbacker, & Winter, 1992). Using the within 1-point guideline was thought to be reasonable for this situation. The credit for items varied from 2 to 15 points and test forms contained from 2 to 11 items; the double scoring of 10 responses with at most one discrepancy ensured agreement in at least 19 out of 20 cases, or greater than 90% reliability. If the criterion for single scoring was never met, the full set of student responses was double scored and reconciled.

Comparing the Performance of CMP and non-CMP Students

Despite careful attempts to match *CMP* students with appropriate comparison students, some differences were found in the initial performance of *CMP* and non-*CMP* students. The correlations between test score gains and initial scores were all small, for all groups. Nevertheless, to ensure that differences between *CMP* and non-*CMP* students could not be attributed to initial score differences, an analysis of covariance (ANCOVA)—with scores from appropriate pretests used as covariates—was used to analyze the data collected in fall and spring, whenever appropriate, to supplement a multivariate analysis of variance (MANOVA) and an analysis of variance (ANOVA). Post hoc comparisons are based on Scheffé's pairwise comparisons.

Student Performance on the BA Tests. Table 9.3 shows pretest and posttest mean raw scores on BA Tests. These data show highly significant benefits of the *CMP* curriculum on tests designed to reflect new educational goals. However, high levels of statistical significance are not to be confused with the size of the differences observed. Practical implications are best judged in terms of effect size—the ratio of the difference between the means and the pooled standard deviation (SD). Starting behind the comparison group mean by 0.15 SD units in sixth grade, *CMP* students finish 0.15 SD units ahead. In other words, the median student in the *CMP* group would be ranked 56 out of a representative sample of 100 students in the non-*CMP* group on the pretest and would be ranked 44 in the non-*CMP* group on the posttest. Considerable gains can be seen at seventh and eighth grade, though these are harder to interpret, because students in later grades have not all been in the *CMP* program for equal amounts of time. An analysis of other variables showed no significant effects, in particular, for gender, teacher, school district, or test form. Effects were surprisingly uniform across variables other than curriculum used.

TABLE 9.3

BA Pretest and Posttest Mean Raw Scores and SDs for *CMP* and Non-*CMP*
Students in Grades 6–8

| | CMP | | | | | | non-CMP | | | | | |
| | Fall | | | Spring | | | Fall | | | Spring | | |
Grade	n	M	SD	n	M	SD	n	M	SD	n	M	SD
6	338	11.7	9.9	338	20.0	12.6	162	13.2	10.3	162	18.1	11.9
7	627	14.5	9.7	627	21.4	11.6	234	12.3	9.5	234	15.4	10.3
8	820	17.7	11.3	820	27.0	14.0	275	11.6	9.6	275	16.3	11.2

Notes. First, the mean raw score (*M*) represents the mean across all five forms. The means for the different forms are comparable because (a) maximum scores across forms were within a few points of each other (maximum 60), (b) difficulties were relatively uniform across the forms, and (c) the same proportion of each of the five forms was given within classes and across the *CMP* and non-*CMP* groups, so different difficulty levels are not relevant to the *CMP* and non-*CMP* comparison. Second, at sixth grade, *CMP* students start behind (Scheffé test, $p < .05$) and finish ahead (Scheffé test, $p < .01$). The interaction is significant; ANOVA, $F(1, 498) = 299.22$, $p < .001$. When an ANCOVA is conducted by using the fall ITBS score as a covariate, the same pattern of results is found; ANCOVA, $F(1, 497) = 19.55$, $p < .001$. Third, at seventh grade, *CMP* students start ahead (Scheffé test, $p < .001$) and finish ahead (Scheffé test, $p < .001$). Students in the *CMP* program gain differentially more and the interaction is significant; ANOVA, $F(1, 859) = 282.60$, $p < .001$. When an ANCOVA is conducted by using the fall ITBS score as a covariate, the same pattern of results is found; ANCOVA, $F(1, 858) = 40.60$, $p < .001$. Fourth, at eighth grade, *CMP* students start ahead (Scheffé test, $p < .001$) and finish ahead (Scheffé test, $p < .001$). Students in the *CMP* program gain differentially more and the interaction is significant; ANOVA, $F(1, 1093) = 41.64$, $p < .001$. The *CMP* students have significantly higher scores in the fall than do the non-*CMP* students in the spring (Scheffé test, $p < .05$). When an ANCOVA is conducted by using the fall ITBS score as a covariate, the same pattern of results is found; ANCOVA, $F(1, 1092) = 41.60$, $p < .001$.

Student Performance on the ITBS Survey Battery.   Table 9.4 shows pretest and posttest Grade Equivalent (GE) scores on ITBS Tests. GE scores reflect the age at which half the students achieve a particular score or better, and they are based on a national sample identified by the test developer, that is, Riverside Testing Company. So, one would expect an average student at the start of sixth grade to have a GE of approximately 6.0, and at the end of sixth grade to have a GE of approximately 7.0; over the course of a year, one would expect to see GE scores increase by approximately 1 year (i.e., 1.0).

The pattern of results on the ITBS test is not completely clear. Starting behind by 0.52 SD units (1 year GE) in sixth grade, *CMP* students finish 0.61 SD units (1.5 years GE) behind their non-*CMP* counterparts. At the end of seventh grade, after either 1 or 2 years of exposure to the new curriculum, *CMP* students are 0.19 SD units (0.5 years GE) behind their non-*CMP*

TABLE 9.4

ITBS GE Pretest and Posttest Scores for Grades 6–8

| | CMP | | | | | | non-CMP | | | | | |
| | Fall | | | Spring | | | Fall | | | Spring | | |
Grade	n	M	SD	n	M	SD	n	M	SD	n	M	SD
6	338	6.1	1.9	338	7.1	2.3	162	7.1	2.0	162	8.6	2.7
7	627	7.4	2.3	627	8.6	2.6	234	7.9	2.6	234	9.1	2.9
8	820	8.2	2.2	820	9.4	2.5	275	7.7	2.3	275	8.6	2.6

Notes. First, at sixth grade, *CMP* students start behind by a full year (Scheffé test, $p < .001$) and finish behind by 1.5 years (Scheffé test, $p < .001$). The interaction is significant; ANOVA, $F(1, 498) = 6.92$, $p < .01$. Non-*CMP* students gain differentially more than *CMP* students. Second, at seventh grade, *CMP* students start behind by 0.5 years (Scheffé test, $p < .001$) and finish behind by 0.5 years (Scheffé test, $p < .01$). The interaction is nonsignificant; ANOVA, $F(1, 859) = 1.17$, $p < .28$. There is no evidence that *CMP* students catch up with non-*CMP* students. Third, at eighth grade, *CMP* students start ahead by 0.5 years (Scheffé test, $p < .001$) and finish ahead by 0.8 years (Scheffé test, $p < .001$). The interaction just fails to reach statistical significance; ANOVA, $F(1, 1093) = 3.74$, $p < .053$.

counterparts. At the end of eighth grade, after either 1, 2, or 3 years of exposure to the new curriculum, *CMP* students are 0.32 SD units (0.8 years GE) ahead of their non-*CMP* counterparts. These data suggest that the *CMP* curriculum has no immediate advantage in the first year of study over conventional curricula in terms of the development of mathematical technique. One might judge the significantly poorer performance of *CMP* students as an indication that *CMP* actually harms the development of technical skills. However, their absolute gain is exactly in line with publisher's data on expected gains on ITBS; the relative differences between *CMP* and comparison students are attributable to excellent gains by the comparison group for which we offer no explanation.

Summary

For this large-scale study, student attainment on a test aligned with the goals of a *Standards*-based curriculum and student attainment on a commonly used norm-referenced test were examined. The *Connected Mathematics* curriculum was effective in raising the attainment of students on challenging open-response items that emphasize reasoning, communication, connections, and problem solving as compared with the attainment of students in curricula less aligned with the *Standards*. Further, the *CMP* students made gains on a traditional multiple-choice, timed standardized test comparable to both the test publisher's representative sample (1 year GE in Grade 6; 1.2 years GE in Grade 7; 1.2 years GE in Grade 8) and in later years to the comparison group. Finally, no significant differences in growth as measured by the BA Test and ITBS Survey were attributable to gender, teacher, school district, test form, or other identifiable variables.

Long-Term Effects of *CMP* on the BA Test, the ITBS, and State Tests

The data in Tables 9.3 and 9.4 raise tantalizing questions about the long-term effects of the *CMP* curriculum on student attainment. If these data were taken from a longitudinal study, inspection of the differences between spring and fall scores would be a measure of forgetting over the summer break. These data appear to show that the *CMP* students forget less over summer, a plausible conjecture given the "connected" nature of the program; further, after 3 years in the program, student performance on technical skills exceeds that of students in the comparison group. However, we cannot be confident about such conjectures because of the changing sample compositions across the 3 years being studied. The populations included some schools where *CMP* was taught only in a few target classes, so many seventh grade students were not in the program during their sixth-grade year. Further, although the sixth- and seventh-grade populations were from the same schools in the same year, the eighth-grade testing occurred 1 year later and was associated with a large number of schools dropping out and another group of students entering the study. Thus, to investigate the question of the sustained and cumulative effect of *Connected Mathematics*, we look more closely at the results from one school that implemented the curriculum in all 3 years. We compare the performance of the students at this school and the performance of the non-*CMP* population on both the BA Tests and ITBS Tests. We also look at the achievement results from this school on the state mathematics test.

Bouck and Wilcox (1996) describe a situation in which districtwide commitment to improving mathematics education was initiated in 1985. All of the sixth- through eighth-grade students at the small school district in rural Michigan were in one school. This homogeneous farming community is made up of families of primarily European descent. Parents typically work as shopkeepers, factory and service workers, and farmers. The number of poor had been growing in the district; in 1995, less than $5,000 per student was expended for education, placing the district fourth from the bottom of the surrounding 36 rural, suburban, and urban districts. Despite the lack of wealth, this district had a vision shared by the faculty and administration to improve the mathematics education program of students. Thus, the district was already addressing many of the issues and themes described in the various NCTM documents as they were released. The faculty was increasingly involved in professional organizations, and a number of them were developing reputations as leaders outside their district. Administration was supportive, facilitating communication with the community, involving the teachers in the hiring of new faculty, and supporting teachers' efforts to reach out to neighboring districts in an effort to pool resources; these efforts resulted in ongoing, countywide staff development programs in mathematics. When Michigan State University became one of the NSF-sponsored curriculum development sites, the district teachers volunteered to become one of the *CMP* field test sites, because they needed curricular materials to support the efforts upon which they had already embarked. Subsequent to the initial pilot, the school has continued to use the more recent versions of the materials, including the most recently published program.

Student Performance on the BA Tests

Table 9.5 shows the performance of students in this school, denoted School R, and the performance of the students from the entire non-*CMP* sample. Considering the performance on BA tasks overall, students in School R start somewhat ahead of the non-*CMP* group and increase their lead. By the end of the first year, they are 0.57 SD units ahead of the non-*CMP* students. At the end of the second year they are 0.80 SD units ahead. At the end of the third year they are 1.46 SD units ahead. In other words, after

TABLE 9.5

BA Pretest and Posttest Mean Raw Scores for School R and Comparison
Students in Grades 6–8

| | School R (CMP) | | | | | | Comparison (non-CMP) | | | | | |
| | Fall | | | Spring | | | Fall | | | Spring | | |
Grade	n	M	SD	n	M	SD	n	M	SD	n	M	SD
6	53	14.8	9.5	53	25.0	12.9	162	13.2	10.3	162	18.1	11.9
7	69	18.5	10.4	69	24.0	11.9	234	12.3	9.5	234	15.4	10.3
8	126	22.3	12.8	126	33.8	13.4	275	11.6	9.6	275	16.3	11.2

Notes. First, at sixth grade, *CMP* students and non-*CMP* students start at about the same level, but *CMP* students finish ahead (Scheffé test, $p < .001$). The interaction is significant; ANOVA, $F(1, 213) = 34.42$, $p < .001$. *CMP* students gain differentially more than non-*CMP* students. Second, at seventh grade, *CMP* students start ahead (Scheffé test, $p < .001$) and finish ahead (Scheffé test, $p < .001$). The interaction is significant; ANOVA, $F(1, 301) = 27.94$, $p < .05$. *CMP* students gain reliably more than non-*CMP* students. Third, at eighth grade, *CMP* students start ahead (Scheffé test, $p < .001$) and finish ahead (Scheffé test, $p < .001$). The interaction is significant; ANOVA, $F(1, 399) = 52.87$, $p < .001$. *CMP* students gain reliably more than non-*CMP* students.

3 years in the *CMP* program, the average student would be in the top 7% of the comparison group in terms of their performance on a *Standards*-based mathematics test.

Student Performance on the ITBS Survey Battery

Table 9.6 shows the performance of students at School R and the comparison students on the ITBS Survey. Considering the performance on ITBS overall, the School R group starts sixth grade at approximately the expected level compared with a national sample, but 1.3 GE years behind the non-*CMP* group. They finish 1.4 GE years behind the non-*CMP* group, but at approximately the expected level. In seventh grade, the School R group starts at the expected GE level and makes good progress (1.8 GE years) over the year; the comparison group starts ahead and makes more than a full year's progress, but it still loses ground relative to the students in School R and loses its superiority. The School R students start eighth grade ahead of where one might expect, and ahead of the comparison group, and they gain 1.4 GE years in eighth grade. Overall, they gain 4.3 GE years over 3 school years. In contrast, the gains in the non-*CMP* group were a modest 1.5 GE years over 3 school years—the modest gain attributable to losing ground between the end of one school year and the start of the next or to problems in

TABLE 9.6

ITBS GE Pretest and Posttest Scores for School R and
Comparison Students in Grades 6–8

| | School R (CMP) | | | | | | Comparison (non-CMP) | | | | | |
| | Fall | | | Spring | | | Fall | | | Spring | | |
Grade	n	M	SD	n	M	SD	n	M	SD	n	M	SD
6	53	5.8	1.3	53	7.2	1.7	162	7.1	2.0	162	8.6	2.7
7	69	7.0	1.8	69	8.8	2.4	234	7.9	2.6	234	9.1	2.9
8	126	8.7	2.3	126	10.1	2.4	275	7.7	2.3	275	8.6	2.6

Notes. First, at sixth grade, *CMP* students start 1.3 GE years behind the non-*CMP* students (Scheffé test, $p < .001$) and finish 1.4 years behind them (Scheffé test, $p < .001$). There are no statistically reliable differential gains for either group; ANOVA, $F(1, 213) = 1.29$, $p < .4$. Second, at seventh grade, *CMP* students start 0.9 years behind (Scheffé test, $p < .001$) but finish just 0.3 years behind (statistically, at about the same level: Scheffé test, $p < .44$). The interaction is significant; ANOVA, $F(1, 300) = 8.72$, $p < .01$. *CMP* students gain reliably more than non-*CMP* students. Third, at eighth grade, *CMP* students start 1.0 years ahead of non-*CMP* students (Scheffé test, $p < .001$) and finish 1.5 years ahead (Scheffé test, $p < .001$). The interaction is significant. *CMP* students gain reliably more than non-*CMP* students; ANOVA, $F(1, 399) = 6.38$, $p < .05$.

identifying appropriate comparison students at each grade level. In School R, there is evidence of steady, better than average performance over each year in mathematical technique, and relatively little slippage between school years.

Student Performance on the State Mathematics Test

The Michigan Educational Assessment Program (MEAP) is administered in the fourth and seventh grades. The test is designed to assess whether students are meeting statewide performance objectives as they appear in the Michigan Essential Goals and Objectives approved by the State Board of Education in the 1980s. The Grades 4 and 7 tests were first given in the fall of 1991, a year prior to the formal sixth-grade pilot (1992–1993). The test addresses basic computation skills and also emphasizes students' understanding of mathematical ideas and the use of computation as a tool to solve problems.

There are three sections to the test, which are composed of multiple-choice questions and are untimed, with the exception of the mental arithmetic portion of the mathematics test. In the mental arithmetic section, students must compute mentally and make estimations without writing in their test booklets. The second section of the test is noncalculator computation, which includes arithmetic problems that students can solve on paper. The third section includes concepts and problem solving and contains the majority of the questions on the mathematics test. Calculators are allowed on this section, but they are not required nor necessary.

The state sets standards for three levels of performance at selected grade levels and reports the percent of students in a district performing at those levels; in descending order, the levels are labeled "satisfactory," "moderate," and "low." Bouck and Wilcox (1996) reported the MEAP results for the seventh-grade students in School R from 1991 to 1995 as shown in Fig. 9.5; the September 1993–1994 test is the first administration to include students who had used *CMP* for 1 year. During that time, the percent of students scoring in the satisfactory category rose from 44.4% to 78.8% and the percent of students scoring in the low category decreased from 20.5% to 6.8%. Here we have added test results for the 1996–1997, the 1997–1998, and 1998–1999 academic years, indicating stabilization and natural fluctuation since the full implementation of the *Connected Mathematics* curriculum.

In contrast, Fig. 9.6 shows the statewide percentages of seventh-grade students scoring in the "satisfactory" and "low" categories during the same time period. The results for School R are consistently better than the average state results.

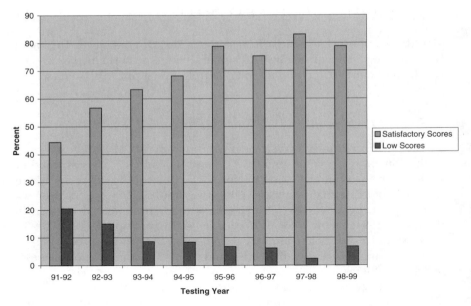

FIG. 9.5. Percent of *CMP* students at School R scoring in different categories on the MEAP. From 1991 to 1997, testing occurred in September; in 1997–1998 and 1998–1999 testing occurred in January.

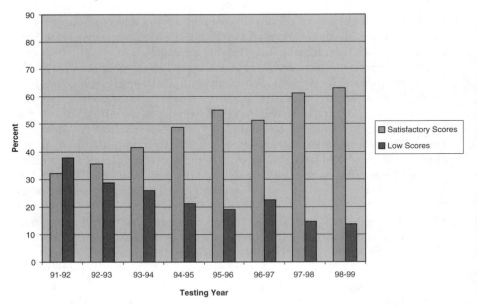

FIG. 9.6. Percentages of students in Michigan scoring in different categories on the MEAP. From 1991 to 1997, testing occurred in September; in 1997–1998 and 1998–1999 testing occurred in January.

Study on Proportional Reasoning

The highest priority goal for the seventh-grade *Connected Mathematics* curriculum is the development of proportional reasoning, which is the primary emphasis of the units *Stretching and Shrinking* and *Comparing and Scaling*, and which is heavily used across the remaining units of study. To understand the character and effectiveness of proportional reasoning by students in *CMP* and not in *CMP*, a focused study was carried out by Ben-Chaim, Fey, Fitzgerald, Benedetto, and Miller (1998). They report on students' understanding of rate problems by using a student population drawn from the sample used in the large-scale study previously described. Ben-Chaim et al. selected a mix of sites representing inner-city urban, urban, suburban, and rural communities: three from the Midwest, one from the West, and one from the East. Of the students they tested with a mixture of ratio and proportion problems, they report on the 124 *CMP* and 91 non-*CMP* seventh-grade students who completed items involving rate. Further, they interviewed approximately 25% of these students, using both contextualized and context-free problems paralleling those on the written tests. The ITBS results for this subsample indicated that the *CMP* students' scores were slightly lower than those of the non-*CMP* students in the fall and slightly higher in the spring.

The testing instrument was made up of 13 items, 5 of which were rate items (the focus of the report by Ben-Chaim et al.). The first two pairs of items were related to a written story situation. The first pair dealt with unit price: the first question involved a numerical comparison, and the second question involved a missing value. The second pair of rate items dealt with proportional relations among distance, time, and speed, and both questions involved numerical comparisons, as illustrated in Fig. 9.7. The first used integers and the second used fractions and decimals for the time given in the problem. The fifth problem dealt with population density in a numerical comparison involving relatively large numbers.

The student work was coded on a rating form by first classifying responses as correct, incorrect, and no response. Correct work was then coded as accompanied by no support, correct support work, and incorrect support work. Incorrect answers were then coded as accompanied by no support, support indicating partial understanding, and incorrect thinking. Ben-Chaim et al. report that the most difficult subcategory to code was incorrect answers with partial understanding. Responses in this category included incorrect responses in which the thinking appeared to be correct but computational mistakes were made, or correct relationships were used but mistakes were made with units, or the problem was completed correctly with a minor mistake near the end. Although the authors did not provide rubrics for classifying responses in their report, they did provide sample responses to selected response categories, which are found in Fig. 9.8 (based on Item 3 in Fig. 9.7).

A Trip To The Zoo

Max, Eliza, Alex, and Cosima planned a bicycle trip to the zoo as a year-end outing

for their class. Students gathered at the school parking lot and rode together on the bicycle path

to the zoo. After looking at the animals for a few hours, they met at the picnic tables near the

duck pond for a snack and cold drink before riding back to school.

Item 3. Cosima and Alex decided to have a contest to see who rode the fastest on the way home.

Cozi rode 5 miles to her house in 20 min. Alex rode 7 miles to his house in 25 min. Who

rode the fastest? How do you know?

Item 4. On the next Saturday, Max and Eliza rode their bikes the long way around the lake to a

park. It was 30 miles and it took them 1.4 h of riding time. After lunch, they rode back

by the short way. It was 20 miles and they made it in $\frac{3}{4}$ of an hour of riding time. On

which part of their round trip did they have the fastest riding rate? How do you know?

FIG. 9.7. Sample items on proportional reasoning from Ben-Chaim, D., Fey, J. T., Fitzgerald, W. M., Benedetto, C., and Miller, J. Proportional reasoning among 7th grade students with different curricular experiences. *Educational Studies in Mathematics, 36* (p. 255) ©1998. Reprinted with kind permission of Kluwer Academic Publishers.

Correct with correct support work.

"Cozi: 20 min ÷ 5 miles = 4 min per mile.
Alex: 25 min ÷ 7 miles = 3.57 min per mile.
Alex rode the fastest because he rode 0.43 min a mile faster.
He had a longer way, but it took him less time."

Correct with incorrect support work.

"Alex. Because he went farther because of all the straight roads"

Incorrect with partial understanding.

"Cozi rode the fastest. I divided 20 by 5 and got 4 miles per minute for Cozi.
Then I divided 25 by 7 = 3.5 miles per minute."

FIG. 9.8. Sample responses to Item 3 (Fig. 9.7) illustrating selected response classifications (Ben-Chaim, et al., 1998, p. 266). Reprinted with kind permission of Kluwer Academic Publishers.

Ben-Chaim et al. report that *CMP* seventh-grade students performed markedly better than non-*CMP* students in their overall performance. Table 9.7 shows that more than half of the *CMP* students gave correct support to correct answers. In contrast, only approximately a quarter of the non-*CMP* students were able to do this. A related point they make is that 80–90% of both groups of students are providing written support for their

TABLE 9.7

Percent of Total Grade 7 Responses Falling Into Each of Seven Response
Classifications for Rate Problems

| Group | Correct Answer | | | Incorrect Answer | | | |
	Corr. Answer Only	Corr. Support Work	Incorr. Support Work	Incorr. Answer Only	Partial Understand.	Incorr. Thinking	No Response
7th-Grade CMP[a]	3	53	9	2	15	10	8
7th-Grade non-CMP[b]	6	28	21	4	10	23	8

Note. From Ben Chaim et al. (1998, p. 253). Reprinted with kind permission of Kluwer
Academic Publishers.
[a] $n = 124$; [b] $n = 91$.

answers. However, it was the authors' opinion, based on examination of all
of the student responses, that the *CMP* students produced higher-quality
written responses and were better able to articulate their responses during
the interviews than the non-*CMP* students.

Ben-Chaim et al. conjecture that the superior performance of the *CMP*
students might be attributed to characteristics of the *CMP*: its problem-
solving approach and its expectation that students will present their different approaches to solving problems to each other, as well as compare, justify,
and debate those approaches. They also point out that the connected nature
of the curriculum may provide more time for students to work with proportional reasoning compared to curricula in which proportions comprise only
one or two chapters during the school year. They recommend further study,
particularly with the finalized *CMP* curriculum and with classroom observations, in order to link *Connected Mathematics* students' performance to the
nature of their classroom experiences.

SUMMARY AND IMPLICATIONS

The three studies provide findings concerning the effects of the *Connected
Mathematics* curriculum on student achievement, yet these findings also raise
issues about curriculum evaluation, especially when the curriculum broad-
ens and heightens the expectations from what has previously been expected
from students.

One major finding was that *Connected Mathematics* students made very
large gains on a broad range of curriculum topics and processes compared
with students in curricula less aligned with the NCTM *Standards*. Another
finding is that students studying the *Connected Mathematics* curriculum made
reasonable gains on technical skills of mathematics, as indicated by the

performance on the ITBS Survey Battery when the ITBS national sample was used.[6] Finally, there was evidence of long-term gains afforded by the *CMP* curriculum when performance over time was studied in School R, where *CMP* was the sole curriculum for all of the middle grades. This evidence was conclusively supported by the longitudinal study of the state test results. Thus, there seems to be reason to believe that gains afforded by the *CMP* curriculum are likely to be long term and sustainable.

However, there are still a number of questions pending as a result of these studies. A first question is: Exactly what sorts of implementation of the *CMP* curriculum are responsible for the student achievement findings reported here? Of all the variables in the large-scale study database (including teacher, class, school, site, gender, and fall test achievement levels), the only one associated with gains in attainment was curriculum (*CMP* vs. non-*CMP*). However none of the three studies included in-depth information about *how* the *CMP* was actually used in the schools. Although all of the *CMP* teachers had promised to use the *CMP* materials as their "core" curriculum, no classroom observations were made during the years of the student testing. The *CMP* did conduct extensive classroom observations in a wide variety of classrooms throughout the country for purposes of formative evaluation of the curriculum, but these observations occurred during the early development phases of the materials, at least a year or more prior to the collection of student achievement data. The formative evaluation observations uncovered wide variations in how the materials were actually used in *CMP* classrooms. Variability of outcome measures across classrooms using *CMP* is beyond the scope of this chapter, but is disussed elsewhere (Ridgway, Zawojewski, & Hoover, 2000).

Another question that remains is how revision of the *Connected Mathematics* materials subsequent to the large-scale study would affect student achievement findings. Data for the large-scale study were gathered before the curriculum was finalized because the study was designed, in part, to provide feedback to the authors' efforts to make final revisions to the curriculum. Perhaps a comparison of the technical skills of students studying the revised curriculum, as compared with the skills of non-*CMP* students, would yield more definitive results than the comparison study reported in this chapter. For example, the most significant revision to the curriculum as a result of field testing was made to a sixth-grade unit on fractions that serves as the foundation of basic computations for the sixth-grade curriculum.

A third question that emerges is whether there are differential effects of the *Connected Mathematics* curriculum on different populations. The state testing data of School R seems to indicate that more students have entered the highest levels of performance after studying *Connected Mathematics*, and at the same time many students have moved out of the lowest levels of performance. This is an encouraging finding, inviting more investigation of the possibility that the *Connected Mathematics* curriculum does, in fact, work well for promoting mathematical growth in *all* students. Additionally, supporting evidence comes from the very weak relationships between fall test scores and the gain scores from fall to spring in the large-scale study.

A final question still pending is whether the suggestion of long-term gains indicated by School R is generalizable to other schools. The case study of School R revealed a complex network of conditions in that district that apparently were quite supportive of long-term improvement when the *Connected Mathematics* curriculum was adopted.

Indeed, the study at School R suggests that curriculum reform is a complicated process likely to be idiosyncratic to individual sites. Simply importing curriculum materials into the classroom is not sufficient to implement change that can lead to improvement. Simply providing professional development is not sufficient alone. Simply providing leadership that supports reform is insufficient without materials, professional development, and accompanying resources. Simply implementing high-stakes state testing that is reasonably aligned with higher expectations will not necessarily change practice; without professional development, materials, resources, and leadership, the only alternative often left to teachers is to "teach to the test," which can have detrimental effects on a program by narrowing its focus to only what is on the test. Efforts to improve a district's (or school's) mathematics education program have to address all of these aspects in a coherent manner. A collection of longitudinal case studies might bring issues and themes to the surface that inform other schools and districts engaged in systemic reform and improvement. Such research is currently underway through a series of district self-studies of *Connected Mathematics* implementation, although the results are not yet available.

When an attempt is made to evaluate the impact of a curriculum such as *Connected Mathematics* that is intended to broaden and strengthen the mathematics education of students beyond that of conventional curricula, a number of issues emerge. One is the need to document the nature of the instruction occurring in the classrooms so that student attainment can be more tightly linked to the entire curricular experience. This was not accomplished in any of these three studies but definitely has to be addressed in future studies. Another issue that emerges is the need to create or identify assessment instruments that actually capture the intended goals of the curriculum. In the large-scale study, two instruments were used to capture both the narrower goals of conventional curricula (by means of the ITBS Survey Battery) and the broader curriculum and processes recommended by the NCTM *Standards* (by means of the BA Test).

Some of the varied assessment methods described in this chapter might themselves serve to support curriculum change, giving teachers multiple sources of information on which to judge the success of their own implementation efforts and supporting them in their role as reflective practitioners. A "map" of the normative progress made over the course of several years of working with a new curriculum is likely to aid teacher reflections as well as to help in planning systemic change. For example, if short-term decrements in pure computation are real, yet are compensated for later, this knowledge is useful in teachers' planning and in discussions with concerned parents and with students themselves. If more mathematics is retained for long periods of time, this has important consequences for planning curricular articulation during educational reform in mathematics. Overall, there is clear evidence that students learn both high-level thinking and basic skills as a result of experiences with the *Connected Mathematics* curriculum. However, questions about how *Connected Mathematics* can be a curriculum for all students, all teachers, and in all situations still have to be pursued.

APPENDIX A

Title and Description of the *Connected Mathematics* Units by Grade Level

Grade 6	Grade 7	Grade 8
Prime Time	*Variables and Patterns*	*Thinking With Mathematical Models*
Number theory: factors, multiples, primes, and composites	Introducing algebra: understanding variables and representations of relationships, such as tables, graphs, and simple symbolic forms	Representing relationships: introduction to functions and modeling; slope and finding the equation of a line
Data About Us Statistics: formulating questions, gathering, organizing and representing data, and interpreting results from data	*Stretching and Shrinking* Similarity: finding missing side lengths in similar figures, using scale factors, and understanding basic transformations and their algebraic rules	*Looking for Pythagoras* The Pythagorean theorem: investigating the Pythagorean theorem, area, irrational numbers, slope, and distance
Shapes and Designs Two-dimensional geometry: relationships among lengths, angle measures, and how shapes fit together	*Comparing and Scaling* Proportional reasoning: ratio, proportion, rate, and percent	*Growing, Growing, Growing...* Exponential relationships: exponential growth and decay through data tables, graphs, and simple symbolic forms
Bits and Pieces, Part I Understanding rational numbers: fractions, decimals, and percents; equivalence and order	*Accentuate the Negative* Integers: understanding and using integers with various models, including a number line	*Frogs, Fleas, and Painted Cubes* Quadratic relationships: growth and quadratic functions through data tables, graphs, and simple symbolic forms

Grade 6	Grade 7	Grade 8
Covering and Surrounding Two-dimensional measurement: relationships between area and perimeter and finding area and perimeter of various polygons and circles	*Moving Straight Ahead* Linear relationships: connecting tables, graphs, and simple symbolic forms	*Say It With Symbols* Algebraic reasoning: investigating equivalent expressions; solving linear and simple quadratic equations
How Likely Is It? Probability: understanding and using expected value	*Filling and Wrapping* Three-dimensional geometry and measurement: relationships of volume and surface area and finding volume and surface area of various solids	*Hubcaps, Kaleidoscopes, and Mirrors* Symmetry and transformational geometry: connecting geometry and algebra
Bits and Pieces, Part II Using rational numbers: meaning of and skill in addition, subtraction, and multiplication of fractions and decimals	*What Do You Expect?* Probability: understanding and using expected value	*Samples and Populations* Statistics and probability: using samples to reason about populations and make predictions; comparing samples and sample distributions
Ruins of Montarek Spatial visualization and reasoning: architectural and isometric forms of representation	*Data Around Us* Number sense: developing quantitative reasoning with large numbers, scientific notation	*Clever Counting* Combinatorics: ways to count in application situations; using combinations, trees, and other representations

Note. From *Connected Mathematics Series*, by G. Lappan, J. T. Fey, W. Fitzgerald, S. N. Friel, and E. D. Phillips, 1998, Palo Alto, CA: Dale Seymour. Copyright 1998 by Dale Seymour. Adapted with permission.

APPENDIX B: AN INVESTIGATION OF THE AREA OF TRIANGLES[7]

Deborah Taylor is a sixth-grade teacher in a large urban school. Ms. Taylor taught the *Connected Mathematics* unit, Covering and Surrounding, which is about the measurement concepts of perimeter and area and the relationship between them, in her mathematics class. In the first five investigations of the unit, students build a conceptual understanding of perimeter as the number of linear units required to surround a figure and area as the number of square units needed to cover a figure. In the fifth and sixth investigations, students begin to use their understanding of area of rectangles to explore the area of triangles and parallelograms. After working on Problem 6.3 for a while, a group of three students, Matt, Trevor, and Alecia, were eager to share something with Ms. Taylor. They were excited about a discovery they made.

Problem 6.3: Draw two triangles on a sheet of grid paper. Make sure the triangles are very different from one another. For each triangle, complete parts A–C.
A. Record the base, height, area, and perimeter of your triangle.
B. Make a copy of your triangle, and cut out both copies. Experiment with putting the two triangles together to make new polygons. Describe and sketch the polygons that are possible.
C. Can you make a parallelogram by piecing together the two identical triangles? If so, record the base, height, area, and perimeter of the parallelogram. How do these measures compare to the measures of the original triangles?
D. Draw a parallelogram on grid paper, and cut it out. Can you cut the parallelogram into two triangles that are the same shape and size? Describe and sketch what you find.

Matt, Trevor, and Alecia showed Ms. Taylor two congruent right triangles that were pushed together to form a rectangle:

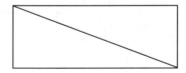

The three students told Ms. Taylor that they had discovered why the area of a triangle was "one-half the base times the height". Ms. Taylor listened closely as the students explained their reasoning to her:

Matt: Basically, you can make a rectangle from two equal right triangles. The base times the height gives you, like, the area of the rectangle.

Trevor: But we want the area of the triangle, not the area of the whole thing—I mean the rectangle. So you just take half of the base times the height because the triangle is half of the rectangle.

Alecia: Yea. You can see that it's (indicating triangle) half of it (indicating the rectangle) so you only need half of it—like half of the area of the rectangle.

Ms. Taylor: This sounds interesting—good work! What I would like each of you to do is sit down and construct your own explanation—in writing—and showing me your diagram, i.e., the rectangle constructed from two congruent triangles—of this discovery. Tomorrow I'll have you share this with the class.

Clearly excited at having their discovery recognized, Matt, Trevor, and Alecia went back to their desks and each began writing a description of the reasoning they had just shared with Ms. Taylor.

APPENDIX C: SAMPLE FOLLOW-UP (ACE) PROBLEMS FROM GRADE 6 COMPARING AND SCALING MODULE[8]

Applications Illustration:

In 8–11, find the perimeter and area of the figure.

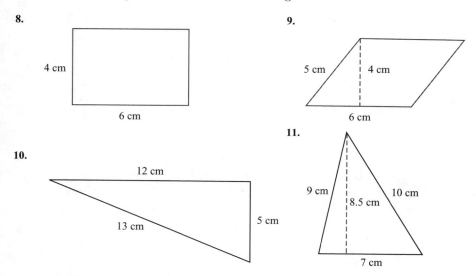

8.

4 cm

6 cm

9.

5 cm   4 cm

6 cm

10.

12 cm

13 cm   5 cm

11.

9 cm   8.5 cm   10 cm

7 cm

Connections Illustration:

19. A **trapezoid** is a polygon with at least two opposite edges parallel. Below are two trapezoids drawn on grid paper.

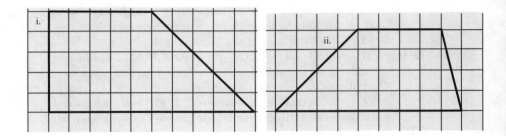

a. Try to find a way to find the area of a trapezoid without having to count each square. Use your method to find the area for each trapezoid. Summarize your method as a rule or a description.

b. How can you find the perimeter of a trapezoid? Use your method to calculate the perimeter of each trapezoid. Summarize your method as a rule or a description.

Extensions Illustration:

23. You saw earlier that in some parallelograms and triangles, the height falls outside of the shape being measured.

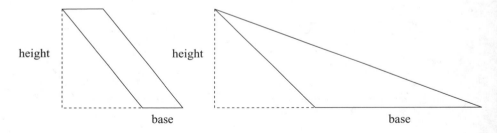

a. The area of the parallelogram can still be calculated by multiplying the base times the height. Write an explanation of why this is true.

b. The area of the triangle can still be calculated by multiplying $1/2$ times the base times the height. Write an explanation of why this is true.

REFERENCES

Balanced Assessment. (1999). *Middle grades assessment package 1*. Palo Alto, CA: Dale Seymour.

Ben-Chaim, D., Fey, J. T., Fitzgerald, W. M., Benedetto, C., & Miller, J. (1998). Proportional reasoning among seventh grade students with different curricular experiences. *Educational Studies in Mathematics, 36*, 247–273.

Bouck, M. K., & Wilcox, S. K. (1996, December). A case study of success. *NCTM Xchange*, pp. 2–4.

Herman, J., Aschbacker, P., & Winter, L. (1992). *A practical guide to alternative assessment.* Arlington, VA: Association for Supervision and Curriculum Development.

Lane, S. (1993). The conceptual framework for the development of a mathematics performance assessment. *Educational Measurement: Issues and Practice, 12*(2), 16–23.

Lappan, G., Fey, J., Fitzgerald, W., Friel, S., & Phillips, E. D. (1996). *A guide to the Connected Mathematics curriculum: Getting to know Connected Mathematics.* Palo Alto, CA: Dale Seymour.

Lappan, G., Fey, J. T., Fitzgerald, W., Friel, S. N., & Phillips, E. D. (1998). *Connected Mathematics series.* Palo Alto, CA: Dale Seymour.

National Council of Teachers of Mathematics. (1989). *Curriculum and evaluation standards for school mathematics.* Reston, VA: Author.

National Council of Teachers of Mathematics. (1991). *Professional teaching standards for school mathematics.* Reston, VA: Author.

National Council of Teachers of Mathematics. (1995). *Assessment standards for school mathematics.* Reston, VA: Author.

Ridgway, J., Zawojewski, J., & Hoover, M. (2000). Problematising evidence based policy and practice. *Evaluation and Research in Education, 14*(3, 4), 181–192.

Riverside Publishing Company. (1994). *Riverside 94 assessments, scoring, guidance systems, software.* Chicago: Author.

Silver, E. A., & Lane, S. (1993). Assessment in the context of mathematics instruction reform: The design of assessment in the QUASAR Project. In M. Niss (Ed.), *Cases of assessment in mathematics education* (pp. 59–69). The Netherlands: Kluwer.

Zawojewski, J. S., Robinson, M., & Hoover, M. (1999). Innovations in curriculum: Reflections on developing formal mathematics and the *Connected Mathematics Project. Mathematics Teaching in the Middle School, 4*(5), 324–331.

ENDNOTES

1. The *CMP* was conducted at Michigan State University from 1991 through 1996, funded by the National Science Foundation under Grant MDR 9150217. This work ultimately led to the publication of *Connected Mathematics* by Dale Seymour Publications.

2. BA was an assessment development project conducted at the University of California at Berkeley, the Shell Centre for Mathematics Education at the University of Nottingham, Harvard University, and Michigan State University from 1993 to 1996 with the support of the NSF under Grant MDR 9252902. BA packages, comprising assessment tasks and instructional support, are published by Dale Seymour.

3. Two of the tasks in the collection were adapted from released items developed for the QUASAR Cognitive Assessment Instrument (see Lane, 1993; Silver & Lane, 1993).

4. The analysis done here for the ITBS is consistent with the publisher's description that the Concepts and Estimation subtest emphasizes "the logic of the computational process and students' understanding of algorithms . . . [and] computational estimation" (Riverside, 1994, p. 6). There is also a Computation subtest.

5. Actual items from the ITBS Survey Battery are secure, so similar items were created by the authors as illustrations of the types of items on this test.

6. When the large-scale study non-*CMP* comparison group was considered, the sixth-grade *CMP* students did not improve on technical skills as much as the non-*CMP* students (although they did gain as much as would be expected from national norms), but gains were not significantly different in seventh and eighth grades. However, when the performance of students in School R was considered, in which the curriculum was implemented with all

students for all 3 years, there was no significant difference in gains in sixth grade, but School R made significantly larger gains in the seventh and eighth grades.

7. This vignette originally appeared in *Getting to Know CMP: An Introduction to the Connected Mathematics Curriculum* (Dale Seymour, 1996, pp. 9–13), which was available in prepublication form. Copyright 1996 by Michigan State University. Published by Dale Seymour. Used by permission.

8. From *Connected Mathematics*. Copyright 1998 by Michigan State University. Published by Dale Seymour. Used by permission.

10

Mathematics in Context (MiC)—Preliminary Evidence About Student Outcomes

Thomas A. Romberg
National Center for Improving Student Learning and Achievement in Mathematics and Science

Mary C. Shafer
Northern Illinois University

From 1991 until 1998, research and development teams from the Wisconsin Center for Education Research at the University of Wisconsin–Madison and the Freudenthal Institute at the University of Utrecht in The Netherlands, together with a group of U.S. middle school teachers, collaborated on the development of the *Mathematics in Context (MiC)* curriculum (National Center for Research in Mathematical Sciences Education & Freudenthal Institute, 1997–1998). The *MiC* materials (including 40 units [10 at each grade level, 5–8], detailed teacher's guides for each unit, a resource guide for the entire program, and various supplementary materials) are now being commercially produced by Encyclopædia Britannica.

Over the course of the 4-year *MiC* curriculum, middle school students explore and connect the following mathematical strands:

- number (whole numbers, common fractions, ratio, decimal fractions, percents, and integers),
- algebra (creation of expressions, tables, graphs, and formulas from patterns and functions),
- geometry (measurement, spatial visualization, synthetic geometry, and coordinate and transformational geometry), and
- statistics and probability (data visualization, chance, distribution and variability, and quantification of expectations).

TABLE 10.1

MiC Units by Grade Level and Strand

		Strand		
Grade	Number	Algebra	Geometry	Statistics and Probability
5	Some of the Parts Measure for Measure Per Sense Grasping Sizes	Patterns and Symbols Dry and Wet Numbers	Side Seeing Figuring All the Angles	Picturing Numbers Take a Chance
6	Fraction Times More or Less Ratios and Rates	Expressions and Formulas Tracking Graphs Comparing Quantities Operations	Reallotment Made to Measure	Dealing With Data
7	Cereal Numbers Powers of Ten	Ups and Downs Building Formulas Decision Making	Packages and Polygons Triangles and Beyond Looking at an Angle	Ways To Go Statistics and the Environment
8	Reflections on Number	Graphing Equations Get the Most Out of It Patterns and Figures Growth	Triangles and Patchwork Going the Distance	Insights Into Data Digging Numbers Great Expectations

The organization of the units by strand and grade level is shown in Table 10.1. Within a strand, the units generally are to be used in the order indicated, but the sequence can be organized flexibly across strands and grades.

For each strand, the developmental question was, "How could we design a set of activities over the 4 years (Grades 5–8) that would provide students an opportunity to progress from informal notions in that strand toward using formal mathematical reasoning and representations to model and solve nonroutine problems?" To answer this question, we began by specifying a set of goals. For example, by the end of Grade 8, a goal for students is that they be able to use algebraic representations (both graphical and symbolic) to model a variety of problem situations. A nonroutine problem students might be expected to solve by the end of Grade 8 is shown in Fig. 10.1.

For this problem, students need to be able to write algebraic equations to represent both the area and perimeter of rectangles, to graph those

Here are two constraints for all rectangles with two sides along the axes.

I. The area is at least 900 square meters, and it is at most 1,200 square meters.

II. The horizontal side is at least 20 meters, and it is at most 60 meters.

13. a. Graph the feasible region for these constraints.

b. Graph the line for the upper-right vertices for all rectangles with perimeters of 180 meters.

c. Use the rolling line strategy to find the rectangle that satisfies constraints I and II and minimizes the perimeter.

d. Do the same thing to find the rectangle with the maximum perimeter.

FIG. 10.1. An area–perimeter constraint problem. *Note.* From *Get the Most Out of It*, in *Mathematics in Context*, by the National Center for Research in Mathematical Sciences Education and Freudenthal Institute (Eds.), 1997–1998, Chicago: Encyclopædia Brittanica. © 2001 by the Encyclopædia Brittanica. Reprinted with permission.

equations, to consider the constraints given in the particular problem, and to use those ideas to answer the questions raised. To reach this goal, 13 algebra units were created (see Fig. 10.2).

To illustrate how units in *MiC* are organized, we look more closely at this set of algebra units. At the simplest level, algebra can be thought of as the generalization of arithmetic. Symbols replace numbers for various purposes. First, symbols can be used to describe calculations (e.g., $12n + 8$ means multiply by 12, then add 8). Symbols can be used to represent relationships and provide ways to solve problems in the real word (e.g., $t = 12n$, meaning, to find the total cost of several items that cost $12 each,

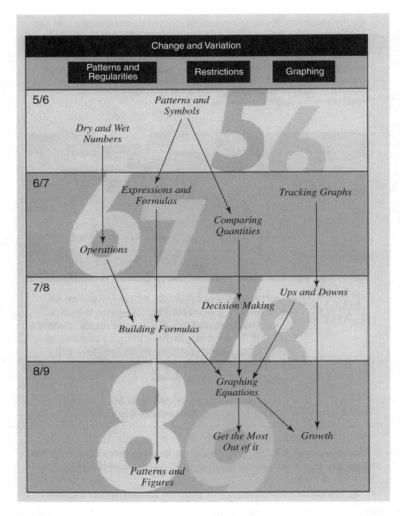

FIG. 10.2. *MiC* map of algebra strand units by grade level. *Note.* From *Teacher Resource and Implementation Guide,* in *Mathematics in Context,* by the National Center for Research in Mathematical Sciences Education and Freudenthal Institute (Eds.), 1997–1998, Chicago: Encyclopædia Brittanica. © 2001 by the Encyclopædia Brittanica. Reprinted with permission.

multiply the number of items purchased by the cost of one item). Algebra uses symbols to generalize and express relationships that are always true (e.g., $x + x = 2x$, meaning a number plus itself is the same as multiplying the number by 2; or $d = rt$, expressing the relationship among distance traveled, rate of speed, and time spent traveling). We can also use algebraic symbols to represent relationships that are true only under certain circumstances or constraints (e.g., $C = 75x + 18$ represents the cost of building a small shop, but only if a minimum number of shops are to be built).

To capture these different algebraic ideas, three themes run throughout the algebra units: (a) the study of change, (b) consideration of constraints, and (c) the study of patterns. Similar to themes in a symphony, sometimes one theme is stronger than the others; sometimes the themes are evident simultaneously.

Students study change in water levels in Dry and Wet Numbers (Streefland, Roodhardt, Simon, Burrill, & Middleton, 1997) as a basis for developing notation and ways of computing with positive and negative numbers. In Operations (Abels, Wijers, Burrill, Simon, & Cole, 1998), students build on their informal understanding of positive and negative numbers and use these numbers in comparison, addition, subtraction, multiplication, and division. In Tracking Graphs (de Jong, Querelle, Meyer, & Simon, 1998), students produce graphs by analyzing phenomena that change over time (e.g., temperature). Studying change plays a central role in Ups and Downs (Abels, de Jong, Meyer, Shew, Burrill, & Simon, 1998), as students graph and describe different kinds of change (e.g., linear, exponential, or periodic). It is also central in one of the culminating units, Growth (Roodhardt, Spence, Burrill, & Christiansen, 1998).

In Comparing Quantities (Kindt, Abels, Meyer, & Pligge, 1998), students informally explore systems of equations using reasoning and ways of organizing information. Considering constraints becomes more prominent in Decision Making (Roodhardt, Middleton, Burrill, & Simon, 1998) as students solve a realistic problem about building housing on a reclaimed landfill. It is again prominent in Graphing Equations (Kindt et al., 1998) as students develop the understanding and skills needed to graph linear inequalities and as they learn to use these graphs to define restricted regions on the coordinate system. Considering constraints is again prominent in Get the Most Out of It (Roodhardt, Kindt, Pligge, & Simon, 1998), when students tackle a complicated problem in which they use all of their graphing skills and accumulated knowledge of linear programming.

It is through the study of patterns in Patterns and Symbols (Roodhardt, Kindt, Burrill, & Spence, 1997) that students begin using symbols to represent patterns they see in such things as growth rings of a tree or in blocks used to make a border along a garden. For example, in one lesson students are given information about the red and black growth rings that develop

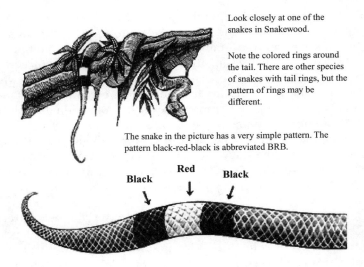

Look closely at one of the
snakes in Snakewood.

Note the colored rings around
the tail. There are other species
of snakes with tail rings, but the
pattern of rings may be
different.

The snake in the picture has a very simple pattern. The
pattern black-red-black is abbreviated BRB.

Black   Red   Black

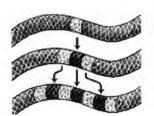

Some snakes in Snakewood have a changing
pattern. As a snake grows older, the pattern
extends. There is a system to the way the
pattern grows.

It starts with a red ring.

In the next stage, the same thing happens with
each red ring, but the black rings stay the same.

The process continues in the same way as the
snake grows older.

FIG. 10.3. Patterns in Snakewood. *Note.* From *Patterns and Symbols*, in *Mathematics in Context*, by the National Center for Research in Mathematical Sciences Education and Freudenthal Institute (Eds.), 1997–1998, Chicago: Encyclopædia Brittanica. © 2001 by the Encyclopædia Brittanica. Reprinted with permission.

on a snake (see Fig. 10.3). They describe this growth pattern symbolically and systematically record the number of red and black rings for a snake's first five growth cycles. They then predict the number of red and black rings a snake would have after a certain number of growth cycles or determine the age of a snake with a given number of red and black rings. Recognizing and describing patterns is important as students write algebraic formulas in Expressions and Formulas (Gravemeijer, Roodhardt, Wijers, Cole, & Burrill, 1998) and Building Formulas (Wijers et al., 1998).

The Patterns and Figures unit (Kindt, Roodhardt, Spence, Simon, & Pligge, 1998) centers on the study of patterns as students analyze sequences

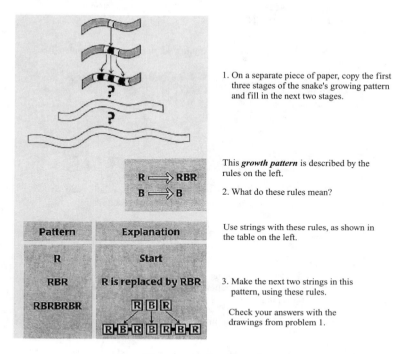

1. On a separate piece of paper, copy the first three stages of the snake's growing pattern and fill in the next two stages.

This **growth pattern** is described by the rules on the left.

2. What do these rules mean?

Use strings with these rules, as shown in the table on the left.

3. Make the next two strings in this pattern, using these rules.

Check your answers with the drawings from problem 1.

FIG. 10.3. (Continued)

and write formulas for finding terms in the sequence. In this unit, they encounter several classic topics in mathematics that deal with patterns (e.g., Pascal's triangle). Patterns also play an important part as students write formulas and equations, work on graphing, describe various kinds of change, and make and use symbols as an efficient way to represent real situations.

The design of units for the other strands (number, geometry, and statistics and probability) followed a similar pattern. As a consequence of studying the problems in the sequence of algebra units, students have the opportunity to reason, reflect on, and use the terms, symbols, and rules of algebra to solve problems. Students first use words, pictures, or diagrams of their invention to describe mathematical situations, organize their own knowledge and work, solve problems, and explain their strategies. In the later units, students learn and use standard, conventional algebraic notation for writing expressions and equations, for manipulating algebraic expressions and solving equations, and for graphing equations. Movement along this continuum is not necessarily smooth or all in one direction. Students move back and forth among levels of formality depending on the problem situation or on the mathematics involved. Although they are actually doing algebra less formally

Numbers of Rings

4. a. Study the table below. Copy it into your notebook and complete it.

Pattern	Number of Red Rings	Number of Black Rings	Number of Rings
1. R	1	0	1
2. RBR	2	1	3
3. RBRBRBR	4	3	7
4. ?	8	?	?
5. ?	?	15	?

   b. Look at the table you just completed. What is the relationship between the numbers of red and black rings in each string?

   c. Look at the numbers in the table. Predict the ring numbers for the sixth snake.

5. Of course the number of rings for any snake is limited. But if there were no length restrictions, would it be possible to find a snake of this kind with an even number of rings?

6. A snake has 128 red rings. How many rings does the snake have in total?

7. Another snake has 255 black rings. How many total rings does this snake have?

8. Is it possible for this kind of snake to have 499 rings? Why or why not?

FIG. 10.3. (Continued)

in the earlier grades, students are not forced to generalize their knowledge to a more formal level, or to operate at a more formal level, before they have had sufficient experience with the underlying concepts.

REALISTIC MATHEMATICS EDUCATION

MiC was developed as a consequence of the publication of the *Curriculum and Evaluation Standards for School Mathematics* (National Council of Teachers of Mathematics [NCTM], 1989). In NCTM's vision, students are seen as individuals who tackle problems with a confidence based on a combination of coherent mathematical knowledge that has emerged from working experience and on the collaborative support that comes from membership in a learning community. The developers of *MiC* attempted to create an existence proof that a program could be created with NCTM's vision in mind.

The Dutch Realistic Mathematics Education (RME; Freudenthal, 1983) approach was selected as the development model for three reasons. First, the approach is epistemologically similar to that envisioned by the NCTM. The Dutch believe that students make sense of a situation by seeing and extracting the mathematics embedded within it. This involves learning to represent quantitative and spatial relationships in a broad range of situations; to express those relations by using the terms, signs, and symbols of mathematics; to use procedures with those signs and symbols, following understood rules, to carry out numerical and symbolic calculations; and to make predictions and interpret results based on the use of those procedures. This belief also implies that the sequence of contextual activities should help students gradually develop methods for symbolizing problem situations. All activities are seen as helping students in their transition from informal to formal use of mathematical concepts and procedures. This implies that instruction, as is too commonly done in mathematics classes, should not start with presenting students with the formal terms, signs, symbols, and rules and later expecting them to use these formal ideas to solve problems. Instead, the activities should lead students to the need for the formal concepts and procedures of mathematics. The implication for students is that they should gradually develop more formal ways of representing complex problems. Psychologically, this process is called "progressive formalization."

Second, the Dutch have been designing instructional materials relying on realistic problem situations for nearly two decades. As a consequence, they have a lot of experience in developing activities and have gathered considerable evidence about student performance as a consequence of using materials based on their approach.

Third, in 1988 the U.S. National Center for Research in Mathematical Sciences Education funded the Freudenthal Institute to conduct an initial design study in a U.S. school. The experiment involved six algebra teachers at a high school in Greenfield, Wisconsin (see de Lange, Burrill, Romberg, & van Reeuwijk, 1993). One conclusion was as follows:

> All students had the opportunity to succeed and, in doing so, exceeded our expectations. Consistently there was evidence of higher-order thinking and analysis in all of the classes, not just the honors class. One teacher commented that some of the student work on the final test demonstrated a level of maturity about mathematical reasoning that is rarely evident in first-year algebra. (de Lange, Burrill, & Romberg, 1993, p. 158)

The experiment was impressive, and both teacher reaction and student achievement strongly influenced our choice of RME as a foundation for *MiC* units.

EVIDENCE ABOUT STUDENT OUTCOMES

Designing a new set of curricular materials, no matter how well conceived, is a difficult process. For *MiC*, the process involved developing a blueprint for a middle school curriculum based on NCTM's *Standards*, creating an initial version of each student unit, pilot testing the unit in a few classrooms, revising the unit, field-testing the unit with other units, developing a teacher's guide for each unit, and having the units reviewed by content experts. Based on this formative information, the student units and teacher's guides were revised for commercial production and marketing. Throughout this process of development, evidence that students learn with understanding the mathematical concepts and procedures was considered. The actual data that students use the ideas in the four strands to solve nonroutine problems come from six sources: Dutch research, the pilot test, the actual field test, external evidence, case studies, and the *MiC* longitudinal–cross-sectional study.

Dutch Research

In 1992, The Netherlands National Institute for Educational Measurement (CITO) compared the performance of students using realistic text materials with those using traditional materials on 29 mathematics scales. The results were based on a random survey of all students at the end of Dutch primary education (Grade 8). In Fig. 10.4, the level of achievement of students using traditional textbooks is indicated by the "0" line, and differences are indicated along the vertical axis. Students who used realistic materials scored significantly higher (at least a 7-point difference in scaled scores) on 12 scales, whereas students using the traditional texts were significantly higher on just 3 scales (Bokhove, 1995). Although these student outcome data are not on U.S. students using *MiC*, the Dutch traditional textbooks are similar in many ways to U.S. traditional texts. Hence, these data lend credence to the potential of the RME approach to school mathematics instruction.

Pilot Test

Data were collected during 1992–1993 and 1993–1994 as each initial version of a student unit was piloted in one or more middle school classrooms in the Wisconsin communities of Dodgeville, Madison, Milwaukee, Stoughton, and Waukesha. *MiC* staff spent at least 2 weeks in pilot-test classrooms, observing students as they used each of the 40 pilot versions of the units and collecting notes on the sections of the units that were particularly successful or problematic.

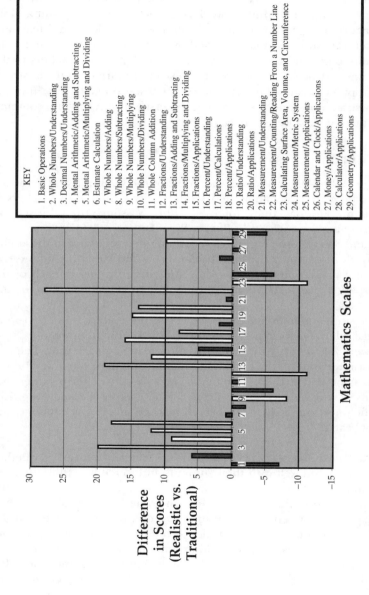

KEY

1. Basic Operations
2. Whole Numbers/Understanding
3. Decimal Numbers/Understanding
4. Mental Arithmetic/Adding and Subtracting
5. Mental Arithmetic/Multiplying and Dividing
6. Estimate Calculation
7. Whole Numbers/Adding
8. Whole Numbers/Subtracting
9. Whole Numbers/Multiplying
10. Whole Numbers/Dividing
11. Whole Column Addition
12. Fractions/Understanding
13. Fractions/Adding and Subtracting
14. Fractions/Multiplying and Dividing
15. Fractions/Applications
16. Percent/Understanding
17. Percent/Calculations
18. Percent/Applications
19. Ratio/Understanding
20. Ratio/Applications
21. Measurement/Understanding
22. Measurement/Counting/Reading From a Number Line
23. Calculating Surface Area, Volume, and Circumference
24. Measurement/Metric System
25. Measurement/Applications
26. Calendar and Clock/Applications
27. Money/Applications
28. Calculator/Applications
29. Geometry/Applications

Mathematics Scales

FIG. 10.4. Difference in student performance: realistic versus traditional texts. *Note.* Traditional scores are set to zero. White bars indicate significant difference.

Assessment tasks developed for every unit were designed to assess both the content students had learned in that unit and how they could use that knowledge in new contexts. The teachers, however, usually adapted these tasks for use in their classrooms. As a result, there was considerable variation in the summary data on student outcomes for any unit. Nevertheless, staff collected samples of student work completed during the unit and interview data on each unit from a small number of students and teachers. The overall student performance varied by unit, but in general the results were encouraging, and the response of both students and teachers to the materials was very positive. However, because of the variations in classroom assessment practices and the fact that the focus was on gathering information to revise an initial and very preliminary version of any unit, no common student outcome data were collected.

Field Test

During the 1993–1994 academic year, most of the Grades 5 and 7 revised units were used in a recommended sequence by a sample of teachers at sites in Miami, Florida; Ames, Iowa; St. Louis, Missouri; the pilot schools in Wisconsin; and one school in Puerto Rico. During 1994–1996, units for Grades 6 and 8 were also taught in a recommended sequence at those sites and at two additional sites, Culver City, California and Memphis, Tennessee. During these years, one member of the *MiC* staff traveled to each of the sites and spent 1 week each month of the school year collecting survey and interview data.

At these sites, general data about the use of the materials in classrooms and about student performance were formally gathered in three ways. First, teachers were asked to fill out two forms after teaching each unit. The first teacher form focused on the construction and content of the unit, and the second form focused on the assessment strategies used with the unit. Second, site liaisons were asked to prepare a report after each of the weeklong visits made to field-test sites. Third, an overall teacher survey was conducted at the end of Year 2.

Construction–Content Form. On this form, teachers were asked whether the activities worked well with their students and to identify those that did not, whether their students were able to make connections between the mathematics in this and previous units, and whether their students had the prerequisite knowledge for the unit. Overall, the teachers found the units to be challenging for their students, but they saw their students get excited about problems, able to build arguments, and so forth. However, one teacher's review of an early algebra unit, Expressions and Formulas, brought the following remarks: "No, students did not make connections between the mathematics in this unit and that in other units" and "students were missing knowledge of basic multiplication and order of operations."

Assessment Form.   Teachers were asked about the forms of assessment they used during and at the end of the unit, the amount of time allowed for the assessment activities, and the results they obtained. In response to the question, "How successful were students in understanding the mathematics in the unit?," one teacher of Expressions and Formulas responded, "I was very pleased with the [students'] understanding of the mathematics in this unit. Students understood the concepts and were able to apply them on the assessment [activity]."

Teachers were also asked to provide one or more copies of student work, specifically examples of low, medium, and high performances. Some comments from teachers about Expressions and Formulas were negative: "Formulas were generally hard for students"; "this unit needed teacher direction"; and "there were no parts my students could accomplish in small groups." Others were positive: "Students as a whole were quite successful as exhibited by their discussions, journals, and assessments" and "content was presented in such a way that it was meaningful and related to a variety of situations in everyday life." Finally, all of the teachers who participated in the field test completed an overall survey at the end of Year 2. Some insight into student performance was obtained from the survey.

Teachers, for example, were asked whether students understood the mathematics in each unit taught. Again, some comments were positive: "Most students did well, especially where they had to think"; "students were able to apply the concepts on the assessment"; and "I noticed several [students] using procedures used in this unit to solve other math problems after we completed the unit." Others were negative: "Students were confused and anxious but demonstrated effort to understand. Towards the end they 'clicked'" and "occasionally the students would not understand how a problem was worded, and we would have to discuss it as a group."

Teachers' lists of scores for end-of-unit assessment activities identified students by gender and grade level. Copies of these forms allowed staff members who were revising units to study the ways teachers graded student work and the differences in student achievement, both within a classroom at a single site and across classrooms at one or several sites. As in the pilot testing of units, teachers in the field test rarely used the unit assessment materials as intended. Again, traditional test items were commonly added, and the tasks designed to let students show what they could do in a new situation were skipped or drastically modified.

In summary, although the project staff gathered student achievement data at the unit level, because of the variation in classroom testing no summary information across units within strands was feasible. Again, all of the information obtained during the field test was summarized for each unit and the related teacher's guide, and it was used by the staff members to make final revisions for commercial publication.

External Evidence

The project staff did not gather standardized test data during the pilot and field tests of the units. In fact, we felt that information from such tests did not reflect our instructional goals. However, several school districts using the *MiC* materials have shared district-collected student performance data.

The most extensive data came from Ames, Iowa, a university community committed to reforming their mathematics program in spite of a history of being a high-scoring district on standardized tests. *MiC* was used experimentally in a few classrooms as a field-test site from 1993 through 1995. In 1995, the district formally adopted *MiC* as its curriculum for Grades 5–8 and began to use *MiC* districtwide during the 1995–1996 school year. The curriculum was gradually implemented, and by the 1997–1998 school year most teachers were teaching 8 or more of the 10 units per grade.

The data reported in Table 10.2 were offered voluntarily by the Ames School District and were not part of a formal evaluation study of *MiC*. The Iowa Tests of Basic Skills (ITBS) are administered to all students in the district annually and reported to the general public by the school district. From the district data, we selected the Grade 6 students with complete data who had used *MiC* in the 1995–1996 school year. Table 10.2 shows the national percentile ranking of this set of students from Grade 4 through Grade 8 ($N = 385$). Note that in Grade 4, prior to the use of *MiC*, the percentile ranking was high. In Grade 5 during the 1994–1995 school year, 35% of the students began to study some *MiC* units as part of the field test. The lower ranking on computation that year was surprising but consistent across all students, not just those using *MiC*. In Grade 6, all students in this cohort used *MiC*. The significant, sustained gain in computation is

TABLE 10.2

ITBS National Percentile Ranking for One *MiC* Cohort Group

Academic Year	Grade	Mathematics Concepts	Problem Solving	Computation
1993–1994	4	81	88	60
1994–1995	5	78	87	40
1995–1996	6	89	98	75
1996–1997	7	90	94	72
1997–1998	8	90	95	79

Notes. $N = 385$. Scores are reported as a district average for Ames, Iowa schools. *MiC* was adopted districtwide in the spring of 1995.

noteworthy given that *MiC* does not stress arithmetic computation as a goal. Instead, after several number units in Grades 5 and 6, students reinforce their number skills in the context of problem solving, modeling, and learning about other significant mathematics such as algebra, geometry, statistics and probability.

Until 1997, the ITBS was the only external assessment used to measure student achievement in Ames. Although the ITBS continues to be used, in 1997 the district also began to use the New Standards Reference Exam (NSRE; University of Pittsburgh & National Center on Education and the Economy, 1997) to provide a deeper look at students' conceptual understanding and problem-solving ability, district goals that were not being adequately assessed by the ITBS. The NSRE is designed to show student achievement in mathematics in three areas: skills, concepts, and problem solving. Unlike the ITBS, which consists of multiple-choice items, the NSRE consists of constructed-response items scored by using rubrics. Thus, although the scores are labeled similarly to those in the ITBS, the questions are more complex and the scores reflect the kind of strategies used. For example, Part 2 of the exam (to be completed in 45 minutes) contains three tasks, with two questions in each task. The questions not only expect students to produce an answer but also to illustrate or explain their work. Results of the NSRE are reported in five achievement levels: little evidence of achievement, below standard, nearly achieved standard, achieved standard, and achieved standard with honors. Table 10.3 shows the percentage of all Grade 8 students in 1997 and 1998 achieving the standard or standard with honors compared to students across the nation. Note that ITBS data on many of these students in 1998 are reported in Table 10.2.

The results on the NSRE demonstrate superior achievement of eighth-grade Ames students in mathematical skills, concepts, and problem solving after 4 years of using *MiC*. This demonstrates that *MiC*, a curriculum that emphasizes the development of mathematics concepts and provides students with extensive experiences solving nonroutine problems, can facilitate achievement in these areas without compromising the development of mathematical skills.

TABLE 10.3

New Standards Reference Exam: Percentage of Grade 8 *MiC* Students
Achieving Standard in Ames, Iowa Schools

Academic Year	Skills		Concepts		Problem Solving	
	MiC	*National*	*MiC*	*National*	*MiC*	*National*
1996–1997	79	33	57	20	50	11
1997–1998	79	33	56	20	51	11

In summary, the information from Ames, Iowa, is encouraging but not conclusive. The data also do not reflect the variations in content coverage or instructional patterns that have been documented in classrooms attempting to implement a *Standards*-based curriculum.

Case Studies

From the initiation of the project to develop *MiC*, we considered the materials to be research tools to study the problems of transition from traditional mathematics instruction toward *Standards*-based instruction, and the creation of *MiC* units to be design experiments. Teachers in some pilot and field-test schools collectively agreed to participate in this research, and a series of case studies of teachers using *MiC* was carried out. (For a summary of the impact of *MiC* on the teachers in these case studies, see Romberg, 1997.)

Although the focus in these studies was on teachers and the challenges they faced when teaching the draft *MiC* materials, the challenges often had implications for students and their mathematical performances. For example, initially teachers were challenged by new definitions for instructional practice, authority, and expectations. Traditional classrooms had been built around a review, presentation, and study–assistance sequence. As one *MiC* teacher found, "there was little to 'teach'" in a traditional sense. *MiC* student units contained tasks for students to read, discuss, and carry out with "guidance" from their teacher. In providing guidance, teachers had to move to an approach that occasionally clarified but reserved for students the mathematizing and solving of problems.

Changes in the distribution of power and expertise in *MiC* classes affected both teachers and students. Although some teachers wanted to lessen students' discomfort as they struggled to solve problems, others were concerned about the "boisterous interactions" that occurred during task-oriented group activities. All teachers in the studies were "surprised by what their students were able to do." Sometimes students who had been labeled as "poor in math" or "quiet" were able to display their understanding or found they could succeed. Students who had considered themselves "good" in mathematics often sought a return to the approach that had earned them the "good" label.

Unmoored from traditional assessments of student progress—quizzes, homework, and tests that emphasize one correct answer—case study teachers voiced frustration. They were not yet familiar with the mathematics in a unit and the connections that could be made with the mathematics in other units. Thus, it was difficult for them to use assessment activities that looked at students' thought processes and their development by using some form of rubric. When these teachers created their own assessment activities, they tended to develop problems that focused on computation closely related to classroom content and that, typically, had one right answer.

Finally, mathematics, more than other middle school subjects, has been used to track students—to provide them with opportunities based on standardized test scores, mathematics grades, and the subjective views of parents and counselors. A reform approach challenges tracking. One field-test teacher wrote, "This is when we first found out that this math is really successful, because at-risk learners or LD students were doing really well. . . . We thought it was a good tool for opening up communication between the students" (Romberg & Shafer, 1995, p. 10).

In summary, the case studies provided the project staff with in-depth accounts of the struggles that teachers, and occasionally students, were having with content and instruction different from that to which they had been accustomed. Although students were observed to do well on the units and were enthusiastic about the *MiC* approach, they were sometimes confused about the "two maths" (*MiC* and the one needed for the standardized test).

Longitudinal–Cross-Sectional Study

Both the pilot test and the field test provided substantial evidence about student performance on particular units and sequences of units, and the school district standardized test data and information from the case studies were encouraging. Nevertheless, because the commercial versions of the *MiC* materials were not fully available until 1998, few students to date have used the program for the full 4 years as intended, and it is premature to report on *MiC* student outcomes when the program is used as intended.

In 1996, however, the National Science Foundation (NSF) funded the Wisconsin Center for Education Research to conduct a longitudinal–cross-sectional study of the impact of *MiC* on student mathematical performance. This study was designed to meet two goals: to determine the mathematical knowledge and understanding, attitudes, and levels of performance of students as a consequence of studying units in each of four content strands over 1, 2, and 3 years, and to compare the performance of students using *MiC* with that of students using conventional middle school mathematics programs.[1]

The Project. During the initial year of this project (1996–1997), instruments were developed related to a "model for monitoring school mathematics" (see Fig. 10.5). The prior variables include background (gender, ethnicity, and primary language) and prior knowledge of students (standardized test scores, mathematical reasoning profiles, and attitudes toward mathematics), teacher background (mathematics preparation, teaching experience, and conceptions about mathematics teaching and learning), and the social context or culture in which particular schools operate and support or hinder change (demographic information and school vision for student learning). The independent variables include curricular content and materials, the

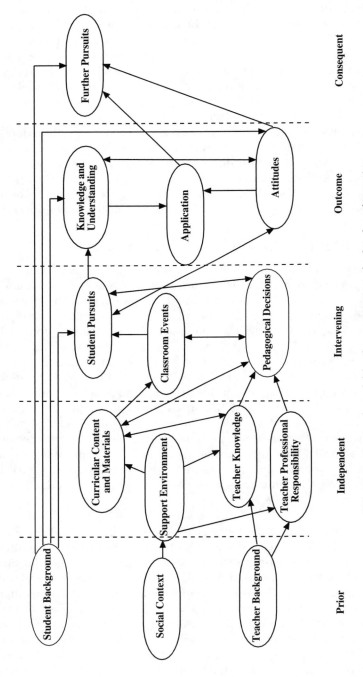

FIG. 10.5. Revised model for the monitoring of school mathematics.

242

support environment available for students and teachers, teacher knowledge, and teacher professional opportunities (reading of professional literature and participation in professional development). The three intervening variables include pedagogical decisions (including decisions prior to instruction, interactive decisions, and classroom assessment practices), classroom events, and student pursuits (including substantive conversation among students and student collaborative working relationships). The three outcome variables include student knowledge of mathematics, students' abilities to apply that knowledge, and students' attitudes toward mathematics. The consequent variable, further pursuit of mathematics, includes information about students' transition into high school and the number and type of mathematics courses they plan to take during high school.

Four sites agreed to participate in the longitudinal study, two in urban locations and two in small suburban areas. Evidence on all the variables (with the exception of the consequent variable) was gathered for Grades 5, 6, and 7 during 1997–1998; Grades 6, 7, and 8 during 1998–1999; and Grades 7 and 8 during 1999–2000. A limited amount of data on Grade 9 students who participated in the study during previous years was also collected during 1999 and 2000. During the first year of data collection, 54 teachers and 2,225 students in 17 schools participated in the study. Approximately 80% of the students studied *MiC*; the remaining students studied the conventional mathematics curricula already in place in the schools.

Variation. Evidence for the student outcome variable (related to knowledge and application of mathematics) is based on three sources: scores on the standardized tests used by each district; an "external assessment" (EA) composed of items from the National Assessment of Educational Progress (NAEP) and Third International Mathematics and Science Study (TIMSS) tests; and a newly developed "problem-solving assessment" (PSA) that examines three levels of mathematical thinking in relation to four content strands (number, algebra, geometry, and probability–statistics). Student performance, aggregated at the classroom level, will be summarized by content strand and by level of reasoning by combining results of the EA and the PSA. Complete information on student outcomes as a consequence of studying mathematics by using *MiC* for a period of years will not be available until sometime in 2002.

As we scored and coded the data, set up data files, and began to examine the information gathered from classrooms, some consequences of conducting such a comprehensive evaluation study became clear. First, although the units of treatment and analysis were classrooms, not individual students, the between-class variance on most of the variables in the model was quite large. For example, in one district, the class mean percentile on the TerraNova test (CTB/McGraw-Hill, 1997) for prior mathematical performance at Grade 5 varied within *MiC* classrooms from 24.09 to 92.37. This recently published standardized test includes multiple-choice items and a few open-response items, with most of the items being set in some context. Computational fluency is tested only in a supplementary test and was not reported by the district. Given the nature of the items, performance on this test could be influenced by reading proficiency as well as by prior mathematics achievement. Tracking by ability was prevalent in some schools, and the study classes differed in prior mathematics achievement as well as in ethnic composition, socioeconomic status, and so on.

Second, teachers inevitably adapt the lessons or add to the lessons in a new program. Given the uncertainty of the student outcomes, the limits of the teachers' individual understanding of the content, *MiC*'s pedagogical approach, the concerns about external assessments, and so on, the degree of teacher implementation of *MiC* varied in all four districts. In 1997–1998, the number (and content) of units taught during the school year varied from 2 to 7 (of the prescribed 10 per grade level). Some teachers chose to emphasize one or two content strands, particularly number and algebra, and skipped work in geometry and probability–statistics. Other teachers used units from more than one grade level, or just used some problems or activities from some units; most supplemented *MiC* units with conventional resources.

Variation was also documented in the instructional methods used. In some classes, *MiC* was taught in ways consistent with the philosophy of the curriculum. In other classes, *MiC* was taught by using conventional teaching methods. Also, some "conventional" teachers taught in reform-oriented ways and supplemented their teaching with curricular materials that emphasized mathematical problem solving and communication.

What these aspects illustrate is the complex nature of classroom research. What might naively be seen as a simple comparative experiment in fact takes place within a complex social context with considerable variation in prior, independent, intervening, and outcome variables. Controlling potential sources of possible variation, as is done in laboratory experiments, is more difficult in student and school settings. That such phenomena often do not lend themselves to classical experimental procedures does not mean quality research cannot be done. Rather, as in other social sciences, in carrying out multivariate social interventions (such as classroom research), formal models identifying the key variables and locating paths between the variables must be built. Specification, measurement, estimation, and statistical inference become paramount in such work.

Although the variation in each set of variables in the monitoring model for the *MiC* study shown in Fig. 10.5 could be examined by using structural equations, the number of classes at a given grade level is small and collinearity across variables is a serious interpretation problem. For this reason, a simplified model was posited for the longitudinal–cross-sectional study. Variation in classroom achievement, CA, aggregated by strand, level, or total performance, can be attributed to variations in opportunity to learn with understanding, $OTL_{(u)}$, preceding achievement, PA, and method of instruction, I. This relationship can be expressed as classroom achievement = opportunity to learn(with understanding) + preceding achievement + method of instruction, or

$$CA = OTL_{(u)} + PA + I.$$

Currently, each of these composite variables is being specified from information collected for the different variables in the original model, and scales are being developed.

For CA, a one-parameter logistic model will be used to develop one or more progress maps from item information taken from the EA and PSA. Such maps are intended to describe the nature of development in an area of learning and provide a frame of reference for monitoring growth (Masters & Forster, 1996, p. 1). Having a progress map, for example, for the prealgebra domain would facilitate the awareness or recognition of individual students' preconceptions, the understanding of students' progress from informal to formal thinking, and the documentation of progress.

In the simplified model, the scale $OTL_{(u)}$ will include information about mathematical content taught, the processes students experienced in learning that content, and the school context (e.g., the vision for student learning established and enacted in schools, the content of curricular materials, and teacher beliefs about the best ways for students to learn mathematics).

For the initial year of the study, PA for classes was determined by examining the relationship between the distribution of scores in each class on the district's standardized test from the prior year and the distribution of scores on the *Collis–Romberg Mathematical Problem Solving Profiles* (Collis & Romberg, 1992). The latter test assesses the level of reasoning as a consequence of responding to several tasks that ask increasingly complex questions. From this information, preceding class achievement can be characterized as low, low average, average, high average, and high.

Finally, a scale for instruction, I, is being developed from data on each class taken from observation reports, teacher log entries, and journal entries. We are focusing on the instructional experiences that affect students learning mathematics with understanding (e.g., emphasis on conceptual understanding and connections among mathematical ideas) and student engagement in the lesson (e.g., substantive conversation among students and student collaborative working relationships).

The importance of examining classroom outcome data in this manner can be illustrated with the following example from the 1997–1998 data from 3 of 10 fifth-grade classes in District 1. The three classes were characterized

TABLE 10.4

Class Results as Percentages on the External Assessment and the Problem
Solving Assessment for Three Fifth-Grade Classes

	Class		
Assessment Results	High Average 1 (MiC)	High Average 2 (MiC)	High Average 3 (Conventional)
External Assessment			
Mean	43	44	33
Number	51	51	34
Geometry	37	30	22
Algebra	46	42	33
Statistics–Probability	40	55	42
Problem-Solving Assessment			
Mean	54	48	42
Number	50	48	42
Geometry	46	30	29
Algebra	56	33	41
Statistics–Probability	55	57	45

Note. The three fifth-grade classes were in District 1 and were characterized as high average preceding achievement.

as high average (HA) on PA; two were *MiC* classes and the other was a conventional class. Table 10.4 shows the achievement data, reported as class
means for each assessment and for the content subsections of each assessment. The class means were higher for the two *MiC* classes on both tests,
but the percentages of correct responses to the items in the four domains
on both tests varied across all three classes.

It is simplistic to claim that the differences in classroom achievement are
due merely to the differences in the curricula used. A detailed examination
of the results from these three classes on the number-strand items on the
two tests suggests that students in the two *MiC* classes selected appropriate operations for problems and, in most cases, outperformed students in
the conventional class on both constructed-response and multiple-choice
number-strand assessment items. Even though the conventional class spent
most of the school year studying the number strand, the students in the conventional class did not perform as well on assessment items in the number
strand as the students in the two *MiC* classes did.

The class means for the two *MiC* classes were higher on assessment items
that involved the following:

- division of whole numbers with the answer expressed as a fraction;
- multiplication of a whole number by a decimal;
- fraction–decimal use in calculation of a quantity represented by a sector
  of a circle;

- reading a decimal from a scale (vertical number line);
- placement of a decimal number on a scale (vertical number line); and
- problem solving by using ratio and scale.

To understand differences such as these, we need to examine the content that students had an opportunity to learn with understanding $OTL_{(u)}$ and the type of instruction, I, planned and carried out in each class. Although these composite variables have not yet been scaled, there are differences between these classes on the content covered, the way it was covered, the social context of the school, and so on. The *MiC* teacher in HA1, for example, taught six *MiC* units: two geometry, two number, one algebra, and one statistics. The *MiC* teacher in HA2 taught those same six, but added two more: a number unit and a probability unit. The teacher in HA3 did not teach any *MiC* units but used a conventional fifth-grade mathematics textbook as a basis for instruction.

In the *MiC* units, the mathematical tasks and questions were situated in contexts designed to stimulate mathematical thinking and promote discussion among students. Students were expected to explore mathematical relationships, develop and explain their own reasoning and solution strategies, select and use mathematical tools (such as the fraction bar and ratio table), think deeply about mathematical content, and solve nonroutine problems that involved increasingly complex thinking. By contrast, the mathematical tasks in the conventional text lacked emphasis on connections among mathematical ideas and reasoning in nonroutine or complex problems, were devoid of contexts, and expected students to calculate in specific, algorithmic ways. In contrast to the *MiC* classes, the conventional class did not study ratio, algebra, or many of the geometric concepts presented in the two *MiC* geometry units. The social context of the schools and the beliefs of the teachers about mathematics also differed. The teacher of the conventional class, for example, felt it was more important to cover the textbook than to cover fewer topics in greater depth. Data from these areas, however, have yet to be scaled.

The variability of the data on instruction, I, also has not yet been scaled, but in the raw data the instructional differences are apparent. The *MiC* teacher in HA1, for example, generally planned to supplement *MiC* so that her program met the district curriculum standards and the state testing standards. She valued small-group work because it helped students learn to rely on each other, not just on the teacher. Students were able to share ideas, pool their thinking, and question each other. This teacher also planned for individual work time because she wanted the students to learn to be responsible for their own work. Whole-class discussion was usually planned for the end of each day or activity.

Similarly, the *MiC* teacher in HA2 also checked whether the *MiC* units met the new state standards. She had reservations that fractions were not addressed completely enough for the expectations of sixth-grade teachers, and she resolved this issue by using *MiC* ancillary materials and supplementary worksheets from other resources. Whole-class discussions, used routinely, either took place amid other forms of instruction that were given equal emphasis during the class period or lasted for more than half of the class period. Small-group work was used during fewer than half as many class periods as in HA1 and was generally used in combination with other instructional formats. Students in this class were actively involved in investigating problems, discussing answers and solution strategies, and participating in whole-class discussions. Practice of computation received far less attention than in the conventional class, and students' listening to the teacher or taking notes and beginning homework were given virtually no attention.

In contrast to the two *MiC* teachers, in the conventional class, teacher presentation and student independent practice were important elements. Review of previous material and small-group work was reported approximately one fourth of the days, and whole-class discussion was reported infrequently. On most days, the activities students engaged in during at least half of the class period involved listening to the teacher, taking notes, or practicing computation. Students began homework on few occasions. Although at times students explained their solution strategies and multiple strategies were elicited, conceptual understanding was generally not fostered during class. As noted by the observer on one occasion, "The teacher was interested in the students doing her procedure, which is the only correct method in this class. The lesson did not foster any conceptual understanding. Many topics were presented, but they were presented in isolation of one another. Although students were seated in small groups, they were not allowed to work together or discuss the mathematics and solutions to problems."

Given this preliminary picture of the information being gathered through the use of the simplified model, we are confident we will be able to demonstrate growth of mathematical knowledge in a strand (or in a composite of strands) by groups over time. Furthermore, we believe the pattern of variations in such achievement can be associated with variations in opportunity to learn with understanding, instruction, and preceding achievement.

SUMMARY

Mathematics in Context materials and materials from other reform curricula include substantial mathematical content in major domains of school mathematics (in *MiC*, in number, algebra, geometry, and statistics–probability), and reform instructional activities motivate and challenge both teachers and students. The evidence from the pilot and field tests of *MiC*, from the early case studies of teachers implementing *MiC,* and from early (and limited) external assessment of the impact of *MiC* on student achievement, suggests that middle school students being taught a reform curriculum can and do learn important mathematics. We emphasize, however, that outcome evidence on *MiC* is still preliminary.

Although the data suggest that students using *MiC* do achieve, that evidence is strongly influenced by factors other than the curriculum itself. The NSF-funded longitudinal–cross-sectional study of the impact of *MiC* is designed to gather substantial, corroborative evidence of *MiC* impact on student achievement, but we note the influence of prior student achievement, classroom opportunity to learn with understanding, and the method of instruction used with the curriculum. Although our preliminary evidence is encouraging and supports broader implementation of *MiC* (and by association, of other reform curricula), we also note the need for more complex research and analysis of classroom culture and its impact on student achievement and curriculum implementation.

REFERENCES

Abels, M., de Jong, J. A., Meyer, M. R., Shew, J. A., Burrill, G., & Simon, A. N. (1998). Ups and downs. In National Center for Research in Mathematical Sciences Education & Freudenthal Institute (Eds.), *Mathematics in context.* Chicago: Encyclopædia Britannica.

Abels, M., Wijers, M., Burrill, G., Simon, A. N., & Cole, B. R. (1998). Operations. In National Center for Research in Mathematical Sciences Education & Freudenthal Institute (Eds.), *Mathematics in context.* Chicago: Encyclopædia Britannica.

Bokhove, J. (1995). Brief sketch of results of assessment research on mathematics in primary education (E. Feijs, Trans.). *Journal for Mathematics Education in The Netherlands, 14*(4), 4–9.

Collis, K. F., & Romberg, T. A. (1992). *Collis-Romberg mathematical problem solving profiles.* Hawthorn, Victoria, Australia: Australian Council for Educational Research.

CTB/McGraw-Hill. (1997). *TerraNova.* Monterey, CA: Author.

de Jong, J. A., Querelle, N., Meyer, M. R., & Simon, A. N. (1998). Tracking graphs. In National Center for Research in Mathematical Sciences Education & Freudenthal Institute (Eds.), *Mathematics in context.* Chicago: Encyclopædia Britannica.

de Lange, J., Burrill, G., & Romberg, T. (1993). Looking back: Some retrospective comments. In J. de Lange, G. Burrill, T. Romberg, & M. van Reeuwijk (Eds.), *Learning and testing mathematics in context* (pp. 147–160). Pleasantview, NY: Wings for Learning.

de Lange, J., Burrill, G., Romberg, T., & van Reeuwijk, M. (1993). *Learning and testing mathematics in context.* Pleasantview, NY: Wings for Learning.

Freudenthal, H. (1983). *Didactical phenomenology of mathematical structures.* Dordrecht: Reidel.

Gravemeijer, K., Roodhardt, A., Wijers, M., Cole, B. R., & Burrill, G. (1998). Expressions and formulas. In National Center for Research in Mathematical Sciences Education & Freudenthal Institute (Eds.), *Mathematics in context.* Chicago: Encyclopædia Britannica.

Kindt, M., Abels, M., Meyer, M. R., & Pligge, M. A. (1998). Comparing quantities. In National Center for Research in Mathematical Sciences Education & Freudenthal Institute (Eds.), *Mathematics in context.* Chicago: Encyclopædia Britannica.

Kindt, M., Roodhardt, A., Spence, M. S., Simon, A. N., & Pligge, M. A. (1998). Patterns and figures. In National Center for Research in Mathematical Sciences Education & Freudenthal Institute (Eds.), *Mathematics in context*. Chicago: Encyclopædia Britannica.

Kindt, M., Wijers, M., Spence, M. S., Brinker, L. J., Pligge, M. A., & Burrill, J. (1998). Graphing equations. In National Center for Research in Mathematical Sciences Education & Freudenthal Institute (Eds.), *Mathematics in context*. Chicago: Encyclopædia Britannica.

Masters, G., & Forster, M. (1996). *Progress maps*. Melbourne, Australia: Australian Council for Educational Research.

National Council of Teachers of Mathematics. (1989).*Curriculum and evaluation standards for school mathematics*. Reston, VA: Author.

National Center for Research in Mathematical Sciences Education & Freudenthal Institute. (Eds.). (1997–1998). *Mathematics in context*. Chicago: Encyclopaedia Britannica.

Romberg, T. (1997). *Mathematics in context*: Impact on teachers. In B. Nelson & E. Fennema (Eds.), *Mathematics teachers in transition* (pp. 357–380). Mahwah, NJ: Lawrence Erlbaum Associates.

Romberg, T., & Shafer, M. (1995). Results of assessment. Unpublished manuscript, National Center for Research in Mathematical Sciences Education, University of Wisconsin–Madison.

Roodhardt, A., Kindt, M., Burrill, G., & Spence, M. S. (1997). Patterns and symbols. In National Center for Research in Mathematical Sciences Education & Freudenthal Institute (Eds.), *Mathematics in context*. Chicago: Encyclopædia Britannica.

Roodhardt, A., Kindt, M., Pligge, M. A., & Simon, A. N. (1998). Get the most out of it. In National Center for Research in Mathematical Sciences Education & Freudenthal Institute (Eds.), *Mathematics in context*. Chicago: Encyclopædia Britannica.

Roodhardt, A., Middleton, J. A., Burrill, G., & Simon, A. N. (1998). Decision making. In National Center for Research in Mathematical Sciences Education & Freudenthal Institute (Eds.), *Mathematics in context*. Chicago: Encyclopædia Britannica.

Roodhardt, A., Spence, M. S., Burrill, J., & Christiansen, P. (1998). Growth. In National Center for Research in Mathematical Sciences Education & Freudenthal Institute (Eds.), *Mathematics in context*. Chicago: Encyclopædia Britannica.

Streefland, L., Roodhardt, A., Simon, A. N., Burrill, G., & Middleton, J. A. (1997). Dry and wet numbers. In National Center for Research in Mathematical Sciences Education & Freudenthal Institute (Eds.), *Mathematics in context*. Chicago: Encyclopædia Britannica.

University of Pittsburgh & National Center on Education and the Economy. (Eds.). (1997). *New standards reference exam: Mathematics*. Orlando, FL: Harcourt Brace.

Wijers, M., Roodhardt, A., van Reeuwijk, M., Burrill, G., Cole, B. R., & Pligge, M. A. (1998). Building formulas. In National Center for Research in Mathematical Sciences Education & Freudenthal Institute (Eds.), *Mathematics in context*. Chicago: Encyclopædia Britannica.

ENDNOTE

1. In the original proposal, the study design included data collection over a 4-year period in order to follow a fifth-grade cohort of students as they studied *MiC* through eighth grade. As funded, however, the study was limited to a 3-year data-collection period. Three cohorts of students were studied: one beginning in Grade 5 and followed through Grade 7; one beginning in Grade 6 and followed through Grade 8; and one beginning in Grade 7 and followed through Grade 8 with limited data collection, specifically a survey about transition into high school in Grade 9.

11

Middle Grades MATH Thematics: The STEM Project

Rick Billstein
Jim Williamson
The University of Montana

Middle Grades MATH Thematics is a complete middle school (Grades 6–8) mathematics curriculum designed to implement the recommendations outlined in the National Council of Teachers of Mathematics (NCTM) *Standards* documents (1989, 1991, 1995). The *MATH Thematics* curriculum was developed by the *Six Through Eight Mathematics* (STEM) *Project*,[1] a National Science Foundation sponsored curriculum development project at The University of Montana. The goal of the curriculum is to help all students develop their abilities to

- reason logically;
- apply mathematics to real-life activities;
- communicate about and through mathematics;
- make connections among mathematical concepts and relate them to other content areas;
- use quantitative and spatial information and problem solving to make decisions; and
- become independent learners who are well prepared for the real world and future mathematics courses.

The *MATH Thematics* curriculum is published by McDougal Littell, a Houghton Mifflin Company (Billstein & Williamson, 1999).

THE CURRICULUM: CONTENT, INSTRUCTION, AND ASSESSMENT

Mathematics Content

The mathematics content was selected with the goal of involving students who have learned the basic number structure in a K–5 curriculum in doing mathematics that is new, interactive, meaningful, and interesting. The content is organized around two components: Content Strands and Unifying Concepts.

Content Strands

To ensure that the 3-year curriculum is broad and balanced at each grade level, learner outcomes are organized in the following strands: Number, Measurement, Geometry, Statistics, Probability, Algebra, and Discrete Mathematics. The content within each strand emphasizes problem solving, critical thinking, and reasoning over rote procedural drill. Overall, the curriculum decreases the emphasis on the review of elementary topics such as whole number computation, and it increases the emphasis on data analysis and statistics, proportional reasoning, algebra, geometry, and discrete mathematics.

Unifying Concepts

Four unifying concepts, Proportional Reasoning, Multiple Representations, Patterns and Generalizations, and Modeling, are used throughout the curriculum to help students develop mathematical concepts and make connections among mathematical ideas and between mathematics and the real world.

Proportional reasoning is the ability to express one number as a certain multiple of another. It provides the basis for understanding ratio, rate, percent, proportions, slope, similarity, scale, linear functions, and probability.

Exploring different representations of concepts helps students understand mathematical ideas by making connections among concepts and accommodating different learning styles. Multiple representations connect topics such as coordinate systems and functions, fraction–decimal–percent representations, and geometric representations of arithmetic concepts.

Identifying and describing numeric and geometric patterns and making, testing, and applying generalizations about the data gathered from problem situations are the tools students use to develop algorithms and construct mathematical meaning.

Modeling is the tool students use to connect mathematics to the real world. It is the process of taking a real-life problem, expressing it mathematically, finding a mathematical solution, and then interpreting the solution in the real-world context. Examples of problems that are modeled include decision making, population growth, time–motion problems, and games.

Organization and Instructional Approach

The mathematics content for each grade level of *MATH Thematics* is presented in eight thematic modules that develop mathematical ideas in relevant and meaningful contexts. The mathematics content of each module is integrated and includes cross-curricular connections to other content areas such as science, language arts, and social studies. The themes and primary mathematics content of the modules for each grade level are summarized in Table 11.1.

Each module is divided into four to six Sections, each requiring 1–3 days to complete. Every section begins with a Setting the Stage—a reading, game, visual display, or activity—designed to pique students' interest and create a context for learning the mathematics. The example in Fig. 11.1 contains a science connection.

Each section contains one to three Explorations in which students are actively involved in learning new mathematics. Each exploration may be completed by students working individually, in cooperative groups, or as a class. The activities in the explorations range from guided discovery to open-ended investigations. Many involve the use of concrete, hands-on materials. In an exploration, students investigate a question or problem by doing one or more of the following:

- collecting, generating, researching, and presenting data;
- using concrete or visual models;
- applying problem-solving strategies;
- looking for patterns and relations;
- exploring alternative methods and solutions;
- making and testing conjectures;
- using number sense; and
- applying prior knowledge.

An exploration from the sixth-grade materials that illustrates how students construct their own algorithm for integer addition is shown in Fig. 11.2. The Setting the Stage in Fig. 11.1 introduces this activity.

TABLE 11.1
MATH Thematics: Module Themes and Content

Grade 6	Grade 7	Grade 8
Tools for Success Patterns and Sequences; Lines, Angles, and Triangles; Problem Solving; Estimation; Mental Math	*Making Choices* Data Displays; Sequences; Exponents; Probability; Problem Solving; Evaluating Expressions	*Amazing Feats, Facts, and Fictions* Problem Solving; Data Displays; Fitted Lines; Perimeter; Circumference; Area; Volume; Equations
Patterns and Designs Polygons; Transformations; Symmetry; Fractions and Mixed Numbers; Decimal Addition and Subtraction	*Search and Rescue* Angles; Integers; Coordinate Graphing; Functions; Addition and Subtraction Equations	*At the Mall* Proportions; Percents; Probability; Operations with Integers and Fractions; Inequalities; Data Displays
Statistical Safari Fractions; Percents; Data Displays; Mean, Median, and Mode; Dividing Decimals; Mental Math; Metric Measurement	*A Universal Language* Number Theory; Fractions and Mixed Numbers; Tree Diagrams; Probability; Decimals; Exponents; Equations; Metric Length	*The Mystery of Blacktail Canyon* Measurement; Equations, Graphs, and Slope; Similar Figures; Constructions; Scientific Notation
Mind Games Probability; Number Theory; Fraction and Decimal Multiplication; Equations and Graphs	*The Art of Motion* Circumference; Similarity; Transformations; Fraction, Decimal, and Integer Operations; Equations	*Patterns and Discoveries* Fractals; Classifying Quadrilaterals; Rotations; Pythagorean Theorem; Geometric Probabilities
Creating Things Customary Measurement; Operations with Fractions and Mixed Numbers	*Recreation* Ratio and Proportion; Data Displays; Percent; Probability	*Inventions* Surface Area and Volume; Slope; Equations of Lines; Exponents; Permutations; Combinations; Probability
Comparisons and Predictions Ratios; Rates; Proportions; Percents; Similarity; Tree Diagrams and Probability	*Flights of Fancy* Inequalities; Probability; Surface Area and Volume; Circles; Similarity; Parallel Lines; Metric Measurement	*Architects and Engineers* Constructions; Surface Area and Volume; Parallel Lines and Transversals; Inequalities; Similarity
Wonders of the World Area; Space Figures; Nets; Circles and Cylinders; Temperature; Integers; Coordinate Graphs	*Health and Fitness* Cylinders; Percent; Customary Capacity; Circle Graphs; Quadrilaterals	*Visualizing Change* Graphs; Functions; Linear Equations; Exponential Change; Quadratic Change; Transformations
Our Environment Integer Operations; Percent; Probability; Misleading Graphs and Averages; Scientific Notation	*Heart of the City* Volume; Permutations; Combinations; Spatial Visualization; Tessellations	*Making an Impact* Collecting Data; Choosing and Making Data Displays; Misleading Graphs

Section 1 Adding and Subtracting Integers

IN THIS SECTION

EXPLORATION 1
• Adding Integers

EXPLORATION 2
• Subtracting Integers

---•Setting the Stage

Lightning is caused by the movement of electrical charges within a cloud, between two clouds, or between a cloud and the ground.

You may think it is almost impossible to be hit by lightning, but Virginia park ranger Ray Sullivan would surely disagree. Ray was struck by lightning seven different times! The lightning knocked him out, burned off his hair, damaged his hearing, tore off a toenail, threw him in the air, melted his watch, and burned his clothing. Amazingly, Ray survived all seven lightning strikes.

A lightning bolt typically involves over 100,000,000 volts and can have enough power to light up all of New York City!

Think About It

1 Shuffling your feet on a carpet can produce up to a hundred thousand volts—enough to give you quite a shock. About how many times as many volts are there when lightning strikes?

2 **Estimation** Lightning strikes the United States about 40 million times each year. On average, about how often does it strike the United States each day?

▶ Lightning is one of nature's most powerful forces. In this module you'll learn about how the power of nature affects people and how people affect nature.

FIG. 11.1. Setting the Stage (Sixth Grade Module, Our Environment). *Note.* From *Math Thematics, Book 1* (p. 526), by R. Billstein and J. Williamson, 1999, Evanston, IL: McDougal Littell. Copyright 1999 by McDougal Littell. Reprinted with permission.

Exploration 1

Adding
+ Integers

GOAL

LEARN HOW TO...
• add integers

AS YOU...
• play the game
  Thunderbolt!

KEY TERM
• opposites

SET UP *Work with a partner. You will need:* • *Labsheet 1A*
• *12 beans, each marked with a "+" on one side and a "–"
on the other side* • *paper cup* • *2 game pieces*

▶ **Like other sparks of static electricity, lightning gets its power from
the difference in the electrical charges of two objects. You will
simulate the changing charges in a cloud by playing the game
Thunderbolt! When the difference in charges is 10 or more—Zap!**

3 **Use Labsheet 1A.** Follow the directions
on the labsheet to play *Thunderbolt!*
Play the game two times.

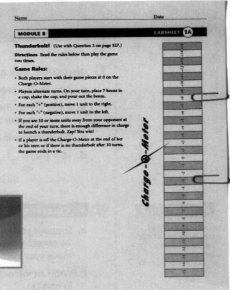

4 **a.** Did you find a way to quickly
determine where to place your game
piece after a bean toss? Explain.

b. At the end of a turn, can your game
piece ever be an even number of units
away from where it was at the start of
your turn? Why?

c. At the end of a turn, can your game
piece ever be in the same place it was
when you started the turn? Why?

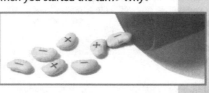

5 **a.** If you played *Thunderbolt!* with only six
beans, what moves would be possible?

b. Would playing with only six beans change your answers
to Questions 4(b) and 4(c)? Explain.

FIG. 11.2. An exploration from the section introduced in
Fig. 11.1 (Our Environment). *Note.* From *Math Thematics, Book 1*
(pp. 527–529), by R. Billstein and J. Williamson, 1999, Evanston,
IL: McDougal Littell. Copyright 1999 by McDougal Littell. Reprinted
with permission.

▶ One strategy for quickly finding how far to move your game piece is to pair positive beans with negative beans. This strategy can also be used to model addition of integers.

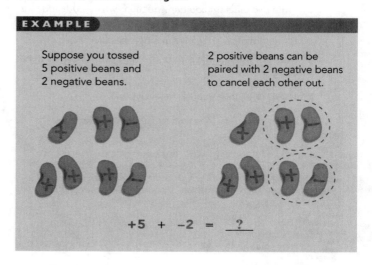

EXAMPLE

Suppose you tossed 5 positive beans and 2 negative beans.

2 positive beans can be paired with 2 negative beans to cancel each other out.

+5 + −2 = __?__

6 Discussion Look at the addition in the Example.

a. Why do the paired beans cancel each other out?

b. If you tossed the combination of beans shown, how far would you move your game piece and in what direction?

c. What integer is represented by the combination of beans?

d. +5 + (−2) = __?__

 To avoid confusion a negative integer can be shown in parentheses.

 QUESTION 7

...checks that you can represent integer addition using a bean model.

7 ✔ CHECKPOINT

a. Suppose you had 24 beans in your cup and you tossed 14 negative beans and 10 positive beans. How would you move your game piece?

b. Write an integer addition equation for the combination of beans in part (a).

8 Use a bean model to find each sum.

a. +1 + (−5)   **b.** +6 + (−4)   **c.** +3 + (−3)   **d.** −5 + (−2)

FIG. 11.2. (Continued)

Use beans to help answer Questions 9–11.

9 **Try This As a Class**

  a. Write two different addition equations where both addends (the numbers that are added) are negative.

  b. Is the sum of two negative numbers positive or negative?

  c. How can you find the sum of two negative numbers without using beans?

10 Write two different examples for each case.

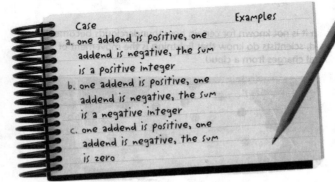

```
                                    Examples
    Case
    a. one addend is positive, one
       addend is negative, the sum
       is a positive integer
    b. one addend is positive, one
       addend is negative, the sum
       is a negative integer
    c. one addend is positive, one
       addend is negative, the sum
       is zero
```

11 **Discussion** When will the sum of a positive and a negative integer be positive? negative? equal to 0?

12 How can you find the sum of a positive and a negative integer without using beans?

13 **Try This as a Class** The numbers you used to answer Question 10(c) are *opposites*. What do think it means for two numbers to be **opposites**?

▶ **It is not necessary to label positive integers with a "+" sign. For example, +3 is the same as 3.**

14 ✔ **CHECKPOINT** Find each sum without using beans.

  a. −17 + 25   **b.** 13 + (−7)   **c.** −36 + (−9)

  d. −11 + 11   **e.** −24 + 19   **f.** 12 + (−17)

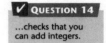

✔ **QUESTION 14**

...checks that you can add integers.

HOMEWORK EXERCISES ▶ See Exs. 1–21 on pp. 534–535.

FIG. 11.2. (Continued)

Following the explorations, each section contains a Key Concepts page. This page provides a summary of the mathematics content developed in the section, gives examples to illustrate the content, highlights the most important content, and gives references to the applicable pages in the explorations.

Each section concludes with a set of Practice and Application Exercises that range from skill level to application and from single answer to open ended. They include a Reflecting on the Section question that requires students to summarize and extend the ideas in the section; Spiral Review questions provide ongoing practice to maintain previously acquired knowledge and skills and bring them to long-term memory.

The instructional approach in *MATH Thematics* is designed to involve students in doing mathematics. Throughout the program, students are actively engaged in the following activities: investigating, discovering, and applying mathematics; using concrete materials to explore mathematical properties and relationships; working cooperatively; communicating their ideas orally and in writing; using technological tools when appropriate; and integrating mathematical strands to solve real-life problems.

The *STEM* vision is that middle school should be a time when students are actively involved in doing mathematics that is new and meaningful, not just a period of review. As a result, the *MATH Thematics* materials portray a different view of mathematics and mathematics learning than traditional textbooks. A sixth-grade *STEM* student from Chicago described the curriculum in the following way:

> Mainly, the STEM program asks one question, why? Why does it work? Why does it do that? In regular math, they tell you how to do it, what to do, and that's it. They don't explain to you why it works. The STEM program is a whole new approach to math. It shows kids that math does not have to be boring and not fun. It can be interesting, informative and fun.

Assessment

The *MATH Thematics* curriculum includes a comprehensive assessment package that is designed to be an integral part of the instructional process, rather than an add-on to it. Not only is assessment information drawn from instructional tasks, but the assessment tools themselves help students master concepts and develop skills.

Purposes of Assessment

The *MATH Thematics* assessment package serves four major purposes: monitoring student progress in problem solving, reasoning, and communication; assessing student proficiency in content areas; helping teachers make instructional decisions; and documenting student progress for students, parents, and teachers.

Assessment Tools

During the prepilot of the *STEM* sixth-grade materials, it became apparent that teachers needed guidance on how and when to interact with students. To accomplish this, Checkpoints, Discussion Questions, and Try This As A Class exercises were included in the materials.

Checkpoints are questions or problems that are used by the teacher to check understanding of a concept or skill before students continue with the exploration. Checkpoints appear after students have explored a concept and when some level of mastery is expected. Discussion questions enable students to check their understanding of a concept by sharing or generating ideas within their group or as a class. Try This As A Class questions appear at points where direct instruction is needed to summarize key ideas or to bring closure to a line of inquiry. They are similar to Discussion questions, except that the teacher directs the discussion or activity and guides the learning. Examples of Checkpoints, Discussion Questions, and Try This As A Class exercises can be seen in the exploration in Fig. 11.2.

Reflecting on the Section questions provide an opportunity for students to look back on the whole section and refine, describe, summarize, and extend the mathematical ideas they have explored. A reflecting exercise may take the form of a Discussion, Research, Oral Report, Journal, or Visual Thinking question. The Reflecting on the Section question in Fig. 11.3 is from the section containing the Setting the Stage and the Exploration shown in Fig. 11.1 and 11.2.

Each module includes a Module Project, which students typically work on in groups. The project provides a focused opportunity for students to apply the mathematics being developed in the module to a real-world situation, such as designing a pop-up greeting card, preparing an investigative report, designing a model town, planning and carrying out a search for a missing pilot, and creating a world travel poster. Students work on the project throughout the module as part of their homework and write a report or do a presentation of the results at the end of the module.

In contrast, Extended Explorations (E^2) are typically open-ended or open-response problems that students complete independently, or occasionally in small groups, outside of class. Each module contains one E^2. E^2s apply a variety of mathematical concepts, may be solved in different ways, and usually take 1–2 weeks to complete. Solutions to E^2s are assessed by using a multidimensional generalized assessment rubric. A sixth-grade student from Massachusetts commented on the E^2s as follows: "The E^2s are

Oral Report

Exercise 44 checks that you understand integer addition and subtraction.

Reflecting on the Section

Be prepared to report on the following topic in class.

44. Explain how each situation could occur. You may want to draw a model for an example of each situation.

   a. adding an integer to a number and getting a sum that is less than the original number

   b. subtracting an integer from a number and getting a difference that is greater than the original number.

 From Module 8, Our Environment, Page 536

FIG. 11.3. A Reflecting on the Section question from the section represented in Figs. 11.1 and 11.2 (Our Environment). *Note.* From *Math Thematics, Book 1* (p. 536), by R. Billstein and J. Williamson, 1999, Evanston, IL: McDougal Littell. Copyright 1999 by McDougal Littell. Reprinted with permission.

good for your mind. It makes you work hard for the answer but can be fun learning." A sixth-grade student from Chicago reported, "I have always had problem solving, but not the way you teach it. All the other teachers only care for the answer. But you only care for the process of getting the answer." An example of an Extended Exploration is given in Fig. 11.4.

Portfolios provide comprehensive documentation of students' progress in, attitude toward, and understanding of mathematics over a period of time. A portfolio is a collection of representative samples of a student's work. It may include assignments, answers to Reflecting exercises, solutions to E^2s (to document growth in problem solving, reasoning, and communication), and Module Projects (to demonstrate understanding of mathematical concepts and the ability to apply them).

Assessment Scales

Assessment scales are a unique feature of the *MATH Thematics* curriculum. The scales help students answer the question, "How can I improve my problem solving, reasoning, and communication skills?" Combined, they provide a generalized rubric that defines the dimensions of mathematical investigation. The scales are applied to open-ended questions, projects, reflecting exercises, and *especially* Extended Explorations. Students are encouraged to write their solutions to these items using appropriate mathematical language and representations to communicate how they solved the problem, the decisions they made as they solved it, and any connections they made.

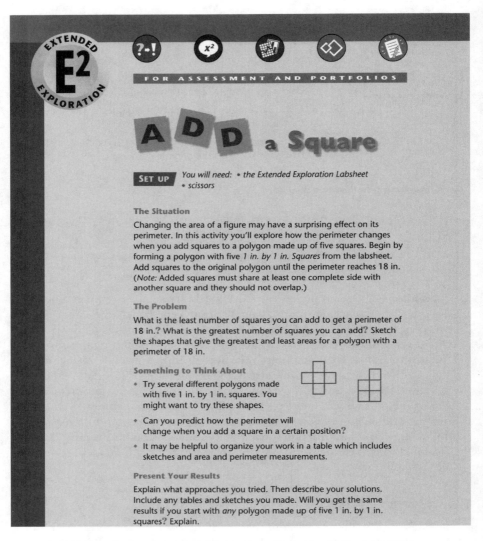

ADD a Square

SET UP *You will need: • the Extended Exploration Labsheet • scissors*

The Situation

Changing the area of a figure may have a surprising effect on its perimeter. In this activity you'll explore how the perimeter changes when you add squares to a polygon made up of five squares. Begin by forming a polygon with five *1 in. by 1 in. Squares* from the labsheet. Add squares to the original polygon until the perimeter reaches 18 in. (*Note:* Added squares must share at least one complete side with another square and they should not overlap.)

The Problem

What is the least number of squares you can add to get a perimeter of 18 in.? What is the greatest number of squares you can add? Sketch the shapes that give the greatest and least areas for a polygon with a perimeter of 18 in.

Something to Think About

• Try several different polygons made with five 1 in. by 1 in. squares. You might want to try these shapes.

• Can you predict how the perimeter will change when you add a square in a certain position?

• It may be helpful to organize your work in a table which includes sketches and area and perimeter measurements.

Present Your Results

Explain what approaches you tried. Then describe your solutions. Include any tables and sketches you made. Will you get the same results if you start with *any* polygon made up of five 1 in. by 1 in. squares? Explain.

FIG. 11.4. An Extended Exploration (Sixth Grade Module, Wonders of the World). *Note.* From *Math Thematics, Book 1* (p. 466), by R. Billstein and J. Williamson, 1999, Evanston, IL: McDougal Littell. Copyright 1999 by McDougal Littell. Reprinted with permission.

Their solutions are assessed using five scales: Problem Solving, Mathematical Language, Representations, Connections, and Presentation.

One key to raising student performance is to actively involve the students in assessing their own work, such as through use of Student Self-Assessment Scales (see Fig. 11.5). Student self-assessment has not been a part of the traditional curriculum, and yet it is an important part of student learning. As students become familiar with the scales, they understand what they need to do to improve their problem solving, reasoning, and communication skills. A student in Vermont had this reaction to using assessment scales: "I know what is expected of my work and it makes me stride [sic] harder to do better. I like it better than any other grading system I ever had. I think it is easier to get the grade you want because you have to work harder."

Teachers assess students' work by using the same scales written from a teacher's point of view. The assessment scales allow the teacher to recognize a student's strengths and help the student focus on areas where growth is needed. The combination of student and teacher assessment provides important feedback to help students improve.

EVIDENCE OF STUDENT ACHIEVEMENT

Since *Middle Grades MATH Thematics,* the commercial version of the *STEM Project* curriculum, only became available in April 1998, research regarding its impact is limited. The research reported here is based on the field-test versions of the *STEM* curriculum materials. Changes were made in the commercial version to enhance the materials and address any problems identified in the field tests.

Evidence from External Sources

Evidence from three external sources is reported in this paper: research conducted at the University of Missouri—Columbia; research conducted as part of a high school study; and research conducted by a school district.

Research Conducted in Missouri on Middle School Curricula

Researchers at the University of Missouri—Columbia (Lapan, Reys, Barnes, & Reys, 1998) compared the mathematics achievement of two groups of students using *Standards*-based curricula (one using the *STEM* curriculum and one using the *Connected Mathematics Project* curriculum) and a control group using a mathematics curriculum with a 1993 copyright that the

FIG. 11.5. The Student Self-Assessment Scales. *Note.* From *Math Thematics, Book 1* (p. 21), by R. Billstein and J. Williamson, 1999, Evanston, IL: McDougal Littell. Copyright 1999 by McDougal Littell. Reprinted with permission.

publisher said was "based on the NCTM *Standards.*" The study examined the results of a yearlong implementation of the *Standards*-based curricula and involved 255 sixth-grade students. Only the results comparing students in the *STEM* and control groups are reported here.

The *STEM* students were from a K–12 school district of approximately 5,000 students in a middle-class suburban community within a large midwestern city. After a year review of curriculum materials, teachers in the two middle schools in the district had selected *STEM* for use in sixth grade during the 1996–1997 school year. The control group was from a K–12 school district of approximately 14,000 students in an upper-middle-class midsized university town with a strong academic program. Their text was the sixth grade text from the series used in Grades 3–6.

Several different measures of mathematics achievement and problem solving were used in the study. Fifth-grade mathematics scores on the Missouri Mastery and Achievement Tests (MMAT) were used to check for preexisting mathematics achievement differences among the treatment and control groups. The mathematics portion of this battery of tests measures achievement in number concepts, geometry and measurement, and interpretation and problem solving. As part of a state-mandated testing program, sixth graders in the district using the *STEM* curriculum took the mathematics subtest of the Stanford Achievement Test (SAT) and students in the control group took the mathematics subtest of the California Achievement Test (CAT). According to the test developers, the SAT assesses achievement with number systems, theory, and relationships, prealgebra, probability, patterns and functions, statistics, geometry, measurement, estimation, and problem-solving strategies. As indicated in Lapan et al., the SAT and CAT are highly correlated, with $r = 0.85$ at the sixth grade. A linear transformation was used to convert CAT scores on the mathematics subtest to SAT scores for use in statistical tests. Finally, the SAT Open-Ended Mathematics Problem Solving Test (MPST), a standardized measure of mathematics problem solving, was used to assess problem-solving ability. This test contains nine problems, with problems covering three content areas (Number Concepts, Patterns and Relationships, and Concepts of Shape and Space) and three process areas (Problem Solving, Reasoning, and Communication). Items are open ended, requiring students to write solutions and support answers with additional information. Scoring was completed by the Psychological Corporation with trained raters. On each subscale, each student is given a single score (a 0, 1, 2, or 3).

Table 11.2 contains the means and standard deviations on the achievement tests for the *STEM* and the control students. There are no statistically significant differences between groups with respect to measures of traditional mathematics achievement (SAT; $t = -1.420$, $p < .158$) or in

TABLE 11.2
Means and Standard Deviations on Mathematics Achievement Tests:
STEM and Control Students

Test Measure	STEM (n = 115)		Control (n = 46)	
	Mean	SD	Mean	SD
MMAT	59.1	29.3	62.7	26.1
SAT	56.3	28.2	63.0[a]	23.9
MPST	59.8	18.9	53.4	18.4

Note. Table is based on results reported in Lapan et al. (1998).
[a]SAT scores for the control group result from a linear transformation applied to CAT scores.

mathematics problem solving ($t = 1.9566$, $p < .052$).[2] Lapan et al. note that performance of *STEM* and control groups differed on four subtests of the MPST: Problem Solving, Communication, Patterns, and Shapes and Space. For example, on the Problem Solving subscale, 25% of the control group scored 0 compared with 11% of the *STEM* group. In contrast, 15% of the control group and 33% of the *STEM* group earned the highest score possible (3). Lapan et al. conclude that "*STEM* students were both more likely to at least earn partial credit for each subscale and to excel at the highest level of achievement" (1998, p. 30).

Research on Middle School Curricula Conducted as Part of a High School Study

Researchers at the University of Iowa (Schoen, 1997) are conducting a longitudinal study of the impact of *Standards*-based curricula in three schools: a rural midwestern school, a rural western school, and a suburban midwestern school. As part of the study, the Ability to Do Quantitative Thinking test, the mathematics subtest of the Iowa Tests of Educational Development, was administered to ninth graders in the schools in September 1993 and again in September 1997, but not in the intervening years. The students tested in 1993 had used a traditional curriculum in Grades 6–8, and those tested in 1997 had used one of the new *Standards*-based middle school curricula in those three grades. The *STEM* curriculum was only used in the rural western school. In 1993, the mean for ninth graders in this school was at the 44th national percentile for school means. In 1997, after the *STEM* field-test materials were used for 3 years, the mean was at the 89th percentile for school means. As one of the researchers (H. L. Schoen, personal communication, September 16, 1998) expressed it, "Other factors might be contributing to this improvement, but surely *STEM* is one important factor."

Research Conducted by School Districts

Schools involved in field-testing the *STEM* materials were not asked to supply results on district- or state-mandated standardized tests. However, some schools did, and the results document not only the impact of the *STEM* curriculum on students' mathematics achievement but also the spin-off effect in other content areas. The following is typical of the results reported.

A field-test site in a middle-class suburban Minnesota community had used the *STEM* curriculum with its seventh-grade students for 4 years. The test site was one of two middle schools in the district and served the lower socioeconomic population of the two schools, with 26% of the school's students receiving free or reduced-price lunches. A traditional mathematics curriculum was used with all sixth-grade students in the district as well as with the seventh-grade students in the non-*STEM* school. The Iowa Test of Basic Skills (ITBS) is administered to all students in the district in early October of their sixth- and eighth-grade school years. The district reported the following results for students who were in the *STEM* program during the 1996–1997 academic year; no specific data for the non-*STEM* group were provided by the district.

1. The *STEM* students scored 12% higher in mathematics than the non-*STEM* group in the other school.
2. The same group scored 18% higher in reading than the non-*STEM* group, which seems to indicate that the emphasis on communication in the *STEM* curriculum has a positive impact in other content areas.

The positive impact of the *STEM* curriculum also seems evident when the change in mathematics achievement, language achievement, and the national percentile distributions of the ITBS scores of students at the Minnesota field-test site are examined. Results are shown in Table 11.3.

The increase in the percent of students scoring in the 51st to 75th and 76th to 99th percentiles in mathematics, and the corresponding decline in the percent scoring in the 1st to 25th and 26th to 50th percentiles, seems to show that the *STEM* curriculum had a positive effect on the mathematics achievement of most of the students who used it. The corresponding change in the distribution of the language arts scores of these students suggests that the use of the *STEM* curriculum may also have had a positive spin-off effect on achievement in that content area. However, a more detailed study comparing these results with historic data from the district and isolating and controlling other variables is needed to verify these impressions.

TABLE 11.3
Mathematics Achievement, Language Achievement, and Percentile
Distributions of ITBS Scores at the Minnesota *STEM* Field-Test Site

	ITBS Math. Achievement		*ITBS Lang. Achievement*	
	6th Grade (1995–1996)	8th Grade (1997–1998)	6th Grade (1995–1996)	8th Grade (1997–1998)
	Grade Equivalents			
Mean G. E.	7.2	10.6	6.8	9.6
Median G. E.	7	11	6.4	9.4
Percentile Range	Distribution of Scores			
1st–25th	15%	7%	23%	14%
26th–50th	25%	14%	26%	23%
51st–75th	27%	32%	27%	29%
76th–99th	33%	47%	24%	34%

Evidence from Internal Sources

During its development, the *STEM* curriculum underwent extensive field testing. Over a 5-year period, 250 teachers in 25 states used the curriculum with approximately 35,000 students. The field-test schools were chosen by Research Communications Limited (1994, 1995, 1996, 1997), the project's outside evaluator, to assess the effectiveness of the *STEM* materials in different types of schools and in a variety of classroom settings throughout the country. The information provided by the evaluator and by the teachers and students involved in the prepilots and field tests was used to revise, edit, and rewrite the materials prior to commercial publication.

At the end of each year of the field test, a criterion referenced test (CRT), developed by Dr. James Schultz from Ohio State University and the *STEM Project* staff, was administered to *STEM* students and non-*STEM* (control group) students. The CRTs assessed student achievement on the content-specific learner outcomes specified in the project curriculum. Each outcome was related to one of the NCTM Curriculum *Standards* for Grades 5–8.

The *STEM* sixth-grade CRT measured 40 learner outcomes. The items measuring the outcomes were divided between two forms: A and B. Each form consisted of approximately 70 short answer, open-response items that assessed 20 of the learner outcomes. In addition, each form included one essay question designed to measure students' abilities to communicate with and about mathematics, do arithmetic, and solve problems. Testing was completed in two class periods. Both forms of the test were used in each class tested, and they were randomly distributed within classes.

The CRT was administered in 31 of the 95 classes participating in the *STEM* sixth-grade field test, resulting in tests for 720 *STEM* students. The

STEM sample was chosen from classes at random, to represent the school size, geographic area, and student ability levels of the total sixth-grade *STEM* field-test population. Fifteen classes of students who had not used the *STEM* curriculum were chosen to serve as a control group. Although no pretest was given, the control group classes were chosen to match the *STEM* CRT classes as closely as possible in terms of geographic location, type of area, and student ability level. Twelve of the 15 tested classes were from the same school as a *STEM* class; 320 non-*STEM* students participated in the testing.

Trained mathematics teachers under the direction of Dr. James Schultz, the test designer, graded all CRT tests in a central location. Each objective was tested by three to seven items. The criteria for judging student mastery of the objectives on the CRT were two items correct on those objectives measured by three test items (67%); three items correct on those objectives measured by four items (75%); and five correct on those objectives measured by seven items (71%). All scores were converted to a percent in order to normalize scores on open-ended responses and to allow for comparisons across objectives with different mastery criteria. The results on the sixth-grade CRT are shown in Table 11.4. The relatively low levels of mastery and the level of missing data caused by noncompletion suggest that the CRT was too long or too difficult for some students to complete within the time frame allowed.

Doing straightforward statistical tests results in significant differences on 24 of the 40 objectives, 18 favoring *STEM* and 6 favoring the control group. Because of multiple planned comparisons with the same sample, the Bonferonni correction was used to reduce the level of significance. With this correction, significant differences in performance between *STEM* and non-*STEM* students were found on percent reaching mastery for 11 of the 40 objectives, all in favor of the *STEM* students. Although the results of applying this correction may be seen as less favorable to the *STEM* students, they are more robust. The 11 objectives on which *STEM* students performed significantly better than non-*STEM* students measure performance on operations with whole numbers, fractions, decimals, and percents; describing rules for sequences; recognizing geometric transformations; and displaying and interpreting statistical graphs. Non-*STEM* students did not perform significantly better than *STEM* students on any objectives.

The seventh-grade CRT measured 42 learner outcomes. To limit the number of questions each student would answer, the items measuring the outcomes were divided among six tests. Forms A through D each consisted of 30 short answer, open-response items that assessed 10 of the learner outcomes; Forms F and G each included six open-response items designed to assess Mathematics as Problem-Solving, Mathematics as Communication, and Mathematics as Reasoning. Forms A, B, C, and D were randomly distributed within classes and completed in one class period; Forms F and G

TABLE 11.4

Percent of *STEM* and Control Students Achieving Mastery on the Sixth-Grade CRT

Objective	No. of CRT Items	STEM		Control		p
		n	% Mastery	n	% Mastery	
		Mathematics as Problem Solving				
Use problem-solving strategies to solve open-response problems	4	391	26	131	18	.072
		Number and Number Relationships				
Identify the fractional part of a region	4	393	37	133	24	.007
Convert fractions to equivalent fractions including fractions in lowest terms	3	323	59	186	72	.004
Identify decimal place value to ten thousandths and use explanded notation	4	391	35	130	25	.042
Order fractions and decimals	3	324	19	183	22	.463
Recognize and use positive integer exponents	3	300	33	177	39	.186
Order integers and find opposites of integers	3	358	47	114	18	6×10^{-8}*
Convert between fractions and mixed numbers	4	349	35	113	19	.0011*
Solve ratio problems by using proportional reasoning or developing ratio tables	3	280	13	173	15	.513
Convert among ratios, fractions, decimals, and percents	4	273	21	172	24	.463
Set up and solve proportions by using equivalent fractions and mental math	3	331	47	105	32	.008

Use percent to make comparisons and predictions	4	323	21	98	4	9×10^{-5}*
Number Systems and Number Theory						
Understand the concept of divisibility and its applications	3	383	36	116	16	6×10^{-5}*
Find common factors, common multiples, the GCF, and the LCM of a set of numbers and apply them in problem situations	7	309	13	176	21	.019
Determine if a given number is prime or composite	4	376	10	115	1	.0013*
Computation and Estimation						
Use order of operations	3	326	33	184	22	.006
Compute with decimals	4	378	23	127	9	4×10^{-4}*
Apply mental math and estimation techniques with whole numbers, fractions, and decimals	4	310	8	169	10	.461
Compute with fractions and mixed numbers	4	292	14	174	21	.043
Patterns and Functions						
Find subsequent terms of a sequence given initial terms	3	308	36	177	42	.208
Describe rules for simple numeric and shape sequences	3	369	48	115	31	.0017*
Algebra						
Describe situations with variables and mathematical expressions	3	303	37	176	50	.005

(Continued)

TABLE 11.4
(Continued)

Objective	No. of CRT Items	STEM		Control		p
		n	% Mastery	n	% Mastery	
Evaluate expressions by substituting values for variables	3	362	16	114	4	9×10^{-10}*
Plot data on a coordinate plane and use a coordinate graph to make predictions	3	344	7	105	4	.240
Statistics						
Display statistics using bar graphs, line plots, and stem-and-leaf plots	3	384	52	127	31	2×10^{-5}*
Interpret bar graphs, line plots, and stem-and-leaf plots	3	321	42	183	23	1×10^{-5}*
Calculate and use statistical measures of average (mean, median, and mode) and the range for data	4	383	5	122	0	.012
Probability						
Recognize common vocabulary and understand concepts of probability	3	290	10	73	1	.017
Determine experimental and theoretical probabilities and use them to make predictions	5	274	8	67	3	.148
Geometry						
Identify and classify polygons	4	325	3	183	3	.826
Apply line symmetry	3	393	62	131	47	.003

Objective						p
Draw, measure, estimate, and classify angles	4	323	25	185	34	.031
Classify pairs of lines as parallel, perpendicular, or intersecting	3	317	21	184	31	.014
Identify similar and congruent figures and their corresponding parts	4	258	8	162	11	.307
Recognize and use transformations	3	199	51	151	24	3×10^{-7}*
Measurement						
Estimate length, area, capacity, weight, and mass by using an appropriate unit within the customary and metric systems	3	253	60	165	65	.326
Convert units of length, area, capacity, and mass within the customary and metric systems	3	317	18	84	20	.635
Find the perimeter and area of polygons and circles	5	219	2	160	0	.086
Find the volume and surface area of a rectangular prism	3	302	1	80	0	.371
Add and subtract times and determine elapsed time	3	213	15	154	12	.358

Note. N varies depending on the form of the test used and the number of students completing each item. A Bonferroni correction was used to adjust the significance level for multiple planned comparisons. Because each form of the test assessed 20 objectives, resulting in 20 comparisons, the significance level was set at $\alpha = .05/20 = .0025$. The Bonferroni correction results in significant differences on 11 objectives; the evaluation report by Research Communications Limited (1994) used a significance level of $\alpha = .05$, resulting in significant differences on 24 objectives. GCF = Greatest Common Factor; LCM = Least Common Multiple.

*Indicates differences significant at $\alpha < .0025$.

were also randomly distributed and administered during the second class period. The results were compared across the following groups of students.

1. Control Group Students: These students used a curriculum other than *STEM* in both Grades 6 and 7. The control group was initially larger, but several of the classes originally selected did not return completed CRTs.
2. *STEM* students: These students had used the *STEM* curriculum for at least 1 year. Roughly 66% of these students were taught seventh-grade mathematics with *STEM* but had been taught with a different curriculum in sixth grade; the other 34% used the *STEM* curriculum in both sixth and seventh grades.

Most of the items on the CRT were graded as *correct* (1 point) or *incorrect* (0 points). However, on some open-response items and on items for which more than one response was required, students could get more than 1 point. To allow for comparisons across objectives, all item scores were normalized. For example, an item with a possibility of 0, 1, 2, or 3 points was converted to scores of 0, 0.33, 0.66, or 1 point to be comparable with an item with a score of 0 or 1 point. All scores were then converted to a scale from 0 to 100. This normalization process made it possible to average scores across items measuring the same outcome and across outcomes related to the same NCTM *Standard*.

Table 11.5 summarizes the achievement on CRT items related to each NCTM *Standard*. Straightforward statistical tests show significant differences on 15 of the 42 objectives, 14 of which favor *STEM*. With the Bonferonni correction, *STEM* students showed significantly higher mastery levels on five measured outcomes:

1. Make and evaluate conjectures based on observations and accumulated data.
2. Recognize and use integer exponents.
3. Analyze, extend, and generalize patterns and sequences.
4. Analyze, interpret, and make inferences from data displayed in single- and double-bar graphs, stem-and-leaf plots, circle graphs, and box-and-whisker plots.
5. Convert between measures of length, area, mass, and capacity within the conventional system.

Control group students had a significantly higher level of mastery on one outcome.

1. Determine the areas of triangles and trapezoids.

TABLE 11.5

Percent of *STEM* and Control Students Achieving Mastery on the Seventh-Grade CRT

Objective	No. of CRT Items	STEM		Control		p
		n	% Mastery	n	% Mastery	
Mathematics as Problem Solving						
Select and apply appropriate problem-solving strategies to solve open-response problems						
Form F	3	269	9	75	4	.161
Form G	3	315	36	98	21	.008
Mathematics as Communication						
Construct, analyze, and make conjectures about networks and trees	3	139	25	40	15	.177
Mathematics as Reasoning						
Make and evaluate conjectures based on observations and accumulated data						
Form F	3	269	32	75	17	.013
Form G	3	315	20	98	5	$5 \times 10^{-4*}$
Number and Number Relationships						
Illustrate and apply relationships among ratios, fractions, decimals, and percents	3	151	35	42	31	.351
Apply number sense and estimation concepts with multiplication and division of fractions and decimals	3	139	20	40	13	.272
Apply the concept of inverse in mental math and estimation contexts	3	151	25	42	24	.857

(Continued)

TABLE 11.5
(Continued)

Objective	No. of CRT Items	STEM		Control		p
		n	% Mastery	n	% Mastery	
Set up and solve proportion problems	3	151	35	42	33	.832
Set up and solve percent problems	3	134	37	51	43	.468
Number Systems and Number Theory						
Apply primes, composites, LCM, GCF, and prime factorization	3	134	28	51	18	.135
Recognize and use integer exponents	3	151	82	43	51	3×10^{-5}*
Computation and Estimation						
Apply decimal place value and rounding and perform operations with decimals	3	139	28	40	25	.702
Add and subtract mixed numbers	3	151	31	43	21	.193
Multiply and divide fractions and mixed numbers	3	134	13	51	8	.353
Apply mental math techniques including applications of the distributive property	3	151	17	43	7	.097
Perform operations with integers	3	151	20	43	5	.018
Use order of operations including negative numbers and whole number exponents	3	139	12	40	3	.071
Patterns and Functions						
Generate tables, graphs, rules, expressions, and equations to model real-world situations	3	151	25	43	7	.010

	3					
Use permutations and combinations in counting situations (focus on finding permutations by listing and counting arguments rather than with a formula)	3	151	41	42	26	.079
Analyze, extend, and generalize patterns and sequences	3	151	34	43	9	.002*
Algebra						
Choose appropriate scales to graph linear functions and make predictions based on the graph	3	139	31	40	15	.046
Evaluate expressions for given values of the variable(s)	3	151	58	42	48	.218
Solve one- and two-step equations and check the solutions	3	134	36	51	22	.063
Demonstrate an understanding of slope	3	134	27	51	26	.850
Statistics						
Determine which average (mean, median, or mode) is appropriate	3	151	16	42	10	.300
Construct double-bar graphs, line plots, and stem-and-leaf plots to display data	3	151	43	43	26	.008
Analyze, interpret and make inferences from data displayed in single- and double-bar graphs, stem-and-leaf plots, circle graphs, and box-and-whisker plots	3	139	46	40	20	.003
Recognize and explain misleading uses of statistical displays	3	134	13	51	16	.594

(Continued)

TABLE 11.5
(Continued)

Objective	No. of CRT Items	STEM		Control		p
		n	% Mastery	n	% Mastery	
			Probability			
Recognize and use common vocabulary and understand the concepts of probability	3	151	22	42	14	.280
Determine experimental and theoretical probabilities of outcomes and events	3	139	58	40	38	.020
Make predictions based on probabilities	3	151	34	43	16	.027
			Geometry			
Identify and use the distinguishing properties of quadrilaterals	3	139	28	40	28	.945
Construct perpendicular lines and the bisectors of segments and angles by using a straightedge and compass	3	151	8	42	5	.481
Identify similar and congruent figures, identify their corresponding parts, and use proportionality to determine missing measures in them	3	151	38	43	23	.078
Reflect, translate, and rotate figures by using appropriate tools and methods including coordinates and apply the properties of the transformations	3	134	40	51	26	.061
Apply rotational and line symmetry	3	134	77	51	79	.820

			Measurement			
Determine the area of triangles and trapezoids	3	134	7	51	22	.004*
Determine the circumference and area of circles	3	151	32	42	29	.690
Demonstrate an understanding of surface area and determine the surface area of prisms	3	139	6	40	5	.855
Demonstrate an understanding of volume and determine the volume of prisms and cylinders	3	134	11	51	4	.126
Convert between measures of length, area, mass, and capacity within the metric system	3	151	17	42	17	.933
Convert between measures of length, area, mass, and capacity within the conventional system	3	139	31	40	8	.003*
Identify vertical, complementary, and supplementary angles and determine their measures	3	151	12	43	0	.017

Note. *N* varies depending on the form of the test used and the number of students completing each item. A Bonferroni correction was used to adjust the significance level for multiple planned comparisons. Because each form of the test assessed 10 objectives, resulting in 10 comparisons, the significance level was set at $\alpha = .05/10 = .005$. The Bonferroni correction results in significant differences on 6 objectives; the evaluation report prepared by Research Communications Limited (1995) used a significance level of $\alpha = .05$, resulting in significant differences on 18 objectives. GCF = Greatest Common Factor; LCM = Least Common Multiple.

*Indicates differences significant at $\alpha < .005$.

279

IMPACT ON STUDENT ATTITUDES

In addition to addressing mathematics curriculum objectives outlined by the NCTM, a major goal of the *STEM* curriculum was to help students develop a positive attitude toward mathematics. At the beginning of each year of the field test, *STEM* and control group students completed a 52-item survey to assess their initial attitudes toward mathematics in terms of motivation, perceptions of gender differences, problem-solving ability, future interest in studying mathematics, interactions with teachers, communication with and about mathematics, relevance of mathematics to careers and adulthood, and use of calculators. At the end of the year, students completed the same questionnaire to determine the affective areas in which *STEM* had an impact. Research Communications Limited, the outside evaluator, collected the attitude data, analyzed it, and reported the results.

On the attitude assessment, students rated their agreement with numerous statements on a five-point scale from strongly disagree to strongly agree. To prevent a positive skew in responses, approximately half of the statements were negatively phrased, with the scale reversed. Correlated t tests were conducted across pretest and posttest items to determine whether significant shifts in attitude had occurred over the year. Table 11.6 contains those statements for which *STEM* students demonstrated significant change in attitude.

TABLE 11.6
Mean Scores on Items on the Sixth-Grade Attitude Survey for Which *STEM*
Students Demonstrated a Significant Change in Attitude

Item	Pre	Post
I am usually comfortable in math class.	3.68	3.58
Math does not scare me at all.	3.54	3.72
I think I could handle more difficult mathematics.	3.07	2.96
There are different ways to solve most mathematics problems.	3.90	4.08
I am challenged by math problems I can't understand immediately.	3.72	3.93
Learning mathematics [does not involve] mostly memorizing.	2.91	3.17
It is important to know mathematics in order to get a good job.	4.29	4.43
I will use mathematics in many ways as an adult.	3.96	4.12
Most of mathematics has [a lot of] practical use on the job.	3.76	3.92
I feel comfortable using graphs, tables, drawings, and equations when I try to show others how I solved a math problem.	3.11	3.29
I would like to continue taking math courses all the way through high school.	3.85	4.06
Girls can do difficult math problems just as well as boys.	4.29	4.48
Mathematics helps one to think logically.	3.80	3.91

Note. $N = 1061$ students. Item ratings are based on a 5-point scale from strongly disagree (1) to strongly agree (5), with a 3 indicating a neutral response. Differences between pretest and posttest scores in the table are significant ($p \leq .05$). Brackets in the table indicate positive rephrasing of an originally negative statement that was recorded for analysis.

Statistically significant shifts were found in approximately one fourth of the items, indicating a strong level of measurable impact of the *STEM* curriculum after only 1 year. Positive shifts were most notable in student attitudes toward their problem-solving abilities, interest in mathematics, and the perception of the importance of mathematics for their future. Negative shifts were mainly with measures of student self-confidence and comfort level with using mathematics in the classroom.

Although this shift in positive attitudes toward mathematics was found among both girls and boys, there was evidence that *STEM* may have benefited girls by helping to close a "gap" in attitudes between girls and boys that was evident on the initial survey. Table 11.7 contains those statements for which there was a significant difference in attitude between boys and girls on either the pretest or posttest survey.

Research has shown that declines in positive attitudes toward mathematics are common among students in the middle school years. The attitude data presented here suggest that *STEM* can be a successful form of intervention in curbing the growth of negative attitudes toward mathematics.

Summary

Because *Middle Grades MATH Thematics*, the commercial version of *STEM*, has only been available since April 1998, little research has been done regarding its impact on students. However, the data that are available from the field tests of the materials are encouraging. They seem to indicate the following.

1. Students studying from the *STEM* curriculum do as well as students studying from more traditional curricula as measured by standardized tests of traditional content. *STEM* students perform better than comparison students on items measuring students' reasoning, communication, and mathematics problem-solving abilities.
2. Use of the curriculum has a positive impact on students' attitudes toward mathematics.
3. The curriculum is effective with all students.
4. There may be a spin-off effect that results in improved reading and language arts achievement.

Nevertheless, more thorough and detailed studies are necessary to verify these impressions.

Effective instructional materials are now available for students, but this is only the first step in the process of achieving change. Because *Standards*-based curricula such as *Middle Grades MATH Thematics* emphasize new mathematical content, new ways to help students learn this content, and new ways to assess students' knowledge and understanding, teachers need time, resources, and assistance to prepare them to use the curricula. If successful,

TABLE 11.7
Sixth-Grade Attitude Survey Items on Which There Were Significant
Gender Differences

	Pre		Post	
Item	Girls (n = 550)	Boys (n = 511)	Girls (n = 550)	Boys (n = 511)
General				
How interesting was the math class you took this past school year?	2.81	2.72	3.05*	2.90*
Career/Adulthood				
Most of mathematics has [a lot of] practical use on the job.	3.91*	3.60*	3.94	3.85
Motivation				
[When I try hard,] I [can] understand mathematics.	2.80*	3.30*	2.95	3.02
I [understand] how some people can spend so much time on math and seem to enjoy it.	3.36*	3.13*	3.30	3.15
I am [not] often discouraged with my mathematics school work.	2.79*	3.06*	2.78	2.93
I can get good grades in math.	3.07*	3.25*	3.19	3.08
Communication				
When I do math problems, I usually [do not] have problems with mathematical language and symbols.	3.80*	3.43*	3.75	3.58
Future Interest				
I would like to continue taking math courses all the way through high school.	3.95*	3.75*	4.13*	3.98*
Problem Solving/Challenge				
I am challenged by math problems I can't understand immediately.	3.84*	3.58*	3.99	3.87
I would rather work on a hard math problem by myself than have someone tell me the answer.	2.79*	3.22*	2.84	3.01
Learning mathematics [does not] involve] mostly memorizing.	3.02*	2.80*	3.21	3.12
Gender				
Girls can do difficult math problems just as well as boys.	4.43*	4.15*	4.59*	4.33*
Jobs that use mathematics are [not] better suited for men than for women.	4.25*	3.79*	4.32*	3.87*
Taking advanced math is [not] a waste of time for girls.	3.85*	3.63*	3.81*	3.59*

(Continued)

TABLE 11.7
(Continued)

	Pre		Post	
Item	Girls (n = 550)	Boys (n = 511)	Girls (n = 550)	Boys (n = 511)
Boys [do not] have more natural ability in mathematics than girls.	3.91*	3.31*	3.93*	3.43*
		Teacher Reaction		
My teachers [do not] think advanced math is a waste of time for me.	3.78	3.63	3.77*	3.62*
My math teachers have encouraged me to solve problems on my own.	3.40*	3.58*	3.49	3.49
		Daily Relevance		
Mathematics helps one to think logically.	3.67*	3.81*	3.70	3.77
Math is something that is used in everyday life.	4.07	4.01	4.12*	3.98*
		Calculators		
Using a calculator makes math more enjoyable.	3.42*	3.62*	3.45*	3.63*
Calculators help me understand math better.	3.52*	3.67*	3.51*	3.76*

Note. Brackets in the table indicate positive rephrasing of an originally negative statement that was recorded for analysis. The first question under General had four choices: 1, not at all interesting; 2, a little interesting; 3, somewhat interesting; 4, very interesting. Other items were answered by using a 5-point scale from strongly disagree (1) to strongly agree (5), with a 3 indicating a neutral response.
*Differences are significant ($p \leq .05$).

sustained implementation of *Standards*-based curricula and improved mathematics instruction are to be achieved, teacher preparation and professional development must accompany the new materials. Research is needed to determine the additional support teachers need in order to use these materials effectively for high levels of student achievement.

REFERENCES

Billstein, R., & Williamson, J. (1999). *Middle grades Math Thematics* (Books 1–3). Evanston, IL: McDougal Littell.

Denny, R., & Williamson, J. (1999). *Middle grades MATH Thematics professional development handbook* (Books 1–3). Evanston, IL: McDougal Littell.

Lapan, R. T., Reys, B. J., Barnes, D. E., & Reys, R. E. (1998). *Standards-based middle grade mathematics curricula: Impact on student achievement.* Unpublished manuscript, University of Missouri at Columbia.

National Council of Teachers of Mathematics. (1989). *Curriculum and evaluation standards for school mathematics.* Reston, VA: Author.

National Council of Teachers of Mathematics. (1991). *Professional standards for teaching mathematics.* Reston, VA: Author.

National Council of Teachers of Mathematics. (1995). *Assessment standards for school mathematics.* Reston, VA: Author.

Research Communications Limited. (1994, November). *An assessment of the sixth grade STEM curriculum* (Final Report). Dedham, MA: Author.

Research Communications Limited. (1995, October). *An evaluation of the STEM seventh grade modules* (Final Report). Dedham, MA: Author.

Research Communications Limited. (1996, October). *An evaluation of the STEM eighth grade modules* (Final Report). Dedham, MA: Author.

Research Communications Limited. (1997, January). *An evaluation of the STEM curriculum: Sixth, seventh, and eighth grade modules* (Summary). Dedham, MA: Author.

Schoen, H. L. (1997). *Core-Plus Mathematics Phase II longitudinal study brief status report.* Unpublished paper, University of Iowa, Iowa City.

ENDNOTES

1. *Middle Grades MATH Thematics* is based on the field-test versions of The *STEM Project* curriculum. The *STEM Project* was supported in part by the National Science Foundation under Grant ESI-9150114. Opinions expressed in this paper are those of the authors and not necessarily those of the National Science Foundation.

2. Because of large differences on the MMAT among the *CMP*, *STEM*, and control samples, Lapan et al. (1998) used an analysis of covariance to adjust posttest scores for initial pretest differences. However, the scores of the *STEM* and control samples did not differ significantly on the MMAT. Hence, in an examination of just the data from the *STEM* and control groups, an analysis of covariance is not used. Rather, in this chapter we use simple two-sample t tests to compare the scores on the posttests given in Table 11.2.

12

Keeping Mathematics Front and Center: Reaction to Middle-Grades Curriculum Projects Research

Michaele F. Chappell

Middle Tennessee State University

In years past, trends such as "too much skill and drill" or "algebra for all" have influenced mathematics education and have prompted debate about the middle-grades mathematics curriculum and how it is taught (e.g., see Mathematical Sciences Education Board, 2000). The projects featured in this section, *Connected Mathematics (CMP)*, *Mathematics in Context (MiC)*, and *Six Through Eight Mathematics* (now published as *MATH Thematics*), have developed curricula intended to foster significant mathematics learning for all middle-grades students. These programs are designed to support and extend the experiences encountered by students in elementary schools and to serve as a bridge between middle school mathematics and more formal and rigorous high school mathematics.

Because the curricula are relatively new, certain questions pertaining to their characteristics and their influence remain unanswered. For example, to what extent are these curricula similar to or different from each other? What are the strengths and possible shortcomings in their background research? More important, what impact do these curricula have on middle-grades students' mathematics learning? This chapter examines these questions, drawing on evidence provided in Chapters 9–11. Implications for teacher education and issues for future research are also considered.

COMMONALITIES AND DIFFERENCES
AMONG THE CURRICULA

Essential Commonalities

Vision and Purpose

All three programs seem to have a definite vision of a mathematically sound curriculum organized in a manner that students might find meaningful and enjoyable. The programs envision a middle school learning environment that highlights problem-based mathematics and varied forms of classroom discourse. The vision held by each project has strongly guided its program structure and follow-up evaluation.

Mathematics Content

Influenced largely by the National Council of Teachers of Mathematics (NCTM) *Standards* (1989), the content in all three curricula is very similar. Composed of strong, deeply connected mathematics, each program includes topics not typically featured in conventional middle school texts, such as transformational geometry and discrete mathematics (i.e., data analysis and probability). The content is organized in chunks of modules or units. Each curriculum assigns to these content modules somewhat catchy titles, such as Accentuate the Negative (*CMP*), Per Sense (*MiC*), or At the Mall (*MATH Thematics*). This feature seems carefully crafted with the intent to capture middle school students' attention and enable them to maintain interest and enthusiasm in the mathematics task at hand.

Additionally, the curricula approach the content through a variety of processes, such as multiple representations and modeling. Instructional and assessment strategies, as identified in the *Professional Teaching Standards* (NCTM, 1991) and the *Assessment Standards* (NCTM, 1995), are elicited as students conduct problem-based investigations and follow-up exercises. Each curriculum supports hands-on experiences, technology tools, applications and nonroutine problems, cooperative groups, mathematics discourse, and other techniques that scholarly literature generally has indicated, when used appropriately, are key characteristics of an effective middle school mathematics classroom (e.g., see Leutzinger, 1998; Owens, 1993).

"Real-Time" Dilemma

The developers of the curriculum projects allude to dilemmas encountered when curriculum research is conducted in real classrooms with real students and teachers. In each chapter, the authors cite issues that surfaced during curriculum evaluation, such as the recruitment of classroom volunteers for evaluation purposes, proper handling and distribution of test materials, concerns about overtesting, and implementing the curriculum as intended by the developers. In curriculum research, the reality is that participants can have different intents and agendas; "things" happen in schools and classrooms. Thus, even with the best planning and organization, pilot testing and field testing large-scale curriculum projects are difficult to conduct without road blocks arising in the process. Complications that surface are rarely easy to resolve, if at all. Nevertheless, the potential dilemmas should not deter individuals from developing curriculum and conducting evaluation efforts in schools. Well thought out, high-quality curriculum research is certainly possible and, in fact, is absolutely vital if we are to understand the extent to which curricula impact students' achievement in mathematics.

Essential Differences

Structure and Design

Differences among the three curricula are apparent in their structure and design. Whereas the *CMP* and *MATH Thematics* programs begin at Grade 6, the *MiC* program includes Grade 5. Also, the number of content modules or units differs slightly. The *CMP* program comprises eight modules each at three grade levels, yielding 24 modules altogether; similarly, the *MATH Thematics* curriculum contains 24 content modules for Grades 6–8; the *MiC* program is composed of 40 units—10 each at Grades 5–8. The individual modules are quite detailed; they are usually subdivided into multiple investigations containing, for example, story-problems, projects, application exercises, extensions, and reflection questions. These differences merely add uniqueness to each program and should not suggest that any one curriculum is superior to another.

Overarching Emphasis

Each curriculum program seems to have a special emphasis that distinguishes it from the others. The trade name of each curriculum reflects its overarching emphasis. For example, *CMP* emphasizes multifaceted connections. *MiC* maintains a focus on informal-to-formal progressions of different mathematical ideas with emphasis on the context in which these ideas are learned. *MATH Thematics* emphasizes unifying themes that thread the content together and aid in monitoring assessment by the student and teacher. Accenting the curriculum in this manner enables each program to actualize its vision and purpose.

In summary, the three curricula share some similarities, as they all aim to improve the teaching and learning of mathematics in the middle grades.

Although similar, they certainly are not carbon-copy versions of each other. Particular features unique to each curriculum—the structure, the emphasis, and especially the modules themselves—contribute to a degree of distinction in each program.

IMPACT ON STUDENT OUTCOMES

Conceptual Understanding

From the onset, each middle-grades project was committed to developing a comprehensive mathematics curriculum, featuring rich topics and connections not typically addressed in traditional middle school curricula. Throughout development and evaluation stages, students' conceptual understanding of mathematics was important. So how do middle school students fare in this conceptual understanding of mathematics? Both short- and long-term results from the evaluation research offer insights to this question.

Within the *CMP* chapter, for example, it is reported that the Balanced Assessment (BA) scores for sixth-, seventh-, and eighth-grade students who used *CMP* (for at least 1 year) increased significantly within 1 year from pretest to posttest. Although the comparison (non-*CMP*) students, who used commercially available texts, also improved during the year, their gains were not as substantial. Furthermore, the separate study on the proportional reasoning of seventh-grade students revealed that the performance of *CMP* students far surpassed that of non-*CMP* students on items involving rate, where more than half of the *CMP* group—and only around one quarter of non-*CMP* students—provided correct responses with correct explanations.

Students' conceptual understanding is also discussed in the *MATH Thematics* chapter, in which the authors share results of an external comparison study that solely involved sixth-grade students. The treatment group studied from the *STEM* curriculum over 1 year; the control group studied from a recent commercial text and was part of a school district with a strong academic program. Performance on standardized tests, including the multiple-choice Stanford Achievement Test (SAT) and the open-ended Mathematics Problem Solving Test (MPST), indicated no significant differences between the two groups. However, achievement differences, favoring the treatment group, were noted on four of six subtests of the MPST.

The longitudinal data of student performance are rather impressive. In the *CMP* chapter, authors report significant cumulative gains on the BA test by *CMP* students over non-*CMP* students in School R, a school using the *CMP* materials at Grades 6–8. Similarly, data displayed in the *MiC* chapter show superior performance by the eighth-grade students in Ames, Iowa who had studied from the *MiC* curriculum for 4 years in comparison to a national eighth-grade sample on the New Standards Reference Exam (NSRE). Their achievement is recognized not only in nonroutine problem solving but also in the area of mathematical skills.

Procedural Understanding

As noted in Chapter 1 of this volume, debates about school mathematics curricula raise questions about the need to learn the basics (e.g., facts, computational algorithms, definitions, properties). The evaluation research reported in Chapters 9–11 shows that while studying from curricula oriented toward problem solving, students indeed can develop their procedural understanding of mathematics. Evidence provided suggests both short-term and long-term benefits.

Results from a specially designed criterion referenced test (CRT), which included traditional objectives, show that sixth-grade students who used the *MATH Thematics* (*STEM*) curriculum for 1 year significantly outperformed control-group students on 11 of the 40 CRT objectives. The non-*STEM* sixth-grade students did not significantly outperform the *STEM* group on any of the CRT objectives. Similarly the seventh-grade students, including more than one third who had experienced the *STEM* program for 2 years, achieved a significantly greater mastery level on 12 of the 42 CRT objectives at this level. For only one objective did the non-*STEM* group significantly outperform the *STEM* group. These results occurred after a statistical correction was applied to make significance more difficult to obtain, thus giving more meaning to the differences. Hence, students using *Standards*-based curricula can learn the basics of mathematics as well as the problem solving.

Long-term evidence about students' procedural understanding of mathematics is discussed in both the *CMP* and *STEM* chapters in terms of grade-equivalent years. These data offer a new dimension to the notion of "being promoted from one grade to the next" in middle school. For example, the authors note that over 3 school years *CMP* students in School R gained 4.3 grade-equivalent years (with respect to the ITBS) compared to 1.5 grade-equivalent years for the non-*CMP* group. Similar findings from a field-test site are reported in the *MATH Thematics* chapter. Whereas the sixth-grade students at the site used a traditional mathematics curriculum, the *STEM* curriculum had been used with seventh-grade students for 4 years. ITBS scores show a mean gain of 3.4 grade-equivalent years from the beginning of Grade 6 to the beginning of Grade 8. The site provided no comparison data for the non-*STEM* group. The implication is that the growth over 2 middle school years (sixth and seventh) is attributed to the seventh-grade students' involvement with the *STEM* curriculum.

The *CMP* chapter also mentions the performance of Schools R's seventh-grade students on the Michigan Educational Assessment Program (MEAP). Over an 8-year period, the percent of students at School R in the lowest level decreased more rapidly, and the percent of students in the satisfactory level increased more rapidly than the statewide averages. Parallel to these results, the *MATH Thematics* field-test school site disclosed that, over 2 academic years, the seventh-grade *STEM* students decreased their rankings in the lower percentiles of the ITBS; simultaneously, they increased their rankings in the upper percentiles.

Lastly, *MiC* reports the ITBS percentile performance over a 5-year period of sixth-grade students in the Ames school district. The significant increase and consistent rank in computation after 1-year implementation of *MiC* as well as the overall percentile increase are impressive. In totality, these data indicate a longitudinal influence that these curricula can have on students' learning of mathematics skills related to computation, problem solving, and other basic ideas.

Other Benefits

Some findings hint at other benefits students may have gained from interacting with the middle-grades curricula. These hints are often presented as researchers' intuitions, but nevertheless they could be useful when the overall impact on student outcomes is considered. For instance, authors of the proportional reasoning study note that the *CMP* students demonstrated a better quality in writing their responses and better articulated their thinking than did the non-*CMP* students. As reported in the *MATH Thematics* chapter, district data on the field-test site revealed corresponding gains in ITBS grade-equivalent means and percentile distribution on the language subtests for the *STEM*-group seventh-grade students; the school district posited that the *STEM* curriculum affected the students' achievement in other content areas.

There is some hint that the curricula favor at-risk students or those who have learning disorders. In a cursory manner, the *MiC* chapter suggests such in its discussion of the case studies. Finally, the *MATH Thematics* curriculum found that its use had a positive impact on students' attitudes toward mathematics and especially may have benefited the attitudes of females.

Summary of Impact on Student Outcomes

Collectively, the evaluation results provide converging evidence that *Standards*-based curricula may positively affect middle school students' mathematics achievement, in both conceptual and procedural understanding.

One could argue that, given the design of each project, conceptual understanding should occur automatically. However, when any mathematics curriculum is implemented, there simply are no guarantees. Growth of any type, short or long term, is not automatic; careful planning and implementation are required to achieve it.

The short-term benefits outlined herein are commendable; however, the ultimate aim of these curricula is to generate more lasting, long-term advantages for middle school learners of mathematics. With respect to long-term benefits, the findings identified are convincing. They reveal that the curricula indeed can push students beyond the basics to more in-depth problem-oriented mathematical thinking without jeopardizing their learning in either area. This message seems especially critical given the current educational climate that impinges on how mathematics is taught and assessed in schools.

STRENGTHS AND SHORTCOMINGS OF THE EVALUATION RESEARCH

As with all major research endeavors, there exist certain strengths and shortcomings within the evaluation research presented by the curriculum projects. One strong aspect is the variety of the data sources. In total, the curriculum projects have drawn from over a dozen sources of evaluation data, both internal and external to the projects themselves. This point is highlighted, not just to focus on the quantity of sources, but to call attention to the immenseness of the curriculum research process. Many participants have been involved; as can best be determined from the data, the number of students participating in the research is at least 40,000 students in schools located throughout every geographic region in the country, including Puerto Rico. Furthermore, the research was conducted by various groups of individuals (e.g., curriculum developers, university researchers, and school district personnel). Although certain research methods are common (e.g., large-scale comparison studies involving field-test sites and longitudinal studies of standardized test performance), others are unique in design (e.g., a content-focused study on proportional reasoning, teacher case-studies, or a special classroom achievement model). Numerous measures are included, featuring national (e.g., BA, ITBS, MPST, NSRE and SAT), state (e.g., MEAP, MMAT), and specially designed (e.g., the CRT) instruments. Surely, behind this immense source of data are efforts, in terms of time and lessons learned, that cannot be seen or accurately measured by the instruments or by those who engaged in any phase of the research experience.

The authors of each curriculum recognize certain shortcomings in their own evaluation research. Therefore, my comments focus on broad concerns found in the data or evaluation process, pointing to some specific examples from the curriculum projects. For example, one shortcoming pertains to monitoring how the curriculum is actually implemented in the classrooms. In the chapters about *CMP* and *MiC*, authors raise the issue; but it seems particularly problematic in certain *MiC* sites in which teachers varied the implementation of the materials or supplemented assessment with traditional items. Perhaps other research methods are needed to capture what is actually happening in classrooms as the materials are being used. This suggests a need to understand why teachers might feel compelled to supplement their teaching with other curricula or with other types of assessments. Mathematically speaking, are there levels of maturation and sophistication on which a teacher must operate in order to "juggle" the merging of curricula without jeopardizing students' mathematics learning? Obviously, inappropriate implementation can jeopardize the integrity of the evaluation. Therefore, it behooves project developers to design methods that will help detect how the curricula are being implemented in classroom settings.

Another shortcoming pertains to the inconclusive or irrelevant evidence associated with some data sources. For example, in the chapter about *MATH Thematics*, too little information is provided about the middle school study affiliated with the larger high school study to make any conclusions about how the curricula affected these students. Moreover, in the *MiC* chapter there is a description of how the Dutch Realistic Mathematics Education research is used to frame the *MiC* curriculum; however, it is unclear how that research directly affects student achievement. Yet, this data source was included as evidence of student outcomes. Also, more information about the case studies is warranted to assess the benefits of the *MiC* curriculum to student outcomes.

Within the discussions of the evaluation research, it was difficult to ascertain the extent to which the curricula were good for *all* students. Exactly who is *all*? There is some indication from the reports that, for *CMP*, *all* includes poor students; for *MiC*, it includes at risk students or those with learning disorders; for *MATH Thematics*, it includes students of lower socioeconomic status. The authors fail to clarify explicitly how *all* learners benefit from the curricula. Additionally, in the *CMP* and *MiC* chapters, strong student outcomes were recorded from the efforts of a seemingly small school and a small eclectic school district. What then can schools situated in other locales (e.g., inner city or urban) take from these conclusions? Detailing student and school demographics helps to understand how representative field-test sites are and to what degree the findings may be generalized.

IMPLICATIONS FOR TEACHER EDUCATION

For this book, the curriculum projects were charged to focus primarily on student achievement. Therefore, their discussions on teacher education are limited. Nevertheless, the projects speak to the mathematics teacher education community because their respective programs elicit a need for innovative instructional strategies. As teachers participated in the various stages of evaluation research, it was necessary for them to engage in professional development activities. For example, teachers involved with the *CMP* evaluation attended summer workshops where they interacted with the curriculum as students themselves. Within the *MiC* evaluation, teachers seemed more involved in the research process by regularly completing different survey forms and by serving as the subjects under investigation in the case studies. Assuredly, inservice teachers will need to experience these types of professional development activities to maximize their fluency in teaching mathematics from these *Standards*-based curricula.

Major implications exist for the initial preparation of middle school mathematics teachers. Preservice teachers should compare *Standards*-based curricula with more traditional texts; they should explore the depth of the mathematics found in *Standards*-based curricula to extend their own understanding of mathematics. Moreover, in order to teach with these innovative curricula, they should experience the mathematics and instructional pedagogy in the same manner as suggested within the curricula.

Implementing these recommendations is problematic because middle school teachers' preparation is so varied. Some teachers are prepared initially as elementary teachers, usually with limited emphasis in several disciplines; others are prepared as secondary teachers with a specialty in mathematics. Still others are specifically prepared as middle school specialists and tend to be generalists in their fields. The content background for these different groups varies widely and, hence, teachers approach mathematics instruction by using these curricula in very different ways and with different levels of sophistication. Thus, ongoing dialogues between teacher educators and clinical teachers requiring thoughtful and systematic plans of action are imperative to equip beginning teachers with the skills to teach from innovative curricula such as those presented in this document.

Regardless of a teacher's experience, teaching from *Standards*-based curricula may require a different role than is typically expected of teachers in conventional classrooms. Teachers involved in the curriculum projects found themselves in this situation. The *CMP* teachers had to teach differently and overcome urges to just tell students what to do. Yet, there may be appropriate times to do just this when these curricula are used. In the *MiC* case studies, teachers grappled with what they perceived as novel ideas about their teaching practice and expectations; they labored over the different presentations of the content. Thus, in order to teach from *Standards*-based curricula, a teacher should have a willing and committed posture as well as a mathematics disposition that is open to change.

SUGGESTIONS FOR FUTURE RESEARCH

The authors of the curriculum chapters raise a number of suggestions for further research. I elaborate on recommendations that, perhaps, represent the intersection between issues raised in the curriculum reports and the current state of affairs of mathematics teaching and learning in middle schools. Hence, future research related to middle-grades curricula should aim to include more about the following ideas.

First, future research should include a substantive component on teacher preparation and development. Though a discussion of teacher preparation and development goes beyond the intent of the chapters, the three curriculum programs imply that the teacher is critical in ensuring that the curriculum is implemented as intended. Related issues might pertain to how much preparation a teacher needs to feel comfortable implementing *Standards*-based curricula or what array of activities comprises the teacher-development component. Fully understanding the teacher's role in curriculum implementation can broaden our perspectives of the impact of the teacher on student achievement. Moreover, given the level of sophistication of the mathematics contained in these curricula, it is imperative to understand the extent to which teachers know and learn mathematics in order to teach it well. Efforts along these lines have begun (e.g., see Mathematical Sciences Education Board, 2001); however, curriculum evaluation research can offer another perspective on this matter.

Second, future research should study the impact of policy-related school issues on curriculum evaluation. The critical shortages of K–12 mathematics teachers around the country are causing alarming concern. To address the need, state boards of education and school districts may create policies that affect the classroom directly but may counteract what is perceived best for students. For example, individuals without sufficient backgrounds in mathematics or mathematics pedagogy are being placed in middle school mathematics classrooms to teach. Granted this situation, how easy will it be to get teachers to take on the challenges associated with using these *Standards*-based curricula? Further, given the growing focus on school and teacher accountability, implementing new curricula may not be of high priority in many schools, regardless of what these curricula say about student outcomes.

How will the focus on school and teacher accountability affect curriculum research? What influences will there be as policy, social, and educational trends change? Political leaders and the general public desire to see better student outcomes, usually as assessed on standardized measures. However, they are not always willing to provide monetary and time resources that might encourage teachers to implement best practices that yield substantive short- and long-term results.

Third, future research should study the impact of the curricula on students from more diverse populations. Little is known about the effects of using traditional curricula with diverse ethnic or racial student populations, and even less is known about *Standards*-based curricula. Do the curricula help in closing the achievement gap between various ethnic and racial groups? Are they changing teachers' perceptions of mathematics abilities of students from diverse populations? In this area, more data collection is warranted and more promising evidence is desired.

Fourth, future research should closely examine affective factors (e.g., attitudes) as students interact with different curricula. Although attitudinal research can be difficult to interpret, it is important that middle school students' attitudes be monitored. Too much "math unpopularity" is advertised throughout society and the media; middle school students are prime candidates for developing unpopular mindsets toward mathematics. Because *Standards*-based curricula focus on purposeful mathematics, curriculum evaluation research should include a comprehensive investigation of students' attitudes over time.

CLOSING REMARKS

This chapter has presented a reaction to the three middle-grades projects featured in this section, discussing student outcomes, both from short- and long-term perspectives. The evidence is compelling and I wish to highlight two points of interest here. First, middle school students appeared to benefit in procedural understanding of mathematics and in conceptual understanding of mathematics. This suggests that problem-oriented *Standards*-based curricula can help students learn facts and skills as they learn more abstract content. Second, the long-term benefits seem more impressive than the short-term benefits. Perhaps, then, all stakeholders may need more patience in order to see the ultimate gains from using these curricula.

How do middle-grades students fare with these curricula and others like them? Surely, they do not fare worse. In fact, the evidence offered in Chapters 9–11 indicates that students fare quite well. Hence, for *Standards*-based curriculum projects, the goal to keep mathematics front and center in middle grades has been a worthwhile effort. Let us remain hopeful that middle school students will strive to keep mathematics front and center as they continue their growth as users and thinkers of mathematics.

REFERENCES

Leutzinger, L. (Ed.). (1998). *Mathematics in the middle.* Reston, VA: National Council of Teachers of Mathematics and National Middle School Association.

Mathematical Sciences Education Board of the National Research Council. (2000). *Mathematics education in the middle grades: Teaching to meet the needs of middle grades learners and to maintain high expectations.* Washington, DC: National Academy Press.

Mathematical Sciences Education Board of the National Research Council. (2001). *Knowing and learning mathematics for teaching.* Washington, DC: National Academy Press.

National Council of Teachers of Mathematics. (1989). *Curriculum and evaluation standards for school mathematics.* Reston, VA: Author.

National Council of Teachers of Mathematics. (1991). *Professional standards for teaching mathematics.* Reston, VA: Author.

National Council of Teachers of Mathematics. (1995). *Assessment standards for school mathematics.* Reston, VA: Author.

Owens, D. T. (Ed.). (1993). *Research ideas for the classroom: Middle grades mathematics.* New York: Macmillan.

PART IV

High School
Curriculum Projects

13

High School Mathematics Curriculum Reform

Denisse R. Thompson
University of South Florida

Sharon L. Senk
Michigan State University

This part of the book is devoted to research regarding what students learn and can do after studying from *Standards*-based mathematics curriculum materials in high school. The purpose of this chapter, like Chapters 2 and 8, is to provide a context for the research and development of these high school projects. In particular, we describe the typical high school mathematics curriculum used in schools prior to the development of the *Curriculum and Evaluation Standards* (National Council of Teachers of Mathematics [NCTM], 1989), and the state of high school mathematics achievement during the 1980s as measured by national and international assessments. We also discuss the recommendations made by the NCTM for a reformed curriculum in Grades 9–12, as well as the call for the development of instructional materials at this level from the National Science Foundation.

THE HIGH SCHOOL
MATHEMATICS CURRICULUM

During the decade of the 1980s, the high school curriculum in the United States was highly influenced by the ability track in which students were enrolled. Weiss (1987) reported that in a 1985–1986 survey,

299

approximately 70% of mathematics classes in Grades 10–12 were tracked; 11% were considered to be of high ability, 46% of average ability, and 12% of low ability. The other 30% of classes were of widely differing abilities.

During this period most schools had distinct programs for college-bound and non-college-bound students. In the mid-1980s, the typical college preparatory high school mathematics curriculum was a 3-year sequence of algebra I, Euclidean geometry, and algebra II, followed by 1 year of precalculus mathematics consisting of trigonometry, analytic geometry, and elementary functions. In some schools, a year of calculus was also offered. Weiss (1987) reports that although 99% of schools with Grades 10–12 offered a first course in algebra, only 31% offered a calculus course in 1985–1986.

Students may begin the college-preparatory sequence in 8th, 9th, or 10th grade. The aptitude and interests of students determine how many courses they complete in the traditional sequence.

The calculus courses offered were of two types: either a general introduction to calculus or an Advanced Placement course that follows a set syllabus with a nationally administered exam (Kenelly, Henry, & Jones, 1985). Students completing the Advanced Placement calculus and scoring at a given level are often able to obtain one or two semesters of college calculus credit. Generally, students need to begin the college-preparatory sequence in Grade 8 in order to complete the Advanced Placement course in their senior year.

Fey and Good (1985) note that the curriculum for the college-bound students was dominated by the "transformation of symbolic expressions" with "objectives of comprehension, problem solving, and analysis" not prominently emphasized (p. 44).

Students not in the college-bound program typically studied either general mathematics or consumer mathematics for 1 or 2 years (Sonnabend, 1985). General mathematics often included more work with arithmetic skills and computational algorithms. Consumer mathematics dealt with practical applications of mathematics, such as home loans, buying insurance, budgets, and taxes.

Table 13.1 contains the percentages of 17-year-olds reporting various mathematics courses as the highest level of mathematics studied. During the 1980s and 1990s, enrollment patterns in the third and fourth years of college preparatory courses rose, with the percentage of students stopping their mathematics course taking with prealgebra or general mathematics dropping from 15% in 1990 to 9% in 1994 (Dossey & Usiskin, 2000, p. 15).

TABLE 13.1

Percent of 17-Year-Olds Reporting the Given Mathematics Course as the Highest Level Course Studied

Course	1986	1990	1994
Algebra I	18	15	15
Geometry	17	15	15
Algebra II	40	44	47
Precalculus/calculus	7	8	13

Note. Data for 1986 are from Carpenter and Lindquist (1989, p. 162); data for 1990 and 1994 are from Dossey and Usiskin (2000, p. 15).

Achievement of 12th-Grade Students in the Second International Mathematics Study

During the 1981–1982 school year, the Second International Mathematics Study (SIMS) assessed the achievement of roughly 5,000 12th-grade students in the United States who were still taking college-preparatory mathematics, that is, precalculus or calculus. Although 82% of this age-group population was still in school, only 13% of the age cohort was still taking college-preparatory mathematics (McKnight et al., 1987).

Twelfth graders were assessed on six topics: sets and relations, number systems, algebra, geometry, functions and calculus, and probability and statistics. On the topic of sets and relations, the U.S. results "were midway between the bottom quarter of the countries and the international average. On the remaining five topics, our scores were generally among those of the bottom one-fourth of the countries" (McKnight et al., p. 23). The following comments by McKnight et al. (1987) summarize students' performance:

> the achievement of the Calculus classes, the nation's **best** mathematics students, was at or near the average achievement of the advanced secondary school mathematics students in other countries.... The achievement of the U.S. Precalculus students (the majority of twelfth grade college-preparatory mathematics students) was substantially below the international average. (p. vii; bold in original)

Given the importance of precalculus and calculus for success in college work, particularly in scientific and technical fields, this level of performance was cause for concern.

As was the case at Grade 8, the precalculus curriculum was considered to be of "low intensity," with many topics receiving a small amount of attention rather than giving students opportunities to study fewer topics in depth. In contrast, 12th-grade mathematics students spent more time listening to teachers' explanations than did eighth-grade students. A study of "effective" classes examined classroom processes in classes in which achievement was better than would have been predicted statistically. The researchers found that in these classes teachers used more diverse teaching methods, spent more time teaching new material, discussed difficulties with previously studied material more frequently, and offered more opportunities for supervised study than teachers in less effective classes (McKnight et al., 1987).

High School Students' Achievement on the National Assessment of Educational Progress

Results from the Fourth National Assessment of Educational Progress (NAEP) conducted in 1985–1986 showed a similar pattern of achievement to that observed from the SIMS. As indicated in Chapter 8, some items from the various assessments have remained secure so that they can be used repeatedly to assess mathematical performance over time. To be consistent with previous assessments, these trend items were administered to 17-year-olds. In addition, the Fourth NAEP administered items to students in the 11th grade. Altogether, approximately 32,000 students in the 11th grade participated in the Fourth NAEP; because of the sampling methods used with the items, approximately 2,000 students responded to each item (Carpenter, 1989, p. 6).

An analysis of the trend data from the Fourth NAEP indicated that 96% of 17-year-olds were at or above the level at which they know the four basic operations, can compare information in charts and graphs, and can analyze simple logical relations. However, only 51% were at or above the level at which they can compute with rational numbers as fractions, decimals, or percents, can identify geometric figures and determine areas of rectangles, use logical reasoning, and operate with integers, exponents, and square roots. Only 6% were at or above the level at which they can solve two-step problems with variables, identify functions, and understand coordinate systems (Dossey, Mullis, Lindquist, & Chambers, 1989, pp. 118–119).

Analysis of the results from the 11th-grade students indicated that few were able to deal with mathematical proof (Silver & Carpenter, 1989). Further, few could handle any but the simplest probability items, such as probability of getting a particular number on the roll of a single die, and students could not work with permutations or combinations (Brown & Silver, 1989). Levels of performance on specific items about number, geometry, and algebra are indicated as follows.

1. Only 38% of 11th-grade students understood that one way to determine $\frac{3}{4}$ of a number is to "divide by 4 and multiply by 3" (Silver & Carpenter, 1989, p. 13).
2. Slightly more than 70% were successful on fraction multiplication and subtraction of mixed numbers with no regrouping; only 45% were successful at subtracting two mixed numbers when regrouping was required (Kouba, Carpenter, & Swafford, 1989, p. 81).
3. The achievement of 11th-grade students on units of measurement, area, and volume was higher than for seventh-grade students. However, 11th-grade students did not demonstrate a conceptual understanding of area. "Although three-fourths of the 11th-grade students can find the area of a rectangle, fewer than half can use this skill in related problems" (Lindquist & Kouba, 1989b, p. 35).
4. "Few differences in performance were found between 11th-grade students who had and had not taken geometry on items that depended mainly on visualization [e.g., identifying perpendicular lines, sphere, diameter], some differences were found on items involving geometric terms, and great differences were found on items requiring a knowledge of geometric properties or applications" (Lindquist & Kouba, 1989a, p. 44).
5. Of 11th-grade students with geometry, 71% could find the missing degree measure of an angle to form a linear pair, compared with 14% of those with no geometry (see Fig. 13.1; Lindquist & Kouba, 1989a, p. 49).
6. Among students with algebra II, 91% could solve $6x + 5 = 4x + 7$; 83% of those with just algebra I could solve the equation; and 43% of those with no algebra were successful. Simplifying $3x + 2y + 5x$ was answered correctly by 93% of those with algebra II, 86% of those with algebra I, and 26% of those with no algebra (Swafford & Brown, 1989, pp. 57, 59).

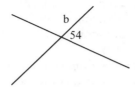

Find the measure of angle b.

FIG. 13.1. Geometry item from the fourth NAEP. *Note.* From *Results from the Fourth Mathematics Assessment of the National Assessment of Educational Progress* (p. 49), by M. M. Lindquist (Ed.), Reston, VA: National Council of Teachers of Mathematics. © 1989 by the National Council of Teachers of Mathematics.

In summary comments to the 1986 NAEP results, Carpenter and Lindquist (1989) raise the concern that many students are only learning mathematics at a very superficial level, with gaps in their understanding and their ability to apply mathematics.

OTHER STUDIES ABOUT HIGH SCHOOL MATHEMATICS

Space does not permit a comprehensive review of the research on learning and teaching mathematics in high school known at the time of the development of the standards for high school mathematics (NCTM, 1989). In the paragraphs that follow, we report on several studies and recommendations that appear to have had an impact on the calls for changes in the high school mathematics curriculum.

In 1985, Usiskin called for a revolution in secondary school mathematics. He noted that recommendations in the reports of the early 1980s, such as *A Nation at Risk*, suggested two changes that needed to occur simultaneously. First, students' performance needed to be upgraded to include more problem solving instead of rote memorization. Second, the curriculum needed to be updated to include more applications, statistics, probability, and the use of computers. He argued that the changes needed were so massive that the needs of students could not be met without a major overhaul of the secondary curriculum.

In the same volume, Fey and Good (1985) argued that technology could perform many of the manipulative skills that students spend considerable time learning. As a result, the algebra curriculum should take advantage of that technology. Practicing manipulative skills should be replaced with the study of families of elementary functions. Applications of mathematics and modeling real-life data should play a more central role in the curriculum. This shift "places the function concept at the heart of the curriculum, preparing students for the dynamic, global quantitative thinking that typifies most models they will encounter in future mathematics and its applications" (pp. 49–50).

The views of Usiskin and Fey and Good about the value of students learning mathematics set in real-world contexts were supported by decades of research and development in the Netherlands on realistic mathematics education (Freudenthal, 1987).

The first calculators with graphing capabilities had been developed in the mid-1980s, and they soon began to be used in some high school mathematics classes. Fey's (1984, 1989) calls for the use of technology as a tool for teaching and learning mathematics in secondary school also were supported by other researchers. Kaput (1989) recommended that new technology-based learning environments be developed that link the various forms of algebraic representation—graphs, tables, and equations.

Computer technology developed during the 1980s also suggested a major shift in the way geometry might be approached. The Geometric Supposer, a piece of software capable of running on microcomputers, enabled students to do Euclidean constructions electronically. Hence, rather than the teacher determining the theorems to be proved, the Geometric Supposer enabled a student to "become a potent and nimble conjecture maker" (Schwartz & Yerushalmy, 1987, p. 623).

Research on the van Hiele model (Burger & Shaughnessy, 1986; Senk, 1989) concluded that students pass through a sequence of up to five levels when learning geometry. This research validated Wirszup's (1976) conjecture that the mismatch between the level of teachers' explanations and students' levels of thinking explained why so many students have trouble learning to write proofs in geometry. Senk's (1985) research verified that many students were not successful with proof, despite spending an entire year working on this task. Only about 30% of those who studied a proof-oriented geometry course for an entire year were able to reach a 75% mastery level with proof. In discussing the implications of this research, Senk suggested that the content of a traditional geometry curriculum be examined to determine if it was appropriate for preparing students for future options.

The burgeoning field of computer science in the 1980s also suggested changes in the high school curriculum. Rather than having a curriculum leading primarily to calculus, some argued for a more balanced mathematics curriculum to include topics from discrete mathematics that would be important for the study of applied mathematics, including the area of computer science. Such topics might include combinatorics, discrete probability, mathematical induction, graph theory, difference equations and recurrence relations, and mathematical logic (Ralston, 1985).

NCTM's STANDARDS FOR CURRICULUM IN GRADES 9–12

As was the case at elementary and middle school levels, standards for high school students set goals for *all* students. However, unlike the standards at the elementary and middle school levels, the curriculum standards for high school establish a framework for a "core curriculum differentiated by the depth and breadth of the treatment of topics and by the nature of applications" (NCTM, 1989, p. 125). At least 3 years of the core curriculum were recommended for all high school students, with 4 years of mathematical study recommended for all college-intending students. These 4 years of mathematics were expected to "revolve around a broadened curriculum that includes extensions of the core topics and for which calculus is no longer viewed as *the* capstone experience" (p. 125, italics in original).

The ten content standards for Grades 9–12 are listed here:

- Algebra
- Functions
- Geometry From a Synthetic Perspective
- Geometry From an Algebraic Perspective
- Trigonometry
- Statistics
- Probability
- Discrete Mathematics
- Conceptual Underpinnings of Calculus
- Mathematical Structure

Within the description of the standards for Problem Solving, Reasoning, Communication, and Connections, no distinction was made between the needs of college-intending or non-college intending students. However, within each content standard, the authors distinguish between expectations for all students and additional expectations for those students who are college intending. For instance, the algebra standard states that the mathematics curriculum should prepare all students to "represent situations that involve variable quantities with expressions, equations, inequalities, and matrices." In addition, college-intending students are expected to "use matrices to solve linear systems" (p. 150).

The curriculum based on these content strands is expected to move away from rote memorization of skills and procedures and toward an emphasis on "conceptual understandings, multiple representations and connections, mathematical modeling, and mathematical problem solving. . . . In addition, topics from statistics, probability, and discrete mathematics are elevated to a more central position in the curriculum for all students" (p. 125). Increased attention was to be given to real-world problems, the use of calculators and computers to foster conceptual understanding and to solve equations and inequalities, and connections between various forms of a function (symbolic, graphical, and contextual). Decreased attention was to be paid to paper-and-pencil manipulations, the use of factoring to solve equations and simplify rational expressions, and graphing by hand by using a table of values.

The standards at this level also discuss expectations for instruction. To prepare students for the workplace or for higher education, classroom experiences should help students become more independent so that they are "self-directed learners who routinely engage in constructing, symbolizing, applying, and generalizing mathematical ideas. Such experiences are essential in order for students to develop the capability for their own lifelong learning and to internalize the view that mathematics is a process, a body of knowledge, and a human creation" (p. 128). Thus, the *Standards* suggest placing less of an emphasis on teacher-directed lecture as the primary means of learning.

The recommendation for a core curriculum appropriate for all students represented a significant shift from the practice of the time, which essentially provided one program of study for college-bound students (at least 2 years of algebra and a year of geometry) and a very different program for non-college-bound students (general or consumer mathematics).

The 9–12 *Standards* assume that high school students will have experienced the broad mathematics curriculum envisioned at both the elementary and middle school levels. Until all students have experienced such a K–8 curriculum, high school educators will be faced with the challenge of implementing the high expectations of the 9–12 *Standards* while simultaneously enhancing the K–8 prerequisite knowledge of entering students.

The core curriculum for all students outlined in the 9–12 *Standards* highlighted several issues. First, the core curriculum deemphasizes, but does not eliminate, much of the focus on manipulative skill that had been a hallmark of traditional algebra and precalculus courses. Would students studying from a core curriculum be prepared for placement exams in college and university mathematics departments? Second, what would a set of high school courses based on a core curriculum look like? Third, what impact would the core curriculum have on the Advanced Placement calculus program in a school? Fourth, if all students studied the same curriculum, how would students and parents of those previously in the advanced track react?

NATIONAL SCIENCE FOUNDATION SOLICITATION FOR CURRICULUM DEVELOPMENT

The call in the *Standards* for a core curriculum accessible to all students was reflected in the National Science Foundation's (NSF's) program solicitation for the development of secondary instructional materials in mathematics, for which proposals were due in March 1992. The introduction acknowledged that current secondary curricula prepared college-intending students for calculus whereas the non-college-intending students continued to study a curriculum dominated by arithmetic. Furthermore, topics in statistics, probability, and discrete mathematics were not widely studied, even though they were important for many majors.

Proposals submitted in response to the solicitation were expected to meet a number of objectives (NSF, 1991):

- to increase access to and achievement in mathematics for all students, particularly those from underrepresented groups;
- to align instructional materials with national standards for curriculum, teaching, and evaluation;
- to integrate calculators, computers, and other technologies into the classroom as essential components of the materials and pedagogy of mathematics;
- to incorporate situations from the natural and social sciences and from other parts of the school curriculum as contexts for developing and using mathematics;
- to develop student assessment strategies as integral components of instruction; and ultimately,
- to improve the quality of learning and teaching of mathematics in classrooms. (p. 1)

Given these objectives, this solicitation proposed to support several comprehensive projects that would

- prepare and disseminate course materials for at least a three-year core curriculum, designed to serve all students and reflecting the full range of mathematical sciences, beginning in grade 9;
- develop strategies and materials for teachers that acknowledge cultural diversity and fully engage all students in mathematical thinking;
- formulate assessment methods and materials that will enable teachers to evaluate and adjust learning environments to best suit the needs of their students. (p. 1)

In addition, the solicitation would support preparing "materials for fourth-year course options supporting students' varied curricular goals."

STANDARDS-BASED HIGH SCHOOL CURRICULUM PROJECTS

Four projects were funded from this solicitation. Three would create new mathematics curricula: the Core-Plus Mathematics Project, the Secondary Mathematics Core Curriculum Initiative (currently *MATH Connections*), and Applications/Reform in Secondary Mathematics (ARISE). A fourth, the Interactive Mathematics Program, received funding to complete the development of a curriculum for Grades 9–12 that had been begun earlier.

At about the same time, the Systemic Initiative for Montana Mathematics and Science (SIMMS) also received funding to develop a high school mathematics curriculum in response to a different solicitation from the NSF.

The University of Chicago School Mathematics Project (UCSMP) Secondary curriculum had begun to develop materials for Grades 7–12 in 1983, with support from private funding. When the NSF began to hold yearly Gateways conferences in 1992 to facilitate discussion of common issues across the K–12 funded curriculum projects, representatives of UCSMP were invited to the conferences, perhaps to offer advice as other projects began their curriculum development.

At the time that chapters for this volume were written, the ARISE project staff had only collected preliminary data on student outcomes; hence, no chapter about the work of the ARISE project is included in this book. Thus, this part of the book contains information only about the results of the other five curriculum development projects mentioned earlier. Chapter 19, by Jane Swafford, is a commentary on the research reported in Chapters 14–18.

REFERENCES

Brown, C. A., & Silver, E. A. (1989). Discrete mathematics. In M. M. Lindquist (Ed.), *Results from the fourth mathematics assessment of the national assessment of educational progress* (pp. 19–27). Reston, VA: National Council of Teachers of Mathematics.

Burger, W., & Shaughnessy, J. M. (1986). Characterizing the van Hiele levels of development in geometry. *Journal for Research in Mathematics Education, 17,* 31–48.

Carpenter, T. P. (1989). Introduction. In M. M. Lindquist (Ed.), *Results from the fourth mathematics assessment of the national assessment of educational progress* (pp. 1–9). Reston, VA: National Council of Teachers of Mathematics.

Carpenter, T. P., & Lindquist, M. M. (1989). Summary and conclusions. In M. M. Lindquist (Ed.), *Results from the fourth mathematics assessment of the national assessment of educational progress* (pp. 160–169). Reston, VA: National Council of Teachers of Mathematics.

Dossey, J. A., Mullis, I. V. S., Lindquist, M. M., & Chambers, D. L. (1989). What can students do? (Levels of mathematics proficiency for the nation and demographic subgroups.) In M. M. Lindquist (Ed.), *Results from the fourth mathematics assessment of the national assessment of educational progress* (pp. 117–134). Reston, VA: National Council of Teachers of Mathematics.

Dossey, J., & Usiskin, Z. (2000). *Mathematics education in the United States 2000: A capsule summary written for the Ninth International Congress on Mathematical Education.* Reston, VA: National Council of Teachers of Mathematics.

Fey, J. (1984). *Computing and mathematics: The impact on secondary school curricula.* Reston, VA: National Council of Teachers of Mathematics.

Fey, J. T. (1989). School algebra for the year 2000. In S. Wagner & C. Kieran (Eds.), *Research issues in the learning and teaching of algebra* (pp. 199–213). Mahwah, NJ: Lawrence Erlbaum Associates.

Fey, J. T., & Good, R. A. (1985). Rethinking the sequence and priorities of high school mathematics curricula. In C. R. Hirsch & M. J. Zweng (Eds.), *The secondary school mathematics curriculum* (pp. 43–52). Reston, VA: National Council of Teachers of Mathematics.

Freudenthal, H. (1987). Mathematics starting and staying in reality. In I. Wirszup & R. Streit (Eds.), *Developments in school mathematics education around the world: Applications-oriented curricula and technology-supported learning for all students* (pp. 279–295). Reston, VA: National Council of Teachers of Mathematics.

Kaput, J. J. (1989). Linking representations in the symbol systems of algebra. In S. Wagner & C. Kieran (Eds.), *Research issues in the learning and teaching of algebra* (pp. 167–194). Mahwah, NJ: Lawrence Erlbaum Associates.

Kenelly, J., Henry, P., & Jones, C. O. (1985). The advanced placement program in calculus. In C. R. Hirsch & M. J. Zweng (Eds.), *The secondary school mathematics curriculum* (pp. 166–176). Reston, VA: National Council of Teachers of Mathematics.

Kouba, V. L., Carpenter, T. P., & Swafford, J. O. (1989). Number and operations. In M. M. Lindquist (Ed.), *Results from the fourth mathematics assessment of the national assessment of educational progress* (pp. 64–93). Reston, VA: National Council of Teachers of Mathematics.

Lindquist, M. M., & Kouba, V. L. (1989a). Geometry. In M. M. Lindquist (Ed.), *Results from the fourth mathematics assessment of the national assessment of educational progress* (pp. 44–54). Reston, VA: National Council of Teachers of Mathematics.

Lindquist, M. M., & Kouba, V. L. (1989b). Measurement. In M. M. Lindquist (Ed.), *Results from the fourth mathematics assessment of the national assessment of educational progress* (pp. 35–43). Reston, VA: National Council of Teachers of Mathematics.

McKnight, C. C., Crosswhite, F. J., Dossey, J. A., Kifer, E., Swafford, J. O., Travers, K. J., & Cooney, T. J. (1987). *The underachieving curriculum: assessing U.S. school mathematics from an international perspective.* Champaign, IL: Stipes.

National Council of Teachers of Mathematics. (1989). *Curriculum and evaluation standards for school mathematics.* Reston, VA: Author.

National Science Foundation. (1991). *Instructional materials for secondary school mathematics: Program solicitation and guidelines.* Washington, DC: Directorate for Education and Human Resources, National Science Foundation.

Ralston, A. (1985). The really new college mathematics and its impact on the high school curriculum. In C. R. Hirsch & M. J. Zweng (Eds.), *The secondary school mathematics curriculum* (pp. 29–42). Reston, VA: National Council of Teachers of Mathematics.

Schwartz, J. L., & Yerushalmy, M. (1987). The GEOMETRIC SUPPOSER: Using microcomputers to restore invention to the learning of mathematics. In I. Wirszup & R. Streit (Eds.), *Developments in school mathematics education around the world: applications-oriented curricula and technology-supported learning for all students* (pp. 623–636). Reston, VA: National Council of Teachers of Mathematics.

Senk, S. L. (1985). How well do students write geometry proofs? *Mathematics Teacher, 78*(6), 448–456.

Senk, S. L. (1989). Van Hiele levels and achievement in writing geometry proofs. *Journal for Research in Mathematics Education, 20,* 309–321.

Silver, E. A., & Carpenter, T. P. (1989). Mathematical methods. In M. M. Lindquist (Ed.), *Results from the fourth mathematics assessment of the national assessment of educational progress* (pp. 10–18). Reston, VA: National Council of Teachers of Mathematics.

Sonnabend, T. (1985). Non-career mathematics: the mathematics we all need. In C. R. Hirsch & M. J. Zweng (Eds.), *The secondary school mathematics curriculum* (pp. 107–118). Reston, VA: National Council of Teachers of Mathematics.

Swafford, J. O., & Brown, C. A. (1989). Variables and relations. In M. M. Lindquist (Ed.), *Results from the fourth mathematics assessment of the national assessment of educational progress* (pp. 55–63). Reston, VA: National Council of Teachers of Mathematics.

Usiskin, Z. (1985). We need another revolution in secondary school mathematics. In C. R. Hirsch & M. J. Zweng (Eds.), *The secondary school mathematics curriculum* (pp. 1–21). Reston, VA: National Council of Teachers of Mathematics.

Weiss, I. R. (1987). *Report of the 1985–86 national survey of science and mathematics education.* Research Triangle Park, NC: Research Triangle Institute.

Wirszup, I. (1976). Breakthroughs in the psychology of learning and teaching geometry. In J. L. Martin & D. A. Bradbard (Eds.), *Space and geometry: Papers from a research workshop* (pp. 75–97). Columbus, OH: ERIC Center for Science, Mathematics and Environmental Education.

14

The *Core-Plus Mathematics Project*: Perspectives and Student Achievement

Harold L. Schoen
University of Iowa

Christian R. Hirsch
Western Michigan University

The *Core-Plus Mathematics Project* (*CPMP*) curriculum is designed to make important and broadly useful mathematics meaningful and accessible to a wide range of students. The curriculum consists of a single core sequence for both college-bound and employment-bound students during the first 3 years of high school. This organization is intended to keep post-high school education and career options open for all students. A flexible fourth-year course continues the preparation of students for college mathematics. The completed curriculum is published under the title *Contemporary Mathematics in Context: A Unified Approach* (Coxford, Fey, Hirsch, Schoen, Burrill et al., 1997, 1998, 1999; Coxford, Fey, Hirsch, Schoen, Hart et al., 2001).

This chapter provides a brief overview of the *CPMP* curriculum in terms of its design and theoretical framework, and a profile of the mathematical achievement of students who participated in the national field test of the curriculum.[1] Other focused research studies conducted in *CPMP* classrooms are reported elsewhere (cf. Huntley, Rasmussen, Villarubi, Sangtong, & Fey, 2000; Kett, 1997/1998; Lloyd & Wilson, 1998; Truitt, 1998/1999; Walker, 1999/2000).

The profile of *CPMP* student achievement continues to evolve over time. In Fall 1997, *CPMP* embarked on a longitudinal summative evaluation of the complete curriculum implemented with students who have completed middle school mathematics programs funded by the National Science Foundation and described elsewhere in this volume. Mathematical performance and attitudes of Fall 1997 high school freshmen have been monitored from Grade 9 through their first year of post-high school education or work. A summary of the findings from the longitudinal study is in preparation.

BACKGROUND AND PERSPECTIVES

Each *CPMP* course was developed in consultation with an international advisory board, mathematicians, instructional specialists, and classroom teachers. In creating the *CPMP* 3-year core curriculum (typically completed by students in Grades 9–11), the authors used a "zero-based" process (Mathematical Sciences Education Board, 1990) in which the inclusion of a topic was based on it own merits. In designing each course, we always asked and debated: "If this is the last mathematics students will have the opportunity to learn, is the most important mathematics included?" This approach resulted in the elimination or deemphasis of some topics found in traditional curricula, a reordering of other topics, and the inclusion of what the authors believed to be the most broadly useful and important mathematical ideas. As a result, statistics, probability, and discrete mathematics have assumed a central position in each year of the curriculum. Course 4 formalizes and extends the core program with a focus on the mathematics needed to be successful in college mathematics and statistics courses.

In each year of the *CPMP* curriculum, mathematics is developed along interwoven strands of algebra and functions, geometry and trigonometry, statistics and probability, and discrete mathematics. Each of these strands is developed in focused units connected by common topics such as symmetry, functions, matrices, and data analysis and curve fitting. The strands also are connected across units by mathematical habits of mind such as visual thinking, recursive thinking, searching for and explaining patterns, making and checking conjectures, reasoning with multiple representations, inventing mathematics, and providing convincing arguments and proofs. The strands are unified further by fundamental themes of data, representation, shape, and change. The choice of curriculum organization was influenced by the importance of connections among related concepts and procedures in developing deep understanding of mathematics (Skemp, 1987). This curriculum organization breaks down the artificial compartmentalization of traditional "layer cake" curricula in the United States and addresses weaknesses identified (Schmidt, 1998) in the findings from the Third International Mathematics and Science Study (TIMSS). In addition, developing mathematics each year along multiple strands capitalizes on the different interests and talents of students and helps to develop diverse mathematical insights (Hirsch & Coxford, 1997).

Tables 14.1 and 14.2 provide an overview of the scope and sequence of the *CPMP* 4-year curriculum. Recognizing that increasing numbers of college major programs involve the study of mathematics, though not necessarily calculus, *CPMP* Course 4 consists of a core of units for all college-bound students, plus additional units supporting a variety of collegiate majors.

TABLE 14.1
The *CPMP* Core Curriculum

Unit No.	Course 1	Course 2	Course 3
1	Patterns in Data	Matrix Models	Multiple-Variable Models
2	Patterns of Change	Patterns of Location, Shape, and Size	Modeling Public Opinion
3	Linear Models	Patterns of Association	Symbol Sense and Algebraic Reasoning
4	Graph Models	Power Models	Shapes and Geometric Reasoning
5	Patterns in Space and Visualization	Network Optimization	Patterns in Variation
6	Exponential Models	Geometric Form and Its Function	Families of Functions
7	Simulation Models	Patterns in Chance	Discrete Models of Change
Capstone	Planning a Benefits Carnival	Forests, the Environment, and Mathematics	Making the Best of It: Optimal Forms and Strategies

TABLE 14.2
CPMP Course 4 Units

Core Units	Additional Units for Students Intending to Pursue Programs in:	
	Mathematical, Physical and Biological Sciences or Engineering	*Social, Management, and Health Sciences or Humanities*
1. Rates of Change	6. Polynomial and Rational Functions	5. Binomial Distributions and Statistical Inference
2. Modeling Motion	7. Functions and Symbolic Reasoning	9. Informatics
3. Logarithmic Functions and Data Models	8. Space Geometry	10. Problem Solving, Algorithms, and Spreadsheets
4. Counting Models		

Curriculum Development Principles

Several key principles guided the design of the *CPMP* curriculum. First and foremost is the belief that mathematics is a vibrant and broadly useful subject that should be explored and understood as an active science of patterns (Steen, 1990). As a result, experimentation, data analysis, and seeking and verifying patterns are pervasive in the curriculum. For instance, in Course 1 (Unit 2), *CPMP* students conduct experiments that simulate bungee jumping and analyze patterns in the relation between jumper weight and bungee cord stretch as a prelude to the study of algebraic expressions and equations. In Course 1 (Unit 7), they explore patterns in gender distribution of juries and multichild families as an entrée to the concepts and techniques of probability and statistics. In Course 2 (Unit 2), they study patterns in computer graphic images and then the related ideas of coordinate geometry, transformations, congruence, and similarity. An analysis of patterns in transportation and communication networks in Course 2 (Unit 5) leads to important concepts in graph theory that are widely used in computer and management sciences.

A second principle underlying the curriculum is that problems provide a context for developing student understanding of mathematics (Hiebert et al., 1996; Schoenfeld, 1992). As suggested by the unit titles, mathematical modeling and related concepts of data collection, representation, interpretation, prediction, and simulation are emphasized.

Third, consistent with our view of mathematics as a science of patterns, exploration and experimentation necessarily precede and complement theory. Investigations are always accompanied by opportunities for students to analyze and abstract underlying mathematical structures that can be applied in other contexts and that, themselves, often are the subject of further investigations.

A fourth underlying principle is the incorporation of graphics calculators and project-developed calculator software as tools for developing mathematical understanding and for solving authentic problems. Graphics calculators permit the *CPMP* curriculum and instruction to emphasize multiple representations (verbal, numerical, graphical, and symbolic) and to focus on goals in which mathematical thinking is central. The use of graphics calculators promotes versatile ways of dealing with realistic situations and, for some students, reduces the manipulative skill filter that would have prevented them from studying significant mathematics.

The design of the *CPMP* curriculum was also informed by pedagogical principles, the most central of which is that classroom cultures of sense-making shape students' understanding of the nature of mathematics as well as the ways in which they can use the mathematics they have learned (Lave, Smith, & Butler, 1988; Resnick, 1987, 1988). Investigations of real-life contexts lead to (re)invention of important mathematics that makes sense to students and that, in turn, enables them to make sense of new situations and problems.

Integrated Instruction and Assessment

The *CPMP* curriculum was developed not only to reshape what mathematics all students have an opportunity to learn but also to influence the manner in which learning occurs and is assessed. Each unit in the curriculum is developed around a series of four or five lessons in which major ideas are developed through student investigations of rich applied problem situations. Each lesson focuses on several interrelated mathematical concepts and often spans 4 or 5 days.

The *CPMP* instructional materials recognize the pivotal roles played by small-group collaborative learning, social interaction, and communication in the construction of mathematical ideas, particularly in cases involving females and underrepresented minorities. Each *CPMP* lesson is introduced by a problem situation which the entire class is asked to think about, such as that in Fig. 14.1. In this case, the context is an experiment that simulates pollution of a lake by some contaminant and the following clean-up efforts.

Once launched, a lesson usually involves students working together collaboratively in small groups or pairs as they investigate more focused problems and questions related to the launching situation. This investigative work is followed by a teacher-moderated class discussion in which students share mathematical ideas developed by their groups and together construct a common understanding of important mathematical concepts, methods, and approaches. Sharing, and agreeing as a class, on the mathematical ideas groups are developing is promoted by Checkpoints in the instructional materials. The sample Checkpoint in Fig. 14.2 is the third of three Checkpoints in the lesson referenced in Fig. 14.1. (In Courses 1 and 2, students use NOW-NEXT language to describe linear and exponential patterns of change recursively.) Each Checkpoint is followed by a related On Your Own assessment task to be completed individually by students.

Each lesson is accompanied by additional tasks to engage students in modeling with (M), organizing (O), reflecting on (R), and extending (E) their mathematical understanding developed through the investigations. MORE tasks are primarily for individual work outside of class.

Assessment is embedded in the *CPMP* curriculum materials and is an integral part of instruction. The instructional materials support continuous assessment of group and individual progress through observing and listening to students during the exploring and summarizing phases of instruction. In addition, there are individual assessments that measure understanding of mathematical concepts, methods, and skills. Each of the core courses also includes a thematic capstone as seen in Table 14.1. These project-oriented capstones provide rich mathematical problems whose solutions require the

Think About This Situation

One of the problems of our complex modern society is the risk of chemical or sewage spills that can pollute rivers and lakes. Correction requires action of natural or human cleanup processes, but both take time. The graphs below show two possible outcomes of a pollution cleanup effort following an oil spill.

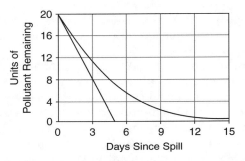

(a).   What pattern of change in pollution level is shown by each graph?

(b).   Which graph shows the pattern of change that you would expect from a pollution cleanup effort? Test your idea by running the pollution cleanup experiment several times and plotting the (*time, pollutant remaining*) data.

(c).   What sort of equations relating pollution *P* and time *t* would you expect to match your plot of data? Test your idea using a graphing calculator or computer.

FIG. 14.1.   Launching the study of exponential decay (Exponential Models unit, Course 1).

use of mathematics from each of the four strands studied during the year. This is an opportunity for students to review and consolidate their learning as well as demonstrate their mathematical growth over the year. For more detail on *CPMP* pedagogical perspectives and on the instructional model embedded in the curriculum, see Hirsch, Coxford, Fey, and Schoen (1995) and Schoen, Bean, and Ziebarth (1996).

SELECTED STUDIES
OF STUDENT OUTCOMES

The *CPMP* evaluation has three interrelated goals: first, to provide a data-based guide for the development of the curriculum; second, to test the feasibility of the curriculum; and third, to identify strengths and weaknesses

---

Checkpoint

In this lesson, you have seen that patterns of exponential change can be modeled by equations of the form $y = a(b^x)$.

(a).   What equation relates *NOW* and *NEXT y* values of this model?

(b).   What does the value of a tell you about the situation being modeled? About the tables and graphs of (x, y) values?

(c).   What does the value of b tell you about the situation being modeled? About the tables and graphs of (x, y) values?

(d).   How is the information provided by values of a and b in exponential equations like $y = a(b^x)$ similar to, and different from, that provided by a and b in linear equations like $y = a + bx$?

Be prepared to compare your responses with those from other groups.

FIG. 14.2. Summarizing and formalizing mathematical discoveries.

of the curriculum. Following the initial development and small-scale local tryouts of each course, the materials were pilot tested for 1 year, revised, and then field tested in the following year. The pilot test focused on providing data to guide the development of the curriculum.

Feasibility, strengths, and weaknesses were the focus of the field test, although field-test data continued to guide the revisions of each course until publication. The feasibility of the *CPMP* curriculum was determined by how easily teachers and students could use the materials and by the impact of the materials on students' learning of important mathematical content. Strengths and weaknesses were addressed by measuring a variety of student outcomes and by analyzing those outcomes in comparison to those of students using more traditional curricula.

The *CPMP* evaluation model combines a large-scale field test with more focused research studies. In this chapter, results are drawn from the evaluation in order to paint a picture of students' mathematical achievement after completing each course in the *CPMP* curriculum. The outcomes for *CPMP* students are compared with those of students in more traditional mathematics curricula in some of the same field-test schools or to nationally representative norm groups.

Each of the first three *CPMP* courses was field tested in 36 high schools, and Course 4 was field tested in 28 high schools. Field-test schools were located in 11 states—Alaska, California, Colorado, Georgia, Idaho, Iowa, Kentucky, Michigan, Ohio, South Carolina, and Texas. A broad cross section of students from urban, suburban, and rural communities with ethnic and cultural diversity was represented. The field-test schools were encouraged to include students with a wide range of achievement and interest in mathematics and, where possible, to group students heterogeneously. Limitations at local sites did not always make this possible. Approximately one fifth of the Course 1 teachers reported that their classes included all ninth-grade students, including honors students. The most common *CPMP* class (as reported by 43.0% of the teachers) was composed of students with a wide range of prior mathematics achievement and interest; however, accelerated students were generally not included because they completed a traditional ninth-grade course in Grade 8 and continued with the next course in the sequence in Grade 9. Thus, accelerated students are probably underrepresented in the *CPMP* field-test sample.

Comparative Studies of Courses 1 and 2

Design and Methodology

The goal of these studies was to compare the mathematical achievement of students experiencing the *CPMP* curriculum with that of students with similar mathematical aptitude and interest who were studying more traditional high school mathematics curricula. We administered some of the same pretests and end-of-year posttests to both *CPMP* students and to comparison students in more traditional curricula. The pretest provided a baseline for matching students in the two groups on their entering aptitude, and the posttests served as outcome measures following the different curricular experiences.

Population

At the beginning of the first field-test year (1994–1995), invitations were issued to lead teachers in each *CPMP* field-test school inviting them to identify, if possible, a set of students in more traditional ninth-grade mathematics courses in their school who were comparable in mathematical background and aptitude to their *CPMP* Course 1 students. For the first year, we envisioned comparison students coming mostly from ninth-grade Algebra courses with some from Prealgebra. Thus, participation was limited to schools that offered both *CPMP* and a more traditional mathematics curriculum and that were willing to devote a class period in comparison classes for pretesting in September and two periods for posttesting in May or early June.

Eleven schools accepted the invitation. Six were from the Midwest, one urban, one rural and four suburban; three were from the West, one urban and two rural; one was urban and from the East; and the last was rural and from the South. At each site there were from two to five *CPMP* teachers and from one to three comparison teachers. The comparison classes for the Course 1 study were composed of 20 Algebra, five Prealgebra, three General Mathematics, and two ninth-grade Accelerated Geometry classes.

For the Course 2 study, we asked these 11 schools to posttest as many of the same comparison students as was feasible in May or June of the second year. This proved to be problematic for many schools because the comparison students had enrolled in a variety of mathematics classes in their sophomore year and were difficult to locate and posttest at the end of the second year. As a result, only 5 of the 11 schools who had comparison groups in year 1 agreed to test their comparison students at the end of the second year—two suburban Midwestern schools and three urban schools, one from the South and two from the West. The comparison students for the Course 2 study were a subset of the Course 1 comparison students and were enrolled in either Algebra, Geometry, or Accelerated Advanced Algebra.

Classroom Instruction

Because the *CPMP* curriculum and its teaching and assessment methods were new, at least one *CPMP* teacher from each school attended a 2-week workshop during the summer prior to teaching a *CPMP* course. In this workshop, teachers worked through the *CPMP* course materials by using a small-group investigative approach similar to that they would be using with their own students in the Fall. The comparison teachers had no special inservice program, because they were presumably accustomed to the curriculum and teaching method that they used.

Although what is reported are naturalistic studies occurring in classrooms with intact groups of students, the primary explanatory variable is the nature of the curriculum, including the curriculum-inspired pedagogy and assessment methods. The *CPMP* classes were composed of students with a wide range of entering mathematics achievement, including ninth graders who normally would not have taken Algebra. Consequently, teachers commonly finished five or six of the seven units in Course 1, failing to complete Exponential Models in some cases and Simulation Models in nearly all cases. Survey data from 27 *CPMP* Course 1 teachers in these 11 schools indicate that a mean of 48.9% of class time (min. = 17%; max. = 80%) was spent in small group work. Approximately 80% indicated that calculators were available 100% of the time, and the most common restriction on calculator use was their unavailability for homework.

The nature of the instruction in the comparison classes was not specified in advance, but at the end of the year comparison teachers described what transpired. Approximately 80% of the comparison teachers reported small group work was used either not at all or less than once a week. Approximately 74% of the comparison teachers reported that their students used a calculator more than once per week, although there are no data about how it was used. Understanding and solving linear equations in one variable was the main instructional goal for Course 1 comparison classes; teachers indicated a mean of 23% of the yearly class time spent on this topic and up to 50% of the time in some algebra classes.

Instruments

Two main instruments were used in the Course 1 and Course 2 comparative studies: first, a nationally standardized high school mathematics achievement test, and second, project-developed open-ended posttests for each *CPMP* course measuring important *CPMP* outcomes judged to overlap with goals of the comparison curricula.

Standardized Achievement. The standardized test was the mathematics subtest of the Iowa Tests of Educational Development (ITED), called Ability to Do Quantitative Thinking, or ITED-Q (Feldt, Forsyth, Ansley, & Alnot, 1993). Rather than testing outcomes of a particular high school curriculum, the focus of ITED-Q is on quantitative thinking processes that are important for anyone with at least a high school education. In particular, the ITED-Q assesses high school students' ability to use appropriate mathematical reasoning in situations requiring the interpretation of data, charts, or graphs that represent information related to business, social and political issues, medicine, and science. It consists of three subtests:

1. Understanding Mathematical Concepts and Procedures (UMCP): These items require students to select appropriate procedures, make connections among various concepts, and identify examples and counterexamples of concepts.
2. Interpreting Information (Int. Inf.): These items require students to make inferences or predictions based on data or information often given in graphs or tables.
3. Solving Problems (Solve Probs.): These items require students to apply quantitative procedures to relatively novel situations, reason quantitatively, and evaluate reasonableness of solutions.

The mathematical content includes whole numbers, exponents, fractions, decimals, percents, ratios, geometry, measurement, estimation, rounding, statistics, probability, tables, and graphs. Although very little symbolic algebra is required, the ITED-Q is quite demanding for the full range of high school students. For example, on ITED-Q (Form K, Level 16) the median of the nationally representative norm group in Spring of Grade 10 is approximately 15 of 40 items correct, and the 99th percentile is approximately 35 of 40 items correct.

The ITED-Q correlates highly with other well-known measures of mathematical achievement, such as the Iowa Test of Basic Skills (ITBS), the ACT Mathematics test, and the Scholastic Achievement Test (SAT) Mathematics test.[2] A form of the ITED-Q was administered as a pretest to all *CPMP* and comparison students at the beginning of Course 1, and alternative forms as posttests at the end of Courses 1 and 2.

CPMP Posttests. In order to obtain a measure of students' attainment of specific curriculum objectives, the *CPMP* evaluation team developed open-ended achievement tests, called the Course 1 Posttest and Course 2 Posttest, each in two parts. Part 1 was designed to be a test of content that both *CPMP* and comparison students would have had an opportunity to learn that year, namely algebraic content for Course 1 and both algebraic and geometric content for Course 2. Part 2 of each *CPMP* Posttest included subtests of Data Analysis, Discrete Mathematics, Probability, and (in Course 1) Geometry; that is, content that the comparison students probably did not have the opportunity to study. Comparison students completed only Part 1 of the *CPMP* Posttest at the end of each year, and *CPMP* students completed both parts. These tests required students to construct their responses and to show and often explain their work. Only results from Part 1 are reported here.

Course 1 Posttest (Part 1) is composed of two contextual subtests, each requiring algebraic methods, and a third subtest of procedural algebra. The first two *Standards*-oriented subtests require students to show that they understand algebraic concepts by applying them in realistic settings and interpreting their meaning in those settings. In particular, students translate between problem situations and algebraic representations, including linear equations and inequalities, tables, and graphs. These subtests also require students to rewrite algebraic expressions, solve equations that provide insights into the problem context, and explain how solutions or equivalent forms represent new information in the problem context. The third, more traditional, subtest requires students to solve linear equations in one variable and simplify linear expressions with no context.

The Course 2 Posttest (Part 1) also contains two contextual subtests, one algebraic and the other geometric, and a procedural algebra subtest. The contextual algebra and procedural algebra subtests are similar in design to their counterparts on the Course 1 Posttest but include some work with exponents and quadratic expressions. The geometry subtest presents a situation overlaid on a coordinate system; students are required to apply concepts and methods of coordinate geometry and explain the meaning of the results. Concepts and methods include finding an equation of a line given two points on it, the point of intersection of a vertical line and a second line, the midpoint of a segment, the distance between two points, an estimate of the area of an irregular closed region, and the reflection image of a figure across a given line. A related contextual problem requires the use of right triangle trigonometry to solve a triangle for the unknown length of a side.

Data Collection and Analysis

The lead teacher in each field-test school was responsible for testing at that site. Pretests were administered during regular class periods within the first 2 weeks of school and posttests during the last 2 weeks of school. Students had 40 minutes to complete the 40 item, multiple-choice ITED-Q, and 45 minutes to complete each part of the open-ended *CPMP* Posttests. Graphics calculators were allowed on all tests.

For the *CPMP* Posttests, a 5-point general scoring rubric was used:

- 4 for a "complete, correct response with clear unambiguous work or explanation";
- 3 for a "good response with minor error of execution but not of understanding";
- 2 for a "complete response showing understanding of some important ideas but misunderstanding of other ideas";
- 1 for an "incomplete response that omitted important parts or included major errors"; and
- 0 for "no response or an irrelevant response."

Graduate and advanced undergraduate Secondary Mathematics Education students were trained to use the rubrics to score the posttests. Training and practice on the scoring of each task continued until the interscorer agreement was 90% or higher. No scorers were aware of whether a particular test paper belonged to a *CPMP* or to a comparison student.

Matching CPMP and Comparison Groups

It makes sense to compare outcomes of groups whose previous achievement and aptitude are similar. To establish this similarity in the Course 1 study, the comparison students were separated into three subgroups according to whether they were just completing Prealgebra–General Mathematics, Algebra, or Accelerated Geometry. Each of these subgroups was matched to a subgroup of the *CPMP* Course 1 students. The matching variables were ITED-Q pretest score, school, and gender, in that order. If a match on pretest score could not be made with the same gender, then a student of opposite gender in the same school was chosen. If a match could not be made in the same school, a student of the same gender was chosen randomly from among potential pretest score matches in one of the other 10 schools. Only two comparison students could not be well matched in this way.

A similar process was used to match *CPMP* Course 2 students to the comparison students who were enrolled in Algebra, Geometry, or Accelerated Advanced Algebra in Grade 10. All but seven comparison students were well matched with *CPMP* Course 2 students. As Tables 14.3 and 14.4 show, pretest means and standard deviations for matched groups were nearly identical.

Matching on one preachievement measure has the limitation that outcomes and characteristics not tested by the matching measure do not enter into the match. For example, the Accelerated Geometry students had completed 2 years of college-preparatory high school mathematics, whereas the *CPMP* Course 1 matched students were just completing their first high school mathematics course.

Matched Group Comparisons

ITED-Q Posttests. The ITED-Q Posttest (Form L, Level 15) results for the three matched groups of students in the Course 1 study are given in Table 14.3. The test developers provide standard scores for the entire test but not for the subtests, so means and standard deviations of the number of

TABLE 14.3

ITED-Q Pretest and Posttest Information for Matched Groups of *CPMP* Course 1 and Comparison Students

Course	n	ITED-Q Pretest Mean	SD	ITED-Q Posttest Total Mean	SD	UMCP (5 Items) No.[a]	SD	Int. Inf. (18 Items) No.[a]	SD	Solve Probs. (17 Items) No.[a]	SD
Prealgebra	109	230.8	31.0	218.8	40.2	1.6	1.3	3.9	2.5	5.4	3.0
CPMP 1 (Match)	109	230.8	31.0	240.4*	35.5	2.0	1.4	5.1*	2.2	6.9*	3.0
Algebra	367	261.5	33.2	262.2	42.0	2.6	1.4	6.5	3.0	8.6	3.8
CPMP 1 (Match)	367	261.5	33.2	269.2*	37.9	2.7	1.2	6.9*	3.0	9.1	3.6
Acc. Geometry	49	294.6	22.1	304.0	21.6	3.6	1.0	9.4	3.0	12.6	2.6
CPMP 1 (Match)	49	294.6	21.8	299.1	23.7	3.6	0.8	9.3	3.1	11.6	2.9
All Comparison	525	258.3	36.1	257.1	46.2	2.5	1.4	6.2	3.3	8.3	4.0
All *CPMP* 1 (Match)	525	258.3	36.1	266.0*	39.5	2.7	1.3	6.8*	3.0	8.9*	3.6

Note. ITED-Q results were obtained by converting each student's raw score to a standard score, using conversion tables for norm groups who took the test with a calculator. The standard score describes a student's location on an achievement continuum, regardless of the ITED-Q test form or the student's grade level. As an example, on the ITED-Q Pretest (Form K, Level 15) the maximum standard score is 353, the minimum is 154, and the median is 255. The standard deviation is ~25 standard score points.

[a]The values in this column represent the mean number of items correct.

*The t statistics for significant matched group mean comparisons are as follows. Prealgebra: ITED-Q Posttest Total, $t = -4.19$, $p < .001$; Interpreting Information, $t = -3.86$, $p < .001$; Solving Problems, $t = -3.80$, $p < .001$. Algebra: ITED-Q Posttest Total, $t = -2.38$, $p = .017$; Interpreting Information, $t = -1.96$, $p = .05$. All matched students: ITED-Q Posttest Total, $t = -3.37$, $p = .001$; Interpreting Information, $t = -2.80$, $p = .005$; Solving Problems, $t = -2.50$, $p = .013$.

TABLE 14.4

ITED-Q Pretest and Posttest Information for Matched Groups of *CPMP*
Course 2 and Comparison Students

Course	n	ITED-Q Pretest		ITED-Q Posttest Total		UMCP (7 Items)		Int. Inf. (18 Items)		Solve Probs. (15 Items)	
		Mean	SD	Mean	SD	No.[a]	SD	No.[a]	SD	No.[a]	SD
Algebra	31	227.4	29.2	248.6	22.0	2.7	1.2	5.4	2.3	5.0	1.7
CPMP 2 (Match)	31	227.3	29.2	252.0	33.2	2.6	1.4	6.2	2.4	4.9	2.7
Geometry	139	265.0	29.8	281.4	30.1	3.5	1.4	8.2	3.0	7.6	2.9
CPMP 2 (Match)	139	265.0	30.4	283.7	28.3	3.4	1.3	8.4	3.0	7.8	2.7
Acc. Adv. Algebra	25	291.9	17.6	311.4	17.5	4.6	1.5	11.3	2.5	10.4	2.5
CPMP 2 (Match)	25	291.8	17.5	305.0	23.8	4.4	1.5	10.6	2.8	9.8	2.5
All Comparison	195	262.5	33.4	280.0	32.3	3.5	1.5	8.1	3.3	7.5	3.0
All *CPMP* 2 (Match)	195	262.4	33.8	281.4	32.0	3.4	1.4	8.4	3.1	7.6	3.0

[a]The values in this column represent the mean number of items correct.

items correct on each subtest are presented. For the Prealgebra students and their *CPMP* matched sample, the mean scores of the *CPMP* students were significantly higher on the entire test, Interpreting Information Subtest, and Solving Problems Subtest. For the Algebra students and their *CPMP* matched sample, the mean scores of the *CPMP* students were significantly higher on the entire test and Interpreting Information Subtest. The Accelerated Geometry students' ITED-Q and subtest means did not differ significantly from those of the matched group of *CPMP* students.

The ITED-Q Posttest (Form K, Level 16) results for the three matched groups of students in the Course 2 study are given in Table 14.4. The results for the Algebra and Accelerated Advanced Algebra students should be viewed with caution because they are each based on a small number of students. With that caution, the available data show no significant differences in matched group means on the ITED-Q or any of its subtests.

It is important to note that the samples for the Course 1 and Course 2 studies are different from one another. The results in Table 14.3 are for one study and those in Table 14.4 are for another study with a different student sample. No inferences about 2 years of growth on the ITED-Q can be made from the two tables.

Table 14.5 contains data from all students in the five schools that had Course 2 comparison classes who completed the ITED-Q Pretest, the ITED-Q Posttest for Course 1, and the ITED-Q Posttest for Course 2. The 2-year trends in the means show that the comparison students started at a higher level on the pretest (59th compared with 46th national student percentile). The *CPMP* students grew 10 percentile points on the posttest administered after Course 1, compared to a 2-point increase for the comparison students. Both groups maintained their first-year increase in the second year.

ITED-Q Means and Standard Deviations for All *CPMP*
and Comparison Students

Group	n	ITED-Q Pretest			ITED-Q Posttest (Course 1)			ITED-Q Posttest (Course 2)		
		Percentile	Mean	SD	Percentile	Mean	SD	Percentile	Mean	SD
Comparison	186	59	264.7	35.3	61	272.5	43.9	61	281.6	33.8
CPMP	287	46	250.9	35.4	56	266.8	36.5	56	274.9	33.1

Note. Means are standard scores. Percentiles are national student percentiles. Data are for all students in the 5 schools with comparison classes who completed the ITED-Q pretest, the ITED-Q posttest for Course 1, and the ITED-Q posttest for Course 2.

A similar 3-year pattern emerges when the ITED-Q pretest and ITED-Q posttest means for Courses 1, 2, and 3 are analyzed for all 1,457 *CPMP* field-test students with complete data. There was no Course 3 comparison group. For students with 3 years of *CPMP*, means over the 3 years are compared with the growth of the nationally representative norm group's growth at the 62nd percentile, the pretest level of the *CPMP* students. As Fig. 14.3 indicates, *CPMP* growth was strong in the first year, and the first-year increase was

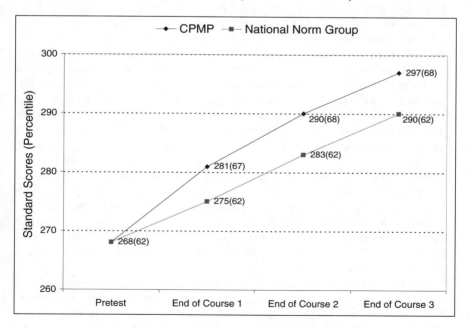

FIG. 14.3.   Three-year trends in ITED-Q standard scores and national student percentiles (based on all 1,457 *CPMP* students with complete data).

built on slightly in Course 2 and maintained in Course 3. This 3-year pattern is consistent, on average, in rural, urban, and suburban schools, for males and females, for various minority groups traditionally underrepresented in mathematics-related occupations, and for students for whom English was not their first language (Schoen, Hirsch, & Ziebarth, 1998).

In summary, the *CPMP* curriculum appears to have a positive effect on quantitative thinking as measured by the ITED-Q, with the greatest effect occurring in the first year of *CPMP* use. The particularly strong *CPMP* effect on the ITED-Q Interpreting Information and Solving Problems Subtests suggests that the impact of the curriculum is greatest in the areas of making inferences and predictions from data given in tables and graphs, applying quantitative procedures to relatively novel problems, reasoning quantitatively, and evaluating reasonableness of solutions.

It is not surprising that the largest mean differences occurred when *CPMP* students were compared with other nonaccelerated students. Two findings that may seem surprising are that: the accelerated Geometry students' means were not significantly greater than those of the matched *CPMP* students in spite of the former's extra year of high school mathematics and, the positive effect of *CPMP* measured by the ITED-Q was mainly realized in the first year. The likely explanation for both of these results lies in the non-curriculum-specific content of the ITED-Q. Because the specific content of the extra year of traditional mathematics is not measured by the ITED-Q, the advantage of having that year is not reflected in the posttest scores. However, the curriculum-based experiences of reading, analyzing, and reasoning about problem situations enabled *CPMP* students to approach the dense verbal load of the ITED-Q as a sense-making activity. We conjecture that this learning occurred within the first year of *CPMP*, and that the further learning of more specific mathematics in future years of *CPMP*, as with the accelerated traditional students, may not be measured by the ITED-Q.

Course 1 CPMP Posttest. Although the matched groups were formed from the set of all students who had completed both the ITED-Q Pretest and the ITED-Q Posttest for each course, not all students in the matched groups completed the *CPMP* Posttests. Rather than make new matches, the following results are presented for all students in the matched groups who also completed the Course 1 *CPMP* Posttest. The groups formed in this way were still well matched on the ITED-Q Pretest.

The algebra strand of the *CPMP* curriculum emphasizes development of algebraic ideas through modeling of quantitative relationships in contextual problems, so it might be expected that *CPMP* students would perform well on such tasks. Similarly, the comparison students might be expected to be fluent in algebraic symbolic manipulation with no context given. With some exceptions, the pattern of results in Table 14.6 aligns well with these

TABLE 14.6
Subtest Means and Standard Deviations for Matched Groups of *CPMP*
Course 1 and Comparison Students

Course	n	ITED-Q Pretest		Context. Alg. I		Context. Alg. II		Proced.Alg.	
		Mean	SD	Mean	SD	Mean	SD	Mean	SD
Prealgebra	100	228.99	30.61	3.07	2.42	1.37	1.16	5.53	3.94
CPMP 1 (Match)	101	231.20	31.14	7.51*	4.04	2.95*	2.34	6.13	3.93
Algebra	338	262.76	32.47	6.98	4.07	3.43	2.25	11.90*	4.74
CPMP 1 (Match)	317	263.40	32.73	10.60*	3.99	4.56*	2.49	9.41	5.04
Acc. Geometry	47	295.00	22.44	9.60	4.14	4.23	2.29	14.89*	3.77
CPMP 1 (Match)	44	295.16	21.44	12.48*	3.33	5.91*	3.05	11.75	4.80
All Comparison	485	258.91	36.03	6.42	4.22	3.09	2.26	10.87*	5.32
All *CPMP* 1 (Match)	462	259.39	35.98	10.11*	4.20	4.34*	2.64	8.92	5.05

Note. Subtest means and standard deviations are on the Course 1 Posttest. Maximum scores are as follows: Contextual Algebra I, 16; Contextual Algebra II, 12; and Procedural Algebra, 20.

*The t statistics for significant matched group mean comparisons are as follows. Prealgebra: Contextual Algebra I, $t = -9.45$, $p < .001$; Contextual Algebra II, $t = -6.06$, $p < .001$. Algebra: Contextual Algebra I, $t = -11.47$, $p < .001$; Contextual Algebra II, $t = -6.06$, $p < .001$; Procedural Algebra, $t = 6.51$, $p < .001$. Accelerated Geometry: Contextual Algebra I, $t = -3.64$, $p < .001$; Contextual Algebra II, $t = -2.98$, $p = .004$; Procedural Algebra, $t = 3.48$, $p = .001$. All matched students: Contextual Algebra I, $t = -13.44$, $p < .001$; Contextual Algebra II, $t = -7.84$, $p < .001$; Procedural Algebra, $t = 5.80$, $p < .001$.

expectations. Notice that mean differences on the contextual algebra subtests are approximately 0.5–1.0 standard deviation, favoring *CPMP* students. Mean differences on the procedural algebra subtests are approximately 0.5 standard deviation, favoring the comparison group for all but the Prealgebra students.

A more detailed analysis of particular tasks may illuminate the pattern of results and suggest ways that curriculum developers can refine materials and teachers can modify implementation to improve student learning. As an illustration of the nature of the group differences in algebraic understanding and reasoning, the four-part task referred to in Table 14.6 as Contextual Algebra I is given in Fig. 14.4. Means of the matched groups on each part of this task are also given. Numbers of students in the groups are the same as those given in Table 14.6.

In part (a) of this task, the intent was for students to indicate that 18 is the number of gallons of gasoline the boat had on board at the start and −2 indicates that 2 gallons of gasoline are used by the boat for each mile it travels. Such a response was given a score of 4. A score of 3 means either that both parts of the question were answered but with some vagueness such as "18 is the starting point" or "−2 is the slope" or that one question was answered at a 4 level and the other was vague or incorrect. A score of 2 was

The number of gallons (y) of gasoline left in a large motor boat after traveling x miles since filling the tank is given by $y = 18 - 2x$.

	Prealg	CPMP Match	Alg.	CPMP Match	Acc. Geo.	CPMP Match
(a). Explain what 18 and -2 in the equation tell about the number of gallons.	1.1	2.2	2.1	2.8	2.6	3.2
(b). Graph this equation. Explain the role of 18 and -2 in the graph.	0.4	1.6	1.3	2.3	1.4	2.8
(c). After filling the gasoline tank, Helen drove the boat until there were 10 gallons left. How many miles had she driven? Explain how you can tell from the equation and how you can tell from the graph.	0.6	1.7	1.5	2.6	2.4	3.2
(d). How many gallons of gasoline were left after Helen had driven the boat 8 miles? Show or explain your work.	1.0	2.1	2.1	2.9	3.1	3.2

FIG. 14.4. Contextual Algebra 1 task from the CPMP Course 1 Posttest (means based on 4 points for each part).

assigned if one part of the response was vague but relevant, that is, at the 3 level, but the other part was incorrect, or if one part of the question was answered at the 4 level but the other part was missing. Parts (b), (c), and (d) can be interpreted in a similar manner.

The CPMP means are generally much higher than those of the matched comparison group. However, there is room for improvement by all student groups.

Course 2 CPMP Posttest. As in Course 1, rather than form new matched groups the following results are presented for all students in the original matched groups who also completed the Course 2 CPMP Posttest. The groups formed in this way were still well matched on the ITED-Q Pretest. Unfortunately, one of the five schools that administered the ITED-Q Posttest to comparison students in the Course 2 field test decided not to disrupt classes for a second day to administer the Course 2 CPMP Posttest to comparison students. This accounts for the large decrease in numbers in the geometry matched groups.

As indicated in Table 14.7, Course 2 CPMP students performed much better than matched comparison students on the contextual tasks and not as well on the procedural tasks, although the latter differences were only statistically significant in comparison to the Accelerated Advanced Algebra students who were completing their second full year of Algebra.

The procedural algebra tasks from the CPMP Course 2 Posttest are given in Fig. 14.5, together with means of the CPMP and comparison groups. Numbers of students in the groups are the same as those given in Table 14.7. Again, there is room for improvement for all groups of students, but

TABLE 14.7
Subtest Means and Standard Deviations for Matched Groups of *CPMP*
Course 2 and Comparison Students

Course	n	ITED-Q Pretest		Coord. Geom.		Context. Alg.		Proced. Alg.	
		Mean	SD	Mean	SD	Mean	SD	Mean	SD
Algebra	31	227.35	29.17	8.26	3.41	2.54	2.05	6.26	2.86
CPMP 2 (Match)	27	227.33	30.72	13.15*	3.75	7.04*	4.05	7.23	4.41
Geometry	67	261.52	30.76	10.97	4.19	3.99	2.83	7.51	3.19
CPMP 2 (Match)	69	260.72	33.05	16.84*	4.66	6.70*	3.99	7.23	4.41
Acc. Adv. Algebra	25	291.88	17.57	15.16	3.70	5.64	2.36	12.88*	3.43
CPMP 2 (Match)	18	289.50	16.48	17.33	4.33	8.83*	3.62	9.50	2.83
All Comparison	123	259.08	35.51	11.13	4.53	3.94	2.74	8.30	3.94
All *CPMP* 2 (Match)	114	257.36	36.09	16.10*	4.70	7.14*	3.97	7.54	4.05

Note. Subtest means and standard deviations are on the Course 2 Posttest. Maximum scores are as follows: Coordinate Geometry, 24; Contextual Algebra, 12; and Procedural Algebra, 16.

*The t statistics for significant matched group mean comparisons are as follows. Algebra: Coordinate Geometry, $t = -5.20$, $p < .001$; Contextual Algebra, $t = -5.43$, $p < .001$. Geometry: Coordinate Geometry, $t = -7.72$, $p < .001$; Contextual Algebra, $t = -4.56$, $p < .001$. Accelerated Advanced Algebra: Contextual Algebra, $t = -3.50$, $p = .001$; Procedural Algebra, $t = 3.42$, $p = .001$. All matched students: Coordinate Geometry, $t = -8.25$, $p < .001$; Contextual Algebra, $t = -7.27$, $p < .001$.

	Alg.	CPMP Match	Geo.	CPMP Match	Adv. Alg.	CPMP Match
Solve $126 = 84 - 14x$. Explain your work and how to check it.	1.9	2.2	2.6	2.3	3.6	2.9
For the equation below, write an equivalent equation in the form $y = a + bx$. Explain how you are sure that the new equation is equivalent to the given one. $y = 52 + 20\,(x - 4)$	1.2	0.7	1.0	1.1	2.8	1.4
If $2^3 = 8$, $2^5 = 32$, and $(8)(32) = 2^n$, then $n = \_\_\_\_$.	1.5	2.0	1.8	1.9	3.3	2.4
(0 - 2 points for each part) • Find $3(2^x)$ if $x = 4$.	1.1	1.2	1.5	1.2	1.9	1.7
• Does $3(2^x) = 6^x$ for any given x? Explain.	0.6	1.0	0.6	0.7	1.2	1.0

FIG. 14.5. Sample algebraic procedural tasks from the *CPMP* Course 2 Posttest (means based on 4 points for each task).

differences in Course 2 group means are small. Consistent with the data presented in Table 14.7, means of the Accelerated Advanced Algebra group are greater than those of the *CPMP* matched group on the procedural algebra subtest; means of the Algebra and Geometry groups are similar to those of their *CPMP* matched group.

The results on the Course 1 and Course 2 Posttests are consistent with the differing emphases of the *CPMP* and traditional curricula. *CPMP* students probably had an advantage on the contextual problems as they were in a familiar form. However, individual interviews of *CPMP* and comparison students suggest that *CPMP* students are indeed better able to handle mathematical ideas in context and that *CPMP* students are less automatic and efficient with paper-and-pencil algebra procedures than some comparison students (Schoen, Hirsch, & Ziebarth, 1998). The finding on contextual problem solving is consistent with extensive research evidence documenting the inability of many traditionally-educated students to move between symbolic and contextual situations and to solve verbally stated mathematics problems (Boaler, 1997; Schoenfeld, 1988, 1992).

Course 3 NAEP-Based Achievement Results

Procedures

The National Assessment of Educational Progress (NAEP) is administered periodically to monitor U.S. students' achievement levels in various subject areas. In 1990 and 1992, a NAEP mathematics assessment was administered at several grades, including Grade 12. As another measure of *CPMP* students' achievement, a 30-item test was constructed by using released NAEP items from five content categories and three process categories.

The NAEP-based test was administered in May 1997 to *CPMP* students at the end of Course 3. A total of 1,292 students in 22 *CPMP* field-test schools completed this test.[3] Six of the schools were urban, six were rural, and 10 were suburban. In the presentation of the results, comparisons are made between the *CPMP* students and students in the nationally representative sample of 8,499 twelfth-grade students who took the NAEP in Fall 1990 or 1992 (Kenney & Silver, 1997).

The pattern of mathematics course taking of the NAEP sample and the *CPMP* Course 3 group differed considerably. Students in the NAEP sample reported having taken the following mathematics courses: Calculus (10%), Precalculus (19%), Advanced Algebra (61%), Geometry (76%), or Algebra (87%). Thus, the sample included some students who had not enrolled in a mathematics course within the year prior to the NAEP testing and others

TABLE 14.8

Mean Percent Correct and Mean Percent Differences by Group on
NAEP-Based Test

Calculator, Content, or Process Type	No. of Items	National (% correct)	CPMP 3 (% correct)	% Difference (CPMP–Nat.)	CPMP 3 SD
		Content Categories			
Data, Statistics, & Probability	4	44.5	67.0	22.5	24.5
Measurement	8	42.9	58.6	15.7	23.3
Algebra & Functions	6	41.5	53.2	11.7	21.8
Geometry	7	48.6	59.6	11.0	22.7
Numbers & Operations	5	34.1	43.8	9.7	25.7
		Process Categories			
Conceptual	10	44.3	60.8	16.5	18.4
Problem Solving	12	39.5	53.3	13.8	21.2
Procedural	8	45.4	55.6	10.2	23.4
		Calculator Access			
Calculator Available (all)	11	39.1	56.4	17.3	22.7
No Calculator (NAEP sample)	19	44.7	56.4	11.7	17.3
Total	30	42.7	56.4	13.7	17.9

Note. For *CPMP*, $N = 1,292$; for the national NAEP sample, $N = 8,499$.

who were taking calculus. In contrast, all of the *CPMP* students were just completing *CPMP* Course 3.

Testing conditions were not equivalent to the original administration of these same items by NAEP. For example, items were not administered in the same order, possibly affecting the item statistics. Further, the *CPMP* students had a graphics calculator available for the entire test; for the NAEP sample, a calculator was required for 11 of the 30 items and was not available for the others. Instead of a focus on comparing means, the item data from the NAEP sample are used as a benchmark of the difficulty of an item or of all items in a content, process, or NAEP-sample calculator category.

Results

The results from the NAEP-based test are given in Table 14.8.

Of the five content categories, the mean percent differences between *CPMP* and NAEP sample students was greatest on data analysis, statistics, and probability, a content strand of the *CPMP* curriculum that is not emphasized in most of the more traditional mathematics curricula.

Of the process categories, *CPMP* students' performance relative to the NAEP sample was best on conceptual items. This outcome is consistent with *CPMP*'s emphasis on sense making, applications, and problem solving with an accompanying deemphasis on procedural skill practice.

It might be expected that *CPMP* students would be relatively advantaged on the 19 items for which students in the national NAEP sample had no calculator available, but the data suggest the opposite. In fact, the difference between the performance of *CPMP* students and the national NAEP sample is greater on those items for which a calculator was permitted in the NAEP testing. Perhaps part of the explanation is that a graphics calculator is an essential tool in the *CPMP* curriculum, and students are taught its various uses as the need arises. Thus, *CPMP* students may become more proficient at using a calculator than students in many traditional classes in which the calculator often has a supplementary or enrichment role. This greater calculator proficiency is likely a positive factor for *CPMP* students on items for which a calculator is needed or potentially useful.

Sample tasks with percent correct for the *CPMP* and NAEP sample are presented in Fig. 14.6 to illustrate the content, process, and NAEP sample calculator-availability categories.

The NAEP-based test results show a pattern similar to the one that emerged from the ITED-Q and *CPMP* Posttest results. *CPMP* students demonstrate strengths in areas of conceptual understanding and problem solving in realistic contexts; they demonstrate somewhat lesser success with paper-and-pencil procedures and memory-based tasks.

Performance on College Entrance Examinations

Most universities and colleges require applicants to complete either the SAT or the ACT college entrance examinations, and the results are usually used in the admission process as one indicator of potential for success in college. Such examinations are important to both students and their parents.

The SAT college entrance examination (SAT I) comprises two subtests, Verbal and Mathematics. The SAT Mathematics test measures mathematical reasoning and symbol sense, drawing on content from arithmetic, algebra, and geometry. It requires understanding of basic algebraic and geometric concepts typical of the first 2 years of traditional high school mathematics but measures little standard paper-and-pencil algebraic symbolic manipulation. The scores on both subtests are standardized with a mean of 500 and standard deviation of 100.

The ACT college entrance examination consists of four subtests: English, Mathematics, Reading, and Science Reasoning. The ACT also reports a Composite score, the average of the four subtest scores. The ACT Mathematics subtest measures achievement on the content of a traditional college preparatory mathematics curriculum, including topics from elementary algebra, intermediate algebra, coordinate geometry, plane geometry, and trigonometry. ACT Mathematics items test algebraic, geometric, and

Sample NAEP Item	CPMP	NAEP
[*Data, Statistics & Probability, Problem Solving, NC*] From a shipment of 500 batteries, a sample of 25 was selected at random and tested. If 2 batteries in the sample were found to be dead, how many dead batteries would be expected to be in the sample?	80%	51%

(a) 10   b) 20   (c) 30   *(d) 40   (e) 50

| [*Measurement, Problem Solving, C*] In the figure above, a circle with center O and radius of length 3 is inscribed in a square. What is the area of the shaded region? | 64% | 37% |

(a) 3.86   *(b) 7.73   (c) 28.27   (d) 32.86   (e) 36.00

| [*Algebra & Functions, Conceptual, C*] For what value of x is $8^{12} = 16^x$? | 82% | 34% |

(a) 3   (b) 4   (c) 8   *(d) 9   (e) 12

| [*Algebra & Functions, Procedural, NC*] In right triangle ABC above, cos A = | 34% | 30% |

*(a) $\dfrac{3}{5}$ (b) $\dfrac{3}{4}$ (c) $\dfrac{4}{5}$ (d) $\dfrac{4}{3}$ (e) $\dfrac{5}{3}$

| [*Geometry, Conceptual, NC*] Which of the following is NOT a property of every rectangle? | 86% | 71% |

(a) The opposite sides are equal in length.   (b) The opposite sides are parallel.

(c) All angles are equal in measure.   *(d) All sides are equal in length.

(e) The diagonals are equal in length.

| [*Number & Operations, Procedural, C*] A savings account earns 1 percent per month on the sum of the initial amount deposited plus any accumulated interest. If a savings account is opened with an initial deposit of $1,000 and no other deposits or withdrawals are made, what will be the amount in this account at the end of 6 months? | 36% | 15% |

(a) $1,060.00   *(b) $1,061.52   (c) $1,072.14   (d) $1,600.00   (e) $6,000.00

FIG. 14.6. Sample NAEP-based items of various types with average percent correct by group. (C means students in the NAEP sample used a calculator on that item; NC means that they did not. The asterisks mark the correct answers.).

trigonometric concepts and procedures and standard word problems usually intended to be solved by using equations or inequalities. ACT subtest and composite scores are reported on a scale ranging from 1 to 36.

Both the ACT and SAT allow, but do not require, students to use graphics calculators. Virtually no statistics, probability, or discrete mathematics are tested on either test.

TABLE 14.9
ITBS and SAT Information for *CPMP* and Traditional Students

Group	n	ITBS Math (Percentile)		SAT Math	
		Mean	SD	Mean	SD
CPMP	54	57.1	20.4	484.6	53.8
Traditional	44	57.5	17.9	467.0	67.5

Note. Information is for students at Southeast High School.

Comparative Studies

One field-test school, referred to by the pseudonym Southeast High School, provided eighth-grade ITBS scores as baseline data. This school is in a suburban district in the South in which families are primarily middle to upper-middle income and parents are well educated. Approximately 89% of students are Caucasian and others are from various minority groups. Three years of high school mathematics are required for graduation.

At the beginning of the *CPMP* field test, Fall 1994, all students who qualified for Prealgebra or nonhonors Algebra were randomly assigned to *CPMP* Course 1 or to the appropriate Prealgebra or Algebra class. Many of these students completed Advanced Algebra or *CPMP* Course 3 in their junior year and took the SAT either in Spring or Summer of their junior year or in Fall of their senior year. Results for this set of *CPMP* and traditional students are given in Table 14.9. Both groups of students were comparable in mathematics achievement at the beginning of Grade 9. The difference between SAT Mathematics means is not statistically significant at the 0.05 level for students studying from the two different curricula.

One urban school district in the Midwest provided ACT Mathematics and ACT Composite scores along with sixth-grade California Achievement Test (CAT) scores. This district does not give standardized mathematics tests to students in Grades 7 or 8. The pseudonym, Midwest High School, is used, although the data come from two similar high schools in the same district in a city with a population of several hundred thousand. The students come from a mix of socioeconomic backgrounds, and approximately 30% of students are either Hispanic or African American. Midwest High School requires 3 years of high school mathematics for graduation.

At the beginning of the *CPMP* field test (Fall 1994), all students who qualified for remedial mathematics through algebra were randomly assigned by computer to *CPMP* Course 1 or to the appropriate traditional class. Many of these students completed Advanced Algebra or *CPMP* Course 3 in their junior year and took the ACT either in Spring or Summer of their junior year or in Fall of their senior year. Results for these students are given in Table 14.10. Students in the two curricula had comparable mathematical

TABLE 14.10

Sixth-Grade Information for *CPMP* and Traditional Students

Group	n	CAT Math (Percentile)		ACT Math		ACT Composite	
		Mean	SD	Mean	SD	Mean	SD
CPMP	71	66.3	24.2	18.3	3.1	20.3	3.6
Traditional	42	68.5	26.4	18.4	3.5	19.1	3.6

Note. Information is for Students at Midwest High School.

backgrounds at the beginning of high school. The ACT Mathematics mean for the *CPMP* group was almost identical to that of the traditional group.

In both Southeast and Midwest High Schools, the *CPMP* and traditional students were well matched on before-high school standardized mathematics test means. At each site, the only apparent systematic difference is that one group learned high school mathematics in the context of the *CPMP* curriculum and the active learning environment it promotes. Class observations, student and teacher interviews, and teacher surveys provide evidence that teachers in both schools implemented *CPMP* in a way that was well aligned with the project team's recommendations. Together the SAT and ACT Mathematics results suggest that well-matched *CPMP* and traditional students do not differ significantly on these college entrance examinations.

ACT Trends

By Fall 1999, eight *CPMP* field-test schools had adopted *CPMP* for all their Grade 9–12 students. Seven of the eight schools are midwestern schools where most of the students who plan to attend college take the ACT. Three of the eight schools are rural, two are urban, and three are suburban. Seven of the eight schools were also pilot-test schools, so beginning in 1995–1996 nearly all their students (mainly juniors) who took the ACT college entrance examination had experienced *CPMP* as their high school mathematics program. By 1996–1997, all students in all eight schools had experienced *CPMP* rather than the traditional mathematics program that had been in place in previous years.

The trend data in Table 14.11 are compiled from the 1997–1998 ACT school reports from these eight schools. ACT Science Reasoning scores are reported because this subtest requires reasoning in contextual, quantitative, and graphical settings. The decrease in the number of *CPMP* students taking the ACT in 1997–1998 was due to the opening of a new high school in the town with the largest of the eight schools, thereby cutting enrollment in the *CPMP* school by nearly one half. National means are those of all students

TABLE 14.11
Five-year Trends of ACT Means

Year	CPMP N	ACT Mathematics		ACT Science Reasoning		ACT Composite	
		CPMP	National	CPMP	National	CPMP	National
1993–1994	1,067	21.3	20.2	22.2	20.9	21.9	20.8
1994–1995	1,107	21.8	20.2	22.4	21.0	22.1	20.8
1995–1996	1,040	21.9	20.2	22.7	21.1	22.3	20.9
1996–1997	1,150	21.5	20.6	22.6	21.1	22.3	21.0
1997–1998	971	21.6	20.8	22.8	21.1	22.4	21.0

Note. ACT means are across eight schools, using the *CPMP* curriculum with all students beginning in either 1995–1996 or 1996–1997.

who took the ACT each year, a number that has steadily increased over the 5 years from 891,714 in 1993–1994 to 995,039 in 1997–1998.

The all-*CPMP* schools may differ demographically from those in the national ACT sample, so the magnitude of a mean difference on a particular subtest at any given time is of little interest. However, a comparison of the annual trends for the *CPMP* students and the national ACT sample is informative. First, mean scores in the *CPMP* schools nearly all held steady or increased since 1995–1996 when examinees in those schools first completed *CPMP* rather than a traditional program. Second, the annual ACT Mathematics trends in *CPMP* schools are similar to those in the ACT national sample. ACT Mathematics means in *CPMP* schools increased by 0.3 points from 1993–1994 to 1997–1998 compared with 0.6 in the national ACT sample. Over the same period, ACT Science Reasoning and ACT Composite means increased more in the all-*CPMP* schools than in the national sample (increases of 0.6 and 0.5, respectively, compared with an increase of 0.2). Although student populations may have changed in ways that affect ACT scores over this 5-year period, these longitudinal trends are consistent with a conclusion that the *CPMP* curriculum prepares students for the ACT at least as well as traditional mathematics curricula.

Performance on a College Mathematics Placement Test

A mathematics placement test that is currently used at a major university was administered to students in field-test schools in May 1999 at the end of *CPMP* Course 4 and at the end of traditional Precalculus. The university's mathematics department uses this placement test, compiled from a bank of items developed by the Mathematical Association of America, to make recommendations to entering freshmen concerning the college mathematics course in which they should enroll. This test contains three subtests—Basic

Algebra (15 items), Advanced Algebra (15 items), and Calculus Readiness (20 items). The first two subtests consist almost entirely of symbolic manipulation tasks such as simplifying and factoring algebraic expressions, solving equations and inequalities, and finding equations for lines given sufficient conditions. The third subtest measures some of the important concepts and processes that underlie calculus, such as logarithmic and exponential equations, trigonometric functions and identities, composition of functions, rational functions and their domains, systems of nonlinear equations, and area of a rectangle under a curve. A graphing calculator (that does not do symbolic manipulation) is allowed on this test.

The *CPMP* Course 4 students included in the comparison that follows are all those in the 1998–1999 Course 4 field test who completed at least six of the seven "preparation for calculus" units of Course 4 as the last course in their sequence of *CPMP* Courses 1–4. The Precalculus students, also from field-test schools, competed a traditional Precalculus course to end a sequence of Algebra, Geometry, and Advanced Algebra. The two groups were restricted to those students who indicated on a written survey their intention to attend a 4-year college or university in the next school year. Both groups are composed of students who fell mainly in the 75th to 95th national percentiles, on average approximately 85th, on standardized mathematical achievement tests at the beginning of high school. Means and standard deviations by group and subtest are reported in Table 14.12.

The *CPMP* Course 4 mean is significantly greater than the Precalculus mean on the Calculus Readiness subtest, whereas the group means do not differ significantly on the Basic Algebra and Advanced Algebra subtests. This is more content-specific evidence to combine with the SAT and ACT findings presented earlier that *CPMP* students are at least as well prepared for entering college mathematics as students from more traditional curricula. An area of particular strength for the *CPMP* Course 4 students is understanding of the concepts and processes that underlie Calculus.

TABLE 14.12

Placement Subtest Information for *CPMP* and Traditional
Precalculus Students

Group	n	Basic Algebra		Intermediate Algebra		Calculus Readiness	
		Mean	SD	Mean	SD	Mean	SD
Precalculus	177	11.4	2.3	9.6	3.2	10.5	4.3
CPMP 4	164	11.5	2.6	9.2	3.4	12.9*	4.7

*The t statistics for the significant Calculus Readiness group mean comparison are $t = -4.93$, $p < .001$.

Performance in College Mathematics Courses

The first students who have experienced the entire four courses of *CPMP* in the field-test version entered college in Fall 1999. However, some preliminary evidence on how high school graduates who studied the *CPMP* curriculum in its pilot version perform in collegiate mathematics courses is available. Freshmen college mathematics course grade data for each year from 1995–1996 through 1998–1999 were gathered for all graduates of two similar high schools in one midwestern, suburban school district who enrolled at the University of Michigan. For purposes of this report, the pseudonyms East High School and West High School are used. Both East and West High Schools' 1995 and 1996 graduates experienced a traditional high school college-preparatory mathematics program with offerings through AP Calculus. This program continued at West High School. At East High School, all 1997 graduates who were not in an accelerated mathematics program and all 1998 graduates completed the *CPMP* pilot curriculum. Accelerated students among 1998 East graduates took AP Calculus as seniors after completing *CPMP* Courses 1–4 in previous years.

Located in a suburb with many affluent, well-educated residents, East and West High Schools (enrollments of approximately 840 and 1,070, respectively) are 2 miles apart and demographically similar. Many adults in the community are professionals in upper management positions. Over 80% of the students are White, with Asian Americans comprising the largest of several minority groups. Fewer than 10 students in each school are eligible for the free lunch program. Freshman college mathematics course grades of graduates from these two schools who matriculated at the University of Michigan were analyzed by using computer data files with school names, but no student names, attached. Thus, the form of the data precludes any connecting of data to individual students, but it allows for analysis of 4-year school trends in college mathematics course-taking and grades.

Pertinent mathematics courses at the university are Precalculus, Calculus I, Calculus II, Calculus III, Introduction to Differential Equations, and honors (all honors math courses open to freshmen). Precalculus is the most basic mathematics course offered. Typically, freshmen enrolled in Precalculus have completed 3–4 years of college-preparatory high school mathematics but not AP Calculus. Freshmen enrolled in Calculus I in fall semester have usually completed at least 4 years of high school mathematics through Precalculus or *CPMP* Course 4, and some may have taken a high school AP Calculus course. Spring-semester Calculus I classes include some students who successfully completed Precalculus in the Fall semester. Freshmen in Calculus II or Calculus III are placed there mainly because of high AP Calculus Examination scores or success in the preceding college

TABLE 14.13

College Mathematics Mean Grade-Point Averages by School, Course,
and Year

	East High School				West High School			
College Class	*1995* (50)	*1996* (74)	*1997* (87)	*1998* (72)	*1995* (34)	*1996* (57)	*1997* (45)	*1998* (35)
Precalculus	3.18	2.29	2.74	2.98	1.46	3.00	2.60	2.97
	(4)	(6)	(13)	(6)	(7)	(4)	(5)	(3)
Calculus I	2.86	2.60	3.08	2.89	2.33	2.82	2.58	2.87
	(14)	(19)	(32)	(25)	(7)	(13)	(15)	(7)
Calculus II	2.67	3.33	3.17	3.49	2.45	3.21	2.63	2.29
	(14)	(12)	(19)	(12)	(6)	(18)	(8)	(8)
Calculus III	2.66	3.10	2.95	2.99	2.50	3.17	3.34	2.34
	(5)	(4)	(6)	(8)	(2)	(11)	(6)	(5)
Intro. To Diff. Eqn.	2.15	4.00	4.00	3.30	—	3.67	3.65	—
	(2)	(1)	(2)	(2)		(3)	(2)	
Honors	—	3.28	—	—	3.30	3.77	4.23	—
		(5)			(1)	(3)	(4)	
All Courses	2.76	2.89	3.06	3.07	2.15	3.15	2.92	2.57
	(39)	(47)	(72)	(53)	(23)	(52)	(40)	(23)

Note. Number of students is shown parenthetically; years denote year of graduation. East High School used *CPMP* in 1997 and 1998; West High School used traditional curricula in all 4 years.

calculus course in the Fall semester. Freshmen with exceptionally strong high school mathematics backgrounds and high AP Calculus Examination scores may take Calculus III in the Fall semester and Differential Equations in the Spring semester.

Table 14.13 gives the number of matriculants at the University of Michigan among the 1995, 1996, 1997, and 1998 graduates of East and West High Schools, the numbers of these graduates completing each mathematics course in their freshman year, together with grade point averages, and course averages. The grade point averages were calculated by using the university's system: A + (4.3), A (4), A − (3.7), B + (3.3), B (3), . . . , D (1), D − (0.7), E + (0.3), and E (0).

University mathematics course grades of East High School graduates for 1997 and 1998, when the *CPMP* pilot curriculum was in place, are generally higher than both pre-*CPMP* (that is, 1995 and 1996) East graduates and 1997 and 1998 West High School graduates. The number of 1997 and 1998 East High School graduates matriculating at the University of Michigan is greater than for the previous 2 years. As for courses in Calculus I and above, school trends in grade point averages (GPA) are shown in Fig. 14.7.

While West High's grade averages varied greatly from year to year, those of East High were higher in 1997 and 1998 after using the *CPMP* curriculum

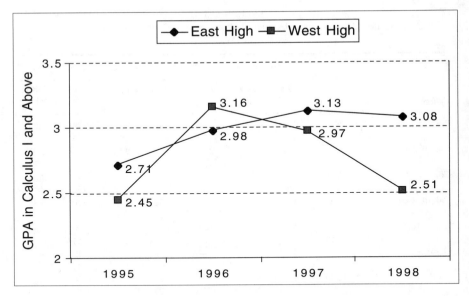

FIG. 14.7.   Mean grade point averages in Calculus I courses and above.

than in the previous two years when a traditional curriculum was in place. The percent of course enrollments in Calculus I and above is greater for West High School in 1997 (88% compared with 82% for East High); but in 1998 when all East High graduates had completed the *CPMP* curriculum, these percents were 89% for East High and 87% for West High. More information concerning the relationship between individual students' high school and college mathematics records would allow for a more detailed interpretation of these data. However, this preliminary evidence suggests that students who experienced the pilot *CPMP* curriculum were at least as well prepared for calculus (AP or college level) as students in a more traditional curriculum.

DISCUSSION

The primary goals of *CPMP* were to design, develop, and evaluate a four-year high school mathematics program that embodies the content, processes, and teaching principles recommended by the NCTM *Standards.* Evaluation data were used both to guide the development of the curriculum and to provide evidence of its impact on student learning. The *CPMP* curriculum seems to be particularly effective in developing students' conceptual understanding, quantitative thinking, and ability to solve contextualized problems. *CPMP* students perform well on tasks involving statistics and probability; content that was emphasized throughout the curriculum. At the same time, there is evidence that they are at least as well prepared for the SAT and the ACT college entrance examinations as similar students in more traditional curricula. *CPMP* students also perform well on calculus readiness tasks, which is consistent with the curriculum's focus on functions and patterns of change beginning in Course 1.

Symbolic manipulation in algebra is an area of concern for critics of *Standards*-oriented curricula. Results of the *CPMP* Posttests in Courses 1 and 2 and the NAEP-based test in Course 3 consistently show that *CPMP* students are stronger than comparison students in more traditional curricula in conceptual understanding, interpretation of algebraic representations and calculations, and problem solving in realistic contexts, but somewhat weaker in out of context, paper-and-pencil symbolic manipulation. This general pattern of algebraic learning is also confirmed by a study of matched groups of *CPMP* Course 3 and comparison students in Advanced Algebra in six field-test schools who were tested with a researcher-developed measure of a broad range of algebraic outcomes (Huntley et al., 2000).

The *CPMP* development team used this evidence in the development of the field-test version of Course 4. For example, a section providing additional symbolic manipulation skill practice was included at the end of each lesson of each unit. The intent was to improve the procedural algebra outcomes while maintaining the curriculum's identified strengths. The college mathematics placement test results presented earlier suggest that this goal was achieved.

Evidence from the field tests of Courses 1–3 was also used to shape the final published version of each of these courses. As part of *CPMP*'s longitudinal study of the published curriculum mentioned at the beginning of this chapter, the Educational Testing Services's Algebra End-of-Course Examination was administered to 586 *CPMP* Course 2 students in May 1999. This test is developed, distributed, and scored by the Educational Testing Service. The *CPMP* students were all the Course 2 students in the three longitudinal study schools (one suburban and two rural) in which all students have experienced a *Standards*-oriented mathematics curriculum in middle school and the *CPMP* curriculum in high school. Compared with 7,235 first-time Algebra students using traditional curricula who took this test in May 1999, the scores of *CPMP* students were 9% higher in Concepts, 7% higher in Process, 10% higher in Algebraic Representations, and 6% higher in Functions. However, *CPMP* students were just 1% higher in both Algebraic Skills and Algebraic Expressions and Equations.

We believe that the *CPMP* evaluation provides strong evidence in support of the feasibility of the curriculum and of *Standards*-oriented reform generally. Nonetheless, because potentially important changes were made in the *CPMP* curriculum following its field test, new research is needed to study the effect of the "final" curriculum on student achievement outcomes in high school and post-high school settings. Ideally, such research would involve schools that have used *CPMP* for at least a few years so that teachers understand the full scope and sequence of the curriculum and that both teachers and students are accustomed to the expectations of the *CPMP* classroom environment.

REFERENCES

Boaler, J. (1997). *Experiencing school mathematics: Teaching styles, sex and setting.* Bristol, PA: Open University Press.

Coxford, A. F., Fey, J. T., Hirsch, C. R., Schoen, H. L., Burrill, G., Hart, E. W., Watkins, A. E., with Messenger, M. J., & Ritsema, B. (1997). *Contemporary mathematics in context: A unified approach* (Course 1). Columbus, OH: Glencoe/McGraw-Hill.

Coxford, A. F., Fey, J. T., Hirsch, C. R., Schoen, H. L., Burrill, G., Hart, E. W., Watkins, A. E., with Messenger, M. J., & Ritsema, B. (1998). *Contemporary mathematics in context: A unified approach* (Course 2). Columbus, OH: Glencoe/McGraw-Hill.

Coxford, A. F., Fey, J. T., Hirsch, C. R., Schoen, H. L., Burrill, G., Hart, E. W., Watkins, A. E., with Messenger, M. J., & Ritsema, B. (1999). *Contemporary mathematics in context: A unified approach* (Course 3). Columbus, OH: Glencoe/McGraw-Hill.

Coxford, A. F., Fey, J. T., Hirsch, C. R., Schoen, H. L., Hart, E. W., Keller, B. A., Watkins, A. E., with Ritsema, B., & Walker, R. K. (2001). *Contemporary mathematics in context: A unified approach* (Course 4). Columbus, OH: Glencoe/McGraw-Hill.

Feldt, L. S., Forsyth, R. A., Ansley, T. N., & Alnot, S. D. (1993). *Iowa tests of educational development (Forms K & L).* Chicago: Riverside.

Hiebert, J., Carpenter, T. P., Fennema, E., Fuson, K., Human, P., Murray, H., Olivier, A., & Wearne, D. (1996). Problem solving as a basis for reform in curriculum and instruction: The case of mathematics. *Educational Researcher, 25*(4), 12–21.

Hirsch, C. R., Coxford A. F., Fey, J. T., & Schoen, H. L. (1995). Teaching sensible mathematics in sense-making ways with the CPMP. *Mathematics Teacher, 88,* 694–700.

Hirsch, C. R., & Coxford, A. F. (1997). Mathematics for all: Perspectives and promising practices. *School Science and Mathematics, 97,* 232–241.

Huntley, M. A., Rasmussen, C. L., Villarubi, R. S., Sangtong, J., & Fey, J. T. (2000). Effects of Standards-based mathematics education: A study of the Core-Plus Mathematics Project algebra and functions strand. *Journal for Research in Mathematics Education, 31*(3), 328–361.

Kenney, P. A., & Silver, E. A. (1997). *Results from the sixth mathematics assessment of the national assessment of educational progress.* Reston, VA: National Council of Teachers of Mathematics.

Kett, J. R. (1998). A portrait of assessment in mathematics reform classrooms. (Doctoral dissertation, Western Michigan University, 1997). *Dissertation Abstracts International, 58*(12), 4591.

Lave, J., Smith, S., & Butler, M. (1988). Problem solving as everyday practice. In R. I. Charles & E. A. Silver (Eds.), *The teaching and assessing of mathematical problem solving* (pp. 61–81). Reston, VA: National Council of Teachers of Mathematics.

Lloyd, G., & Wilson, M. R. (1998). Supporting innovation: The impact of a teacher's conceptions of functions on his implementation of a reform curriculum. *Journal for Research in Mathematics Education, 29*(3), 248–274.

Mathematical Sciences Education Board. (1990). *Reshaping school mathematics: A philosophy and framework for curriculum.* Washington, DC: National Academy Press.

Resnick, L. B. (1987). Education and learning to think. Washington, DC: National Academy Press.

Resnick, L. B. (1988). Treating mathematics as an ill-structured discipline. In R. I. Charles & E. A. Silver (Eds.), *The teaching and assessing of mathematical problem solving* (pp. 32–60). Reston, VA: National Council of Teachers of Mathematics.

Schmidt, W. H. (1998). *Facing the consequences: Using TIMSS for a closer look at United States mathematics education.* Boston, MA: Kluwer.

Schoen, H. L., Bean, D. L., & Ziebarth, S. W. (1996). Embedding communication throughout the curriculum. In P. C. Elliott & M. J. Kenney (Eds.), *Communication in mathematics: K–12 and beyond* (pp. 170–179). Reston, VA: National Council of Teachers of Mathematics.

Schoen, H. L., Hirsch, C. R., & Ziebarth, S. W. (1998). *An emerging profile of the mathematical achievement of students in the Core-Plus Mathematics Project.* Paper presented at the annual meeting of the American Educational Research Association, San Diego, CA. (ERIC Document Reproduction Service No. ED 421 351)

Schoenfeld, A. H. (1988). Problem solving in context(s). In R. I. Charles & E. A. Silver (Eds.), *The teaching and assessing of mathematical problem solving* (pp. 82–92). Reston, VA: National Council of Teachers of Mathematics.

Schoenfeld, A. H. (1992). Learning to think mathematically: Problem solving, metacognition, and sense making in mathematics. In D. A. Grouws (Ed.), *Handbook of research on mathematics teaching and learning* (pp. 334–370). Reston, VA: National Council of Teachers of Mathematics.

Skemp, R. R. (1987). *The psychology of learning mathematics.* Hillsdale, NJ: Lawrence Erlbaum Associates.

Steen, L. A. (Ed.). (1990). *On the shoulders of giants: New approaches to numeracy.* Washington, DC: National Academy Press.

Truitt, B. A. (1999). How teachers implement the instructional model in a reformed high school mathematics classroom. (Doctoral dissertation, University of Iowa, 1998). *Dissertation Abstracts International, 59*(09), 3385.

Walker, R. K. (2000). Students' conceptions of mathematics and the transition from a Standards-based reform curriculum to college mathematics. (Doctoral dissertation, Western Michigan University, 1999). *Dissertation Abstracts International, 61*(02B), 887.

ENDNOTES

1. The research and development was funded in part by grants from the National Science Foundation (MDR-9255257 and ESI-9618193).

2. When given in Grade 9, correlation of the ITED-Q with the ITBS Mathematics total score in Grade 8 is 0.81, with students' final cumulative high school grade point average in mathematics courses is 0.59, with the ACT Mathematics test is 0.84, and with the SAT Mathematics test is 0.82. The ACT and SAT are college entrance examinations, usually completed in 11th or 12th grade.

3. Of these 1,292 students, 1,104 (85.4%) also took the ITED-Q Pretest at the beginning of Grade 9, indicating they had completed all of *CPMP* Courses 1–3. It is likely that most of the remaining 188 students transferred into *CPMP* sometime during Courses 1–3. The 1,104 students' mean score on the total NAEP-based test differed very little from that of all 1,292 students (56.1% compared with 56.4% as given in Table 14.9). Furthermore, means on the various subtests for the two groups of *CPMP* students all differed by less than 1 percentage point.

15

The Effects of MATH *Connections* on Student Achievement, Confidence, and Perception

Donald Cichon
Donald Cichon Research Consultants

June G. Ellis
MATH Connections *Implementation Center*

MATH *Connections*: A Secondary Mathematics Core Curriculum, funded by the National Science Foundation in 1992, is designed to introduce the concepts of higher mathematics to *all* students. It shows students mathematics as a vital, powerful, relevant, flexible tool for interacting with their world in many ways and at many levels, from the commonplace settings of everyday life and work to the frontiers of science, technology, and human understanding.

Vision and mission statements express the underlying philosophy of the project.

The Vision that spurred the development of **MATH** *Connections*: *All* students can learn mathematics, be critical thinkers and problem solvers.

The Mission that became the mantra of **MATH** *Connections*: The conceptual understanding of the student.

Five primary goals of **MATH** *Connections* were also established by the principal investigators, the developers, and the Advisory Council (mathematicians, scientists, mathematics and science educators, business people, and industrialists):

- to bridge the worlds of education, students, and business through mathematics;
- to increase the mathematical power of all students;
- to empower students for their own learning;
- to develop a core curriculum that reflects the National Council of Teachers of Mathematics (NCTM) *Curriculum and Evaluation Standards for School Mathematics* (1989); and
- to empower teachers to meet the *Professional Standards for Teaching Mathematics* (NCTM, 1991).

In keeping with its vision, its mission, and its primary goals, **MATH** *Connections* is concept driven and built around connections between mathematics and the real world of people, business, and everyday life. **MATH** *Connections* builds bridges between different mathematical areas, between mathematics and science, and between mathematics and other subject areas such as history, geography, language, and art.

DESCRIPTION OF THE CURRICULUM

MATH *Connections* is an integrated curriculum. The integration of topics is not just the juxtaposition of an algebra topic with a related topic from geometry, statistics, or discrete mathematics. Rather, it is the *blending* of ideas from these traditionally separate fields in ways that make it difficult, and often impossible, to say where one field begins and another ends. The curriculum presents mathematics as the subject is used, bringing ideas from a wide range of areas to bear on a question. In this sense, **MATH** *Connections* approaches mathematics as a seamless fabric, perhaps with different patterns or colors in different areas. In a survey of the content of *Standards*-based curriculum materials, Robinson and Robinson (1998) describe the curriculum as follows:

> The development approach most often used in **MATH** *Connections* is for the students to actively explore a concept in order to develop experimental evidence and or recognize a pattern, be assured the pattern is accurate, represent the pattern by a formula. . . . It is the philosophy of the developers that a great deal of mathematical power comes from being able to understand formulas and being able to transfer them in a variety of contexts. (p. 2)

The 3-year curriculum replaces the traditional Algebra I, Geometry, Algebra II sequence and is designed for all students in Grades 9, 10, and 11, with honors students beginning the curriculum in Grade 8. Each year of the curriculum is built around a general theme, which serves as a unifying thread connecting and blending mathematical topics that traditionally have been taught independently. This approach emphasizes the unity and inter-connectedness among mathematical ideas; it prepares students for Calculus, AP Statistics, or other senior level courses as well as for college and the work-place. Appendix A contains an abbreviated scope of the **MATH** *Connections* curriculum.

The general theme for Year 1 is Data, Numbers, and Patterns. In the first semester, students use data, linear equations, and the regression capa-bilities of a graphing calculator to forecast real-world settings. Figure 15.1 contains a situation from the materials for Year 1 that blends mathematics with botany and studies from space. It gives students valuable experience in using experimental data and a chance to learn about the frustrations of doing science in the real world. Students use statistics to determine the me-dian, range, and quartiles, construct boxplots, and compare data. Students deal with and adjust to changes as they unfold. Understanding the limita-tion of mathematical tools in the real world is as important as understanding their power.

Later, the discussion of carbon dating uses first-degree equations (alge-bra), straight line graphs (geometry), least-squares differences (algebra and statistics), and a graphing calculator (technology) to solve a problem in ar-chaeology (natural science). All these tools come together naturally in this context. Although the concept of function may be traditionally included in a course on Precalculus, the topic of functions appears throughout the entire **MATH** *Connections* curriculum, beginning with Year 1.

For Year 2, the general theme is Shapes in Space. As the description in Appendix A indicates, the curriculum in this year focuses on properties and measurements of figures in two and three dimensions, and includes work with transformations, trigonometry, and matrices. Standard principles of congruence and triangulation of polygons are developed and employed in innovative ways to make clear their applicability to real-world problems. Students solve linear equations using matrices by solving problems that re-quire finding the most efficient use of resources for a manufacturing com-pany, a crucial need for business and industry. This understanding transfers to other real-world situations involving chemistry, scheduling of resources, financial business, and ecology. Algebra, geometry (the volume of a cone), and Cavalieri's Principle (usually in Precalculus) are combined to calculate the volume of a sphere. Figure 15.2 contains a sample task from the Year 2 curriculum.

Mathematical Models is the general theme for Year 3. Properties of ax-iomatic systems (logic) are introduced by examining the rules of a simple card game and the probabilities of certain kinds of outcomes. Axiomatic systems are related to physics by means of the Law of the Lever and also to the arithmetic properties of the number systems. Euclid's plane geome-try is studied from axiomatic and historical perspectives. The story of two

To learn the ways long trips in space might affect living things, NASA sent 13,000 tomato seeds into an orbiting platform for five years. The seeds were identical to the Rutgers tomato seeds you can buy in any hardware or department store, except that they were launched on the shuttle, orbited for five years, and then recovered. The seeds were next sent to schools all over the country to grow and to be observed. The first seedlings grown from the space seeds and seedlings from usual seeds were measured (in centimeters). Display 1.43 shows the measurements from one school.

(a) Make dotplots of the four lists of measurements. Mark the mean on the number line of each one.

(b) Make boxplots of the four lists of measurements.

(c) Are the stem lengths different between the earth seeds and the space seeds?

(d) Are the numbers of leaves different between the earth seeds and the space seeds?

(e) Suppose that the next generation of plants (grown from the seeds made by the plants just described) has the boxplots shown in Display 1.44. What can you say about these plants? Are they similar to their "parents" or have they changed? If they have changed, what do you observe about their numbers?

Three Week Old Seedlings			
Earth-bound Seeds		**Space-exposed seeds**	
Stem length	No. of leaves	Stem length	No. of leaves
29	8	26	6
20	9	29	10
23	10	22	7
23	6	26	9
26	10	28	7
27	8	17	6
22	10	25	7
18	9	21	10
30	10	30	7
28	7	16	8

Display 1.43

Three Week Old Seedlings

Display 1.44

FIG. 15.1. Sample task from **MATH** *Connections*, Book 1.a, *Note.* From **MATH** *Connections*: A Secondary Mathematics Core Curriculum (pp. 51–52). by W. P. Berlinghoff, C. Sloyer, and R. W. Hayden, 2000, Armonk, NY: IT'S ABOUT TIME. Copyright 2000 by MATHconx, LLC. Reprinted with permission.

Toon Town Trucking Co. is installing a large fuel tank in a level field next to its main terminal. The tank is a right cylinder 30 feet in diameter, mostly buried underground. The top 10 feet of the cylinder are above ground. Local safety regulations require that the part above ground be surrounded by a collar of earth that slopes from the top of the tank to the level of the field. A 30° angle is the steepest angle that the bulldozer operator will allow. Your job is to estimate the number of cubic yards of earth that will be needed for this earthen collar. (*Hint:* The earth needed is the volume formed by revolving a triangular region around the centerline of the cylinder.)

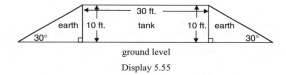

ground level

Display 5.55

FIG. 15.2. Sample task from **MATH** *Connections*, Book 2.b. *Note.* From **MATH** *Connections*: A Secondary Mathematics Core Curriculum (p. 436), by W. P. Berlinghoff, C. Sloyer, R. W. Hayden, and E. F. Wood, 2000, Armonk, NY: IT'S ABOUT TIME. Copyright 2000 by MATHconx, LLC. Reprinted with permission.

Draw an equilateral triangle and think of its area as 1 square unit. Join the midpoints of all three sides to make a new equilateral triangle. Then join the midpoints to form another smaller triangle inside it. If this process were continued indefinitely, what would be the sum of all the combined areas of all of the smaller triangles in the diagram? Treat each area as a separate one, ignore that it is contained in other triangles.

FIG. 15.3. Sample task from **MATH** *Connections*, Book 3.b. *Note.* From **MATH** *Connections*: A Secondary Mathematics Core Curriculum (p. 522), by W. P. Berlinghoff, C. Sloyer, and E. F. Wood, 2000, Armonk, NY: IT'S ABOUT TIME. Copyright 2000 by MATHconx, LLC. Reprinted with permission.

non-Euclidean geometries provides a view of their significance in reshaping our perspective of the way mathematics is related to the real world. Students are engaged in ideas about population growth, physics, integer arithmetic, and concepts of infinity and integral calculus. The sample task in Fig. 15.3 from the Year 3 curriculum highlights foreshadowing the concept of limit, a topic often not introduced until Calculus.

Your task is to enter parametric equations that will produce the following picture. The head, nose, mouth and eyes are circles; the ears are semicircles. The center of the nose is at the origin.

A BALD CHOIR BOY

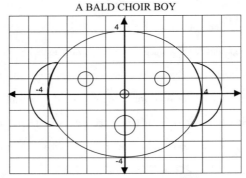

- Use your graphing calculator to assist you to recreate the picture without the ears. You may use parametric equations or the DRAW menu to complete this question.

- If you choose parametric equations, answer part a. of each section. If you choose to use the DRAW menu, answer part b. for each section.

Head: a. Parametric Equations: _____   _____
              b. Center: _____   Radius: _____

Nose: a. Parametric Equations: _____   _____
              b. Center: _____   Radius: _____

Mouth: a. Parametric Equations: _____   _____
              b. Center: _____   Radius: _____

Right Eye: a. Parametric Equations: _____   _____
              b. Center: _____   Radius: _____

Left Eye: a. Parametric Equations: _____   _____
              b. Center: _____   Radius: _____

EXTRA CREDIT: How would you construct the two ears, which are semicircles?

Right Ear: Parametric Equations: _____   _____
              T_{min}: _____ T_{max}: _____
              Center: _____   Radius: _____

Left Ear: Parametric Equations: _____   _____
              T_{min}: _____ T_{max}: _____
              Center: _____   Radius: _____

FIG. 15.4. Assessment quiz, A Bald Choir Boy, Section 4.3, Problem 3, Year 2. *Note.* From **MATH** *Connections*: A Secondary Mathematics Core Curriculum Assessments by D. Hastings, 2000, Armonk, NY: IT'S ABOUT TIME. Copyright 2000 by MATHconx, LLC. Reprinted with permission.

The examples from each year of the curriculum illustrate that problems typically combine ideas from at least two traditionally separate mathematical areas. They illustrate the blended nature of the curriculum.

In order to provide teachers with the flexibility of working with students of different mathematical backgrounds, Supplementary Materials to enhance students' mathematical skills and Extensions for further discovery have been developed to augment all 3 years of the program.

Student Assessments

The curriculum-specific assessments, embedded in the text and as quizzes, reflect the intent of the *Assessment Standards for School Mathematics* (NCTM, 1995) in several ways.

1. The assessments allow students to use a variety of formats—graphs, diagrams, essays, processes, equations, formulas, functions, etc.—to demonstrate their knowledge of mathematics concepts and skills.
2. Students are consistently required to analyze problems, determine solutions, and write justifications for their solutions. There are quizzes with performance assessment items that a teacher might assign to a group.

Figure 15.4 contains a sample performance assessment that incorporates technology, trigonometry, functions, parameters, and the use of parametric equations or the DRAW menu of a graphing calculator.

Professional Development

Professional Development is an important component to the successful implementation of **MATH** *Connections*. It consists of an extensive Teacher Commentary, Summer and Academic Year Leadership Institutes, follow-up support visitations and videos, and e-mail discussions with teachers and developers. Implementation support is provided by **MATH** *Connections* staff, teachers, and administrators.

RESEARCH ON STUDENT OUTCOMES

A number of studies about the impact of the curriculum have been conducted, including studies done as part of the evaluation of **MATH** *Connections* as well as studies completed by school districts using the curriculum materials.

Research Conducted as Part of the Evaluation of MATH *Connections*

A multifaceted evaluation of the **MATH** *Connections* program was an integral part of the initial proposal to the National Science Foundation. Independent external evaluators conducted this ongoing research. The **MATH** *Connections* staff only had access to the data, recommendations, and conclusions each quarter and at the end of the year.

Methodology

The evaluation of **MATH** *Connections* was designed to answer the following questions.

1. How do **MATH** *Connections* students perform on independent, standardized mathematics achievement measures in comparison with nonparticipants?
2. To what extent do the participating students achieve the objectives of the **MATH** *Connections* curriculum, as indicated by their scores on curriculum-specific tests?
3. How is achievement on **MATH** *Connections* curriculum related to the characteristics of student gender, ethnicity, and special education levels?
4. How do **MATH** *Connections* students' attitudes toward mathematics and mathematics learning compare with those of students not in the program? How do the attitudes differ for females, or for different ethnic groups?[1]
5. What do **MATH** *Connections* classrooms look like in terms of their basic structural characteristics, student grouping practices, extent of cooperative learning, gender participation, and nature of student mathematical thinking and applications?

Student Sample

The **MATH** *Connections* student population is diverse, consisting of Caucasian, Asian, African American, and Hispanic students. The population represents inner-city, urban, suburban, and rural communities, as well as heterogeneity of ethnic and financial environments. There is a variety of class compositions: homogeneous and heterogeneous; honors middle school; honors high school; multilevel and mainstream Special Education students.

Instruments

Independent test measures were used to answer the central question: "How do **MATH** *Connections* students perform on independent, standardized math achievement measures in comparison with nonparticipants?" The evaluators requested information from all participating schools for their students in the graduating classes of 1997, 1998, and 1999 on three tests:

1. the Connecticut Academic Performance Test (CAPT), taken in the spring of Grade 10;
2. the Preliminary Scholastic Aptitude Test (PSAT), generally taken in Grade 10 or 11; and
3. the Scholastic Aptitude Test (SAT), generally taken in Grades 11 and 12.

The first test is from the Connecticut State Department of Education's testing program. The CAPT is a statewide performance test in language arts, mathematics, science, and interdisciplinary assessment. It emphasizes "the application and integration of skills and knowledge in realistic contexts," provides data regarding students' strengths and weaknesses, and uses "performance tasks, to also measure what students *can do* with what they know" (Cichon, 1998, p. 2). Figure 15.5 contains a sample CAPT performance assessment; the suggested rubric can be found in Fig. 15.6.

Achievement on the CAPT

The evaluators obtained and analyzed scores for **MATH** *Connections* students and comparison students in the graduating classes of 1997, 1998, and 1999 in eight schools (inner city, urban, suburban, and rural) that implemented **MATH** *Connections*. Students in both groups were matched on their standardized Connecticut Mastery Test (CMT) mathematics test scores taken in the fall of Grade 8. The CMT is a statewide assessment given to all nonexempt students in Grades 4, 6, and 8 to assess students' mastery of specific objectives in mathematics and language arts. The Grade 8 test is used as a placement criterion for entering high school students' course selections. For this evaluation, the CMT mathematics scaled scores were used to measure if **MATH** *Connections* and comparison students were of comparable mathematics ability. Students in the comparison classes were in the same grade levels as the **MATH** *Connections* students and were studying in the conventional Algebra I, Geometry, and Algebra II sequence.

The CAPT scores were examined in three ways. The first was a comparison of the percent of students in **MATH** *Connections* and those not in **MATH** *Connections* who met or exceeded the statewide CAPT mathematics goal of 266. This comparison is based on a subset of the total sample matched on their Grade 8 CMT mathematics scores so that the comparison is of students with comparable mathematics ability at the start of their high school tenure. Sixty (60) percent of the 558 **MATH** *Connections* students met or exceeded the state goal compared with 55% of the 745 non-**MATH**

DOUBLE DISCOUNT

At a department store sale, you are buying a $50 sweater that you selected

from a table that says "25% OFF." You also have a coupon for an additional

10% off on any purchase.

The cashier takes 25% off the original price and then takes an additional 10%

off. She asks you for $33.75. Write what you would explain to the cashier to

justify why this price is not as good as the bargain claimed in the coupon.

Sunday, December 23rd	**10 - 5**

Take an additional
        10% OFF EVERYTHING*
                    in the store.

Most Merchandise Storewide Already Reduced 20-50%!

      For Example:
Regular price merchandise: = $60.00
Less 25% already discounted   = $45.00
Less additional 10% discount (today): = $39.00

FIG. 15.5. Sample mathematics assessment from CAPT, Component II, Item Number D26 (Connecticut Common Core of Learning Assessment Project).

Connections students, a statistically significant difference (Chi square 4.255, 1 *df, p* < .039).

A second method of comparison uses the mean scores of students from both groups who had matching CMT scores. As indicated in Table 15.1, no significant difference exists between the two groups on the mean CAPT score.

A third comparison uses the mean scores of the **MATH** *Connections* and comparison students with the CMT score as a covariate to control for incoming high school mathematics ability. As Table 15.1 indicates, there is a significant difference in the means, in favor of the **MATH** *Connections* group.

When the results on CAPT performance are considered, the **MATH** *Connections* students perform at least as well, if not better, on the CAPT than their nonparticipating peers. The difference in the mean CAPT scores between the two groups is statistically significant in favor of the **MATH** *Connections* students.

Explanation for Scoring Mathematics Open-ended Items

Each score category contains a range of student responses on the CAPT which reflect the descriptions given below.

Score 3
The student has demonstrated a full and complete understanding of all concepts and processes embodied in this application. The student has addressed the task in a mathematically sound manner. The response contains evidence of the student's competence in problem-solving and reasoning, computing and estimating and communicating to the full extent that these processes apply to the specified task. The response may, however, contain minor arithmetic errors that do not detract from a demonstration of full understanding.

Score 2
The student has demonstrated a reasonable understanding of the essential mathematical concepts and processes embodied in this application. The student's response contains most of the attributes of an appropriate response including a mathematically sound approach and evidence of competence with applicable mathematical processes, but contains flaws that do not diminish countervailing evidence that the student comprehends the essential mathematical ideas addressed by this task. Such flaws include errors ascribable to faulty reading, writing, or drawing skills; errors ascribable to insufficient, non-mathematical knowledge; and errors ascribable to negligent or inattentive execution of mathematical processes or algorithms.

Score 1
The student has demonstrated a limited understanding of some of the concepts and processes embodied in this application. The student's response contains some of the attributes of an appropriate response, but lacks convincing evidence that the student fully comprehends the essential mathematical ideas addressed by this task. Such deficits include evidence of insufficient mathematical knowledge; errors in fundamental mathematical procedures; and other omissions or anomalies that bring into question the extent of the student's ability to solve problems of this general type.

Score 0
The student has demonstrated merely an acquaintance with the topic. The student's response is associated with the task in the item, but contains few attributes of an appropriate response. There are significant omissions or anomalies that indicate a basic lack of comprehension in regard to the mathematical ideas and procedures necessary to adequately address the specified task. No evidence is present to suggest that the student has the ability to solve problems of this general type.

FIG. 15.6.   Scoring rubric for task in Fig. 15.5.

An independent study, conducted by the State of Connecticut mathematics supervisor (Leinwand, 1996) looked at two different classes of students in one suburban high school. One group took Prealgebra and Algebra in Grades 9 and 10; the other group took **MATH** *Connections* Year 1 and Year 2 in Grades 9 and 10. For the 26 students in the traditional program and the 30 students in the "alternative" (**MATH** *Connections*) program, each student's scores in the fall of 1992 on the Grade 8 CMT and in the spring of 1995 on the Grade 10 CAPT were examined. Table 15.2 shows the means and standard deviations for both groups. Although the two groups of students had essentially equivalent mean test scores in Grade 8, there were significantly stronger scores at the end of Grade 10 for students in the **MATH** *Connections* program.

TABLE 15.1

Mean CAPT Score Comparisons for **MATH** *Connections* and
Comparison Group Students

	MATH *Connections*			*Non-***MATH** *Connections*			
	n	*Mean*	*SD*	*n*	*Mean*	*SD*	*p*
Matched sample	558	269	31.2	745	266	34.6	.107
Total sample	748	265	33.0	1,340	260	38.4	.047

Note. More than one comparison student was matched to a **MATH**
Connections student on the basis of Grade 8 CMT scores. Hence, the numbers of students in the two groups are different. The maximum scale score
on the CAPT is 400. The matched sample uses a *t* test; the total sample uses
an analysis of covariance to control for incoming high school mathematics
ability.

TABLE 15.2

Means and Standard Deviations for **MATH** *Connections* and
Comparison Students on Two Tests

Test	**MATH** *Connections*			*Comparison Program*			
	n	*Mean*	*SD*[a]	*n*	*Mean*	*SD*[a]	*p*
Grade 8 CMT	30	101.2	12.0	26	97.9	16.1	.38
Grade 10 CAPT	30	237.0	24.9	26	212.3	27.4	.001

Note. The maximum score for the Grade 8 CMT was 172; that of the Grade
10 CAPT was 400. These results are based on Leinwand (1996).

[a]Standard deviations are approximated from the data values in Fig. 15.7.

Figure 15.7 indicates the relationship between the CAPT score and
eighth-grade achievement, as measured by the CMT, for students in the
traditional program and in the **MATH** *Connections* program. Students in the
MATH *Connections* program generally score higher than those in the traditional program on the CAPT, regardless of whether their initial eighth-grade
CMT score represented a high or low level of achievement.

Achievement on the PSAT and SAT

Comparison of achievement on the PSAT and SAT used the same an-
alytical method described for the CAPT. That is, achievement of **MATH**
Connections students and non-**MATH** *Connections* students who were in the
Algebra I, Geometry, and Algebra II sequence were compared, using their
scores on the Grade 8 CMT as a covariate. On the PSAT, mean mathematics
scores of the **MATH** *Connections* and non-**MATH** *Connections* students were
48 and 46, respectively, on a score range of 20 to 80. On the SAT, mean
mathematics scores for the two groups were 522 and 502, respectively, on
a score range of 200 to 800. According to the external evaluator (Cichon,

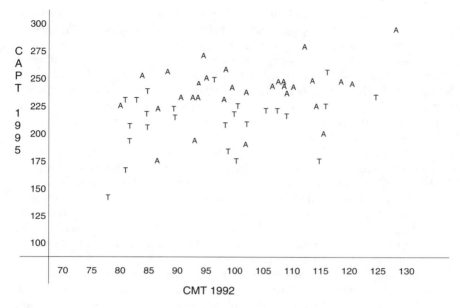

T = Traditional (Algebra)
A = Alternative (**MATH** *Connections*)

FIG. 15.7.　Grade 8 CMT scores versus Grade 10 CAPT scores for students receiving traditional or alternative (**MATH** *Connections*) mathematics instruction (Leinwand, 1996, p. 2).

1998), "The PSAT mean scores show mixed results, though more favorable than not in the comparisons between the **MATH** *Connections* students and the non-**MATH** *Connections* students; the SAT means favor the **MATH** *Connections* students in a clear pattern" on both the mathematics and verbal subtests (p. iv).

The schools represented in the analysis of the PSAT and the SAT scores constituted 80% of the schools implementing **MATH** *Connections* in a substantial manner for 3 years. The results on the PSAT and SAT suggest that students studying from the **MATH** *Connections* curriculum perform at least as well, if not better, than students studying from a traditional curriculum on these important tests for college admission.

Achievement on Curriculum-Specific Assessments

The **MATH** *Connections* program assessment specialist designed quizzes for each subchapter unit of the curriculum. Overall, across the 65 quizzes analyzed for the 1996–1997 school year, the average scores ranged from a high of 91 (out of 100) to a low of 69, with a fairly even distribution across the range. If the criteria of 70 as passing and 80 as average are considered, then the **MATH** *Connections* students achieved the program's objectives of mastering the content at a passing to a high level.

In an examination of the quiz score averages to see how results differed across gender, ethnicity, or special education status, the findings indicate that **MATH** *Connections* is gender free—that is, females and males achieved at about the same levels overall. As for ethnicity, the mean difference in scores was not statistically significant among groups for those quizzes taken by substantial numbers of ethnic minorities.

Approximately 5% of the total population of students on whom there was quiz assessment data were designated as being in Special Education. These students almost all have learning or emotional disabilities and were mainstreamed in the **MATH** *Connections* classes. Because the proportion of Special Education students was small in comparison with the total sample, the evaluator focused on the 35 quizzes on which there were scores from more than 10 Special Education students. These quizzes were mostly in Year 1 and in the earlier part of Year 2.

Special Education students scored at a passing level to an average or above-average level on 30 of the 35 quizzes. Of 20 quizzes from **MATH** *Connections* Year 1 with at least 10 student scores reported from each group, Special Education and non-Special Education, only 7 quiz scores had means that were different at a statistically significant level. These were in favor of the non-Special Education students. An example of this is the Graphical Estimation Quiz in Fig. 15.8. On this quiz, the mean score of the non-Special Education students was 79% and that of the Special Education students was 71%, a statistically significant difference in favor of the non-Special Education students ($p < .003$).

In Year 2 of **MATH** *Connections,* for quizzes with 10 or more student scores reported in each group, there was no statistical significance in the mean score differences. However, the mean scores of the Special Education students were higher than those of the non-Special Education students on 8 of the 15 quizzes. On the quiz in Fig. 15.9, the mean score of the Special Education students was 90% and that of the non-Special Education students was 85%.

There are some factors to be considered in understanding these results. In looking at the composition of the teachers in Year 1, eight had not previously experienced Special Education students mainstreamed in their classes. Some Special Education students did not seem to assimilate to the new curriculum or to the new classroom environment as quickly as the non-Special Education students. By Year 2, the Special Education students seemed more attuned to the classroom environment, as did the teachers.

Another study is needed to determine the specific factors that resulted in Special Education students performing at passing (70%) to at least average

(80%) during Year 1 and Year 2 of **MATH** *Connections,* given that in conventional mathematics courses they did not score in that range. The ability of Special Education students to be successful with the broad mathematical curriculum of **MATH** *Connections* needs to be explored as a means of helping all students to be successful with higher mathematics.

1. The number of Catholic clergy that reside in the six states that contain the geographical area of Southern New England and the Northern Mid-Atlantic States is listed in the table below:

| | CATHOLIC CLERGY | |
State	Number of Priests	Number of Nuns
Connecticut	1298	2450
Massachusetts	3630	6715
New Jersey	2784	5102
New York	7334	14665
Pennsylvania	4600	12785
Rhode Island	580	1105

   a. Use the following directions:
      • Make a scattergram for this data.
      • Use the horizontal axis for the number of priests and choose a scale from 500 to 7,500.
      • Use the vertical axis for the number of nuns and choose a scale from 1000 to 15,000.

   b. Is there a pattern displayed by the points on the scattergram? Explain your answer.

2. MADD (Mothers Against Drunk Driving) is a national organization that provides information and educational programs to assist local groups and governments. It provides programs to make the public aware of the problems created by drunk drivers. Melissa Hargrove, local president of MADD, researched the fatalities from automobile accidents from 1966 to 1990. She presented the following data to her local organization.

TRAFFIC FATALITIES	
Year	Fatality Rates per 100,000 Drivers
1966	50
1970	47
1974	36
1978	36
1982	29
1986	29
1990	27

The scattergram for this data is displayed below:

FIG. 15.8. Graphical estimation quiz, Year 1, Chapter 4, Section 4.1–4.3. *Note.* From **MATH** *Connections*: A Secondary Mathematics Core Curriculum Assessments by D. Hastings, 2000, Armonk, NY: IT'S ABOUT TIME. Copyright 2000 by MATHconx, LLC. Reprinted with permission.

TRAFFIC FATALITIES PER 100,000 DRIVERS

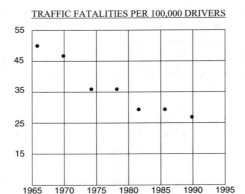

a. Lucy Winfield wondered what the fatality rate was in 1973. In order to find this from the
    graph, linear interpolation was used. Use a ruler to demonstrate how you can find an estimate
    for the number of fatalities in 1973 using linear interpolation. What estimate did you find?

b. Find the equation of the line that contains the line segment connecting (70, 47) to (74, 36).
    Show your work.

c. Use the equation from part b. to find an estimate for the number of fatalities in 1973 by
    substituting 73 into the equation. Show your work.

d. How did your estimates from Parts a and c compare? Be as specific as you can.

e. Write **at least two reasons** why you think fatalities decreased from 1966 to 1990.

FIG. 15.8. (Continued)

1. Clean-Up Janitorial Services has the contract to maintain the new gymnasium at the Swamplands
    Sports Complex. The gymnasium measures 200 feet by 160 feet. The electrical outlets for the
    cleaning and refinishing machine are located at the center of each wall. Since the machine is very
    expensive, the Clean-Up Janitorial Services can only afford to buy one. Your job is to determine the
    smallest length of cord on the machine in order to cover the entire surface of the gymnasium. (The
    cord is very expensive.)

    •   Sketch the gym in the space below. Indicate where the electrical outlets are located.

    •   You decide that the cord on the machine to be purchased could be 110 feet long and cover the
        entire surface of the gym from the four outlets.

    a. Write the center and radius of each circle with the center at an outlet and the cord length
        equal to 110 feet.

        Center: _____   Radius: _____

        Center: _____   Radius: _____

        Center: _____   Radius: _____

        Center: _____   Radius: _____

    •   Set-up the gym dimensions on the window of your TI-82 and draw the four circles from
        part a.

    b. Are you correct? _____Discuss if a machine with a cord less than
        110 feet could be purchased.

2. Given: x = 3 cos T
            y = 3 sin T

    (a) What do you expect the graph will be?
    (b) Enter the pair of parametric equations on the TI-82.
    (c) Write settings for the "best" window:

    T_{Min} _____ T_{Max} _____ T_{Step} _____

    X_{Min} _____ X_{Max} _____ X_{Step} _____

    Y_{Min} _____ Y_{Max} _____ Y_{Step} _____

3. This item is the *Bald Choir Boy* task of Figure 15.4.

FIG. 15.9. Circles and disks quiz, Year 2, Section 4.3. *Note.* From **MATH** *Connections*: A Secondary Mathematics Core Curriculum, Assessments by D. Hastings, 2000, Armonk, NY: IT'S ABOUT TIME. Copyright 2000 by MATHconx, LLC. Reprinted with permission.

Confidence in and Usefulness of Mathematics

In 1996, a study was conducted on students' confidence in learning mathematics and students' perception of the usefulness of mathematics, using an adaptation of the Fennema–Sherman Mathematics Attitude Scales. Two scales were administered: confidence in learning mathematics and perceived usefulness of mathematics. The scales were developed in the mid-1970s and their psychometric properties are well established. A full description of the instrument and its psychometric characteristics is found in Fennema and Sherman (1975). Figure 15.10 contains five sample statements.

The study was included in the evaluation because research on the variables in the affective domain indicates that students' beliefs, attitudes, confidence, perseverance, and emotions play a central role in mathematics learning (Fennema & Sherman, 1975; Hirschhorn, 1993; McLeod, 1992, 1994; Merkel–Keller, 1977; Schoenfeld, 1989). These surveys have shown that attitudes towards mathematics have an effect on students' decisions to enroll in higher-level math courses (Fennema & Sherman, 1975; Merkel–Keller, 1977). Also taken into account were two of the five general goals of the NCTM *Standards*: first, students learn to value mathematics, and second, students become confident in their ability to do mathematics.

The study took place in a diverse urban residential community with a population of about 51,000 and a high school with approximately 1,900 students. Upon entering high school, students are placed into one of three levels of mathematics: level I (honors—not included in this study), level II (college preparatory), or level III (postsecondary preparatory). Within both

A professional form of the Fennema-Sherman Attitude Index was used. On the first page students were asked their gender (male or female), Grade (8, 9, 10, 11, or 12) and ethnicity (African-American, Asian, Hispanic, White, non-Hispanic or Other). Students were asked to rate 30 statements about their attitudes towards mathematics based upon five categories: Strongly Agree, Agree, Undecided, Disagree and Strongly Disagree. Five typical questions from this Survey are listed here.

I can get good grades in mathematics.	SA	A	U	D	SD
I'll need a firm background in mathematics for my future work.	SA	A	U	D	SD
The challenge of math problems doesn't appeal to me.	SA	A	U	D	SD
I do as little work in math as possible.	SA	A	U	D	SD
I am challenged by math problems I can't immediately understand.	SA	A	U	D	SD

FIG. 15.10. Sample items from the **MATH** *Connections* student survey.

the college preparatory (CP) and postsecondary preparatory (PSP), there were two options: first, **MATH** *Connections*: A Secondary Mathematics Core Curriculum; and second, the traditional Algebra I, Geometry, and Algebra II sequence. Students were placed in **MATH** *Connections* on a voluntary basis, having the opportunity to sign up for the program during the eighth grade. In this 1996 study, 131 students in CP and PSP completed a formal survey of their confidence in mathematics and their perception of the usefulness of mathematics.

Three groups of classes were studied.

Group I consisted of students in **MATH** *Connections* classes with teachers trained in and teaching **MATH** *Connections*;

Group II consisted of students in conventional Algebra II classes with teachers trained in and teaching **MATH** *Connections* but teaching traditional Algebra II as well;

Group III consisted of students in Algebra II classes with teachers not trained in nor teaching **MATH** *Connections*.

Table 15.3 contains the mean score, by group, for each of the two attitude scales. A one-way analysis of covariance, with students' Grade 8 CMT scores as the covariate, indicated a statistically significant difference among the three groups with respect to their confidence in learning mathematics and in their perception of the usefulness of mathematics. In order to determine which group means differ significantly from one another, pairwise comparisons were conducted on Groups I, II, and III using the Scheffé post hoc comparison test. The results indicated that significant differences occurred between Groups I and II, Groups I and III, and Groups II and III, all at the $p < .01$ level in favor of the students with **MATH** *Connections* teachers.

TABLE 15.3

Mean Scores By Groups for Two Fennema-Sherman Scales

Scale	Group I		Group II		Group III		df	F	p
	n	Mean	n	Mean	n	Mean			
Confidence	34	3.90	68	3.61	29	3.27	2	3.71	.025
Usefulness	34	4.06	68	3.71	29	3.49	2	3.49	.031

Note. Group I consists of students in the **MATH** *Connections* program with teachers trained in the program. Group II consists of students in Algebra II classes but with teachers trained in **MATH** *Connections*. Group III consists of students in Algebra II classes whose teachers had not been trained in **MATH** *Connections*. The two scales are students' confidence in mathematics and students' perception of the usefulness of mathematics. Results are based on Staffaroni (1996). The maximum score on each scale is 5, with SA coded as 5.

(See Staffaroni, 1996, for further details.) These results seem to suggest that teachers who have received professional development in the philosophy and approach of **MATH** *Connections* are better able to help students develop confidence in mathematics and recognize the usefulness of mathematics than teachers without this training.

Characteristics of **MATH** Connections *Classrooms*

In order to answer the question "What is the influence of **MATH** *Connections* participation on students?," evaluators conducted structured observations of classrooms with participating students and teachers in 13 schools. Of the 13 schools visited (inner-city, urban, suburban, and rural), 6 schools permitted observation of nonparticipating classes. Among the 13 schools visited, 47 **MATH** *Connections* classes were observed three times in the fall, and 42 of the same classes were observed three times in the spring. These included observations of almost every participating teacher, about half the **MATH** *Connections* classes, and 16 non-**MATH** *Connections* classes of students with comparable ability in conventional Algebra, Geometry, Algebra II, and Algebra II Honors courses. The sampling of classes was well representative of the **MATH** *Connections* population at the time of the study.

The evaluators adapted the Hiebert and Wearne framework (1993) for classifying and analyzing the teachers' and students' statements. Some of the categories and statement types were refined or modified for use at the secondary school level. See Appendix B for the actual instrument used. One of the main intentions in using rating scales for the classroom observations was to provide a systematic basis for comparisons across classes. Such quantitative data would serve as a more objective indicator of the reliability of the observation data than qualitative observations would allow.

The observations were set up to cover a wide range of students with two observers in one day at the school; a pool of three observers with rotating pair combinations completed the observations across the 13 schools. The observers were trained and experienced in behavior research. Whenever possible, the observers also observed one or two non-**MATH** *Connections* classes with students of comparable mathematics ability to the **MATH** *Connections* students.

Observers first mapped the basic classroom structural characteristics, determining whether activities were for the whole class, small groups, or for individuals. The evaluators rated features observed in the classrooms on a 5-point Likert type scale, with 5 indicating the most frequent occurrence of the feature. The paired observers' ratings for all common episodes were held to two criteria: first, the ratings should be within ±1 of each other; second, the correlations between the two observers' ratings should be above 0.6. Using this modified scale, the observers collected and analyzed data on levels of discourse, gender interaction, cooperative learning, and on-task student behavior in the **MATH** *Connections* and comparable nonparticipating classes.

Both the **MATH** *Connections* classes and the non-**MATH** *Connections* classes had an average small group interaction rating of 2.0 (with 1 = none and 5 = extensive). **MATH** *Connections* classes had significantly more on-task student behavior than did non-**MATH** *Connections* classes, with mean ratings of 4.4 and 3.8, respectively ($p < .01$, 1 = off task and 5 = on task). **MATH** *Connections* classes also used more complex cognitive levels of discourse than comparison classes, with mean ratings of 2.3 and 1.9, respectively ($p < .04$, 1 = fact–right answer and stop and 5 = complex cognitive process). **MATH** *Connections* classes provided the same types of opportunities for both genders. The review of the class observations in this category strongly suggests a few patterns.

One, **MATH** *Connections* teachers and their students made statements and asked questions that evoked a broad range of reasoning, communicating, and problem-solving skills.

Two, this wide range appeared more uniformly among the **MATH** *Connections* classes than it did in non-**MATH** *Connections* classes with students of comparable mathematics ability. That such activity is built into the **MATH** *Connections* curriculum is evident in the classrooms: in problem-solving tasks; in classroom and small group discussions; and in the nature and amount of writing and explaining expected of students. Several classroom features appeared to foster an environment in which students were expected to attain both an understanding of concepts and significant successful problem-solving experience. These features include: routine incorporation of graphing calculators; frequent use of multiple representations of mathematical phenomena (visual and symbolic); the use of real-world problem-solving activities; and the focus on argument and open-ended questions with possible multiple answers.

Three, discourse in most of the non-**MATH** *Connections* classrooms was at lower cognitive levels than in **MATH** *Connections* classrooms. The observers' rating on the "types of thinking scale" showed a statistically significant difference in means in favor of the **MATH** *Connections* students.

As a result of the philosophy and development of the **MATH** *Connections* program, students are provided with the resources necessary for the development of reasoning, communication, problem solving, and critical thinking skills. Also, through leadership institutes and workshops in **MATH** *Connections* and through notes in the Teacher Commentary, teacher professional development has included various ways for teachers to encourage students to elicit these attributes, as well as providing teachers with a greater understanding of the mathematics. The material in the conventional Algebra I, Geometry, and Algebra II sequence does not fit this model. Although teachers vary in their questioning techniques and teaching skills, the development of reasoning and communication skills through the student materials and the encouragement for teachers to try new teaching strategies likely contributes to the success of the **MATH** *Connections* students in comparison to their non-**MATH** *Connections* counterparts.

Research Conducted by School Districts

Several studies about the impact of **MATH** *Connections* on achievement or retention have been conducted by school districts using the curriculum materials.

Research on Achievement on College Admission Tests

In one midsized suburban school system, students self-select their mathematics courses. A number of students began **MATH** *Connections* in their freshmen year. Although there are no data on the initial comparability of **MATH** *Connections* students and students in the more traditional mathematics program (but not in Honors courses), an examination of SAT scores for students in the Class of 1999 suggests that concerns about students in the **MATH** *Connections* program being unprepared for college admission tests are unwarranted. Figure 15.11 contains boxplots of the score distribution for students studying from **MATH** *Connections* and from traditional mathematics programs. Eleven of the 103 **MATH** *Connections* students scored at least 700, with 4 scoring 800; in contrast, 6 of the 110 non-**MATH** *Connections* students scored at least 700, with 1 scoring 800.

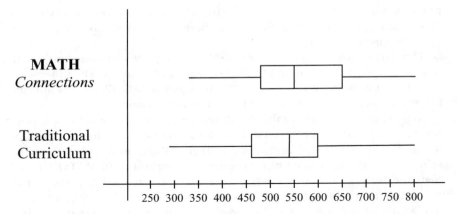

FIG. 15.11. Boxplots comparing SAT performance from MATH *Connections* students and students in a traditional mathematics program (Class of 1999).

TABLE 15.4
Table Comparing SAT Mathematics Means from 1997–2001 for One School District. Coppola (2001)

	Class of 1997	Class of 1998	Class of 1999	Class of 2000	Class of 2001
School District	419	504	500	501	528
State	504	509	509	509	510
National	508	512	511	514	514

In a second school district study the mean mathematics SAT scores of students in a suburban high school of 2000 students were tracked from 1997 to 2001. Table 15.4 shows an increase of 37 points over the 5-year period, an increase far greater than the state and national scores during the same time period.

In his summary to the Board of Education, the Associate Superintendent reports,

> A significant factor in the rise of the math scores is the **MATH** *Connections* curriculum (Coppola, 2001). The class of 2001 is the first to have spent their entire high school years with this curriculum. . . . A somewhat unexpected factor of the **MATH** *Connections* program is the number of students who take four rather than three math courses [only three required by the state] during their high school years. In the past, students enrolled in the Algebra I, Geometry, Algebra II sequence, ending their high school involvement with math in their junior year. Many **MATH** *Connections* students continue on to a fourth year of high school mathematics. Fully 65% of the graduating seniors of the class

of 2001 took 4 or 5 math courses. Prior to the introduction of the **MATH** *Connections* program, only 32% of the graduating seniors were enrolled in a 4th or 5th math course.

Research on Retention

A case study of **MATH** *Connections* was completed in 1998–1999. The objective was to look at and report on possible changes in student academic results and behavior which could be attributed to **MATH** *Connections* according to school district administrators. This study, conducted in an inner-city school, was designed to determine whether these Hispanic and African American at-risk students from an inner-city environment would opt to take a fourth year of mathematics if only 3 years were required for graduation. Further, would any of those students completing a fourth year have an interest in applying to schools of higher education and, upon applying, would they be admitted?

The school was in the first group of field-test sites. The students were placed in **MATH** *Connections* as their performance prior to entering Grade 9 was so low that the personnel responsible for student placement were unable to find a mathematics course where their grades would be accepted for entry. Without knowledge of the **MATH** *Connections* curriculum and as no prerequisites had been set for entry, placement personnel decided to schedule them for the program.

These at-risk students got off to a slow start, as did their teachers, who were also in their first year of the program. Consequently, students and teachers had not completed the 3-year curriculum by the end of the junior year; they had completed only the first semester and a small part of the second semester of Year 3. Of the 30 students in the study, 20 requested to continue **MATH** *Connections* in their senior year (1996–1997) and complete the curriculum, although only 3 years of mathematics were required for graduation.

In the senior year, students finished the Year 3 curriculum and worked on extra material. Of those 20 students who continued **MATH** *Connections*, 6 students applied for, were accepted to, and will graduate from 4-year colleges; of the remaining students, all but one attended and graduated from community technical colleges (1998–1999). On average, only 74% of the graduating class at this school continues to postsecondary education.

CONCLUSIONS

The research reported in this chapter was conducted from 1996 to 2001. In the 1996–1997 school year, **MATH** *Connections* had just completed its fourth year of field testing, having expanded each successive year with more students and higher-grade levels. By all available evidence and in keeping with its vision, its mission, and its goals, **MATH** *Connections* has been and continues to be successful. On what might be taken as the strongest and most direct evidence—the independent test scores of the CAPT, the PSAT, and the SAT—**MATH** *Connections* students perform as well as or better than their nonparticipating peers who had comparable mathematical ability on entering high school. These achievements by **MATH** *Connections* students are important on two counts. One, at the onset of field-testing in 1993, a common concern about the program among parents, teachers, and students was whether the participating students would be sufficiently prepared for conventional scholastic academic measures and college entrance requirements. The scores of **MATH** *Connections* students on these independent tests compared with the scores of their nonparticipating peers should allay such fears, as **MATH** *Connections* graduates are attending colleges and universities throughout the country.

Two, the results from the PSAT and SAT tests are from students in the program's early years of implementation. The teachers were teaching the curriculum for the first time and so were often not able to complete all of the material. Also, the material was being revised during these early years as areas for improvement suggested by teachers and students were implemented by the curriculum developers. The participating students showed that they learned the content and achieved the program's objectives at a passing to high level overall.

The results of the survey of students' confidence in learning mathematics and their perception of the usefulness of mathematics suggest that teachers trained to use **MATH** *Connections* transfer that training to their teaching of non-**MATH** *Connections* courses. Students in classes with teachers trained in **MATH** *Connections* have greater confidence in learning mathematics and see the usefulness of mathematics to a greater degree than nonparticipating students in classes with teachers not trained in **MATH** *Connections*.

Classroom observations suggest that the program was implemented in line with its goals. That is, students in its classes were observed to work cooperatively with other students on mathematics tasks, engage more actively on task in the mathematics content, and work at higher cognitive levels than nonparticipating students in comparable classes. The mathematical applications and sense of the "reality" of mathematics came through clearly to participants.

The results of the case study of the Hispanic and African American at-risk students in an inner-city school, in conjunction with the independent standardized test results and the **MATH** *Connections* curriculum-specific tests, suggest that *all* students can successfully meet the challenge of a mathematically rigorous course. When provided with an interesting, exciting, real-world curriculum, students, upon graduation, can and do move on to higher education and are prepared for careers and the workplace of the 21st Century.

APPENDIX A: ABBREVIATED SCOPE OF THE MATH *CONNECTIONS* CURRICULUM

Year 1—Data, Numbers, and Patterns

Book 1.a. Begins and ends with data analysis. It starts with hands-on data gathering, presentation, and analysis and then poses questions about correlating two sets of data. This establishes the goal of the term—that students be able to use the linear regression capabilities of a graphing calculator to do defensible forecasting in real-world settings. Students reach this goal by mastering the algebra of first-degree equations and the coordinate geometry of straight lines, gaining familiarity with graphing calculators along the way.

Chapter 1.   Turning Facts into Ideas
Chapter 2.   Welcome to Algebra
Chapter 3.   The Algebra of Straight Lines
Chapter 4.   Graphical Estimation

Book 1.b. Generalizes and expands the ideas of Book 1.a. It begins with techniques for solving two linear equations in two unknowns and interpreting such solutions in real-world contexts. Functional relationships in everyday life are identified, generalized, brought into mathematical focus, and linked with the algebra and coordinate geometry already developed. These ideas are then linked to an examination of the fundamental counting principles of discrete mathematics and to the basic ideas of probability.

Chapter 5.   Using Lines and Equations
Chapter 6.   How Functions Function
Chapter 7.   Counting Beyond 1, 2, 3
Chapter 8.   Introduction to Probability: What Are the Chances?

Year 2—Shapes in Space

Book 2.a. Starts with the most basic ways of measuring length and area. It uses symmetries of planar shapes to ask and answer questions about polygonal figures. Algebraic ideas from Year 1 are elaborated by providing them with geometric interpretations. Scaling opens the door to similarity and then to angular measure, which builds on the concept of slope. Extensive work with angles and triangles lays the groundwork for right-angle trigonometry, the last main topic of this book. Standard principles of congruence and triangulation of polygons are developed and employed in innovative ways to make clear their applicability to real-world problems.

Chapter 1.   The Building Blocks of Geometry: Making and Measuring
             Polygons
Chapter 2.   Similarity and Scaling: Growing and Shrinking Carefully
Chapter 3.   Introduction to Trigonometry: Tangles with Angles

Book 2.b.   Begins by exploring the role of circles in the world of spatial relationships. It then generalizes the two-dimensional ideas and thought patterns of Book 2.a to three dimensions, starting with fold-up patterns and contour lines on topographical maps. This leads to some fundamental properties of three-dimensional shapes. Coordinate geometry connects this spatial world of three dimensions to the powerful tools of algebra. That two-way connection is then used to explore systems of equations in three variables, extending the treatment of two-variable equations. In addition, matrices are shown to be a convenient way to organize, store, and manipulate information.

Chapter 4.   Circles and Disks
Chapter 5.   Shapes in Space
Chapter 6.   Linear Algebra and Matrices

Year 3—Mathematical Modeling

Book 3.a.   Examines mathematical models of real-world situations from several viewpoints, providing innovative settings and a unifying theme for the discussion of algebraic, periodic, exponential, and logarithmic functions. These chapters develop many ideas whose seeds were planted in Years 1 and 2. The emphasis throughout this material is the utility of mathematical tools for describing and clarifying what we observe. The modeling theme is then used to revisit and extend the ideas of discrete mathematics and probability that were introduced in Year 1.

Chapter 1.   Algebraic Functions
Chapter 2.   Exponential Functions and Logarithms

Chapter 3. The Trigonometric Functions
Chapter 4. Counting, Probability and Statistics

Book 3.b. Begins by extending the modeling theme to Linear Programming, optimization, and topics from graph theory. Then the idea of modeling itself is examined in some depth by considering the purpose of axioms and axiomatic systems, logic, and proof. Various forms of logical argument, already used informally throughout Years 1 and 2, are explained and used to explore small axiomatic systems, including groups. These logical tools then provide guidance for a mathematical exploration of infinity, an area in which commonsense intuition is often unreliable. The final chapter explores Euclid's plane geometry, connecting his system with many geometric concepts from Year 2. It culminates in a brief historical explanation of Euclidean and non-Euclidean geometries as alternative models for the spatial structure of our universe.

Chapter 5. Math Does It Better
Chapter 6. Playing By the Rules: Logic and Axiomatic Systems
Chapter 7. Infinity—The Final Frontier?
Chapter 8. Axioms, Geometry and Choice

Appendices

A. Using a TI-82 (TI-83) Graphing Calculator. This appendix provides a gentle introduction to this technology and also serves as a convenient student reference for the commonly used elementary procedures.

B. Using a Spreadsheet. Although a spreadsheet is not explicitly required anywhere in **MATH** *Connections,* it is very handy for doing many problems or explorations and should be considered as a legitimate, optional tool.

C. Programming the TI-82 (TI-83). Students can use it to learn useful general principles of programming, as well as techniques specific to the TI-82 and TI-83.

D. Linear Programming with Excel. This appendix is not primarily a tool for doing problems within the chapters. Rather, it describes a technological approach to ideas that come up from time to time in various chapters. Linear Programming itself is discussed in detail in Chapter 5 of Year 3. This appendix can be used either as a precursor to that discussion or as an extension of it.

APPENDIX B
MATH *Connections* Classroom Observation Instrument

Date: _____	Observer: _____	Book: _____
School: _____	Teacher: _____	Grade: _____
Period: _____	Heterogeneous/Homogeneous	# Males: ___ # Females _____

	Behavioral Category	*Observation*
I. Structure	A. Grouping (whole class, small groups (2–6), individual, other (describe); if small group, describe gender mix)	
	B. Teacher Activity (lecture/demonstration, lecture/discussion/question, monitoring, assistance, other [describe])	
	C. Student Activity (listen, discuss, practice, read/write, use calculator or computer, use other objects, student presentations, sharing, other [describe])	
II. Cooperative Student Learning	A. Use of Small groups? How formed? How conducted?	
	B. Types of questions and responses in student-student interactions (fact, open-ended, hypotheses, help, challenge, on or off task, etc.)	
	C. Types of teacher guidance and interaction with students (group process v. math content, work with individuals vs. small group, etc.)	
	D. Judgment of extent of student-student interaction None Moderate Extensive 1 2 3 4 5 off task equal mix on task 1 2 3 4 5	
III. Types of Thinking	A. Types of teacher questions (facts or right answers vs. explain, why?, what does this mean?, etc.), or statements (to give answer, to stimulate higher-order thinking)	

APPENDIX B
(Continued)

	B. Types of questions students initiate (promote further thinking, lead to class discussion vs. factual or right/wrong answer)	
	C. Judgment of extent of teacher questions & statements Fact/right answer complex cognitive & stop process 1 2 3 4 5	
IV. Gender Interaction	A. Teacher favors Males Females 1 2 3 4 5	
	B. Female involvement/initiative Low High 1 2 3 4 5	
	C. Male involvement–initiative Low High 1 2 3 4 5	

V. Other Striking Features:

REFERENCES

Berlinghoff, W. P., Sloyer, C., & Hayden, R. W. (2000). **MATH** *Connections*: A Secondary Mathematics Core Curriculum (Book 1.a). Armonk, NY: IT'S ABOUT TIME.

Berlinghoff, W. P., Sloyer, C., Hayden, R. W., & Wood, E. F. (2000). **MATH** *Connections*: A Secondary Mathematics Core Curriculum (Book 2.b). Armonk, NY: IT'S ABOUT TIME.

Berlinghoff, W. P., Sloyer, C., & Wood, E. F. (2000). **MATH** *Connections*: A Secondary Mathematics Core Curriculum (Book 3.b). Armonk, NY: IT'S ABOUT TIME.

Berlinghoff, W. P., Sloyer, C., Hayden, R. W., & Wood, E. F. (2000). **MATH** *Connections*: A Secondary Mathematics Core Curriculum. Assessments by D. Hastings. Armonk, NY: IT'S ABOUT TIME.

Cichon, D. (1998). **MATH** *Connection*: A Secondary Mathematics Core Curriculum Evaluation Results. Dover, NH: Donald Cichon Research Consultants.

Connecticut Common Core of Learning Assessment Project. (1990). Mathematics assessment items. Hartford, CT: Connecticut State Department of Education.

Coppola, A. J. (2001). *Summary Report, Scholastic Assessment Test, 2000–2001*. Southington, CT: Southington School District.

Fennema, E., & Sherman, J. A. (1975). Fennema-Sherman Mathematics Attitudes Scales. *Journal for Research in Mathematics Education, 7*(5), 324–326.

Hiebert, J., & Wearne, D. (1993). Instructional Tasks, Classroom Discourse and Students' Learn-ing in Second Grade Arithmetic. *American Educational Research Journal, 20*, 393–425.

Hirschhorn, D. B. (1993). A Longitudinal Study of Students Completing Four Years of UCSMP Mathematics. *Journal for Research in Mathematics Education, 24*(2), 136–158.

Leinwand, S. (1996). Capturing and Sharing Success Stories. *NCSM Newsletter, 25*, 1–2.

McLeod, D. B. (1992). Research on Affect in Mathematics Education: A Reconceptualization. In D. A. Grouws (Ed.), *Handbook for Research on Mathematics Teaching and Learning* (pp. 575–596). New York: Macmillan.

McLeod, D. B. (1994). Research on Affect and Mathematics Learning in the JRME: 1970 to the Present. *Journal for Research in Mathematics Education, 25*(6), 637–647.

Merkel–Keller, C. (1977). *An Investigation of Sex-differentiated Attitudes Toward Mathematics and Sex-differentiated Achievement in Mathematics on the Ninth Grade Level in Eight Schools in New Jersey.* (ERIC Document Reproduction Service No. ED 143)

National Council of Teachers of Mathematics. (1989). *Curriculum and Evaluation Standards for School Mathematics.* Reston, VA: Author.

National Council of Teachers of Mathematics. (1991). *Professional Standards for Teaching Mathe-matics.* Reston, VA: Author.

National Council of Teachers of Mathematics. (1995). *Assessment Standards for School Mathematics.* Reston, VA: Author.

Robinson, E., & Robinson, M. (1998). **MATH** *Connections:* A Secondary Mathematics Core Curriculum Content Overview. In *Guide to Standards-based Instructional Materials in Secondary Mathematics* (1st ed.). Ithaca, New York: COMPASS, Ithaca College (also available on the Internet: www.ithaca.edu/compass: Curriculum Descriptions).

Schoenfeld, A. H. (1989). Explorations of Students' Mathematical Beliefs and Behavior. *Journal for Research in Mathematics Education, 20*(4), 338–355.

Staffaroni, M. A. (1996). **MATH** *Connections Program: A Study of Students' Confidence in and Perceived Usefulness of Mathematics.* Hartford, CT: Connecticut State Department of Education.

ENDNOTES

1. **MATH** *Connections* student textbooks were reviewed (favorably) for Access and Equity by Drs. Ray Shiflett, California Polytechnic Institute at Pomona and Leo Edwards, Fayetteville State University, NC.

2. **MATH** *Connections*: A Secondary Mathematics Core Curriculum Years 1 and 2 have been certified by the National Collegiate Athletic Association (NCAA) eligibility clearinghouse as fulfilling the NCAA mathematics requirements for Level 1. **MATH** *Connections* Year 3 has been certified as fulfilling the requirements for Level 2.

3. A Project 2061 research study conducted by the American Association for the Advancement of Science (AAAS) ranked **MATH** *Connections* as one of the highest among other high school mathematics curricula evaluated.

16

The Impact of the *Interactive Mathematics Program* on Student Learning

Norman L. Webb
Wisconsin Center for Education Research

Development of the *Interactive Mathematics Program* (*IMP*) began in 1989 with initial funding from the California Postsecondary Education Commission, and it continued in 1992 with major funding from the National Science Foundation (Schoen, 1993). The curriculum is designed to be aligned with the core curriculum recommended in the *Curriculum and Evaluation Standards* (National Council of Teachers of Mathematics [NCTM], 1989). *IMP* was one of the first high school mathematics curricula to try to embody the vision of the NCTM *Standards*. Students who complete the 4-year *IMP* are to be prepared both for the continued study of mathematics in college and for the world of work (Fendel, Resek, Alper, & Fraser, 1997, 1998, 1999a, 1999b). The problem-based curriculum incorporates traditional branches of mathematics that include algebra, geometry, and trigonometry, as well as topics that have been given little attention in the traditional high school program, especially statistics and probability. Students learn to experiment, investigate, ask questions, make and test conjectures, reflect, and accurately communicate their ideas and conclusions.

THE *IMP* CURRICULUM

The *IMP* curriculum is a 4-year college-preparatory sequence of courses designed for Grades 9–12. The units for each year are included in Table 16.1. It is a curriculum that integrates algebra, geometry, and trigonometry with probability, statistics, discrete mathematics, and matrix algebra. Technology instruction and applications are incorporated throughout the program.

Algebra and geometry, traditionally taught in self-contained courses, are interspersed over the 4 years. In Year 1, the curriculum exposes students to algebraic ideas of variables, equations, proportional equations, graphical representations, and data fitting. In Year 2, the curriculum builds on students' growing knowledge of algebra by developing their capacity to solve problems involving linear and quadratic equations, exponents, linear inequalities, and linear programming, and to use both symbols and graphs. Year 3 of *IMP* extends students' understanding of algebra by having them work with functions (exponential, logarithmic, and inverse), systems of equations including the use of matrices, and multivariable linear programming. In Year 4, students prove and use the quadratic formula and properties of quadratic equations.

As in the case with algebra, geometry is woven into the curriculum throughout the 4 years. In Year 1, students study angles, angular measurements, polygons, and similarity. In Year 2, *IMP* is designed to further students' understanding of area and volume, including area of polygons, surface area, an area proof of the Pythagorean Theorem, areas of similar figures, and tessellations. In Year 3, *IMP* incorporates work on analytic and coordinate geometry, including slope in relation to rate of change, equations using points and slope, the concept of a derivative, and standard formulas, including those for distance, midpoint, circles, and planes. Students also study properties of circles, polygonal approximation of circular areas, congruence, geometric constructions (straight edge and compass), finding loci of points, parallel lines, and planes in 3-space. In Year 4, *IMP* students study polar coordinates, geometric transformations (including using matrices), projections, and linear representations in 3-space.

IMP places strong emphasis on probability and statistics, in part because of the increasing importance these areas have in the work place. In Year 1, students engage in data collection and analysis, apply means and standard deviations to describe data sets, study the distinctions between theoretical and experimental probabilities, use different representations of probabilistic situations, and learn about normal distributions and the normal curve. In Year 2, students' work turns to designing, conducting, and interpreting statistical experiments, using null hypotheses, using and understanding the χ^2 statistic, testing statistical significance, and conditional probability. In Year 3, students analyze more complex probability problems, combinatorics,

TABLE 16.1
Course Topics in the Interactive Mathematics Program Curriculum

Unit Name	Mathematical Content and Contexts
IMP—Year 1	
1: Patterns	Basic ideas of functions, integers, angles, and polygons; mathematical investigations
2: The Game of Pig	A mathematical analysis based on an area model for probability in the context of a complex probability game call Pig
3: The Overland Trail	Linear relationships in the context of western migration
4: The Pit and the Pendulum	Data analysis and development of statistical ideas, including standard deviation in the context of developing a formula for the period of a pendulum
5: Shadows	Similar triangles and basic trigonometry in the context of developing formulas for finding the length of a shadow
IMP—Year 2	
1: Solve It!	Represent real-world situations and solve equations in different ways
2: Is There Really a Difference?	Expand understanding of statistical analysis through sampling and an understanding of the chi-square statistic in the context of analyzing data from real-world situations
3: Do Bees Build It Best?	Surface area, volume, and trigonometry in the context of developing the best shape for a honeycomb
4: Cookies	Relationships among equations, inequalities, and their graphs in the context of profit maximization problems
5: All About Alice	Principles for working with exponents in the context of a model based on *Alice's Adventures in Wonderland*
IMP—Year 3	
1: Fireworks	Algebraic investigations using quadratic expressions, equations, and functions in the context of the trajectory of a rocket
2: Orchard Hideout	Circles and coordinate geometry in the context of trees growing in a circular orchard
3: Meadows or Malls?	Graphing systems of linear inequalities and solving systems of linear equations in the context of making decisions about land use
4: Small World, Isn't It?	Study of the rates of growth, development of the concept of slope, and generalization of the idea of derivative in the context of world population

(Continued)

TABLE 16.1

(Continued)

Unit Name	Mathematical Content and Contexts
5: Pennant Fever	Development of the binomial distribution and use of combinatorics in the context of determining the probability of a team winning a pennant race
IMP—Year 4	
1: High Dive	Extension of right-triangle trigonometry to circular functions and use of the quadratic formula in the context of the physics of falling objects in a circus act
2: As the Cube Turns	Geometric transformations of translations, rotations, and reflections for two and three dimensions, trigonometric functions, polar coordinates, and matrices in the context of constructing a program for rotating a cube
3: Know How	Radian measures, ellipses, the quadratic formula, laws of sines and cosines, and complex numbers in the context of students' independent study of mathematics
4: The World of Functions	Representation and composition of the family of functions using tables, graphs, symbols, and other models in the context of an automobile braking problem
5: The Pollster's Dilemma	Central limit theorem, confidence intervals, and margin of error in the context of election polls

permutations, Pascal's Triangle, and the binomial distribution. Year 4 *IMP* students study sampling with and without replacement, the Central Limit Theorem, procedures for characterizing probability distributions, binomial sampling, confidence intervals, and margin of error.

The *IMP* requires students to experiment with examples, look for and articulate patterns, and make, test, and prove conjectures. They are challenged to explore open-ended situations in a way that closely resembles the inquiry methods used by mathematicians and scientists (Alper, Fendel, Fraser, & Resek, 1995, 1997; Ohanian, 1997). The problem-based curriculum is organized into 5- to 8-week units that focus on a central problem or theme. Students engage in solving both routine and nonroutine problems, use graphing calculators, and are encouraged to work cooperatively. For example, in the Year 1 unit, Pit and the Pendulum, students are presented a problem at the beginning of the unit based on Edgar Allan Poe's story, *The Pit and the Pendulum.* Students determine whether the amount of time the prisoner has to escape from a swinging blade on a 30-foot pendulum fits the reality of how pendulums work. Students extrapolate from data collected by experimenting with smaller pendulums. During the course of the unit, students engage in a number of activities that require them to collect data and analyze the degree of accuracy, including measuring strides, pulse rates, and the weights of pennies. They learn how to use mean and standard deviation to analyze variations in measurements. In the culminating activity of the unit, students develop a function that will describe the time required for 12 swings of a 30-foot pendulum.

Teaching techniques used in the *IMP* are designed to help students gain deep understanding of mathematical ideas, reason mathematically, and apply mathematics to solve problems. For example, in the Pit and the Pendulum unit, one night's homework involves four sets of data about which students are to respond to a number of questions, including spread from the mean, standard deviation, and the similarity among the data sets (Fendel et al., 1997, p. 343). One purpose of the curriculum is to enhance students' abilities to reason in many ways. For instance, students are asked to design experiments, to state their conclusions based on evidence and analysis, to compare mathematical ideas, and to explain general cases of specific situations.

Students are also assigned Problems of the Week (POWs) to work on for as many as 5 or more days. In the Pit and the Pendulum unit, Problems of the Week include one on determining whether four chess knights placed at the corner of a 3-square by 3-square board can switch places, and one on how many weighings on a balance scale are needed to detect the one bag out of eight identical bags that weighs less than the others.

Classroom experiences such as presentations, written explanations, and small-group activities are structured to encourage students to verbalize their thinking. This verbalization is designed to increase students' understanding and to improve their communication of mathematics. Students are encouraged to become independent learners as a result of using multiple sources of information, including their teachers, the textbook, classmates, and other resources.

IMPLEMENTATION AND EVALUATION OF *IMP*

During the 1990s, the number of schools with one or more *IMP* classes increased steadily. The *IMP* curriculum was taught during the 1992–1993 school year in 28 schools in the United States; during 1993–1994, in 56 schools; during 1994–1995, in 100 schools; during 1995–1996, in 140 schools; during 1996–1997, in 178 schools; during 1997–1998, in 243 schools; and during 1999–2000, in 500 schools. In 1999–2000, 1,700 teachers attended inservices on *IMP*.

A range of evaluation procedures was used to determine what mathematics students enrolled in *IMP* classes were learning. The results reported here were derived from three studies that are labeled Study 1, Study 2, and Study 3. Study 1 compared grades, mathematics courses taken, and test scores of students who had taken *IMP* with students who had had a traditional college preparatory mathematics course sequence. Study 2 analyzed the performance of students in *IMP* and traditional classes on probability, statistics, and quantitative reasoning, content emphasized in the *IMP* curriculum. Study 3 was a replication of Study 2, using the same instruments but in different schools. A replication study helps to establish the conditions under which results hold and contributes to the generalizability of findings (Shaver & Norton, 1980). Evaluators are seldom afforded the opportunity to control conditions sufficiently to establish attested results. Replication, in a different setting, of the effects attributed to curriculum helps to validate the findings and extend them to a larger population.

Over the course of the three studies, data were collected from students enrolled in nine public high schools from 1989 to 1997. Five of the high schools are in California. The other four high schools are in different states: two in the east, one in a midwestern state, and one in a mountain state. Five of the high schools are in large urban areas and one is an inner-city school; the other four are in middle-size communities or suburban areas. Nearly all of the high schools had diverse student bodies, with the percentage of non-White students ranging from nearly 100% to 17%. In five of the high schools, more than half of the students were from "underrepresented" groups. Two of the high schools were select high schools that required students to meet specific requirements to enroll in the school.

In general, the high schools in the studies offered from two to four classes of *IMP* at the grade levels studied. Each high school used different procedures for assigning students to *IMP* classes. Staff from many of the high schools made presentations to eighth graders in feeder middle schools to interest them in enrolling in *IMP* classes. Students and parents were told that *IMP* was designed to be a college-preparatory mathematics curriculum for all students. They were informed of *IMP*'s emphasis on learning how to solve problems and to apply mathematics to real-life situations. As a result, some entering Grade 9 students enrolled in *IMP* classes indicated they would probably have taken a prealgebra class or a general mathematics class.

Data were not available from all high schools that made a clear distinction in the proportion of *IMP* students who would have enrolled in courses below the first course in Algebra. However, one California high school gave students entering in the fall of 1989 the opportunity to enroll in the *IMP* Year 1 course. All students who volunteered to take *IMP* were accepted, regardless of their mathematics experience in Grade 8. Twelve percent of the population at this school enrolled in *IMP* classes, 14% enrolled in Algebra classes, and 61% enrolled in basic mathematics courses that included prealgebra and remedial mathematics.

Because the selection process varied greatly, it was difficult to form clear comparisons between students enrolled in *IMP* classes and those enrolled in the traditional college-preparatory mathematics sequence of Algebra I, Geometry, and Algebra II–Trigonometry. For this reason, great efforts were made in each of the studies conducted to obtain some measure of the students' mathematics achievement prior to entering high school.

Study 1: A Transcript Analysis in Three Schools

The primary objectives of the transcript analysis were to investigate whether enrollment in *IMP* courses (a) increases the percentages of students who take college-qualifying high school mathematics courses and (b) has an impact on student achievement. The population for the transcript analysis consisted of students in the only three high schools at which students had had the opportunity to complete 3 years of *IMP* at the time of this study. For the effects of curriculum to be determined, the transcripts of all of the students who were in the Class of 1993 in those three California schools were analyzed.

Studying transcripts is tedious, but it offers the advantage that it is possible to get information on all of the students, track the courses they took, and note the grades they achieved. The problems faced in transcript analysis include inconsistent labeling of courses among the schools, reporting by different schools of different information on transcripts, the necessity of entering all information into an electronic database, and the need to address how data from transfer students would be analyzed.

A total of 1,121 student transcripts were analyzed from the three California high schools—Brooks, Hill, and Valley (all pseudonyms). Brooks High School serves a middle-sized community and had a school enrollment in 1992–1993 of 2,075 students. Less than 20% of those students were from families that received Aid to Families with Dependent Children (AFDC) or participated in a government-funded meal program. English was the second language of 20% to 35% of the students in the school. Students came from a variety of ethnic heritages: approximately 63% were White, 28% were Hispanic, 4% were Black, 3% were Asian, Filipino, or Pacific Islanders, and the rest were American Indians or others. A full range of mathematics courses, in addition to *IMP*, was offered, from basic mathematics through Advanced Placement Calculus. The school proudly reported that in 1992–1993, 95% of the students were enrolled in some mathematics class.

Hill High School, located in a community within a large metropolitan area, enrolled approximately 2,000 students at the time of this study. The Class of 1993 included an ethnically diverse group: 43% were White, 30% were Black, 12% were Asian, Filipino, or Pacific Islanders, 7% were Hispanic,

5% were interracial, 0.4% were American Indian, and 2% were classified as "other." Hill High School offered a full range of mathematics courses, from basic mathematics to Advanced Placement Calculus. Approximately one of every five students entering Grade 9 enrolled in geometry or a higher mathematics course. These students formed the Accelerated Mathematics group.

Valley High School was one of eight comprehensive 4-year high schools in a city of approximately 700,000. The school serves a very diverse and mobile population. Nearly half of the 1,600 students enrolled at any one time dropped out or transferred from the high school before completing 4 years. Of the 500 students who enrolled as ninth graders in 1989, 219 graduated in 1993. The Class of 1993 was ethnically diverse: 37% Hispanic, 33% Chinese, 11% other non-White, 11% Filipino, 6% Black, and 2% White. Two of every three students in Grade 9 took a basic mathematics course such as Math A, Prealgebra, or some other computation-based course. As did the other two high schools, Valley High School's mathematics department offered a full range of courses from basic mathematics through Advanced Placement Calculus.

Across the three high schools, 53% of the 1,121 students in the Class of 1993 were female. By ethnic heritage, 42% were White, 20% were Hispanic, 16% were Black, 16% were Asian, Filipino, or Pacific Islanders, 5% were classified as "other," and 0.6% were American Indian. In ninth grade, 16% of the Class of 1993 enrolled in *IMP*, 26% took Algebra, 42% took a Basic Mathematics course, 15% were in the accelerated group, and less than 1% took no mathematics. During the 4 years from 1989 to 1993, 27% of the Class of 1993 at the three high schools took at least some *IMP* courses.

Without random assignment between the *IMP* and the traditional college-preparatory mathematics sequence, it is difficult to ensure that the makeup of the cohorts of students who took each program was similar when they began. Each school had developed its own criteria for assigning students to the *IMP* course sequence. In general, students volunteered to take *IMP*. Valley High School, which had a large number of students studying English as a second language, also required a minimal score on a reading test for entry into *IMP*. At Hill High School, a greater number of students volunteered to take *IMP* in ninth grade than could be served by the available classes, so some random selection was used to assign students to *IMP* classes.

Completion of College-Preparatory Mathematics Courses

One of the most powerful predictors of ultimate completion of college degrees is the highest level of mathematics an individual studies in high school (Adelman, 1999). The level of high school mathematics is a better predictor of college completion than high school grades or standardized

TABLE 16.2
Percent of *IMP* and Comparison Students Completing College-Qualifying
Mathematics Courses by Gender

Gender	IMP				Traditional College Preparatory			
	N	Math 3 Years[a]	Math 3+ Years	Calculus[b]	N	Math 3 Years[a]	Math 3+ Years	Calculus[b]
Female	97	78	66	18	156	72	34	18
Male	81	84	62	27	131	76	43	27
Total	178	81	64*	22	287	74	38*	23

[a]This is the percent of students who began *IMP* in Grade 9 and who completed 3 years of *IMP* by the end of 4 years. A total of 9% of the Brooks High School students (10 females and 6 males) who took *IMP* in Grade 9 transferred to the traditional mathematics course sequence and completed it through Algebra II.

[b]This is the percent of students who took at least one semester of Precalculus or Calculus in high school.

*Difference is significant at the $p < .01$ level.

test scores. An important goal for *IMP* is to increase the number of high school students who take college-preparatory mathematics.

Analyses of the transcripts from the three high schools indicate that a slightly higher percentage of students who began their high school career in Grade 9 by taking *IMP* Year 1 completed 3 years of college-preparatory mathematics than did students who took Algebra I in Grade 9 (Table 16.2). For those beginning high school mathematics courses in Grade 9, 81% of *IMP* students compared with 74% of students in the traditional program (Algebra I, Geometry, and Algebra II) completed 3 years of their respective programs. For both programs, a slightly higher percentage of male students than female students completed 3 years in the program they began in Grade 9.

A higher percentage of *IMP* students than students in the traditional curriculum went on to take advanced high school mathematics after they completed 3 years of college-qualifying mathematics. Across the three high schools, of the 178 students who started *IMP* in Grade 9, 114 (64%) went on to take more advanced mathematics courses. This is compared with 110 (38%) of the 287 students who began the traditional sequence with Algebra. This difference is statistically significant ($p < .01$). The students who completed 3 years of *IMP* went on to take advanced classes, including courses entitled Mathematics Analysis (a course based on preliminary materials from *IMP* Year 4), Trigonometry–Analytic Geometry, Precalculus, and Calculus. Students in the traditional program took classes in advanced high school mathematics, including Trigonometry, Analytic Geometry, Precalculus, and Calculus.

Among *IMP* students, 4% more females than males took more than 3 years of mathematics. In contrast, among students in the traditional

TABLE 16.3

Percent of *IMP* and Comparison Students by Highest College-Qualifying
Mathematics Courses Completed by Ethnicity

Ethnicity	IMP				Traditional College Preparatory			
	N	Math 3 Years [a]	Math 3+ Years	Calculus	N	Math 3 Years	Math 3+ Years	Calculus
Asian, Pacific Islander, or Filipino	24	88	83	33	41	88	58	32
Black	19	53	53	10	68	51	20	6
Hispanic	30	80	43	23	37	62	19	11
White	96	83	64	22	119	82	48	36
Total	169	80	62*	22	265	72	38*	24

Note. The total *N* reported in this table is different from that reported in Table 16.2 because of small numbers of students, Native American students and "other" categories have been omitted from this analysis.

[a]This is the percent of students who began *IMP* in Grade 9 and who completed 3 years of *IMP* by the end of 4 years. A total of 9% of the Brooks High School students (10 females and 6 males) who took *IMP* in Grade 9 transferred to the traditional mathematics course sequence and completed it through Algebra II.

*Difference is significant at the $p < .01$ level.

program, 9% more males than females took more than 3 years of mathematics. The percentages of students who took Precalculus or at least one semester of Calculus was the same for both the *IMP* program and the traditional mathematics curriculum sequence, about one out of five students. For both *IMP* and the traditional curriculum sequence, a higher percentage of male students than female students took Precalculus or Calculus.

In each ethnic group (Asian, Pacific Islander, or Filipino; Black; Hispanic; and White), a higher percentage of *IMP* students than of those who took the traditional sequence completed more than 3 years of mathematics while in high school (see Table 16.3). For all ethnic groups except Hispanic students, nearly equal percentages in both the *IMP* program and the traditional course sequence completed 3 years of their respective mathematics programs. Among Hispanic students, a higher percentage of *IMP* students than students in the traditional sequence completed 3 years of their respective programs.

Achievement on Traditional Standardized Tests

Transcripts from the different schools included different information and data on mathematics achievement test scores, including the Comprehensive Test of Basic Skills (CTBS) administered in Grade 11 and the Scholastic Aptitude Test (SAT) Mathematics score. Not all information on all of the tests was recorded on the transcripts. Therefore, we do not have scores on the two tests from all three high schools. An analysis was performed on the data that were available that differed among the three high schools.

Whenever they were available, measures of prior mathematics achievement were used to compare *IMP* students with those in the traditional course sequence. For instance, at Hill High School, seventh-grade CTBS mathematics scores were available. For the other two high schools, ninth-grade Prealgebra grade-point averages were used to compare the prior achievement of students who began *IMP* Year 1 in 10th grade with students who began Algebra I in 10th grade. Such data provide opportunities to control for prior achievement when one is making comparisons. From the analysis of seventh- and ninth-grade scores, there was no firm evidence from any of the three high schools that students who took *IMP* were a select group; however, it must be noted that students who volunteer to enroll in a new mathematics program under development are, if nothing else, adventurous.

As shown in Table 16.4, students who had enrolled in *IMP* in Grade 9 generally performed comparably with students enrolled in the traditional college-preparatory mathematics course sequence on common measures of mathematics. *IMP* and traditional students had no significant difference in means on the CTBS administered to students in Grade 11. The only significant difference for any of the contrasts occurred at Brooks High School, where students who started *IMP* in Grade 9 and who took the SAT scored significantly higher on the mathematics section than did students who started in the traditional sequence in Grade 9 and took the test.

At two high schools, students could begin taking the college-preparatory mathematics course sequence (either *IMP* or the traditional sequence) in either Grade 9 or Grade 10. Those students who began the college-preparatory sequence in Grade 10, as would be expected, had more difficulty in mathematics. Students who began the college-preparatory sequence in Grade 10, both those who took the *IMP* course(s) and those in traditional mathematics, had lower mathematics scores than students who had begun the college-preparatory mathematics courses as ninth graders.

Data reported in Table 16.4 do not account for any differences in prior mathematics achievement before students began their high school college-preparatory courses. Consequently, a special study was conducted at Hill High School, the only school that included on its transcripts both a mathematics achievement score prior to high school (Grade 7 CTBS Mathematics) and an SAT Mathematics score. Another purpose of the Hill High School analysis was to consider how higher-achieving students were performing in a mathematics curriculum designed to provide a quality mathematics curriculum for all students. At the time, there was some concern among parents and others that higher-achieving students would be disadvantaged by taking mathematics in heterogeneous classes, as compared with tracking by ability.

TABLE 16.4

Performances of *IMP* and Traditional Curriculum Students on Two Tests

| | | IMP | | | | Traditional | | | | |
School	Grade Began [a]	N	% of Total [b]	Mean	SD	N	% of Total [b]	Mean	SD	ΔSD Units [c]
					CTBS Mathematics Grade 11					
Brooks	9	58	93	823.81	30.45	51	82	819.88	30.90	+.13
Brooks	10	37	92	801.19	20.84	38	90	796.76	25.54	+.19
Valley	9	22	85	809.41	30.73	21	81	825.62	39.99	−.45
Valley	10	34	87	771.85	42.86	43	86	789.26	44.77	−.39
					SAT Mathematics					
Brooks	9	21	34	513.33*	73.30	16	26	453.75*	78.13	+.74
Brooks	10	7	18	365.71	55.33	7	17	360.00	52.28	+.11
Hill	9	71	79	519.58	122.09	111	56	501.98	120.09	+.14

Note. Performances are for students in the Class of 1993 at the three high schools listed.

[a] Grade level at which college-preparatory sequence was begun.

[b] Percent of grade level group in each curriculum with CTBS or SAT scores available. For example, 62 students from Brooks began *IMP* in Grade 9. Of these students, 58 or 93% of them had CTBS scores available.

[c] Mean for the *IMP* group less the mean for the traditional group divided by the standard deviation for the combined group.

*Statistically significant differences, using an analysis of variance ($p < .01$).

TABLE 16.5
Performances of *IMP* and Traditional Curriculum Students on SAT
Mathematics and GPAs

Item	IMP			Traditional		
	N	Mean	SD	N	Mean	SD
CTBS Math Grade 7	58	92.00	6.09	58	90.50	6.41
SAT Math	48	544.79	109.37	43	530.93	94.44
Overall GPA	58	3.11*	0.52	58	2.69*	0.56
Math GPA	58	3.24*	0.73	58	2.44*	0.64

Note. Performances are for students in a matched group in the classs of 1993 at Hill High School. The traditional group was matched to the 58 *IMP* students by gender, ability level, etc. Not all students in both groups took the SAT. GPA = grade-point average.

*The difference between the means of the *IMP* and traditional groups is statistically significant ($p < .01$).

With the use of CTBS Mathematics Grade 7 scores, as well as ethnicity and gender data for Hill High School students, high-scoring students from the traditional group were matched with the *IMP* group. Only students who scored in the 76th percentile or higher, using the national norms on the Grade 7 CTBS Mathematics test, were included in the analysis. Also, for both the *IMP* and traditional groups, only those students who had completed at least $2\frac{1}{2}$ years of mathematics were included.

In the Class of 1993 of Hill High School, 58 students in each group met these criteria, and thus, two matched groups were created. The two groups were very similar demographically and on Grade 7 scores. The *IMP* group was 66% female; the traditional group was 57% female. The *IMP* group was 7% Asian, Filipino, or Pacific Islander; 16% Black; 12% other; and 66% White. The traditional group was 9% Asian, Filipino, or Pacific Islander; 19% Black; 12% other; and 59% White. The two matched groups were compared on their SAT Mathematics scores. As shown in Table 16.5, the *IMP* group had a slightly higher mean SAT Mathematics score; however, the difference was not statistically significant.

The *IMP* students did achieve a significantly higher overall high school grade-point average, as well as a significantly higher mathematics grade-point average. Because grades can be subjective, another analysis was performed to determine whether *IMP* students' higher mean overall grade-point average was mainly explained by their higher grades in mathematics. This analysis eliminated students' mathematics grades from their overall grade-point average and only used grades from courses other than mathematics. This was based on the assumption that students from both programs would have taken nonmathematics courses from the same pool of teachers and were as equally likely to get the same grades. Even when their mathematics grades were adjusted for, *IMP* students had higher grade-point averages than students who had taken the traditional curriculum ($p < .07$).

Studies 2 and 3: Student Performance on Content Emphasized by the *IMP*

The intent of these studies was to evaluate the *IMP*'s claim that *IMP* students achieve at a higher level on statistics, probability, and complex problem solving than students in traditional college-preparatory mathematics. There are multiple reasons for this claim. A primary reason is that *IMP* gives more emphasis to statistics, probability, and solving extended problems than most traditional Algebra I, Geometry, and Algebra II curricula. Another factor is that students in *IMP* classes have the opportunity to use statistics and probability in the context of realistic situations and to understand the mathematics better as a result of having to apply it to solve real-world problems.

As in the Transcript Study, students from the traditional college-preparatory courses were used as contrasting groups. However, students were not randomly assigned between *IMP* and the traditional college-preparatory curriculum, an impossibility under the available conditions. Without random assignment, the studies cannot absolutely attribute any findings to the curriculum because other variables such as teacher differences, motivation of students, and other mathematical experiences not tested could not be strictly controlled. Any positive findings for *IMP* do increase the likelihood that *IMP* is having an effect.

At the end of the 1995–1996 school year, three studies were conducted, in three different high schools, each at a different grade level, and with a different outcome measure and instrument.

Schools selected for each of the three studies were located in different regions of the country and were considered sites where the *IMP* curriculum was being implemented as intended. An adequate number of students with pretest scores had to be available to participate. The school participating in the study of students in Grade 10 was a select urban high school from the midwest. Nearly 50% of the sample at this site were Black (not of Hispanic origin), 16% were Hispanic, 13% were White (not of Hispanic origin), and 11% were Asian or Pacific Islander. The school participating in the study of students in Grade 9 served a midsize city in a western state. Of the approximately 2,500 students enrolled in the school, nearly 50% of the students were White (not of Hispanic origin), 19% Asian, 13% Hispanic, 8% Black (not of Hispanic origin), 7% Filipino, and 3% other. The school participating in the study of students in Grade 11 was one of the oldest high schools in a long-established eastern city. The school is a magnet school with admission requirements for all incoming students. At the time of the study, the school enrolled approximately 2,200 students of whom nearly 45% were White (not of Hispanic origin), 33% Black (not of Hispanic origin), 18% Asian, and 4% Hispanic and others.

In each of the three schools, IMP students were matched with participating students from the traditional course sequence on the basis of Grade 8 achievement test scores. Gender and ethnicity were also used in matching student groups, when it was possible to include these factors and also match scores. Such matched group analyses for each test ensure that students in the groups being compared had comparable mathematics abilities and skills when they entered high school.

Grade 9 students were tested on statistics, Grade 10 students on problem solving, and Grade 11 students on quantitative reasoning. This design allows for valid comparisons of the IMP curriculum with the traditional curriculum, with minimal interference within any one school. The Grade 9 test was composed of all statistics items (a total of four) released from the Second International Mathematics Study (SIMS; Crosswhite et al., 1986). In the SIMS, these items were administered to Grade 12 students in the 1981–1982 school year. For the IMP study, the items were modified from the multiple-choice format used in SIMS to an open-response format. In this process, the two parts of Item 3 were scored separately. Thus, the total possible score on the four statistics items is five (see Fig. 16.1).

The Grade 10 test consisted of two performance assessment activities prepared for the Wisconsin Student Assessment System under the auspices of the Wisconsin Department of Public Instruction (Fig. 16.2). Each activity requires students to construct a response by solving a multistep mathematics problem, generalizing the results obtained, and writing an explanation of the reasoning and procedures used. One activity requires some knowledge of probability and one activity requires knowledge of combinatorics. Each item was graded by using a five-point rubric; thus, the maximum possible score on the problem-solving test was 10.

The Grade 11 test consisted of 10 multiple-choice items from a practice version of a quantitative reasoning test (QRT) developed by a prestigious university for its first-year students. Students at this university were required to pass the QRT, or another specified course, as a graduation requirement. Permission was not received from the university to disclose its name or the test items. The items from the QRT focused mainly on data interpretation and sought evidence of how students used mathematics, probability, statistics, and computation to solve problems. Items address the standard deviation and the mean of a distribution, data and graph interpretation, probability, and basic understanding of statistical concepts. To answer items correctly, students are required to understand and apply arguments supported by numerical data. Even though the items were multiple-choice items, they were difficult items as indicated by the fact that the university gave

1. In the graph, rainfall (in centimeters) is plotted for 13 weeks. What was the approximate

    average weekly rainfall during the period?

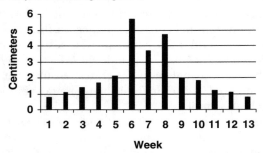

    Answer 1: _____

2. The same test was given in two classes. The first class, with 20 pupils, obtained an average

    score of 12.3 points. The second class, which had 30 pupils, obtained an average score of

    14.8 points. What was the average score for the whole group of 50 pupils?

    Answer 2: _____

3. The mean of a population is 5 and its standard deviation is 1. If 10 is added to each element

    of the population, what will be the new mean and standard deviation?

    Answer 3: New mean: _____

                   New standard deviation: _____

4. A test is taken by all first year university students in a country. The mean is 50 and the

    standard deviation 20. Assuming the scores are normally distributed, approximately what

    percentage of students scores more than 30?

      Answer 4: _____

    FIG. 16.1. Modified SIMS items about statistics administered to
    Grade 9 students.

students nearly 4 minutes, on the average, to work each item. The QRT has
a reliability of 0.65, which is reasonably high for a 10-item test.
   At the end of the 1996–1997 school year, replication studies for Grades 9
and 10 were conducted in three different high schools. At these three high
schools, *IMP* students and students enrolled in the traditional mathematics
course (Algebra in Grade 9, Geometry in Grade 10) were administered the
same tests used in the original studies.

CONNECTING NODES

Melinda and Harvey are teaching assistants at the University of Wisconsin in Milwaukee. One day they posed a problem called Connecting Nodes for their classes to solve.

- A node is just like a point.

- Each node is connected with every other node only once.

- A connection can be straight or curved.

- Connections can cross each other without creating a node.

- Any single connection has only two nodes on it, one at each end.

- Find the number of connections existing between nodes, no matter how many nodes there are.

The diagram below illustrates the number of connections that exist between the first four nodes.

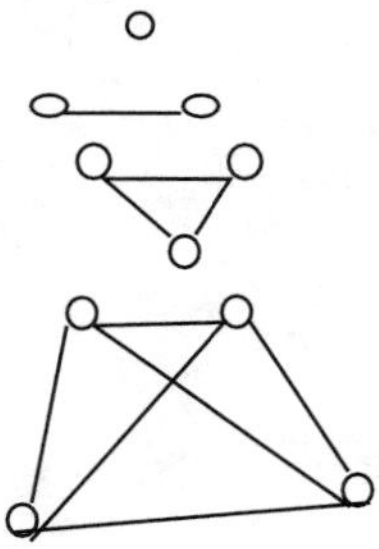

Diagram	Number of Nodes	Number of Connections
○	1	0
○——○	2	1
(triangle)	3	3
(complete quadrilateral)	4	6

1. How many connections will there be if there are 5 nodes? _____

2 How many connections will there be if there are 50 nodes? _____

   Explain in detail how your determined your answer.

3. Write a generalization to find the number of connections for *n* nodes.

> FIG. 16.2. Two performance assessment items administered to Grade 10 students as a test of problem solving.

NEW CUBES

Your school is planning a casino night to raise funds to construct a wall aquarium in your school.

As a mathematics student, you are given the job of developing a dice game for this event.

A regular pair of "number dice" consists of two cubes, each with its faces numbered 1 through 6.

Often dice games are played by rolling the two dice and then finding the sum of the two numbers

turned upward.

1. Show that, with a regular pair of number dice, the probability of rolling a sum of 7 is greater

    than the probability of rolling any other sum.

You decide to call your casino game "New Cubes." To make it interesting, you decide to

construct new dice that have different numbers on their faces than regular dice. Here is how you

will construct them:

- Only the single digits 0 through 9 can be used.

- Any digit can be used more than once.

- When the dice are rolled, every sum from 4 to 14 must be possible and

  no other sums can occur.

- The two dice do not have to be identical.

2. What numbers would you put on the 6 faces of each of the two dice so that the above

    conditions are met?

    Die 1:   _____   _____   _____   _____   _____   _____

    Die 2:   _____   _____   _____   _____   _____   _____

3. Which sum(s) do you think would turn up most frequently if your New Cubes were

    rolled 1000 times? Explain why.

FIG. 16.2. (Continued)

   The replication study took an interesting twist at one of the schools. During the 1996–1997 school year, teachers of the traditional courses had given their students instructional material on content directly related to what was included on the tests. These teachers had supplemented the traditional curriculum by incorporating a unit on statistics (e.g., properties of the normal distribution) in the Grade 9 Algebra course and a unit on problem solving (including some work on combinatorics) in the Grade 10 Geometry course. The instructional experience varied enough from the traditional course so that the curriculum in that school was labeled as "enhanced traditional" and the data were analyzed and are reported separately.

Thus, the sample for the original study consists of students from one school at each of Grades 9, 10, and 11. In contrast, the sample for the replication study consists of students from three schools at each of Grades 9 and 10, two of which used a traditional curriculum, and one of which used an enhanced traditional Curriculum.

Results on Achievement

Results on the tests of statistics, problem solving, and quantitative reasoning for both the original and replication studies are presented in Tables 16.6, 16.7, and 16.8, respectively. As shown in Table 16.6, *IMP* Year 1 students in Grade 9 in the original study performed significantly higher on the four statistics items than did students who were enrolled in Algebra I. *IMP* students demonstrated they had knowledge of statistical concepts, including mean, standard deviation, and the normal distribution. This finding was replicated at two of three high schools when *IMP* students were

TABLE 16.6
Performances of Grade 9 *IMP* Year 1 and Algebra I Students

	IMP			*Traditional*[a]			
Grade	N	Mean	SD	N	Mean	SD	$\Delta SD\ Units$[b]
			Original Study: 1995–1996				
8	60	70.45	23.34	55	62.40	22.85	
9	60	3.07*	1.41	55	1.00	0.92	+1.31
			Replication Study: 1996–1997 (*IMP* & Trad.)				
8	56	70.68	21.84	40	65.98	21.26	
9	73	1.70*	1.11	63	0.87	0.71	+0.83
			Replication Study: 1996–1997 (*IMP* & Enhanced Trad.[c])				
8	27	68.56	17.80	35	64.60	23.04	
9	32	1.78	1.24	40	2.68*	0.97	−0.76

Note. Performances are on the SIMS statistics items, using the Grade 8 covariate: original study and replication. Mean scores are raw mean scores.

[a]Traditional includes the Grade 9 college-preparatory course *IMP* students had the opportunity to take if they had not taken *IMP*. Generally, the traditional course was Algebra I. At one high school in the replication study, Grade 9 students traditionally took Geometry.

[b]Mean for *IMP* group less the mean for the traditional group divided by the standard deviation for the combined group.

[c]Enhanced traditional indicates that the traditional Algebra I course was supplemented with a unit on statistics.

*$p < .01$, using an analysis of covariance with Grade 8 mathematics national percentiles as covariate.

TABLE 16.7
Performances of Grade 10 *IMP* Year 2 and Geometry Students

	IMP			Traditional [a]			
Grade	N	Mean	SD	N	Mean	SD	ΔSD Units[b]
			Original Study: 1995–1996				
8	71	77.43	15.13	80	79.53	16.24	
10	87	6.44*	1.66	97	4.56	1.44	+1.04
			Replication Study: 1996–1997 (*IMP* & Trad.)				
8	69	80.20	14.66	56	79.27	21.12	
10	97	5.34*	2.07	77	3.88	1.53	+0.74
			Replication Study: 1996–1997 (*IMP* & Enhanced Trad.[c])				
8	32	58.31	24.99	40	51.73	19.80	
10	35	5.74	2.29	45	5.56	2.18	+0.08

Note. Performances are measured on two items testing problem solving, using the Grade 8 covariate: original study and replication.

[a]The traditional curriculum includes the Grades 9 and 10 college-preparatory courses *IMP* students had the opportunity to take if they had not taken *IMP*. At the high school in the original study, the traditional courses used the *UCSMP Algebra* and *Geometry* textbooks. No information about comparison texts is available for the schools in the replication study.

[b]Mean for *IMP* group less the mean for the traditional group divided by the standard deviation for the combined group.

[c]Enhanced traditional indicates that the traditional Algebra I course was supplemented with a unit on statistics and the traditional Geometry course was supplemented with a unit on combinatorics and probability.

*$p < .01$, using an analysis of covariance with Grade 8 mathematics national percentiles as covariate.

compared with students enrolled in Algebra, the traditional Grade 9 mathematics course. However, in the replication study with the enhanced traditional course, the *IMP* students did not perform as high as did the *IMP* students in the original study. When the traditional course was supplemented by instructional experiences directly related to the statistical ideas tested, students in the traditional course performed significantly higher than the *IMP* students at Grade 9. Grade 9 students in the enhanced traditional course at this one school outperformed the students enrolled in the *IMP* Year 1 at the same school by approximately one point on a five-point test.

The findings from the original study and its replication indicated that *IMP* students in the study were learning more about statistics, as is the intent of the curriculum, than students in traditional Algebra. When students are given the opportunity to learn statistical ideas in the traditional class, they also were able to demonstrate their knowledge of this area.

As indicated in Table 16.7, Grade 10 *IMP* students, when compared with students in the traditional Grade 10 Geometry classes, performed significantly higher on two items requiring students to engage in reasoning, problem solving, and application of their knowledge. The difference in

TABLE 16.8
Performances of Grade 11 *IMP* Year 3 and Algebra II Students

		IMP			*Traditional*[a]		
Grade	N	Mean	SD	N	Mean	SD	ΔSD Units[b]
			Total Group				
8	91	94.53	4.18	35	92.71	4.67	
11	93	5.04*	2.12	40	2.40	1.52	+1.15
			Matched-Group Analysis				
8	31	93.71	3.75	31	93.68	3.77	
11	31	5.42**	2.20	31	2.39	1.61	+1.24

Note. Performances are measured on QRT items, using the Grade 8 covariate.

[a]The Houghton Mifflin *Algebra 1, Geometry,* and *Algebra II Structure and Method* textbooks were used at this high school.

[b]Mean for *IMP* group less the mean for the traditional group divided by the standard deviation for the combined group.

*$p < .01$, using an analysis of covariance with Grade 8 mathematics national percentiles as covariate.

**$p < .01$, using a large-sample matched-group Wilcoxon test analysis.

mean scores was larger in the original study than in the replication study in the two schools using traditional curricula. When the traditional course was enhanced, the difference between *IMP* students and those in the traditional course was small.

The Grade 9 and Grade 10 studies indicate that *IMP* students were learning mathematics not typically included in the traditional college-preparatory Grade 9 and Grade 10 mathematics courses. *IMP* students demonstrated greater understanding of statistics as measured by SIMS items and a greater ability to apply reasoning when asked to solve problems requiring them to apply mathematics and give an explanation of their work. It was concluded that the main reason for these differences was that content included in the *IMP* curriculum was aligned with national standards, but was not normally included in the traditional courses at Grades 9 and 10.

Only one school participated in the Grade 11 study on quantitative reasoning. This school was different from all of the schools in the other studies. In addition to the use of an analysis of covariance to control for prior achievement, a matched-group analysis was performed to establish some statistical controls. A matched-group Wilcoxon test was used to determine statistical significance. For this test, students from both groups were matched according to prior achievement. Only students in both groups who had taken the California Achievement Test (CAT) in Grade 8 were included in the analysis. After the students were ranked on CAT scores, the two groups (*IMP* and Algebra II) were matched, with the two highest and comparable-scoring students paired, the next two comparable-scoring students paired, and so on, with the two lowest and comparable-scoring students forming the last pair. A total of 31 pairs were formed. Additionally, the groups were formed taking into account ethnicity, sex, and the middle school attended. The main purpose of the pairing process was to form two groups (*IMP* Year 3 and Algebra II) that matched as closely as possible on mean CAT scores and by sex and ethnicity.

Data in Table 16.8 indicate that the *IMP* Year 3 students performed significantly higher than Algebra II students on the QRT, whether one considers the results for the whole sample or the results from the matched-group analysis.

Item analysis indicates that the proportion of *IMP* students answering an item correctly ranged from 18% to 75%, compared with 3% to 53% for the Algebra II students. Items related to the application of the normal curve properties, especially standard deviation, were relatively difficult for both groups; only 18% of *IMP* students and 3% of Algebra II students answered correctly. Other relatively difficult items, especially for the Algebra II students, were those related to extrapolation by using rates and percentages. The percent correct on these items ranged from 43% to 54% for the *IMP* group and from 10% to 23% for the Algebra II group. *IMP* Year 3 students did considerably better on items related to probability concepts than did Algebra II students (75% and 67% compared with 53% and 38%). The Grade 11 study, without a replication, represents the findings only for this particular school, teachers, and the students tested. The findings are consistent, except for the low percentage of *IMP* students correctly answering the standard deviation question, with the findings of the studies at the other two grade levels. The *IMP* students outperformed students in the traditional college-preparatory mathematics course on content emphasized in their curriculum and generally not addressed in the traditional college-preparatory mathematics curriculum.

DISCUSSION

Our studies produced evidence that students who had taken *IMP* performed as well as students who had taken the traditional college-preparatory mathematics sequence on common standardized tests, including the mathematics portion of the SAT and the mathematics part of the Grade 11 CTBS. Neither of these tests fully measured the *IMP* curriculum's objective to provide students with some understanding of statistics and probability, two topics not normally included in the traditional curriculum, or the *IMP* goal of making students more effective problem solvers. On tests more aligned with these goals, *IMP* students outperformed students in the traditional mathematics courses, a finding that was replicated in Study 3. This result was attributed to the inclusion of content by *IMP* not normally presented in the traditional curriculum. When the traditional curriculum was enhanced to provide students with instruction on statistics and specific problem-solving activities, students in these classes show increased performance.

Data reported here are quantitative and cannot fully represent the experiences students have while enrolled in *IMP* for 3 or 4 years in high school. Students interviewed revealed some of their experiences in *IMP* when asked to reflect on their high school mathematics career after graduating from high school:

> It was interactive, it was interesting, and I wasn't bored.

> I learned how to think differently; more in terms of the real world, and working with others to solve a problem. It made you think about math in terms of not formulas, but rather thinking of things as they have to do with the world.

> The IMP program helped me to just think of the reasons why a formula worked instead of just memorizing. It helped me to remember things better; to look at things in real life situations. It also taught me how to use a calculator.

> I enjoyed working in groups. It helped me to become a better problem solver and be more open to divergent ideas.

> It totally made us look at where we started from, not just memorization, but dissecting what we already knew so we could apply it later.

> It also helped me with critical analysis; it made me less afraid to approach different problems.

This evaluation of *IMP* faced a number of issues. Legitimate control groups were very difficult to identify. Even in schools implementing both *IMP* and traditional programs, students transferred between programs, teachers taught both programs, and teachers in each program communicated with teachers of the other program. Evidence was found that practices in *IMP*, such as students working in small groups, crept into the traditional classes, clouding some of the differences between the curricula. In some schools, teachers of traditional classes were actively opposed to *IMP* and were not interested in having their students compared with *IMP* students. Special effort was made during the evaluation to understand the context within which the study was being made and to obtain baseline data to determine the comparability of students.

IMP places strong emphasis on students learning how to reason and solve problems. Assessment instruments that could be used on a large scale and that were aligned with the *IMP* curriculum were not available. This factor restricted the capacity of the evaluators to do large-scale testing and to measure whether students were achieving important goals of the program. The evaluation was designed to use existing assessment instruments in an effort to counter arguments that only instruments biased toward the curriculum were used to judge outcomes.

Evaluation data clearly indicated that if teachers are to use the curriculum effectively, they need time, experience with the curriculum, reflection, and peer support. It is not unreasonable to expect teachers to at least teach all 4 years of the curriculum before they fully understand it and are in a position to help students gain the most from the curriculum. In addition, the completed curriculum materials were not available to most of the teachers and to the classes that participated in the evaluation studies. Because of these and other reasons, I am aware that the findings reported here do not represent the effectiveness that experienced *IMP* teachers will have with later versions of the *IMP*.

REFERENCES

Adelman, C. (1999). *Answers in the tool box: Academic intensity, attendance patterns, and bachelor's degree attainment.* Washington, DC: U.S. Department of Education.

Alper, L., Fendel, D., Fraser, S., & Resek, D. (1995). Is this a mathematics class? *Mathematics Teacher, 88,* 632–638.

Alper, L., Fendel, D., Fraser, S., & Resek, D. (1997). Designing a high school mathematics curriculum for all students. *American Journal of Education, 106,* 148–179.

Crosswhite, F. J., Dossey, J. A., Swafford, J. O., McKnight, C. C., Cooney, T. J., Downs, F. L., Grouws, D. A., & Weinzweig, A. I. (1986). *Second international mathematics study, detailed report for the United States.* Champaign, IL: Stipes.

Fendel, D., Resek, D., Alper, L., & Fraser, S. (1997). *Interactive mathematics program. Integrated high school mathematics. Year 1.* Berkeley, CA: Key Curriculum Press.

Fendel, D., Resek, D., Alper, L., & Fraser, S. (1998). *Interactive mathematics program. Integrated high school mathematics. Year 2.* Berkeley, CA: Key Curriculum Press.

Fendel, D., Resek, D., Alper, L., & Fraser, S. (1999a). *Interactive mathematics program. Integrated high school mathematics. Year 3.* Berkeley, CA: Key Curriculum Press.

Fendel, D., Resek, D., Alper, L., & Fraser, S. (1999b). *Interactive mathematics program. Integrated high school mathematics. Year 4.* Berkeley, CA: Key Curriculum Press.

National Council of Teachers of Mathematics. (1989). *Curriculum and evaluation standards for school mathematics.* Reston, VA: Author.

Ohanian, S. (1997). Math that measures up. *The American School Board Journal, 184*(6), 25–27.

Schoen, H. (1993). Interactive mathematics program. In N. L. Webb, H. Schoen, & S. D. Whitehurst (Eds.), *Dissemination of nine pre-college mathematics instructional materials projects funded by the National Science Foundation, 1981–91.* Madison: University of Wisconsin—Madison.

Shaver, J. P., & Norton, R. S. (1980). Randomness and replication in ten years of the American Educational Research Journal. *Educational Researcher, 9*(1), 9–15.

ENDNOTE

1. The ethnic categories used for this analysis are those that were given with the transcripts. This is done with the realization that each category can encompass a broad range of students with diverse ethnic backgrounds.

17

Curriculum and Assessment in *SIMMS* Integrated Mathematics

Johnny W. Lott
James Hirstein

The University of Montana

Maurice Burke
Michael Lundin

Montana State University—Bozeman

Glenn Allinger

Formerly of Montana State University— Bozeman

Terry A. Souhrada

The University of Montana

Dean Preble

Formerly of Montana State University— Bozeman

Sharon Walen

Boise State University

From their inceptions the Systemic Initiative for Montana Mathematics and Science (*SIMMS* Project), funded in 1991, and the *SIMMS Integrated Mathematics Project* (*SIMMS IM* Project), funded in 1996, differed from the other curriculum projects funded by the National Science Foundation (NSF). Both NSF awards were made to the Montana Council of Teachers of Mathematics (MCTM). Neither award was solely as a curriculum development project. The *SIMMS* Project was a State Systemic Initiative (SSI) specifically charged with changing mathematics and science education in Montana. The *SIMMS IM* Project had as goals the completion of the 9–12 integrated mathematics curriculum begun in the *SIMMS* Project and the testing of the curriculum in two large urban areas with minority populations.

399

The curriculum is published commercially as *MCTM/SIMMS Integrated Mathematics: A Modeling Approach Using Technology, Levels 1–6* (MCTM/ SIMMS, 1996, 1997, 1998).

HISTORY OF THE CURRICULUM

Conceived in 1991 by members of the MCTM, and with support from state legislators and the governor, the *SIMMS* Project was based on the 1989 national survey, "Integrated Mathematics Project," funded by the Exxon Education Foundation. This survey defined "integrated mathematics" as a holistic mathematical curriculum that consists of topics chosen from a wide variety of mathematical fields and that blends those topics to emphasize the connections and unity among fields (Beal, Dolan, Lott, & Smith, 1990). Further, integrated mathematics emphasizes relationships among topics within mathematics as well as between mathematics and other disciplines.

The *Curriculum and Evaluation Standards for School Mathematics* (National Council of Teachers of Mathematics [NCTM], 1989) stated, "We favor a truly integrated curricular organization in all grades to permit students to develop mathematical power more readily and to allow the necessary flexibility over time to incorporate the content of these standards" (p. 252). Based on the definition of the national survey and encouraged by the NCTM *Standards*, the *SIMMS* Project outlined a complete integrated mathematics curriculum, including assessment and evaluation.

THE CURRICULUM

Unlike other reform curricula, the *SIMMS IM* curriculum was developed by a team of approximately 75 secondary mathematics teachers and 8 university personnel. The 9–12 mathematics curriculum was designed for all students and is

- integrated and interdisciplinary,
- problem centered and applications based,
- technology based,
- sensitive to multiple perspectives and the negative effects of bias and stereotyping, and
- multimodal to accommodate multiple learning styles (Burke & Lott, 1993).

Incorporating the conceptual mathematization of de Lange (1989), the *SIMMS* curricular framework recognized the importance of beginning with situations that can be manipulated, organized, and structured according to their mathematical aspects. Set in constructivist philosophy, problem solving emerges from specific contexts to become a part of a larger process of organizing, understanding, and mathematizing. To knit together mathematics and other subjects, mathematical modeling is the basic thread of the curriculum (Burke & Lott, 1993).

Polya (1973), Skemp (1987), and van Hiele (1959/1984) recognized the importance of the reflective activity of "integration" in producing relational structures and insights in the learner. Without this activity, mathematical concepts are neither learned, completed, long lasting, nor useful. In the *SIMMS* curriculum, the integration process is constructed of such activities as informal organizing of propositions and ideas; relating procedures from one context to another; interpreting, justifying, and evaluating mathematical models, structures, and solutions; and summarizing and communicating mathematical insights in cogent arguments (*SIMMS* Project, 1993).

The *SIMMS IM* curriculum uses computers and calculators as tools, not tutors, in the learning of mathematics. Every student studying from the *SIMMS IM* curriculum should have access to the functionality of a graphing calculator and to either computer utilities or calculators such as the Texas Instruments TI-92 PLUS for exploring geometry, graphing, analyzing data, using spreadsheets, and word processing. In addition, each student and teacher should have access to the Internet.

Both core understandings and core attitudes are expected of all students using the *SIMMS IM* curriculum (Burke & Lott, 1993). The following are core understandings: number, operation, function, graphs, spatial visualization, statistics, modeling, measurement, and computer–algorithm. Among the core attitudes expected of students are the following.

1. Mathematics is useful.
2. Doing mathematics is more than following rules.
3. Doing mathematics is communicating and discussing.
4. I can make mathematically informed decisions.

The *SIMMS IM* curriculum for all secondary students is divided into six levels, each consisting of 1 year of work. Level 1, the first course, is typically offered to ninth-grade students. After Level 2, students may choose between Levels 3 and 4 and then go to either Levels 5 or 6 as illustrated in the schematic of the course sequence in Fig. 17.1. The sequence for students expecting to study mathematics or science in college is 1-2-4-6.

Each level consists of 14 to 16 modules. Table 17.1 gives the number of modules at each level containing the mathematical content area listed. The examples that follow provide additional evidence of the ways in which *SIMMS IM* is an integrated and interdisciplinary curriculum.

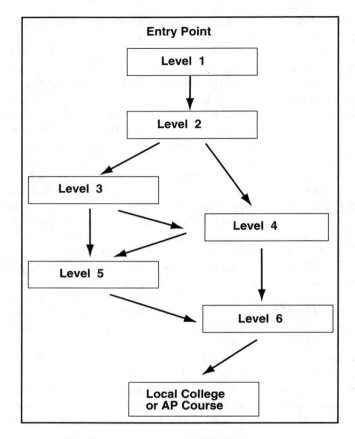

FIG. 17.1. Sequence of *SIMMS IM* courses.

Levels 1 and 2 provide basic mathematical literacy that every educated adult should know, even if no further mathematics is studied formally in school. Because the curriculum was written as part of a state systemic initiative and the primary minority in Montana is Native American, this culture provides contexts for the mathematics in many *SIMMS IM* materials. Figure 17.2 contains several examples from the "Traditional Design" module found in Level 2, Volume 3 (MCTM/SIMMS, 1996). In it, Native American art is used as a context to explore basic geometric concepts.

The examples in Fig. 17.2 illustrate typical technology use in the curriculum. Initial discussions introduce mathematics in context. Explorations use technology to allow students to make and verify mathematical conjectures. In Fig. 17.2, students conjecture that the intersection of the perpendicular bisectors of two chords is the center of the circle. In the *SIMMS IM* curriculum

TABLE 17.1
Number of Modules in Each Level Containing Identified Content

Content	Level 1	Level 2	Level 3	Level 4	Level 5	Level 6
Arithmetic	8	5	3	1	1	1
Algebra	11	7	10	11	8	12
Geometry	6	5	5	5	4	6
Trigonometry	0	2	1	3	2	5
Statistics–Data Anal.	8	3	4	5	6	6
Probability–Combinatorics	3	3	2	2	6	3
Logic–Proof	2	1	2	2	1	2
Discrete Math.	3	4	3	1	3	2
Precalc.–Calc.	0	2	1	3	0	3
No. of modules in level	15	15	14	16	14	15

Note. The sum of the numbers in each column does not equal the total because many modules include work in two or more content areas.

there are no explicit technology lessons. Additional discussions bring closure to mathematics developed by means of the explorations.

For those with nonmathematical or nonscientific aspirations, the *SIMMS* Project developed Levels 3 and 5. An example of the level of mathematics in Levels 3 and 5 is found in Fig. 17.3. This activity involves the use of technology to develop the notion of parabolas by using acceleration due to gravity. Contextual notes, as seen in Fig. 17.3, are used to help students identify connections between mathematics and other areas.

For those interested in mathematics and science careers, Levels 4 and 6 prepare students to complete a postsecondary mathematics curriculum. Figure 17.4 provides an example from a module in Level 4.

Curriculum assessment items apply mathematics in a real-world setting. Assessment items require students to write mathematical explanations. Figure 17.5 shows a summary assessment for a unit in Level 3.

RESEARCH TO SUPPORT
THE CURRICULUM

The success of any curriculum can only be measured through research and assessment of the program in different situations and over time.

Assessment of the *SIMMS* Curriculum in Montana

The *SIMMS* Project used the following principles in the development of student assessment materials.

The medicine wheel in Figure **13** has two **concentric circles** (circles that have the same center), a set of evenly spaced quadrilaterals, and a Cheyenne design in the middle.

Figure 13: A Cheyenne medicine wheel

In this activity, you use geometric properties of a circle to create a medicine wheel.

Discussion 1

a.   Disregarding the tassels and beads, what types of symmetry do you observe in the medicine wheel in Figure **13**?

b.   Explain how you could use reflections, rotations, dilations, and translations to reconstruct this medicine wheel—including tassels and beads—on a geometry utility.

Exploration

a.   Using a geometry utility, draw a circle whose diameter is approximately two-thirds the width of the screen.

b.   **1.** A **chord** is a line segment joining any two points on a circle. Draw two chords of your circle.

        2. Predict where the perpendicular bisectors of the two chords will intersect. Draw a point at that location.

        3. Construct the perpendicular bisectors of the chords. Mark the intersection point (if different from the location predicted in Step **2**).

Discussion 2

a.   Figure **15** shows a fragment of American Indian pottery. Before beginning reconstruction of the circular plate, a museum curator might first make a sketch of the original artifact, including its center. Using your observations from the exploration, describe how to find the center of this circular plate.

Figure 15: Pottery fragment

b.   Describe how to use paper folding to find the center of a circle.

FIG. 17.2. Excerpt from "Traditional Design," *Note.* From *Integrated Mathematics: A Modeling Approach Using Technology, Level 2* (Vol. 3), by MCTM/SIMMS, 1996, Needham Heights, MA: Simon and Schuster. © 1996 by Simon and Schuster. Reprinted with permission.

According to legend, Isaac Newton "discovered" gravity after watching an apple fall from a tree. In this activity you explore how the **acceleration** due to gravity affects the distance-time graphs of freely falling objects.

Science Note

Acceleration is the rate of change in velocity with respect to time.

For example, consider a car driving along a straight section of highway. Over time, the velocity of the car can increase, decrease, or remain the same. When the car's velocity increases, its acceleration is positive. When the car's velocity decreases, its acceleration is negative. If the car's velocity remains constant, its acceleration is 0.

The average acceleration of an object over a particular time interval can be determined by dividing the change in velocity by the change in time. For example, consider a model rocket launched straight into the air. At $t = 3$ sec, its velocity is 48.65 m/sec. At $t = 5$ sec, its velocity is 29.33 m/sec. The rocket's average acceleration during this period can be estimated as follows:

$$\frac{29.33 \text{ m/sec} - 48.65 \text{ m/sec}}{5 \text{ sec} - 3 \text{ sec}} = -9.66 \text{ m/sec}^2$$

This means that, during the time interval [3, 5], the rocket's velocity decreased by an average of 9.66 m/sec for every second that passed.

Exploration

In this exploration, you collect distance-time data for a ball rolling down an incline. You then use polynomial functions to model this data.

a. Obtain a track, a ball, and the range-finder apparatus and set it up as shown in Figure **4**. Use books to raise the end of a track with the range finder on it.

Figure 4: Ball on track with range finder

b. Collect distance-time data as the ball rolls down the ramp.

c. Edit your data set so that it contains only information collected as the ball was actually moving, beginning with the moment of its release. Determine a quadratic equation that appears to model this data set.

d. Recall that a **residual** is the difference between an observed value and the corresponding value predicted by a model, and that the sum of the squares of the residuals can be used to evaluate how well a model fits a data set. Calculate the sum of the squares of the residuals for your model. Adjust the equation until the sum of the squares of the residuals indicates that the model closely approximates the data.

FIG. 17.3. Excerpt from "Graphing the Distance." *Note.* From *Integrated Mathematics: A Modeling Approach Using Technology, Level 3* (Vol. 2), by MCTM/SIMMS, 1997, Needham Heights, MA: Simon and Schuster. © 1997 by Simon and Schuster. Reprinted with permission.

1. Assessment's primary goal should be improvement of student learning.
2. Collecting data on student achievement should be an integral part of instruction, not something external to the teaching process.
3. Assessment should include the active participation of students in open-ended problems.
4. Assessment should reflect the real-world applications used in instruction.
5. Assessment must permit the full use of technology.

Mathematicians have long used functions to model real-world situations. Many of these situations involve events that repeat in predictable cycles. In this module, you investigate the functions required to model these and other **cyclic** events such as the rise and fall of ocean tides and the hours of sunlight in the days of the year.

Exploration

In this Exploration you will create the graph of a function that can model cyclic events.

Figure 2: Placement of number line

a.   Position the can so that the 0 on the number line corresponds with the coordinates (1,0), as shown in Figure **2**. Use the number line to mark the points on the circle that correspond to labeled points on the number line. This process simulates a **wrapping function** that pairs each point on the real number line with a location on the unit circle. Label each point on the circle with all its corresponding real numbers using the wrapping function.

b.   Approximate the ordered pair that corresponds to each labeled point on the circle. Record them in a spreadsheet with headings like those in Table **1**.

Table 1: Real numbers and corresponding xy-coordinates

Real Number	x-coordinate	y-coordinate
0	1	0
$\pi/4$	0.7	0.7
1	0.5	0.8
$\vdots$	$\vdots$	$\vdots$

c.   Create two scatterplots: one with the x-coordinates versus the real numbers and another with the y-coordinates versus the real numbers.

Assignment

4.1   The hours of light in each day change with the seasons. At locations near 40°N latitude, the hours of daylight range from a minimum of about 9 hr to a maximum of approximately 15 hr.

Assuming that the mean number of daylight hours occurs on March 21, the number of daylight hours on any given day can be modeled by the following

$h = 12 + 3\sin\left(\dfrac{2\pi}{365}d\right)$. Based on this model, what is the mean number of daylight

hours in a year? When do the longest and shortest days occur?

4.2   Ordinary household circuits carry alternating current. This current can be modeled by the function $i = I_{max}\sin\theta$, where i is the current, I_{max} is the maximum current, and θ is the angle of rotation measured in the generator.

a.   Write a function that could be used to model alternating current with a maximum of 20 A. Graph the function over the interval $[0, 4\pi]$.

b.   The effective value of an alternating current equals $0.707 \cdot I_{max}$. Determine the values of θ when i equals the effective current.

FIG. 17.4. Excerpt from "Can It." *Note*. From *Integrated Mathematics: A Modeling Approach Using Technology, Level 4* (Vol. 1), by MCTM/SIMMS, 1997, Needham Heights, MA: Simon and Schuster. © 1997 by Simon and Schuster. Reprinted with permission.

Microwave signals are used in a variety of applications, including telephone transmissions. Since microwaves travel in straight lines and weaken considerably over distances greater than 5 km, microwave repeaters must be placed along the transmission path to relay signals.

In this activity, you use topographic maps to create **profiles** of mountainous terrain. Profiles help provide visual images of landscapes between points on a topographic map.

Exploration

On a topographic map, label two points at least 10 km apart and located on different contour lines. As shown in Figure **15**, connect the points with a **profile segment**. Create a profile by connecting the points of intersection of the perpendiculars to the profile segment with the corresponding altitude line as shown in Figure **15**.

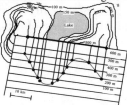

Figure 15: Creating a profile

Summary Assessment

The map shows locations and heights of buildings in a business district in a large city.

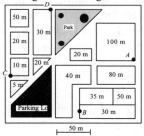

The local telephone company plans to build a microwave transmitter on the top of the building at point *A*. The transmitter will send signals to a receiver located on the top of a building at point *C*.

    a. Determine the distance between points *A* and *C* using the coordinates of ordered triples and the angle of elevation necessary to transmit the signal directly from point *A* to point *B*.

    b. Write a letter to the president of the company describing your findings Include appropriate profiles and mathematical explanations.

FIG. 17.5. A sample assessment from the module "From Here to There." *Note.* From *Integrated Mathematics: A Modeling Approach Using Technology, Level 3* (Vol. 1), by MCTM/SIMMS, 1997, Needham Heights, MA: Simon and Schuster. © 1997 by Simon and Schuster. Reprinted with permission.

Testing the *SIMMS* Project curriculum required the development of new assessment instruments. Traditional mathematics assessments could not completely describe results of using this curriculum.

In the *SIMMS* Project curriculum, students explore topics and make inquiries about both real-world and mathematical contexts. Students confront complex issues in mathematizing a real-world problem and in interpreting and communicating its solutions. Additionally, students reflect on their own performance. Insight into student work was provided through holistic and analytic analyses of such classroom artifacts as written tests, quizzes, homework, journal entries, and measures of student participation and cooperation.

The Prepilot Study in Montana

The *SIMMS* curriculum research involved a two-step process for the trial and testing of the materials. As each level of the curriculum was developed, a prepilot study was conducted the following school year in Montana. Teacher and student feedback during the prepilot year informed revisions of the curriculum. The revised curriculum was then tested in formal pilots, with the results of these studies used for the final revisions. The prepilot studies also served as a testing ground for assessment methods and materials used to evaluate student outcomes.

Schools in the prepilot study of Level 1 had to satisfy three criteria:

1. The necessary technology had to be in place.
2. The school had to be willing to teach at least one class with the *SIMMS* Level 1 curriculum.
3. A teacher from the school must have participated as a writer or teacher–leader during the summer of 1992.

Twelve Montana schools, public and private, were chosen for the initial prepilot study. These schools covered a range of sizes (four schools with more than 500 students, and four with fewer than 100 students), a range of communities (rural and urban), and a wide geographical distribution. Students in 23 classrooms used Level 1 materials during the first year.

At the end of the 1993 school year, two formats of tests were administered: the mathematics section of the Preliminary Scholastic Aptitude Test (1987, Form T) and a series of internally constructed, open-ended questions that were labeled End-of-Year Tasks (EOYT). These tests were given to all *SIMMS* students and to students in a selection of non-*SIMMS* classes in the participating schools.

A major assessment goal of the prepilot study was to develop a scoring mechanism to address student responses on open-ended questions. A modification of the California State Department of Education rubric for

TABLE 17.2
Rubric for Scoring EOYT

Category	Score	Descriptor
Exemplary	6	exemplary; understanding of the general problem
	5	complete; shows understanding and competence
Satisfactory	4	satisfactory; minor flaws
	3	nearly satisfactory; serious flaws
Inadequate	2	unable to complete the problem
	1	did not begin effectively
None	0	no response

Note. From "Student Assessment in the Pilot Study," by J. Hirstein, in *Assessment* (Monograph No. 4, p. 3), 1998, Missoula, MT: The SIMMS Project. Copyright 1998 by The SIMMS Project. Reprinted with permission.

the open-ended mathematics tasks was selected. General descriptors that were applied to student responses are given in Table 17.2.

In the analysis of the prepilot study, the performance of all *SIMMS* classes was compared with the performance of a sample composed of one randomly selected *SIMMS* class from each school. There was no significant difference between sampled *SIMMS* classes and the entire population of *SIMMS* classes, so the pilot studies adopted a design using one *SIMMS* class per school. A complete report of the prepilot year of Level 1 is given in Austin, Hirstein, and Walen (1997).

Pilot Studies in Montana

Pilot studies in Montana were carried out over 4 years, beginning with Level 1 during the 1993–1994 school year. Each year one pilot class was chosen at each *SIMMS* school, using criteria based on technology access, curriculum implementation, and teacher training. Comparison classes were selected in order to have students as close as possible in age and mathematical background to students in *SIMMS* classes. As in the prepilot study, only intact classes were used in the comparison.

During the 1993–1994 school year, 115 classes in 37 schools used the pilot version of *SIMMS* Level 1 materials. Ten schools participated in the pilot study. Five had been prepilot schools; five were new to the project and had satisfied the three previously described criteria. One of these schools was located outside Montana. The testing sample consisted of 171 *SIMMS* students in 10 classrooms and 105 non-*SIMMS* students in 5 classrooms. As in the prepilot study, comparison classes studied either Algebra, Math 1 (first year of a non-*SIMMS* integrated mathematics program), or Prealgebra (Hirstein, 1998).

During the 1994–1995 school year, 73 classrooms in 26 schools used the pilot version of *SIMMS* Level 2 materials. The same 10 schools that had participated in the Level 1 study during the previous year were the sites for the pilot study of *SIMMS* Level 2. The sample contained 163 *SIMMS* students in 10 classes. For comparison, data were collected from 117 non-*SIMMS* students in six classes. Approximately 50% of these students were in Geometry, 25% in Algebra 1, and 25% in Math 2 (the second year of a non-*SIMMS* integrated mathematics program). None of the courses, either *SIMMS* or non-*SIMMS*, was specifically designated as remedial or honors (Hirstein, 1998).

In the fall of 1995, 36 classrooms in 18 schools used the pilot version of *SIMMS* Level 4. One of the 10 pilot schools decided not to offer Level 4 during this year. By the end of the academic year, one additional school had so changed its mathematics offerings that the school's class could not be considered a *SIMMS* class. Therefore, the sample for the 1995–1996 study contained eight *SIMMS* Level 4 classes with 127 students, and four comparison classes with 48 students. The non-*SIMMS* students were enrolled in a third year of college-preparatory mathematics (Hirstein, 1998).

Some schools that offered *SIMMS* Level 4 did not offer Level 6. For the study conducted in 1996–1997, the *SIMMS* sample contained seven *SIMMS* Level 6 classes, consisting of 88 students. The comparison group consisted of six non-*SIMMS* classes of seniors in their fourth year of college-bound mathematics, a total of 80 students. Because of the design of the pilot studies and the selection of samples, most of the schools in the Level 6 study participated in earlier studies. Although most of the students in the *SIMMS* and comparison classes in the Level 6 study had not participated in earlier studies, virtually every *SIMMS* student in the Level 6 study had used the *SIMMS* curriculum for 4 years.

During the spring of each year of the four pilot studies, the *SIMMS* classes and comparison classes took one form of the mathematics portion of the Preliminary Scholastic Aptitude Test (PSAT-M). Consistent with the test developers' guidelines, students were not allowed to use calculators to answer questions on the tests used in the studies of Levels 1, 2, and 4. The form of the PSAT-M used in the Level 6 study permitted calculators to be used. The mean score for each class on the PSAT-M was calculated and the differences in class means for the *SIMMS* and comparison groups were computed. The results are summarized in Table 17.3. In general, they showed no significant differences in the performance of the two groups.

Each spring students in the pilot studies also took EOYT developed by the *SIMMS* staff. The format of the EOYT was similar in all of the pilot years. Scoring was conducted by trained scorers; the reliability of the scoring was checked by using other trained scorers. Each EOYT tested students' knowledge of various content areas, including algebra, geometry, statistics, and probability. Most items involved some realistic context. Each used a free-response format.

TABLE 17.3
Mean Performance of *SIMMS* and Comparison Classes on the PSAT-M
for the Montana Samples

SIMMS Level	Test Form	SIMMS		Comparison		Stat. Test
		No. of Classes	Mean	No. of Classes	Mean	
1	1988 Form T	10	36.85	5	37.87	$t = 0.543$
2	1989 Form T	10	39.50	6	40.71	$t = 0.429$
4	1992 Form T	2	42.48	2	46.54	$F = 1.793^a$
6	1995 Form T	7	15.82	6	15.36	$t = 0.440^b$

Note. Means reported are means of class means. For the studies at Levels 1, 2, and 4 the means are scale scores in the range 20–80. For the Level 6 study, the means are raw scores with a maximum of 25.

[a]In the Level 4 study, one of the schools failed to give the PSAT to non-*SIMMS* classes, resulting in an insufficient number of comparison classes to conduct a t test on the differences in class means. The analysis of the PSAT-M data was modified accordingly. Because the other two schools each tested a *SIMMS* and comparison group, the four classes were compared by using a 2×2 analysis of variance. The F test reported is for the main effect comparing *SIMMS* and non-*SIMMS* students.

[b]The 1995 PSAT-M is substantially different from the earlier versions. Because of the imposition of the test on teacher instructional time, only one of the two mathematics parts was used.

Each year one common question was asked of all students. The common items for Levels 1, 2, 4, and 6 are shown in Fig. 17.6. Additionally, each student responded to two rotated questions chosen from a pool of nine. Responses were scored by using the modified California rubric scale of 0–6 described in Table 17.2.

A sample student response to one question is shown in Fig. 17.7. This response received a rubric score of 4 because the 20% decrease in the question is applied to subsequent steps of the process, but it considers only one dose of the drug. The student's mathematical analysis neglected an important feature of the question, "... to be taken at regular intervals," and therefore it is incomplete. Still, the paper clearly communicates the choice of a mathematical model and the problem-solving processes were logically presented, appropriate to the task, and justified through connections to the real world.

Mean scores were calculated for each item in each class. Then the mean scores of the *SIMMS* classes and comparison classes were compared by using a t test. Results of students' performances on the common questions for the 4 pilot years are shown in Table 17.4.

On the Level 1 common item, the mean score of the *SIMMS* students was significantly higher than the mean score of the comparison students. Among the nine rotated items on the Level 1 EOYT, the *SIMMS* students scored significantly higher than non-*SIMMS* students on five items (Hirstein, 1998).

SIMMS   Common EOYT Item for Level
Level

1   According to a newspaper report, the trees in a certain land area are being
          cut at a rate of 15% per year. The lumber company claims that it replants
          2000 trees every year in this area. Discuss the future tree production of
          this land area if this plan continues.

2   When a drug is taken into the bloodstream, the body works to remove it.
          Suppose the body removes 20% of a certain drug every 4 hours. The
          body needs at least 100 mg of this drug to be effective, but more than
          1000 mg of the drug is dangerous. A doctor wants to prescribe an amount
          of the drug to be taken at regular intervals. How much of the drug should
          be taken? How often should it be taken?

4   The gray wolf has recently been reintroduced to the Yellowstone National
          Park Ecosystem. The project began by releasing 7 breeding pairs into the
          park in March of 1995. A wolf pack is led by an alpha pair who mate and
          produce offspring. An average of 6 pups are born to the pair in early
          spring. Within 1 to 2 years the pups are ready to mate. At this time they
          may leave to form their own [pack]. There are an average of 12 wolves in a
          pack, but this number may vary depending on the season and food supply.
          The range of a wolfpack can be as much as 50 square miles depending on
          the availability of food. Yellowstone National Park has an area of about
          3468 square miles. Discuss the future of the wolves in Yellowstone Park.

6   The owner of a registered female black Labrador retriever wants to make
          some money by selling her pups. A veterinarian's handbook says that the
          average litter size for black Labradors is 9 and that 95% of the litters
          contain 4 to 14 puppies. Locally, the owner expects to be able to sell the
          male puppies for $200 and the female puppies for $250. How likely is it
          that the money received from selling the puppies will be more than
          $2500?

FIG. 17.6.   Common EOYT items for posttests.

Three of the five involve visualization and geometry, one involves probability, and one is a problem involving distance, rate and algebra.

On the other three common items there was no significant difference in the performance of *SIMMS* and comparison students. Among the 27 rotated items used on the EOYT for Levels 2, 4, and 6, only on one item was there a statistically significant difference between the mean scores of *SIMMS* and comparison students.

In later years, a more detailed analysis was used to investigate reasoning, problem solving, and communication. In addition to a holistic score, student papers were judged to be strong, satisfactory, or unsatisfactory based on the following variables:

- communication of reasoning—students give evidence of reasoning by making conjectures, gathering evidence, or building arguments;
- communication of a solution strategy—students give evidence of the solution process by using words or mathematical symbols;
- communication of the context—students give evidence of connections to the real world by providing additional information in the response.

2. When a drug is taken into the bloodstream, the body works to remove it. Suppose the body removes 20% of a certain drug every 4 hours. The body needs at least 100 mg of this drug to be effective, but more than 1000 mg of the drug is dangerous. A doctor wants to prescribe an amount of the drug to be taken at regular intervals. How much of the drug should be taken? How often should it be taken?

You would have to have an amount inbetween 100 mg and 1000 mg, so it stays over 100 mg until the next one is taken, but you have to make the amount a resonable amount so the person doesn't have to take the pill frequently. I feel that a persons weight would be a factor for the amount of medicine. I found that if the person is lighter in wieght they should take a pill of 250 mg twice a day. Here is a chart on what the amount would be.

medicine mg's.	
after 4hr	200 mg's
after 8hr	160 mg's
after 12hr	128 mg's

250 · .2 = 50 $\frac{250}{-50}$ 200
200 · .2 = 40 $\frac{200}{-40}$ 160
160 · .2 = 32 $\frac{160}{-32}$ 128

If it was a larger person I would make the pill a little stronger such as 500 mg twice a day.

	mg's
after 4 hours	400
8	320
12	256

500 · .2 = 100 $\frac{500}{-100}$ 400
400 · .2 = 80 $\frac{400}{-80}$ 320
320 · .2 = 64 $\frac{320}{-64}$ 256

FIG. 17.7.   A sample response to an item on the Level 2 EOYT.

SIMMS students demonstrated stronger reasoning and problem-solving skills than non-*SIMMS* students, with non-*SIMMS* students more likely to use a simple model resulting in incomplete solutions. *SIMMS* students often used more sophisticated mathematical strategies and made clear connections between the problem and the real world (Walen & Hirstein, 1998).

In summary, there were no significant differences in PSAT-M scores of *SIMMS* students and non-*SIMMS* students. On open-response EOYT, *SIMMS* students showed significantly better performance during Level 1.

TABLE 17.4
Mean Performance on Common EOYT Items of *SIMMS* and Comparison
Classes in the Montana Samples

	SIMMS		Comparison		
SIMMS Level	No. of Classes	Mean[a]	No. of Classes	Mean[a]	t
1	10	1.89	5	1.32	3.839*
2	10	2.20	6	1.63	2.020
4	8	2.72	4	2.97	0.921
6	7	1.97	6	1.23	1.479

Note. Maximum score on each EOYT item is 6.

[a]Statistics were computed by using Data Desk, and standard deviations are not explicitly reported.

*There are significant differences.

On the EOYT for Levels 4 and 6, there were no significant differences between scores of *SIMMS* and non-*SIMMS* students. This result may be due in part to the improved abilities of non-*SIMMS* students to approach these types of questions. In addition, non-*SIMMS* comparison classes had become a more homogeneous group of students who were electing advanced mathematics and science. Furthermore, because of the systemic nature of the professional development in the state, approximately 75% of the secondary mathematics teachers had some type of inservice using the *SIMMS* Project curriculum and philosophy. As a result, teaching methods for the two groups may have become more similar as the studies progressed.

A detailed analysis of responses to EOYT indicated that the *SIMMS* curriculum provided the kinds of experiences that develop skills in communication, reasoning, and problem solving. *SIMMS* students gained these skills early and kept them throughout the program. Supplementally, *SIMMS* students were more flexible in their approach to open problem situations. They were more likely than comparison students to make assumptions and to "see what happens." This outcome appears to be an early and lasting feature of the program.

Pilot Studies in Urban Areas

During the 1997–1998 academic year, the *SIMMS IM* Project conducted pilot studies in both El Paso and Cincinnati using the commercially produced Level 1 *SIMMS IM* curriculum.[1] These studies complement the Montana pilot studies. Montana's population is primarily Caucasian; the greatest single minority is Native American (12%) with all other minorities totaling less than 2%. In addition, Montana is primarily rural with only one city having more than 100,000 people. In contrast, both El Paso and Cincinnati qualified for NSF-funded Urban Systemic Initiatives (USI) designed for populations greater than 1,000,000 with schools of primarily minority populations. The school population of Cincinnati is largely African American; in El Paso, it is largely Hispanic.

Both cities agreed to 2 weeks of summer on-site teacher inservices before the studies began and additional inservice and observations during the academic year of the study. They also agreed to provide baseline data from district eighth-grade standardized tests and to administer pretests and posttests for both *SIMMS IM* students and comparison students.

The El Paso pilot study is discussed here for illustrative purposes. Similar results were found in Cincinnati and are available in Allinger, Lundin, and Dalton (1998).

Pilot Study in El Paso

In 1997–1998, eight high schools in three different El Paso school districts implemented the *SIMMS IM* Level 1 curriculum. One high school in each district was selected by the El Paso USI staff to participate in the pilot study. The comparison classes studied Algebra 1 by using the texts *Algebra: Structure and Method, Book 1, Texas Edition* (Dolciani, Brown, & Cole, 1990) or *The University of Chicago School Mathematics Project Algebra* (McConnell, Brown, Eddins, Hackworth, & Usiskin, 1990). All teachers of *SIMMS* and comparison classes held Texas certification in secondary mathematics.

Enrollment in each study school was at least 84% Hispanic. Both *SIMMS* and comparison classes reflected this ethnic composition. Parental support for education is strong in these schools. In general, families expect children to attend school and to respect teachers. Attendance in both *SIMMS* and comparison classes was 90% or greater in all schools.

As a baseline to compare groups, researchers used the Texas Assessment of Academic Skills (TAAS) given in the eighth grade. Of the 74 *SIMMS IM* students who took the TAAS in the eighth grade, 72% passed. Of the 69 control students who took the TAAS in the eighth grade, 68% passed. These results suggest that *SIMMS* and non-*SIMMS* students were of comparable abilities at the start of the study. Originally, a mathematical autobiography and a one-item open-response problem were to have been given as pretests at the beginning of the school year. As a result of scheduling conflicts and changes in the El Paso USI administrative personnel, it was not possible to give all pretests until January 1998. As a result, the amount of growth attained from September to May can only be approximated; thus these data are not reported here. (For further information on these aspects, see Allinger, Lundin, et al., 1998.)

In the spring, students took section 2 of the October 1996 PSAT-M. There were 125 students (60 *SIMMS* and 65 comparison) that participated. The

TABLE 17.5

Mean Performance on EOYT Items for *SIMMS IM* and Comparison
Students in the El Paso Sample

| EOYT Item | SIMMS | | Comparison | | |
	n^a	Mean	n	Mean	t^b
1	60	1.88	65	1.78	0.515
2	21	2.90	21	2.43	0.887
3	21	0.86	23	0.87	0.058
4	18	0.94	20	1.00	−0.310
5	60	1.35	65	1.09	1.299

Note. Maximum score on each EOYT item is 6.

[a]Statistics were computed by using Data Desk, and standard deviations are not explicitly reported.

[b]Based on the *SIMMS* comparison.

mean (and standard deviation) was 6.17 (2.74) for *SIMMS* students and 7.14 (2.85) for comparison students. There was no significant difference between the achievement of the two groups at the 0.05 level.

In the spring students also took a three-item open-response posttest. Figure 17.8 contains items from this test. All students had an opportunity to work Items 1 and 5, and approximately one third of the students were given each of Items 2–4. Items were scored by using the 0 to 6 scale described in Table 17.2. Mean scores on the posttest open-response problems are given in Table 17.5. An independent sample *t* test was used to analyze differences in mean scores for each of the five problems given. None of the differences in performance between *SIMMS* and comparison students are statistically significant.

Other Collected Information.   Direct classroom observation, interviews, and discussions during bimonthly inservice days and follow-up summer institutes indicated that *SIMMS* teachers made many changes in their pedagogical habits. Specifically, teachers increased their understanding of content, applied collaborative learning processes, improved their questioning techniques, gained confidence in using technology, practiced multiple assessment techniques, and developed more advanced time-management techniques.

Both students and teachers obtained a valuable learning experience during the implementation of *SIMMS IM*. However, *SIMMS IM* classes completed only 6–8 modules of the 15 for Level 1.[2] Even though they did not complete the intended curriculum, *SIMMS IM* students at least matched the performance of Algebra 1 students on the PSAT and on the posttest open-response problems.

Item No.   EOYT Item
  1   An entomologist (insect scientist) wants to establish the number of grasshoppers in Prairie Park, a
           region of 25,000 m². She stakes out 5 squares, each 10 m by 10 m, randomly arranged around the
           Park, and carefully counts the grasshoppers in each square. Here are the results:

Square	1	2	3	4	5
No. of Grasshoppers	18	3	12	15	20

           The entomologist would like to be able to say, "On this day, there were at least ___ grasshoppers
           in the Park." What number would you suggest in the blank? Tell how you determined this.

  2   A drugstore sells a brand of cold medicine at these prices:

           A 6-ounce bottle costs $4.00.
           A 10-ounce bottle costs $5.50.
           A 14-ounce bottle costs $7.00.

           At these prices, what will a 20-ounce bottle cost? Explain your answer.

  3   After each fishing trip, a fishing guide takes pictures of the customers with their fish. The guide
           develops the pictures and constructs a wooden frame for each. To make the frame, the guide cuts four
           pieces of wood, sands the wood, and glues it together as shown in the figure. All of the frame boards
           are 5 cm wide and 2 cm thick.

           a.   After the glue dries, the guide paints all of the surfaces of the picture frame (including the back).
                Using the dimensions in the figure, find how much surface the guide paints on each frame.
           b.   After the paint dries, the guide mails the framed picture. The wood has a mass of 0.75 grams
                per cm³. Find the mass of the picture frame.

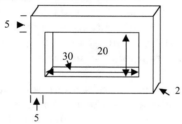

  4   One person started walking along a path at a rate of 2 meters per second. Two minutes later, a
           jogger started down the same path at a rate of 5 meters per second. How long (in minutes) did it
           take the jogger to catch the walker?

  5   Since 1990, the number of subscribers to EVERYWEEK magazine has increased by 10% every
           year. There are 152,000 subscribers in 1994.
           a.   How many subscribers do you expect in 1995?
           b.   How many subscribers were there in 1993?

FIG. 17.8. EOYT items on El Paso study posttest. *Note.* From
The SIMMS Project—The Classroom (Monograph No. 5, pp. 61–74),
1998, Bozeman, MT: The SIMMS Project. © 1998 by The SIMMS
Project. Reprinted with permission.

Montana College Freshmen Study

The staff of the *SIMMS* Project investigated the achievement level and attitudes of students who had passed three or more full-year *SIMMS IM* courses
and enrolled in a fall semester mathematics class immediately upon entering college. A pilot study of May 1996 high school graduates meeting the

criteria just discussed was conducted at the two state universities in Montana. In order to establish baseline data from which the students could be compared, grades were obtained for students enrolled in mathematics courses designed for entering college freshmen. With the use of an established protocol, a subset of the *SIMMS IM* educated freshmen was interviewed. The results were analyzed and used to plan a larger study for 1997–1998.

In the fall of 1997, representatives from the six Montana 4-year public colleges, two universities, seven tribal colleges, and one private 4-year college were enlisted to assist in data gathering following the lines of the pilot study. The following timeline was established.

- From October to December, freshmen meeting the criteria were identified.
- In January, fall semester grades for subjects were collected.
- From February to March, subjects were interviewed.
- In April and May, data were analyzed.

Table 17.6 shows the enrollment patterns of college freshmen students taking mathematics in Montana during the fall semester 1997. The data in Table 17.6 reveal that freshmen who complete at least 3 years of *SIMMS* courses are as likely as their traditional counterparts to take calculus but more likely than their traditional counterparts to take developmental mathematics.

Table 17.7 shows the percentage of students successfully completing various college freshman mathematics courses (Allinger, Lott, & Lundin, 1998). Successfully completing a course is considered to be receiving a passing grade.

Among the entering freshmen, 84 had taken *SIMMS* courses and were identified as meeting the high school course criterion for the study. Of this group, 66 (79%) enrolled in a mathematics course in the fall semester. Of those who enrolled, 56% enrolled in developmental courses, 27% enrolled in courses above the developmental level, and 17% enrolled in calculus. As

TABLE 17.6
Enrollment Patterns of Freshmen Taking Mathematics at Montana Colleges
and Universities in Fall 1997

Group	n	No Math. Course (%)	Developmental Course (%)	Courses Above Develop. Level[a] (%)	Various Calculus Course (%)
All freshmen	4880	21	32	33	14
SIMMS freshmen	84	21	44	21	14

[a]This includes Statistics and Precalculus courses but excludes Calculus.

TABLE 17.7

Percent of Montana Students at Each Level Who Were Successful in
Mathematics in Fall 1997

Group	Developmental Courses	Courses Above Develop. Level[a]	Various Calculus Courses
All students	53	83	76
All freshmen	60	84	83
Other students	43	82	72
SIMMS freshmen	49	94	73

[a]This includes Statistics and Precalculus courses but excludes Calculus.

shown in Table 17.7, freshmen tend to do better than all students in successfully completing freshmen-level courses. Former *SIMMS IM* students had the highest successful completion rate of any group in courses above the developmental level, though they were slightly less successful in the developmental courses when compared with other freshmen. Note that former *SIMMS IM* students were more successful than nonfreshmen students. In the calculus courses, the *SIMMS IM* students mirrored the nonfreshmen students but were less successful than other freshmen. Possible reasons for the success or nonsuccess of the *SIMMS IM* students are seen in their interview comments in the paragraphs that follow.

The majority of freshmen who had taken at least 3 years of *SIMMS* courses enrolled at either the University of Montana or Montana State University. Hence, the interview data reported here are only from interviews at the two state universities.

A total of 33 former *SIMMS IM* students (of the 66 students in the available population) were interviewed in a modified stratified sample. The sample was chosen to include students who took all types of college mathematics courses and who received high, medium, and low grades. In the sample, 73% successfully completed their mathematics courses, 12% failed, 3% withdrew, and 9% received an "N" grade. (On one campus, students who successfully complete a minimum number of curricular units are considered "in progress," receive a "N" grade, and are allowed to continue in the same course in the next semester. Percentages are rounded.) Of the 33 interviewed, 16 took developmental courses with 50% completing the course successfully, 25% failing their course, 6% withdrawing, and 19% receiving "N" grades. Ten students took courses above the developmental level. Of this number, 90% successfully completed their course. Six students took calculus courses with 100% successfully completing their course.

The questions used in each interview are listed as follows with summary data described after each one. Individual comments were written or typed as students shared their views during a 15- to 35-minute interview session.

1. *In what ways did integrated mathematics prepare you for your college course?* Almost half (48%) of the students gave positive responses to this question, mentioning such things as group work, problem solving, or preparation for specific courses such as linear algebra or statistics. Approximately 33% gave mixed responses and 18% gave negative responses, including comments such as "It lacks formulas. The teachers did what they could." (Allinger, Lott, et al., 1998, p. 20).

2. *How could your integrated mathematics high school course content have been more helpful?* Student comments about how *SIMMS IM* could be improved often focused on a perceived need for more emphasis on algebraic skills and procedures.

3. *Do you feel that the integrated mathematics courses empowered you with respect to each of the following: problem solving, reasoning, applications–connections, technology, communicating mathematics (speaking, reading, writing), and independent learning?*

- With regard to problem solving, 79% gave positive responses, 9% indicated negative views, and 9% did not respond.
- With regard to reasoning, 73% gave positive responses; 24% gave neutral or mixed responses.
- With regard to applications–connections, 85% gave positive responses.
- With regard to technology, 85% gave positive responses and 12% were neutral.
- With regard to communicating mathematics, 64% gave positive responses, 27% were neutral, and 9% gave negative responses.
- With regard to independent learning, 42% gave positive responses, 21% gave negative responses, and 36% gave neutral responses.

4. *What advice would you give a high school sibling who anticipates attending college and is trying to decide whether to take integrated mathematics curriculum courses to prepare for college?* Forty-eight percent of the responses conveyed a mix of recommendations concerning *SIMMS IM* and traditional mathematics curricula, with 24% recommending a traditional curriculum, 12% recommending *SIMMS IM*, and 15% with comments too disparate to categorize.

5. *Did you take your college–university placement test? If so, when did you take the test? How many times did you take the test? What course was recommended by the result on the placement test? Did you follow the recommendation? Did you feel prepared in the course you took?* Seventy-nine percent took the placement test and 18% did not. No answer was given for the other 3%. At one university, taking the placement test and placement based upon it are mandatory. Of those who took a placement test, 58% followed the recommendations and 21% did not. No data were available on the remainder. Forty-eight percent

responded that *SIMMS IM* prepared them for their initial course; 30% felt unprepared, primarily because of lack of drill in the *SIMMS IM* program; and 6% made comments difficult to categorize.

Overall, 82% of those interviewed gave either positive or neutral responses when asked if *SIMMS IM* helped them prepare for their first college course. More than 73% stated that the program prepared them well in the areas of problem solving, applications–connections, use of technology, and reasoning. However, 48% would recommend a combination of *SIMMS IM* and traditional curricula to siblings. This contradictory information may be the result of students having taken placement tests that reflect traditional programs and freshmen classes that are presented in the traditional lecture format. The students also found very limited use of technology at the collegiate level.

The results of this study demonstrate that a program of 3 years of *SIMMS IM* in high school prepares students for college mathematics. In fact, the data show that former *SIMMS IM* students who proceed directly to nondevelopmental courses do so with a very high probability of success. In contrast, when former *SIMMS IM* students enter developmental courses, they may experience more difficulties than students who prepared for college by using more traditional high school programs.

CONCLUSIONS

Evidence from most facets of the evaluation shows that study with the *SIMMS IM* curriculum does not limit students' abilities on such standardized tests as the mathematics portion of the PSAT. Teachers of the *SIMMS IM* curriculum are preparing students very well in the areas of problem solving, reasoning, applications, communication, and use of technology. Students do at least as well overall in collegiate classes, especially the nondevelopmental classes. Students who must take developmental classes in college are at a disadvantage when compared with students who studied a more traditional curriculum, though fewer *SIMMS IM* students appeared in those courses when given the option of not taking them.

The collegiate student interviews suggest that the view of collegiate mathematics is not changing as rapidly, specifically in Montana, as the secondary curriculum is changing. Much reform work has to be done at the collegiate level. Until collegiate courses change, teachers at one or both levels must create bridges to help students through the changes found in the two systems.

The student interviews also suggest that teachers at the secondary level need to continue their learning if they are to implement reform curricula. Use of technology, an integrated mathematics curriculum, and new forms of pedagogy provide a basis for needed inservice for current teachers at all levels.

Research is in progress with a 4-year longitudinal study of *SIMMS IM* students from one high school and a separate study to determine whether or not use of the *SIMMS IM* curriculum encourages women and minorities to take more mathematics. Additional research is needed with greater numbers relative to the college freshmen mathematics study and to the use of *SIMMS IM* materials in urban areas.

REFERENCES

Allinger, G., Lott, J. W., & Lundin, M. (1998). Attitudes and performance of college freshmen who used the *SIMMS Integrated Mathematics* curriculum. In *The SIMMS project—The classroom* (Monograph No. 5, pp. 16–30). Bozeman, MT: The SIMMS Project.

Allinger, G., Lundin, M., & Dalton, K. (1998). Pilot studies from El Paso and Cincinnati. In *The SIMMS project—The classroom* (Monograph No. 5, pp. 61–74). Bozeman, MT: The SIMMS Project.

Austin, J. D., Hirstein, J., & Walen, S. (1997). Integrated mathematics interfaced with science. *School Science and Mathematics, 97(1),* 45–49.

Beal, J., Dolan, D., Lott, J. W., & Smith, J. (1990). *Integrated mathematics: Definitions, issues and implications.* Helena, MT: Montana Council of Teachers of Mathematics. (ERIC Document Reproduction Service No. ED 3477071)

Burke, M., & Lott, J. W. (1993). *SIMMS* curriculum development philosophy. In *Philosophies* (Monograph No. 1, pp. 4–17). Missoula, MT: The SIMMS Project.

de Lange, J. (1989). The teaching, learning, and testing of a mathematics for the life and social sciences. In W. Blum, J. S. Berry, R. Biehler, I. D. Huntley, G. Kaiser-Messmer, & L. Profke (Eds.), *Applications and modeling in learning and teaching mathematics* (pp. 98–141). Chinchester, England: Harwood.

Dolciani, M., Brown, R., & Cole, W. (1986). *Algebra structure and method.* Boston: Houghton Mifflin.

Hirstein, J. (1998). Student assessment in the pilot study. In *Assessment* (Monograph No. 4, pp. 1–12). Missoula, MT: The SIMMS Project.

McConnell, J., Brown, S., Eddins, S., Hackworth, M., & Usiskin, Z. (1990). *The University of Chicago School Mathematics Project Algebra.* Glenview, IL: Scott, Foresman.

MCTM/SIMMS. (1996). *Integrated mathematics: A modeling approach using technology. Level 1* (Vols. 1–3). Needham Heights, MA: Simon & Schuster.

MCTM/SIMMS. (1996). *Integrated mathematics: A modeling approach using technology. Level 2* (Vols. 1–3). Needham Heights, MA: Simon & Schuster.

MCTM/SIMMS. (1997). *Integrated mathematics: A modeling approach using technology. Level 3* (Vols. 1–3). Needham Heights, MA: Simon & Schuster.

MCTM/SIMMS. (1997). *Integrated mathematics: A modeling approach using technology. Level 4* (Vols. 1–3). Needham Heights, MA: Simon & Schuster.

MCTM/SIMMS. (1998). *Integrated mathematics: A modeling approach using technology. Level 5* (Vols. 1–3). Needham Heights, MA: Simon & Schuster.

MCTM/SIMMS. (1998). *Integrated mathematics: A modeling approach using technology. Level 6* (Vols. 1–3). Needham Heights, MA: Simon & Schuster.

National Council of Teachers of Mathematics. (1989). *Curriculum and evaluation standards for school mathematics.* Reston, VA: Author.

Polya, G. (1973). *How to solve it.* Princeton, NJ: Princeton University Press.

Skemp, R. (1987). *The psychology of learning mathematics.* Mahwah; NJ: Erlbaum.

The SIMMS Project. (1993). *Philosophies* (Monograph No. 1). Missoula, MT: Author.

Walen, S., & Hirstein, J. (1998). Students completing year two of an integrated mathematics curriculum. In *Assessment* (Monograph No. 4, pp. 13–21). Missoula, MT: The SIMMS Project.

van Hiele, P. (1984). A child's thought and geometry. In D. Geddes, D. Fuys, & R. Tischler (Eds.), *English translation of selected writings of Dina van Hiele-Geldorf and Pierre M. van Hiele* (published as part of the research project, "An Investigation of the van Hiele Model of Thinking in Geometry among Adolescents," Research in Science Education (RISE) Programs of the National Science Foundation, Grant No. SED 7920640). Washington, DC: National Science Foundation. (Original work published 1959)

ENDNOTES

1. The authors distinguish between the *SIMMS* Project curriculum and the commercial version labeled as the *SIMMS IM* curriculum because the latter was revised based on the pilot studies of the former.
2. Some teachers in the Montana pilot studies completed only about half the *SIMMS* modules the first year they taught a course. However, in the second year they taught a course they typically completed at least the expected number of modules for the course.

18

Effects of the UCSMP Secondary School Curriculum on Students' Achievement

Sharon L. Senk

Michigan State University

The University of Chicago School Mathematics Project (UCSMP) was organized in 1983 with support from a 6-year grant awarded by the Amoco Foundation to the Departments of Mathematics and Education at the university.[1] As described by Usiskin (1986), the UCSMP was founded in response to needs in business and industry for a more competent workforce, and to recommendations by government-appointed commissions and professional organizations to update the mathematics curriculum.

The UCSMP consists of several independent, yet interconnected, components whose goal is to improve students' understanding of mathematics in Kindergarten through Grade 12. As noted in Chapter 4 of this volume by Carroll and Isaacs, the Elementary Component of the UCSMP has developed a set of curriculum materials for students in Grades K–6. Similarly, the Secondary Component of UCSMP, under the direction of Zalman Usiskin and Sharon Senk, has developed a set of textbooks and extensive ancillary materials for Grades 7–12.

The UCSMP secondary curriculum consists of six courses called Transition Mathematics; Algebra; Geometry; Advanced Algebra; Functions, Statistics and Trigonometry; and Precalculus and Discrete Mathematics. First editions of the textbooks for these courses were published between 1989

425

and 1991. Further refinements of the instructional materials were made beginning in 1992, resulting in second editions of all six UCSMP secondary school textbooks. In the 2000–2001 school year, approximately 6% of students in Grades 7–12 in the United States were using UCSMP secondary materials.[2]

This chapter contains an overview of the UCSMP secondary curriculum, including its development, content, and main features, and a summary of the results of four research studies conducted about the effects of the curriculum on students' achievement.

THE UCSMP SECONDARY CURRICULUM

Stages of Curriculum Development

The first edition of each book was developed in stages spanning 4 or 5 years. In the planning stage, the UCSMP codirectors and lead authors created overall goals for each course through consultation with a national advisory board of distinguished mathematics educators and through discussion with secondary school teachers and administrators. At the pilot stage, authors or teachers known by the authors taught the first draft of the materials. Based on feedback from pilot teachers, materials were revised and used the following year by a larger number of classes taught by teachers who were not known by the authors. During this formative evaluation stage, independent evaluators monitored classroom implementation and students' learning.

The first three books underwent an additional year of school use as part of large nationwide field studies in which the performance of students using UCSMP materials was compared with the performance of students using so-called traditional materials. After the field studies were completed, manuscripts were revised again and submitted for commercial publication. This development spanned 8 years from the pilot testing of *Transition Mathematics* in 1983–1984 to the final manuscript preparation for the first edition of *Precalculus and Discrete Mathematics* in 1991.

In 1991–1992, UCSMP developers began to plan for revisions of the first editions, taking advantage of the results of the research conducted on the first editions and information gathered from the many users of the published materials. Changes in the availability of technology (particularly graphing calculators) and recent reports about the advantages of writing in mathematics, and working in small groups (Countryman, 1992; Davidson, 1990; Stenmark, 1991) also suggested ways in which the first editions might evolve. Thus, although the work of UCSMP began prior to the publication of the *Curriculum and Evaluation Standards* (National Council of Teachers of Mathematics [NCTM], 1989), continued work on the UCSMP materials has been influenced by the *Standards* movement and the discussions about reform that have resulted from this movement.

Content of the UCSMP Secondary Curriculum

As noted by Flanders (1987), seventh- and eighth-grade mathematics textbooks of the 1970s and 1980s contained little more than a review of the arithmetic taught in Grades 1–6. In contrast, in the first-year algebra textbooks of that period virtually everything was new for students. To address the issue of excessive review at this level, the UCSMP curriculum attempts to smooth out the introduction of new content in secondary schools by creating courses that are challenging to, but attainable by, typical students. In particular, as described by Usiskin (1987), the secondary curriculum aims to prepare students who are achieving at grade level in Grade 7 to succeed in learning algebra in Grade 8.

Consequently, Transition Mathematics (TM) was designed originally for average to above-average seventh graders, and UCSMP Algebra was initially intended for eighth graders who had completed TM or an equivalent course. However, experience has shown that by starting TM earlier or later, or by taking the first two courses at a slower pace, the curriculum sequence accommodates a wide range of students. The UCSMP curriculum is designed so that the first four courses (i.e., through Advanced Algebra) contain the mathematics the developers envision is needed by every high school graduate. Further, the developers recommend that all college-bound students take the first five courses, and that all students who are intending to pursue technical careers, such as engineering or computer science, take all six courses (Usiskin, 1986).

TM weaves together three major content strands—applied arithmetic, prealgebra, and elementary geometry—with approximately equal attention paid to each (Usiskin et al., 1990; Usiskin et al., 1995). For instance, *TM* introduces concepts of algebra by studying variables and three of their elementary uses as described in Usiskin (1988): pattern generalizers, abbreviations in formulas, and unknowns in equations or inequalities. Arithmetic is involved in all three of these aspects of prealgebra. Arithmetic is related to geometry through measurement of length, perimeter, and area; number line models for adding and subtracting positive and negative numbers; graphs in the coordinate plane; and the study of turns, two-dimensional slides, and expansions and contractions.

UCSMP *Algebra* (McConnell et al., 1990; McConnell et al., 1996) builds on the uses of variables introduced in *TM* to develop linear, exponential, and quadratic growth patterns. See Fig. 18.1 for examples of patterns studied in each course.

TM   Describe the pattern using variables.

                One person has 2 eyes.

                Two people have 4 eyes in all.

                Three people have 6 eyes in all.

                Four people have 8 eyes in all. (Lesson 4-2)

Algebra   A cellular phone company charges $69.95 for up to 200 minutes of phone calls

                per month, and 21¢ per minute thereafter.

         a.   Make a table showing the cost of using this phone for 100, 200, 300, 400,

                and 500 minutes during the month.

         b.   Write a formula for the cost c in terms of the number m of minutes the

                phone is used.

         c.   To what values of m does your formula apply? (Lesson 3-8)

FIG. 18.1.   Sample questions from *TM* and UCSMP *Algebra* texts
in which students are asked to generalize patterns (reprinted with
permission).

Connections between algebra and other fields are made explicit in
UCSMP *Algebra.* For instance, formulas for perimeter and work with expressions and formulas for geometric transformations are settings for further
work with linear expressions and sentences. Probability provides a context
for simple algebraic fractions, functions, and set ideas. Considerable attention is given to graphing in the coordinate plane and to developing ideas
of slope. Both paper-and-pencil algorithms, as well as techniques based on
the use of tables and graphs, are developed for solving linear and quadratic
equations. Manipulation with rational algebraic expressions is delayed until
later courses.

UCSMP *Geometry* significantly diverges from the order of topics in many
high school geometry texts by presenting coordinates, transformations, measurement formulas, and three-dimensional figures earlier in the year
(Coxford, Usiskin, & Hirschhorn, 1991; Usiskin et al., 1997). Work with
proof-writing is developed based on the logical and conceptual precursors
to proof identified by research on the van Hiele model of learning geometry.
(See, for instance, Burger & Shaughnessy, 1986; Fuys, Geddes, & Tischler,
1988; Senk, 1985, 1989; Usiskin, 1982.)

Advanced Algebra is primarily a study of functions and related equations
and inequalities (Senk et al., 1990; Senk et al., 1996). Linear, quadratic,

power, and exponential functions are emphasized; logarithmic and trigonometric functions are introduced. All functions are studied both for their abstract properties and as tools for modeling real-world situations. Equivalence of algebraic forms is emphasized. The course applies geometrical ideas learned in the previous years, including transformations and measurement formulas.

Functions, Statistics, and Trigonometry (*FST*) integrates statistical and algebraic concepts (Rubenstein et al., 1992; Senk et al., 1998). Students study descriptive and inferential statistics, combinatorics, and probability; they also do further work with polynomial, exponential, logarithmic, and trigonometric functions. Enough trigonometry is included to constitute a standard precalculus background in circular functions.

Precalculus and Discrete Mathematics (*PDM*) integrates the traditional precalculus topics needed for success in calculus with the discrete mathematics helpful in computer science (Peressini et al., 1992; Peressini et al., 1998). Precalculus topics include further work with properties of elementary functions (including zeros, singularities, and asymptotes), manipulation of rational expressions, polar coordinates, complex numbers, and introductions to the derivative and integral. Discrete mathematics topics include recursion, mathematical induction, combinatorics, vectors, graphs, and circuits. Mathematical thinking, including specific attention to formal logic and proof and comparing structures, is a unifying theme throughout.

Features of the UCSMP Secondary Curriculum

Since the early stages of development of the UCSMP secondary school curriculum, several features have distinguished the UCSMP materials from many of their traditional counterparts. First, the UCSMP curriculum has wider scope than the names of the courses might convey. Algebra, geometry, and some discrete mathematics are integrated in all courses; statistics and probability are included in the first four courses and receive major attention in the last two courses.

Second, uses of mathematics are incorporated into every chapter to motivate topics and to help develop abstract concepts. For instance, in *Advanced Algebra* various forms of linear equations are abstracted from studying specific situations. An examination of the cost of buying A adult tickets at $7 each and S student tickets at $3 each leads to a study of linear combinations; analyses of situations involving a constant increase or decrease lead to the slope-intercept form of a line. As described by Usiskin (1997), applications of mathematics are included as specific objectives in the UCSMP curriculum in a manner analogous to that traditionally reserved for skills, and these objectives are sequenced, reviewed, and tested. Figure 18.2 shows

Algebra   At age 9 Karen was 4'3" tall. At the age of 11 she was 4'9" tall. How fast did she

grow from age 9 to age 11? (Lesson 7-1)

Advanced   [Students are given some data about braking distance in relation to speed.]
Algebra
Find the following rates of change, and explain what each means.

a. r_1, the rate of change from (20, 25) to (40, 100)

b. r_2, the rate of change from (40, 100) to (60, 225) (Lesson 2 – 5)

PDM   For a projectile whose height in feet t seconds after launch is described by the

equation $h(t) = 800\,t - 16\,t^2$, the average velocity between times $t = 10$ and

$t = 10 + \Delta t$ is $480 - 16\,\Delta t$ ft/sec. Find the instantaneous velocity at time $t = 10$

seconds. (Lesson 9-2)

FIG. 18.2. Questions showing a sequence of uses of the concept of rate of change from three UCSMP courses (reprinted with permission).

questions about rates to illustrate one such sequence in the secondary curriculum.

Third, all UCSMP secondary materials are written with the expectation that students will read them. Each lesson includes selections for students to read to develop key ideas in the lesson. Questions Covering the Reading and Notes on Reading are designed to help students learn to read effectively. Questions Applying the Mathematics are designed to encourage students to extend the concepts, algorithms, or contexts presented in the lesson.

Fourth, calculator and computer technology is used as a tool for solving problems. *TM* is written with the assumption that each student has access to a scientific calculator both in and out of class and for use on tests. We believe that it was the first middle school textbook in the United States to make such assumptions. UCSMP *Algebra* and *Geometry* also assume that scientific calculators are available at all times. Users of the second edition of *Algebra* are encouraged to have graphing calculators available for some activities. Similarly, users of the second edition of *Geometry* are encouraged to use a dynamic geometry drawing tool for exploration. The second editions of *Advanced Algebra*, *FST*, and *PDM* are written with the assumption that each student and teacher has technology to use both in and out of class to graph and analyze functions, analyze and display data, find models for data, and operate with matrices.

In the UCSMP secondary curriculum, both paper-and-pencil algorithms and calculator-based algorithms are taught for many situations (e.g., solving a system of 3×3 linear equations or solving a quadratic equation). However, when no algorithm is known to lead to an exact solution, calculator-based algorithms are taught to enable students to solve classes of problems that were previously inaccessible (e.g., solve the equation $\sin x = 0.2x$).

Fifth, in each UCSMP course a multidimensional view of understanding mathematics is emphasized. Secondary school mathematics has at least four dimensions: Skills, Properties, Uses, and Representations. This is what we call the SPUR approach. Most lessons have questions addressing at least two dimensions of understanding; virtually every chapter addresses all four. The SPUR approach is designed to illustrate the breadth of mathematics; it also allows students who might not be proficient in one dimension to show strengths in other areas.[3]

Sixth, continual review and a modified mastery learning strategy are used to support learning. Review questions at the end of each lesson provide distributed practice to help students maintain and improve their proficiency with important content. These questions address content from previous lessons in the given course as well as from previous courses. At the end of each chapter, a summary, self-test, and a set of review questions keyed to objectives organized by the SPUR dimensions are designed to help students monitor their progress toward mastery. Figure 18.3 illustrates the four dimensions of understanding from the end-of-chapter review about circular functions in *FST*.

Seventh, projects in the last two courses of the first-edition materials and in all courses of the second-edition materials offer students an opportunity to work on an extended topic over a period of time and to explore that topic in some depth. Figure 18.4 shows two projects from *Geometry*.

For further details about the UCSMP secondary curriculum, see Hirschhorn, Thompson, Usiskin, and Senk (1995) and Senk (1999).

RESEARCH ABOUT STUDENT OUTCOMES

During the period 1984–1996, an evaluation staff that was at "arm's length" from the curriculum developers conducted studies of the UCSMP secondary curriculum. The curriculum developers were consulted about the design, selection of sample, and choice of instruments for each study. However,

Skills deal with the procedures used to get answers.

Give three values of θ from −2π to 2π such that cos θ = 1.

Properties deal with the principles behind the mathematics.

True or false. Justify your answer.

For all θ, sin (θ + 6 π) = sin θ.

Uses deal with applications of mathematics in real situations.

The length of the day from sunrise or sunset in a city at 30 N° latitude (such as Baton

Rouge, Louisiana or Cairo, Egypt) is given in the table below.

a.   Find an equation using the sine function to model these data.

b.   What is the period of the function used to model these data?

c.   Predict the length of the day on December 21, the winter solstice at 30° N latitude.

Date	Jan 1	Feb 1	Mar 1	Apr 1	May 1	June 1	July 1	Aug 1	Sept 1	Oct 1	Nov 1	Dec 1	Jan 1
Days after January 1	0	31	59	90	120	151	181	212	243	273	304	334	365
Length in hours	10.25	10.77	11.53	12.47	13.32	13.93	14.05	13.58	12.77	11.88	11.00	10.37	10.25

Representations deal with pictures, graphs, or objects that illustrate concepts.

Refer to the unit circle at the right. Which

letter could represent the value given?

cos (-160°)

$\sin\left(\dfrac{26\pi}{9}\right)$

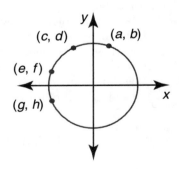

FIG. 18.3. Sample items illustrating the four dimensions of understanding from the review of Chapter 4 of *FST* (reprinted with permission).

Kaleidoscopes. Sir David Brewster (1781 – 1868) invented the first kaleidoscope. Find out how kaleidoscope images use reflections and rotations, and then make your own. Prepare a report for your class on how a kaleidoscope works. (Chapter 4, Project 4)

Geometry on a Sphere. Consider the following postulates and theorems from this book.

>   Point-Line-Plane Postulate

>   Corresponding Angles Postulate

>   Transitivity of Parallelism Postulate

>   Two Perpendiculars Theorem

>   Perpendicular to Parallels Theorem

a. Do these hold true if "points" are locations on a sphere, "lines" are great circles on a sphere, and a "plane" is the surface of a sphere? For each, explain why or why not using diagrams and words.

b. Do the five statements above hold true if great circles and small circles are considered to be the only lines in the "plane" of the sphere? Explain. (Chapter 9, Project 4)

FIG. 18.4. Two projects from *Geometry* (reprinted with permission).

the evaluation staff ran the day-to-day activities of the studies, including oversight of the pretesting and posttesting, and analyses of the data. A brief summary of the applicable evaluation study is given in the Teacher's Edition of each UCSMP textbook.

Detailed reports of two evaluation studies have long been available (Hedges, Stodolsky, Mathison, & Flores, 1986; Mathison, Hedges, Stodolsky, Flores, & Sarther, 1989). These studies showed that students using early editions of *TM* and *Algebra* performed at least as well as comparison students on traditional content and skills, and they outperformed them on new content and on applications of mathematics.

Results from four additional studies are reported in the paragraphs that follow. The first two studies examined the effects of early versions of courses beyond TM and Algebra. The last two studies examined the effects of the field trial versions leading to the second editions of two UCSMP texts. The first two studies summarize results of dissertations written by doctoral students who served as editors of UCSMP secondary materials. The last two studies were supervised by a member of the evaluation staff who had no part in the development of the materials. The studies described herein were chosen to illustrate the variety of research questions, designs, and instruments that have been used to investigate the effects of curriculum on students enrolled in various UCSMP courses.

Research on Early Versions of UCSMP Materials

Hirschhorn's Longitudinal Study

Research Sites and Sample.   Hirschhorn (1993) conducted a longitudinal study to examine the cumulative effects of the use of the first 4 years of the UCSMP curriculum materials. The cohort of students studied consisted of *all* students in the United States who used the first four textbooks in the UCSMP secondary series between 1986–1987 and 1989–1990. These students, who were enrolled in three different school districts, had begun TM as seventh graders and were in the 10th grade at the time of this study. At all three sites students used prepublication versions of *TM, Algebra,* and *Geometry,* and the first edition of UCSMP *Advanced Algebra* (Senk et al., 1990) the first year it was available.

At Site A all UCSMP courses were taught in a single college-preparatory magnet school for Grades 7–12 in a large urban school district. The magnet school population was approximately one third minority, mostly African American. Sites B and C are two affluent suburban areas with largely White populations. At these sites students studied from *TM* and *Algebra* in junior high feeder schools, and from *Geometry* and *Advanced Algebra* in the high schools serving their districts.

Because the treatment of the study, the UCSMP secondary curriculum, had already been implemented, the selection of comparison students was, by necessity, ex post facto. Specifically, Hirschhorn matched the UCSMP students to potential comparison students by using scores on standardized mathematics and reading achievement tests given by their districts in the sixth grade, that is, before any student had studied from any UCSMP materials.[4]

At Site A, all students in the school had taken Geometry as 9th graders in 1988–1989, and all were enrolled as 10th graders in Algebra II in 1989–1990. Hence, the comparison students at site A match on both age and course. In contrast, at the other two sites, whereas the UCSMP students had taken Geometry as 9th graders and were enrolled in algebra II as 10th graders, most of the non-UCSMP students had taken Algebra, not Geometry, in 9th grade. Therefore, at Sites B and C two comparison groups were created. An age cohort comparison group consisted of 10th graders who were enrolled in a mathematics course at the time of the study. At both sites this included a few students in an Advanced Algebra course, and a majority in a Geometry course. A course level cohort comparison group consisted

TABLE 18.1
Number of Students at each Site in the Longitudinal Study

Site	Age Level		Course Level		Students in Both Comparisons	
	UCSMP	Comp.	UCSMP	Comp.	UCSMP	Comp.
A	11	11	11	11	11	11
B	13	13	10	10	10	0
C	18	18	27	27	7	0

Note. From "A Longitudinal Study of Students Completing Four Years of UCSMP Mathematics," by D. B. Hirschhorn, 1993, *Journal for Research in Mathematics Education, 24*, p. 139. © 1993 by the National Council of Teachers of Mathematics. Reprinted with permission. All rights reserved.

of eleventh graders who had taken Geometry and were enrolled in an Advanced Algebra course.

The procedure for forming the comparison groups was based on matching individual UCSMP students to individual comparison students. At Site A, students were matched based on sex, race, and sixth-grade achievement test score. At Sites B and C, because there were very few minority students, only sex and sixth-grade achievement test results were used to match students. In order to get the largest comparison groups possible, some UCSMP students were matched with students in both age and course level comparison groups. For instance, of the 18 UCSMP students at site C who were matched with students in the age cohort, 7 were also in the course level comparison. A total of 141 students participated in the study, as indicated in Table 18.1.

Procedures. All students who satisfied the criteria were asked to complete two posttests and a survey. The Mathematics Level I Achievement Test, Form 3JAC2, consisting of 50 multiple-choice questions, is designed to measure achievement on standard college-preparatory mathematics through Algebra II (The College Board, 1988). Tests were scored by using specifications provided by the College Board, and scores were reported on a scale of 200 to 800.

An Applications Test developed by the UCSMP staff consists of 30 multiple-choice questions about applications of arithmetic, algebra, geometry and advanced algebra. The score on the Applications Test is the number of items the student answered correctly.

Results. Scores on the posttests are displayed in Table 18.2. At Site A the UCSMP students outperformed the age–course level comparison group at a statistically significant level. At Site B UCSMP students performed better than students of comparable ability in the same grade on both the Mathematics Level 1 Achievement Test and the Applications Test. UCSMP

TABLE 18.2

Results on the Equating Tests and Posttests in the Longitudinal Study

Group		Sixth-Grade Equating		Posttests	
		Math	Reading	Level 1 Achiev.	Applications
Site A: Age–Course Level Cohort Tenth Graders ($n = 22$)					
UCSMP	$\bar{X}$		7.12[a]	483.64*	18.18*
	SD		0.56	41.05	5.47
Comparison	$\bar{X}$		7.12[a]	432.73	13.00
	SD		0.56	53.12	3.16
Site B: Age Cohort Tenth Graders ($n = 26$)					
UCSMP	$\bar{X}$	88.85	81.92	514.62*	21.77**
	SD	6.20	12.57	32.82	2.42
Comparison	$\bar{X}$	89.00	82.00	460.00	15.62
	SD	8.01	13.33	73.48	2.79
Site B: Course Level Cohort Eleventh Graders ($n = 20$)					
UCSMP	$\bar{X}$	89.70	80.70	513.00	21.90*
	SD	6.25	13.52	36.53	2.73
Comparison	$\bar{X}$	90.30	80.80	506.00	17.90
	SD	5.56	8.97	37.48	3.41
Site C: Age Cohort Tenth Graders ($n = 36$)					
UCSMP	$\bar{X}$	89.61	77.72	476.11	20.61*
	SD	9.32	16.72	48.77	4.67
Comparison	$\bar{X}$	89.67	77.56	510.00	17.06
	SD	9.07	17.74	77.54	4.60
Site C: Course Level Cohort Eleventh Graders ($n = 54$)					
UCSMP	$\bar{X}$	81.37	80.19	465.93	20.07
	SD	10.75	14.33	47.50	4.27
Comparison	$\bar{X}$	81.52	80.00	525.19**	20.22
	SD	9.94	14.00	63.99	3.34

Note. From "A Longitudinal Study of Students Completing Four Years of UCSMP Mathematics," by D. B. Hirschhorn, 1993, *Journal for Research in Mathematics Education,* 24, p. 145. © 1993 by the National Council of Teachers of Mathematics. Reprinted with permission. All rights reserved.

[a]Grade-level equivalencies based on mathematics, reading, and general intelligence measures.

*$p < .05$; **$p < .01$.

students performed as well as students a year older on the standardized instrument and better than they did on the Applications Test. At Site C the course comparison group outperformed the UCSMP students on the Level 1 Achievement Test; on the Applications Test the UCSMP students performed better than the age cohort, and as well as comparison students in the course cohort.

Thus, on the standardized test the results were mixed. At Sites A and B, the UCSMP students outperformed all but one of their comparison groups at statistically significant levels. At Site C the course level cohort outperformed the UCSMP students. The results on the Applications Test clearly favored the UCSMP students, with the UCSMP students significantly outperforming all but one comparison group. Hirschhorn (1993) notes that the performance at Site A

> is a powerful result because it is the only site in the study where the comparison students were the same age as the UCSMP students and had both geometry and advanced algebra. With students of the same age, ability, and course load, UCSMP students made significant achievement gains over comparable students on both achievement instruments. (p. 150)

Item analyses indicate that on both tests used in this study the curriculum affected what was learned by the students. Students studying from the UCSMP materials were better than comparison students on items related to functions, graphing, and applications of mathematics. Comparison students generally scored higher than UCSMP students on items requiring factoring or polynomial division, two traditional topics deemphasized in the first 4 years of the UCSMP curriculum. (See Hirschhorn, 1993, pp. 146–150 for details.)

Thompson's Study of Precalculus and Discrete Mathematics

Research Sites and Sample. During the 1989–1990 school year, Thompson (1992) investigated several issues related to the PDM course, including the achievement of students on standard precalculus content. Because of its unusual blend of content, PDM does not replace a single course in the traditional high school mathematics curriculum. Hence, no group of students could be found to form a true comparison group. However, in response to a call for volunteers, nine schools in eight states agreed to participate in a study about PDM. Three were private coed schools: two K–12 day schools, and one secondary day school. Students in these schools were largely from middle- and upper-income families. Six public schools also participated: two in midsized cities, two in suburbs (one blue collar and one middle class), and two in urban areas. The latter were both magnet schools: one highly selective; the other not selective.

In four schools, most of the students in the PDM classes had used an early version of *FST* the previous year. In the other five schools none of the students had used UCSMP materials in the past. In six of the schools most of the sample had completed Algebra, Geometry, Algebra II, and one additional course, and were taking PDM as a fifth year of high school mathematics. In the other schools, students were taking PDM as a fourth mathematics course in high school.

In all, 180 students (96 male and 84 female) in 12 classes participated in the study. Approximately 73% were White, 13% were Black, and the rest were other racial minorities or students of mixed race. Approximately 70% of the sample consisted of students in Grade 12, with most of the rest in Grade 11. Approximately 57% of the students in the sample were seniors taking a fifth year of mathematics.

Procedures.   Because no comparison group was available, Thompson used data from the Second International Mathematics Study (SIMS) as a benchmark for the achievement of the PDM students. The SIMS had studied the achievement of two groups of 12th graders in the United States: a precalculus and a calculus sample (McKnight et al., 1987). Students in the SIMS precalculus sample were 12th graders enrolled in college-preparatory precalculus courses; each had taken a minimum of 2 years of Algebra and a year of Geometry. This SIMS sample had studied content that overlapped considerably with the precalculus content studied by the PDM students. In contrast, students in the SIMS calculus sample were enrolled in a full-year calculus class that studied content that assumed much of the content of PDM as a prerequisite. However, like the majority of the PDM sample, the SIMS calculus sample was studying a fifth year of mathematics in high school.

Toward the end of the school year, Thompson administered a 32-item multiple-choice posttest containing 11 multiple-choice items that had been selected from items used by the SIMS. The SIMS items Thompson used test content studied in the PDM course, including polynomial and rational functions, trigonometry, introductory ideas of calculus, and combinatorics. (Consult Chang & Ruzicka, 1985, for further information about SIMS items.)

Students in the SIMS were not allowed to use calculators when answering the multiple-choice items. Students in Thompson's study were permitted to use scientific, but not graphing, calculators. However, at three schools students had had constant access to graphing calculators during the school year. The investigator and the teachers decided it would be unfair to expect these students to use an unfamiliar calculator on the posttest. Thus these students were allowed to use their graphing calculators, but they were restricted to using the scientific features. Teachers at these schools agreed to monitor students' use of technology (Thompson, 1992, pp. 72–73).

Results.   Table 18.3 contains the items from the posttest and the percent of students in the PDM and SIMS samples who got each item correct.

On 3 of the 11 items, more than 80% of the PDM sample answered the items correctly. In contrast, the SIMS precalculus sample scored less than 50% correct on all 11 items. Two-sample z tests of the proportion of PDM and SIMS precalculus students who got each item correct indicate that on 7 of the 11 items the PDM students significantly outscored the SIMS precalculus

TABLE 18.3

Achievement of PDM Students on SIMS Items

| | | Percent Successful | |
	PDM $N = 180$	SIMS Precalculus (N)	SIMS Calculus (N)
Item Stem			
Functions			
12. Which of the following could be a sketch of the graph of the curve $y = x^4 - x^2$?	87	48* (932)	70* (185)
13. The functions f and g are defined by $f(x) = x - 1$ and $g(x) = (x + 3)^2$. $g(f(x))$ is equal to	87	48* (954)	85 (187)
15. The curve defined by $y = 3x(x - 2)(2x + 1)$ intersects the x axis only at the points	85	43* (955)	73 (183)
25. Which of these is the sketch of the graph of the function f where $f(x) = \frac{x}{(x-2)(x+2)}$?	47	36 (939)	60 (190)
30. The graph of the curve $y = \frac{2x+1}{x^2+2x+3}$ intersects the axes at the points	62	35* (932)	71 (185)
Trigonometry			
6. Which of the following is (are) true for all values of θ for which the functions are defined? I. $\sin(-\theta) = -\sin\theta$ II. $\cos(-\theta) = -\cos\theta$ III. $\tan(-\theta) = -\tan\theta$	48	42 (970)	49 (177)
10. In the interval $2\pi \leq x \leq 4\pi$, the solution set of the equation $\sin x = \frac{1}{2}$ is	56	32* (958)	51 (183)
Calculus			
26. $\lim\limits_{x \to +\infty} \frac{(2x+1)(x+1)}{3x^2-2}$ is equal to	43	34 (958)	57 (183)
31. The line l in the figure is the graph of $y = f(x)$.	35	26 (954)	59* (187)

$\int\limits_{-2}^{3} f(x)\,dx$ is equal to

(Continued)

TABLE 18.3
(Continued)

| | | Percent Successful | |
| | | | |
Item Stem	PDM N = 180	SIMS Precalculus (N)	SIMS Calculus (N)
Discrete Mathematics			
8. Four persons whose names begin with different letters are placed in a row, side by side. What is the probability that they will be placed in alphabetical order from left to right?	74	49* (955)	66 (183)
29. In how many ways can one arrange on a bookshelf 5 thick books, 4 medium-sized books, and 3 thin books so that the books of the same size remain together?	34	15* (939)	22 (190)

Note. The values of N for the SIMS samples vary because not all items were administered to the same students in that study. The table is based on data from Thompson (1992, p. 323) and from Chang and Ruzicka (1985).

*Difference between the percent correct by the PDM sample and the SIMS sample is statistically significant at $p < .05/11$, approximately equal to .0046.

sample; on the other 4 items their performance was comparable. In contrast, two-sample z tests showed that on 9 of the 11 items the PDM sample and the SIMS calculus sample performed comparably, with the PDM sample scoring higher on Item 12 and the SIMS calculus sample scoring higher on Item 31.

Thus, overall, on these 11 items the performance of the PDM students is comparable to that of the calculus sample and higher than that of the pre-calculus sample from the SIMS. However, the extent to which the difference in the access to technology by the PDM and SIMS samples contributed to these results cannot be determined from the data Thompson reports.

Research on the Second Editions of UCSMP Materials

During the 1993–1994 school year, UCSMP evaluation staff conducted studies to examine the effects of the field-trial versions of the second editions of *Geometry* and *Advanced Algebra*. Participants were recruited through advertisements in UCSMP and NCTM publications. From among schools that met the selection criteria, four schools were chosen to participate in each study. In each school one teacher was assigned by local school personnel to two sections of the UCSMP course and the other to two sections of the standard course using the textbook currently in place at that school. This resulted in an initial sample of 16 classes in each study, 8 using the UCSMP curriculum and 8 using curricula perceived as more traditional. The classes were either heterogeneous in schools with no tracking or designated "average" in schools with tracking.[5]

In each school, students were given a pretest of prerequisite knowledge, and classes were matched on the basis of mean scores on the pretest. In such a design each matched pair is considered a ministudy, and results are aggregated across the ministudies. Thus, for each study the primary unit of analysis is the class.

Some posttests had multiple-choice items and some had free response items. Rubrics were developed for scoring the free response items by using a 0 to 4 scale, as applied in earlier work by Malone, Douglas, Kissane, and Mortlock (1980), Senk (1985, 1989), and Thompson and Senk (1993). Students attaining scores of 3 and 4 were considered successful, with a 4 indicating a model response and a 3 indicating a solution that contained some minor error(s). Students scoring 0, 1, or 2 were considered unsuccessful, with a score of 1 indicating some entry into the problem but no chain of reasoning and a score of 2 indicating a chain of reasoning but some conceptual error. Items were scored with no knowledge of the student's name or the curriculum from which the student had studied.

Although each study examined multiple research questions, because of space limitations only results of students' achievement are reported in this chapter. For further details about the studies, including copies of all instruments used, see Witonsky et al. (2002), Thompson and Senk (2001), and Thompson et al. (2001).

Many scholars (e.g., Burstein, 1993; Shavelson, McDonnell, & Oakes, 1989) have noted the importance of opportunity to learn (OTL) as a factor in determining students' achievement. Consequently, in the Geometry and Advanced Algebra studies, the teachers were asked to indicate whether the students in their classes had the opportunity to learn the mathematics needed for each item on each posttest. In each study the teachers' responses on some instruments varied considerably.

As a way to try to understand the extent to which OTL affects achievement, results on posttests were analyzed in two ways. First, scores were calculated on the entire test, regardless of whether or not the teachers indicated that their students had an opportunity to learn the needed content. Second, for each instrument, achievement was also calculated on a subtest consisting of only those items for which both teachers in each school reported that their students had the opportunity to learn the needed content. Because both the Second Edition and comparison teachers at the school viewed these items as fair to their students, this subtest is called the Fair Test. Note that the Fair Tests control for differences in OTL at each school, and thus, each Fair Test is potentially unique for each school.

A Study of the Second Edition of UCSMP Geometry

Research Sites and Sample. The four schools chosen for the Geometry study were called I, J, K, and L. School I, located in a city in Indiana, had approximately 2,000 students. The majority of its students were African American. Most students in the geometry classes were sophomores. Some students in both UCSMP and comparison classes had previously used UCSMP *Transition Mathematics.*

Schools J and K were located in two different communities in Oregon. Most students at each school were White. School J was larger (1,100 students vs. 700 students) and sent a larger percent of students to college (65% vs. 35%). The geometry classes in each school contained students in each of Grades 9–12. Many students in both UCSMP and comparison geometry classes in School J had previously used *TM* and UCSMP *Algebra.* None of the students in School K had previously studied from UCSMP materials.

School L, located in a middle-class suburb in South Carolina, had approximately 1,500 students. The school was between 20% and 30% African American, with most of the rest being White. Geometry classes consisted of students in Grades 10–12. Students had not previously studied from UCSMP materials.

The textbooks used by the comparison classes were *Discovering Geometry* (Serra, 1989) at School I, *Geometry* (Jurgensen, Brown, & Jurgensen, 1988) at Schools J and K, and *Merrill Geometry* (Yunker, 1990) at School L. According to Weiss, Matti, and Smith (1994) these were among the most widely used geometry textbooks at the time of this study.

The final sample consists of all students in the eight matched pairs of classes who had taken the pretest and all posttests. There were 139 students in UCSMP classes; 24% of the students were in Grade 9, 48% were in Grade 10, and 21% were in Grade 11. There were 115 students in the comparison classes; 23% were in Grade 9, 49% in Grade 10, and 22% in Grade 11.

Procedures. The Entering Geometry Student Test was given as a pretest in the fall. It consists of 49 multiple-choice items, 35 on Part I and 14 on Part II. The test, developed by the UCSMP, covers material from middle school Geometry and first-year Algebra courses, including such topics as names and properties of polygons and circles, area formulas, elementary coordinate geometry, solutions of linear and quadratic equations, and graphs of lines. Items on this test had been used in several previous studies conducted at the University of Chicago, including a study on geometry achievement (Usiskin, 1982) and the evaluation study of the First Edition of UCSMP *Algebra* (Mathison et al., 1989).

Scores of each class on the Entering Geometry Student Test indicated that at the beginning of the school year there were no significant differences between the prerequisite knowledge of students entering UCSMP *Geometry* and comparison classes.

In the spring, three posttests were administered. The first was the High School Subject Tests (HSST)—Geometry Form B, a standardized test with 40 items (Wick & Gatta, 1988). It includes items about lines and angles, properties of triangles and other polygons, congruence and similarity theorems, the Pythagorean theorem, perimeter and area of polygons, circles, and sectors, coordinate geometry, surface area and volume, and other content.

The second posttest was a 35-item multiple-choice instrument developed by UCSMP authors and staff, called the UCSMP Geometry Posttest. This test includes items about concepts or applications included in the UCSMP *Geometry* curriculum, but not tested or only minimally tested on the HSST Geometry Test, such as reasoning and proof, three-dimensional geometry, and transformations.

The third posttest was the Geometry Problem Solving and Understanding (PSU) Test, available in two forms and developed by UCSMP authors and staff. The forms were alternated among students in each class, so that approximately half of each class took each form. Each form of the Geometry PSU Test contains three different free-response items. Among the six items on the two forms, three ask students to write short essays about their understanding of congruence, similarity, or proof, and three ask students to write proofs or to explain their reasoning about geometric figures. The proof items are shown in Fig. 18.5.

Results. Table 18.4 gives the mean percent of items correct by class on the HSST Geometry Posttest. The mean score for the students is at the 47th percentile nationally in the UCSMP classes and is at the 46th percentile nationally for the comparison classes. Overall, the UCSMP teachers reported less opportunity to learn the mathematics on this standardized test than did the comparison teachers. However, a matched-pairs *t* test on the mean of the pair differences indicates that the difference in performance between UCSMP and comparison classes is not statistically significant.

Teachers' reports on their students' opportunity to learn the mathematics needed to solve the items on the UCSMP Geometry Posttest varied widely. For instance, at School I the UCSMP teacher reported that students had the opportunity to learn the content for all 35 items on the test; in contrast, the comparison teacher reported that students had the opportunity to learn the content for less than half of the test items. Hence, results on the entire UCSMP Geometry Posttest are not reported here; rather, only results for the Fair Tests are reported.

Table 18.5 contains the achievement results for the Fair UCSMP Geometry Posttests. Among the eight pairs of classes, the difference in the mean percent correct between UCSMP and non-UCSMP classes varies from 4.5% (pair I1) to 30% (pair J2). Statistically significant differences in the mean

TABLE 18.4
Mean Percent Correct on the HSST Geometry Test by UCSMP Geometry
and Comparison Matched Pairs

School Code & Pair ID	UCSMP Geometry				Comparison				p
	n	M (%)	SD	OTL (%)	n	M (%)	SD	OTL (%)	
I1	9	34.4	10.1	83	7	39.3	13.7	90	.427
I2	5	29.0	8.9	83	9	36.7	14.1	90	.299
J1	22	50.3	12.7	78	13	43.5	12.7	90	.132
J2	20	48.3	9.3	78	17	42.2	12.3	90	.097
K1	20	46.8	15.0	90	19	48.4	14.8	90	.728
K2	17	47.5	10.7	90	15	49.7	10.2	90	.564
L1	25	40.4	10.0	70	14	38.6	15.0	93	.651
L2	21	33.8	10.8	70	21	38.8	17.1	93	.265
Overall	139	43.1	12.9	80.2	115	42.7	14.4	91.8	

Note. The mean percent correct is based on a 40-item multiple-choice posttest. A matched-pairs t test indicates that the differences in achievement between the two curricula are not statistically significant: $\bar{x} = -0.824$, $s_{\bar{x}} = 5.298$, $t = -0.44$, and $p < .673$.

ODD Form

1. Can a convex quadrilateral have four obtuse angles? If so, draw such a quadrilateral. If not, explain why this cannot be.

2. Given: Points N, O, P, and Q with
   coordinates as shown at the right.

   Prove: NOPQ is a parallelogram.

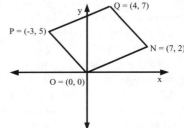

EVEN Form

2. Write a proof in the space provided.

   Given: M is the midpoint of $\overline{AB}$.

   M is the midpoint of $\overline{CD}$.

   Prove: $\overline{AC} \parallel \overline{BD}$

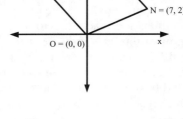

FIG. 18.5. Proof items from the Geometry PSU Test.

TABLE 18.5

Mean Percent Correct on the Fair UCSMP Geometry Posttest: UCSMP Geometry and Comparison Matched Pairs

School Code & Pair ID	UCSMP Geometry			Comparison			
	n	$M\,(\%)$	SD	n	$M\,(\%)$	SD	p
I1	9	34.1	13.7	7	29.6	14.5	0.533
I2	5	34.3	17.8	9	22.2	11.0	0.139
J1	22	71.0	17.0	13	49.0	20.1	0.002*
J2	20	71.9	18.5	17	41.9	20.7	0.000*
K1	20	58.9	19.8	19	48.5	22.4	0.130
K2	17	57.9	12.1	15	50.5	14.5	0.126
L1	25	56.6	13.8	14	44.0	17.2	0.016*
L2	21	51.6	15.1	21	40.9	15.0	0.026*

Note. The number of items comprising each Fair Test is as follows: for School I, 14 items (3, 11, 13, 17, 18, 21–23, 26, 27, 29, 31–33); for School J, 8 items (3, 5, 17, 21, 28, 29, 31, 35); for School K, 19 items (3–5, 8–11, 13, 15, 17, 18, 21–23, 26–29, 33); and for School L, 19 items (1, 3–5, 9–11, 13, 14, 17, 20–23, 26–29, 32). A matched-pairs t test indicates that the difference in achievement of the UCSMP and comparison students is significantly different: $\bar{x} = 13.726$, $s_{\bar{x}} = 8.280$, $t = 4.689$, and $p < .002$.

*There is a statistically significant difference at $p < .05$.

percent correct, all in favor of UCSMP *Geometry Second Edition* classes, occur for four pairs. A matched-pairs t test shows that the differences in the achievement of the students studying from the two curricula are statistically significant. That is, even when OTL is controlled, students studying from the UCSMP *Geometry* text outperform students studying from the comparison texts on a multiple choice test about applications of geometry and concepts such as reasoning and proof, three-dimensional geometry, and transformations.

Because two forms of the PSU Tests were given in each class, the number of students answering each item was quite small for several classes. For this reason, results on the PSU Test by class are not reported here; rather, the scores for the students in the two classes taught by each teacher have been combined to produce a single score for each teacher's students in the school.[6] Table 18.6 shows the results for each teacher's students on the proof items.

Neither group of students did particularly well at writing proofs in geometry. The performance of the UCSMP and comparison classes is roughly comparable on the item requiring an indirect argument. The UCSMP students outperformed the comparison students on both the coordinate and synthetic geometry proofs. However, the UCSMP teacher at School J and all of the comparison teachers indicated that their students had not had an

TABLE 18.6

Achievement on the Proof Items on the Geometry PSU Tests by UCSMP
and Comparison Students

School Code	Item No.	UCSMP Geometry			Comparison			
		n	M	SD	n	M	SD	p
I	Odd 1	9	1.3	1.2	7	1.0	0.6	.557
	Odd 2	9	0.6	1.1	7	0.0	0.0	
	Even 2	5	0.8	0.4	9	0.2	0.7	.167
J	Odd 1	22	2.0	0.9	13	1.8	1.7	.652
	Odd 2	22	1.7	1.4	13	0.5	0.9	.009*
	Even	20	2.1	1.5	17	0.6	0.9	.001*
K	Odd 1	18	2.1	1.5	16	2.1	1.5	1
	Odd 2	18	1.7	1.4	16	1.2	1.4	.306
	Even 2	19	1.4	1.3	18	1.4	0.8	1
L	Odd 1	22	2.0	1.0	17	1.5	1.1	.47
	Odd 2	22	2.0	1.7	17	0.5	1.2	.0038*
	Even 2	24	0.8	0.8	18	1.0	0.8	.427
Overall	Odd 1	71	1.9	1.2	53	1.7	1.1	.343
	Odd 2	71	1.6	1.5	53	0.7	1.1	.001*
	Even 2	68	1.4	1.3	62	0.9	0.9	.012*

Note. The mean score for each item is based on a maximum of 4 points. Underlined numbers indicate results for classes in which the teacher indicated that
students did not have the opportunity to learn the content needed to answer the
item.

opportunity to learn the mathematics needed to do the coordinate geometry
proof (Item 2 on the Odd Form).

Overall, regardless of whether or not OTL is controlled, classes using
UCSMP and comparison texts perform comparably on a standardized geometry test, and classes using UCSMP *Geometry* outperform comparison classes
on a multiple-choice test about reasoning, transformations, and applications
of geometry not covered on the standardized test.

A Study of the Second Edition of UCSMP
Advanced Algebra

Research Sites and Sample. The four schools participating in this study,
labeled W, X, Y, and Z, represent a variety of educational and socioeconomic
conditions. School W is a high school with a population of approximately
2,200 in a predominantly White middle-class suburb of Atlanta. Most students in each class were in Grade 11.

School X is a high school with a population of approximately 800, located
in a rural area that is in transition toward becoming a suburb of Chicago.

Approximately half the students in each class were in Grade 10 and half in Grade 11. Virtually all students were White.

School Y, with a population of approximately 500 students, is located in a small community in Mississippi. Most students were in Grade 10. Approximately three fourths of the students were White and one fourth were African American.

School Z is a high school of between 900 and 1,000 students located in an affluent suburb of Philadelphia. Most students were in Grade 11. Virtually all were White.

Most schools had not previously used any UCSMP materials. However, a few students in UCSMP classes in School W had used UCSMP *Algebra* prior to this study.

The comparison classes used *Addison-Wesley Algebra and Trigonometry* (Smith, Charles, Keedy, Bittinger, & Olfan, 1988) in School W, *Algebra and Trigonometry: Structure and Method: Book 2* (Dolciani, Sorgenfrey, Brown, & Kane, 1986) in Schools X and Z, and *Merrill Algebra 2 With Trigonometry* (Foster, Rath, & Winters, 1983) in School Y. According to Weiss et al. (1994), they represent the three most widely used second-year algebra texts at the time the study was conducted.

Overall, 150 students in the UCSMP classes and 156 students in the comparison classes took all tests. Among the UCSMP sample, 19% were in Grade 10, 76% in Grade 11, and 5% in Grade 12; 84% of these students were White, 1% Hispanic, 3% African American, and the rest were Other or Unknown. Among the comparison sample, 28% were in Grade 10, 65% in Grade 11, and 7% in Grade 12; 80% of these students were Caucasian, 1% were Hispanic, 5% were African American, and the rest were Other or Unknown.

Students in all UCSMP classes had access to graphing calculators. In each of Schools W and Z, more than 90% of UCSMP students purchased graphing calculators. In the other two schools, graphing calculators were purchased by the school and were available for use by students during class time. At the end of the school year, 96% of UCSMP students reported having access to a graphing calculator on the posttests.

Even though there were no references to graphing technology in their textbooks, three comparison teachers reported using graphing calculators. The comparison teacher at School X did not have access to graphing calculators and did not use them. At the end of the school year, 93% of the comparison students at Schools W, Y, and Z reported having access to graphing calculators on the posttests; only 4% of the comparison students at School X reported access to graphing calculators, but 60% reported access to scientific calculators.

Procedures. In the fall, students took the Entering Advanced Algebra Student Test. This test, developed by UCSMP staff, is composed of 46 multiple-choice items, 32 on Part I and 14 on Part II. Its content samples core ideas of first-year algebra and geometry including solving linear and quadratic equations, finding slopes of lines, and calculating perimeters, areas, and volumes of familiar geometric figures. It also has questions about topics taught in prerequisite UCSMP courses that may not be emphasized in non-UCSMP classes, for instance, finding equations to describe data in tables or recognizing transformations of figures. Many items on this test had been used in other studies conducted at the University of Chicago (e.g., Mathison et al., 1989).

Scores of each class on the Entering Advanced Algebra Student Test indicated that in the beginning of the school year there were no significant differences in the prerequisite knowledge between students entering UCSMP *Advanced Algebra* and comparison classes.

Although project personnel desired to assess students' knowledge of the content of second-year algebra by using a standardized test, no such test was found for the evaluation study. Hence, the project personnel created their own posttests of content knowledge. The Advanced Algebra Multiple-Choice Posttest has 36 items designed to assess knowledge of core content of second-year algebra. Most questions had been used in an earlier research study, so issues such as neutrality of language and the nature of distracters had already been resolved. Students were given 40 minutes to complete the test. With the exception of several application items unique to the UCSMP curriculum, the content of the items is common to both the UCSMP and comparison texts. The test includes items about linear, quadratic, and higher degree polynomials, exponents and logarithms, general properties of functions, variation, sequences, matrices, and trigonometry.

Students also took a six-item posttest called the Advanced Algebra PSU Test. This test is designed to measure students' abilities to solve multistep problems. The items were chosen because each can be solved by using several strategies, including numeric, symbolic, and graphical methods, and each requires students to explain their reasoning. With the exception of the last item on the test, the mathematics tested is standard content for a second-year algebra curriculum, whether it is perceived as traditional or more in the vein of *Standards*-based reform. Also, with the exception of Item 6, all questions can be solved fairly easily without a graphing calculator. The complete PSU Test appears in Thompson and Senk (2001) and Thompson et al. (2001). Sample work from students who took this test appears in Thompson and Senk (1998). Figure 18.6 shows the three items on the PSU Test about polynomial functions.

Results.   As noted in Thompson and Senk (2001, pp. 71–72), students using the UCSMP *Advanced Algebra* text outperformed the students using comparison texts on the Multiple-Choice Test at a statistically significant

SHOW YOUR WORK! IF YOU USE A CALCULATOR, EXPLAIN WHAT YOU'RE
DOING.

Item 2.   On a test, one student found an equation for a parabola to be $y - 5 = 4(x + 3)^2$.

                For the same parabola, a second student found the equation $y = 4x^2 + 24x + 31$.

                Can both students be right? Explain your answer.

Item 3.   Consider the function f, where $f(x) = x^4$. For what values of x between -3 and 3

                is $f(x) > 10$?

Item 4.   When a baseball is thrown straight up from a height of 5 feet with an initial

                velocity of 50 ft/sec, its height h in feet after t seconds is given by the equation

                    $h = -16t^2 + 50t + 5$.

                Assuming that no one catches the ball, after how many seconds will the ball hit

                the ground?

FIG. 18.6.   Items about polynomial functions from the Advanced
Algebra PSU Test.

level. However, teachers' responses on the OTL forms indicate major
differences in content coverage among these classes. The mean OTL percentage was approximately 94% for the teachers of UCSMP classes and
approximately 64% for the teachers of comparison classes. Hence, results
on the entire Multiple-Choice Posttest are not reported here.

Table 18.7 reports achievement for the Fair Tests. Among the eight pairs,
the difference in the mean percentage correct between UCSMP and comparison classes varies from −0.4% (Pair W2) to 17.1% (Pair X4). Significant
differences in the mean percentage correct, all in favor of UCSMP classes,
occur for four pairs. A matched-pairs t test shows that on these Fair Tests,
which control for OTL, the mean percent correct for the UCSMP classes is
statistically higher than for the comparison classes.

Additional analyses of the items all eight teachers considered to be fair
showed that both UCSMP and comparison students performed comparably on the skill items; the mean score of each group was 59% correct on
eight items covering linear, quadratic, cubic, and exponential equations and
functions. Results on the items testing graphical representations favored the
UCSMP students (Thompson & Senk, 2001, p. 75).

Results on the entire PSU are reported in Thompson and Senk (2001,
p. 75). Table 18.8 gives the item scores for the items from the PSU that
deal with polynomial functions. On each item the UCSMP students outperformed the comparison students at a statistically significant level. The most

TABLE 18.7

Mean Percentages Correct on the Fair Tests of the Multiple-Choice
Advanced Algebra Posttest by UCSMP and Comparison Matched Pairs

School Code	UCSMP Advanced Algebra			Comparison			
& Pair ID	n	M (%)	SD	n	M (%)	SD	p
W1	18	63.8	10.8	14	61.7	9.9	.576
W2	11	59.6	12.7	15	60.0	14.7	.943
X3	22	66.8	12.8	24	53.5	12.9	.001*
X4	16	68.3	15.6	23	51.2	14.1	.001*
Y5	19	61.5	18.0	20	46.5	10.8	.003*
Y6	13	50.9	11.0	15	45.4	14.8	.281
Z7	29	59.6	13.6	22	46.0	19.6	.005*
Z8	22	39.6	17.3	23	36.8	14.0	.553

Note. For School W, the Fair Test consists of 25 items (1–3, 5, 7–20, 22–27).
For School X, the Fair Test consists of 26 items (1–16, 18, 20–23, 25, 26, 28–30).
For School Y, the Fair Test consists of 26 items (1–16, 18–20, 22, 23, 25–29). For
School Z, the Fair Test consists of 17 items (1, 2, 7–13, 15, 16, 18–21, 23, 25). A
matched-pair t test shows that the difference in achievement of the UCSMP
and comparison students is significant ($\bar{x} = 8.825$, $\bar{s}_{\bar{x}} = 6.833$, $t = 3.57$, and
$p < .009$). From "The Effects of Curriculum on Achievement in Second-Year
Algebra: The Example of the University of Chicago School Mathematics Project,"
by D. R. Thompson and S. L. Senk, 2001, *Journal for Research in Mathematics
Education, 32,* p. 72. © 2001 by the National Council of Teachers of Mathematics. Reprinted with permission. All rights reserved.
   *There are statistically significant differences between the mean percentages
correct for the pair.

striking differences in performance between the two groups of students
were on Item 4, a classic application of quadratic functions to the height
of a projectile. However, two of the four comparison teachers reported that
their students did not have the opportunity to learn the content needed for
this item, even though they taught quadratic functions. On this item, the
mean score of the UCSMP students was almost 1.8 points higher than that of
the comparison students. Even at School W, where the comparison teacher
reported that the item was fair, there are large differences in performance
between UCSMP and comparison students.

SUMMARY AND DISCUSSION

The four studies described in this chapter report effects of the UCSMP
secondary curriculum on students' achievement in high school. Three studies used comparison groups. In Hirschhorn's longitudinal study students
were matched on demographic characteristics, current mathematics course
or grade in school, and prior mathematics achievement as determined by

TABLE 18.8

Achievement on the Function Items on the Advanced Algebra PSU Test
by UCSMP and Comparison Students

School Code	Item No.	UCSMP Advanced Algebra			Comparison			
		n	M	SD	n	M	SD	p
W	2	29	3.34	0.72	29	3.10	1.29	.385
	3	29	1.28	0.75	29	1.00	0.65	.134
	4	29	2.59	1.5	29	0.28	0.70	.001*
X	2	38	3.21	1.19	47	2.85	1.4	.212
	3	38	1.13	0.41	47	0.91	0.46	.024
	4	38	2.32	1.51	47	0.11	0.31	.001*
Y	2	32	2.59	1.56	35	2.31	1.62	.475
	3	32	1.00	0.77	35	0.77	0.60	.143
	4	32	1.50	1.70	35	0.14	0.55	.001*
Z	2	51	2.90	1.32	45	1.53	1.66	.001*
	3	51	1.22	1.01	45	0.58	0.62	.001*
	4	51	1.53	1.64	45	0.13	0.40	.001*
Overall	2	150	3.00	1.27	156	2.40	1.62	.001*
	3	150	1.16	0.77	156	0.80	0.60	.001*
	4	150	1.93	1.65	156	0.15	0.48	.001*

Note. The mean score for each item is based on a maximum of 4 points. Underlined results indicate classes in which the teacher reported that students did not have the opportunity to learn the content needed to answer the item. The comparison teacher at School Y did not respond to the OTL form for the PSU Test. From "The Effects of Curriculum on Achievement in Second-Year Algebra: The Example of the University of Chicago School Mathematics Project," by D. R. Thompson and S. L. Senk, 2001, *Journal for Research in Mathematics Education, 32,* p. 76. © 2001 by the National Council of Teachers of Mathematics. Adapted with permission. All rights reserved.

standardized test scores before the study began. In the studies of *Geometry* and *Advanced Algebra*, classes were matched on the basis of current mathematics course and scores on a pretest given at the start of the study. In Thompson's study of *PDM*, because no comparison course could be found, the performance of UCSMP students was compared to data from two sets of students who participated in the SIMS. The techniques used in these studies to match students or classes illustrate how the investigators tried to ensure that the students using the two curricula were comparable.

Although the number of students involved in Hirschhorn's longitudinal study was relatively small, it involved *all* students who had studied from the first 4 years of the UCSMP curriculum at that time. Samples in the other studies were large and diverse. Collectively, the longitudinal study and the studies of *Geometry* and *Advanced Algebra* involved approximately 350 UCSMP and 350 comparison students in 11 schools in 7 states. Thompson's study involved 180 additional UCSMP students.

Across the studies, achievement was measured by standardized tests, tests created by staff of the UCSMP, and items from the SIMS. The longitudinal study and the studies of *Geometry* and *Advanced Algebra* measured the impact of the curricula on students' achievement with multiple measures. All studies used multiple-choice tests to measure students' performance; the *Geometry* and *Advanced Algebra* studies also used tests with free-response items.[7]

The results from these studies show that when students were matched by both course and grade, the UCSMP students achieved at least as well as the comparison students on every test administered. Thus, at minimum, these studies show that UCSMP secondary curriculum does no harm. Further, the longitudinal study and the studies of *Geometry* and *Advanced Algebra* show that students using the UCSMP curriculum perform better on tests of applications of mathematics than do students studying from so-called traditional materials. Thus, the UCSMP secondary curriculum has positive effects on students' ability to learn advanced mathematics, to solve multistep problems, and to use mathematics in realistic contexts.

The studies of the first editions of the UCSMP materials did not examine how OTL influenced the achievement of students in either the UCSMP or comparison classes. Hence, we cannot determine what accounts for the performance of the students in Hirschhorn's longitudinal study. However, studies of the second editions of UCSMP materials did investigate relations between OTL and achievement. In general, even when teachers used the same textbooks, students' opportunities to learn varied quite a bit. This was true for classes using both UCSMP *Geometry* and *Advanced Algebra* and for comparison classes. In some cases, differences in OTL seemed to have little or no effect on students' achievement. For instance, even though the comparison teachers in the *Geometry* study reported a higher opportunity to learn the material on the HSST Geometry Test than the UCSMP teachers, UCSMP and comparison students performed equally well on this standardized test. In other cases, differences in OTL were associated with large differences in achievement. For instance, three of the four UCSMP teachers but none of the comparison teachers reported that their students had studied coordinate geometry. This difference in OTL, no doubt, accounts for much of the fact that the UCSMP students outperformed the comparison students on a proof about a figure set on a coordinate grid.

The use of OTL measures allowed investigators in the *Geometry* and *Advanced Algebra* studies to examine performance on subsets of questions that teachers of both UCSMP and comparison classes said their students had studied. When achievement on such Fair Tests is examined, the UCSMP students outperform the comparison students on all tests except the standardized geometry test. UCSMP students do particularly well on questions involving graphical representations or applications of mathematics.

Thus, the emphasis of the UCSMP courses on realistic uses of mathematics and on multiple dimensions of understanding influences students' achievement in a positive way. However, there are many variables other than curriculum that influence students' achievement. Teachers' knowledge of mathematics, their pedagogical skills, the ways in which they implement the curriculum, and their expectations of their students also vary. Students' entering knowledge and motivation also vary considerably. Additional research is needed to understand how these variables influence students' achievement. In particular, longitudinal research examining curricular effects on students' performance in schools that have been using *Standards*-based materials for several years is recommended.

REFERENCES

Burger, W. F., & Shaughnessy, J. M. (1986). Characterizing the van Hiele levels of development in geometry. *Journal for Research in Mathematics Education, 17*, 31–48.

Burstein, L. (Ed.). (1993). *The IEA study of mathematics III: Student growth and classroom processes.* Tarrytown, NY: Pergamon.

Campbell, D. T., & Stanley, J. C. (1963). Experimental and quasi-experimental designs for research on teaching. In N. L. Gage (Ed.), *Handbook of research on teaching* (pp. 171–246). Chicago: Rand McNally.

Chang, L. C., & Ruzicka, J. (1985). *Second International Mathematics Study, United States technical report I: Item level achievement data, eighth and twelfth grades.* Champaign, IL: Stipes.

The College Board. (1988). *Four popular achievement tests.* New York: The College Entrance Examination Board.

Cook, T. D., & Campbell, D. T. (1979). *Quasi-experimentation: Design and analysis issues for field settings.* Boston: Houghton Mifflin.

Countryman, J. (1992). *Writing to learn mathematics: Strategies that work, K–12.* Portsmouth, NH: Heinemann.

Coxford, A., Usiskin, Z., & Hirschhorn, D. (1991). *Geometry.* Glenview, IL: Scott, Foresman.

Davidson, N. (Ed.). (1990). *Cooperative learning in mathematics: A handbook for teachers.* New York: Addison-Wesley.

Dolciani, M. P., Sorgenfrey, R. H., Brown, R. H., & Kane, R. B. (1986). *Algebra and trigonometry: Structure and method: Book 2.* Boston: Houghton Mifflin.

Flanders, J. R. (1987). How much of the content in mathematics textbooks is new? *Arithmetic Teacher, 35*, 18–23.

Foster, A. G., Rath, J. N., & Winters, L. J. (1983). *Merrill algebra 2 with trigonometry.* Columbus, OH: Merrill.

Fuys, D., Geddes, D., & Tischler, R. (1988). The van Hiele model of thinking in geometry among adolescents. *Journal for Research in Mathematics Education* (Monograph Series No. 3). Reston, VA: National Council of Teachers of Mathematics.

Hedges, L. V., Stodolsky, S. S., Mathison, S., & Flores, P. (1986). *Transition mathematics field study.* Chicago: The University of Chicago School Mathematics Project.

Hirschhorn, D. B. (1993). A longitudinal study of students completing four years of UCSMP mathematics. *Journal for Research in Mathematics Education, 24*, 136–158.

Hirschhorn, D. B., Thompson, D. R., Usiskin, Z., & Senk, S. L. (1995). Rethinking the first two years of high school mathematics with UCSMP. *The Mathematics Teacher, 88*, 640–647.

Jurgensen, R. C., Brown, G., & Jurgensen, J. W. (1988). *Geometry.* Boston: Houghton Mifflin.

Krutetskii, V. A. (1976). *The psychology of mathematical abilities in schoolchildren* (J. Kilpatrick & I. Wirszup, Eds.). Chicago: University of Chicago Press.

Malone, J. A., Douglas, G. A., Kissane, B. V., & Mortlock, R. S. (1980). Measuring problem solving ability. In S. Krulik & R. Reys (Eds.), *Problem solving in school mathematics, 1980 Yearbook of the National Council of Teachers of Mathematics* (pp. 204–215). Reston, VA: National Council of Teachers of Mathematics.

Mathison, S., Hedges, L. V., Stodolsky, S. S., Flores, P., & Sarther, C. (1989). *Teaching and learning algebra: An evaluation of UCSMP Algebra.* Chicago: University of Chicago School Mathematics Project.

McConnell, J. W., Brown, S., Eddins, S., Hackworth, M., Sachs, L., Woodward, E., Flanders, J., Hirschhorn, D., Polonsky, L., & Usiskin, Z. (1990). *UCSMP algebra.* Glenview, IL: Scott, Foresman.

McConnell, J. W., Brown, S., Usiskin, Z., Senk, S. L., Widerski, T., Anderson, S., Eddins, S., Hynes Feldman, C., Flanders, J., Hackworth, M., Hirschhorn, D., Polonsky, L., Sachs, L., & Woodward, E. (1996). *Algebra* (2nd ed.). Glenview, IL: Scott, Foresman.

McKnight, C. C., Crosswhite, F. J., Dossey, J. A., Kifer, E., Swafford, J. O., Travers, K. J., & Cooney, T. J. (1987). *The underachieving curriculm: Assessing U.S. school mathematics from an international perspective.* Champaign, IL: Stipes.

National Council of Teachers of Mathematics. (1989). *Curriculum and evaluation standards for school mathematics.* Reston, VA: Author.

Peressini, A. L., Epp, S. S., Hollowell, K. A., Brown, S., Ellis, W. Jr., McConnell, J. W., Sorteberg, J., Thompson, D. R., Aksoy, D., Birky, G. D., McRill, G. A., & Usiskin, Z. (1992). *Precalculus and discrete mathematics.* Glenview, IL: Scott, Foresman.

Peressini, A. L., McConnell, J. W., Usiskin, Z., Epp, S. S., Ahbel, N. P., Witonsky, D., Hollowell, K. A., Brown, S., Ellis, W., Sorteberg, J., Thompson, D. R., Aksoy, D., Birky, G. D., & McRill, G. A. (1998). *Precalculus and discrete mathematics* (2nd ed.). Glenview, IL: Scott, Foresman–Addison Wesley.

Rubenstein, R. N., Schultz, J., Senk, S. L., Hackworth, M., McConnell, J., Viktora, S. S., Aksoy, D., Flanders, J., Kissane, B., & Usiskin, Z. (1992). *Functions, statistics, and trigonometry.* Glenview, IL: Scott, Foresman.

Senk, S. L. (1985). How well do students write geometry proofs? *Mathematics Teacher, 78*, 448–456.

Senk, S. L. (1989). Van Hiele levels and achievement in writing geometry proofs. *Journal for Research in Mathematics Education, 30*, 309–321.

Senk, S. L. (1999). The UCSMP secondary curriculum second edition. In Z. Usiskin (Ed.), *Developments in school mathematics education around the world* (Vol. 4, pp. 380–384). Reston, VA: National Council of Teachers of Mathematics.

Senk, S. L., Thompson, D. R., Viktora, S. S., Rubenstein, R. N., Halvorson, J., Flanders, J., Jakucyn, N., Pillsbury, G., & Usiskin, Z. (1990). *Advanced algebra.* Glenview, IL: Scott, Foresman.

Senk, S. L., Thompson, D. R., Viktora, S. S., Usiskin, Z., Ahbel, N., Levin, S., Weinhold, M. L., Rubenstein, R. N., Jaskowiak, J. H., Flanders, J., Jakucyn, N., & Pillsbury, G. (1996). *Advanced algebra* (2nd ed.). Glenview, IL: Scott, Foresman.

Senk, S. L., Viktora, S. S., Usiskin, Z., Ahbel, N. P., Highstone, V., Witonsky, D., Rubenstein, R. N., Schultz, J., Hackworth, M., McConnell, J., Aksoy, D., Flanders, J., & Kissane, B. (1998). *Functions, statistics, and trigonometry* (2nd ed.). Glenview, IL: Scott, Foresman–Addison Wesley.

Serra, M. (1989). *Discovering geometry: An inductive approach.* Emeryville, CA: Key Curriculum Press.

Shavelson, R. J., McDonnell, L. M., & Oakes J. (Eds.). (1989). *Indicators for monitoring mathematics and science education.* Santa Monica, CA: RAND.

Smith, S. A., Charles, R. I., Keedy, M. L., Bittinger, M. L., & Orfan, L. J. (1988). *Addison-Wesley algebra and trigonometry.* Menlo Park, CA: Addison-Wesley.

Stenmark, J. K. (Ed.). (1991). *Mathematics assessment: Myths, models, good questions, and practical suggestions.* Reston, VA: National Council of Teachers of Mathematics.

Thompson, D. R. (1992). *An evaluation of a new course in precalculus and discrete mathematics.* Unpublished doctoral dissertation, The University of Chicago.

Thompson, D. R., & Senk, S. L. (1993). Assessing reasoning and proof in high school. In N. L. Webb & A. F. Coxford (Eds.), *Assessment in the mathematics classroom* (1993 Yearbook of the National Council of Teachers of Mathematics) (pp. 167–176). Reston, VA: National Council of Teachers of Mathematics.

Thompson, D. R., & Senk, S. L. (1998). Using rubrics in high school mathematics courses. *Mathematics Teacher, 91,* 786–793.

Thompson, D. R., & Senk, S. L. (2001). The effects of curriculum on achievement in second-year algebra: The example of the University of Chicago School Mathematics Project. *Journal for Research in Mathematics Education, 32,* 58–84.

Thompson, D. R., Senk, S. L., Usiskin, Z., Kaely, G., & Witonsky, D. (2001). *An evaluation of the second edition of UCSMP Advanced Algebra.* Chicago: The University of Chicago School Mathematics Project.

Usiskin, Z. (1982). Van Hiele levels and achievement in secondary school geometry. (Final report of the Cognitive Development and Achievement in Secondary School Geometry Project.) Chicago: The University of Chicago, Department of Education. (ERIC Document Reproduction Service No. ED 220 288)

Usiskin, Z. (1986). The UCSMP: Translating grades 7–12 mathematics recommendations into reality. *Educational Leadership, 4,* 430–435.

Usiskin, Z. (1987). Why elementary algebra can, should, and must be an eighth-grade course for average students. *Mathematics Teacher, 80,* 428–438.

Usiskin, Z. (1988). Conceptions of algebra and uses of variables. In A. F. Coxford & A. P. Shulte (Eds.), *The ideas of algebra, K–12* (pp. 8–19). Reston, VA: National Council of Teachers of Mathematics.

Usiskin, Z. (1997). Applications in the secondary school mathematics curriculum: A generation of change. *American Journal of Education, 106,* 62–84.

Usiskin, Z., Feldman, C. H., Davis, S., Mallo, S. Sanders, G., Witonsky, D., Flanders, J., Polonsky, L., Porter, S., & Viktora, S. (1995). *Transition mathematics* (2nd ed.). Glenview, IL: Scott, Foresman.

Usiskin, Z., Flanders, J., Hynes, C., Polonsky, L., Porter, S., & Viktora, S. (1990). *Transition mathematics.* Glenview, IL: Scott, Foresman.

Usiskin, Z., Hirschhorn, D., Coxford, A., Highstone, V., Lewellen, H., Oppong, N., DiBianca, R., & Maeir, M. (1997). *Geometry* (2nd ed.). Glenview, IL: Scott, Foresman.

Usiskin, Z., Hirschhorn, D., Highstone, V., Lewellen, H., Oppong, N., & Coxford, A. (1993). *Geometry* (2nd ed.). Field Trial Version. Chicago: University of Chicago School Mathematics Project.

Weiss, I. R., Matti, M. C., & Smith, P. S. (1994). *Report of the 1993 survey of science and mathematics education.* Chapel Hill, NC: Horizon Research.

Wick, J. W., & Gatta, L. A. (1988). *High school subjects tests, geometry form B.* Iowa City, IA: American Testronics.

Witonsky, D., Senk, S. L., Usiskin, Z., & Kaely, G. (2002). *An evaluation of the second edition of UCSMP geometry.* Chicago: The University of Chicago School Mathematics Project. Manuscript in preparation.

Yunker, L. E. (1990). *Merrill geometry.* Columbus, OH: Merrill.

ENDNOTES

1. Additional support for the UCSMP Secondary Component was provided by the Carnegie Corporation of New York, the Ford Motor Company, the General Electric Fund, and the UCSMP Secondary Curriculum Royalties.
2. Zalman Usiskin, personal communication, February 17, 2000.
3. For a related discussion of dimensions of mathematical abilities, see Krutetskii (1976).
4. Hirschhorn described this design as an untreated equivalent control group design with a retrospective pretest and posttest (Campbell & Stanley, 1963; Cook & Campbell, 1979).
5. Each study also contained schools in which the performance of students using the Second Edition, Field-Trial Version was compared with that of students using the First Edition. Those results are not included here but are available in Thompson, Senk, Usiskin, Kaely, and Witonsky (2001) and Witonsky, Senk, Usiskin, and Kaely (2002).
6. Notice that the results in Table 18.6 shift the unit of analysis from the class to the teacher. The fact that the OTL measures reported were identical for each par of classes taught by each teacher is further justification for this shift.
7. Thompson's (1992) study also included a free-response Proof Test and interviews of students, but because of space limitations the results are not discussed here.

19

Reaction To High School Curriculum Projects Research

Jane Swafford

Illinois State University

Not since the 1950s, with the introduction of new math, has there been a major attempt to transform the high school mathematics curriculum in the United States. The five curricula described in this section represent such an attempt. They seek to update the content and improve instruction, to downplay memorization and practice of procedures, and to emphasize developing conceptual understanding and solving problems in realistic settings. New content such as probability, statistics, and discrete mathematics is introduced; and, in some cases, new and traditional topics are integrated across the grades.

On the surface, one would think that such changes would be welcomed. However, fears from parents and professional mathematicians that the new curricula do not adequately prepare students in the necessary basics to be successful in college or higher mathematics have led to what has aptly been called the "math wars" (Jackson, June/July, 1997; August, 1997; "Math Wars," 2000). One assault in the war was the publication of an open letter to then-Secretary of Education Richard Riley in *The Washington Post* requesting that the designation of "exemplary" or "promising" be withdrawn from the 10 K–12 mathematics programs, including 3 described in this section (*Core Plus*, *Interactive Mathematics Program*, and University of Chicago School

Mathematics Project Secondary Curriculum) ("Mr. Secretary," 1999; U.S. Department of Education, 1999). In a congressional hearing following the publication of the open letter, one critic of reform claimed that valid research on the effectiveness of these new curricula was nonexistent (*Federal Role* in *K–12*, 2000). What has been presented in this section is not only extensive research on five reform curricula, but also considerable evidence that the promises of reform mathematics are real and the fears of the anti-reformers unjustified.

FINDINGS FROM THE FIVE
CURRICULUM PROJECTS

Achievement on Traditional Measures

The five high school curricula presented in this section have goals that differ from those of a traditional high school curriculum consisting of 2 years of Algebra and 1 year of Geometry; but they also share many of the same goals of a traditional curriculum. Although they may differ with respect to the emphasis given to common content, both reform and traditional curricula expect reasonable levels of skills and understanding on this common content. Therefore, it is not just in response to the fears of the opponents that evaluations of the new curricula look at achievement on traditional measures of mathematics achievement. These tests also measure important goals of the reform curricula. Each of the five curriculum projects gathered data on student performance on some standard measures of mathematics achievement and compared it with that of students in traditional programs. Overall, students in the reform programs performed as well as students in traditional programs on tests designed to measure traditional content.

Students from the *Interactive Mathematics Program* (*IMP*) did not score significantly different on a standardized test (Comprehensive Test of Basic Skills, or CTBS) taken in Grade 11 from students coming from a traditional curriculum. Similarly, students in the *Systematic Initiative for Montana Mathematics and Science* (*SIMMS*) curriculum were not significantly different from comparison students on the Preliminary Scholastic Aptitude Test (PSAT), a traditional measure of achievement. Scores for students from the pilot testing of the *SIMMS* materials in Montana at all four levels and a pilot study of the commercial version of *SIMMS* Level 1 in a large city outside of Montana were not significantly different from scores of students in comparison classes. Likewise, the achievement of the University of Chicago School Mathematics Project (UCSMP) Geometry classes was virtually identical to the achievement of comparison classes on a standardized test of high school geometry (High School Subject Tests—Geometry Form B).

Both *Core-Plus* and *MATH Connections* students performed at least as well, if not better, than students from a traditional curriculum on standardized or state assessments. *Core-Plus* Course 1 students scored significantly higher overall on a standardized test of quantitative thinking than comparison students, but *Core-Plus* Course 2 students did not score significantly different from comparison students. There was no comparison group for the *Core-Plus* Course 3 students, but their growth over 3 years on the quantitative thinking test, when compared with the national norm, was strong in the first year and built slightly in each successive year. However, on a test designed to measure the curriculum, *Core-Plus* students in Course 1, but not Course 2, performed significantly less well than comparison students on procedural algebra tasks. On the Connecticut statewide assessment, *MATH Connections* students performed comparably to their matched peers in a traditional curriculum. Although some would argue that the quantitative thinking test used in the *Core-Plus* evaluation (Iowa Tests of Educational Development, Ability to Do Quantitative Thinking, or ITED-Q) and the statewide assessment test used in Connecticut reflect a more reform view of mathematics than tests such as the PSAT or CTBS, these findings show that students' achievement on conventional measures is, by and large, not harmed by using the reform curricula.

Students in reform curricula also outperformed the national sample on released items from the National Assessment of Educational Progress (NAEP) and from the Second International Mathematics Study (SIMS). *Core-Plus* Course 3 students from the 22 field-test schools performed higher on all categories of items than the national sample on a 30-item test taken from NAEP. UCSMP Precalculus and Discrete Mathematics students scored significantly higher than the U.S. sample of students enrolled in Precalculus on 7 of the 11 multiple-choice SIMS items administered and comparable with the U.S. sample of high school Calculus students on the same items. It should be noted, however, that neither national nor international assessments are high-stakes tests for U.S. students.

On the longitudinal study of students with 4 years of UCSMP mathematics, the results were mixed on a standardized measure of traditional content (Level I Mathematics Achievement Test), with the performance of UCSMP students being higher in two of five comparisons, comparable in two, and lower in one.

Overall, it would seem from the evidence reported that reform curricula do not hamper student performance on traditional content. Although in one case, initial skill with algebraic manipulations was not as good as that acquired in a traditional curriculum, by the second course this gap had been closed.

Achievement on Reform Measures

Because the goals of the reform curricula are broader than those of a traditional curriculum, any attempt to assess the effectiveness of these materials
would be incomplete if it did not also try to gauge what students from these
programs actually know and are able to do. Therefore, each of the evaluations used tests or tasks designed to measure the content and processes
emphasized in their materials. As might be expected, students from the reform curricula tend to outperform students in traditional curricula on these
measures.

Core-Plus students in both Course 1 and Course 2 outperformed comparison students on contextual algebra tasks. Similarly, Level 1 *SIMMS* students
performed significantly better than comparison students on the open response, end-of-year-tasks designed to assess the goals of the curriculum. At
the other three levels, students from *SIMMS* classes did not score significantly
different from students in comparison classes. *SIMMS* students, however, did
demonstrate stronger reasoning and problem-solving skills.

The *IMP* evaluation used a different test at each of the three grade levels
tested. *IMP* Grade 9 students outperformed Grade 9 comparison students in
a traditional Grade 9 college-preparatory course on a test of statistical ideas;
IMP Grade 10 students outperformed Grade 10 Geometry students on a
two-item problem-solving test; and *IMP* Grade 11 students outperformed
Grade 11 Algebra II students on a quantitative reasoning test. However, in
the replication study, when the traditional college-preparatory mathematics
courses were enhanced to provide students with the opportunity to learn the
content covered by these tests, the *IMP* students no longer demonstrated
an advantage.

In the studies reported on the UCSMP, students using UCSMP clearly
outperformed the comparison students on tests developed by the UCSMP
evaluators. The longitudinal study of students in their fourth year of UCSMP
showed that these students performed better on tests of applications of
mathematics than comparison students in traditional classes. Students using the UCSMP Geometry and UCSMP Advanced Algebra curricula scored
higher in four out of eight classes matched to classes using a traditional
program. In both the Geometry and Advanced Algebra studies, data were
reported only for the items in the project-developed test that covered content that both teachers of UCSMP and comparison classes indicated that
their students had had an opportunity to learn. Therefore, the reform measures used were considered fair to both the UCSMP and the comparison
classes. On tests of problem solving and understanding, UCSMP classes
outperformed the comparison classes, although neither group performed
well and the comparison classes had little opportunity to learn the content
tested.

Subchapter unit quizzes, many of which were performance tasks, were used to measure achievement on the content in *MATH Connections* and thus were not administered to a comparison group. From their performance on these quizzes, the *MATH Connections* students were judged to have achieved the program's objectives. However, it is not known how their performance would compare with the performance of students in traditional programs on these quizzes.

Overall, the preceding five chapters present ample evidence that students in reform curricula are experiencing and profiting from a broader, richer curriculum. Many would argue that it is precisely these problem-solving and reasoning skills as well as a knowledge of statistics, probability, and discrete mathematics that are needed, not only for future success in mathematics, but for life.

Retention in Mathematics

That students will elect to take more mathematics beyond the minimum required is a goal of both traditional and reform curricula. The advocates of reform hope that by developing deeper understandings and providing engaging contexts, students will find mathematics more interesting and approachable and hence want to take more of it. Only one program looked at the issue of retention in high school mathematics beyond the minimal requirements. A transcript study was conducted in three high schools at which *IMP* students had completed 3 years of the curriculum. The investigator found that the percentage of students who completed 3 years of a college-preparatory mathematics curriculum was higher for students who began Grade 9 in the *IMP* curriculum than in the traditional curriculum. Further, a higher percentage of these *IMP* students, when compared with students in the traditional curriculum, also went on to take a fourth year of advanced high school mathematics. The percentages of students who took Precalculus or Calculus, however, were the same for both groups. Although there is some evidence that a reform curriculum can have a positive impact on retaining students in mathematics, more research in this area is needed.

It might be said that the motto of the reform movement is "Mathematics for All." Making mathematics accessible to a broader population, particularly in high school, is certainly one of the goals of the reform movement. Only one of the programs, *MATH Connections*, looked at this issue. Their evaluators conducted a case study of at-risk students and an analysis of *MATH Connections* quiz results by gender and ethnicity and for mainstream special education students. The lack of differences by gender and ethnicity and the success of the high-risk and special education students suggests that reform curricula can, indeed, foster mathematics learning for all students.

Student Disposition Toward Mathematics

Whether or not students will be favorably disposed to mathematics after their school experience with mathematics is another contention in the debates over the curriculum. Only one of the programs, *MATH Connections*, reported data on students' attitudes. Students with *MATH Connections* teachers were found to be significantly more confident in their ability to do mathematics and to perceive mathematics as more useful than students with non-*MATH Connections* teachers. Interview data from former *SIMMS* students were also reported. However, the interviews focused on the students' reactions to the *SIMMS* curriculum, not their attitudes about mathematics in general. Consequently, there is limited evidence that the reform curricula have a positive impact on students' attitudes toward mathematics; but here again, more research is needed.

College Entrance Examinations and Mathematics Courses

Perhaps the greatest concern of opponents of the reform movement is whether or not the new curricula will adequately prepare students for college mathematics. The research reported in this section indicates that students in the reform curriculum are at least as well prepared for college entrance examinations as similar students from a more traditional curriculum. No differences were found between *Core-Plus* students and traditional students on Scholastic Aptitude Test (SAT) Math scores in one study or on American College Test (ACT) scores in another study. Students who started *IMP* in Grade 9 and took the SAT scored significantly higher on it than students who started in the traditional curriculum in Grade 9 and took the SAT in Grade 11. Similarly, SAT means in a suburban Connecticut high school favored the students in *MATH Connections*.

A study of college freshman mathematics course performance at a large Midwestern university of graduates from two comparable high schools, one using *Core-Plus* and the other a traditional curriculum, showed similar patterns of performance. A study of Montana college freshmen found students who completed 3 years of *SIMMS* were as likely as their traditional counterparts to take calculus, but more likely than their traditional counterparts to take developmental mathematics. Further, *SIMMS* students were less successful in these developmental courses than non-*SIMMS* students. Therefore, it would appear from the pilot test that *SIMMS* students are not as well prepared for college mathematics as students from a traditional curriculum. However, the results may be a reflection of the highly traditional nature of college mathematics placement tests and mathematics courses in Montana rather than the actual mathematics preparation of the students.

Neither *IMP*, *MATH Connections*, nor UCSMP report following students into college.

The research on the five high school curricula presented in this section offers considerable evidence that reform mathematics has a positive impact on student achievement. Students in the reform classes generally perform as well as students in traditional classes on traditional measures, although in one case weakness on procedural tasks was evidenced. More important, students in the reform classes generally demonstrated strengths on measures of conceptual understanding, problem solving in realistic contexts, and other measures designed to test a broader view of mathematics. There is also some evidence that students in reform curricula are at least as well prepared for college entrance exams as students from traditional mathematics classes and do as well in some, but not all, freshman college mathematics courses. Clearly the results reported here should give advocates of reform substantial evidence to put forward for their cause.

COMMON CHARACTERISTICS ACROSS THE EVALUATIONS

The five evaluations all point to strengths in students' performance that were achieved through reform curricula at little cost to performance on traditional measures. Although the evaluations shared common findings, they also shared a number of design characteristics.

Subjects

Each of the projects collected data on students using their curriculum and made a heroic effort to identify comparison students and collect data on them. The comparison students were found in a variety of ways, making some comparison groups more comparable than others. For the investigation of achievement on traditional content, *Core-Plus* used three groups for each of Course 1 and Course 2 matched individually based on ITED-Q pretest score, school, and gender. For each *Core-Plus* course, three comparison groups were determined by the level of the course the students in the comparison groups were taking: Prealgebra, Algebra, or Accelerated Geometry for Course 1; and Algebra, Geometry, or Accelerated Advanced algebra for Course 2. In contrast, the *MATH Connections* study of traditional content used groups that were matched individually on the basis of scores on the Grade 8 state mastery test. The analysis of the state assessment test scores, PSAT, and SAT scores for all students in three graduating classes in eight high schools were examined by using the Grade 8 mastery test as a covariate.

In the UCSMP longitudinal study, researchers also used individually matched comparison students. They matched students retrospectively using Grade 6 mathematics and reading achievement, sex, and race. At two of the three sites, two groups of matched pairs were formed, one matched by grade (10th) and one matched by course (Advanced Algebra). At the third site, comparison students in the 10th grade were also enrolled in Advanced Algebra; hence, only one group of pairs was used. In the UCSMP Geometry and Advanced Algebra studies, classes, rather than individuals, were matched at each of the four schools on the basis of a UCSMP-developed test of incoming or prerequisite knowledge.

SIMMS, IMP, and one of the UCSMP studies did not use matched-pair groups. The SIMMS evaluation used SIMMS and non-SIMMS classes in participating schools at each of the four grade levels evaluated. Although researchers attempted to choose the comparison classes based on age and mathematics background, no formal pretest was used to establish their comparability. Likewise in the IMP transcript study investigating retention in high school mathematics, the evaluator had no way of knowing whether the IMP and traditional students were similar when they began their study of high school mathematics. Only for the analysis of SAT scores at one school was the IMP evaluator able to form two matched groups based on Grade 7 CTBS scores. The UCSMP study of Precalculus and Discrete Mathematics used the U.S. precalculus and calculus samples from the SIMS. Once again, there was no way to gauge the comparability of the background of the students in the nine schools studied and that of the two U.S. national samples. Further, it was acknowledged that the UCSMP students were allowed to use calculators, whereas the students in the international study were not.

When the evaluations looked at student performance on content emphasized by the reform curriculum, it was even harder to find comparison groups. MATH Connections used subchapter quizzes to assess whether students attained the objectives of the curriculum and used no comparison students at all. SIMMS used the same informally matched groups for both their assessment of student performance on the PSAT and the curriculum's end-of-year tasks. No comparison students were used for the Core-Plus Course 3 evaluation of either the traditional or reform content. For Core-Plus Course 1 and Course 2, only the first part of the curriculum's end-of-year test was given to the comparison students, who had been carefully matched with Core-Plus students. UCSMP, in contrast, used teachers' indications of opportunity to learn to create "fair tests" that covered the content emphasized both by their reform Geometry and Advanced Algebra curricula and by the traditional geometry and advanced algebra programs at each site. Although IMP used a different high school and a different outcome measure and instrument to assess performance on content emphasized by IMP at each of the three grade levels evaluated, they did form matched pairs at each school based on Grade 8 achievement test scores, gender, and ethnicity.

Across all of the evaluations, there was wide variation in how the samples were identified, especially the comparison students. Only in an isolated case were students randomly assigned to treatments: The SAT and ACT studies of *Core-Plus* at two high schools in which all the prealgebra and non-honors algebra students were randomly assigned to *Core-Plus* or a traditional course. Otherwise, a variety of criteria were used at the participating schools to determine which students would be enrolled in the experimental curriculum. Most often students volunteered. In one case, if students qualified for no other mathematics course, they were assigned to the new program. As the *IMP* evaluator observed, "Viable control groups were very difficult to identify," and he cited a litany of reasons why this is the case: students transfer between programs, teachers teach both programs, teachers communicate across programs, reform pedagogy creeps into traditional classes, or teachers with traditional teaching/learning philosophies refuse to have their students compared to students in a reform curriculum (Webb, Chapter 16, this volume). Overall, the evaluations used creative ways to identify comparable students or classes with which to compare the achievement of students in the reform programs. Although in no case were true comparable groups identified for all grade levels of the program or for all instruments used, the efforts undertaken are commendable.

Outcome Measures and Instruments

Each program used some standard measure of the traditional curriculum, such as the PSAT, SAT, ITED-Q, Mathematics Level 1 Achievement Tests, High School Subject Tests, NAEP and SIMS released items, or state assessments. As in the sampling practices, there was no uniformity across programs in the instruments chosen, although each claimed that the instruments used were measuring the content typically covered by the traditional high school mathematics curriculum. As pointed out earlier, some of the instruments chosen as a measure of the traditional curriculum might be considered as measures of a reform curriculum. For example, the following problem from the Connecticut state assessment was used in the *MATH Connections* evaluation:

> At a department store sale, you are buying a $50 sweater that you selected from a table that says "25% OFF." You also have a coupon for an additional 10% off on any purchase.

> The cashier takes 25% off the original price and then takes an additional 10% off. She asks you for $33.75. Write what you would explain to the cashier to justify why this price is not as good as the bargain claimed in the coupon.

Such an open response, explain-your-reasoning question is a hallmark of the reform curriculum. It would be helpful if some standards for control measures could be established.

Each program also used some special measure of the content covered by the curriculum, such as subchapter quizzes, end-of-course tests, tests designed by the developers, or items selected from other instruments that favor content found in the reform curricula. These measures are naturally biased in favor of the reform classes. However, it would be unfair to evaluate reform classes solely on the basis of traditional measures. Each program evaluation attempted to address the bias problem in some way, from not testing comparison classes with the reform measures to developing "fair tests" to use with both groups. Clearly there are limitations with any approach. Nevertheless, it is important to document the mathematical capabilities of students coming from reform classes.

Evaluation Designs

Although evaluators used a wide range of designs from transcript studies to matched-pair comparison studies, for the most part, the data were collected as part of the pilot or field testing of the materials. A field test is not a true test, but more a feasibility test. Across all five programs, it appears that volunteer teachers, volunteer students, or both were used. Often the schools and teachers involved in a field test of innovative materials are those at the margin, schools and teachers who are dissatisfied with the status quo and willing, even eager, to try new things. They are not the rank and file.

QUESTIONS NOT ADDRESSED AND DIRECTIONS FOR FUTURE RESEARCH

Although the efforts undertaken to determine the impact of these materials on student achievement were extensive, there were a number of questions these studies did not address. Because most of the studies were based on the field test of the materials, they give us little insight into how students might fare with teachers who are experienced and comfortable with using these new materials. We might speculate that students' achievement would be better with teachers who have used the materials for a number of years: But the glitter might wear off, enthusiasm wane, and more traditional methods and content creep back into the classroom. The same questions could be raised about how the materials would fare with nonvolunteer teachers and students or how the revised versions of the materials would fare with the same populations. As long as the research on innovative materials is linked to the evaluation of the initial product, we have no clear idea of how final versions will actually play in typical classrooms, with typical teachers, and typical students. Future research has to examine the impact of these curricula under a standard implementation in which a district adopts the materials; and all teachers, reform minded or not, are expected to use them.

Future research on the impact under routine implementation also has to take into account the degree or faithfulness of the implementation and the relationship of the degree to which the materials are implemented to student outcomes. In a pilot or field test, we might assume that the curriculum is being implemented much as the developers intended. However, in an adoption implementation, teachers vary widely in their commitment to the district's chosen curriculum. They may supplement widely, present the new content in a lecture mode, or continue to use the old program. Therefore, unless the faithfulness of the implementation is taken into account at the classroom level, the new curriculum may appear, on average, to have no significant differential impact on student achievement, because the effects in classes where there is a strong implementation are neutralized by those in classes where there is a weak implementation.

Much of the evaluation was done at the course level rather than the program level. Although high school mathematics has traditionally been a collection of distinct courses, the reform curricula make an effort to develop major themes over time, making connections across time and topics. More research is needed that examines the impact of the total program on student achievement, attitude, and future success.

The degree to which these reform curricula open up mathematics to a wider range of students was not well studied. Only one evaluation reported data by gender, ethnicity, or high-risk status. There is reason to believe that mathematics studied in the context of interesting real-world situations will engage a wider audience than conventional high school mathematics has in the past. Further research on these or any materials has to disaggregate data by subpopulations, including race, socioeconomic status, high-risk status, gender, and postsecondary school intent. Also, as mentioned earlier, research on students' attitudes and dispositions toward mathematics as a result of their experience with a reform curriculum should be studied further.

Only two of the evaluations looked at the performance of students from these curricula in college mathematics courses and none explored the success of students in future jobs. These are clearly difficult issues to address, but ones that lie at the very heart of questions about the efficacy of these materials. If students are only at least as well prepared for college entrance examinations and college mathematics courses as students from traditional curricula, why change? The *SIMMS* evaluators argued that the lack of a strong showing on college mathematics placement examinations and in beginning courses of students from the *SIMMS* program is more a reflection of the overly traditional stance of college mathematics than a weakness of the program. The impact of reform mathematics programs on students' future lives requires further research. Although these programs may give students a richer high school mathematics experience, we also need to know whether the programs enable them to be successful in mathematics or live richer, fuller lives.

CLOSING OBSERVATIONS

Taken as a group, these studies offer overwhelming evidence that the reform curricula can have a positive impact on high school mathematics achievement. It is not that students in these curriculum learn traditional content better but that they develop other skills and understandings while not falling behind on traditional content. These evaluations present more solid scientific evidence than has ever before been available about the impact of curriculum materials. They set an example for the developers of all textbooks, both experimental and commercially developed. Critics of reform fear that their children are being used as guinea pigs, but in fact, their children have been recipients of fads and fashions for decades with documented poor results. No curriculum materials have ever been held to the standards that these have: But all should be.

REFERENCES

Jackson, A. (1997, June/July). The math wars: California battles it out over mathematics education reform (Part 1). *Notices of the AMS, 44,* 695–702.

Jackson, A. (1997, August). The math wars: California battles it out over mathematics education reform (Part 2). *Notices of the AMS, 44,* 817–823.

U.S. Department of Education, Mathematics and Science Expert Panel. (1999). *Exemplary and promising mathematics programs.* Washington, DC: Author. Available: http://www.enc.org/professional/federalresources/exemplary/.

Math wars. (2000, January 4). *The Wall Street Journal,* p. 1.

Mr. Secretary, We ask that you withdraw your premature recommendations for mathematics instruction. (1999, November 18). *The Washington Post,* p. A5.

The Federal Role in K–12 Mathematics Reform: Joint Hearing Before the Subcommittees on Early Childhood, Youth and Families and on Postsecondary Education, Training and Life-Long Learning of the House Committee on Education and the Workforce, 106th Cong., 2d Sess. (2000). Available: http://www.house.gov/ed_workforce/hearings/106th/ecyf/fuzzymath2200/milgram.htm/.

PART V

Final Commentary

20

What Works?

Jeremy Kilpatrick
University of Georgia

In 1986, at the direction of Secretary William Bennett, the U.S. Department of Education published a booklet entitled *What Works: Research About Teaching and Learning* to provide "a distillation of a large body of scholarly research in the field of education" (p. v) for the benefit of the American public. Since that time, research on teaching and learning has become a weapon in the so-called math wars over *Standards*-based school mathematics curricula. Advocates of those curricula have reviewed the literature and cited various studies as providing evidence to bolster their proposals. Opponents have argued that the research literature is being misread, that the few available experimental studies do not support the changes advocated, and that new curricula should not replace old ones until experiments show that they yield higher mathematics performance. Disturbed that the authors of the 1989 *Curriculum and Evaluation Standards for School Mathematics* of the National Council of Teachers of Mathematics (NCTM) "do not cite any pilot project or any school district as a model to show that their goals can be achieved in the real world," Sherman Stein (1996) said:

> That means that they are proposing to change the way an entire generation learns mathematics without checking the feasibility of their recommendations.

471

A manufacturer introduces a new soap with more care, first testing its reception in a few stores or towns before committing to mass production. (p. 89)

Politicians have begun to ask that research be conducted before new instructional programs are instituted. The State of California, in Section 60200.c.3 of its Education Code, now insists that instructional materials chosen for Grades K–8 be "factually correct and incorporate principles of instruction reflective of current and confirmed research" (Selection and Adoption, 1995). As the editors of the present volume note in Chapter 1, the U.S. Congress mandated in 1994 that the Office of Educational Research and Improvement establish expert panels that would identify exemplary and promising programs, and the first report, for mathematics, was published in 1999 (U.S. Department of Education, 1999). Opening the February 2000 joint hearing before two subcommittees of the U.S. House Committee on Education and the Workforce on the federal role in K–12 mathematics reform, the chairman, Michael Castle (*Federal Role in K–12*), declared that "federal math research [*sic*] must be based on sound scientific research and these studies must be completed before program recommendations are disseminated nationwide."

In the face of the growing demand for research to support *Standards*-based curricula, the studies reported in this book provide much needed evidence that the new programs work. In this case, "work" means primarily "lead to satisfactory student achievement." As the authors of Chapters 7, 12, and 19 note, students studying from *Standards*-based curricula do as well as students studying from traditional curricula on standardized mathematics tests and other measures of traditional content. They score higher than those who have studied from traditional curricula on tests of newer content and processes highlighted in the *Standards* document. These results indicate that *Standards*-based curricula are working in classrooms in ways their designers intended for them to work.

One might be tempted to say that the *Standards*-based curricula "lead to higher student achievement overall," but that would require that reliable and valid comparisons be made on comprehensive, agreed-upon measures of achievement. For reasons to be discussed in the paragraphs that follow, such comparisons have proved virtually impossible to accomplish in a satisfactory way. Nonetheless, the evidence at hand is both promising and substantial. It will not quiet the critics (lack of evidence is not the true source of their complaints), but it should encourage those who welcome improvements in school mathematics and understand the difficulty of evaluating something as complex as a curriculum.

Because Putnam, Chappell, and Swafford have discussed comparisons of achievement at specific grade levels in their commentary chapters, in this chapter I will focus on a set of problematic issues that cut across curriculum research at all levels.

CURRICULUM EVALUATION

The dozen projects featured in this book have all attempted to change the teaching and learning of school mathematics in the United States by providing curriculum materials and professional development activities that are in line with the recommendations made by the NCTM in the documents described in Chapter 1. In each chapter, studies are described of attempts to evaluate the project's curriculum by examining student outcomes—what students apparently learned as a consequence of being in classrooms in which the curriculum was used. Before considering some of the issues involved in such a curriculum evaluation, I will try to clarify what it means to evaluate a curriculum.

Evaluation is the process of judging the value or worth of something. It requires an object, a scale of value, and some way of collecting information about the object to which the scale of value can be applied. For example, the magazine *Consumer Reports* evaluates different brands of appliances by choosing a scale for each of several features such as durability, ease of operation, repair record, safety features, or price, and by applying each scale to the appliances being tested. In many cases, a weighted combination of scales is used to provide a ranking of brands or of clusters of brands, but in some cases, a chart is provided to indicate how the appliances performed on the various scales, leaving it to the reader to decide how to weight the features.

Curriculum evaluation is intrinsically more difficult than consumer product evaluation for a number of reasons. The most obvious is that a curriculum is not a tangible object like a washing machine whose performance can be studied under specified conditions. A school mathematics curriculum is an abstraction that can only be glimpsed through such means as examining statements of goals, analyzing mathematical and pedagogical features of materials, observing lessons, finding out how teachers understand the curriculum, and assessing what students have learned. Two classrooms in which the same curriculum is supposedly being "implemented" may look very different; the activities of teacher and students in each room may be quite dissimilar, with different learning opportunities available, different mathematical ideas under consideration, and different outcomes achieved.

By focusing on student outcomes, the authors of the chapters in this book have simplified somewhat the evaluation task; there is obviously much more to be said about the nature and quality of these curricula than can be found by sharpening the focus in this way. Even with a focus on outcomes, however, the task of evaluating curricula is still exceedingly complex. It requires engaging in careful and thorough planning, solving a host of logistical problems, collecting and analyzing fallible data, and interpreting findings in ways that are fair to the data and helpful to those using the evaluation. The history of curriculum evaluation, although short, reveals that others have had to deal with similar complexity.

LOOKING BACKWARD

Curriculum evaluation as we know it today began during the new math era of the mid-1950s to mid-1970s (Howson, Keitel, & Kilpatrick, 1981):

> Just as the curriculum had not been widely perceived as something to be "developed" until the middle of [the twentieth] century, with the advent of curriculum development projects, so the need for an explicit, formal evaluation of the curriculum did not arise until people began to ask whether the projects had been worthwhile. The job of curriculum evaluator, like the job of curriculum developer, is a twentieth-century invention. (p. 182)

Like today's *Standards*-based curricula, the new math curricula tended to deemphasize procedural skill and to emphasize conceptual understanding, albeit through a rather different approach—through exposition and use of mathematical structure rather than through applications of mathematics to realistic problems. Some curriculum developers at that time believed that if students understood number systems, for example, they would not need much practice in calculation. They assumed that students who had studied from the new textbooks produced by the projects would calculate as well as or better than students studying from conventional textbooks. Looking back at those heady days, E. G. Begle (1973), director of the School Mathematics Study Group (SMSG), said, "I remember that when SMSG started many of us were convinced that texts which concentrated on the structure of mathematics would solve all the problems of mathematics education" (p. 209). Early studies were encouraging. They suggested, as the present studies do, that students in project classes performed about as well as students in conventional classes on standardized tests and did better on specially constructed tests (SMSG, 1961). Some reformers continued to maintain the view that students in the new programs would not need much practice in, say, multiplying fractions or factoring polynomials. These were trivial skills that would be learned incidentally as the students solved more challenging problems that made use of the skills. Later, however, when the results came in from the more thorough and extensive National Longitudinal Study of Mathematical Abilities (NLSMA; see Begle & Wilson, 1970; Howson et al., 1981, pp. 189–195), the researchers found that students were not able both to learn the new content and to develop and maintain skill in the older content when such skill was not emphasized.

Reviewing NLSMA and similar curriculum evaluation studies, Walker and Shaffarzick (1974) concluded:

> What these studies show, apparently is *not* that the new curricula are uniformly superior to the old ones, though this may be true, but rather that *different curricula are associated with different patterns of achievement.* Furthermore, these different patterns of achievement seem generally to follow patterns apparent in the curricula. Students using each curriculum do better than their fellow students on tests which include items not covered at all in the other curriculum or given less emphasis there. (p. 97; italics in original)

Or as Begle (1973) put it more bluntly, "If a mathematical topic is in the text, then students do learn it. If the topic is not in the text, then, on the average, students do not learn it" (p. 209). Walker and Schaffarzick argue that after examining patterns of outcomes produced by different curricula, evaluators should test hypotheses about what elements in the curricula are responsible for the differences found. They then say, "whatever strategy is adopted for comparing different curricula, the achievement measure should permit the derivation of a pattern of scores rather than simply one conglomerate score" (p. 104). Consequently, conventional achievement tests are unsatisfactory for comparisons

> because the items on the test are drawn in an unspecified way from an unspecified universe of content and skill, and because scores on the individual items are combined in an arbitrary way that obscures the meaning of the separate performances. (p. 105)

The studies reported in the present volume make some attempt to include multiple measures of mathematics achievement, but they also rely very heavily on achievement tests that give conglomerate scores.

EVALUATION PURPOSES, FORMS, AND METAPHORS

In his classic paper on the methodology of evaluation, Michael Scriven (1967) distinguished between goals and roles of evaluation. He argued that the goals are relatively straightforward: In education, they are to get information for answering certain questions about educational "instruments"— processes, personnel, procedures, programs, and so forth. How well does this instrument perform? Is its performance better or worse than another? How does it work? Is it worth what it costs? The roles of evaluation, however, are, in his words, "enormously various": for example, to assist the professional development of teachers, to inform a decision about purchasing instructional materials, to shape the process of curriculum development, or to support a request for a tax increase or subsequent research. In Scriven's view, a persistent failure to distinguish between goals and roles has helped dilute the evaluation process to the point where goals have been sacrificed to roles. That the roles an evaluation plays are sometimes inappropriate does not invalidate the goals of undertaking it. One may not like the uses to which evaluation data may be put, but there are important purposes to be served by finding out whether a curriculum project's work has been beneficial and whether its products are effective. Because the project has incurred costs of various sorts, its benefits must be ascertained.

Scriven (1967) drew a number of contrasts between various roles for evaluation, but the most influential was his contrast between "formative" evaluation, which attempts to provide direction to a curriculum development project's work, and "summative" evaluation, which looks at the final products of the project. In the present volume, the reader sees evaluators attempting to juggle these roles, sometimes supplying information that developers could use in revising materials but most of the time attempting to assess outcomes of the final or all-but-final products. The line between the two roles is often rather blurred. As Scriven observed, elaborate field tests, often undertaken as primarily formative, may amount to summative evaluations of early forms of a new curriculum. That seems to have been the case with most of the studies reported here. The evaluators are usually quick to note that subsequent changes in the curriculum either have already been made or are planned as a consequence of the findings.

Scriven's (1967) approach is in the American vein: education is production, curriculum development is designing and manufacturing the means of production, and curriculum evaluation is quality control. This engineering metaphor has dominated educational thought in the United States ever since the early twentieth century, when Frederick Taylor founded systems engineering and Franklin Bobbitt applied Taylor's ideas about efficiency and job analysis to the study of curriculum. This metaphor is clearly still with us; it permeates the studies reported in the present volume.

During the wave of curriculum development that marked the 1960s and 1970s, metaphors other than engineering quality control were explored for the evaluation of curriculum. Some evaluators adopted the medical model (Anderson, Ball, Murphy, & Associates, 1975, pp. 245–247), in which one studies the process more than the product, looks for long-term outcomes and unintended side effects, and employs multiple comparison groups to assess the effects of the therapist's enthusiasm. Other evaluators acted like journalists, tracking down leads and using interviews and observations to put together a terse and timely report. Still others took the law as the controlling metaphor and assumed the role of a lawyer putting together a case against an adversary (Anderson et al., pp. 21–22). Examples of projects that took innovative approaches to evaluation, even if they did not follow these metaphors exactly, include Erlwanger's (1974/1975) evaluation of the Individually Prescribed Instruction program, Crawford's (1975) evaluation of the Scottish Fife Mathematics Project, and Cundy's (1976) evaluation of the Caribbean Mathematics Project. Today, such metaphors may have faded from view, but the notion is still viable that curriculum evaluation might be a comprehensive portrayal of the curriculum in operation rather than the appraisal of a product. It would be helpful to have portrayals of the *Standards*-based curricula discussed herein that would go further than the studies reported. Such portrayals, however, do not typically lean very heavily on cross-curriculum comparison, which is the engine driving most summative evaluation studies.

CURRICULUM COMPARISON

Anyone proposing a new school mathematics curriculum faces the task of justifying its adoption. Teachers, parents, and students themselves may be dissatisfied with the current situation, but that does not mean they necessarily welcome change of the sort the new curriculum might demand. Curriculum developers are always in the position of "selling" their product by convincing their potential clients that the change it entails is both manageable and for the better. Research showing improved performance, or at least performance that is no worse than at present, is often used to bolster arguments being made on other grounds.

Devising a research study that can yield adequate information on the comparative performance of students using the new curriculum and students not using it requires attention to several critical issues. The learning goals being addressed have to be identified, appropriate measures of learning have to be located or devised, and comparable groups of students have to be located. Unless each of these issues is handled appropriately, the information provided by the study will be difficult to interpret at best and may be invalid.

Identification of Goals

The projects reported in this volume undertook the development of *Standards*-based curricula because the standards are seen as providing an improved framework for school mathematics. The nature of this improvement is well described in Chapter 1 and echoed in the subsequent chapters.

A *Standards*-based reconstitution of school mathematics entails adopting different learning goals for students. For example, although all curricula presumably aim at developing some conceptual understanding as well as procedural skill, *Standards*-based curricula attempt to place greater emphasis on the understanding of mathematical concepts through the provision of problems and situations in which students use their developing mathematical knowledge. Students are presumably expected to be more active learners, to take more responsibility for their learning, and to do more communicating with each other and their teacher about their mathematical work. Topics such as mathematical modeling are added to the curriculum as a means of helping students increase their understanding and apply what they have learned to new situations. Such changes mean that the goals for a given year or course are different than they were before.

But then the problem becomes, How do we compare curricula that are aiming at different learning goals? Do we, for example, assess only the goals they have in common, thereby failing to address important new goals the project has adopted? Or do we assess all goals, common or not, thereby asking students to respond to assessment tasks for which they have had little or no preparation? The chapter authors have clearly struggled with these questions, typically settling for a middle-of-the-road approach. They appear to have gone primarily after goals that seemed to be reasonable for both curricula, but often they have constructed special assessments aimed at unique goals of the new project.

The reader gets the sense, however, that several projects had aimed at ambitious learning goals that were either never addressed by the research studies or addressed in a cursory fashion. For example, the *Interactive Mathematics Program* requires students to make, test, and prove conjectures, but none of the instruments used in the studies of student performance on content emphasized by *IMP* appears to have assessed anything to do with conjectures. *Everyday Mathematics* has students engage in investigations in geometry, data and statistics, and algebra; students' abilities to conduct and report on such investigations have apparently not been evaluated to date. *MATH Thematics* wants students to use technological tools when appropriate, yet how and how effectively they use such tools seem not to have been examined. Every project discussed in the book seems to have been able to evaluate at best only a few of the learning goals it set for the students who have used the materials it produced. Perhaps the evaluators had insufficient time or other resources to study whether those ambitious goals were met, perhaps instruments could not be devised to assess outcomes related to those goals, or perhaps the project's goals had not been spelled out clearly enough to allow the evaluators to assess them. There is plenty of room for additional study of whether these other goals are being met in classrooms in which these curricula are being used.

Appropriateness of Measures

The most common measures used in the studies were standardized tests of mathematics achievement, items from national and international assessments, and, in the case of the high school projects, college entrance examinations, apparently on the assumption that these measures tap learning goals suitable to both new and traditional curricula. The reader sometimes gets the impression, however, that many of these measures were being used more to reassure parents and the public that the new curricula were not harming students than to assess common learning goals. And in fact, the authors are sometimes at pains to point out that the standardized tests used in the studies do not provide very good information on what the new curriculum has sought. That is certainly true of the college entrance examinations, the College Board's Scholastic Assessment Test (SAT) in particular, which are not linked to curricula and therefore unlikely to be sensitive to curriculum differences. In other words, the tests were not appropriate but were being used in the studies anyway for other purposes.

One of the most valuable purposes an evaluation can serve is to reassure anxious parents that their children are not being harmed by an experimental curriculum. During the new math era, for example, the Secondary School Mathematics Curriculum Improvement Study (SSMCIS) undertook studies of possible "bias" of the SAT for students who had completed the SSMCIS curriculum for Grades 7–12 (Fehr, 1974); the studies showed that those students were in no way handicapped by having participated in the new program. Moreover, SSMCIS was able to arrange for a special examination for those students in New York State so that they could obtain Regents Credit for their mathematics courses. Such evaluation activities, though not especially helpful in improving the quality of the curriculum, are necessary if it is to be accepted and used. There is nothing wrong with conducting evaluation activities that are designed to make a curriculum more acceptable, but they should not be confused with activities designed to address common curriculum goals in a deep and thorough way.

Standardized achievement tests, in particular, are exceedingly blunt instruments for measuring what students might learn in a given year from a given curriculum. They are designed to give a global picture of what students know and can do in mathematics. Leaving aside the criticisms one might have of how well the multiple-choice questions that dominate such instruments measure certain learning goals, standardized achievement tests are designed to be used across several grades. They contain, at best, only a few items on any mathematical topic. So if Curriculum A introduces the multiplication of fractions one way and Curriculum B introduces it another way, there might be only a couple of items on the test that could be used to see which curriculum did the better job of teaching the operation. The test would not be able to assess different facets of students' knowledge and understanding: Do they think that the product will always be larger than either of the fractions being multiplied? Can they estimate the relative size of two indicated products without doing the multiplication? Can they explain the steps in the algorithm they are using? No achievement test given in one or two class periods can possibly provide adequate data on these questions while simultaneously assessing the spectrum of other topics that students are learning. To study how well two curricula with different approaches taught a year's worth of school mathematics requires a battery of measures specifically designed to sample the content of that year's course.

In quite a few of the studies reported here, assessments were located or specially devised to tap learning goals unique to, or at least more prominent in, the new curriculum. In some cases, these special assessments were given only to students using the new curriculum; in others, parts of the assessment considered "fair" to both curricula were administered to all students. For example, Mokros reports a study by Flowers in which a written test and follow-up interviews addressed specific skills and understanding emphasized in the *Investigations* curriculum; these were administered to students in both the new program and the comparison one. Schoen and Hirsch divided the *Core-Plus* posttest into two parts, administering to both groups only the part comprising items assessing content seen as common to both curricula (full disclosure: I served on the *Core-Plus* Advisory Board). Senk reports studies of the second editions of *UCSMP* materials that looked at comparisons on items that teachers judged their students as having an opportunity to learn. Despite the importance of assessing students on content that they have had an opportunity to learn, it seems fair to say that in their eagerness to make comparisons with a regular curriculum, the evaluators of the programs under consideration tended not to use a wide range of measures appropriate to the new curriculum. Moreover, they often used open-ended measures or small clusters of items. Because information on the internal consistency and stability of these measures is not always reported, one needs to be concerned that unreliability of measurement might have affected some of the results.

Comparability of Groups

The usual approach in comparative studies such as those reported in the present volume is to measure the performance of students using the new curriculum against that of students using "more traditional" curricula. A problem seldom addressed adequately in this case is defining what is meant by *traditional*. When disparate approaches and materials are lumped together under the same term, differential outcomes are obscured and opportunities to sharpen comparisons are lost. Some of the reports herein contain information on the textbooks the students in the "traditional" groups were using, if not information on what their teachers were doing in class; but other reports make little attempt to go below the label. Many teachers who are not involved in new curriculum programs, however, have heard about *Standards*-based reforms and may be attempting to use some of the ideas and practices in their own teaching. It seems inappropriate to label such teachers "traditional" and to lump them with others who are not making such attempts, an unfortunate occurrence in comparison studies that fail to look inside the classroom.

A serious problem with many of the studies reported herein is that of the "equivalence" of groups being compared. Ideally, one would like the groups of students to be equivalent in all respects other than the curriculum they received. To the extent that they fall short of such equivalence, the ensuing differences in performance may be attributable to other factors and are not "outcomes" in the sense intended. The standard way of ensuring that other factors are not operating is random assignment of students or classes to curriculum groups, as was done with students in the study at Southeast High School reported by Schoen and Hirsch. In other studies, however, it seems fairly clear not only that random assignment was not used (it is seldom feasible under field conditions) but also that the teachers of the new curriculum—who often have elected to use it and therefore might be especially enthusiastic, experienced, well prepared, or more inclined to change their teaching and their curriculum—differed in systematic ways from their counterparts teaching the other curriculum. Teachers of the new curriculum, often with a reputation as being innovative, might have attracted a different group of students than other teachers, for example, students whose parents wanted them in that teachers' class. When teachers in one school are contrasted with teachers in another school, factors associated with the school's participation in the project, as well as the teachers' participation, need to be considered. The principal of the participating school, compared with the principal of the corresponding nonparticipating school, might have placed more emphasis on the mathematics curriculum, or might have been more inclined to select and reward teachers on the basis of their perceived competence in mathematics teaching. A host of selection factors beyond the curriculum itself might account for, or at least contribute to, superior performance by students in the project classes. When only one project class is studied, as happened in some cases, there is no way to disentangle curriculum effects from teacher effects or other circumstances unique to that class.

Comparisons with various reference groups do virtually nothing to compensate for the effects of selection factors. Their value is descriptive, helping to place the group using the new curriculum on some well-known scale. These include comparisons with the group used to norm a standardized test, with a national sample of students taking the National Association of Educational Progress (NAEP) or the Second International Mathematics Study (SIMS) tests, or with cohorts of students from the same school who took a test before the curriculum was instituted. In particular, increases in performance compared with "historical averages" for the same school might be as easily attributable to factors such as changes in the school population or a growing familiarity with the test as to an improved curriculum. Increases on both the verbal and the mathematical scores on a test like the SAT that is virtually curriculum neutral should not be attributed to changes in the mathematics curriculum unless other factors have been ruled out.

In many of the studies reported herein, the evaluators attempted to "equate" students by giving a pretest in mathematics and then either "matching" students on pretest scores and possibly other characteristics or by using analysis of covariance (ANCOVA) with pretest scores as a covariate. There are problems with either approach.

According to Campbell and Stanley (1963), "matching is no real help when used to overcome initial group differences" (p. 15). If the means of the groups on the pretest are substantially different, the process of matching does not simply fail to equate the groups; it ensures the occurrence of undesirable regression effects. The two groups will differ on their posttest scores independently of any effects of the curriculum they encountered because each will tend to regress toward the mean of the population from which it was chosen. A particularly questionable tactic is matching students individually, with no attention to the teacher they had or the mathematics class they were in.

Techniques such as an ANCOVA, although not as problematic as matching, are still tricky, particularly when used in the absence of random assignment to groups. For one thing, an ANCOVA is a powerful technique and requires strong assumptions, including reliable covariates, multivariate normality of distributions, homogeneity of variance, and homogeneity of regression. There are techniques for dealing with certain violations of these assumptions, but the authors of these reports either were not concerned about possible violations, did not have space to discuss them, or thought such a discussion might be too technical for this book. Further, an ANCOVA requires good measurement of each group's performance on both pretests and posttests, and it is not always clear that happened in these studies. When reporting ANCOVA results, one should indicate the reliability of the measures used and give both adjusted and unadjusted scores so that the reader has some sense of the direction and magnitude of the adjustments. The reader of the present volume looks in vain for information on tests of assumptions, instrumentation properties, and nature of score adjustment.

THEMES OF THE REPORTS

I do not see any common themes of curriculum content beyond those that Putnam, Chappell, and Swafford have identified in their respective chapters. There was considerable variation in evaluation methods across the studies, which makes it difficult to identify common themes in mathematics learning or teaching, whether within or across grade levels. One possible theme confirming the findings of curriculum evaluation during the new math era has already been suggested: the tendency of students in new curricula to perform at the same level as comparison students on standardized tests and to perform at higher levels on specially designed tests. Another might be that these new curricula were ordinarily so ambitious that many teachers using them for the first time were unable to complete in a year what had been planned as a year's work. This problem tended to disappear as the teachers gained more experience with the curriculum and as it was revised in light of pilot work. A third theme might be that teachers tended to adapt (or distort) the curriculum to fit their situation. Many evaluators did not report having looked for such adaptation, but when the evaluators reported having looked for it, it was there.

Variation across studies was also true at each of the levels—elementary grades, middle grades, and high school—which makes the identification of common themes at any one level problematic too. In general, the studies of elementary grades curriculum projects seemed somewhat more likely than the others to include attention to how the teachers were handling the new curriculum materials in class, perhaps because of concerns that teachers of elementary grades might have a less-sure command of the mathematical ideas in those materials. In contrast, the studies of the high school projects tended to rely somewhat more than the others on data from standardized achievement tests. Researchers studying projects at the high school level, when students begin to get more choices about the curriculum they will pursue, naturally tended to be more concerned than those studying projects at lower grades with the mathematics courses students went on to take and their subsequent experiences in those courses. In particular, evaluators more often noted lack of skill in algebra by students completing a new high school curriculum than they noted lack of arithmetic skill by students in new elementary and middle school curricula. Also, Webb's study of transcripts for the *Interactive Mathematics Program* does not have any parallel at the lower grades. However, both case studies and large-scale comparisons involving standardized tests can be found at all three levels.

An intriguing finding of the NLSMA, which involved three cohorts of students followed for 5 years, was a trend toward differences in achievement among groups of students using different textbooks becoming smaller as the students went from the lower grades to the higher grades (Begle & Wilson, 1970, p. 400). By Grades 11 and 12, the differences were quite small. Unfortunately, the variation across the present group of studies in what was measured and how it was measured does not permit any such trend to be detected in the evidence presented.

WHAT'S NEXT?

The curriculum projects are now much further along than they were when the data reported in this volume were collected. Most have published final versions of their materials, and some have undertaken revisions. The numbers of schools using the materials have grown, with new cohorts of teachers either being trained to use the materials or simply picking them up and using them. The kinds of studies that can now be undertaken on these curricula have moved beyond what Burkhardt, Fraser, and Ridgway (1990) call "**realizable teaching**—studies of what can actually be achieved with typical teachers under realistic circumstances [to] **curriculum change on a large scale**—studies of how curriculum change can be effected and what other school or social factors affect it" (p. 6; bold in original).

Among the studies that come next should be an examination of the effects of moving from one curriculum to another. Each of the projects reported in this book has taken a segment of the school mathematics curriculum and done its best to reorient it around new learning goals and infuse it with both new content and new ways of addressing that content. However, students experience school mathematics in sequence from kindergarten through high school and then often into further study of mathematics. The U.S. educational system does not ordinarily make the transition from one level of schooling to another exactly seamless, and students often encounter a vastly different mathematic curriculum when they enter a new school or even a new grade in the same school. What are the learning difficulties encountered by students from a traditional curriculum who enter a *Standards*-based one? Can those be detailed so that users of the new curriculum can deal with them? Students who move in another direction, from one *Standards*-based curriculum to another, presumably encounter fewer disruptions and consequently learn more mathematics than those who move on to a more traditional curriculum. Can that presumption be explored? According to the evaluators, the experience of college students who had completed 3 years of the *Systematic Initiative for Montana Mathematics and Science* (*SIMMS*) curriculum only to be apparently less prepared for college mathematics than their non-S*IMMS* peers was more an indication that the college mathematics was too traditional than that the *SIMMS* curriculum is weak. As Swafford suggests, however, that argument does not encourage high schools to change their mathematics curriculum. Developers and evaluators of curricula at one level of the educational system are under no obligation to see that changes are made at other levels. However, if their efforts are to be successful, they need to document the effects of moving from one level, and one curriculum, to another so that those who are seeking change at the higher level have evidence with which to work.

When the next generation of studies is conducted, several features not characteristic of the present studies have to be considered. These include a deeper examination of how teachers are using the curriculum, the inclusion of comparisons across new curricula, and the development of more instruments to measure ambitious learning goals.

Teacher Effects

The new curricula all depend critically for their effectiveness on how they are understood and handled by the teacher. The variability in how teachers use the materials is likely to increase as more teachers who were neither involved in the project nor know much about it end up teaching the curriculum. Several of the studies in the present volume attempted to look at that variability. For example, Mokros reports a study by Goodrow in which a teacher used the *Investigations* curriculum with a "didactic" teaching style and a study by Flowers in which one group of teachers used *Investigations* along with an introduction to procedures that included standard algorithms. These so-called mixed approaches were judged not as effective as the approach of using the curriculum as intended. Given a history of the school mathematics curriculum message becoming garbled when it moves from paper to practice (Griffiths & Howson, 1974, chap. 15; see also Wilson & Floden, 2001), these results are not surprising. What is surprising is that in Ridgway, Zawojewski, Hoover, and Lambdin's large-scale study of the *Connected Mathematics* curriculum, there was no association between gains in achievement and either the teacher the student had or the class he or she was in.

When statistical analyses, whether simple t tests or heavy duty ANCOVA, are performed that take the student as the unit of analysis, the researchers are essentially saying that each student had an independent experience with the curriculum—which is not true. The appropriate unit for such analyses is the class, a point that appears to have been recognized only by Romberg and Shafer in their report on *Mathematics in Context* and by Senk in her report of studies of the second editions of the University of Chicago School Mathematics Project books on geometry and advanced algebra. Further evaluations of the project curricula must look more closely at how the teachers were using the curricula and then analyze the data in appropriate ways that take into account the students' class and their teacher.

Common Goals

Studies of curriculum change on a larger scale will be strengthened if, instead of looking only at how project classes compare with "traditional classes" or with classes using project materials and a variant of project instruction, the evaluators look as well at outcomes across several *Standards*-based curricula. Because different *Standards*-based curricula are aiming at the same or quite similar learning goals, studies that compare outcomes of these curricula can illuminate the strengths and weaknesses of each curriculum in ways that are not feasible when the only comparisons being made are with a traditional curriculum. In each case, the teachers are working with a curriculum that is relatively new to them, which mitigates effects of novelty and of taking part in an experimental program.

Profiles of Achievement

When several *Standards*-based curricula are compared, it becomes even more important to look at patterns of outcomes than just whether one curriculum is better overall than another. Such patterns can be detected only when a battery of outcome measures is used, each targeted at a specific learning goal. As the reports in the present volume indicate, such measures are not easily obtainable and will need to be constructed. Instruments such as the geometry test devised by Carroll for the *Everyday Mathematics* field test, the interview tasks used in the *Investigations* studies, the Balanced Assessment tasks used by the *Connected Mathematics Project*, and the so-called contextual subtests constructed by the *Core-Plus Mathematics Project* evaluation team all make a good start in that direction. The next generation of curriculum evaluation studies is clearly going to have to invest in much more extensive development and construction of instruments to measure *Standards*-based learning goals than has been the case to date.

DO WE WANT MORE EVIDENCE?

The difficulties of changing school mathematics are especially formidable in the United States, with its system of state and local control of education. Teachers and schools are continually beset by conflicting mandates, so they keep their heads down. Wilson and Floden (2001) quote a state official as saying, "What keeps us from absolute sea-sickness is that locals don't jump as quickly onto some new reform bandwagon" (p. 214). Consequently, reform efforts tend to be either ignored or absorbed into traditional practice.

Anyone reading the reports in the present volume will note the difficulty some authors report in getting comparison classes to participate in the field tests. In one case, teachers reported that they felt overwhelmed by district and state tests. In another, a school simply decided not to disrupt classes for a second day of testing. Curriculum developers and evaluators appear to be caught between politicians, on the one hand, who are mandating that research be done to validate programs before they are implemented, and school people, on the other hand, who are required to give tests for other purposes than research and who may consider participating in a research project a luxury they cannot afford. Unwillingness to participate in research projects that require time away from instruction for testing is a big and growing problem in the United States. In other countries, the ministry of education might simply order schools to participate in studies designed to evaluate an experimental mathematics curriculum; here, they have to be cajoled into participating—and they are becoming more resistant to such requests.

A second generation of evaluation of *Standards*-based curricula in school mathematics will have to cope with these problems and pressures. Much more time, effort, and money will have to be invested if the public wants definitive evidence on what students are learning from these curricula. Until that investment is made, the imaginative, varied, and informative first generation of studies reported in this volume offer the best evidence we have that *Standards*-based reform works.

REFERENCES

Anderson, S. B., Ball, S., Murphy, R. T., & Associates. (1975). *Encyclopedia of educational evaluation*. San Francisco: Jossey-Bass.

Begle, E. G. (1973). Some lessons learned by SMSG. *Mathematics Teacher, 66*, 207–214.

Begle, E. G., & Wilson, J. W. (1970). Evaluation of mathematics programs. In E. G. Begle (Ed.), *Mathematics education* (Sixty-ninth Yearbook of the National Society for the Study of Education, Part 1) (pp. 367–404). Chicago: University of Chicago Press.

Burkhardt, H., Fraser, R., & Ridgway, J. (1990). The dynamics of curriculum change. In I. Wirszup & R. Streit (Eds.), *Developments in school mathematics education around the world* (Vol. 2, pp. 3–30). Reston, VA: National Council of Teachers of Mathematics.

Campbell, D. T., & Stanley, J. C. (1963). *Experimental and quasi-experimental designs for research*. Chicago: Rand McNally.

Crawford, D. (Ed.). (1975). *The Fife mathematics project*. Oxford, England: Oxford University Press.

Cundy, M. (1976). *Caribbean mathematics project: An evaluation*. London: British Council.

Erlwanger, S. H. (1975). Case studies of children's conceptions of mathematics (Doctoral dissertation, University of Illinois, 1974). *Dissertation Abstracts International, 35*, 7121A.

Fehr, H. (1974). SSMCIS: A unified mathematics program. *Mathematics Teacher, 67*, 25–33.

Griffiths, H. B., & Howson, A. G. (1974). *Mathematics: Society and curricula*. Cambridge: Cambridge University Press.

Howson, G., Keitel, C., & Kilpatrick, J. (1981). *Curriculum development in mathematics*. Cambridge, England: Cambridge University Press.

National Council of Teachers of Mathematics. (1989). *Curriculum and evaluation standards for school mathematics*. Reston, VA: Author.

School Mathematics Study Group. (1961, November). *Reports on student achievement in SMSG courses* (SMSG Newsletter, No. 10). Stanford, CA: Author.

Scriven, M. (1967). The methodology of evaluation. In *Perspectives of curriculum evaluation* (AERA Monograph Series on Curriculum Evaluation, No. 1, pp. 39–83). Chicago: Rand McNally.

Selection and Adoption of Elementary School Materials, California Educational Code §60200.c.3. (1995). Available: http://www.leginfo.ca.gov/calaw.html.

Stein, S. K. (1996). *Strength in numbers: Discovering the joy and power of mathematics in everyday life*. New York: Wiley.

The Federal Role in K–12 Mathematics Reform: Joint Hearing Before the Subcommittees on Early Childhood, Youth and Families and on Postsecondary Education, Training and Life-Long Learning of the House Committee on Education and the Workforce, 106th Cong., 2d Sess. (2000) (opening statement by M. N. Castle). Available: http://www.house.gov/ed_workforce/hearings/106th/ecyf/fuzzymath2200/oscastle.htm.

U.S. Department of Education. (1986). *What works: Research about learning and teaching*. Washington, DC: Author.

U.S. Department of Education, Mathematics and Science Expert Panel. (1999). *Exemplary and promising mathematics programs*. Washington, DC: Author. Available: http://www.enc.org/professional/federalresources/exemplary/.

Walker, D. F., & Schaffarzick, J. (1974). Comparing curricula. *Review of Educational Research, 44*, 83–111.

Wilson, S. M., & Floden, R. E. (2001). Hedging bets: Standards-based reform in classrooms. In S. H. Fuhrman (Ed.), *From the capitol to the classroom: Standards-based reform in the states* (One Hundredth Yearbook of the National Society for the Study of Education, Part 2, pp. 193–216). Chicago: University of Chicago Press.

Bibliography for Further Reading

Chapter 3 — Trailblazers

Flevares, L. M., & Perry, M. (2001). How many do you see? The use of nonspoken representations in first-grade mathematics lessons. *Journal of Educational Psychology, 93*, 330–345.

Hamm, J. V., & Perry, M. (2002). Learning mathematics in first-grade classrooms: On whose authority? *Journal of Educational Psychology, 94*, 126–137.

Isaacs, A., & Kelso, C. (1996). Pictures, tables, graphs and questions: Statistical processes. *Teaching Children Mathematics, 2*(6), 340–345.

Chapter 4 — Everyday Mathematics

Carroll, W. M. (2000). Invented computational procedures of students in a standards-based curriculum. *Journal of Mathematical Behavior, 18*(2), 111–121.

Carroll, W. M., Fuson, K. C., & Diamond, A. (2000). Use of student-constructed number stories in a reform-based curriculum. *Journal of Mathematical Behavior, 19*, 49–62.

Carroll, W. M. (1998). Polygon capture: A geometry game. *Mathematics Teaching in the Middle School, 4*(2), 90–94.

Carroll, W. M. (1998). Geometric knowledge of middle school students in a reform-based mathematics curriculum. *School Science and Mathematics, 98*(4), 188–197.

Carroll, W., & Porter, D. (1998). Alternative algorithms for whole-number operations. In L. J. Morrow & M. J. Kenney (Eds.), *The teaching and learning of algorithms in school mathematics: 1998 yearbook* (pp. 106–114). Reston, VA: National Council of Teachers of Mathematics.

Carroll, W., & Porter, D. (1998). Invented algorithms can develop meaningful mathematical procedures. *Teaching Children Mathematics, 3*(7), 370–374.

Fuson, K., Carroll, W. M., & Landis, J. (1996). Levels in conceptualizing and solving addition and subtraction compare word problems. *Cognition and Instruction, 14*(3), 345–371.

Hawkes, M., Kimmelman, P., & Kroeze, D. (1997, September). Becoming 'first in the world' in math and science. *Phi Delta Kappan, 79*(1), 30–33.

Isaacs, A. C., & Carroll, W. M. (1999). Strategies for basic-facts instruction. *Teaching Children Mathematics, 5*(9), 508–515.

Riordan, J. E., & Noyce, P. E. (2001). The impact of two standards-based mathematics curricula on student achievement in Massachusetts. *Journal for Research in Mathematics Education, 32*(4), 368–398.

Woodward, J., & Baxter, J. (1997). The effects of an innovative approach to mathematics on academically low-achieving students in inclusive settings. *Exceptional Children, 63*(3), 373–388.

Chapter 6 — Number Power

Davidson, N., Weissglass, J., & Robertson, L. (1990). Staff development for cooperative learning in mathematics. *Journal of Staff Development, 11*(3), 12–17.

Chapter 9 — Connected Mathematics

Keiser, J. J., & Lambdin, D. V. (1996). The clock is ticking: Time constraint issues in mathematics teaching reform. *Journal of Educational Research, 90*(1), 23–31.

Lambdin, D. V., & Preston, R. V. (1995). Caricatures in innovation. Teacher adaptation to an investigation-oriented middle school mathematics curriculum. *Journal of Teacher Education, 45,* 130–140.

Lubienski, S. T. (2000). A clash of social class cultures? Students' experiences in a discussion-intensive seventh-grade mathematics classroom. *The Elementary School Journal, 100*(4), 377–403.

Lubienski, S. T. (2000). Problem solving as a means toward mathematics for all: an exploratory look through a class lens. *Journal for Research in Mathematics Education, 31*(4), 454–482.

Ridgway, J., Zawojewski, J., & Hoover, M. (2000). Problematising evidence based policy and practice. *Evaluation and Research in Education, 14*(3,4), 181–192.

Chapter 10 — Mathematics in Context

Burrill, G., & Romberg, T. A. (1998). Statistics and probability for the middle grades: Examples from *Mathematics in Context.* In S. P. LaJoie (Ed.), *Reflections on Statistics: Learning, Teaching, and Assessment in Grades K-12* (pp. 33–59). Mahwah, NJ: Lawrence Erlbaum Associates.

de Lange, J., Burrill, G., Romberg, T., & van Reeuwijk, M. (Eds.). (1993). *Learning and testing Mathematics in Context.* Pleasantview, NY: Wings for Learning.

Meyer, M. R. (1999). Multiple strategies = multiple challenges. *Mathematics Teaching in the Middle School, 4*(8), 519–523.

Romberg, T. A. (1999). Realistic instruction in mathematics. In J. Block, S. Everson, & T. Guskey (Eds.), *Comprehensive school reform* (pp. 287–314). Dubuque, IA: Kendall/Hunt.

Romberg, T. A. (1998). Designing middle school mathematics materials using problems created to help students progress from informal to formal mathematical reasoning. In L. Leutzinger (Ed.), *Mathematics in the middle* (pp. 117–119). Reston, VA: National Council of Teachers of Mathematics.

Romberg, T. A. (1997). The influence of programs from other countries on the school mathematics reform curriculum in the United States. *American Journal of Education, 106*(1), 127–147.

Romberg, T. A. (1997). *Mathematics in Context*: impact on teachers. In B. Nelson & E. Fennema (Eds.), *Mathematics teachers in transition* (pp. 357–380). Mahwah, NJ: Lawrence Erlbaum Associates.

Shafer, M., & Romberg, T. A. (2001). Assessment in classrooms that promote understanding. In E. Fennema & T. A. Romberg (Eds.), *Classrooms that promote mathematical understanding* (pp. 159–184). Mahwah, NJ: Lawrence Erlbaum Associates.

Chapter 11 — Middle Grades Math Thematics

Billstein, R. (1997). The STEM experience: some things we've learned and their implications for teacher preparation and inservice. *NCSM Journal of Mathematics Education Leadership, 1*(3), 3–8.

Billstein, R. (1998). You are cleared to land. *Mathematics Teaching in the Middle School, 3*(7), 452–456.

Billstein, R. (1998). Assessment: The STEM Model. *Mathematics Teaching in the Middle School, 3*(1), 282–286, 294–296.

Billstein, R. (1998). Middle Grades Math Thematics: the STEM project—a look at developing a middle school mathematics curriculum. In L. Leutzinger (Ed.), *Mathematics in the middle* (pp. 93–106). Reston, VA: National Council of Teachers of Mathematics.

Tetley, L. (1998). Implementing change: rewards and challenges. *Mathematics Teaching in the Middle School, 4*(3), 160–167.

Van Boening, L. (1999). Growth through change. *Mathematics Teaching in the Middle School, 5*(1), 27–33.

Chapter 14 — Core-Plus

Coxford, A. F., & Hirsch, C. R. (1996). A common core of math for all. *Educational Leadership, 53*(8), 22–25.

Hart, E. W. (1997). Discrete mathematical modeling in the secondary curriculum: Rationale and examples from the Core-Plus Mathematics Project. In J. Rosenstein, D. Franzblau, & F. Roberts (Eds.), *Discrete mathematics in the schools* (pp. 265–280). Providence, RI: DIMACS Series in Theoretical Computer Science and Discrete Mathematics, American Mathematical Society.

Hart, E. W. (1998). Algorithmic problem solving in discrete mathematics. In L. Morrow & M. J. Kenney (Eds.), *Teaching and learning of algorithms in school mathematics*, 1998 Yearbook of the National Council of Teachers of Mathematics (pp. 251–267). Reston, VA: National Council of Teachers of Mathematics.

Hart, E. W., & Stewart, J. (1998). Reflections on high school reform and implications for middle schools. In L. Leutzinger (Ed.), *Mathematics in the middle* (pp. 65–71). Reston, VA: National Council of Teachers of Mathematics.

Hirsch, C. R. (2001). The Core-Plus Mathematics Project (CPMP). In L. S. Grinstein & S. I. Lipsey (Eds.), *Encyclopedia of mathematics education* (pp. 159–161). New York: Routledge Falmer.

Hirsch, C. R., & Weinhold, M. L. W. (1999). Everybody counts—including the mathematically promising. In L. Sheffield (Ed.), *Developing mathematically promising students* (pp. 233–241). Reston, VA: National Council of Teachers of Mathematics.

Lloyd, G. M. (1999). Two teachers' conceptions of a reform-oriented curriculum: Implications for mathematics teacher development. *Journal of Mathematics Teacher Education, 2*, 227–252.

Schoen, H. L., Fey, J. T., Hirsch, C. R., & Coxford, A. F. (1999). Issues and options in the math wars. *Phi Delta Kappan, 80*(6), 444–453.

Schoen, H. L., & Ziebarth, S. W. (1997). A progress report on student achievement in the Core-Plus Mathematics Project field test. *NCSM Journal of Mathematics Education Leadership, 1*(3), 15–23.

Schoen, H. L., & Ziebarth, S. W. (1998). High school mathematics curriculum reform: Rationale, research, and recent developments. In P. S. Hlebowitsh & W. G. Wraga (Eds.), *Annual Review of Research for School Leaders* (pp. 141–191). New York: Macmillan Publishing Company.

Van Zoest, L. R., & Ritsema, B. E. (1998). Fulfilling the call for mathematics education reform. *NCSM Journal of Mathematics Education Leadership, 1*(4), 5–15.

Wilson, M. R., & Lloyd, G. M. (2000). The challenge to share mathematical authority with students: High school teachers reforming classroom roles and activities through curriculum implementation. *Journal of Curriculum and Supervision, 15*, 146–169.

Chapter 17 — SIMMS

Barta, J. A. (1999). *Relation between SIMMS integrated mathematics curriculum and enrollment of females and American Indians in Montana secondary schools.* Unpublished masters thesis, The University of Montana.

Buhl, D. (1995). *Student teaching: Opportunities for observing, experimenting with, and implementing assessment practices recommended by the NCTM Standards documents (mathematics).* (Doctoral dissertation, Montana State University-Bozeman). *Dissertation Abstracts International, 56*(12A), 4729.

Dapples, B. (1994). *Comparison of teacher-student interaction in SIMMS and non-SIMMS classrooms.* (Doctoral dissertation, Montana State University-Bozeman). *Dissertation Abstracts International, 55*(04A), 0934.

Hirstein, J. (1995). Assessment and mathematical modeling. In C. Sloyer, W. Blum, & I. Huntley (Eds.), *Advances and perspectives in the teaching of mathematical modeling and applications.* Newark, DE: University of Delaware.

Keck, H. L. (1996). *The development of an analytic scoring scale to assess mathematical modeling projects.* (Doctoral dissertation, The University of Montana-Missoula). *Dissertation Abstracts International, 57*(07A), 2925.

Lott, J. W. (1997). View on high school mathematics education. *Notices of the American Mathematical Society, 44*, 197–206.

Lott, J. W., & Burke, M. J. (1994). Systemic Initiative for Montana Mathematics and Science (SIMMS). *Mathematics Teacher, 87*, 462–465.

Souhrada, T. A. (2001). *Secondary school mathematics in transition: A comparative study of mathematics curricula and student results.* (Doctoral dissertation, The University of Montana). *Dissertation Abstracts International, 62*(04A), 1355.

Walen, S., & Hirstein, J. (1995). *Restructuring mathematics assessment: Suggestions from the classroom.* Needham Heights, MA: Simon & Schuster Custom Publishing Company.

Zuuring, B. (1995). *Attitudes of ninth grade male and female students who participated in the Montana mathematics and science project.* Unpublished masters thesis, The University of Montana.

Chapter 18 — UCSMP

Hirschhorn, D. B. (1991). *Implementation of the first four years of the UCSMP secondary curriculum.* (Doctoral dissertation, The University of Chicago). *Dissertation Abstracts International, 53*(01A), 0092.

Hirschhorn, D. B., & Senk, S. (1992). Calculators in the UCSMP curriculum for grades 7 and 8. In J. T. Fey & C. R. Hirsch (Eds.), *Calculators in mathematics education* (pp. 79–90). Reston, VA: National Council of Teachers of Mathematics.

McConnell, J. W., Brown, S., Usiskin, Z., Senk, S. L., Widerski, T., Anderson, S., Eddins, S., Hynes-Feldman, C., Flanders, J., Hackworth, M., Hirschhorn, D., Polonsky, L., Sachs, L., & Woodward, E. (1996). Research and development of *UCSMP Algebra.* In Teacher's Edition of *Algebra* Second Edition (pp. T54–T59). Glenview, IL: Scott, Foresman.

Peressini, A. L., McConnell, J. W., Usiskin, Z., Epp, S. S., Ahbel, N. P., Witonsky, D., Hollowell, K. A., Brown, S., Ellis, W., Jr., Sorteberg, J., Thompson, D. R., Aksoy, D., Birky, G. D., & McRill, G. A. (1998). Research and development of UCSMP *Precalculus and Discrete Mathematics.* In Teacher's Edition of *Precalculus and Discrete Mathematics* Second Edition (pp. T56–T61). Glenview, IL: Scott Foresman, Addison Wesley.

Senk, S. L., Thompson, D. R., Viktora, S. S., Usiskin, Z., Ahbel, N. P., Levin, S., Weinhold, M. L., Rubenstein, R. N., Jaskowiak, J. H., Flanders, J., Jakucyn, N., & Pillsbury, G. (1996). Research and development of UCSMP *Advanced Algebra*. In Teacher's Edition of *Advanced Algebra* Second Edition (pp. T54–T58). Glenview, IL: Scott Foresman.

Senk, S. L., Viktora, S. S., Usiskin, Z., Ahbel, N. P., Highstone, V., Witonsky, D., Rubenstein, R. N., Schultz, J. E., Hackworth, M., McConnell, J. W., Aksoy, D., Flanders, J., & Kissane, B. (1998). Research and development of UCSMP *Functions, Statistics, and Trigonometry*. In Teacher's Edition of *Functions, Statistics, and Trigonometry* (pp. T55–T60). Glenview, IL: Scott Foresman, Addison Wesley.

Thompson, D. R. (1996). Learning and teaching indirect proof. *Mathematics Teacher, 89,* 474–482.

Usiskin, Z., Hirschhorn, D., Coxford, A., Highstone, V., Lewellen, H., Oppong, N., DiBianca, R., & Maeir, M. (1997). Research and development of UCSMP *Geometry*. In Teacher's Edition of *Geometry* Second Edition (pp. T54–T59). Glenview, IL: Scott Foresman.

Usiskin, Z., Hynes-Feldman, C., Davis, S., Mallo, S., Sanders, G., Witonsky, D., Flanders, J., Polonsky, L., Porter, S., & Viktora, S. (1995). Research and development of *Transition Mathematics*. In Teacher's Edition of *Transition Mathematics* Second Edition (pp. T52–T56). Glenview, IL: Scott Foresman.

Author Index

495

Subject Index